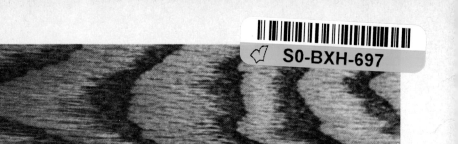
S0-BXH-697

CABINETMAKING: DESIGN AND CONSTRUCTION

CABINETMAKING:
DESIGN AND
CONSTRUCTION

William P. Spence
L. Duane Griffiths

PRENTICE HALL, Englewood Cliffs, New Jersey 07632

Library of Congress Cataloging-in-Publication Data

Spence, William Perkins, [date]
    Cabinetmaking: design and construction/William P. Spence,
L. Duane Griffiths.
      p. cm.
    Includes bibliographical references and index.
    ISBN 0–13–109489–0
    1. Cabinet-work. 2. Furniture making. I. Griffiths, L. Duane.
II. Title.
TT197.S66 1990
684.1'6—dc20
                                 90–44167
                                 CIP

Editorial/production supervision: Fred Dahl and Rose Kernan
Interior design: Meryl Poweski
Page layout: Robert J. Wullen
Manufacturing buyer: Lori Bolwin

For information about our audio products, write us at:
Newbridge Book Clubs, 3000 Cindel Drive, Delran, NJ 08370

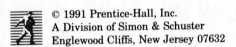 © 1991 Prentice-Hall, Inc.
A Division of Simon & Schuster
Englewood Cliffs, New Jersey 07632

All rights reserved. No part of this book may be
reproduced, in any form or by any means,
without permission in writing from the publisher.

Printed in the United States of America
10 9 8 7 6 5 4 3 2 1

ISBN 0-13-109489-0

Prentice-Hall International (UK) Limited, *London*
Prentice-Hall of Australia Pty. Limited, *Sydney*
Prentice-Hall Canada Inc., *Toronto*
Prentice-Hall Hispanoamericana, S.A., *Mexico*
Prentice-Hall of India Private Limited, *New Delhi*
Prentice-Hall of Japan, Inc., *Tokyo*
Simon & Schuster Asia Pte. Ltd., *Singapore*
Editora Prentice-Hall do Brasil, Ltda., *Rio de Janeiro*

CONTENTS

PREFACE

This book is a handbook for the professional woodworker, the advanced home craftsman, or student. Detailed explanations plus liberal use of photographs and illustrations make it easy to understand even the more difficult constructions and machining techniques. A second color is used to highlight the important features on the illustrations. All of the figures emphasize the hands-on approach utilized throughout the book.

The text gives detailed instructions on how to design cabinets including custom-built and mass-produced units. Special emphasis is placed on the design of kitchens.

Detailed technical information accompanied by many photos and drawings show how to build cabinets including the latest joining techniques such as the European influences on cabinet design and construction. One chapter shows how to properly install the cabinets after they have been built.

Considerable technical information is given about the materials used in cabinet construction. This includes hardwoods, softwoods, reconstituted wood products, plastic laminates, and hardware. An entire chapter is devoted to the application of plastic laminates.

One section gives detailed information about traditional or contemporary construction techniques such as the 32-millimeter system and the use of the lemon splines. The instructions are broken down much the way the units would be built by discussing each part separately. The chapters in this section include basic joinery and show how to construct doors, drawers, and shelves.

The procedure for assemblying the units and using the proper bonding agent is covered in detail.

Another section covers the safe use of portable woodworking tools. These versatile tools can perform a wide range of machining tasks and the procedures are carefully detailed. Safe use of each power tool is stressed.

One of the major sections of the book is the safe and correct use of stationary power woodworking machines. In addition to the basic processes, advanced setups are explained and shown in carefully staged photographs. In addition, selected industrial production machinery is shown and explained. These power tools each have an entire chapter devoted to them. These include chapters covering the table saw, radial arm saw, bandsaw, scroll saw, jointer, and planer. Other tools covered in detail include the drill press, pin router, and a variety of sanders. Safe operating procedures are stressed in each chapter.

No project is completed until it is properly finished. A series of chapters covers the processes of preparing a product for the finishing, staining, filling, sealing, and a protective coating.

As you examine this book you will quickly see that help was received from many companies representing all aspects of the cabinet industry. Their contributions are noted by each item developed with their assistance. Their part in making this book a reality is acknowledged and appreciated. Also, the help of the many students who so willingly assisted when help was needed is appreciated.

William P. Spence
L. Duane Griffiths

CABINETMAKING: DESIGN AND CONSTRUCTION

PART **1**

Introduction

1

DESIGNING CABINETS

When selecting cabinets for a new kitchen, the homeowner has the choice of using custom-made cabinets or production or modular casework.

Custom-made cabinets are those produced by a cabinetmaker in his shop especially for a specific job. They are sized to meet the specific desires of the owner and made to fit the available space.

Production or modular casework is mass produced in a manufacturing plant. It is made in a variety of standard sizes and designs. The homeowner chooses the units from these to be placed in the kitchen.

KITCHEN PLANNING

A kitchen is planned around three activities—food storage, cooking, preparation and clean-up. The food-storage area includes the refrigerator–freezer and cabinets for storage of canned and dry foods. The cooking area includes the range, an oven, and a microwave unit. If a separate oven is to be used, it need not be located near the range because it does not require constant attention. The preparation and clean-up area includes a sink, a compactor, and a dishwasher.

The basic kitchen arrangements include the I-shape, L-shape, U-shape, and corridor (Fig. 1-1). Sometimes an island counter is used. This can contain a sink, cooking unit, or can simply be extra counter space (Fig. 1-2).

To make a kitchen efficient, it is wise to plan it around a work triangle. A *work triangle* is formed by measuring the straight line distances between the refrigerator, cooking unit and sink (Fig. 1-1). This distance should not exceed 22 ft. When planning the counter space allow 3 to 4 ft on each side of the sink. Allow 2 ft or more of counter space on each side of the cooking unit. Allow at least 1 ft of counter beside the refrigerator–freezer so you have somewhere to place things. A minimum of 15 lineal ft of cabinet (including stove and sink) is considered minimum for typical residential kitchens. Standards for multi-family housing are found in "Minimum Property Standards for Housing", U.S. Department of Housing and Urban Development.

Developing the Cabinet Layout

First make a drawing of the floor plan of the room locating the doors and windows that are in the walls to receive cabinets. Then locate the sink, refrigera-

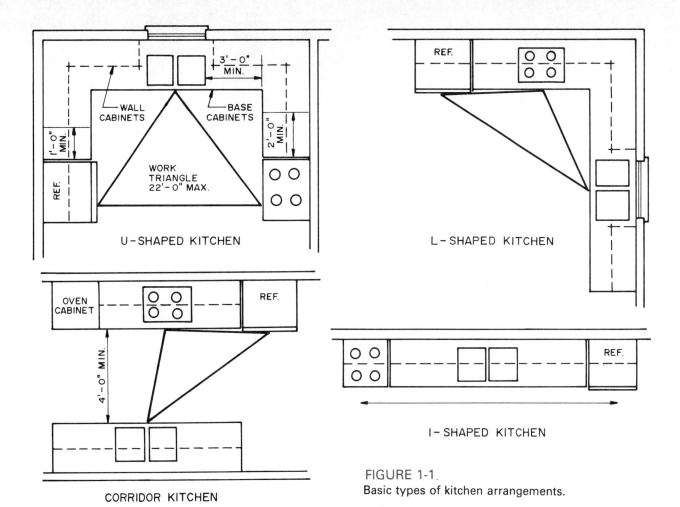

U-SHAPED KITCHEN

WALL CABINETS

BASE CABINETS

3'-0" MIN.

1'-0" MIN.

2'-0" MIN.

REF.

WORK TRIANGLE 22'-0" MAX.

L-SHAPED KITCHEN

REF.

OVEN CABINET

REF.

4'-0" MIN.

CORRIDOR KITCHEN

I-SHAPED KITCHEN

FIGURE 1-1
Basic types of kitchen arrangements.

FIGURE 1-2
An island counter helps improve the efficiency of a kitchen. (Courtesy of Kleweno of Kansas City.)

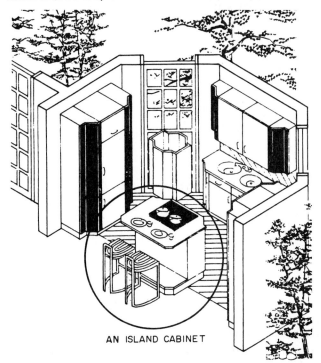

AN ISLAND CABINET

tor, and range (or surface unit and oven). Then draw elevations of each wall (Fig. 1-3).

Next draw the base cabinets and wall cabinets on these drawings (Fig. 1-4). Record the overall length of each cabinet in inches. The cabinetmaker does his/her measurements in inches rather than feet and inches. It is helpful to number each cabinet so there is some way of identifying them when you make a parts list or cut stock to size. Now draw the elevations of each cabinet on the wall elevations prepared. Decide on the location and size of drawers and doors. Notice the dashed lines on each door. The point indicates the hinge side. Be certain to locate appliances that fit below the counter top such as a dishwasher or trash compactor. When sizing cabinets that end next to a door or window, remember allowance must be made for the casing around them. Using these sizes you can have cabinets custom built to fit the space or select units from standard size production cabinets that most nearly fit. The design of this kitchen using production units is shown in Fig. 1-5. If a production cabinet is a little bit short of reaching the wall, a piece can be added to the stile to fill in the space (Fig. 1-6).

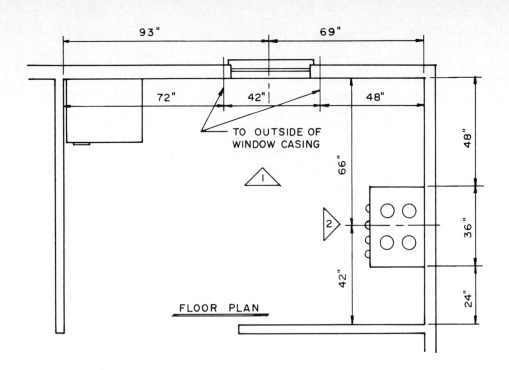

FLOOR PLAN

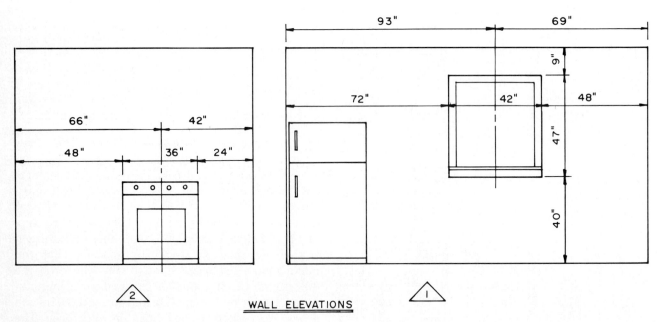

WALL ELEVATIONS

FIGURE 1-3
Begin planning a kitchen by making scale drawings of each wall.

Dividing Cabinets into Buildable Units

The designer must be certain that the cabinets are built in lengths that are easy to move and that will fit through the doorways and hallways of the building. The unit must be light enough to be carried and small enough to turn corners in a hall or room. Production units pose no problems because they are made in standard sizes ranging from 12 in. (305 mm) to 48 in. (1220 mm). They are assembled into long sections after being put in place. (See Chapter 3, Installing Cabinets.)

Custom-built units are assembled in the shop and moved to the job. They can be made to fit any length desired. It is necessary for the cabinetmaker to build units that can be moved easily into place,

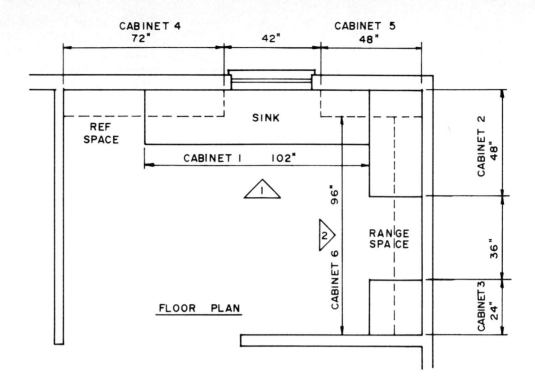

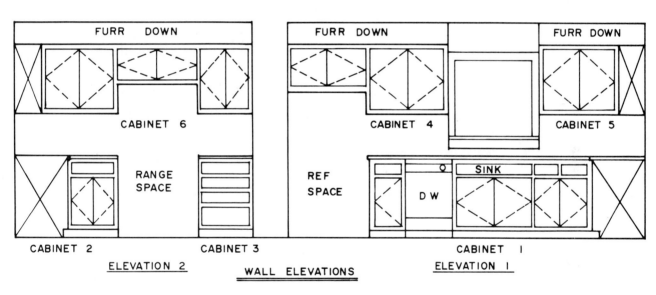

FIGURE 1-4
Draw the cabinets on each wall elevation.

though. This means a long cabinet should be built in two parts and joined on the job. For example, if the cabinet in Fig. 1-7 is determined to be too long, it can be built in two units using a split stile. A split stile is shown in Fig. 1-7.

Handling Corners

When designing cabinets, the corner presents a special challenge. There are three ways to handle the cabinets in a corner. One is to butt the ends of two cabinets together filling between them with a filler strip. This completely wastes the corner for storage (Fig. 1-8). A second way is to use a rectangular cabinet designed to fill the corner space. The cabinet on the other wall butts into it. While the space provided is hard to reach, it does provide good storage (Fig. 1-9). A third way is to use a corner cabinet with a door on a 45° angle or a 90° angle and prepare the corner cabinet to butt the adjoining cabinets. This

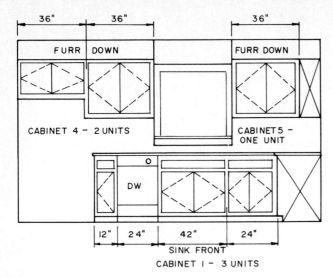

FIGURE 1-5
Give the sizes of each cabinet on the elevation of the wall.

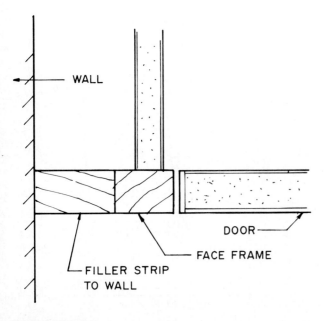

FIGURE 1-6
A filler strip is used to close the space between the wall and the stile.

space is easier to reach and is the best solution (Fig. 1-10). A lazy susan or a unit with revolving circular shelves can also be utilized in this style of corner cabinet.

Styling

The choice of the exterior appearance of cabinets is influenced somewhat by the type of house. A period-style house might use cabinets with faceframes and wood doors with recessed panels, applied molding and shaped drawer fronts (Fig. 1-11). A more contemporary house might choose frameless cabinets with a plastic laminate veneer exterior in some solid color (Fig. 1-12). Regardless of the style of house, the appearance of the cabinets is influenced by:

1. the choice of the exterior material (wood, plastic laminate, and so on);
2. the color and protective finish;
3. the use of moldings, panel construction, routed decorative edges, and banding material;
4. whether faceframes are used or some form of frameless cabinet is chosen;
5. whether the cabinets run to the ceiling or are furred down (a boxed-in area extending from the ceiling to the top of the wall cabinets); and
6. the selection of hinges, pulls, and other decorative hardware (Fig. 1-13).

Considerations as to the texture of the exterior material, the shadows cast by molding and recessed areas, and the shape of the recessed panels and molding are important to the total solution. Companies mass producing units have catalogs showing the many designs available. Retail outlets, such as your local building materials dealer, will have many of these units on display on the sales floor. Custom cabinet companies will also have examples of the jobs they have completed. They can also build to your design or reproduce cabinets you found in a magazine or other source.

CUSTOM-BUILT CABINET SIZES

Custom-built cabinets can be sized to suit the desires of the customer. Most shops have basic sizes they recommend. A typical custom-built cabinet would have the following specifications:

1. the lower cabinet is 24 in. deep and $35\frac{1}{4}$ in. high (a $\frac{3}{4}$ in. thick top makes the total base 36 in. high);
2. the top is 25 in. wide;
3. the faceframe is $\frac{3}{4}$ in. by 2 in.;
4. the upper cabinets are 12 in. deep and from 30 in. to 42 in. high except for special units above a sink or stove;
5. the wall cabinets are 18 in. above the base cabinet; and bathroom sink vanities are 21 in. deep and 32 in. from the floor to the top [The top is 22 in. wide (Fig. 1-14).]

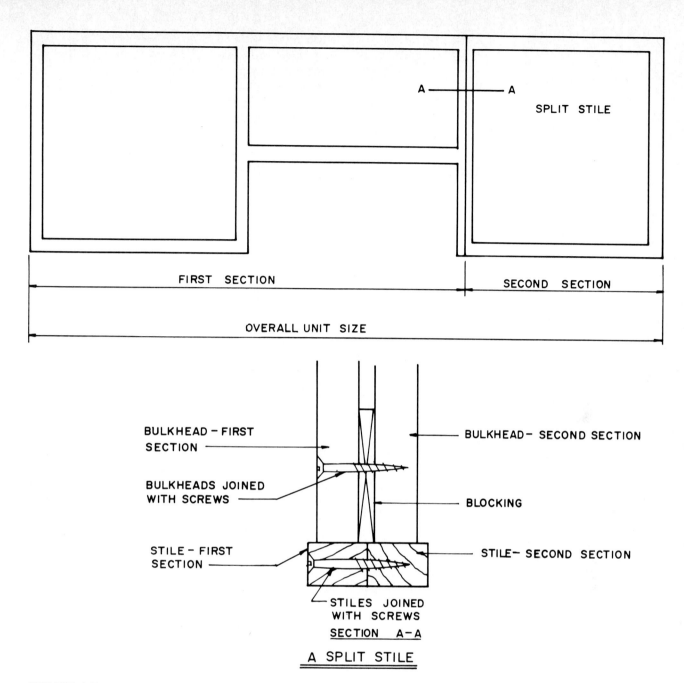

SPLIT STILE

FIRST SECTION

SECOND SECTION

OVERALL UNIT SIZE

BULKHEAD – FIRST SECTION

BULKHEADS JOINED WITH SCREWS

STILE – FIRST SECTION

BULKHEAD – SECOND SECTION

BLOCKING

STILE – SECOND SECTION

STILES JOINED WITH SCREWS

SECTION A–A

A SPLIT STILE

FIGURE 1-7
A split stile is used to separate long cabinets into two parts that can be easily joined on the job.

STANDARD PRODUCTION CABINET SIZES

The standard sizes of American modular cabinet units are shown in Fig. 1-15. *Modular cabinets* are those built to standard sizes that have been agreed upon by a trade organization representing cabinet manufacturers such as the National Kitchen Cabinet Association. All cabinets built by members of

this organization are certified by the NKCA and must meet the standards set forth in the American National Standards Institute Standard ANSI A161.1-1980. Their certification label is placed on cabinets meeting these standards (Fig. 1-16). Certified cabinets are also subject to flame spread ratings. These ratings are established by testing materials used in cabinet construction to determine the rate at which they will burn. The tests compare to the rate

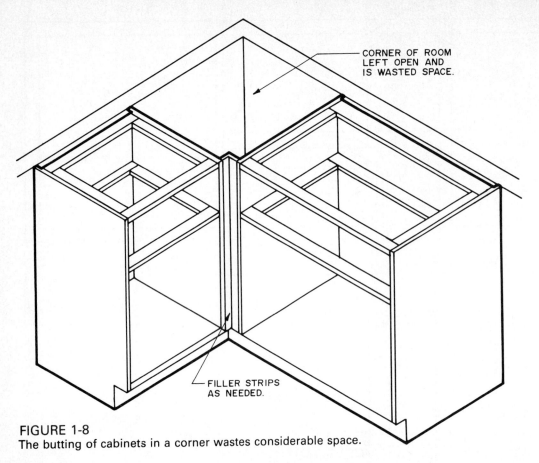

CORNER OF ROOM
LEFT OPEN AND
IS WASTED SPACE.

FILLER STRIPS
AS NEEDED.

FIGURE 1-8
The butting of cabinets in a corner wastes considerable space.

FIGURE 1-9
One base unit is built to fill the corner. The adjoining unit butts against it. A filler strip is used as needed. Note that these units use a faceframe.

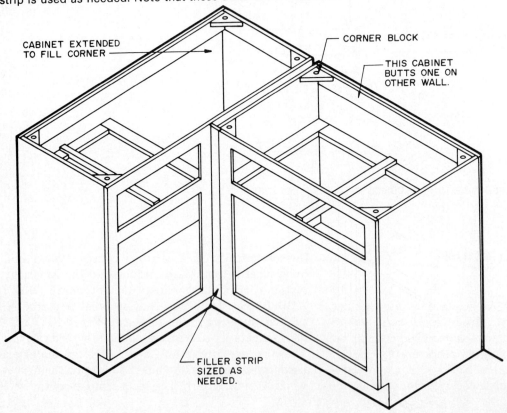

CABINET EXTENDED
TO FILL CORNER

CORNER BLOCK

THIS CABINET
BUTTS ONE ON
OTHER WALL.

FILLER STRIP
SIZED AS
NEEDED.

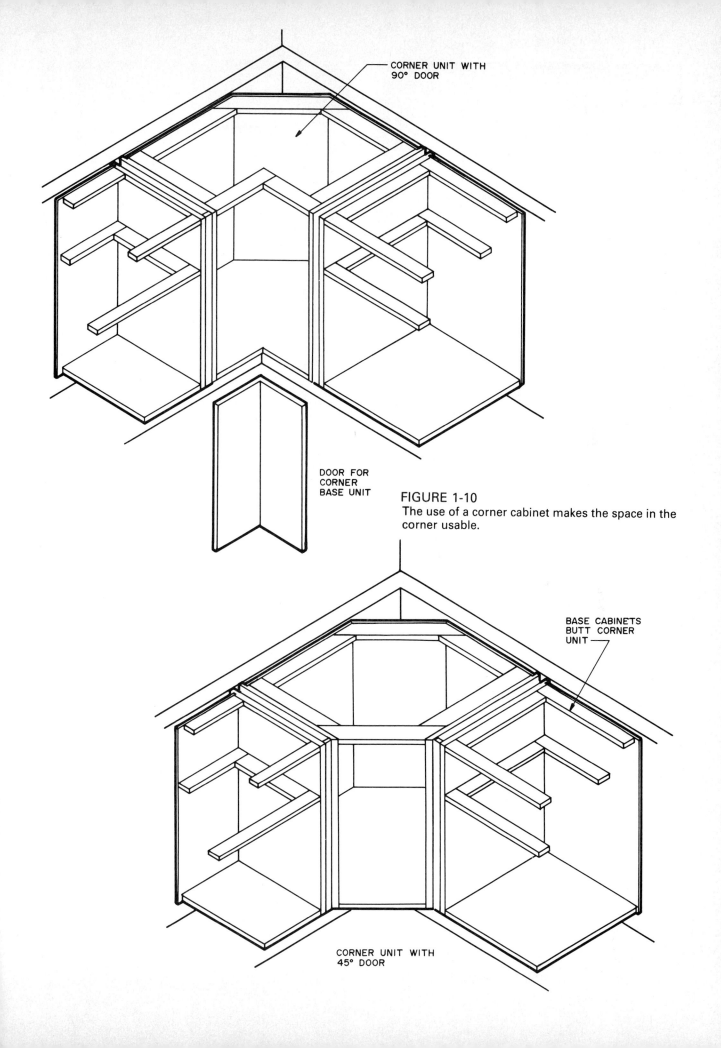

CORNER UNIT WITH
90° DOOR

DOOR FOR
CORNER
BASE UNIT

FIGURE 1-10
The use of a corner cabinet makes the space in the
corner usable.

BASE CABINETS
BUTT CORNER
UNIT

CORNER UNIT WITH
45° DOOR

FIGURE 1-11
This wall of cabinets exhibits informal balance. The side with the stove has the most cabinets and is the heaviest. However, it is balanced by the long sink counter and the refrigerator with cabinets above it. (*Courtesy of Connor Forest Products.*)

FIGURE 1-12
These cabinets are built without faceframes. (Courtesy of Kleweno of Kansas City.)

FIGURE 1-14
Standard sizes for kitchen cabinets and bath lavatories.

FIGURE 1-13
Pulls are designed to blend with the style of furniture.

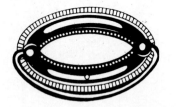

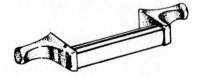

BATH VANITY   KITCHEN CABINETS

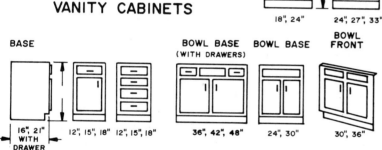

WALL CABINETS

12"

30"

9", 12", 15"
18", 21", 24"

27", 30", 33"
36", 42", 48"

18"

24", 27", 30"
33", 36", 39", 42"

15"

30", 33", 36", 39"

12"

30", 33", 36"

CORNER WALL CABINETS

24"   24"

30"

24", 30", 36"
42", 48"

BASE CABINETS

ALSO OFFERED AS SINK BASES WITHOUT DRAWERS

34 1/2"

24"

9", 12", 15"
18", 21", 24"

27", 30", 33"
36", 42", 48"

12", 15", 18"
21", 24"

CORNER BASE

OPEN

30", 36"
42", 48"

LAZY SUSAN

34 1/2"

36" REQUIRED ALONG EACH WALL

UTILITY
12", 24", DEPTH

84"

18", 24"

OVEN CABINET
24" DEPTH

CUT OPENING TO SUIT

24", 27", 33"

VANITY CABINETS

BASE

16", 21"
WITH DRAWER

12", 15", 18"

12", 15", 18"

BOWL BASE
(WITH DRAWERS)

36", 42", 48"

BOWL BASE

24", 30"

BOWL FRONT

30", 36"

FIGURE 1-15
Standard modular kitchen cabinet sizes.

FIGURE 1-16
Cabinets manufactured to ANSI A161.1-1980 requirements are certified by the National Kitchen Cabinet Association.

at which flame spreads on a material with the rate of untreated red oak. Following are the classes of flame spread:

Classification	Flame Spread
Class I or A	0–25
Class II or B	26–75
Class III or C	76–200

Certified cabinets must have a Class C flame spread rating of 200 or less. This relates to combustible doors, exposed end panels, bottoms and countertops. Cabinet faceframes, mullions, and toe strips are exempted. Those meeting this standard have a certifying seal placed on them (Fig. 1-17). Wood can be treated with chemicals to improve its flame spread rating.

Cabinets are divided into wall cabinets, base cabinets, vanity cabinets, and tall oven and utility

FLAME RATING OF 200 OR LESS ON ALL EXPOSED SURFACES

MANUFACTURER COMPLIES

FIGURE 1-17
This seal certifies the cabinet has a flame spread rating of 200 or less. (Courtesy of National Kitchen Cabinet Association.)

FIGURE 1-18
Standard cabinet heights and widths. (Courtesy of Architectural Woodwork Institute.)

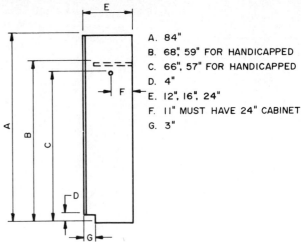

A. 84"
B. 68", 59" FOR HANDICAPPED
C. 66", 57" FOR HANDICAPPED
D. 4"
E. 12", 16", 24"
F. 11" MUST HAVE 24" CABINET
G. 3"

TALL CABINETS

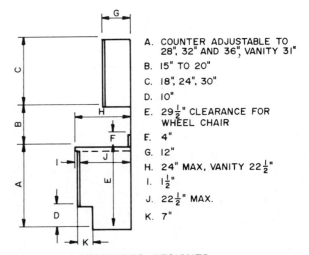

A. COUNTER ADJUSTABLE TO 28", 32" AND 36", VANITY 31"
B. 15" TO 20"
C. 18", 24", 30"
D. 10"
E. 29½" CLEARANCE FOR WHEEL CHAIR
F. 4"
G. 12"
H. 24" MAX, VANITY 22½"
I. 1½"
J. 22½" MAX.
K. 7"

CABINETS DESIGNED FOR THE HANDICAPPED

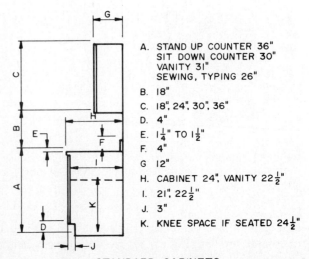

A. STAND UP COUNTER 36" SIT DOWN COUNTER 30" VANITY 31" SEWING, TYPING 26"
B. 18"
C. 18", 24", 30", 36"
D. 4"
E. 1¼" TO 1½"
F. 4"
G. 12"
H. CABINET 24", VANITY 22½"
I. 21", 22½"
J. 3"
K. KNEE SPACE IF SEATED 24½"

STANDARD CABINETS

cabinets. The main components making up these units are drawers, doors, front frames, shelves, unit sides, backs and bottoms, bases, tops, and hardware.

Doors are made from plywood, particleboard, medium-density fiberboard and lumber. They may be flat, have designs routed in them, have molding overlays, or raised panels and inserts such as glass or woven reed or wood slats. Doors are discussed in Chapter 12.

Facefr900s are usually ¾ in. thick when finished. They are usually solid wood and make what is called a *bound cabinet*. Some cabinet styles do not use a faceframe. They are referred to as *unbound cabinets*.

Drawer fronts usually match the doors and faceframes. Sometimes doors and drawers are made of a material that sharply contrasts with the faceframe such as white plastic laminated door and drawer fronts over a natural finished wood faceframe.

Cabinet sides are usually $\frac{3}{16}$ to $\frac{3}{4}$ in. thick plywood, particleboard, or medium-density fiberboard. Exposed sides are finished to match the faceframe.

Shelves are ½ to ¾ in. thick and made from plywood, lumber, particleboard or medium-density fiberboard. All exposed surfaces are finished to protect against moisture. Sometimes the shelves are dadoed into the sides of cabinets while others are made adjustable. Shelves are discussed in Chapter 14.

The standard dimensions for cabinets are shown in Fig. 1-18. These represent the most comfortable height for the majority of people. Custom-built cabinets can be higher or lower as desired by the owner. Special considerations for accommodating the handicapped are necessary.

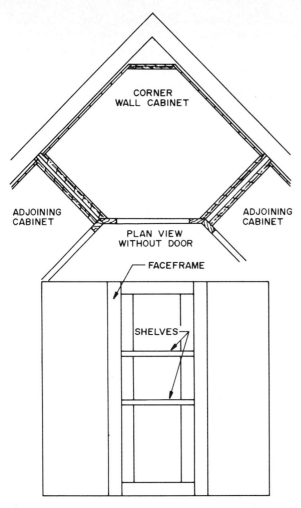

FIGURE 1-19
A special wall cabinet is used when they have to turn a corner.

Base Units

The base cabinet supports sinks, surface cooking units, and many small portable appliances. Below the top is considerable storage in the form of drawers, shelves, or special accessory storage units. Base cabinets at the sink or range may contain only a front and bottom. Special units are built to fit in the corner. The corner has a lot of dead space and requires special planning. See Figs. 1-8, 1-9, and 1-10.

The widths of modular cabinets are based on a 3 in. module and can range from 9 to 48 in. Custom-built cabinets are made to fit the exact wallspace. Both types have a variety of drawer and door combinations. Base cabinets are usually $22\frac{1}{2}$ in. to 24 in. deep from the back to the front of the faceframe, with the top being 24 to 25 in. deep. Bathroom vanities are $22\frac{1}{2}$ in. deep. Standard kitchen cabinet base units are $34\frac{1}{2}$ in. high without the top. Any counter to be used from a chair is 30 in. high. For people in a wheelchair the kitchen counter should be adjustable or replaceable to provide alternative heights of 28, 32, and 36 in. measured from the floor to the top of the counter. (This includes the sink cabinets.) The door handles in base units should be placed as near the top of the door as possible. One 30 in. section of base cabinet should be clear below so a wheelchair can move under it allowing a person to work on the counter. Standards for planning for the handicapped can be found in ANSI A117.1-1980, *Specifications For Making Buildings and Facilities Accessible To, And Usable By, Physical Handicapped People*. See Fig. 1-18 for sizes.

FIGURE 1-20
Many special accessories are used to improve the efficient use of cabinet space. (Courtesy of American Woodmark Corp.)

Wall Cabinets

Wall cabinets are securely mounted on the wall above the base cabinet. They are usually 12 in. deep from the back to the front of the faceframe. They are made in standard widths from 9 in. to 48 in. A variety of heights are available, but 30 in. is the most common. A special corner unit is made for use when they have to turn a corner (Fig. 1-19).

To serve the handicapped at least one shelf must be not more than 48 in. above the floor. Door pulls on the wall cabinets should be mounted as close to the bottom of the door as possible.

Oven and Utility Cabinets

These are tall cabinets generally 84 in. high. Oven cabinets are designed to hold an oven which is separated from the surface cooking unit. They are 24, 27, and 33 in. wide and 24 to 25 in. deep. Space above and below the oven opening is used for shelves and serves as a pantry or for general storage purposes. Utility cabinets are usually 12, 16, or 24 in. deep and 18 or 24 in. wide.

Special Accessories

Cabinet manufacturers provide a wide array of special storage units to increase the efficiency of the space. These include drawers for holding silverware, wire racks for pots and pans as well as units to hold canned goods, spices, and cleaning materials (Fig. 1-20). Hardware and accessories used in cabinets certified by the National Kitchen Cabinet Association must meet the standards set forth in the American National Standards on cabinet hardware.

2

CABINET CONSTRUCTION

While there are a number of ways cabinets are built, the techniques illustrated in this chapter are recommended by professional organizations whose members mass produce cabinets of all kinds. There is always room for individual initiative and creative solutions, but the end result should always be a well-designed, functional, and structurally sound cabinet.

SURFACE VISIBILITY

The parts of cabinets can be identified by surface visibility. *Exposed surfaces* are those that are visible when doors and drawers are closed, behind glass doors, cabinet bottoms more than 42 in. (1066 mm) off the floor, and tops of cabinets lower than 78 in. (1980 mm) above the floor. They require good-guality materials because they will be seen. *Semiexposed surfaces* are surfaces that become visible when opaque doors are open or drawers are extended and cabinet bottoms more than 30 in. (762 mm) and less than 42 in. (1066 mm) above the floor. They should also be good-quality materials. *Concealed surfaces* include surfaces not visible after installation, such as bottoms of cabinets less than 30 in. (762 mm)

above the floor, cabinet tops more than 78 in. (1980 mm) above the floor, and stretchers, blocking, and components concealed by drawers. These parts can be made from any species of wood that is adequate for the job. In some cases metal and plastic parts are used instead of wood.

CONSTRUCTION WITH A FACEFRAME

Cabinets can be constructed in several ways. In this chapter you will be shown several different construction methods. One type that is widely used has an exposed faceframe (Fig. 2-1, page 16). The carcass of this type of cabinet is ¾-in. (18-mm) plywood or reconstituted wood panels. The faceframe, doors, and drawer fronts are solid wood.

Construction details and identification of the parts of this type of cabinet are shown in Fig. 2-2. *Exterior bulkheads* are those that are visible. *Interior bulkheads* are those that meet another cabinet or butt against a wall or appliance. *Partitions* are vertical interior dividers. The *faceframe* is a solid wood frame nailed or glued to the front edges of the carcass. Horizontal members of the faceframe are called *rails* and vertical members or *stiles. Mullions*

15

FIGURE 2-1
These bathroom cabinets have a faceframe and doors with raised panels. (Courtesy of American Woodmark Corp.)

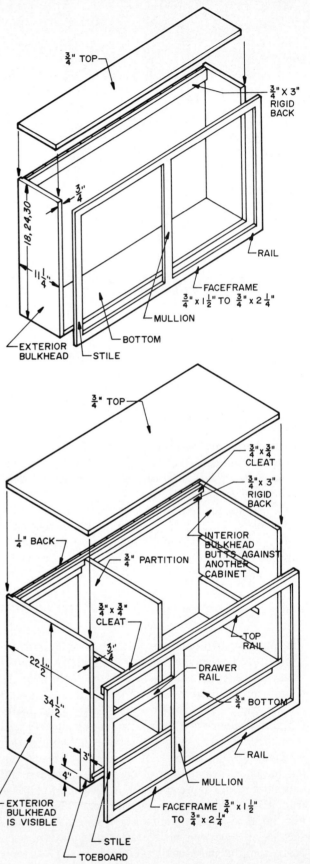

FIGURE 2-2
Conventionally built cabinet with faceframes.

are vertical members that run between doors or drawers. The *rigid back* is a brace used to strengthen the cabinet. The *cleats* are used to fasten the top to the base. Corner blocks can be used instead of cleats.

The base unit is built by cutting the bottom, bulkheads, and partitions to size, cutting $\frac{1}{4}$ in. (6-mm)-deep dadoes for the bottom and shelves. A rabbet $\frac{1}{4} \times \frac{1}{2}$ in. is made in the back edge of the exterior bulkhead for the back. A typical set of bulkheads and a partition are shown in Fig. 2-3. The exterior bulkhead is the full width of the cabinet. The partition and interior bulkhead are $\frac{1}{2}$ in. (12 mm) narrower because the cabinet back is nailed directly on to them rather than having a rabbet as is the case with the exterior bulkhead. Although the base unit can be assembled without dadoes by using nailed butt joints, the dadoes produce a stronger cabinet. The exterior bulkheads are glued to the bottom and shelves. They may be nailed with finishing nails. If this is done, set the nailheads and fill the holes with a filler that matches the color of the finished cabinet. Premium-quality cabinets should be glued and clamped with no exposed nail holes. The interior bulkheads and partitions are nailed to the shelves and bottom with 6d finishing nails. Interior-bulkheads and partitions are nailed to the shelves and bottom. No glue is necessary.

Faceframe construction can be used with lipped, flush, and overlay doors and drawers (Fig. 2-4). The lip used is normally $\frac{3}{8} \times \frac{3}{8}$ in. (9 × 9 mm). Flush construction places the outer face of the doors and drawers flush with the outer surface of the faceframe (Fig. 2-5). *Overlay doors* may be of the flush overlay or reveal overlay types. The flush overlay door and draw front hide the faceframe completely. The reveal overlay design permits some of the faceframe to be seen.

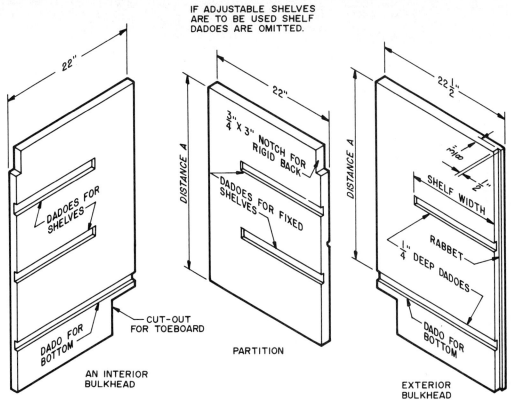

IF ADJUSTABLE SHELVES
ARE TO BE USED SHELF
DADOES ARE OMITTED.

22"

DISTANCE A

DADOES FOR
SHELVES

DADO FOR
BOTTOM

CUT-OUT
FOR TOEBOARD

AN INTERIOR
BULKHEAD

22"

DISTANCE A

3/4" X 3" NOTCH FOR
RIGID BACK

DADOES FOR FIXED
SHELVES

PARTITION

22 1/2"

DISTANCE A

3/8"

1/2"

SHELF WIDTH

RABBET

1/4" DEEP DADOES

DADO FOR
BOTTOM

EXTERIOR
BULKHEAD

FIGURE 2-3
Typical bulkheads and partitions.

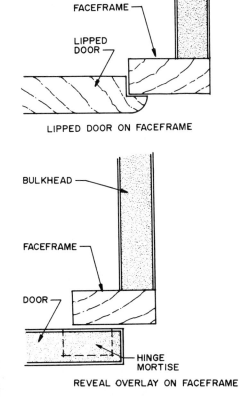

BULKHEAD

FACEFRAME

LIPPED
DOOR

LIPPED DOOR ON FACEFRAME

BULKHEAD

FACEFRAME

DOOR

REVEAL OVERLAY ON FACEFRAME

HINGE
MORTISE

BULKHEAD

FACEFRAME

DOOR

OVERLAY ON FACEFRAME

DOOR

FACEFRAME

FACEFRAME HINGE

FIGURE 2-4
Types of door and drawer construction used with faceframe
construction.

Conventional flush construction with face frame ■

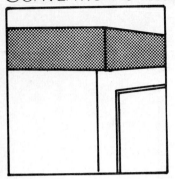

With this style of construction, all door and drawer faces are flush with the face of the cabinet. This style is highly functional and allows the use of different thicknesses of door and drawer fronts. Conventional as well as concealed hinges are available for a variety of door thicknesses.

This is the most expensive of the four styles shown in this publication due to the increased care necessary in the fitting and aligning of the doors and drawers plus the cost of providing the face frame. This style does not lend itself to the economical use of plastic laminate covering.

Note: A, B, C, D, E designates appropriate hardware compatible to particular cabinet construction.
SEE FIG. 2-20

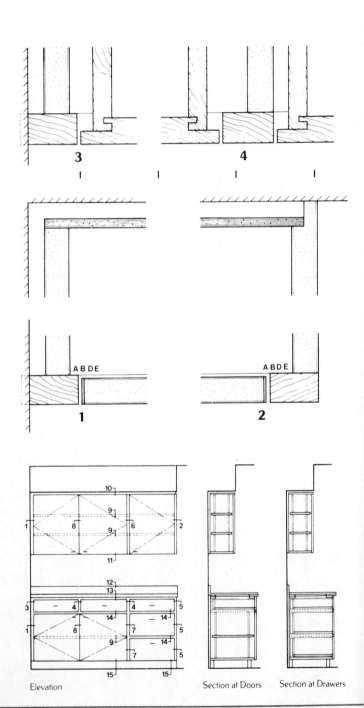

FIGURE 2-5
Conventional flush construction with a faceframe. (Courtesy of Architectural Woodwork Institute.)

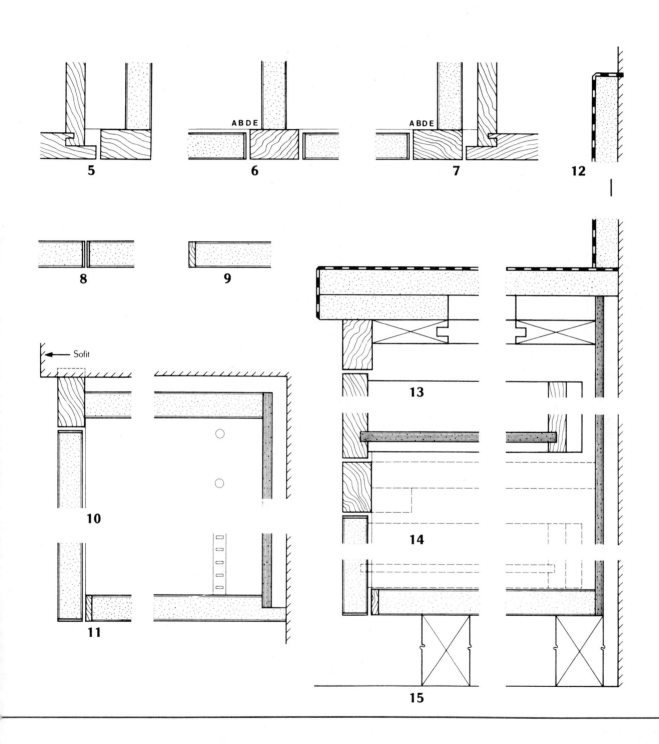

5 6 7 12

ABDE

ABDE

8 9

Sofit

10

11

13

14

15

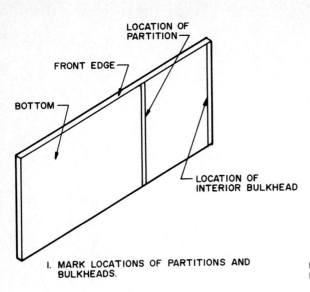

I. MARK LOCATIONS OF PARTITIONS AND BULKHEADS.

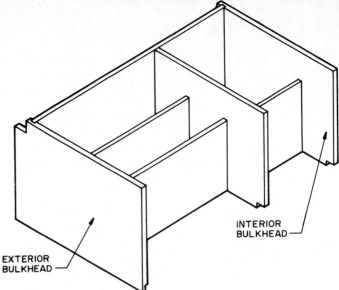

3. JOIN THE INTERIOR AND EXTERIOR BULKHEAD TO THE CARCASS.

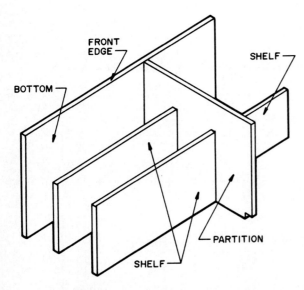

2. NAIL PARTITION TO BOTTOM. NAIL SHELVES TO PARTITION.

FIGURE 2-6
Steps to assemble a cabinet.

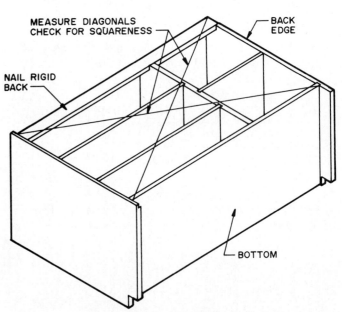

4. TURN CARCASS OVER AND NAIL RIGID BACK, CHECK FOR SQUARENESS AND NAIL $\frac{1}{4}$" BACK IN PLACE.

Assembling the Base Unit

Start by marking the location of partitions on the bottom. Then stand the bottom on its back edge. Nail the partition to the bottom with 6d finishing nails (Fig. 2-6). Then insert the shelves into the dadoes in the partition and nail. Next join the interior and exterior bulkheads to the bottom. Make cer-

tain that they are flush with the front edge of the cabinet bottom. Turn the unit over and nail the rigid back in place. Measure the diagonals to be certain that the unit is square as the rigid back is being nailed. Then place the back on the unit and nail or staple. Use 2d finishing nails or $\frac{3}{4}$-in. staples. Again make absolutely certain that the unit is square before nailing the back in place. Turn the unit over and nail the toe board in place. The unit is now ready for the faceframe.

Assembling the Faceframe

The faceframe is usually assembled using $\frac{3}{8}$-in. (10-mm) dowels. After the faceframe members are cut to length, locate and bore the dowel holes. Assemble on a large flat surface such as a table or on the floor. Begin by putting glue in the dowel holes with a small brush. Join the inside pieces first and work toward the outer rails and stiles (Fig. 2-7). Then clamp using long bar clamps. Clamp just tight enough to close the joints. Check to make certain that the faceframe is square and flat on the clamps. If the clamps cause the faceframe to bow, clamp it to the table or the bar clamp with C-clamps so that it stays flat.

Attaching the Faceframe

The faceframe can be attached to the carcass with finishing nails. However, its appearance is improved if it is glued instead.

Place the carcass on its back on two sawhorses. Place the assembled faceframe on the carcass and check to see that it fits. If it fits properly, remove the faceframe and apply adhesive to the front edges of the carcass. Lay the faceframe in position and begin clamping it to the carcass with bar clamps. Begin at one end of the carcass and apply clamps toward the other end. Make certain that the faceframe is flat

against the edge of the carcass. Use as many clamps as necessary to assure good contact (Fig. 2-8).

If you decide to nail the faceframe instead of clamping, follow the steps just mentioned except that you nail it to the carcass with 6d finishing nails. Begin nailing at a lower corner and nail one end. Then work your way to the other end, nailing into the top and bottom rails and partitions (Fig. 2-9).

Cleaning Up after Assembly

After the adhesive has dried, the faceframe and exterior panels can be sanded and excess glue removed. Sanding can also reduce slight variations in the joint so that the faceframe is flat and doors and drawers fit tightly against them. Sanding must be done very carefully or more damage than good might occur. Since the grain of the stock in the faceframe meets at right angles, careless sanding can produce across-grain scratches. To minimize these, sand the horizontal members first, sanding lightly across the joint as shown in Fig. 2-10. Then sand the vertical rail, removing any scratches. Work lightly back and forth in each direction until the joint is flush. Then give the vertical member a final sanding, being very careful not to run over on the horizontal member.

Constructing a Wall Cabinet

The bathroom wall cabinet in Fig. 2-11 is typical of units having solid wood faceframes. The doors are

FIGURE 2-7
Assemble and clamp the faceframe.

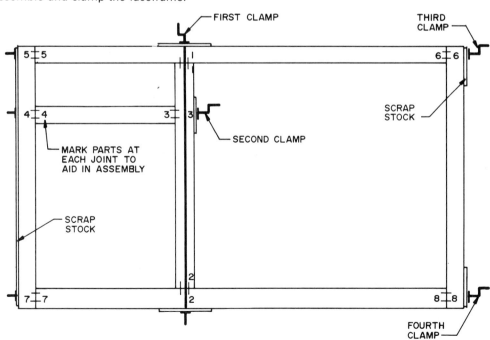

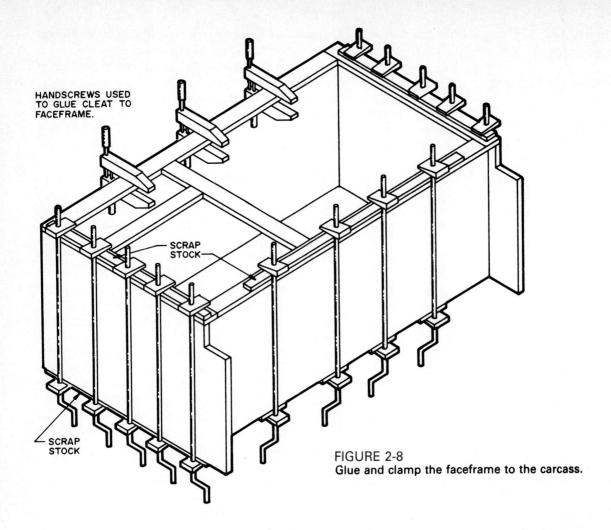

HANDSCREWS USED
TO GLUE CLEAT TO
FACEFRAME.

SCRAP
STOCK

SCRAP
STOCK

FIGURE 2-8
Glue and clamp the faceframe to the carcass.

FIGURE 2-9
Suggested order for nailing a faceframe to the carcass.

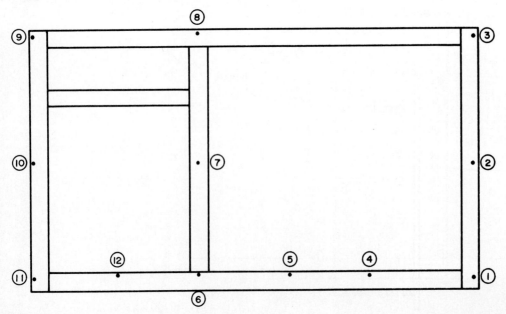

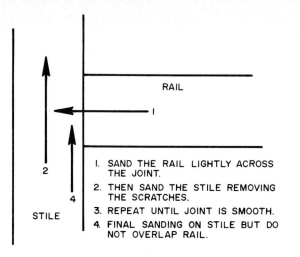

RAIL

STILE

1. SAND THE RAIL LIGHTLY ACROSS THE JOINT.
2. THEN SAND THE STILE REMOVING THE SCRATCHES.
3. REPEAT UNTIL JOINT IS SMOOTH.
4. FINAL SANDING ON STILE BUT DO NOT OVERLAP RAIL.

FIGURE 2-10
Steps to sand faceframe joints so that the surfaces are flush.

FIGURE 2-11
The bathroom wall cabinet has a faceframe and lipped doors. (Courtesy of American Woodmark Corp.)

lipped and hung with semiconcealed hinges. Several designs for wall cabinets using faceframes are shown in Fig. 2-12. These designs can use lipped, flush, or overlay doors. The design of the wall cabinet generally is the same as used for the base cabinet.

Doors and Drawers

If it is desired to have a continuous grain, cut as many doors and drawer fronts as possible from a single sheet of plywood (Fig. 2-13). If drawer fronts are to be from solid wood, try to find stock long enough to enable you to cut all the drawer fronts from one board.

Cabinets with faceframes can have flush or overlay-type doors and drawers (Fig. 2-4) or lipped or overlay doors and drawers (Fig. 2-5). The lipped door uses a semiconcealed or wraparound hinge. The overlay door may use a faceframe hinge that is set into a 35-mm-diameter hole in the door. The flush style has all the doors and drawers flush with the front of the faceframe. This permits the use of drawer fronts and doors that are different thicknesses. Conventional as well as concealed hinges can be used. (See Chapter 12 for more information on hinges.)

The flush style is more expensive than most because of the extra care necessary to fit and align the doors and drawers into the openings in the faceframe. The crack between these must be uniform and parallel on all sides. The faceframe adds to the cost when compared to units without faceframes. This style does not lend itself to the economical use

FIGURE 2-12
Typical construction details for wall cabinets with faceframes.

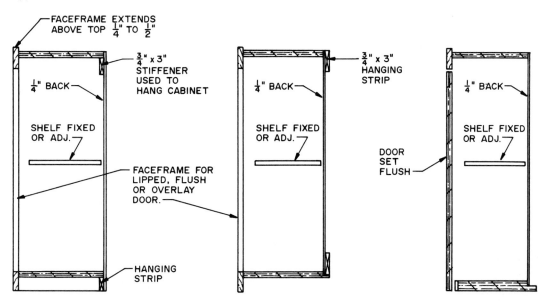

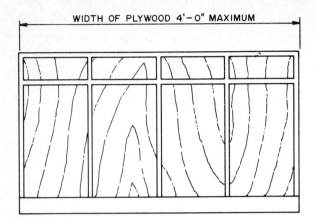

WIDTH OF PLYWOOD 4'–0" MAXIMUM

FIGURE 2-13
To have a continuous grain pattern cut the doors and drawers from a single sheet of plywood.

of plastic laminate covering. Hardwood plywood and solid wood are commonly used.

Lipped drawer and door fronts are usually $\frac{3}{4}$ in. (18 mm) thick and have a $\frac{3}{8}$-in. (9-mm) lip. The lip should be planned so that it clears the faceframe at least $\frac{1}{8}$ in. (3 mm) on all sides.

The overlay door is set over the faceframe a distance recommended by the hinge manufacturer. This is generally about $1\frac{13}{32}$ in. (36 mm).

Lipped doors often are made with a solid wood frame to avoid the problem of seeing the edge grain of the plywood, particleboard ,or medium-density fiberboard that is often used (Fig. 2-14).

Drawers are usually hung using metal side-mounted slides or a single center-mounted slide. Detailed information on drawers and doors is given in Chapters 12 and 13.

FIGURE 2-14
This lavatory cabinet uses solid wood drawer fronts and doors. (Courtesy of American Woodmark Corp.)

Shelves

Shelves may be fixed or adjustable. Fixed shelves are strongest if set in a $\frac{1}{4}$-in. (6-mm) dado, but can be butted to a partition and nailed. If plywood or a reconstituted wood product is used, the front edge is often banded with solid wood, metal, or plastic. Details on shelf construction are given in Chapter 14.

Making a Split Stile

When a cabinet is too long to be made easily as a single unit, it can be made as two units and joined with a split stile. The details for this are shown in Fig. 2-15. When installing the wood screws, be certain to drill shank and pilot holes. Bolts can also be used. However, the nut must be counterbored. To join the cabinets, locate three screws or bolts vertically about $1\frac{1}{2}$ in. (38 mm) behind the faceframe and three more in the rear about $1\frac{1}{2}$ in. (38 mm) in from the cabinet back.

Prepare the faceframe so that it overlaps the adjoining interior bulkheads $\frac{1}{8}$ in. (3 mm). This will allow the faceframes to be tightly joined by the screws or bolts. It is easiest to join the cabinets if

FIGURE 2-15
A split stile is used when two cabinets are joined to form a single long unit.

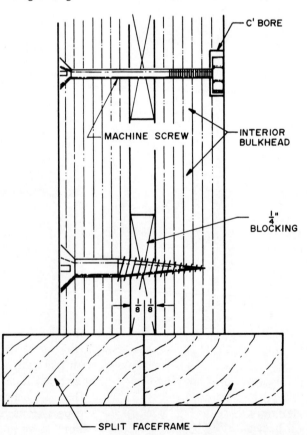

they are lying on their backs on sawhorses. The cabinets can now be separated if they have to be moved to a distant location and rejoined at that point.

An increasing number of cabinets are being built without a faceframe. These types include flush construction without a faceframe, flush overlay, and reveal overlay.

CONSTRUCTION WITHOUT A FACEFRAME

This type of construction is often called European style. The cabinets have a sleeker look (Fig. 2-16). The end panels and bulkheads have their exposed edges banded. The cost is less because the faceframe, which is time consuming to build and install, is eliminated. The common types of cabinets using this construction are the flush, flush overlay, and reveal overlay.

FIGURE 2-16
These cabinets are built without faceframes. (Courtesy of Kleweno of Kansas City.)

Flush Construction

Details for flush construction without a faceframe are shown in Fig. 2-17. The overall design is the same as that described for cabinets with faceframes. The cabinet must be accurately built and the doors and drawer fronts carefully sized so that the space between them and the bulkheads and partitions is uniform on all sides. This style of cabinet does not lend itself to the economical use of plastic laminate covering.

Flush Overlay Construction

Flush overlay construction does not use the conventional faceframe (Fig. 2-18, pages 28, 29). It is built much like the conventional construction without a faceframe. It offers a clean, contemporary look because only the drawer fronts and doors are visible. This style lends itself to the economical use of plastic laminates. When hardwood plywood is used, the grain matching of the fronts can be achieved by cutting all the pieces from the same panel. Conventional or concealed hinges can be used (Fig. 2-18).

Reveal Overlay Construction

In this style the drawer fronts and doors are sized so that the edge of the end panels and bulkheads is revealed. This provides an interesting depth and shadow lines around each drawer and door. It can be built using hardwood plywood or plastic laminate construction. The reveal is usually $\frac{3}{8}$ in., although it could be a maximum of $\frac{1}{2}$ in. if desired. Conventional or concealed hinges can be used (Fig. 2-19, pages 30, 31).

HARDWARE

The chart in Fig. 2-20, page 32, will assist in the selection of hinges generally used for commercial construction.

32-MILLIMETER CARCASS SYSTEM

The European 32-mm system is finding increasing use in cabinet construction as a replacement for the more traditional dado and rabbet methods. It is a much faster way to prepare to join two parts of a cabinet together. The system involves drilling dowel holes spaced 32, 64, or 96 mm center to center along the butting edges of the carcass. These are drilled using a multiple drilling machine that makes it possible to drill simultaneously many holes uniformly spaced (Fig. 2-21, page 33). It also makes it easy to install the many special accessories and interior hardware used in cabinets. It eliminates the need for elaborate jigs and fixtures to hold the cabinet during the assembly operation.

This system requires the use of precision woodworking machinery which permits fast setups and accurate machining. Specially designed hardware

Conventional flush construction without face frame ■

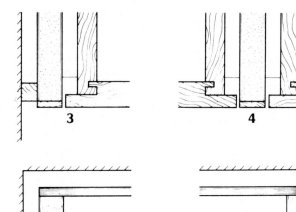

The design features of this casework style are the same as conventional flush with face frame except that the face frame has been eliminated resulting in a cost savings. This style also does not lend itself to the economical use of plastic laminate covering.

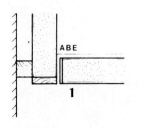

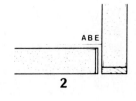

Note: A, B, C, D, E designates appropriate hardware compatible to particular cabinet construction.
SEE FIG. 2-20.

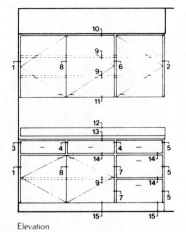

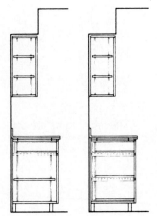

Elevation Section at Doors Section at Drawers

FIGURE 2-17
Conventional flush construction without a faceframe. (Courtesy of Architectural Woodwork Institute.)

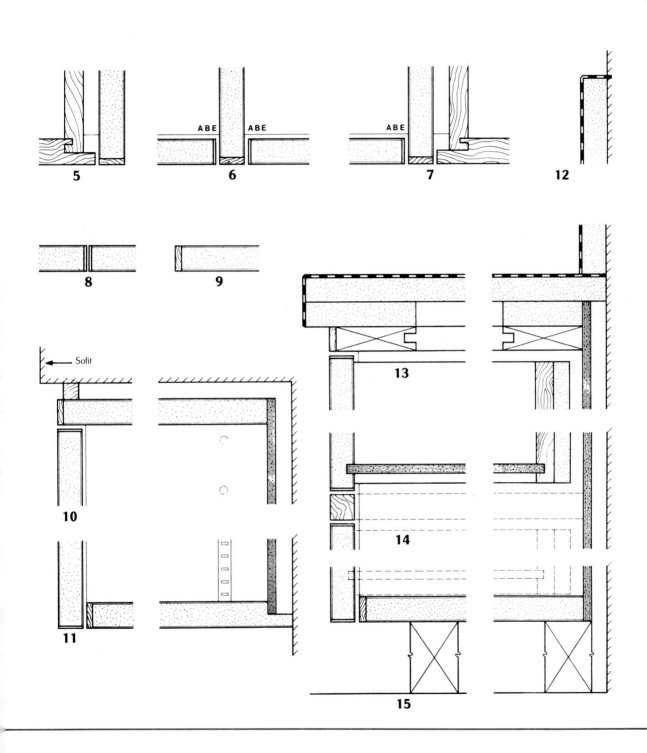

5

6

ABE   ABE

7

ABE

12

8

9

Sofit

10

11

13

14

15

Flush overlay construction ■

Flush overlay construction offers a very clean, contemporary look since only the doors and drawer fronts are visible in elevation. When specified, grain matching between doors and drawer fronts can be achieved by having all pieces cut from the same panel. This style is increasingly popular and lends itself well to the use of plastic laminate for exposed surfaces. Conventional as well as concealed hinges are available for a variety of door thicknesses.

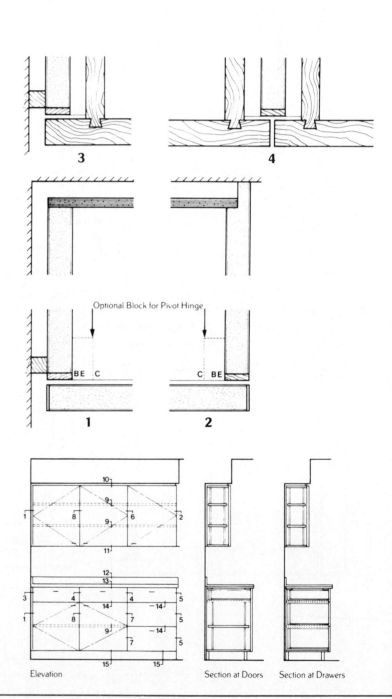

Note: A, B, C, D, E designates appropriate hardware compatible to particular cabinet construction. SEE FIG. 2-20.

FIGURE 2-18
Flush overlay construction. (Courtesy of Architectural Woodwork Institute.)

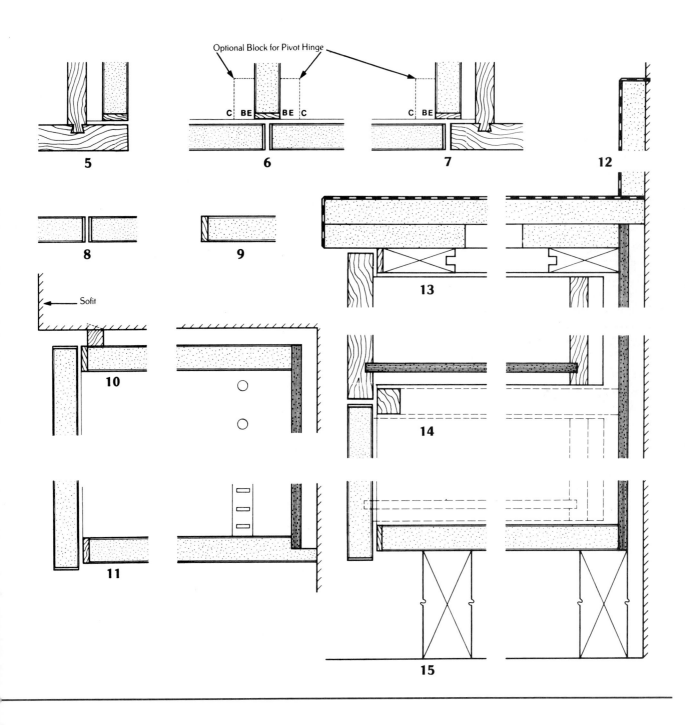

Optional Block for Pivot Hinge

5

C BE BE C

6

C BE

7

12

8

9

Sofit

10

13

14

11

15

Reveal overlay construction ■

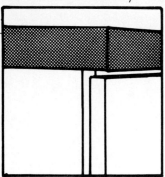

In this style, the separation between doors and drawer fronts is accented by the reveal. The style is equally suited to either wood or plastic laminate construction. Although the detail shown here incorporates a reveal at all horizontal and vertical joints, this can be varied by the designer. It should be noted that a reveal over ½ inch would require the addition of a face frame and, therefore, increases the cost. The addition of a face frame would also change the hinge requirements. With or without a face frame, this style allows the use of conventional or concealed hinges.

Note: A, B, C, D, E designates appropriate hardware compatible to particular cabinet construction.
SEE FIG. 2-20.

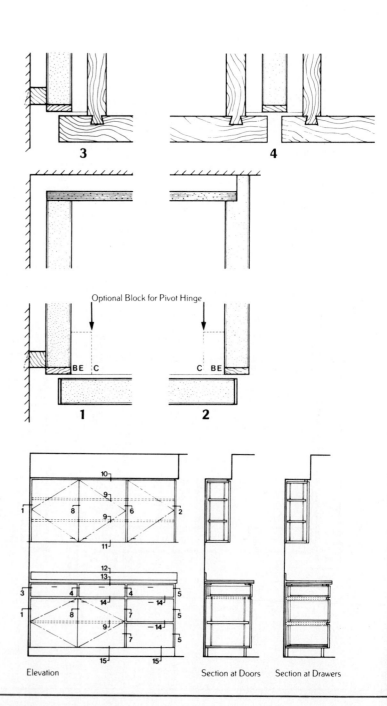

FIGURE 2-19
Reveal overlay construction. (Courtesy of Architectural Woodwork Institute.)

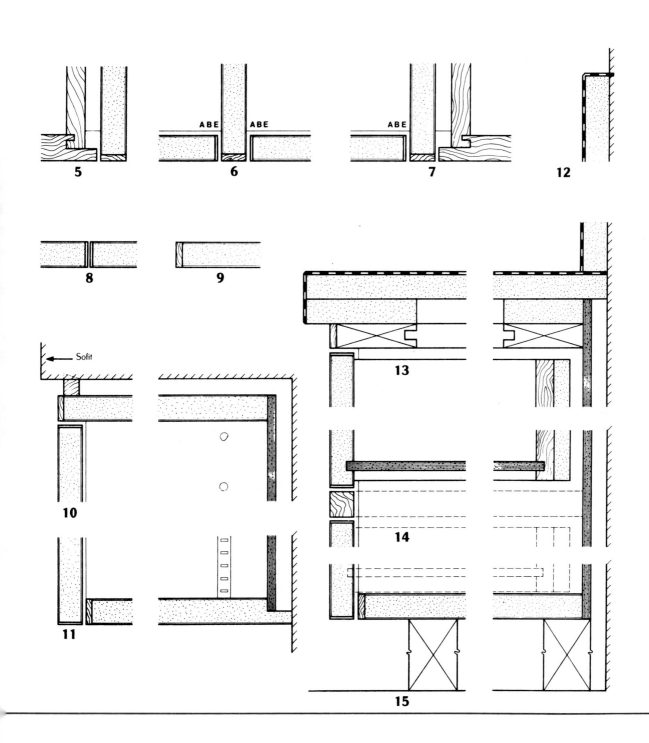

5

ABE   ABE

6

ABE

7

12

8

9

← Sofit

10

11

13

14

15

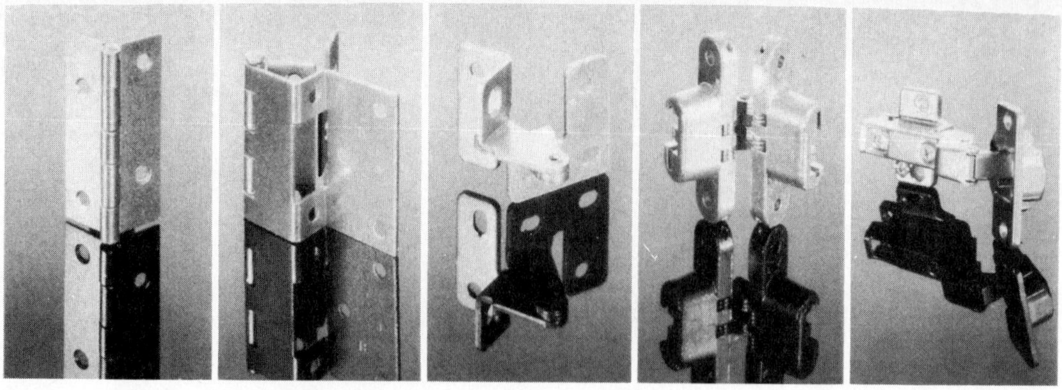

	A BUTT	**B** WRAP AROUND	**C** PIVOT	**D** INVISIBLE	**E** EUROPEAN STYLE
Hinge Type					
Applications	Conventional Flush Front with Face Frame	Conventional Flush Front Reveal Overlay Flush Overlay	Reveal Overlay Flush Overlay	Conventional Flush with Face Frame	Reveal Overlay Flush Overlay Conventional Flush without Face Frame
Strength	High	Very High	Moderate	Low	Moderate
Concealed when closed	No	No	Semi	Yes	Yes
Requires Mortising	Yes	Occasionally	Usually	Yes	Yes
Cost of Hinge	Low	Moderate	Low	High	High
Ease of Installation (cost)	Moderate	Easy	Moderate	Difficult	Very Easy
Can be easily adjusted after installation	No	No	No	No	Yes
Remarks	door requires hardwood edge			door requires hardwood edge	1. Specify degree of opening 2. No catch required

FIGURE 2-20
This chart can be used to evaluate the hinges commonly used in commercial and institutional cabinets. (Courtesy of Architectural Woodwork Institute, Architectural Caseworker General Detail and Specification Guide, Copyright 1984, AWI.)

used with this system enables cabinets to be produced much faster and at less cost than by using the traditional methods used with faceframe cabinets. It must be noted that all panels must be cut very accurately and all drilling and machining operations be carefully performed or doors and drawers will not align properly in the carcass.

Preliminary Machining

After the various parts of the carcass (top, sides, bottom) are accurately cut to size, the cut for the toeboard on the side panels is made. The back of the cabinet is set in grooves which are now cut in the side panels (Fig. 2-22). Edge banding is then per-

DRILLING HEADS

FIGURE 2-21
This multiple-spindle boring machine has one horizontal head with 21 spindles and two vertical heads with 15 spindles each. This permits it to drill a single line of 30 holes or parallel lines of holes, 15 in each line. (Courtesy of Altendorf America.)

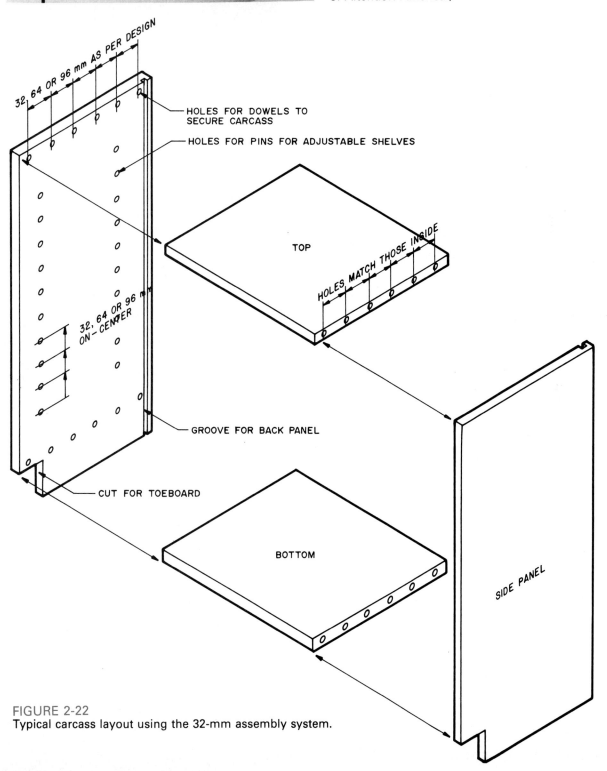

32, 64 OR 96 mm AS PER DESIGN

HOLES FOR DOWELS TO SECURE CARCASS

HOLES FOR PINS FOR ADJUSTABLE SHELVES

TOP

HOLES MATCH THOSE INSIDE

32, 64 OR 96 mm ON-CENTER

GROOVE FOR BACK PANEL

CUT FOR TOEBOARD

BOTTOM

SIDE PANEL

FIGURE 2-22
Typical carcass layout using the 32-mm assembly system.

FIGURE 2-23
This edge bander automatically applies high-pressure laminates, veneers, melamines, solid wood, and PVC coil bands to the edges of stock. (Courtesy of Altendorf America.)

formed on panels where it is required. The edge bander applies PVC coil material as well as high-pressure laminate, veneer coil stock, melamines, and solid lumber bands up to $\frac{3}{4}$ in. (18 mm) thick. It has a hot melt glue system. It will straight or bevel end trim the banding on the top and bottom surfaces (Fig. 2-23).

Material Requirements

Particleboard and fiberboard are the most common materials used. A 45-lb density is recommended. They can be used for carcasses, doors, shelves, and frames. They accept plastic laminates and are easily edge banded. Some panel materials come precoated with melamine or an acrylic finish. This saves finishing or laminating the material. Hardboard can also be used but is limited to backs and drawer bottoms.

For kitchen cabinets $\frac{5}{8}$- or $\frac{3}{4}$-in.-(16- or 19-mm)-thick particleboard is recommended. The back can be 3-mm ($\frac{1}{8}$-in.) laminated hardboard or $\frac{3}{16}$- or $\frac{1}{4}$-in. (4- or 6-mm) hardboard. This construction requires a top rail for screwing the cabinet to the wall. If a $\frac{1}{2}$-in.-thick back panel is used, the top rail is not needed.

Drill Pattern Layout

After the panels have been cut and edge banded, they are ready for the hole drilling operation. These involve two factors: (1) holes used for dowels which assemble the cabinet, and (2) holes for hardware.

Two types of holes are used, dowel holes and line holes. *Dowel holes* are those used to join structural members such as a top or bottom to the bulkheads. *Line holes* are those used for installing hardware. They are generally 5 mm in diameter.

Dowel holes are 8 or 10 mm in diameter and spaced 32 or 64 mm on center as required to form the dowel joint. The distance from the end or edge of the panel depends on the thickness and location of each panel. A layout for a side panel is shown in Fig. 2-24. This layout has dowel holes for joining the top and bottom to the sides (A), line holes for securing fixed shelves (B), line holes for pins for adjustable shelves (C), and line holes for base plates of hinges for the doors (D).

Multigroove hardwood dowels are used. On long butting edges dowels should be 96 mm apart. On short pieces, such as a 100-mm top rail, at least two dowels should be used. The dowel hole should penetrate the side panel 9 mm and the end of the adjoining panel 25 mm. The dowel should be 4 to 6 mm shorter than the overall depth of the hole.

In Fig. 2-25 is shown a layout of a side panel for a unit with drawers. Metal side-mounted drawer slides are used. The metal track is fastened to the sides of the cabinet. A second track is fastened to the bottom of the drawer on each side. They run on nylon rollers (Fig. 2-26). The holes in the slide mounted on the cabinet are spaced 32 mm on center. Typical drawer construction and hardware is shown in Fig. 2-27. The layout in Fig. 2-25 shows the holes for the horizontal top stiles (A), the bottom panel (B), and the metal drawer tracks (C). A con-

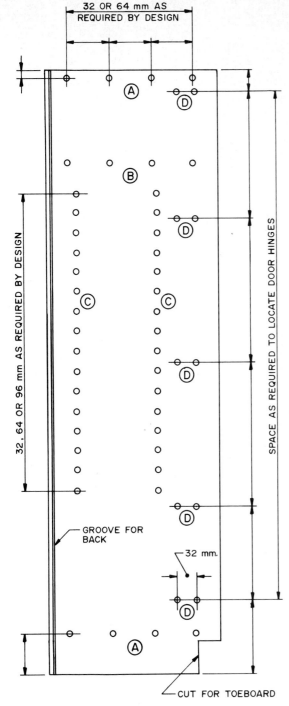

32 OR 64 mm AS REQUIRED BY DESIGN

32, 64 OR 96 mm AS REQUIRED BY DESIGN

SPACE AS REQUIRED TO LOCATE DOOR HINGES

GROOVE FOR BACK

32 mm.

CUT FOR TOEBOARD

(A) 8 mm DIAMETER DOWEL HOLES FOR WOOD DOWELS FOR CARCASS CONSTRUCTION.

(B) 8 mm DIAMETER DOWEL HOLES FOR WOOD DOWELS FOR FIXED SHELF.

(C) 5 mm DIAMETER LINE HOLES FOR PINS FOR ADJUSTABLE SHELVES.

(D) 10 mm DIAMETER HOLES FOR INSERTION OF HINGE BASEPLATES.

NOTE:

HOLES IN COLOR ARE DOWEL HOLES FOR CARCASS ASSEMBLE.

HOLES IN BLACK ARE LINE HOLES FOR HARDWARE.

FIGURE 2-24
Layout for a bulkhead for a cabinet using the 32-mm system. (Courtesy of Grass America, Inc.)

cealed hinge and base plate are shown in Fig. 2-28. Details for installing a hidden hinge are shown in Fig. 2-29. First mount the hinge on the door. Mount the base plate on the cabinet side. The base plate is mounted 32 to 37 mm from the edge of the door opening. Slide the hinge onto the base plate and tighten screw B to secure it to the hinge. Screw A adjusts the door horizontally, and C is the vertical adjustment.

The number of hinges to use depends on the size of the door. Recommendations are shown in Fig. 2-30. The holes drilled for hinge installation are 5 mm in diameter and spaced 32 mm on-center (Fig. 2-31).

Assembling the Cabinet

After all the holes are drilled, the cabinet is assembled using wood dowels and adhesive. The adhesive can be applied using a glue bottle or an automatic dowel-inserter machine. The case itself is assembled with a case clamp or hand clamps (Fig. 2-32, page 38). Unclamp as soon as the glue has reached the manufacturer's set time. Install hardware.

MECHANICALLY JOINED CASEWORK

Furniture and cabinets are increasingly being assembled using mechanical fasteners rather than the traditional joints such as dowels or mortise and tenon. A wide variety of fasteners are available. Some are designed for installation and assembly in the manufacturing plant. Others are designed so that the furniture can be shipped knocked down and assembled by the purchaser. Mechanical fasteners for the knock-down market are designed so that only the simplest tools are needed, such as a screwdriver or Allen wrench.

The joints commonly used for mechanically joined casework include the butt, miter, T and double-T, surface, cross, and end joints. These are explained in Chapter 11. These joints can be secured mechanically in two ways: (1) with rigid nonreleasable fasteners, or (2) with rigid releasable fasteners.

Rigid Nonreleasable Joints

Rigid nonreleasable joints include the traditional joints shown in Chapter 11, such as the mortise-and-tenon or dowel joints. Variations of these include the miter joint using a folding technique, a miter with a flow channel, and the use of H-nails. The folded miter is used in box construction where the box is

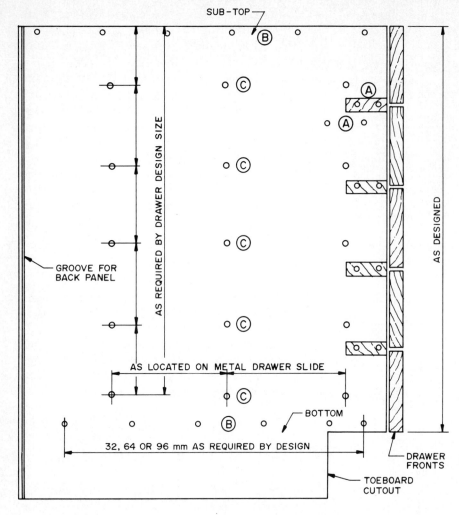

SUB-TOP

(B)

(A) 8 mm DIAMETER DOWEL HOLES
FOR WOOD DOWELS FOR RAILS.

(B) 8 mm DIAMETER DOWEL HOLES
FOR WOOD DOWELS FOR BOTTOM
AND SUB-TOP.

(C) 5 mm DIAMETER LINE HOLES
FOR INSTALLING METAL
DRAWER SLIDES.

NOTE:

HOLES IN COLOR ARE DOWEL
HOLES OR CARCASS ASSEMBLY.

HOLES IN BLACK ARE LINE
HOLES FOR HARDWARE.

AS REQUIRED BY DRAWER DESIGN SIZE

AS DESIGNED

GROOVE FOR
BACK PANEL

AS LOCATED ON METAL DRAWER SLIDE

BOTTOM

(B)

DRAWER
FRONTS

32, 64 OR 96 mm AS REQUIRED BY DESIGN

TOEBOARD
CUTOUT

FIGURE 2-25
Side panel with rail, drawer slide,
and dowel holes for carcass assembly located. (Courtesy of
Grass America, Inc.)

FRONT VIEW OF 6020 and 6040 DRAWER SLIDE

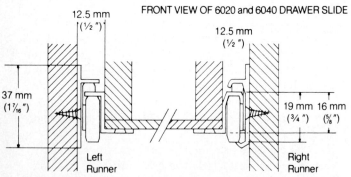

12.5 mm
(½")

12.5 mm
(½")

37 mm
(1 7/16")

19 mm   16 mm
(¾")   (5/8")

Left
Runner

Right
Runner

FIGURE 2-26
Metal drawer slides used with the 32-mm system.
(Courtesy of Grass America, Inc.)

FIGURE 2-27
These drawers slide easily on metal
slides. (Courtesy of Grass America, Inc.)

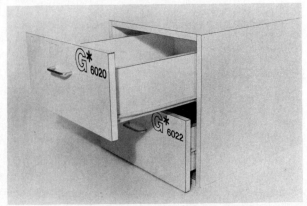

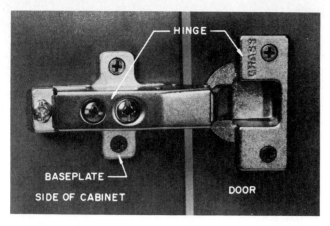

FIGURE 2-28
Concealed hinge. The door can be adjusted by sliding the hinge on the baseplate. (Courtesy of Grass America, Inc.)

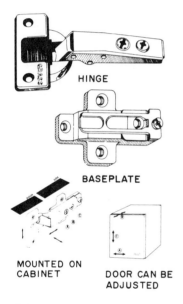

FIGURE 2-29
Installing and adjusting a concealed hinge. (Courtesy of Grass America, Inc.)

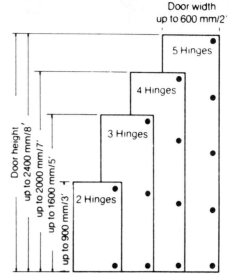

Door width
up to 600 mm/2'

5 Hinges

4 Hinges

3 Hinges

2 Hinges

Door height
up to 2400 mm/8'
up to 2000 mm/7'
up to 1600 mm/5'
up to 900 mm/3'

RECOMMENDED USAGE:
Use the chart to determine number of hinges needed. A trial mounting is advisable due to the variability of quality of material and whether hinge cups are knocked-in or screwed on.

For stabilization, the distance between hinges should be as wide as possible.

For doors up to 24″ wide, weighing
    up to 20 lbs. — 2 hinges
    20 - 40 lbs. — 3 hinges
    40 - 60 lbs. — 4 hinges

FIGURE 2-30
Recommendations for determining the number of concealed hinges to use on various door sizes. (Courtesy of Grass America, Inc.)

FIGURE 2-31
Mounting dimensions for a concealed hinge. (Courtesy of Grass America, Inc.)

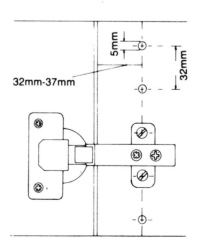

5mm

32mm

32mm-37mm

formed from a single sheet of stock coated with a polyvinyl chloride laminate (Fig. 2-33). The sides of the case are folded to form the box, with the laminate producing a finished corner. The case is then edge banded and end matched along the two long sides.

Another technique is to machine a special miter joint with a channel that receives a molten thermoplastic bonding agent (Fig. 2-34). The channel is filled with polyamide injected by a plastic injection molding machine at 300°F. The plastic penetrates the porous wood in the joint, sealing it and filling the gap between them. As the polyamide cools it shrinks, forcing the panels together to form a rigid nonreleasable joint.

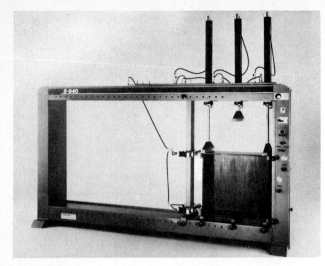

FIGURE 2-32
This power-operated case clamp is used to assemble drawers and carcasses. (Courtesy of Altendorf America.)

THE MITER CUT

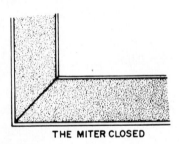

THE MITER CLOSED

FIGURE 2-33
This folded miter uses the PVC laminate to form the finished corner.

FIGURE 2-34
This special miter is joined by injecting polyamide in a machined channel.

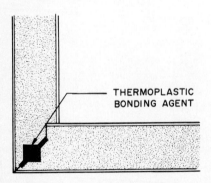

THERMOPLASTIC
BONDING AGENT

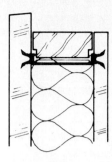

FIGURE 2-35
H-nails can be used to join panels. (Courtesy of H'a'fele America, 203 Feld Ave., High Point, NC 27261.)

H-nails are used to form a drive-in joint that is rigid and nonreleasable (Fig. 2-35). The parts to be joined are stacked with the H-nails between them. They are pressed together, forcing the nails into the wood. There are no nails visible on the exterior of the panel. This type of fastener is stronger than conventional nails or screws. The panels do not require gluing.

Rigid, Releasable Joints

Mechanical fasteners for forming rigid, releasable joints enable a manufacturer to produce furniture and cabinet units that can be assembled without gluing in the factory or shipped in a knocked-down condition. This decreases shipping costs and damage to the units.

These fasteners are available in two types: (1) one-piece fastener, and (2) multipiece fasteners.

A one-piece fastener is shown in Fig. 2-36. The head section is countersunk so that it fits flush with the panel surface. Cover caps can be used to form a button over the head. The threads are designed so that the fastener can be used in wood or

FIGURE 2-36
A boring diagram for one-piece fasteners. (Courtesy of H'a'fele America, 203 Feld Ave., High Point, NC 27261.)

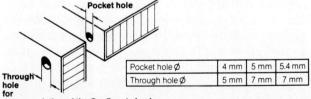

Boring diagram:

Pocket hole

Through hole for accommodation of the Confirmat shank

Pocket hole Ø	4 mm	5 mm	5.4 mm
Through hole Ø	5 mm	7 mm	7 mm

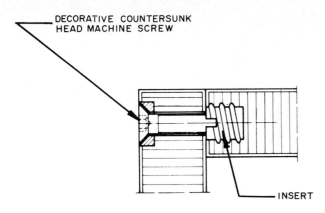

DECORATIVE COUNTERSUNK
HEAD MACHINE SCREW

INSERT

FIGURE 2-37
This multipiece fastener has an insert set into one panel and a screw runs through the joining panel. (Courtesy of H'a'fele America, 203 Feld Ave., High Point, NC 27261.)

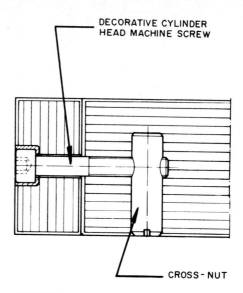

DECORATIVE CYLINDER
HEAD MACHINE SCREW

CROSS - NUT

FIGURE 2-38
This multipiece fastener is secured in the adjoining piece with a cross-nut. (Courtesy of H'a'fele America, 203 Feld Ave., High Point, NC 27261.)

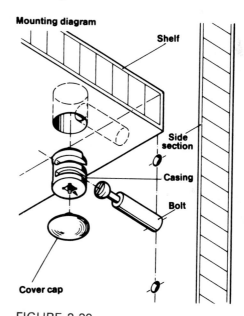

Mounting diagram

Shelf

Side section

Casing

Bolt

Cover cap

FIGURE 2-39
This fastener uses a cam in the casing to lock the shelf to the bolt screwed in the side. (Courtesy of H'a'fele America, 203 Feld Ave., High Point, NC 27261.)

particleboard. They are used in low-stress areas such as lightweight partitions. They may be removed and reinstalled several times. However, if the application is known to require frequent disassembly, a multipiece fastener is recommended. A through hole is bored in the panel and a pocket hole is bored in the material to serve as the anchor. The sawlike screw threads cut internal threads in the pocket hole. The centering tip on the screw guides it through the pocket hole, assuring evenly cut threads in the wood or particleboard. Note that these are metric fasteners with pocket and through-hole diameters given in millimeters.

The following fasteners to be described are multipiece units. One of the simplest uses a decorative countersunk head machine screw which screws into an insert set in the mating part (Fig. 2-37). This fastener has the insert parallel to the axis of the screw. Another type uses a decorative cylinder head machine screw with a cross-nut bolt. Cross-nut bolts are usually steel but some are plastic (Fig. 2-38).

A widely used fastener for knock-down furniture uses an eccentric cam and a mating bolt (Fig. 2-39). Metal eccentric is enclosed in a plastic casing. The casing is set into a hole bored in the shelf or horizontal member. The bolt is available in many designs (Fig. 2-40). Some screw into inserts set into the inside of the bulkhead. Others run through the bulkhead. Various installations are shown in Fig. 2-41. The joint is fastened by inserting the head of the bolt into the casing, which has an eccentric cam. When the casing is rotated, the cam binds tightly against the head and the recessed body below it. The cam can be rotated with a Pozidriv or standard screwdriver or an Allen key (Fig. 2-42). These fasteners are metric and require metric drills to prepare the holes required for installation.

A mechanical shelf fastener is shown in Fig. 2-43. This connector permits rapid connection of shelves to the sides of the carcass. The mating surfaces of the parts are sloped to ensure that the shelf is held firmly. This connector has a high load-carrying capacity and is suitable for heavy wood shelves. It also provides lateral support, which sustains the sides of the carcass. The support is fastened to the bulkhead with special screws. The boss is set in a hole bored in the bottom of the shelf. Typical appli-

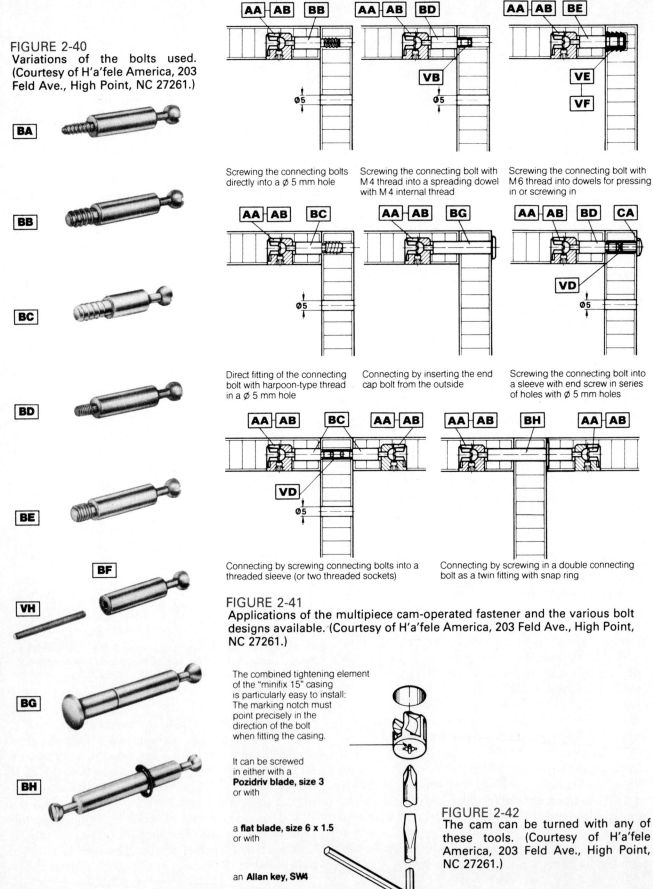

FIGURE 2-40
Variations of the bolts used. (Courtesy of H'a'fele America, 203 Feld Ave., High Point, NC 27261.)

BA

BB

BC

BD

BE

BF

VH

BG

BH

"minifix 15" mounting examples for single or double connections by:

AA AB BB   AA AB BD   AA AB BE

Ø5   VB   VE
              Ø5   VF

Screwing the connecting bolts directly into a ∅ 5 mm hole

Screwing the connecting bolt with M 4 thread into a spreading dowel with M 4 internal thread

Screwing the connecting bolt with M 6 thread into dowels for pressing in or screwing in

AA AB BC   AA AB BG   AA AB BD CA

Ø5   VD
                            Ø5

Direct fitting of the connecting bolt with harpoon-type thread in a ∅ 5 mm hole

Connecting by inserting the end cap bolt from the outside

Screwing the connecting bolt into a sleeve with end screw in series of holes with ∅ 5 mm holes

AA AB BC   AA AB   AA AB BH   AA AB

VD
Ø5

Connecting by screwing connecting bolts into a threaded sleeve (or two threaded sockets)

Connecting by screwing in a double connecting bolt as a twin fitting with snap ring

FIGURE 2-41
Applications of the multipiece cam-operated fastener and the various bolt designs available. (Courtesy of H'a'fele America, 203 Feld Ave., High Point, NC 27261.)

The combined tightening element of the "minifix 15" casing is particularly easy to install: The marking notch must point precisely in the direction of the bolt when fitting the casing.

It can be screwed in either with a **Pozidriv blade, size 3** or with

a **flat blade, size 6 x 1.5** or with

an **Allan key, SW4**

FIGURE 2-42
The cam can be turned with any of these tools. (Courtesy of H'a'fele America, 203 Feld Ave., High Point, NC 27261.)

40

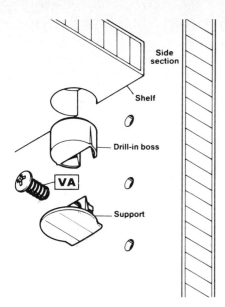

FIGURE 2-43
This shelf connector uses a boss set in a hole in the shelf. (Courtesy of H'a'fele America, 203 Feld Ave., High Point, NC 27261.)

cations are shown in Fig. 2-44. The support, boss, connecting screws, and boring diagram are shown in Fig. 2-45.

Another type of fastener used to join structural panels or shelves has a screw with a cone-shaped head that is installed in the bulkhead. The horizontal panel has a hole bored in the edge to receive an insert. The insert is fastened to the panel with a special screw. The cone head fits into a recess in the insert (Fig. 2-46).

There are mechanical fasteners designed to be used with the 32-millimeter joining system. This system is described in detail in this chapter. One fastener uses a connecting bolt that fits into the holes spaced 32 mm apart in the bulkhead. A housing with an eccentric cam fits into a hole bored in the bottom of the shelf. This system permits shelves to be easily moved when desired and accommodates hinges, catches, and other hardware (Fig. 2-47). Normally, the line of holes in the bulkhead is set in 37 mm from the edge and are 5 mm in diameter.

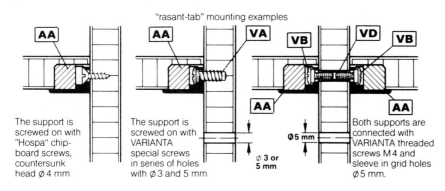

"rasant-tab" mounting examples

The support is screwed on with "Hospa" chip-board screws, countersunk head ⌀ 4 mm

The support is screwed on with VARIANTA special screws in series of holes with ⌀ 3 and 5 mm

⌀ 5 mm
⌀ 3 or 5 mm

Both supports are connected with VARIANTA threaded screws M 4 and sleeve in grid holes ⌀ 5 mm.

FIGURE 2-44
Installation details for the shelf connector. (Courtesy of H'a'fele America, 203 Feld Ave., High Point, NC 27261.)

FIGURE 2-45
The shelf connector parts and its boring diagram. (Courtesy of H'a'fele America, 203 Feld Ave., High Point, NC 27261.)

FIGURE 2-46
This insert is used to join horizontal and vertical panels and shelves. (Courtesy of H'a'fele America, 203 Feld Ave., High Point, NC 27261.)

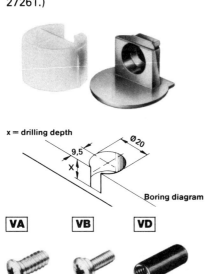

x = drilling depth
9,5
⌀ 20
Boring diagram
VA   VB   VD

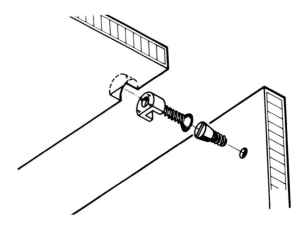

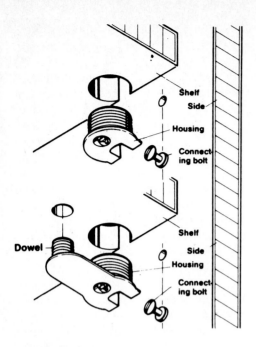

FIGURE 2-47
These shelf connectors are designed to be used with the 32-millimeter system. (Courtesy of H'a'fele America, 203 Feld Ave., High Point, NC 27261.)

FIGURE 2-48
These brackets can be used in many ways to join panels. (Courtesy of H'a'fele America, 203 Feld Ave., High Point, NC 27261.)

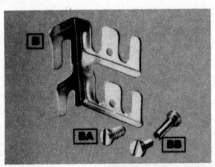

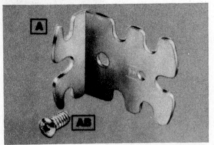

Another system designed for 32-millimeter construction uses brackets and bolts (Fig. 2-48). The brackets can be used to join surface and butt joints. The screws require 5-mm holes in particleboard. Typical applications are shown in Fig. 2-49.

Another application is the use of a multipiece fastener using a threaded sleeve that runs through a hole in the wood section (Fig. 2-50). This makes it possible to secure horizontal panels on both sides of the vertical bulkhead. This system is used in 32-millimeter construction.

Two other knock-down fittings are shown in Figs. 2-51 and 2-52. These secure the sides of the carcass to the top or bottom. The mating wedge-shaped fittings in Fig. 2-51 are fastened to the top and side. When the butt joint is put together, a metal cover is slid in grooves in the wedged parts, locking them together.

FIGURE 2-49
Applications of the brackets being used in connection with the 32-millimeter system. (Courtesy of H'a'fele America, 203 Feld Ave., High Point, NC 27261.)

Application example

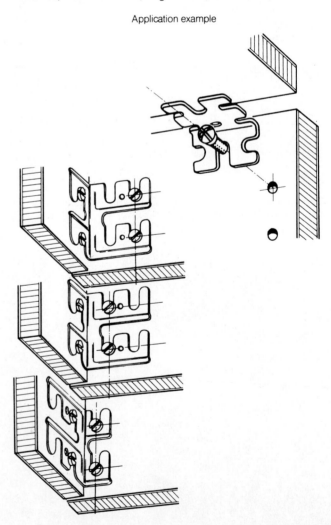

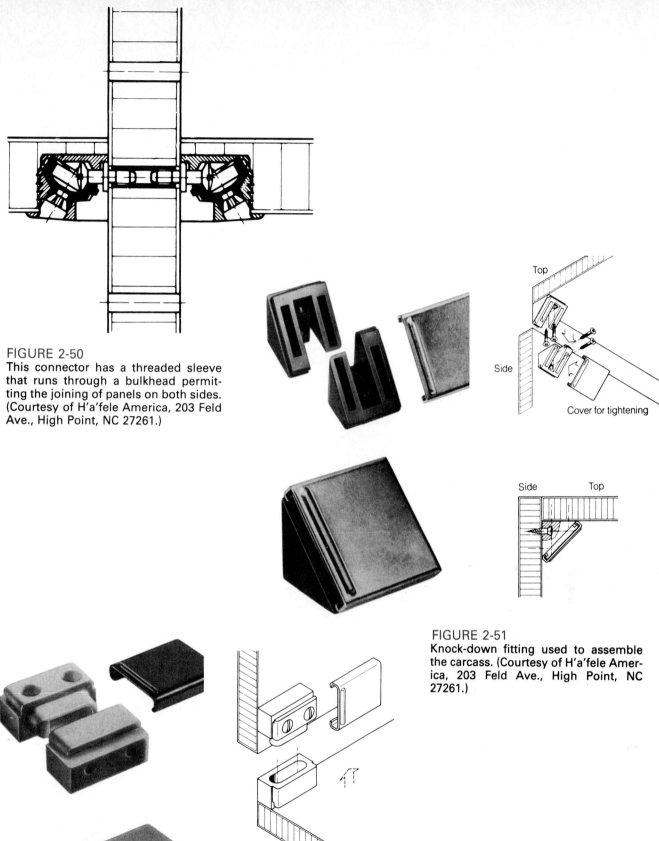

FIGURE 2-50
This connector has a threaded sleeve that runs through a bulkhead permitting the joining of panels on both sides. (Courtesy of H'a'fele America, 203 Feld Ave., High Point, NC 27261.)

Top

Side

Cover for tightening

Side   Top

FIGURE 2-51
Knock-down fitting used to assemble the carcass. (Courtesy of H'a'fele America, 203 Feld Ave., High Point, NC 27261.)

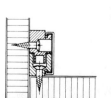

FIGURE 2-52
Another knock-down carcass assembly fitting. (Courtesy of H'a'fele America, 203 Feld Ave., High Point, NC 27261.)

3

INSTALLING CABINETS

The cabinets are delivered to the job safely stored in boxes or protective blankets. The finish carpenter installs them according to the kitchen plan on the working drawings of the house.

The base cabinets are installed first. Begin the installation in a corner. There are three ways to handle a corner. One is to butt the ends of two cabinets together, filling between them with a filler strip. However, the corner is thus completely wasted for storage. A second way is to use a rectangular cabinet designed to fill the corner space. The cabinet on the other wall butts into it. While the space provided is difficult to reach, it provides good storage. A third way is to use a corner cabinet with a door on a 45° angle or a 90° door, butting the adjoining cabinets. This space is easier to reach and is the best solution. Refer to Chapter 1, Figs. 1-8, 1-9, and 1-10.

Preparatory Instructions

1. Make certain that the wall is free of obstructions. In remodeling it may be necessary to remove the old baseboard.
2. Locate the wall studs and mark clearly.
3. Using a level and a long straightedge, find the highest spot on the floor. From this spot mark a line on the wall the height of each unit, $34\frac{1}{2}$ in. for base, 54 in. for wall cabinets, and 84 in. for tall cabinets.

Installing the Base Cabinets

1. Start with a corner unit. Shim it at the floor until it lines up with the $34\frac{1}{2}$-in. mark on the wall (Fig. 3-1, page 45). If the wall is crooked, shim the cabinets at the wall so that they line up straight (Fig. 3-2). Check to make sure that it is level along its length and width.
2. Drill $\frac{1}{4}$-in. holes through the rigid back at each stud.
3. Fasten to the wall using No. 10 sheet metal or wood screws with either washer heads or use a washer. The screws should go at least $\frac{3}{4}$ in. into the stud.
4. Place the next base unit next to the first. Clamp it to the first unit and drill $\frac{1}{8}$-in. pilot holes 6 in. from the top and bottom through the first frame and $\frac{3}{4}$ in. into the second frame. Shim at the floor as necessary to keep level.
5. Drill a $\frac{1}{4}$-in. clearance hole over the pilot hole in the first frame.

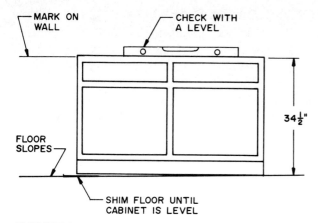

FIGURE 3-1
Start by installing the corner base unit. Shim it at the floor until it is level.

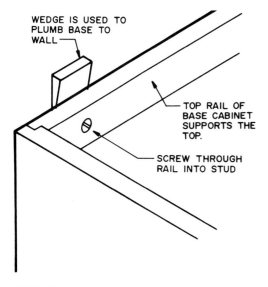

FIGURE 3-2
Shim the cabinet at the wall so that it is straight.

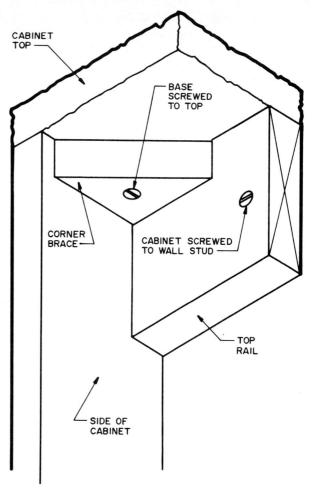

FIGURE 3-3
Fasten the top to the base through cleats or corner blocks.

FIGURE 3-4
Shim out the wall cabinets so they line up straight.

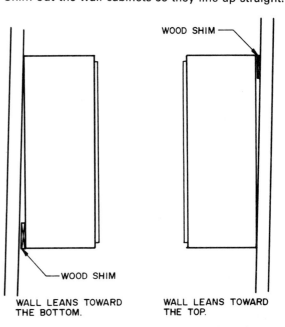

6. Fasten the cabinets together with No. 10 sheet metal or wood screws with either a washer head or washer.

7. Now fasten the second unit to the wall as explained earlier.

Installing the Countertop

Position the counter top and join to the base with screws. Predrill the necessary holes and fasten through the corner blocks or the front and back cleats (Fig. 3-3).

Installing Wall Cabinets

1. Make certain that the wall is free of bows or crooks. If it is not flat, shim it out so that the

cabinets rest on shims, providing a straight wall (Fig. 3-4). If the unit turns a corner, make certain the corner is square. If it is not, shim it out as shown in Fig. 3-5.

2. Start the wall cabinets in a corner. Use blocking resting on the countertop to hold the cabi-

nets in position. Be certain to pad the top so that it is not damaged (Fig. 3-6).

3. Fasten the first cabinent to the wall, being very certain it is level and plumb. Its position will affect all the other cabinets.

4. Fasten each of the other cabinets together and then to the wall as explained for base units.

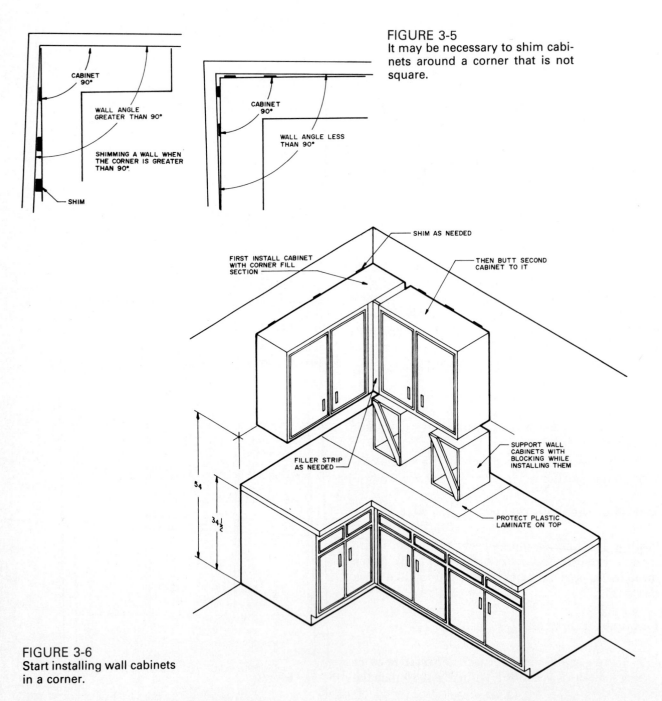

FIGURE 3-5
It may be necessary to shim cabinets around a corner that is not square.

FIGURE 3-6
Start installing wall cabinets in a corner.

4

LAYOUT TOOLS
AND TECHNIQUES

After a product is designed, the next step is to lay out the parts on the materials to be used. The product could be designed using *customary* or *metric units.* Production people in the wood industry must be familiar with both systems. Both systems measure the same quantities but use different units to establish the quantity (Table 4-1, page 48).

CUSTOMARY SYSTEM

The customary system of linear measurement is based on the *yard,* which is divided into three divisions called *feet.* A foot is divided into 12 smaller units called *inches* (Fig. 4-1). Inches are divided into common fractions or decimal fractions. A *common*

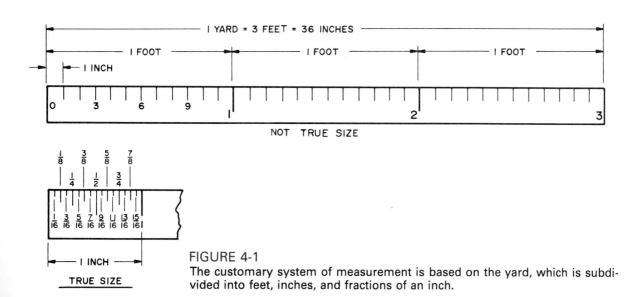

FIGURE 4-1
The customary system of measurement is based on the yard, which is subdivided into feet, inches, and fractions of an inch.

TABLE 4-1
Customary and Metric Units

Measurement	Customary units	Symbol	Metric units	Symbol
Length	yard	yd	meter	m
	foot	ft	decimeter	dm
	inch	in.	centimeter	cm
	mile	mi	millimeter	mm
			kilometer	km
Weight	ton	t	metric ton	t
	pound	lb	kilogram	kg
	ounce	oz	gram	g
Volume	gallon	gal	cubic meter	m^3
	quart	qt	cubic decimeter	dm^3
	pint	pt	cubic centimeter	cm^3
	fluid ounce	oz	cubic millimeter	mm^3
Area	square yard	yd^2	square meter	m^2
	square foot	ft^2	square decimeter	dm^2
	square inch	in^2	square centimeter	cm^2
			square millimeter	mm^2
Temperature	degree Fahrenheit	°F	degree Celsius	°C
Speed, velocity	miles per hour	mph	meters per second	m/s

fraction is when the inch is divided into $\frac{1}{2}$, $\frac{1}{4}$, $\frac{1}{8}$, or $\frac{1}{16}$ of an inch (Fig. 4-1). A *decimal fraction* is when an inch is divided into .1 or .01 (one-tenth or one-hundredth) of an inch (Fig. 4-2). Much of the furniture and cabinets produced by industry is manufactured in decimal inches, which are more accurate and easier to use.

The units for weight are *pounds* and *ounces*. There are 16 ounces in a pound. Some materials, such as nails, are sold by the pound. Finishing materials are often sold by ounces.

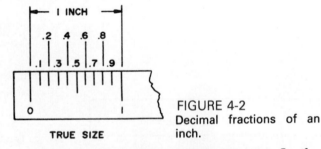

FIGURE 4-2
Decimal fractions of an inch.

Liquids are sold by volume measure. In the customary system this includes gallons, quarts (4 to a gallon), pints (2 to a quart), and fluid ounces (16 to a pint). Paint, varnish, and adhesives are sold by liquid measure.

METRIC SYSTEM

The metric system of linear measurement is based on a unit called a *meter* (m). A meter is a little longer than a yard. The meter is divided into 10 parts called *decimeters* (dm). A decimeter is divided into 10 parts called *centimeters* (cm). A centimeter is divided into 10 parts called *millimeters* (mm) (Fig. 4-3).

Metric units of measure are specified by adding a prefix to the base units, such as a meter (Table 4-2). The prefix *milli* means 1/1000 of the base unit, so a millimeter is 1/1000 of a meter. The prefix *centi* means 1/100 of the base unit, and *deci* is 1/10 of a base unit. The prefix *kilo* means 1000, so a kilometer (km) is 1000 meters.

TABLE 4-2
Prefixes Used on Metric Base Units

Prefix	+ Base unit =	Metric unit of measurement	Means
milli (m)	meter (m)	millimeter (mm)	1/1000
	gram (g)	milligram (mg)	
centi (c)	meter (m)	centimeter (cm)	1/100
	gram (g)	centigram (cg)	
deci (d)	meter (m)	decimeter (dm)	1/10
	gram (g)	decigram (dg)	
kilo (k)	meter (m)	kilometer (km)	1000
	gram (g)	kilogram (kg)	

Since the metric system is based on the unit 10 it is possible to move from one prefix to another simply by moving the decimal point. For example, 5500 mm equals 550.0 cm, which equal 55.00 dm, which equal 5.500 m.

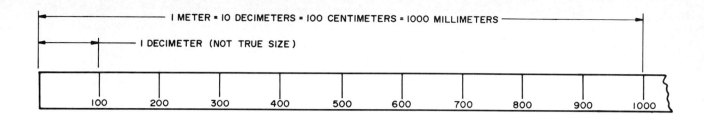

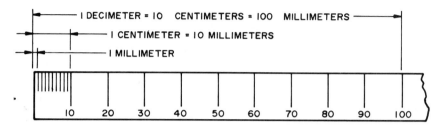

FIGURE 4-3
The metric system of measurement is based on the meter, which is subdivided into decimeters, centimeters, and millimeters.

Working drawings for wood products are dimensioned in *millimeters* (Fig. 4-4). The centimeter and decimeter are not widely used. The meter is used for larger distances, such as a land survey.

The units for *weight* are the *kilogram* (kg) and the gram (g) (1/1000 kilogram). The units for *volume* are derived by multiplying the length by width by height of rectangular objects. The volume is expressed in terms of cubic measure. For example, a cube 1 meter square is 1 cubic meter (m^3). A cubic millimeter is mm^3. The term liter is sometimes used to express a cubic decimeter (dm^3).

Metrics in Product Design

If a product is to be manufactured using metric units, it should be originally designed with these units. To take a product originally designed in inches and convert these to millimeters to produce a metric product is an improper procedure. This reduces the value of going to metric units and actually makes the manufacturing process more difficult because you end up with inconvenient measurements. For example, if you convert $3\frac{1}{4}$ in. to millimeters, you multiply it by 25.4 mm and get 82.550 mm. You have to convert $\frac{1}{4}$ in. to a decimal fraction before you multiply. Then the result 82.550 mm is extremely difficult to measure. A designer would probably make this part 80 mm, which is easy to measure. The 2.550 mm dropped is about $\frac{3}{32}$ in., which is not of importance for most parts of furniture or cabinets. When designing using metric units, consider keeping all measurements based on units of 5 or 10 mm (i.e., 30, 35, 40, etc.).

MEASURING TOOLS

There are a variety of measuring tools used to lay out parts for production. To achieve the desired results, the proper tool must be correctly used.

FIGURE 4-4
Typical metric working drawing of a cabinet door.

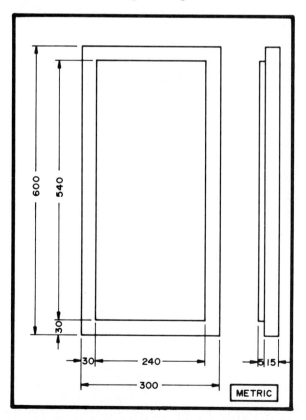

Rules

The bench rule, folding rule, and tape rule are most often used for linear measurements (Fig. 4-5). The *bench rule* is used for measuring short distances and is available in lengths of 1, 2, and 3 ft and 1 m. The *folding rule* is usually 6 ft and 1 and 2-m long. It is used for measuring longer distances. The *tape rule* is used for measuring very long distances. Those used

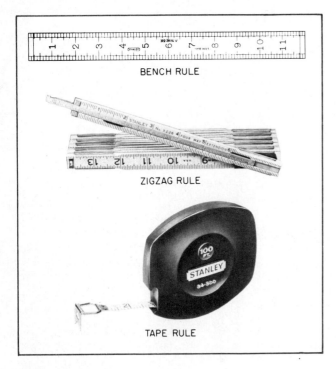

FIGURE 4-5
Rules used for linear layout. (*Courtesy of The Stanley Works.*)

in furniture and cabinet production are usually 8, 10 and 12 ft long and 2 and 3 m long. They are available in 25-, 50- and 100-ft and 15-, 20-, 25- and 30-m lengths.

Squares

The squares most often used are the try square, combination square, framing or steel square, and bevel square or T-bevel (Fig. 4-6). They are used to lay out 90° angles and check for squareness.

The *try square* is available with 6-, 8-, 10-, and 12-in. blades. The blade is rigidly fastened to the handle at a 90° angle. Some have a 45° angle, where the blade and handle join, enabling it to be used to lay out both 90° and 45° angles (Fig. 4-7). The try square must be handled carefully so that the 90° angle is not changed. When not being used, place in a holder on your tool rack. Do not pile tools on top of

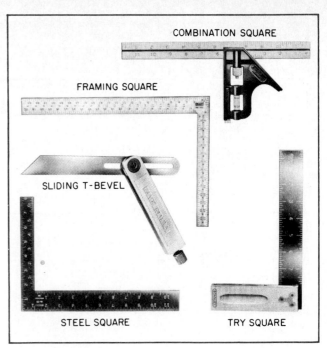

FIGURE 4-6
Squares used for layout and checking stock for squareness and angles. (*Courtesy of The Stanley Works.*)

it or use it as a hammer. The *combination square* has a 12-in. adjustable blade. The length that the blade extends beyond the face of the head can be adjusted. This allows it to be used as a depth gauge. It has a locknut in the head that locks the blade and head together. It can also be used to lay out 45° angles. Some have a steel scriber in the bottom of the head. This is used to scratch a line along the edge of the blade when laying out on wood or metal.

The *steel square* is available with a 12-in. body

FIGURE 4-7
A try square is a basic layout tool.

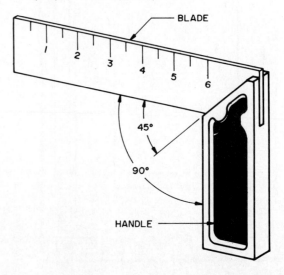

and 8-in. tongue and a 24-in. body and 16-in. tongue. A carpenter's square has a 24-in. body and a 16-in. tongue. Some have rafter tables stamped into the body and tongue. Both are flat metal tools with the body and tongue meeting at right angles. Measurements in inches are marked on both parts. Since they do not have a thick handle like the try square, the tongue is dropped down along the edge of the board as it is used to lay out a 90° angle.

The *bevel square,* sometimes called a T-bevel, has a steel blade 4 to 8 in. long that pivots on a pin through the handle. The blade can be adjusted to any desired angle and is locked to the handle with a thumbscrew. It is used to lay out a series of identical angles and test bevels and chamfers for accuracy.

Marking Tools

The tools most commonly used to lay out on wood are a hard lead pencil with a sharp point, a utility knife, an awl, a compass, and trammel points (Fig. 8-8).

FIGURE 4-9
A utility knife is used for accurate scribing of lines.

FIGURE 4-10
Centers are accurately marked with an awl.

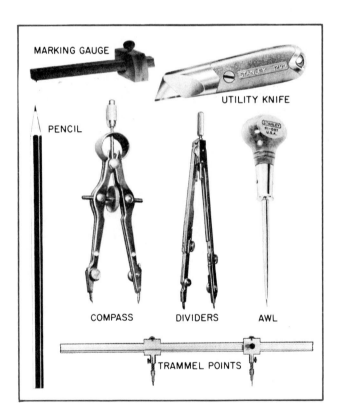

FIGURE 4-8
Commonly used layout tools.

When using the knife, use only the tip of the blade (Fig. 4-9). The centers of holes are located using an awl. The center is located by measurement and the wood is indented by pressing down on the awl with your hand (Fig. 4-10). This helps to accurately locate the point of the bit to be used to bore a hole at this point.

Dividers have two steel legs ending in a point. The distance between these legs is adjustable (Fig. 4-11). Dividers are used to lay out equal distances and transfer measurements from one place to another. They can be used to scribe circles but a compass does a better job.

A *compass* has one steel leg and one leg that holds a pencil or pencil lead. The most accurate work is performed using a drafting compass (Fig. 4-12). Very large diameter circles are drawn using a woodworker's trammel points (Fig. 4-13). One leg is a steel pin and the other holds a pencil. Do not hammer an awl into the wood. An awl can also be used to scribe lines as described for a pencil or utility knife.

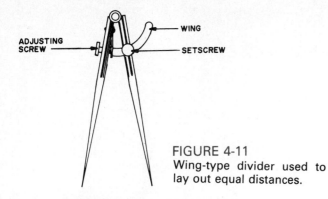

FIGURE 4-11
Wing-type divider used to lay out equal distances.

FIGURE 4-12
Small circles are drawn with a compass.

FIGURE 4-13
Large circles are drawn with trammel points.

STARTING THE LAYOUT

After selecting the stock to be used, the various parts of the product must be laid out. There are several things to consider. One is to avoid the defects in the stock. If knots are not acceptable, you must work

around them. Splits, surface checks, and insect damage must be avoided. Occasionally, the piece can be turned so that minor defects are on the back or are hidden on the inside of a furniture unit. The flatness of the stock must be considered. If it has cup, warp, or twist, the piece might have to be discarded or used for small pieces where these defects can be minimized (Fig. 4-14).

FIGURE 4-14
Stock in crook and cup can be salvaged by cutting into smaller or thinner pieces.

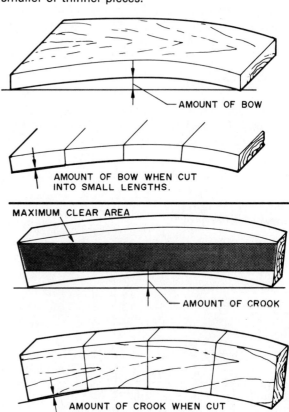

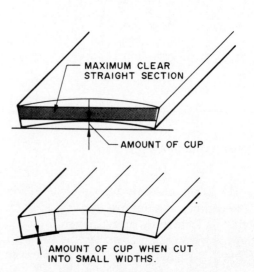

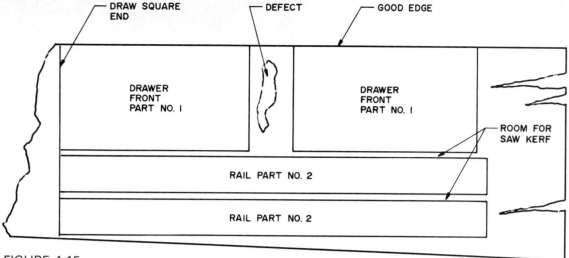

FIGURE 4-15
Avoid defects when making the parts layout on the stock.

Make your layout from a good, straight edge. If necessary, straighten an edge on the jointer. Take all width measurements from this good edge. Length measurements are taken from a good square end or a square line scribed across the end of the stock. Allow extra material between parts for the saw kerf. A typical parts layout is in Fig. 4-15.

When making a layout of parts on stock, make it near the edge and end (Fig. 4-16). This leaves the rest of the stock for other parts. If a part is laid out near the center, much of the stock will become wasted.

Remember to watch the direction and color of the grain. Keep the grain running in the direction desired in the part. A part is stronger with the grain than across the grain (Fig. 4-17). Ideally, all exposed pieces should be close to the same color and general grain pattern.

FIGURE 4-16
Careful planning is necessary when laying out on stock, so that waste is minimized.

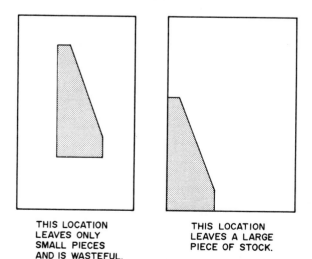

THIS LOCATION LEAVES ONLY SMALL PIECES AND IS WASTEFUL.

THIS LOCATION LEAVES A LARGE PIECE OF STOCK.

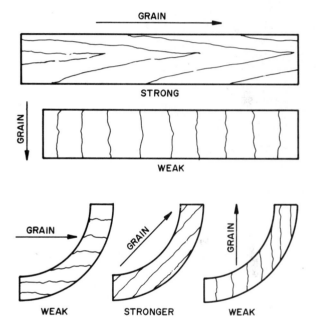

FIGURE 4-17
Consider the direction of the grain and how it affects the strength of each part.

Measuring Linear Distances

Thickness can be measured with a bench rule or try square (Fig. 4-18). *Width* is measured by placing a rule perpendicular to the good edge (Fig. 4-19) or with a try square (Fig. 4-20). Measurements with the bench rule or folding rule are more accurate if the tool is placed on edge. Width can also be measured and marked with a combination square. The blade is extended from the handle the desired width. The head is slid along the good edge and a pencil is held on the end of the blade (Fig. 4-21). A marking

FIGURE 4-18
Thickness can be checked with a try square.

FIGURE 4-21
Width can be marked using a combination square.

FIGURE 4-19
When measuring width, place the rule on edge and keep it perpendicular to the side of the stock.

FIGURE 4-22
A marking gauge is sometimes used to mark stock to width.

FIGURE 4-20
Width can be measured with a try square.

gauge is also used to lay out the width. Set the required distance between the pin and the head. Place the head against the edge of the stock. Roll it until the pin in the end of the beam touches the wood. Then push the gauge away from you (Fig. 4-22).

The length of short pieces can be measured with a bench rule or a folding rule. Longer pieces require a tape rule (Fig. 4-23). Keep the rule parallel with the edge and press it flat against the surface. The tape has a hook on one end that is placed over the good end of the stock.

Laying Out Angles

Angles can be laid out using a protractor. Place the center point on the vertex of the angle and read the degrees on the scale (Fig. 4-24). A T-bevel can also be used (Fig. 4-25) to take the angle from the protractor. It is then drawn on the wood as shown in Fig. 4-26.

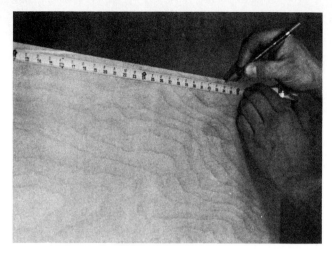

FIGURE 4-23
Long lengths are measured with a tape rule.

FIGURE 4-26
The T-bevel is placed flat on the stock as the angle is drawn.

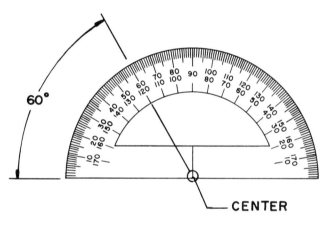

FIGURE 4-24
Angles are measured with a protractor.

FIGURE 4-25
A T-bevel is used to lay out and transfer angles.

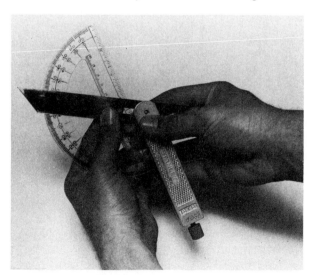

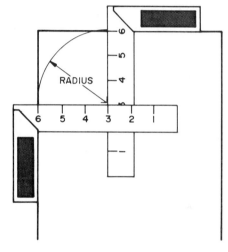

FIGURE 4-27
Round corners are laid out by using the radius to locate the center.

Laying Out a Rounded Corner

First locate the center by measuring the radius from each corner. Then place the pin leg of the compass on this point and swing the arc (Fig. 4-27).

Laying Out Irregular Curves

An irregular curve is one that does not have a fixed radius. It is drawn using a tool called an irregular curve (Fig. 4-28). The line of the curve is indicated by a series of points. These are then connected by placing various sides of the irregular curve along the points until three or more fit the curve. Draw this part. Move the irregular curve until additional

FIGURE 4-28
Irregular curve.

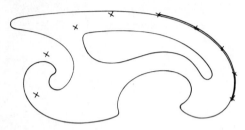

FIGURE 4-29
Irregular curves are drawn by connecting points that are known to be on the curve.

points line up and draw the next section (Fig. 4-29). There are many shapes and sizes of irregular curves, and those working with them will have an entire set.

Enlarging and Reducing Patterns

If you have a drawing of an irregular part and you want to enlarge or reduce it, this can be done by drawing a grid over the drawing. The grid can be any convenient size such as $\frac{1}{2}$ in. If you want to en-

large it 100%, draw another grid with 1-in. squares. Mark where the lines cross the $\frac{1}{2}$-in. grid on the 1-in. grid. Then connect the points with an irregular curve (Fig. 4-30).

If you want to reduce this design 50%, draw another grid with $\frac{1}{4}$-in. squares and repeat the foregoing process.

Template Layouts

Duplicate parts can be laid out using a template. A template is a full-size pattern of the part cut out of cardboard, metal, or hardboard. It is placed on the stock and traced around with a pencil. If a part is symmetrical (same on each side of a centerline), only half a template need be made. It is traced and flipped over to draw the other half (Fig. 4-31).

GEOMETRIC CONSTRUCTIONS

Three basic forms, hexagons, octagons, and ellipses, are used frequently in furniture and cabinet construction. The steps for laying out these forms are in the following examples.

Laying Out a Hexagon

A hexagon has six equal sides and angles. The steps to lay out a hexagon are:

1. Draw a circle with a diameter equal to the distance from one corner of the hexagon to the other (Fig. 4-32).

FIGURE 4-30
Patterns can be enlarged or reduced using this grid method.

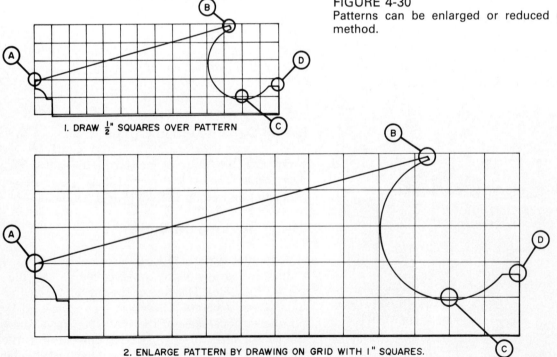

I. DRAW $\frac{1}{2}$" SQUARES OVER PATTERN

2. ENLARGE PATTERN BY DRAWING ON GRID WITH I" SQUARES.

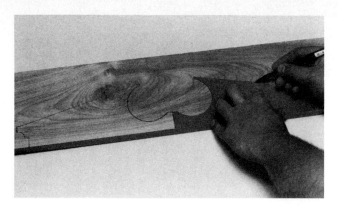

FIGURE 4-31
Templates can be used to lay out patterns on the stock.

Laying Out an Octagon

An octagon has eight equal sides and angles. The steps to lay out an octagon are:

1. Draw a square having sides equal to the desired width of the octagan from one flat side to the other (Fig. 4-33).
2. Locate the center of this square.
3. Set a compass the distance from one corner of the square to the center. Swing arcs from each corner through the center until they cross the sides of the square.
4. Connect these intersections to form the octagon.

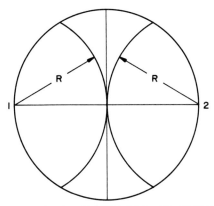

I. DRAW CIRCLE DIAMETER EQUAL TO HEXAGON CORNER TO CORNER DIAMETER. THEN SWING ARCS FROM I AND 2 USING THE RADIUS OF THE CIRCLE.

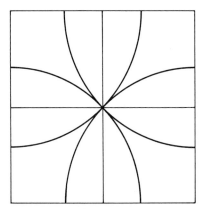

I. DRAW A SQUARE EQUAL TO THE OCTAGON ACROSS THE FLAT SIDES. SWING ARCS FROM EACH CORNER THROUGH THE CENTER UNTIL THEY TOUCH THE SQUARE.

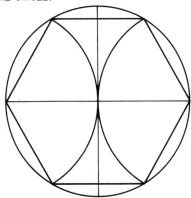

2. CONNECT THE POINTS ON THE CIRCLE LOCATED BY THE ARCS.

FIGURE 4-32
Steps to lay out a hexagon.

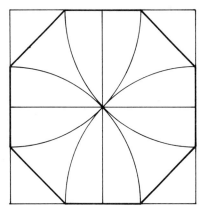

2. CONNECT THE POINTS LOCATED ON THE SQUARE.

FIGURE 4-33
Steps to lay out an octagon.

2. Locate the diameter through the center.
3. From each end of the diameter, swing arcs having a radius equal to the radius of the circle.
4. Connect to points where the arcs meet the circle.

Laying Out an Ellipse

An ellipse is a plane surface formed by looking at a circle with a line of sight that is inclined to the circle. An ellipse has two axes, major and minor. The

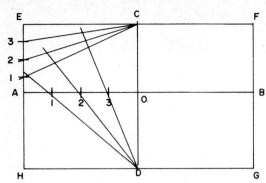

1. DIVIDE OA AND AE INTO AND EQUAL NUMBER OF PARTS. DRAW LINES FROM LIKE – NUMBERED POINTS TILL THEY INTERSECT.

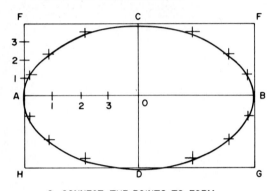

2. CONNECT THE POINTS TO FORM THE ELLIPSE.

FIGURE 4-34
Steps to lay out an ellipse.

major axis is the longest. The steps to lay out an ellipse are:

1. Draw the major axis, *AB,* and minor axis, *CD,* at right angles to each other (Fig. 4-34).
2. Draw a rectangle with its sides parallel with the axes.
3. Divide *OA* and *AE* into the same number of equal parts.
4. Draw lines through these points from *C* and *D* until the like-numbered lines cross. This locates a point on the ellipse.
5. Connect the points with an irregular curve to form the ellipse.

SOME LAYOUT TECHNIQUES

Following are some basic layout techniques that will be helpful.

Bisecting an Arc or Line

The steps are shown in Fig. 4-35.

1. Set a compass on a radius greater than half the length of the line or arc, *AB.*

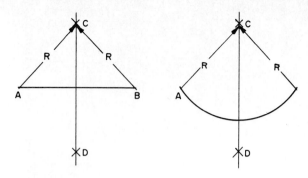

FIGURE 4-35
How to bisect a line or arc.

2. Using *A* and *B* as centers, swing arcs that intersect above and below the line or arc at *C* and *D.*
3. Connect *C* and *D.* This line divides *AB* into two equal parts.

Dividing a Line into Equal Parts

Most wood is in odd widths. It can be divided into equal parts using a rule. For example, to divide a board into three equal parts, place the rule as shown in Fig. 4-36. The zero is on one edge and the 6 is on the other. Place a mark at the 2- and 4-in. locations. This divides the board into three equal parts.

To divide a line into equal parts, first draw a line below it on any angle and length (Fig. 4-37). Divide this into the desired number of parts. Connect the end of the line, *C,* with *B.* Draw lines parallel with *CB* through the other points on *AC.*

Bisecting an Angle

The steps are shown in Fig. 4-38.

1. Set a compass to any radius desired.

FIGURE 4-36
How to divide a board into equal parts.

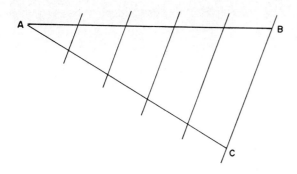

FIGURE 4-37
Lines can be divided in any number of equal parts using this technique.

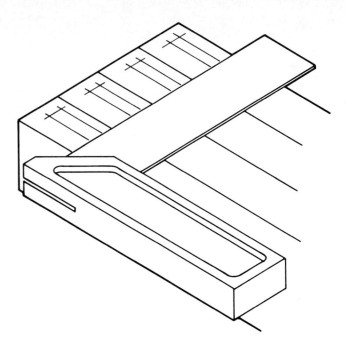

FIGURE 4-39
It is more accurate to lay out duplicate parts together.

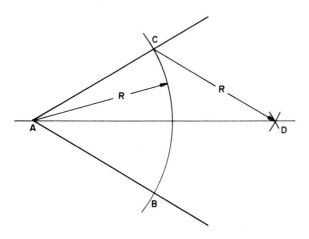

FIGURE 4-38
A compass can be used to bisect an angle.

2. From vertex *A* swing arcs that cross the sides of the angle at *B* and *C*.
3. Swing arcs from *B* and *C* until they intersect at *D*.
4. Connect *A* and *D* to bisect the angle.

Duplicate Parts

If a product has several identical parts or several identical joints, it is more accurate if they are laid out together. Clamp the parts together. Be certain they are flush and square. Mark the locations needed on all at the same time (Fig. 4-39).

Transferring Equal Distances

Accuracy is important when transferring one measurement to several parts. This transfer is made more accurately if a dividers is used rather than a rule. To transfer a distance, set the dividers on the distance to be moved. Move the dividers to the new part and locate the points (Fig. 4-40).

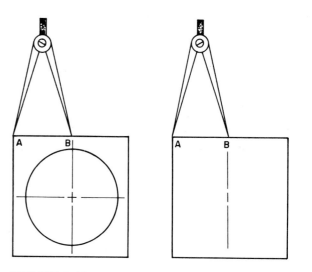

FIGURE 4-40
A divider is used to transfer a distance from one place to another.

The divider can also be used to check dimensions of actual parts or dimensions that are on drawings that are supposed to be the same size. Set the divider on the desired size and use it instead of a rule to check the others for size. This will be faster and more accurate than using a rule. Be careful you do not bump the divider and change its setting.

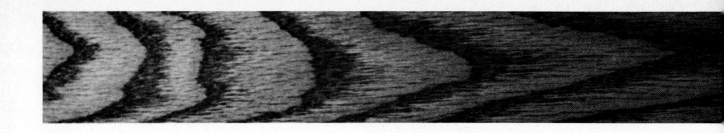

5

GENERAL SAFETY

Safety is everybody's business. If we each develop a positive attitude toward the need for safe working procedures, accidents in woodworking situations would be greatly reduced. Most accidents do not just happen; they are caused by negligence on the part of the operator. Many things enter into the equation for safety. Major factors include our knowledge about proper use of tools, correct dress, a safe working environment, a "safety attitude," good-quality tools kept in good working condition, and stopping work when you begin to feel fatigue. Consideration of these and the other factors mentioned in this chapter will contribute to a safe and happy woodworking experience.

In the other chapters of this book, additional specific safety recommendations are made relating to the tools and materials used in each chapter.

CLOTHING

Wear the required eye, ear, and respiratory protection (Fig. 5-1). Dust and chips will injure the eyes. Wear eye protection the entire time you are working with wood (Fig. 5-2). Prolonged exposure to loud and high-pitched sounds can damage hearing. Wear ear-

plugs or earmuffs (Fig. 5-3). Dust, especially while sanding or working a lathe, clogs the nose and adversely affects the respiratory tract. Wear a respirator or at least a filter. Filters are available at any drugstore (Fig. 5-4). It is recommended that you equip your shop with dust collection equipment connected to each machine. These produce a vacuum and pull dust and chips from the machine into a storage container.

Be certain you do not wear loose clothing that can catch in moving machinery parts. It is best to wear shirts with short, tight-fitting sleeves. Do not wear ties, scarves, or other loose items. If you have long hair, wear a hair net or tie your hair above your shirt collar. Remove all jewelry, including rings, bracelets, necklaces, and earrings. (Fig. 5-5). In industrial situations heavy work shoes are required, and in some cases they must have steel toes. Wear shoes having soles that are least likely to get slippery. Do not wear shoes with open toes.

PHYSICAL CONDITIONS

1. Have a good, strong, steady workbench with a good vise firmly attached.

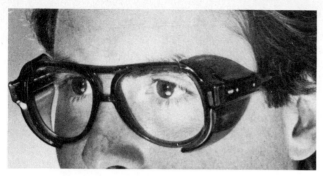

GLASSES WITH SIDE SHIELD

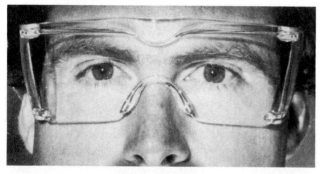

MOLDED EYE SHIELD

SAFETY GLASSES

FIGURE 5-1
Eye protection is required to keep the eyes free of wood chips and dust particles. (*Courtesy of American Optical Safety Products.*)

FIGURE 5-2
A full-face shield is effective for jobs where a considerable amount of chips are produced, as when using a wood lathe. (*Courtesy of American Optical Safety Products.*)

FIGURE 5-3
Ear protection is required for operations producing loud, high-pitched sounds. (*Courtesy of American Optical Safety Products.*)

2. Keep the floor clean of scraps and sawdust. Sweep it often and keep scraps picked up.

3. Store all supplies and tools in proper cabinets. Wood must be neatly stored on racks, finishes in metal fire-resistant cabinets, and tools on racks made especially for them.

4. Provide adequate lighting. Every part of the work area should be fully illuminated.

5. All electrical outlets should be grounded, and better still, should have ground-fault interrupters. *Ground-fault interrupters* (GFIs), detect small electrical leaks that will not cause a circuit breaker to kick off but could cause a shock. When a leak is detected, the GFI breaks the circuit.

HAND TOOL SAFETY RULES

1. Do not use dull or broken tools. They are more likely to require extra pressure or an unusual procedure which can cause them to slip.

2. Keep both hands behind the cutting edge at all times. It is almost impossible to cut yourself this way. Push cutting tools away from you. However, be certain that other people are also in the clear and will not be cut if the tool slips.

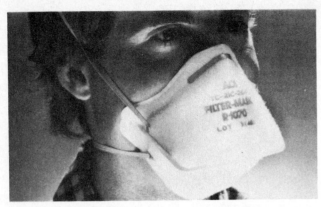

DISPOSABLE FILTER MASK

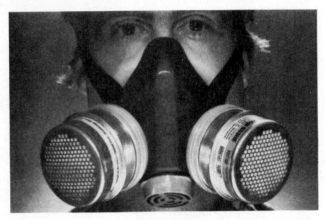

RESPIRATOR

FIGURE 5-4
Respiratory filters are needed to keep the nose and lungs free of wood dust particles. (*Courtesy of American Optical Safety Products.*)

FIGURE 5-5
This person is dressed for safe power tool operation.

3. Clamp your stock to a bench or secure it in a vise before working on it. Loose stock causes accidents.

POWER TOOL SAFETY RULES

1. Never use a power tool unless you have been instructed in its use and you are certain that you understand the instructions completely. Often, you do not get a second chance.
2. Keep all saws and cutters sharp. Destroy heavily chipped or damaged saws and cutters. Make certain that they are properly sharpened and in balance.
3. Install all saws and cutters properly. Make certain that the teeth or bevels are facing in the proper direction as determined by the direction of rotation. If there is any doubt, consult your machine manual.
4. Keep a complete set of power tool manuals available.
5. Do not talk to or get anywhere near someone operating a power tool unless they have asked you to help with the job at hand.
6. After setting up a machine, remove all tools used and replace all guards before giving it a trial startup.
7. Make certain that you know where the switch is located and stay near it so you can shut off the machine if an emergency occurs.
8. Never work in a shop alone if you are planning to use power tools.
9. Make certain that all electrical wires, plugs, and connections are in perfect repair.
10. When using portable power tools, arrange the electrical cord so that it is clear of the work *before* you begin operation.
11. Do not use electrical tools if there are inflammable materials, gases, or vapors present.
12. Before replacing saws or cutters, cut off the electrical power at the fuse box or trip the circuit breaker. If the machine is plugged into a duplex outlet, unplug it.
13. Never run a machine with the guards removed or broken. There are a few cuts that require guards to be removed. These are discussed later in the book.
14. If a piece of wood is badly warped, cupped, twisted, or has large knots or splits, be especially careful. These can cause binding and kickbacks. Consider making some of the pre-

FIGURE 5-6
Always get help when cutting long boards or large panels.

liminary cuts with a handsaw, thus reducing or removing some of the hazards.

15. When cutting long boards or large panels, get help (Fig. 5-6).

16. Do not start to cut with any machine until it is running at full speed.

17. Do not try to force a machine to cut faster than normal. Feed the stock so that the cut proceeds easily without excess pressure or binding. If the blade gets hot and burns the wood, seek the cause. The cut may be too deep, or the saw or cutters may be dull. Either is a hazard. Lighten up the cut and sharpen the tool.

18. Stop the machine and allow the cutter to come to a complete stop before making adjustments.

19. Buy portable power tools that have a threewire cord or have a double-insulated plastic housing (Fig. 5-7). If the tool has a three-prong plug, be certain to plug it into electrical circuits that have the third (ground) wire. They appear as shown in Fig. 5-8.

20. Make and use safety devices to help feed materials, such as featherboards and push sticks. These are covered later in the book (Fig. 5-9).

21. In shops where several people will be working at the same time, paint safety zones around the machines. Only the operator should be in this zone (Fig. 5-10).

22. Plan your shop so that the operator is not standing next to a major aisle of traffic. This will prevent the passerby from distracting or bumping the operator. Arrange equipment so that if a kickback does occur, no one will be in the area behind the machine.

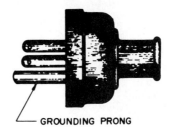

GROUNDING PRONG

FIGURE 5-7
Portable power tools should have a three-prong plug or be of double-insulated construction.

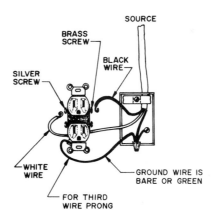

SOURCE
BRASS SCREW
BLACK WIRE
SILVER SCREW
GROUND WIRE IS BARE OR GREEN
WHITE WIRE
FOR THIRD WIRE PRONG

FIGURE 5-8
120-V duplex outlet that has a third (ground) wire.

FINISHING SAFETY RULES

1. Wear eye protection. Finishing materials are liquid and caustic and can easily cause permanent eye damage.

FIGURE 5-9
The use of guards, push sticks, and other safety devices will greatly reduce the chance of an accident.

FIGURE 5-11
This fire extinguisher can be used on type A, B, and C fires.

FIGURE 5-10
Safety zones painted on the floor give the operator safe operating space.

2. When working with caustic materials such as paint remover, wear protective gloves. Inexpensive plastic throwaway gloves are available in any drugstore.

3. Know where the fire extinguishers are kept and the kinds of fires they are designed to extinguish. There are three classes of fires: A, B, and C. Type A refers to combustible materials such as wood or paper. Type B refers to materials such as paints, lacquers, oils, and gasoline. Type C is used on electrical fires. These are marked on the label of the extinguisher. Shown in Fig. 9-11 is a universal extinguisher, often referred to as an ABC because it can be used on all three types of fires.

4. Store dirty rags and paper in metal, fire-resistant containers. Remove them from the building as often as possible.

5. Store flammable finishing materials in metal fire-resistant cabinets. Ground these cabinets and large storage containers to prevent accidental sparking and ignition of materials.

6. Provide mechanical ventilation to remove fumes rapidly. Do everything possible to avoid breathing fumes, including some type of respirator. Keep all containers covered when not in use.

7. Cleanliness is important to safety. Immediately wipe up material spilled on the bench or floor.

8. Do not pour finishing materials down a sink or mix them together.

PART **2**

Materials

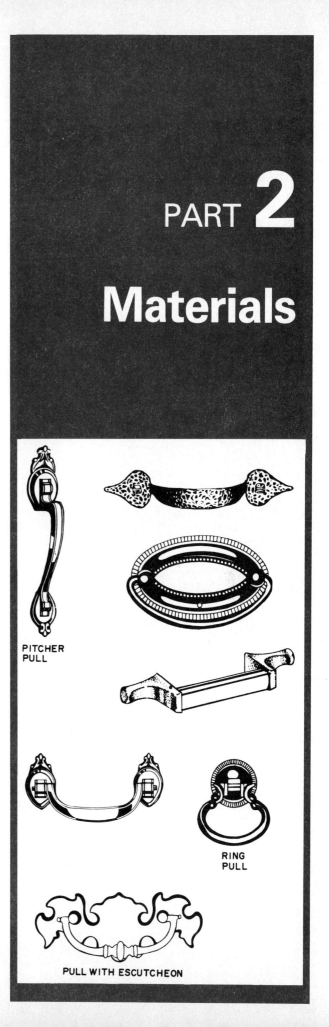

PITCHER PULL

RING PULL

PULL WITH ESCUTCHEON

6

CABINET WOODS

It is the purpose of this chapter to present in brief form information about the solid woods used in the wood products industries.

THE STRUCTURE OF WOOD

A knowledge of the structure of wood is important to those who work with it. The cellular structure and

FIGURE 6-1
A tree begins with the sprouting of a small seed. (*Courtesy of St. Regis Paper Company.*)

grain patterns determine to a large extent how it is machined, how parts are laid out on it, and how it is finished.

The life of a tree begins with the sprouting of a small seed (Fig. 6-1). As this small living plant develops, the characteristics associated with the wood in that species of tree are formed. A very small part of the tree is actually alive. The alive parts include the tips of the roots, the leaves, buds, flowers, seeds, and a thin layer of cells, called the cambium layer, which extends from the root tips to the buds (Fig. 6-2).

Each part of a tree has a specific function (Fig. 6-3). The *outer bark* provides the tree with a protective layer. Beneath it is the *inner bark* or phloem, through which food is passed to the rest of the tree. Next is the *cambium* layer, which produces new bark and new wood. The new wood produced, called the *sapwood*, serves as the pipeline to move water from the roots to the leaves. Beneath the sapwood is the *heartwood*, the central structural part of the tree. It is the mature wood which is dead. It has the color that is characteristic of the particular species of tree.

As a tree grows it adds new layers of wood in the spring and summer. The fast growth in the spring produces a light wood with large cells called

A large tree has hundreds of miles of roots to anchor it to the soil. But most of that length is dead, woody matter. At the very tips of the roots are living, growing cells that push a protective cap of dead cells through the soil. Just behind the tip are the roothairs, tiny, single-cell projections that absorb water and dissolved minerals from the soil, and start it on its way up to the leaves.

Extending from the tips of the roots to the ends of the branches is a single layer of living cells — the cambium layer. They are the only living cells in the trunk. In summer, when the tree grows, these cells divide continually — adding thickness but no height to the tree. The cells that form on the outside of the cambium layer become bark; those that form on the inside become wood.

The leaves — or needles, in coniferous trees — make sugar out of water passed up from the roots and carbon dioxide in the air. In doing this they utilize the energy of light, with the aid of chlorophyll. The sugar is passed back to the other living cells of the tree so that they can breathe — that is, combine the sugar with oxygen to create energy for the infinite processes of life which enable them to grow and develop.

The leaf buds on the twigs are alive, too. It is their growth that gives a tree height, and extends its branches. Cells at the base of the bud divide and elongate, building a new twig behind the developing leaf. This growth is coordinated with the growth in the cambium layer, so that as a tree grows in height, its trunk and its branches are all growing in thickness at the same time.

FIGURE 6-2
A tree has a living system extending from the roots to the leaves or needles. (*Courtesy of St. Regis Paper Company.*)

FIGURE 6-3
The tree trunk serves as the structural part of the tree as well as a pipeline to move water from the roots to the leaves. (*Courtesy of St. Regis Paper Company.*)

The outer bark is the protective outer layer. It develops from inside the tree.

The phloem is the outer layer of the cambium. It is the layer through which food is moved to all parts of the tree.

The xylem is the inner layer of the cambium. It produces new wood and new bark.

The sapwood moves water to the leaves.

The heartwood is the dead wood in the core of the tree. It gives the trunk strength.

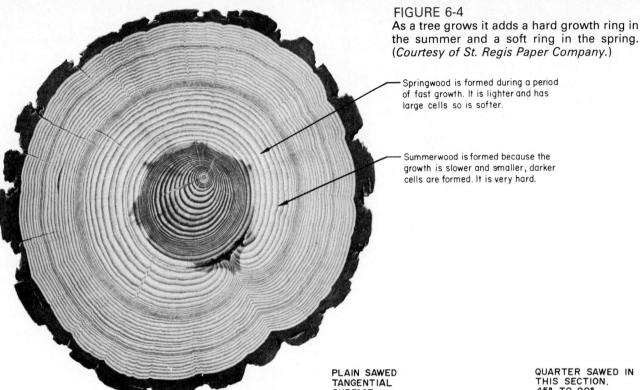

Springwood is formed during a period of fast growth. It is lighter and has large cells so is softer.

Summerwood is formed because the growth is slower and smaller, darker cells are formed. It is very hard.

earlywood or spring wood. In the summer the rate of growth slows and the wood has smaller, darker cells. This band is called latewood or summer wood. A band of earlywood and latewood make up one growth ring. These rings can be seen when a tree is cut. The approximate age of a tree can be ascertained by counting the annual rings. One growth ring is usually added each year (Fig. 6-4).

SAWING LUMBER

Wood is cut to provide tangential, radial, and transverse surfaces. When a log is cut so that the annual rings are tangent with the face, it has a *tangential surface* and is called *plain or flat sawed*. This surface displays the highest figure in its grain pattern. When a board is cut so that the annual rings are at an angle of 45 to 90° to the face, it has a *radial surface* and is called *quarter sawed*. This is the most stable of all cuts of wood. The sides of the hard annual rings are exposed on the face of the board. When a log is cut on an angle of 35 to 45°, it is called *rift sawed*. It is a combination of plain sawed and quarter sawed (Fig. 6-5). The end grain of all three cuts expose the ends of the wood cells. This is called the *transverse surface.*

Softwoods are cut to get the most material from the log that is possible. The cuts are planed to get the various-size members that will produce the least waste. One example is shown in Fig. 6-6.

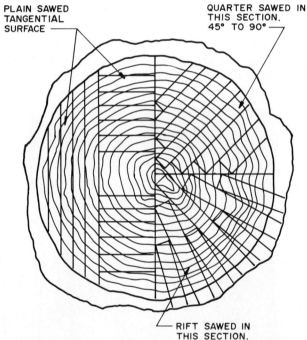

PLAIN SAWED TANGENTIAL SURFACE

QUARTER SAWED IN THIS SECTION. 45° TO 90°

RIFT SAWED IN THIS SECTION.

FIGURE 6-5
These are the ways boards are cut from the tree trunk.

HARDWOODS

Hardwoods come from *deciduous* trees (Fig. 6-7), which shed their broad leaves in the fall. They grow in the northern and southern parts of the United States. Hardwoods are used extensively in furniture and cabinet construction because of their strength

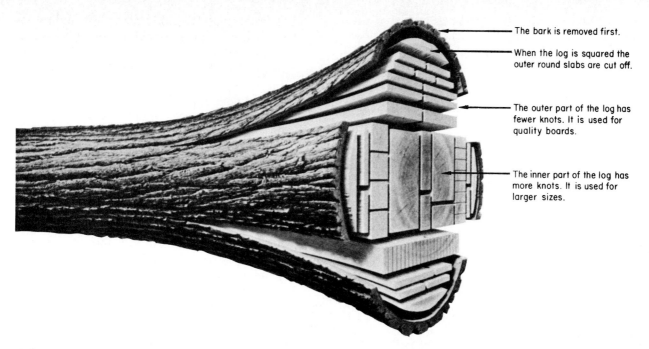

The bark is removed first.

When the log is squared the outer round slabs are cut off.

The outer part of the log has fewer knots. It is used for quality boards.

The inner part of the log has more knots. It is used for larger sizes.

FIGURE 6-6
Softwood is most generally used for construction, so the tree is cut to get the maximum number of standard-sized pieces from it. (*Courtesy of St. Regis Paper Company.*)

and great natural beauty. Most have a highly figured grain and resist dents and abrasion better than most softwoods.

Hardwood Grades

The grades of hardwood lumber are from highest to lowest, firsts, seconds, select, No. 1 common, No. 2 common, and No. 3A common, and No. 3B common.

Firsts and Seconds (FAS) is a combination of the best two grades which are combined for selling purposes. The boards must be at least 6 in. (150 mm) wide and 8 ft (2440 mm) long. The poorest side yields 83% clear wood.

Select Grade must be at least 4 in. (200 mm) wide and 6 ft (1830 mm) long. The best side is as good as the FAS grade. The poorest side is permitted to have more defects.

No. 1 Common must be at least 4 in. (100 mm) wide and 2 ft long (610 mm) or 3 in. (75 mm) wide and 3 ft (915 mm) long. This is an excellent choice for furniture and cabinet work. It is lower in cost

HARDWOODS

SOFTWOODS

FIGURE 6-7
The two classifications of trees are: deciduous and coniferous. (*Courtesy of Fine Hardwoods/ American Walnut Association.*)

Hardwood is primarily decorative — or special wear & impact

Softwood primarily for structural use, with paneling grades

The Deciduous types which bear leaves that fall and that are replaced each season

The Coniferous types which bear needles that remain green the year round, sometimes called evergreen

than the higher grades and has at least 65% of the board clear.

Hardwoods are sold in random widths and lengths (RWL). Common thicknesses are listed in Table 6-1.

TABLE 6-1
Thicknesses of Hardwood Lumber

Nominal (rough) (in.)	Surfaced (S2S)	
	in.	Possible metric size (mm)
$\frac{3}{8}$	$\frac{3}{16}$	5
$\frac{1}{2}$	$\frac{5}{16}$	8
$\frac{5}{8}$	$\frac{7}{16}$	11
$\frac{3}{4}$	$\frac{9}{16}$	14
1	$\frac{13}{16}$	21
$1\frac{1}{4}$	$1\frac{1}{16}$	27
$1\frac{1}{2}$	$1\frac{5}{16}$	33
$1\frac{3}{4}$	$1\frac{1}{2}$	38
2	$1\frac{3}{4}$	44
$2\frac{1}{2}$	$2\frac{1}{4}$	57
3	$2\frac{3}{4}$	70
$3\frac{1}{2}$	$3\frac{1}{4}$	82
4	$3\frac{3}{4}$	95

Source: National Hardwood Lumber Association.

SOFTWOODS

Softwoods come from coniferous or cone-bearing trees which retain their needle-shaped leaves all year. They grow mainly in the south and far western parts of the United States. Common softwoods include cedar, fir, pine, and redwood (Fig. 6-7).

Softwood Grades

Softwood lumber is divided into three size classifications: boards, dimension lumber, and timbers. Boards are used in furniture and cabinet construction.

The grades of softwood lumber from highest to lowest are select, common, factory, and molding.

Select grades are A, B, C, and D. Grades A and B are grouped together under a grade, B and Better. C Select is the second grade board and allows only a few tight pin knots. It is a top-quality paint board. D Select is the lowest select grade and can have obvious defects on the bad face.

Common grades run from No. 1 to No. 5. The higher the grade number, the more defects in the board. These are generally used for building construction work.

Factory grades are used to make doors and windows.

Molding boards are 1 in. (25 mm) and wider and 6 ft (1830 mm) or longer. They are used to manufacture molding.

Softwood lumber is sold in standardized sizes. The nominal size (size before planing) is used when ordering the material. When purchasing a board from a lumberyard you may order a 1 by 4. It will, however, measure $\frac{3}{4}$ by $3\frac{1}{2}$ in. (16 by 88 mm) because it has been planed to remove the saw marks. Standard widths and thicknesses for inch sizes with metric conversions are in Table 6-2.

IDENTIFYING HARDWOODS AND SOFTWOODS

There are several hundred different woods growing over the world. These vary considerably in their physical properties and color. Some are especially well suited for furniture and cabinet construction. Following are brief descriptions of the more popular woods used in the U.S. furniture and cabinet industry.

Selected Hardwoods

Red alder is light in weight compared to other hard woods. It has a fine texture and there is

TABLE 6-2
Standard Sizes of Softwood Lumber

Thickness			Width		
Nominal (in.)	Dressed (in.)	Proposed dressed (mm)	Nominal (in.)	Dressed (in.)	Proposed dressed (mm)
1	$\frac{3}{4}$	16	2	$1\frac{1}{2}$	36
$1\frac{1}{4}$	$1\frac{1}{4}$	27	3	$2\frac{1}{2}$	62
$1\frac{1}{2}$	$1\frac{3}{8}$	40	4	$3\frac{1}{2}$	88
2	$1\frac{1}{2}$	36	5	$4\frac{1}{2}$	114
$2\frac{1}{2}$	2	50	6	$5\frac{1}{2}$	140
3	$2\frac{1}{2}$	62	8	$7\frac{1}{4}$	190
$3\frac{1}{2}$	3	76	10	$9\frac{1}{4}$	233
4	$3\frac{1}{2}$	88	12	$11\frac{1}{4}$	290

little contrast between the spring and summer wood. The heartwood is pale rose colored and the sapwood is lighter. It is easy to machine, stains easily, and is used to blend with more expensive woods.

Ash is heavy, hard, strong, and tough and is straight grained. It is open grained, machines well, and has excellent gluing properties. The sapwood is white and the heartwood is light tan. There are 18 species native to the United States. Of these, white ash is the best known. It can be stained or given a light or natural finish.

Basswood is one of the softest of the hardwoods. It is extremely soft, very light in weight, and pliable. It is used for furniture, picture frame moldings, toys, food containers, drawing boards, and foundry patterns. It is odorless and tasteless. It works easily with hand and power tools, glues well, and can be painted or stained. Basswood is light in color.

Yellow birch is a moderately heavy, hard, strong, close-grained cabinet wood. It has a variety of pleasing grain patterns. Sometimes it is difficult to machine but glues and stains easily. It is often stained with walnut or mahogany stain. Birch is widely used for furniture and cabinets. In color the sapwood is yellow-white and the heartwood is reddish brown.

Cherry is a moderately heavy, strong, close-grained wood that is moderately hard. It is easily worked and finishes well. For hundreds of years it has been a popular cabinet and furniture wood. It is becoming increasingly scarce. It has a rich, reddish heartwood and a figured grain. The sapwood varies from white to yellow-brown.

Cypress resists decay and insects. It is rather coarse in texture, nonporous, soft, light in weight, and stiff. The heartwood is used where the product is in contact with the elements, such as garden furniture, exterior house trim, and trellises. Cypress is pale brown to red in color.

Red gum is an important timber tree in the southern United States. It is one of the softer hardwoods and is strong. The wood is close grained and machines easily and finishes well. It is rated as only fair in stability. The heartwood is reddish brown and the sapwood an off-white. It is often used with more valuable woods such as walnut because it stains and finishes nicely. Much gum is used as outer veneer on plywood.

Honduras mahogany is imported from the tropical regions of Central and South America. It has been a popular cabinet wood for centuries. It has a moderate density and hardness that makes it easy to work. It turns and carves superbly. Mahogany is open grained and is beautifully figured. In color it ranges from a pale to medium reddish brown. It darkens with age.

African mahogany has much the same characteristics as those of genuine mahogany and is related botanically. The African mahogany has a more highly figured open grain and is not quite as good to work as genuine mahogany. It is a fine, first-rate cabinet wood.

Philippine mahogany is native to the Philippine Islands. It has a medium density and hardness and is easy to work. The pores are open and require a filler. There are several species making up the Philippine mahogany group. They range in color from dark red to light pink and are often sold with these color names. It is a fine cabinet wood and is also used to make trim, paneling, and molding.

Northern hard maple is a very hard, stiff, close-grained wood. It is odorless and tasteless and is therefore good for articles used with food. Accidental forms in the grain, called bird's-eye and curly maple, are prized for their unusual appearance. The heartwood is a very light tan and the sapwood is white. It is used in furniture and cabinet construction, woodware, and flooring.

Southern soft maple is really a moderately hard wood. It has medium density and strength. The machining and finishing properties are good and it is very stable. It is a close-grained wood, so does not require filling. The heartwood varies from pale tan to reddish gray. The sapwood is white. It is a very important wood in the manufacture of furniture.

Red oak is found over many parts of the United States. It is coarse textured, open grained, hard, and durable. It can be fairly hard to work. Red oak is used widely in the cabinet and furniture industries. Red oak is reddish brown.

White oak has a uniform strength, is close grained, and has good durability when exposed to weather. It is used in fine cabinet and furniture work and interior trim. It is somewhat difficult to work. White oak has a light brown color that can easily be bleached for furniture requiring a light natural finish.

Pecan/hickory are so closely related it is difficult to identify individual specimens. The wood is hard, heavy, elastic, and strong. The heartwood is light reddish brown and the sapwood is white. It machines well and steam bends nicely.

Yellow poplar is not actually related to the poplar species but to the magnolia family. It is a widely used hardwood because it is soft, straight grained, and easy to work. It can be stained to imitate walnut and mahogany. Because poplar is inexpensive it is frequently utilized for hidden structural parts in furniture and cabinets. The sapwood is light tan to white and the heartwood is yellow-tan.

Rosewood is imported from Asia, Central America, and Brazil. The wood is very hard and dense and has an open grain. When freshly cut it gives off a pleasant fragrance. The grain pattern is very irregular and beautiful. In color the heartwood is usually a deep reddish brown with black streaks. Since it is in limited supply it is usually used as veneer on plywood. It is used on the very best furniture manufactured.

Sycamore is our largest broadleaf tree. It has wood of medium density and is therefore a soft hardwood. It is close grained but has a coarse texture. The heartwood is pink to brownish pink and the sapwood is somewhat lighter.

Teak comes from Burma, India, Java, and Thailand. It is very dense and heavy and will not float. Teak can be worked fairly easily using carbide-tipped tools but will quickly dull ordinary tool-steel cutting devices. It has become one of the most prestigious imported hardwoods. It has a wide range of grain figures and is yellow-brown in color. Since it is expensive it is most often used as veneers on plywood.

North American walnut is one of the most prized American hardwoods. It has a wide range of beautifully figured grain patterns and a deep, rich, brown color. It is relatively hard, open grained, and easy to work. Walnut is durable, stable, easy to carve, and exceptionally nice to finish.

Willow is found in many species, but only the black willow produces trees of timber size. It is one of the softest of the hardwoods. It stains well and is often used to imitate walnut. The color of the heartwood varies from light gray to dark brown. The sapwood varies from white with a gray cast to light tan.

Zebrawood is found in Nigeria, West Africa, Gabon, and Cameroon. It is highly decorative, being light gold in color with narrow streaks of dark brown to black. It is hard and heavy and can be polished to high luster.

Samples of selected examples of these woods are shown in Fig. 6-8.

Selected Softwoods

Aromatic red cedar is not really a cedar but a juniper belonging to the cypress family. The lumber is narrow in width and knotty. The wood is light weight, soft, close grained, and is easily worked except around the knots. It is aromatic and is therefore in demand for cedar chests and clothes closet linings. It is normally left unfinished but can have transparent coatings, as varnish, to protect the natural color. The sapwood is white and the heartwood is reddish purple.

Western red cedar grows in a belt from southern Alaska to northern California. The wood is light in weight and very durable when exposed to the weather. It stains well and is easy to machine. The heartwood is reddish brown. It is used for shingles, windows, doors, tanks, and trim.

Ponderosa pine is used for reproduction of early American cabinets and furniture where small, sound knots are part of the classical appearance. Since it grows over a great part of the western United States, its characteristics differ. From some regions it can be a hardwood with a coarse texture. Grown in other places, it might be softer with a fine texture and grain. It is widely used for doors, windows, and millwork. Most of the time it is painted but can be stained or finished natural. In color it is usually a light tan with white sapwood.

Redwood is a softwood that resists decay and weathers extremely well. It is a softwood that is rather light in weight. It is easy to work and is generally left unfinished or stained. Outdoor furniture and decks are often made from redwood. It has a beautiful reddish color and pleasing grain figure.

KILN DRYING

Wood used in furniture and cabinet construction should have a moisture content of *6 to 8 percent* and must be kiln dried. *Kiln dried wood* is dried in large buildings called kilns, where moisture and temperatures are carefully controlled to reduce the moisture in the wood without causing it to check, split, or warp.

VENEERS

Veneer is a thin sheet of wood, usually about $\frac{1}{28}$ in. thick, which is glued to a base such as plywood or particleboard. It is an economical way of covering a large area with an expensive wood. This costs much less than using solid wood (Fig. 6-9, page 77).

Veneers are sold by the square foot. They are packed in a bundle called a *flitch*. The pieces of veneer in a flitch are stacked in the same order in which they were sliced from the log. The order is important when you want to match the grain on veneer strips used to make a wide panel.

Veneers of different grain patterns are produced by cutting them from different parts of the tree (Fig. 6-10, page 77). Veneer from the crotch contains swirls in the grain pattern. Stump wood produces a wavy grain pattern. Wartlike growths, called burls, have the most complex swirling pattern of all cuts. *Quarter-sliced veneers* are cut from the

Afrormosia	Aider	Apitong	Ash, brown
Ash, white	Balsa	Banak (virola)	Basswood, american
Beech, american	Birch	Butternut	Canalete
Cedar, aromatic red	Cedar, spanish	Cedar, western	Cherry

FIGURE 6-8
Selected wood samples. (*Courtesy of Frank Paxton Company.*)

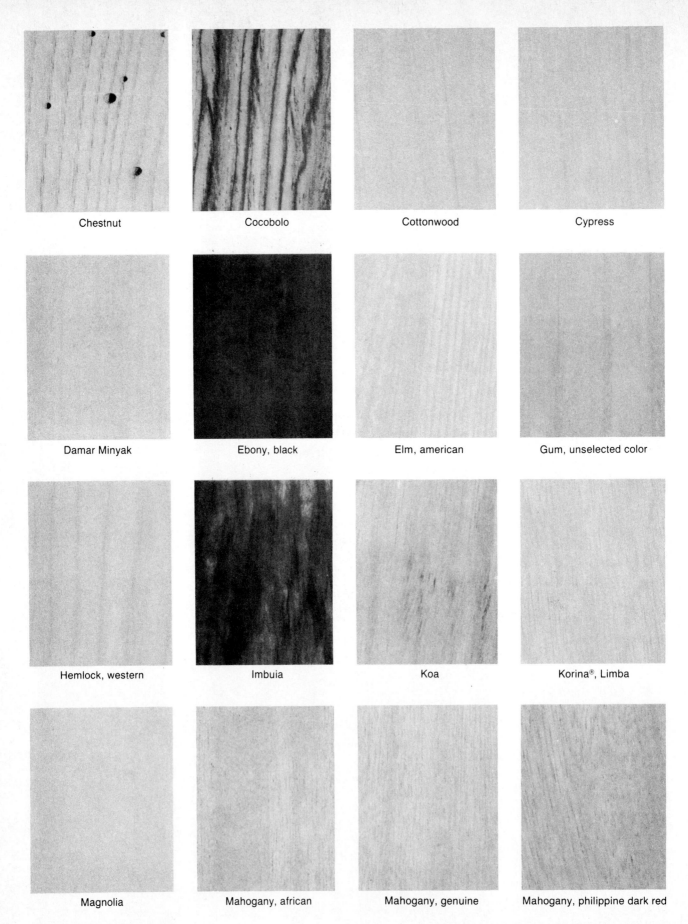

Chestnut

Cocobolo

Cottonwood

Cypress

Damar Minyak

Ebony, black

Elm, american

Gum, unselected color

Hemlock, western

Imbuia

Koa

Korina®, Limba

Magnolia

Mahogany, african

Mahogany, genuine

Mahogany, philippine dark red

FIGURE 6-8 (*Continued*)

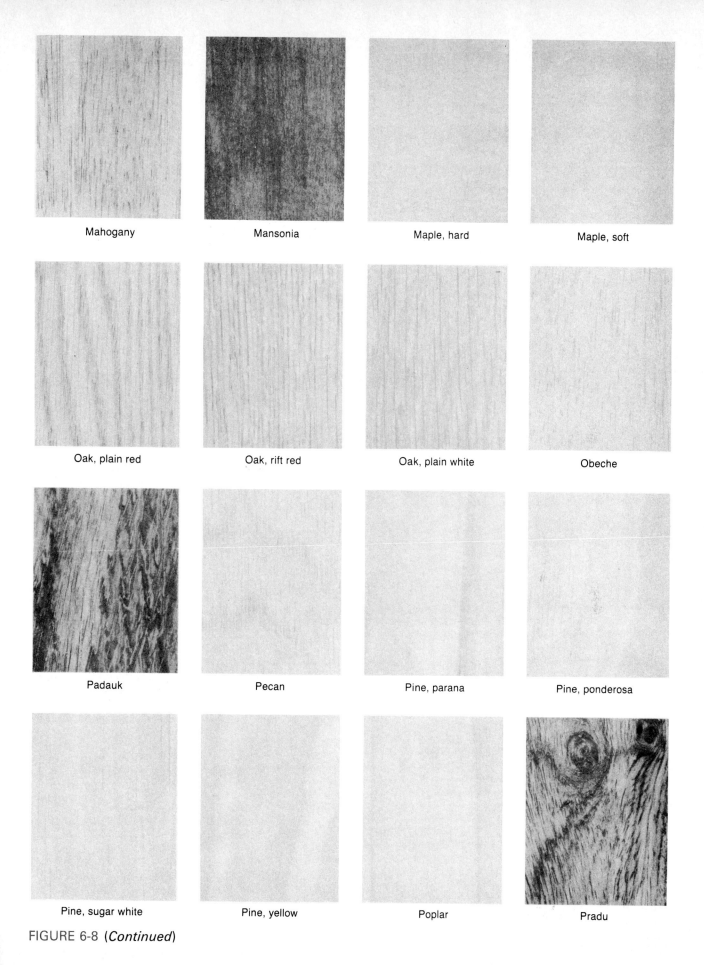

Mahogany

Mansonia

Maple, hard

Maple, soft

Oak, plain red

Oak, rift red

Oak, plain white

Obeche

Padauk

Pecan

Pine, parana

Pine, ponderosa

Pine, sugar white

Pine, yellow

Poplar

Pradu

FIGURE 6-8 (*Continued*)

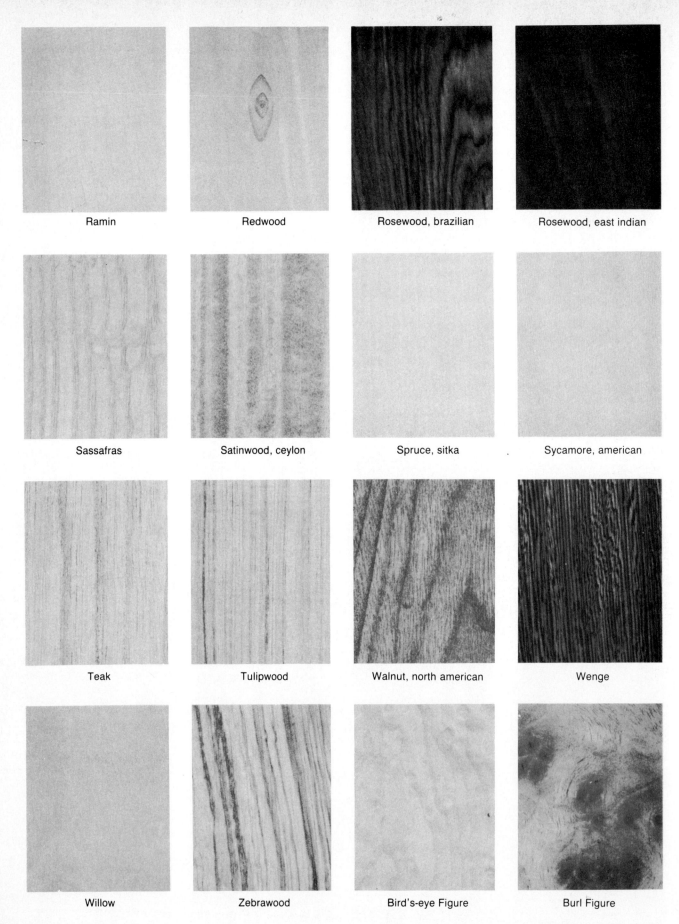

Ramin

Redwood

Rosewood, brazilian

Rosewood, east indian

Sassafras

Satinwood, ceylon

Spruce, sitka

Sycamore, american

Teak

Tulipwood

Walnut, north american

Wenge

Willow

Zebrawood

Bird's-eye Figure

Burl Figure

FIGURE 6-8 (*Continued*)

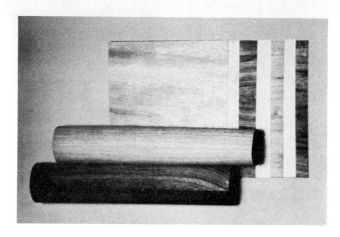

FIGURE 6-9
Wood veneers are glued to less expensive woods.

nual growth ring. This produces figure characteristics similar to rotary- and plain-sliced veneer. A *rift-cut veneer* is produced in this way (Fig. 6-14).

Veneer Matching

When veneers are cut the grain patterns are matched in several ways. The most commonly used match is book matching. When *book matching,* every other sheet in a flitch is turned over just like the pages in a book. The back of one sheet meets the front of the next sheet. This produces a matching design along the joint (Fig. 6-15).

Slip matching places the sheets side by side repeating the figure (Fig. 6-15). This is often used with quarter-sliced veneers.

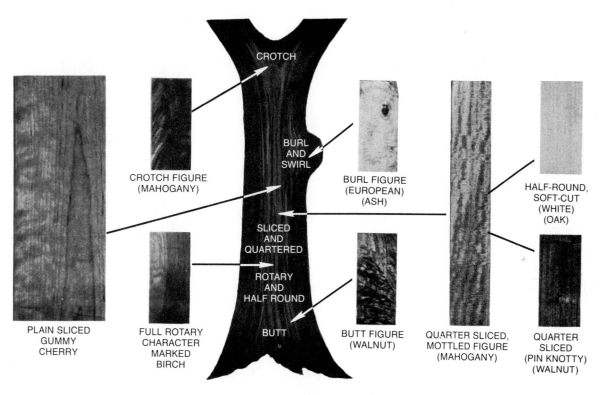

CROTCH

CROTCH FIGURE
(MAHOGANY)

BURL
AND
SWIRL

BURL FIGURE
(EUROPEAN)
(ASH)

HALF-ROUND,
SOFT-CUT
(WHITE)
(OAK)

SLICED
AND
QUARTERED

ROTARY
AND
HALF ROUND

PLAIN SLICED
GUMMY
CHERRY

FULL ROTARY
CHARACTER
MARKED
BIRCH

BUTT

BUTT FIGURE
(WALNUT)

QUARTER SLICED,
MOTTLED FIGURE
(MAHOGANY)

QUARTER
SLICED
(PIN KNOTTY)
(WALNUT)

FIGURE 6-10
The grain pattern of a veneer varies depending on the part of the tree from which it is cut. (*Courtesy of Fine Hardwoods/American Walnut Association.*)

bole (straight trunk). The trunk is first cut into quarters and the veneer cut from each quarter (Fig. 6-11). *Plain-sliced veneers* are also cut from the straight trunk. This trunk is sliced into veneers with large knives (Fig. 6-12). *Rotary-cut veneer* is produced by mounting a log in a veneer lathe and cutting a continuous sheet by feeding a knife into the log (Fig. 6-13). The log is literally unwound much like a roll of paper. *Semirotary slicing* sometimes called half-round slicing cuts across the an-

Random match involves placing sheets so that no repetitive pattern occurs. Sheets may be from several different logs (Fig. 6-16).

Vertical butt and horizontal book leaf match are used when the height of the sheets in a flitch are such that they do not produce the height needed (Fig. 6-16).

Three other matches are shown in Fig. 6-17. These include *diamond, reverse diamond,* and a *four-way center and butt.*

QUARTER SLICED

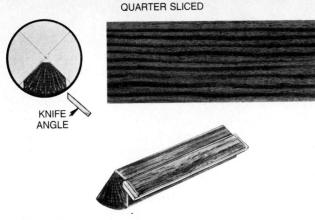

FIGURE 6-11
Quarter-sliced veneers are cut from quartered sections of a log. (*Courtesy of Fine Hardwoods/American Walnut Association.*)

SEMI-ROTARY (HALF-ROUND)

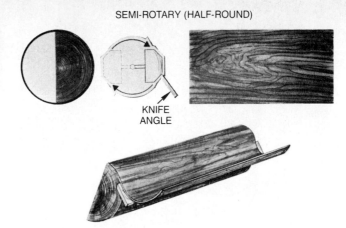

FIGURE 6-14
Semirotary-sliced veneers are made with half-round slicing cuts across the annual growth rings. (*Courtesy of Fine Hardwoods/American Walnut Association.*)

PLAIN SLICED

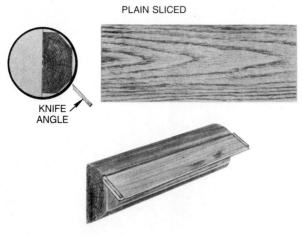

FIGURE 6-12
Plain-sliced veneers are cut from the straight sections of the trunk. (*Courtesy of Fine Hardwoods/American Walnut Association.*)

Veneer Matching
BASIC MATCHING EFFECTS

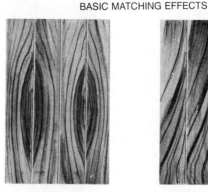

BOOK MATCH   SLIP MATCH

FIGURE 6-15
Book-matched and slip-matched veneers. (*Courtesy of Fine Hardwoods/American Walnut Association.*)

ROTARY

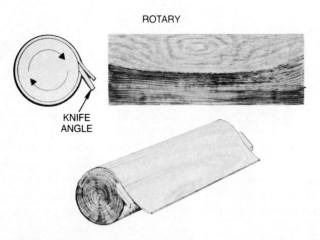

FIGURE 6-13
The log is "unpeeled" to form rotary-cut veneers. (*Courtesy of Fine Hardwoods/American Walnut Association.*)

Veneer Matching
BASIC MATCHING EFFECTS

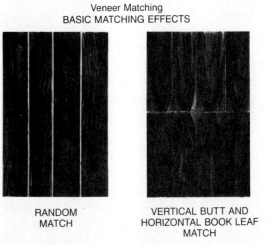

RANDOM
MATCH

VERTICAL BUTT AND
HORIZONTAL BOOK LEAF
MATCH

FIGURE 6-16
Veneer matching: random match and vertical butt and horizontal book lead match. (*Courtesy of Fine Hardwoods/American Walnut Association.*)

Veneer Matching
SPECIAL MATCHING EFFECTS

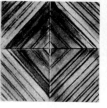

DIAMOND

REVERSE
DIAMOND

FOUR-WAY CENTER
AND BUTT

FIGURE 6-17
Veneer matching: diamond, reverse diamond, and four-way center butt. (*Courtesy of Fine Hardwoods/American Walnut Association.*)

Veneer Matching
SPECIAL MATCHING EFFECTS

"V"

HERRINGBONE

SUNBURST PATTERN

FIGURE 6-18
Veneer matching: vee, herringbone, and sunburst. (*Courtesy of Fine Hardwoods/American Walnut Association.*)

V and herringbone matches are popular. They are especially interesting on large surfaces. A special sunburst pattern is used on tabletops (Fig. 6-18).

ORDERING LUMBER

Solid lumber is sold by the board foot. A board foot is equal to a piece 1 in. thick by 1 ft square. It contains 144 in.^{3}. Stock that is less than 1 in. thick is figured as 1-in. lumber. Board feet is figured on the size of the stock before it was surfaced (the nominal size). For example, a 2-in.-thick piece of hardwood when surfaced is $1\frac{3}{4}$ in. The board feet would be figured on the 2-in. thickness.

Large quantities of lumber are priced per 1000 board feet. The Roman numeral M stands for 1000

and is used to designate this quantity. For example, 1000 board feet at $1500 per M is worth $1500. Divide this by 1000 and the cost per board foot is found to be $1.50 per board foot.

Board feet when the length of the board is in inches can be found with the following formula:

$$\frac{\text{thickness (in.)} \times \text{width (in.)} \times \text{length (in.)}}{144} = \text{bd.ft.}$$

The board feet when the length of the board is in feet can be found with the following formula:

$$\frac{\text{thickness (in.)} \times \text{width (in.)} \times \text{length (ft.)}}{12} = \text{bd.ft.}$$

7

PLYWOOD

Plywood is a manufactured panel widely used when building furniture and cabinets and in construction and industrial applications. It is a very strong product and does not split. Since it is made by joining alternating plies of veneer and in some cases solid wood layers, it resists warping better than solid wood. It is especially useful when large, flat surfaces are required, such as a tabletop or desktop or side panels (Fig. 7-1).

CONSTRUCTION OF PLYWOOD

Plywood is a panel made by gluing together layers of wood, with the grain in each ply perpendicular to the ply below it. A panel always has an odd number of plies; three, five, seven, or nine. Each ply may be a single thickness of veneer or two veneers glued together to form a thicker ply. In this case the grain in these two plies runs in the same direction.

The most common plywood constructions are with a veneer core, lumber core, particleboard core, and medium-density fiberboard core (Fig. 7-2). A *veneer-core* panel typically has three to nine veneer plies. It is the strongest of all panel cores. A *lumber-core panel* has many strips of lumber glued together,

FIGURE 7-1
Hardwood plywood is used extensively in furniture and cabinet construction. (*Courtesy of Fine Hardwoods/American Walnut Association.*)

forming the core and two veneer crossbands on each side. It is often used for cabinet doors where the edge will be exposed. *Particleboard and medium-density fiberboard-core* plywood have a single sheet of one of these as the core, with one veneer sheet glued on each side. These are discussed in detail in Chapter 8.

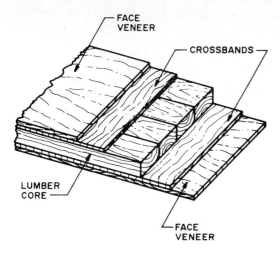

LUMBER CORE PLYWOOD

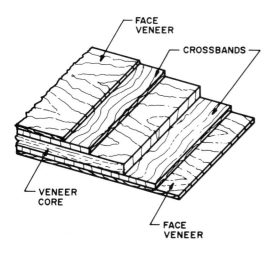

VENEER CORE PLYWOOD

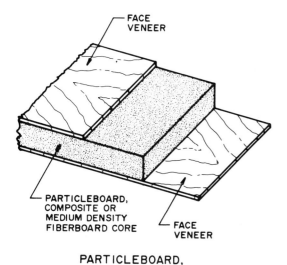

PARTICLEBOARD,
COMPOSITE,
MEDIUM DENSITY
FIBERBOARD OR
HARDBOARD CORE

HARDWOOD PLYWOOD

The standards for hardwood plywood are reported in ANSI/HPMA HP 1983, American National Standard for Hardwood and Decorative Plywood. These standards are published by the Hardwood Plywood Manufacturers Association, P.O. Box 2789, Reston, VA 22090.

Grades of Veneers in Hardwood Plywood

Hardwood plywood is manufactured with six grades of veneers. These grades with their identifying symbols are listed in Table 7-1.

TABLE 7-1
Hardwood Veneer Grades

Grade	Symbol
A grade	A
B grade	B
Sound grade	2
Industrial grade	3
Backing grade	4
Specialty grade	SP

A Grade (A) is the best. The face is made of hardwood veneers carefully matched as to color and grain. This grade is sometimes called *premium.*

B Grade (B) is suitable for a natural finish, but the face veneers are not as carefully matched as on the A grade. This grade is sometimes called *good.*

Sound grade (2) provides a face that is smooth. All defects have been repaired. It is used as a smooth base for a paint finish.

Industrial-grade (3) face veneers can have surface defects. This grade permits knotholes up to 1 in. (25 mm) in diameter, small open joints, and small areas of rough grain.

Backing grade (4) uses unselected veneers having knotholes up to 3 in. in diameter and certain types of splits. Any defect permitted does not affect the strength of the panel.

Specialty grade (SP) includes veneers having characteristics unlike any of those in the other grades. The characteristics are agreed upon between the manufacturer and the purchaser. For example, species such as wormy chestnut or bird's-eye maple are considered as Specialty Grade.

Veneer requirements for softwoods used in hardwood plywood panels are also specified in ANSI/HPMA HP 1983.

FIGURE 7-2
Common types of plywood construction.

Species Used in Hardwood Plywood

A wide range of species of wood are used in hardwood plywood. These are shown in Table 7-2. These species are divided into four categories, A, B, C, and D. The categories reflect the modulus of elasticity (stiffness) of each species. These data are used when

Detailed specifications for each type are in ASNI/HPMA HP 1983. Some of the major requirements are listed in Table 7-4.

Technical type hardwood plywood must withstand a three-cycle boil-shear test. Type I must withstand a two-cycle boil test. A boil test involves following standard procedures in which a sample is

---

TABLE 7-2

Categories of Commonly Used Decorative Species in Hardwood Plywood[a]

Category A	Category B	Category C	Category D
Ash, white	Ash, black	Alder, red	Aspen
Apitong	Avodire	Basswood, American	Cedar, eastern red
Beech, American	Birch, paper	Butternut	Cedar, western red
Birch, yellow, sweet	Cherry, black	Cativo	Fuma
Bubinga	Cypress	Chestnut, American	Willow, black
Hickory	Elm, rock	Cottonwood, black	
Kapur	Fir, Douglas	Cottonwood, eastern	
Keruing	Fir, white	Elm, American (gray,	
Oak (Oregon, red, or	Gum, sweet	red, or white)	
white)	Hemlock, western	Gum, black	
Paldao	Magnolia, cucumber	Hackberry	
Pecan	Sweetbay	Hemlock, eastern	
Rosewood	Maple, sugar (hard)	Lauan	
Sapele	Mahogany, African	Maple, red (soft)	
	Mahogany, Honduras	Maple, silver (soft)	
	Maple, black (hard)	Meranti, red	
	Pine, western white	Pine, ponderosa	
	Poplar, yellow	Pine, sugar	
	Spruce, red, Sitka	Pine, eastern white	
	Sycamore	Prima-vera	
	Tanoak	Redwood	
	Teak	Sassafras	
	Walnut, American	Spruce (black, Engelmann,	
		white)	
		Tupelo, water	

Source: Hardwood Plywood Manufacturers Association.

[a] Based on an evaluation of published modulus of elasticity (MOE) and specific gravity values.

---

establishing the maximum thickness of the veneer. The maximum veneer thickness is listed in Table 7-3.

The species for the *face* of a panel can be any hardwood species. If the face veneer is to be a decorative face, it could be any of the softwood species listed in Table 7-2. The species of the back and inner plies may be any hardwood or softwood species.

Types of Hardwood Plywood

The four types of hardwood plywood listed in decending order of water-resistance capability are:

    Technical (exterior)

    Type I (exterior)

    Type II (interior)

    Type III (interior)

boiled for 4 hours, dried, boiled again, and cooled in cold water. The technical type is tested for shear. Type I is examined to see if the veneers have separated. Any separation over 1 in. (25 mm) is a failure. Basically, this is a test of the glue bond. These panels can be designed to carry very large loads and are actually structural panels.

TABLE 7-3

Thicknesses for Hardwood Plywood Veneer

Category	Maximum veneer thickness (in.)
A	$\frac{1}{12}$
B	$\frac{1}{8}$
C	$\frac{3}{16}$
D	$\frac{3}{16}$

TABLE 7-4

TABLE 7-4
Specifications for Hardwood Plywood

	Technical (exterior)	Type I (exterior)	Type II (interior)	Type III (interior)
Glue bond	Waterproof	Waterproof	Water resistant	Water resistant
Veneer edge joints	No tape	No tape	Tape	Tape
Grade of lumber core	Not suitable	Specify	Specify	Specify
Particleboard or hardboard core	Not suitable	Specify	Specify	Specify

Type II panels must withstand a three-cycle soak test, and type III a two-cycle soak test. The soak test involves immersing samples in 75°F (24°C) water for 4 hours and drying them and resoaking. After the last cycle the sample is examined to see if the veneers have started to separate. A separation greater than 2 in. (50 mm) is a failure.

Construction of Hardwood Plywood

The construction of hardwood plywood is based on the type of core. Following are the standard constructions:

Hardwood veneer core: has an odd number of plies, such as 3-ply, 5-ply, and so on.

Softwood veneer core: has an odd number of plies, as 3-ply, 5-ply, and so on.

Hardwood lumber core: used in 3-ply, 5-ply, and 7-ply constructions.

Softwood lumber core: used in 3-ply, 5-ply, and 7-ply constructions.

Particleboard core: used in 3-ply and 5-ply constructions.

Medium-density fiberboard core: used in 3-ply construction.

Hardboard core: used in 3-ply construction.

Special cores: used in 3-ply construction. Special cores are those made of any other material than those listed above.

Sizes and Thicknesses of Hardwood Plywood

The thickness of the *veneers* varies with the intended use. These are specified in the standard. They range from $\frac{1}{12}$ to $\frac{1}{8}$ in. (2 to 3 mm). Face veneers on decorative plywood are usually $\frac{1}{80}$ in. (0.3 mm).

Hardwood plywood is made in *panels* 48 × 84 in., 48 × 96 in., and 48 × 120 in. The 48 × 96 in. is the most popular size and often is the only available size. Metric sizes have not been established, but the 48 × 96 in. panel will probably be 1200 × 2400 mm. Other sizes can be had by special order.

Standard thickness for veneer-core panels are $\frac{1}{4}$ in (6 mm), $\frac{3}{8}$ in. (9 mm), $\frac{1}{2}$ in. (12 mm), and $\frac{3}{4}$ in. (18 mm). Lumber-core and particleboard-core panels are generally only $\frac{3}{4}$ in. (18 mm) thick.

Product Identification

Hardwood plywood is manufactured to specifications provided by the Hardwood Plywood Manufacturers Association. The panel specifications are indicated with a grade stamp. It identifies the glue bond, the product standard under which it is manufactured, the structural description, the species of wood, the flame spread rating (the lower the number, the slower the flame spread or the more fire resistant), the mill number, and the veneer grade of the face (Fig. 7-3). The backstamp used on the back of prefinished hardwood plywood wall panels is shown in Fig. 7-4. It indicates the flame spread rating as well as formaldehyde emission requiements. The backstamp used on prefinished particleboard panels is shown in Fig. 7-5.

FIGURE 7-3
Grade stamp used on hardwood plywood sold to the furniture industry. (*Courtesy of Hardwood Plywood Manufacturers Association.*)

GLUE BOND
TYPE II
INTERIOR

OAK
A GRADE

HARDWOOD PLYWOOD MANUFACTURERS ASSOCIATION		
FORMALDEHYDE EMISSION 0.2 PPM CONFORMS TO HUD REQUIREMENTS LAY UP 16 3.6MM THICK HP-SG-84	SIMULATED DECORATIVE FINISH ON PLYWOOD **hpma** ® MILL SPECIALTY GRADE	FLAME SPREAD 200 OR LESS ASTM E84 GLUE BOND TYPE II ANSI/HPMA HP 1983

FIGURE 7-4
Backstamp used on sheets of prefinished hardwood plywood wall panels. (*Courtesy of Hardwood Plywood Manufacturers Association.*)

HARDWOOD PLYWOOD MANUFACTURERS ASSOCIATION		
FORMALDEHYDE EMISSION 0.3 PPM CONFORMS TO HUD REQUIREMENTS	**hpma** ® MILL	FLAME SPREAD 200 OR LESS ASTM E84 SIMULATED DECORATIVE FINISH ON **PARTICLEBOARD**

FIGURE 7-5
Backstamp used on sheets of prefinished particleboard wall panels. (*Courtesy of Hardwood Plywood Manufacturers Association.*)

Industrial panels used by furniture manufacturers are shipped in large bundles. Rather than stamp each panel, a bundle grade stamp is used (Fig. 7-6). These panels will most likely be cut up into smaller sizes required for furniture and cabinet construction.

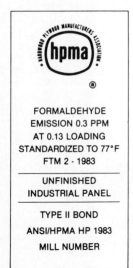

FORMALDEHYDE EMISSION 0.3 PPM AT 0.13 LOADING STANDARDIZED TO 77°F FTM 2 - 1983

UNFINISHED INDUSTRIAL PANEL

TYPE II BOND ANSI/HPMA HP 1983 MILL NUMBER

FIGURE 7-6
The grade stamp used on bundles of hardwood plywood shipped to furniture and cabinet manufacturers. (*Courtesy of Hardwood Plywood Manufacturers Association.*)

MILL (NUMBER)

FLAME SPREAD 200 OR LESS ASTM E162

ON ALL EXPOSED CABINET SURFACES

FIGURE 7-7
This grade stamp is used on hardwood plywood used in the manufacture of kitchen cabinets. (*Courtesy of Hardwood Plywood Manufacturers Association.*)

Hardwood plywood used in kitchen cabinets for mobile homes and conventional houses must meet flame spread ratings set by ASTM E162. All exposed parts of the cabinets must have a flame spread rating of 200 or less (Fig. 7-7). Manufacturers are also meeting the HUD requirements for formaldehyde emissions in cabinets as well as wall panels. See the requirements shown in Fig. 7-6.

Molded Plywood

Molded, curved, or cut to size, hardwood plywood has taken a major place in furniture manufacturing. It is used in many areas, such as in chair backs, seats, legs, arms, stretches, body-shaped parts, and supports. The furniture manufacturer sends to the ply-

FIGURE 7-8
Bent and molded plywood is widely used in furniture construction. This chair and ottoman are made with molded plywood. The legs on the coffee table are also molded plywood. (*Courtesy of Hardwood Plywood Manufacturers Association.*)

wood manufacturer a drawing of the shape desired and the grade and species of veneers wanted. The hardwood plywood manufacturer then uses molds to produce the desired parts. Bent plywood is used in place of bent solid wood frames in overstuffed furniture (Fig. 7-8). This produces a strong, light frame.

CONSTRUCTION AND INDUSTRIAL PLYWOOD

The requirements for the manufacture of plywood for construction and industrial uses are specified in U.S. Product Standard PS 1-83 for Construction and Industrial Plywood. The Office of Product Standards Policy of the National Bureau of Standards works with producers, distributors, consumers, and users (as American Plywood Association) to develop these voluntary product standards.

Although this type of plywood is used mainly for construction and industrial purposes, some types are used for hidden parts of furniture and cabinets.

Grades of Veneers in Construction and Industrial Plywood

The outer veneers are classified in five *appearance groups*, N, A, B, C, and D. N is the best and D is the lowest (Table 7-5). Panel grade designations for interior-type plywood are given in Table 7-6.

TABLE 7-6
Panel Grade Designations for Interior-Type Grades

Panel grade designation	Minimum veneer quality			
	Face	Back	Inner plies	Surface
N-N	N	N	C	Sanded 2 sides
N-A	N	A	C	Sanded 2 sides
N-B	N	B	C	Sanded 2 sides
N-D	N	D	D	Sanded 2 sides
A-A	A	A	D	Sanded 2 sides
A-B	A	B	D	Sanded 2 sides
A-D	A	D	D	Sanded 2 sides
B-B	B	B	D	Sanded 2 sides
B-D	B	D	D	Sanded 2 sides

Source: American Plywood Association.

Species Used in Construction and Industrial Plywood

About 70 species of softwoods and hardwoods are used. They are divided into five groups depending on their strength and stiffness. Group 1 includes those species that are the strongest and stiffest, while Group 5 species have the lowest ratings (Table 7-7). The front and back plies can be from any of the five groups. When they are made of more than one piece,

TABLE 7-5
Veneer Grades

N	Smooth surface ''natural finish'' veneer. Select, all heartwood or all sapwood. Free of open defects. Allows not more than 6 repairs, wood only, per 4 x 8 panel, made parallel to grain and well matched for grain and color.
A	Smooth, paintable. Not more than 18 neatly made repairs, boat, sled, or router type, and parallel to grain, permitted. May be used for natural finish in less demanding applications.
B	Solid surface. Shims, circular repair plugs and tight knots to 1 inch across grain permitted. Some minor splits permitted.
C Plugged	Improved C veneer with splits limited to 1/8-inch width and knotholes and borer holes limited to 1/4 x 1/2 inch. Admits some broken grain. Synthetic repairs permitted.
C	Tight knots to 1-1/2 inch. Knotholes to 1 inch across grain and some to 1-1/2 inch if total width of knots and knotholes is within specified limits. Synthetic or wood repairs. Discoloration and sanding defects that do not impair strength permitted. Limited splits allowed. Stitching permitted.
D	Knots and knotholes to 2-1/2 inch width across grain and 1/2 inch larger within specified limits. Limited splits are permitted. Stitching permitted. Limited to Interior (Exposure 1 or 2) panels.

Source: American Plywood Association.

TABLE 7-7
Classification of Species

Group 1	Group 2	Group 3	Group 4	Group 5
Apitong	Cedar, Port	Alder, Red	Aspen	Basswood
Beech,	Orford	Birch, Paper	Bigtooth	Poplar,
American	Cypress	Cedar, Alaska	Quaking	Balsam
Birch	Douglas	Fir,	Cativo	
Sweet	Fir 2(a)	Subalpine	Cedar	
Yellow	Fir	Hemlock,	Incense	
Douglas	Balsam	Eastern	Western	
Fir 1(a)	California	Maple,	Red	
Kapur	Red	Bigleaf	Cottonwood	
Keruing	Grand	Pine	Eastern	
Larch,	Noble	Jack	Black	
Western	Pacific	Lodgepole	(Western	
Maple, Sugar	Silver	Ponderosa	Poplar)	
Pine	White	Spruce	Pine	
Caribbean	Hemlock,	Redwood	Eastern	
Ocote	Western	Spruce	White	
Pine, South.	Lauan	Engelmann	Sugar	
Loblolly	Almon	White		
Longleaf	Bagtikan			
Shortleaf	Mayapis			
Slash	Red			
Tanoak	Tangile			
	White			
	Maple, Black			
	Mengkulang			
	Meranti,			
	Red(b)			
	Mersawa			
	Pine			
	Pond			
	Red			
	Virginia			
	Western			
	White			
	Spruce			
	Black			
	Red			
	Sitka			
	Sweetgum			
	Tamarack			
	Yellow-			
	Poplar			

(a) Douglas Fir from trees grown in the states of Washington, Oregon, California, Idaho, Montana, Wyoming, and the Canadian Provinces of Alberta and British Columbia shall be classed as Douglas Fir No. 1. Douglas Fir from trees grown in the states of Nevada, Utah, Colorado, Arizona and New Mexico shall be classed as Douglas Fir No. 2.

(b) Red Meranti shall be limited to species having a specific gravity of 0.41 or more based on green volume and oven dry weight.

Source: American Plywood Association.

each piece should be of the same species. Inner plies of Groups 1, 2, 3, or 4 panels may be of any species in Groups 1, 2, 3, or 4. Inner plies of Group 5 panels may be any species listed.

Types of Construction and Industrial Plywood

These plywoods are made in two types, interior and exterior. Following is a description of each.

Interior type bonded with interior glue. These panels are intended for interior applications.

Interior type bonded with intermediate glue. These panels are used where they will be pro-tected from the elements but may be exposed to high humidity or possible water leakage. This bonding is identified as Exposure 2.

Interior type bonded with exterior glue. These panels are used where they will be protected but where they may be exposed to the elements due to long construction delays or other severe conditions. This bonding is identified as Exposure 1.

Exterior type. These panels will retain their glue bond when repeatedly wetted and dried. This bonding is identified as Exposure 1.

Exposure 1 glues are used where exposure to moisture for long periods is severe. Exposure 2 glues are used where the panel will be protected when the construction is finished but will be exposed during construction.

There are other construction and industrial panels that will not find much use in furniture and cabinet construction. Most notable of these are the Performance Rated Panels. These panels are manufactured to provide known load-carrying capacities. There are five performance-rated panels: plywood, composite, waferboard, oriented strand board, and structural particleboard (Fig. 7-9). *Plywood* panels are made from all-veneer cross laminations. *Composite* panels have a core of reconstituted wood with a face and back veneer ply. *Waferboard* is a panel made of large, waferlike flakes of wood randomly or directionally oriented. *Oriented strand board* is a panel of compressed strandlike particles arranged in layers (three to five) oriented at right angles to each other. *Structural particleboard* is a panel comprised of small particles arranged in layers by particle size but not oriented. Table 7-8 lists the panel construction specifications for interior-type plywood.

Sizes and Thicknesses of Construction and Industrial Plywood

Construction and industrial plywood is available in panel widths of 36, 48, and 60 in. (914, 1219, and

TABLE 7-8
Plywood Panel Specifications

Thickness (in.)	Minimum number of plies	Minimum number of layers
Through $\frac{3}{8}$	3	3
Over $\frac{3}{8}$ through $\frac{1}{2}$	4	3
Over $\frac{1}{2}$ through $\frac{7}{8}$	5	5
Over $\frac{7}{8}$	6	5

1524 mm), and lengths from 60 to 144 in. (1524 to 3658 mm) in 12-in. (305-mm) increments. Other sizes are available on special order.

Standard thicknesses of sanded panels range from $\frac{1}{8}$ through $1\frac{1}{4}$ in. (3 through 31 mm) in $\frac{1}{8}$-in. (3-mm) increments. Unsanded panels range from $\frac{5}{16}$ to $1\frac{1}{4}$ in. (8 to 31 mm) in increments of $\frac{1}{8}$ in. (3 mm) for thicknesses over $\frac{3}{8}$ in. (10 mm).

Product Identification

The following trademarks for construction and industrial plywood are from the American Plywood Association. The *sanded grades* are most likely to be used in furniture and cabinet construction. The trademark for sanded grades includes the grade of

APA Performance-Rated
Panel Composition/Configurations

PLYWOOD
All-veneer panels consisting of an odd number of cross-laminated layers, each layer consisting of one or more plies. Many such panels meet all of the prescriptive or performance provisions of U.S. Product Standard PS 1-83/ANSI A199.1 for Construction and Industrial Plywood. Others may include panel constructions, grades and species not currently recognized in PS 1.

COMPOSITE (COMPLY®)
Panels of reconstituted wood cores bonded between veneer face and back plies.

WAFERBOARD
Panels of compressed wafer-like particles or flakes randomly or directionally oriented.

ORIENTED STRAND BOARD
Panels of compressed strand-like particles arranged in layers (usually three to five) oriented at right angles to one another.

STRUCTURAL PARTICLEBOARD
Panels comprised of small particles usually arranged in layers by particle size, but not usually oriented.

FIGURE 7-9
Five types of APA Performance-Rated panels. (*Courtesy of American Plywood Association.*)

veneer on the face and back, the species group number, the type of plywood, the number of the mill producing the plywood, and the product standard followed in making it. The *unsanded grades* are the Performance Rated Panels. Specialty panels include products such as exterior plywood siding. Examples of these trademarks are in Fig. 7-10.

SPECIALTY PLYWOODS

In addition to the plywood products manufactured under the specifications of PS 1-83 and ANSI/HPMA HP 1983, other special products are available.

Overlaid plywood is a high-grade panel of exterior-type plywood that has bonded to one or both

How to read the basic trademarks of the American Plywood Association

Product Standard PS 1-83 is a performance standard for clear understanding between buyer and seller. To identify plywood manufactured by association member mills under the requirements of Product Standard PS 1-83, four types of trademarks and one typical edge mark are used to illustrate the plywood's type, grade, group, class, and Span Rating. Here's how they look together with notations on what each element means.

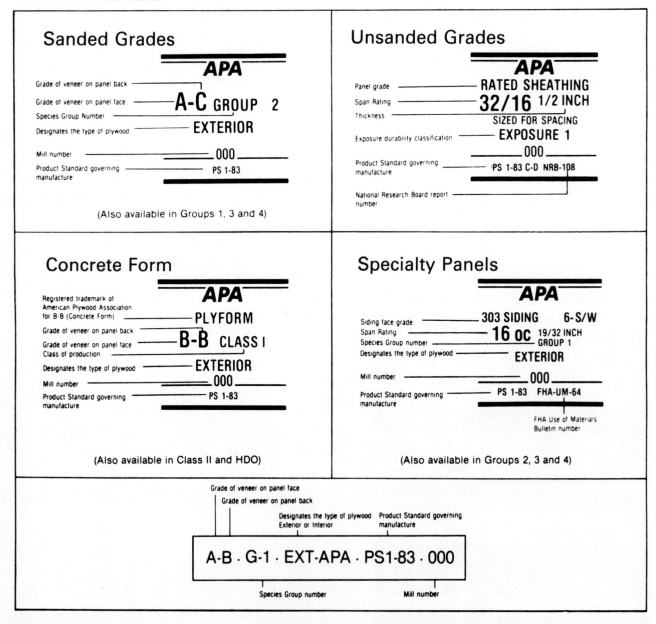

FIGURE 7-10
Basic trademarks of the American Plywood Association. (*Courtesy of American Plywood Association.*)

faces a resin-impregnated fiber sheet. It is available in high density and medium density. *High density* has a hard, smooth chemically resistant surface. It requires no additional finishing. It is available in several colors. It can be painted. *Medium density* has a smooth, opaque, nonglossy surface that hides the grain. It is used where a high-quality paint finish is desired.

Siding panels are used on the exterior of residential and commercial buildings. They are available in a variety of surface finishes, such as a grooved surface, rough-sawed surface, or with a striated design.

Paneling is a prefinished plywood product used on interior walls. Most panels are hardwoods, although some softwoods, such as knotty pine, are available. They are made in a variety of surface textures, such as V-groove, striated, and relief grain.

WORKING WITH PLYWOOD PANELS

Cutting

Plywood can be cut with any saw used to cut solid wood. It is important to prevent the veneer on the good face from chipping as it is cut. Always use a sharp, fine-toothed saw. To cut by hand, use a 10-point crosscut-type handsaw. Cut with the good face up. Support the panel below so that it does not sag.

When using a power circular saw, use a combination or hollow-ground blade, alternating-tip bevel carbide tipped blade, or specialized plywood blade. When using a table saw, keep the good face up. If there is splintering, it will be the bottom face. When cutting with a portable circular saw or radial arm saw, place the good face down. If splintering does occur, it can be reduced by applying masking tape on the face or scoring the face veneer with a sharp knife.

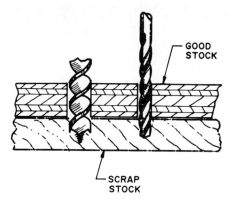

FIGURE 7-11
When drilling or boring through plywood back up the sheet with scrap stock.

Drilling or Boring Holes

Holes in plywood can be drilled or bored using the same tools as for solid wood. It is very important to bore through into a piece of scrap wood to keep the lower veneer from chipping (Fig. 7-11).

Planing

When necessary to plane the edges of plywood, work from each end toward the center. This prevents splitting that occurs if you plane off the ends. Because plywood is difficult to plane, cut the panel to exact size whenever possible.

ORDERING PLYWOOD

Plywood is normally available in sheets 4 ft × 8 ft. A sheet contains 32 ft². Plywood is priced per square foot. If it sells for 80 cents a square foot, a sheet would cost $25.60. The difference in thickness is taken care of by the price per square foot. For example, $\frac{3}{4}$-in.-thick material will cost more per foot than that $\frac{1}{4}$ in. thick.

8

RECONSTITUTED WOOD PANELS

There are a number of different types of reconstituted wood panels that find extensive use in furniture and cabinet construction. These panels include plywood, hardboard, medium-density fiberboard, particleboard, and waferboard. Plywood and related products are discussed in Chapter 7.

HARDBOARD

Hardboard is made from wood chips converted into fibers which are permanently bonded under heat and pressure into a panel. The wood fibers are bonded by their natural lignin and synthetic binders. Other materials are added to improve certain properties as stiffness, hardness, finishing properties, resistance to abrasion and moisture, and to increase strength and durability. Different hardboards have various fiber formulations that enable the product to be used for a wide variety of purposes.

Hardboard is made by chipping wood and wood residues into a chip about the size of your thumbnail. These are cooked under heat and pressure to soften and dissolve some of the natural resin in the wood. They are then reduced to fibers by building up pressure to a high level and then suddenly releasing it. This causes the chips to explode into fiber bun-

dles. These are then shredded into fibers by grinding and the additives needed are added.

The formation of the fibers into a mat can be wet or dry. In the *wet process* the watery pulp flows onto a screen and the water is drawn off through the screen. The mat is run through rollers removing more water. It is then loaded into a press.

In the *dry process* the fibers are rather dry before they are laid on a screen using air instead of water. These are loaded into a press.

The mats are placed in a press under heat of 380 to 550°F (193 to 288°C) and pressure of 500 to 1500 psi (3447 to 10 342 kPa). This welds the fibers back together, producing a product having characteristics unattainable in natural wood.

Hardboard is used for furniture and cabinet backs, drawer bottoms, dust panels, and other applications. It is also manufactured into products such as exterior siding, signs, wall paneling, and cabinet tops.

Hardboard is harder than most natural woods, and since it has no grain, it has nearly equal properties in all directions. It is not as stiff or as strong as natural wood along the grain, but is substantially stronger and stiffer than wood across the grain.

Standards for the manufacture of hardboard products include ANSI/AHA A135.4-1982, Basic

Hardboard; ANSI/AHA A135.5-1982, Prefinished Hardboard Paneling; and ANSI/AHA A135.6-1984, Hardboard Siding.

Hardboard is available in five classes, Tempered, Standard, Service-Tempered, Service, and Industrialite. Data on surface finish thickness and physical properties by class are in Table 8-1.

Class 1: Tempered. It is impregnated with siccative material, and stabilized by heat and spe-cial additives to impart substantially improved properties of stiffness, strength, hardness, and resistance to water and abrasion, as compared with the Standard Class.

Class 2: Standard. It is the form of the material as it comes from the press. It has high strength and water resistance.

Class 3: Service-Tempered. It is impregnated with siccative material, and stabilized by heat

TABLE 8-1
Classification of Hardboard by Surface Finish, Thickness, and Physical Properties

| Class | Nominal thickness (in.) | Water resistance (max. av. per panel) | | Modulus of rupture (min. av. per panel) (psi) | Tensile strength (min. av. per panel, psi) | |
		Water absorption based on weight (%)	Thickness swelling (%)		Parallel to surface	Perpendicular to surface
1 Tempered	$\frac{1}{12}$	30	25			
	$\frac{1}{10}$					
	$\frac{1}{8}$	25	20			
	$\frac{3}{16}$			6000	3000	130
	$\frac{1}{4}$	20	15			
	$\frac{5}{16}$	15	10			
	$\frac{3}{8}$	10	9			
2 Standard	$\frac{1}{12}$	40	30			
	$\frac{1}{10}$					
	$\frac{1}{8}$	35	25			
	$\frac{3}{16}$			4500	2200	90
	$\frac{1}{4}$	25	20			
	$\frac{5}{16}$	20	15			
	$\frac{3}{8}$	15	10			
3 Service-tempered	$\frac{1}{8}$	35	30			
	$\frac{3}{16}$	30	30	4500	2000	75
	$\frac{1}{4}$	30	25			
	$\frac{3}{8}$	20	15			
4 Service	$\frac{1}{8}$	45	35			
	$\frac{3}{16}$	40	35			
	$\frac{1}{4}$	40	30			
	$\frac{3}{8}$	35	25			
	$\frac{7}{16}$	35	25			
	$\frac{1}{2}$	30	20			
	$\frac{5}{8}$	25	20	3000	1500	50
	$\frac{11}{16}$	25	20			
	$\frac{3}{4}$					
	$\frac{13}{16}$					
	$\frac{7}{8}$	20	15			
	1					
	$1\frac{1}{8}$					
5 Industrialite	$\frac{1}{4}$	50	30			
	$\frac{3}{8}$	40	25			
	$\frac{7}{16}$	40	25			
	$\frac{1}{2}$	35	25			
	$\frac{5}{8}$	30	20			
	$\frac{11}{16}$	30	20	2000	1000	25
	$\frac{3}{4}$					
	$\frac{13}{16}$					
	$\frac{7}{8}$	25	20			
	1					
	$1\frac{1}{8}$					

Source: American Hardboard Association.

and additives. Its properties are substantially better than Service Grade.

Class 4: Service. It is basically the same form as it comes from the press but has less strength than Standard Class.

Class 5: Industrialite. It is a medium-density hardboard that has moderate strength and lower unit weight than the other classes.

Standard thickness and manufacturing tolerances are shown in Table 8-2. Hardboard is available in thicknesses from $\frac{1}{12}$ to $1\frac{1}{8}$ in. It is available with one or two sides smooth. A panel with one side smooth will have a textured or screened back. This is utilized when the panel is glued to another surface. The most used panel size is 4 × 8 ft. (1219 × 2438 mm) though widths from 2 to 5 ft (610 to 1524 mm) and lengths from 4 to 16 ft. (1219 to 4877 mm) are available on special order.

Class	Number and color or stripes
Tempered	1 Red
Service Tempered	2 Red
Standard	1 Green
Service	2 Green
Industrialite	1 Blue

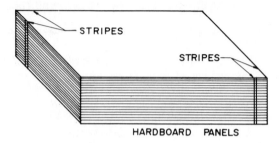

FIGURE 8-1
The classes of hardboard panels are indicated by colored stripes on the edges.

TABLE 8-2
Thickness Tolerances for Hardboard Panels

Nominal thickness (in.)	Thickness tolerance (min.–max., in.)
$\frac{1}{12}$ (0.083)	0.070–0.090
$\frac{1}{10}$ (0.100)	0.091–0.110
$\frac{1}{8}$ (0.125)	0.115–0.155
$\frac{3}{16}$ (0.188)	0.165–0.205
$\frac{1}{4}$ (0.250)	0.210–0.265
$\frac{5}{16}$ (0.312)	0.290–0.335
$\frac{3}{8}$ (0.375)	0.350–0.400
$\frac{7}{16}$ (0.438)	0.410–0.460
$\frac{1}{2}$ (0.500)	0.475–0.525
$\frac{5}{8}$ (0.625)	0.600–0.650
$\frac{11}{16}$ (0.688)	0.660–0.710
$\frac{3}{4}$ (0.750)	0.725–0.775
$\frac{13}{16}$ (0.812)	0.785–0.835
$\frac{7}{8}$ (0.875)	0.850–0.900
1 (1.000)	0.975–1.025
$1\frac{1}{8}$ (1.125)	1.115–1.155

Source: American Hardboard Association.

Basic hardboard is identified by a colored vertical strip which indicates the class of the board (Fig. 8-1).

Working with Hardboard

Hardboard can be worked with standard woodworking tools. If much work is to be done, carbide-tipped cutting tools are recommended. Since there is no grain, the material can be worked in any direction without splitting. Cut edges can be smoothed by sanding or jointing. Faces of panels are very smooth and need no sanding. When drilling, bore from the best face and into a piece of scrap wood to reduce chipping out the back surface.

MEDIUM-DENSITY FIBERBOARD (MDF)

This material is manufactured under ANSI A208.2-1980, which was developed cooperatively by the American Hardboard Association and the National Particleboard Association. Medium-Density fiberboard has moderate strength and lower unit weight than other types of hardboard products.

It is widely used for interior paneling, doors, jambs, cabinets, moldings, interior stair treads, custom cabinet work, and shelves. It is frequently printed with a simulated wood grain for use in commercial furniture and cabinets. The recommended shelf spans for various thicknesses and loads are listed in Table 8-3. A shelf span is the distance between supports such as between bulkheads or partitions. To find the uniform load on the shelf, divide the probable load it will carry by the square footage of the shelf. Using this figure, read across the columns in the chart.

Medium-density fiberboard has smooth flat surfaces and tight edges that can be painted or finished without filling. It has excellent impact strength, is free from knots and voids, and has good screw-holding capacity. It can be worked with standard woodworking tools and does not splinter or chip.

TABLE 8-3
Maximum Shelf Spans for Medium-Density Fiberboard
(in inches for uniform loading)

LOAD	End supported — Maximum span			Multiple supports — Maximum span			Over hanging shelf — Maximum overhang		
	1/2	5/8	3/4	1/2	5/8	3/4	1/2	5/8	3/4
	Maximum Span in Inches								
50.0	15	19	23	20	25	30	7	9	10
45.0	16	19	23	21	26	32	7	9	11
40.0	16	20	24	22	27	33	7	9	11
35.0	17	21	25	23	28	34	8	10	12
30.0	18	22	27	24	30	38	8	10	12
25.0	19	23	28	25	32	38	9	11	13
20.0	20	25	30	27	34	40	9	12	14
17.5	21	26	31	28	35	42	10	12	14
15.0	22	27	33	30	37	44	10	13	15
12.5	23	29	34	31	39	48	11	13	18
10.0	25	31	37	33	41	49	11	14	17
7.5	27	33	39	38	45	53	12	15	18
5.0	30	37	43	40	49	58	14	17	20

Source: National Particleboard Association.

MDF can be nailed in place by driving nails through it. It will not hold nails. When fastening with screws, drill a shank hole through the panel. Thinner panels, as a cabinet back, can be joined to the cabinet with staples. Thicker types of fiberboard will hold screws such as for hinges. Drill a small pilot hole and use sheet metal screws.

MDF will take any of the commonly used finishes. Use the sealer or undercoat recommended by the manufacturer of the finish to be used.

PARTICLEBOARD AND WAFERBOARD

Particleboard is made from wood chips, water, and a synthetic resin binder. The resulting mixture is formed into thick mats which are placed in a heated press. The press applies approximately 1000 psi (6894.7 kPa) forming the panel. The panel is conditioned, sanded, and cut into standard sizes.

Particleboard is generally sold in panels 4 ft wide and 8 ft long and in thicknesses from $\frac{1}{8}$ to 2 in. The most commonly used thicknesses are $\frac{3}{8}$, $\frac{1}{2}$, $\frac{5}{8}$, and $\frac{3}{4}$ in. (10, 13, 16, and 19 mm). Panels are generally marked with a stamp giving the manufacturer's name, ANSI Standard 208.1, the grade, density in pounds per cubic foot, and the thickness in fractions of an inch. For example, ANSI 208.1, 1-H-1, 45, $\frac{5}{8}$ in. Type 2 panels are also marked "Exterior Bond."

Particleboard is available in two grades, 1 and 2. *Type 1, Interior* uses a urea-formaldehyde resin as the bonding agent, which is water resistant and for interior use. *Type 2, Exterior* uses a phenol-formaldehyde resin as the bonding agent, which is waterproof and for exterior use (Table 8-4).

Each grade is divided into density ranges. The grades containing the letter H are higher densities

TABLE 8-4
Grades of Particleboard

Type 1 interior	Type 2 exterior
1-H-1	2-H-1
1-H-2	2-H-2
1-H-3	2-H-3
1-M-1	2-M-1
1-M-2	2-M-2
1-M-3	2-M-3
1-L-1	2-M-W
	2-M-F

Source: National Particleboard Association.

(50 lb per cubic foot and over), M (indicates intermediate densities (37 to 50 lb per cubic foot), and L, lower densities (below 37 lb per cubic foot).

There are four types of particleboard. The *singlelayer* type is the most commonly used and is widely used in construction for underlayment on floors. The *threelayer* type has outer layers made of fines, which are fine wood particles. This produces a panel with a smooth surface suitable for printing. It is also used for doors and tops that are covered with plastic laminates. The *graded density* type is the most expensive and has the smoothest surface and highest density of all four types. It is used for the tops in expensive furniture. The fourth type is *extruded*. It is the least expensive and is commonly used for furniture backs.

Recommended uses for the interior grades, type 1, are shown in Table 8-5.

TABLE 8-5 Recommended Uses for Type 1 Particleboard	
Grade	Use
Shelving	1-M-1
	1-M-2
	1-M-3
Countertops	1-M-2
(with plastic	1-M-3
laminates)	
Kitchen cabinets	1-M-1
(sides, backs, shelves,	1-M-2
front panels)	
Door core	1-L-1
Moldings (vinyl covered)	1-M-3

Working with Particleboard

Particleboard can be worked with standard woodworking tools. If much work is done, carbide-tipped cutting tools are recommended.

Particleboard can be edge banded with solid wood. This can be glued to the particleboard with a butt joint, but it is stronger to use a joint as a tongue and groove or spline. Plastic laminates, veneers, and vinyls can be bonded to particleboard with contact cement (Fig. 8-2).

The nail-holding power of particleboard is less than solid wood. The use of annular threaded nails is recommended. The use of sheet metal screws with

FIGURE 8-2
This library table is constructed of particleboard covered with plastic laminate. (*Courtesy of Worden Company.*)

very small pilot holes is much stronger. There are special screws made just for use with particleboard (Fig. 8-3).

If particleboard is to be painted, enameled, or have a transparent finish, it is recommended that a filler and sealer be applied first.

Waferboard is an exterior grade of particleboard and is used for wall and roof sheathing, single-layer floors, siding, soffits, and other external applications. It is generally made from large thin wafers of aspen.

Particleboard and waferboard are manufactured to the standard ANSI A208.1-1979, Mat-Formed Wood Particleboard.

FIGURE 8-3
Special screw designed for use in particleboard.

A SPECIAL–PURPOSE SCREW DESIGNED FOR USE IN PARTICLE BOARD.

9

HARDWARE AND OTHER PRODUCTS

The selection of the hardware for a product is important to its overall appearance and operation. Hardware should reflect the style of the furniture. For example, Colonial furniture should have hardware designed for that period. It should be of good quality, resist rust and tarnish, and be free of surface blemishes and other defects.

KNOBS AND DRAWER PULLS

Drawers and doors are opened with knobs and pulls (Fig. 9-1). Wood, metal, and porcelain *knobs* are held to the door or drawer front with a screw or bolt (Fig. 9-2). *Pulls* may be held with one or two bolts or screws. Some have a metal escutcheon behind the pull (Fig. 9-3).

HINGES

There are many types of hinges available for use on furniture and cabinets. Some are surface mounted and add to the decorative appearance (Fig. 9-4). Others are designed so that they are hidden or almost entirely hidden (Fig. 9-5). Some of the com-

FIGURE 9-1
A wide variety of drawer knobs are available. (*Courtesy of Amerock Corporation, an Anchor Hocking Company.*)

CRYSTAL

CHROME

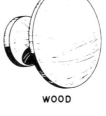

WOOD

BRASS

PORCELAIN

95

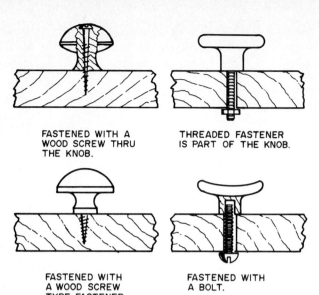

FIGURE 9-2
Drawer knobs are mounted with screws or bolts.

monly used hinges are shown in Fig. 9-5. Additional types of hinges and installation details are described in Chapter 12.

LOCKS, HASPS AND CATCHES

A variety of locks, catches and hasps are available (Fig. 9-6). They serve a functional as well as a deco-

FIGURE 9-3
These surface mounted hinges are part of the overall design of this cabinet. Note the decorative pulls on the door and drawer.

FIGURE 9-4
The hinges on this door are hidden. They are spring loaded and open when the door is pushed inward. No pulls or knobs are needed.

rative purpose. Those that are brass should be mounted with brass screws or escutcheon pins.

DRAWER AND SHELF HARDWARE

There are a variety of metal and plastic *drawer slides* available. It is a good idea to select the type you are going to use before starting a project so that the correct support and spacing is provided (Fig. 9-7). Additional information is given in Chapter 13. Shelves can be permanently installed in a cabinet or be made adjustable by using one of the several types of *shelf hardware* available (Fig. 9-8). More information on shelf construction is presented in Chapter 14.

CARVINGS

A wide variety of mass produced overlays made from compressed wood fibers or solid wood carvings are available. They are glued or nailed to the cabinet doors. They will take stain and filler so their color can match the wood used to make the cabinet (Fig. 9-9).

TRIM MOLDING

Shaped wood trim molding is available in many styles and shapes. They are often glued or nailed to

FIGURE 9-5
These are a few of the many types of hinges available. (*Courtesy of Amerock Corporation, an Anchor Hocking Company.*)

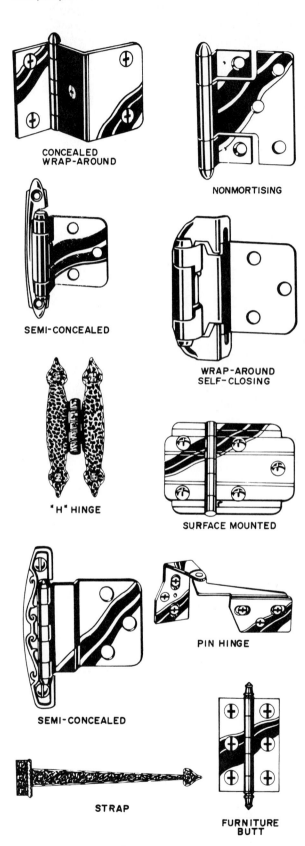

CONCEALED WRAP-AROUND

NONMORTISING

SEMI-CONCEALED

WRAP-AROUND SELF-CLOSING

"H" HINGE

SURFACE MOUNTED

PIN HINGE

SEMI-CONCEALED

STRAP

FURNITURE BUTT

cabinet doors and drawer fronts to give them depth and a decorative touch. Pieces forming corners are precut at 45°. They are available in several different woods and can be stained to match the finish wood on the doors or drawer fronts (Fig. 9-10).

PLASTIC LAMINATES

Cabinets and tabletops are often covered with plastic laminates. A plastic laminate is made of five to seven layers of kraft paper treated with a phenolic resin. A printed layer of kraft paper is applied to the top, which gives the sheets its color and pattern. A translucent topcoat of melamine is applied over the top laminate to form a hard surface.

FIGURE 9-6
Most commonly used door catches. (*Courtesy of Amerock Corporation, an Anchor Hocking Company.*)

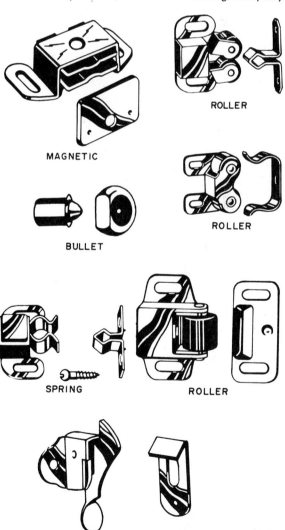

MAGNETIC

ROLLER

BULLET

ROLLER

SPRING

ROLLER

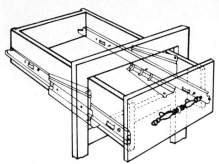

METAL CHANNELS ON EACH SIDE OF
THE DRAWER RUN ON ROLLERS IN
CHANNEL FASTENED TO SIDES OF
THE CABINET.

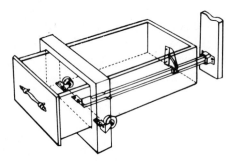

A CENTER TRACK DRAWER GUIDE
WITH THREE NYLON ROLLERS.

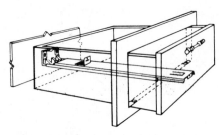

A CENTER TRACK DRAWER GUIDE
WITH A NYLON ROLLER.

FIGURE 9-7
Metal and plastic drawer slides provide stick-free, easy-
sliding drawers. (*Courtesy of Amerock Corporation, an
Anchor Hocking Company.*)

FIGURE 9-8
Adjustable shelves are held on metal clips set in perforated standards. (*Courtesy of Knape and Vogt Manufacturing Co.*)

FIGURE 9-9
There are many carvings and decorative overlays avail-
able for application to drawers and doors. (*Courtesy of
The Woodworkers' Store.*)

Plastic laminates are available in a wide variety of patterns and colors. Solid colors, wood grains,
and other patterns are available.

The grade of plastic laminates applies to the
thickness of the material. Most countertops are
made with *general grade,* which is $\frac{1}{16}$ in. (2 mm)
thick. Walls and cabinet fronts and sides are usually
covered with $\frac{1}{32}$-in. (1-mm)-thick plastic laminates.
Additional information is available in Chapter 16.

CABINET ACCESSORIES

Hardware manufacturers have available a wide array of accessories. These include items such as wood
and plastic trays, wire racks for storage of lids, uten-
sils and other items, lazy susans, trays, and units for
storage of silverware. These accessories greatly improve the efficiency of the use of cabinet space (Fig.
9-11).

In Fig. 9-12 are shown accessories that increase the efficiency of storage space. The built-in
wire baskets have overhanging edges at the top
that slide in U-shaped channels fastened to the
inside of the cabinet bulkhead. The steel baskets
have been surface treated so that any type of material can be stored. The spice racks screw to the inside of cabinet doors, utilizing space that is usually
wasted. The pull-out cupboard is equipped with a
support frame onto which the wire storage components are fastened. These components include
bread baskets, bottle baskets, laundry and cleaning agent baskets, lid racks, and similar storage
units.

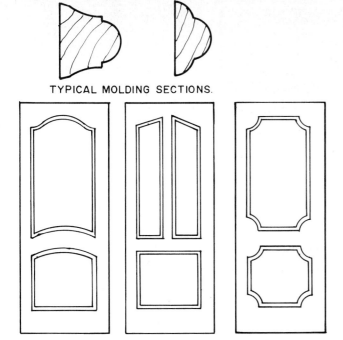

TYPICAL MOLDING SECTIONS.

SAMPLE TRIM MOLD DESIGNS ON CABINET DOORS.

FIGURE 9-10
Doors and drawer fronts can be decorated by applying molding to the surface.

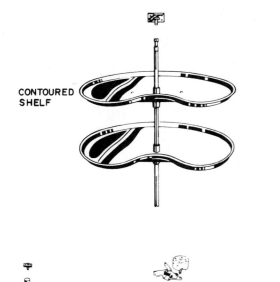

CONTOURED SHELF

WIRE LID RACK AND WOOD TRAYS

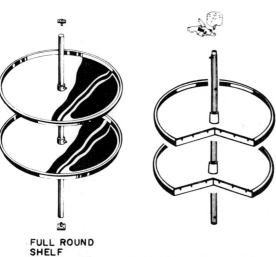

FULL ROUND SHELF

PIE-CUT SHELF

FIGURE 9-11
These shelving and tray units enable lost space in a cabinet to be effectively used. (*Courtesy of Amerock Corporation, an Anchor Hocking Company.*)

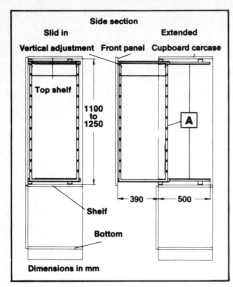

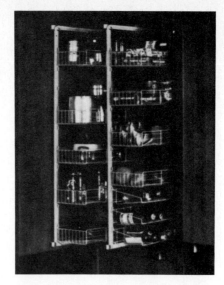

PULL-OUT CUPBOARD UNIT

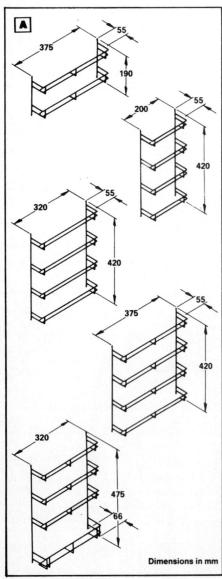

SPICE RACKS

BUILT-IN WIRE BASKETS

FIGURE 9-12
These are a few of the accessories available that can be used to increase the storage capacity and efficiency of kitchen cabinets. (*Courtesy of H'a'fele America, 203 Feld Ave., High Point, NC 27261.*)

10

FASTENERS

Nails and screws are commonly used fastening devices. They are made in a variety of sizes and types. In addition to these, there are many other special-purpose fasteners. A knowledge of fasteners is important to the skilled craftsman and designer.

NAILS

The most commonly available nails are box, common, casing, and finishing (Fig. 10-1). Box and common nails are used in building construction and find limited use in furniture and cabinet construction. Casing nails are designed for the installation of interior trim in buildings. They are much like a finish-

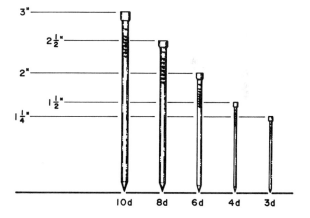

FIGURE 10-2
The length of nails is given by their penny (d) size.

FIGURE 10-1
Common kinds of nails.

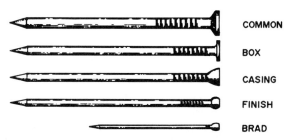

ing nail but are larger in diameter and have a cone-shaped head. The finishing nail is frequently used in furniture and cabinet construction. It is a slender nail with a small head. It is used where it will not be seen or where the head can be set below the surface of the wood and covered with a filler.

The length of nails is indicated by their *penny size* (Fig. 10-2). The small letter d is the symbol used for penny. For example, a 4d nail is a four-penny

101

nail which is 1½ in long. The penny and inch sizes of finishing nails are listed in Table 10-1.

A *wire brad* is another nail often used. It looks much like a finishing nail but is smaller. It is made in lengths of ½ to 1½ in. It is sold by length given in inches and by the diameter given by a gauge number.

TABLE 10-1
Finishing Nail Sizes

Penny size	Inch size	Approximate number of nails per pound
3d	1¼	850
4d	1½	575
6d	2	300
8d	2½	192
10d	3	122

Joining with Nails

For most cabinet work, finishing nails are used. They are driven with a 13-oz curved claw hammer. Brads are driven with a 7-oz hammer. A typical application is nailing a cabinet back to the side (Fig. 10-3). For production work a pneumatic gun can rapidly drive these fasteners (Fig. 10-4).

Wood is joined by face nailing, slant nailing, and toenailing. Face nailing means driving the nail perpendicular to the wood. It does not have the holding power of slanted nailing (Fig. 10-5). When a butt joint is nailed, it can be straight nailed or toenailed

FIGURE 10-3
Finishing nails are commonly used in furniture and cabinet work. (*Courtesy of American Plywood Association.*)

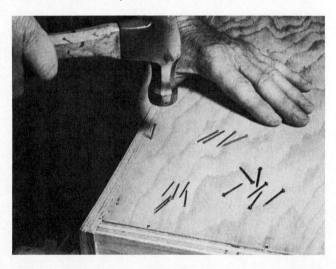

FIGURE 10-4
Various types of nails and staples are power driven. (*Courtesy of Senco Fastening Systems.*)

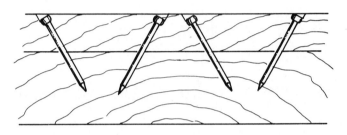

HOLDING POWER IS INCREASED WHEN THE NAILS ARE SLANTED IN OPPOSITE DIRECTIONS.

FIGURE 10-5
Holding power is increased by slanting the nails.

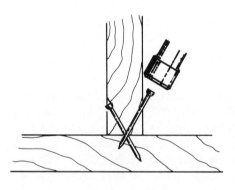

A BUTT JOINT CAN BE TOENAILED

FIGURE 10-6
Butt joints can be joined by toenailing.

(Fig. 10-6). Finishing nails are either nailed flush with the surface or the head is set with a nail set. The head is covered with a filler (Fig. 10-7).

Generally, nails should be placed ¾ in. from the

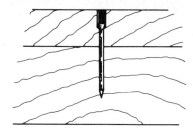

SET THE FINISHING
NAIL. HIDE THE HEAD
WITH FILLER.

FIGURE 10-7
Nails can be hidden by setting the head and filling the hole.

edge of solid wood boards. If they are closer, a hole slightly smaller than the nail should be drilled. This will prevent splitting but may reduce the holding powers slightly (Fig. 10-8). You can usually nail a little closer to the edge of plywood than to solid wood. A major advantage of pneumatic fasteners is that they greatly reduce the tendency to split without diminishing the holding power.

FIGURE 10-8
When nailing close to the edge, drill a hole slightly smaller than the nail. (*Courtesy of American Plywood Association.*)

POWER STAPLING AND NAILING

There are many types of power stapling and nailing tools available. They are designed to use pressurized air to drive fasteners. These fasteners are available with a variety of heads and body sizes (Fig. 10-9).

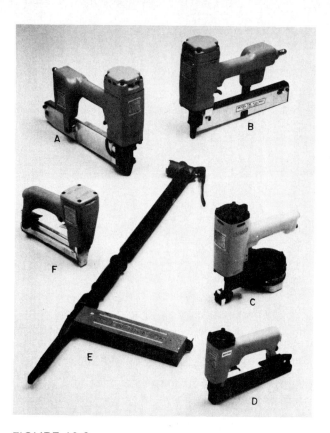

FIGURE 10-9
Power-operated staplers and nailers: (A) staples for skid and case assembly; (B) brad tool for casegoods and subassembly; (C) coil nailers for casebacks and skids; (D) stapler for upholstery; (E) case clamp tool; (F) stapler for subassembly, casebacks, and drawer assembly. (*Courtesy of Bostitch, East Greenwich, RI 02818.*)

This varies from driving brads up to $1\frac{3}{4}$ in. long to small pin tacking machines. The machine in Fig. 10-10 works off a wire coil. It can be adjusted to cut a pin from $\frac{1}{4}$ to 1 in. in length, drive, and countersink it. The hole is so small that it is concealed during the normal finishing operation. One important use is applying decorative molding and panels to drawer fronts and doors.

Power nailing and stapling machines must be properly installed and maintained for maximum effectiveness and long life. The key to this is a properly set-up and maintained air system. A good air system must supply the correct *volume of clean air* at the necessary *pressure*. The air supply may also have to provide *lubrication* to the pneumatic tools.

Air Volume

The air supply system must provide an adequate volume of air *at the air tool*. Consult the manufacturer of the tool for recommended pressures. In most cases this should be 90 psi (63 275 kg/m²). Even

FIGURE 10-10
This power nailer drives small headless pin tacks cut from a wire coil. (*Courtesy of Bostitch, East Greenwich, RI 02818.*)

though the compressor may be of adequate size, restrictions in the air line might reduce the volume at the tool. Restrictions most commonly occur at the quick-disconnect fittings, in hose swivels, and at manifolds, where several air lines are taken off from the main air supply. These should be sized to maintain the needed airflow. The fittings attached to a tool must be of the free-flow type, so that when the air line is disconnected, the pressurized air will be discharged.

Air Filtering

Dirt and water in the air supply are major causes of wear in pneumatic equipment. Dirt, moisture, and oil from the tool exhaust cause objectionable stains on "clean" applications such as upholstery and assemblies which are to be finished. The air filters must be of the correct size and located so that they catch the contaminants before they enter the air lines to the tools. The filter must be cleaned regularly.

The major contaminants are *water, rust, dust, and oil.* Water vapor in the atmosphere condenses into liquid in the receiver tank and piping. These must be drained regularly. Rust and pipe scale are caused by moisture corroding the inside of iron pipe. This produces a creamy sludge that is highly abrasive and damaging to air tools. Filters should be mounted at the end of metal piping and only a flexible line run from the filter to the tool. Dust enters the system through the air compressor air intake. This must have a filter that is cleaned often. Oil is introduced from many compressors as an oil vapor

into the system. This should be filtered out along with the dirt and water.

Air Regulators

Most compressors will produce pressures that exceed the air tool's maximum operating pressure. Air pressure regulators are required to control the operating pressure. Using more air pressure than required for the tool will increase wear on the air tool and waste compressed air. Inadequate pressure will result in inconsistant tool performance and poor driving. Set the pressure as specified in the tool manual. Place the regulator as close to the tool as practical.

Lubrication

Most air tools require frequent but not excessive lubricating by adding small amounts of oil to the air line. This is done by using lubricators mounted downstream from the filters. The lubricators must have adequate flow for the application and be suitable for the cyclical flow of pneumatic fastener drivers. For clean applications, such as upholstery (Fig. 10-11) or work to be painted, be extremely careful to limit the oil added because it could get on the fabric or wood surface. Follow the manufacturer's recommendations.

FIGURE 10-11
Power staples are used in upholstery operations. (*Courtesy of Senco Fastening Systems.*)

Safety

When using air-powered staplers and nailers, wear safety glasses or a face shield (Fig. 10-12). The staples or nails leave the tool under a great deal of pressure, so do not point the tool at anyone. Keep your hands clear of the discharge mouth. Ideally, both hands should be kept on the air tool. Treat it much as you would a loaded gun. Be careful when you are holding a part in place that your hands are not in the direct line of the fastener. When making repairs, disconnect it from the air line.

FIGURE 10-12
Observe all safety regulations when using power staplers and nailers. (*Courtesy of Senco Fastening Systems.*)

Power Nails and Staples

There are a wide variety of nails and staples available for use in power-driven nailing and stapling tools. Some have large heads and resemble box nails. These are used for construction purposes where high holding power is needed. Others have screw threads on their bodies to increase holding power. For furniture and cabinetwork, the finishing nail and headless tack are more common. The headless tack is cut by the nailing tool from a wire coil and driven into place. The head is almost invisible. A variety of staples of various widths, length, and wire diameters are also available. They are used to secure wood parts, as cabinet backs, that will not be seen. They are used extensively for upholstery (Fig. 10-13).

WOOD SCREWS

Wood screws have greater holding power than nails and can easily be removed when necessary. They are used for many purposes, such as installing hinges, hasps, locks, and drawer slides. They are available in a variety of sizes, materials, slot types, head types, and finishes.

The most common head types are flat, round, and oval. Flat-head screws are set flush with the surface or in a counterbore and covered with a wood plug. Round heads are set above the surface and left exposed. Oval heads are most generally used with hinges and other hardware (Fig. 10-14).

The basic types of screw head recesses are slotted, Phillips, Pozidriv, clutch head, and Robertson type (Fig. 10-15). All but the slotted are easier to drive straight and generally drive faster. The head is stronger and the screwdriver is less likely to slip.

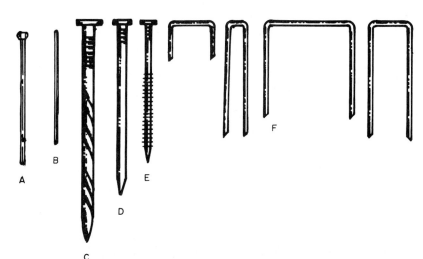

FIGURE 10-13
Examples of power-driven nails and staples: (A) finishing nail; (B) pin; (C) screw shank nail; (D) flat-head nail; (E) ring shank nail; (F) wire staples.

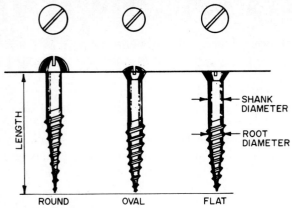

FIGURE 10-14
Common types of wood screws.

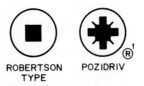

SLOTTED   PHILLIPS   CLUTCH HEAD

ROBERTSON TYPE   POZIDRIV ®

REGISTERED TRADEMARK
OF PHILLIPS SCREW CO.

FIGURE 10-15
Common types of wood screw heads.

TABLE 10-2
Typical Sizes of Wood Screws

Length (in.)	Shank diameter (wire gauge number)
$\frac{1}{4}$	2, 4
$\frac{3}{8}$	2, 3, 4, 5, 6
$\frac{1}{2}$ and $\frac{5}{8}$	2, 3, 4, 5, 6, 7, 8
$\frac{3}{4}$, $\frac{7}{8}$, and 1	4, 5, 6, 7, 8, 9, 10, 11, 12
$1\frac{1}{4}$	4, 5, 6, 7, 8, 9, 10, 11, 12, 14, 16
$1\frac{1}{2}$	6, 7, 8, 9, 10, 11, 12, 14, 16
$1\frac{3}{4}$	6, 8, 9, 10, 12, 14, 16
2	8, 9, 10, 12, 14, 16
$2\frac{1}{4}$	10, 12, 14
$2\frac{1}{2}$	8, 9, 10, 12, 14, 16
3	10, 12, 14, 16

TABLE 10-3
Wood Screw Diameters (inches)
by Gauge Number

Wire gauge number	Decimal size	Fractional size
0	0.060	$\frac{1}{16}$
1	0.073	$\frac{5}{64}$
2	0.086	$\frac{3}{32}$
3	0.099	$\frac{7}{64}$
4	0.112	$\frac{1}{8}$
5	0.125	$\frac{1}{8}$
6	0.138	$\frac{9}{64}$
7	0.151	$\frac{5}{32}$
8	0.164	$\frac{11}{64}$
9	0.177	$\frac{3}{16}$
10	0.190	$\frac{13}{64}$
11	0.203	$\frac{13}{64}$
12	0.216	$\frac{7}{32}$
14	0.242	$\frac{1}{4}$
16	0.268	$\frac{9}{32}$
18	0.294	$\frac{19}{64}$
20	0.320	$\frac{21}{64}$

A SPECIAL-PURPOSE SCREW DESIGNED FOR FACE FRAMING CABINETS.

FIGURE 10-16
This screw is designed to join the faceframe to the carcass.

Wood screws are sold in lengths from $\frac{1}{4}$ to 6 in. The length of a wood screw is that part that enters the wood (see Fig. 10-14).

Wood screws are made in many diameters. The *shank diameters* are given in *gauge numbers*. The larger the number, the larger the diameter of the wire used to make the screw. The diameter is measured just below the head. The *root diameter* varies with the wire diameter. The root diameter is the largest diameter of the core at the threads (Fig. 10-14). Standard wood screw sizes are shown in Table 10-2; the diameter in inches for each gauge is listed in Table 10-3.

Several special-purpose screws for joining the face frame to the carcass and securing materials to particle board are used in furniture and cabinet construction. The *face framing* screw has a Phillips head and a special auger point. This point drills the screw directly into the wood. It is not necessary to drill holes prior to installing the screw (Fig. 10-16). It

has a dry lubricant on the surface that helps its installation. There are different screws for hard and soft woods. The *particleboard screw* is designed for fastening into particleboard. It has widely spaced threads that enable it to be securely set in particleboard (Fig. 10-17). Sheet metal screws have a similar

A SPECIAL-PURPOSE SCREW DESIGNED FOR USE IN PARTICLE BOARD.

FIGURE 10-17
Special screw for use in particleboard.

thread and are sometimes used for this same purpose. There are a variety of special screws used to install hinges and hardware that are usually supplied with them when they are purchased.

Installing Screws

To install a screw properly, a hole the same diameter as the shank must be drilled through the top piece. This is called the shank hole. In the bottom piece a hole must be drilled that is a little smaller

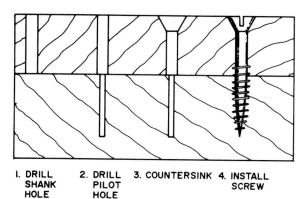

1. DRILL SHANK HOLE 2. DRILL PILOT HOLE 3. COUNTERSINK 4. INSTALL SCREW

FIGURE 10-18
Wood screws are installed by drilling shank and pilot holes.

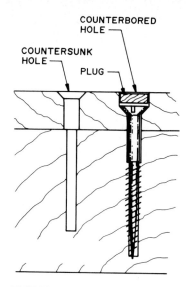

FIGURE 10-19
Flat-head wood screws are set flush with the surface of the wood.

than the root diameter. It is called a pilot hole (Fig. 10-18). In softwood the pilot hole is about 60% of the root diameter. In hardwood it should be about 80%. Recommended hole sizes are shown in Table 10-4.

Flat-head screws can be set flush by countersinking the shank hole after it is drilled (Fig. 10-19). Typical countersinks are in Fig. 10-20. The diameter of the countersink can be checked by placing the head of the screw in the cone-shaped cavity. A Screw Mate can be used to drill the holes and the countersink (Fig. 10-21).

When the head of the screw is to be set below the surface and covered with a plug, a hole slightly larger than the diameter of the screw is bored to the

TABLE 10-4
Recommended Drill Sizes for Shank, Pilot, and Plug Holes

Screw gauge no.	Shank hole: hard and softwood	Pilot hole Softwood	Pilot hole Hardwood	Auger bit size for plug hole
0	$\frac{1}{16}$	$\frac{1}{64}$	$\frac{1}{32}$	—
1	$\frac{5}{64}$	$\frac{1}{32}$	$\frac{1}{32}$	—
2	$\frac{3}{32}$	$\frac{1}{32}$	$\frac{3}{64}$	3
3	$\frac{7}{64}$	$\frac{3}{64}$	$\frac{1}{16}$	4
4	$\frac{7}{64}$	$\frac{3}{64}$	$\frac{1}{16}$	4
5	$\frac{1}{8}$	$\frac{1}{16}$	$\frac{5}{64}$	4
6	$\frac{9}{64}$	$\frac{1}{16}$	$\frac{5}{64}$	5
7	$\frac{5}{32}$	$\frac{1}{16}$	$\frac{3}{32}$	5
8	$\frac{11}{64}$	$\frac{5}{64}$	$\frac{3}{32}$	6
9	$\frac{3}{16}$	$\frac{5}{64}$	$\frac{7}{64}$	6
10	$\frac{3}{16}$	$\frac{3}{32}$	$\frac{7}{64}$	6
11	$\frac{13}{64}$	$\frac{3}{32}$	$\frac{1}{8}$	7
12	$\frac{7}{32}$	$\frac{7}{64}$	$\frac{1}{8}$	7
14	$\frac{1}{4}$	$\frac{7}{64}$	$\frac{9}{64}$	8
16	$\frac{17}{64}$	$\frac{9}{64}$	$\frac{5}{32}$	9

USE IN A HAND OPERATED BRACE

USED IN A POWER DRILL

FIGURE 10-20
Two types of countersinks. (*Courtesy of The Stanley Works.*)

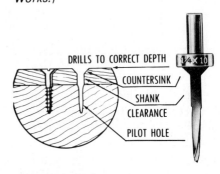

DRILLS TO CORRECT DEPTH

COUNTERSINK

SHANK
CLEARANCE

PILOT HOLE

FIGURE 10-21
The Screw-Mate drills the pilot and shank holes and countersinks all in one operation. (*Courtesy of The Stanley Works.*)

FIGURE 10-22
How to counterbore and install a wood screw.

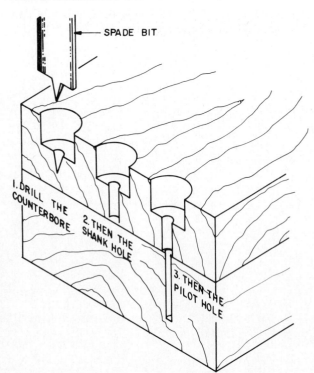

SPADE BIT

1. DRILL THE COUNTERBORE

2. THEN THE SHANK HOLE

3. THEN THE PILOT HOLE

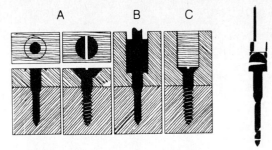

A   B   C

Pic. A Drills accurate pilot hole and clearance hole. Scoring edges cut surface fibres, prevent splintering. Screw head compresses wood fibres exerting clamping force when driven flush.

Pic. B To counterbore, simply add more pressure. Chip remover cleans out screwhole as SCREW SINK™ counterbore is withdrawn.

Pic. C Use Stanley Plug Cutter to form perfectly mated plug; leave as "Button Tip" or sand smooth.

FIGURE 10-23
The Screw-Sink drills the pilot and shank holes and counterbores all in one operation. (*Courtesy of The Stanley Works.*)

desired depth. This is called a counterbore (Fig. 10-22). Then the shank and pilot holes are bored. Counterbores can be made with an auger bit, spade bit, Screw-Sink counterbore, or straight-shank twist drill (Fig. 10-23).

The wood plugs can be bought in a variety of sizes or can be cut from the same wood used in the product. These are cut with a plug cutter (Fig. 10-24). Plugs are usually cut ⅜ in. long. The plug is glued in the hole. Usually, the grain in the plug is lined up with the grain in the board. A contrast can be had by placing the grain perpendicular to the grain in the board using a lighter or darker wood.

When working with oak, use brass screws. The acid in the oak will react with steel screws and eventually may cause a blue-black stain.

When installing screws in hardwood, lubricate the threads of the screw with paraffin, wax, or soap. This eases its installation.

OTHER FASTENING DEVICES

Tee nuts are used for many purposes. One of the most common is the installation of legs. A hole is bored in the furniture base. The tee nut is hammered into the hole. Its prongs hold it in place and keep it from turning or a small brad is placed through the flange. A *hanger bolt* can be screwed into the leg and the end with machine threads is screwed into the tee nut (Fig. 10-25).

FIGURE 10-24
Plug cutter. (*Courtesy of The Stanley Works.*)

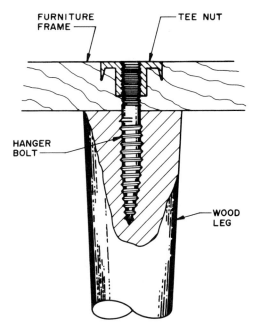

FIGURE 10-25
Legs can be joined to the carcass using tee nuts and hanger bolts.

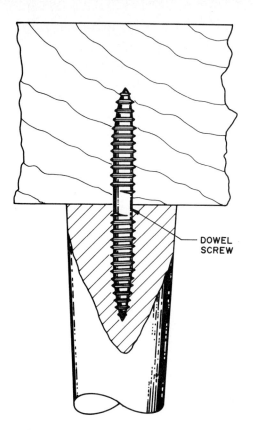

FIGURE 10-26
Dowel screws can be used to join legs and other parts to a carcass.

FIGURE 10-27
Miters can be joined using corrugated fasteners.

A *dowel screw* has wood screw threads on both ends. It is often used to join short legs to the furniture frame (Fig. 10-26).

Edge and butt joints can be held together with corrugated fasteners, clamp nails, chevrons, or Skotch fasteners. These metal fasteners are used where strength and appearance is not a major factor (see Figs. 10-27 to 10-30).

WALL ANCHORS

Various types of cabinets and shelves are hung from the wall. There are a variety of anchors for hollow and masonry walls. Toggle bolts and hollow-wall anchors are used for hollow-wall installations. A *toggle bolt* has either a solid head that pivots flat along the bolt or a spring-loaded head (Fig. 10-31). They require that a hole be drilled in the wall large enough for the fastener to enter.

Hollow-wall fasteners are inserted in a hole drilled in the wall. When the screw is tightened, it

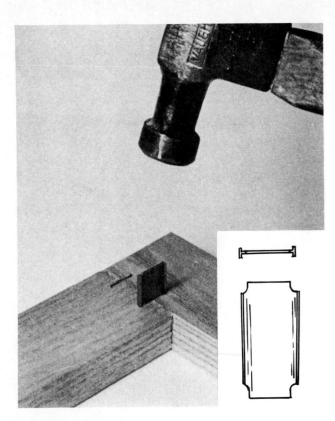

FIGURE 10-28
Clamp nails are driven into slots cut into the wood. They are slightly wedge shaped to pull the joint together.

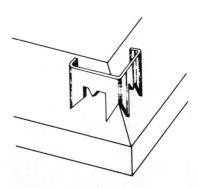

FIGURE 10-29
Miters can be joined using chevron fasteners.

FIGURE 10-30
Skotch fasteners have several legs which are driven into the wood, pulling the joint together.

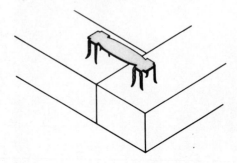

FINISH WALL
MATERIAL

1. BORE HOLE IN FINISH
WALL. PUSH TOGGLE
BOLT THROUGH HOLE.

2. TIGHTEN SCREW TO
PULL BOLT TIGHT
AGAINST OBJECT TO
BE HELD TO WALL.

FIGURE 10-31
Toggle bolts are used to mount lightweight items on walls.

pulls the end toward the head. This squeezes the ribbed center section which expands and binds against the inside of the wall (Fig. 10-32).

Another type of anchor used for hollow walls or in solid masonry is the Poly-Set anchor. It is a polyethylene expansion anchor that forms a knot on the inside of a hollow wall when the screw is tightened. In solid masonry it expands and binds on the side of the drilled hole (Fig. 10-33). They are available for wall thicknesses of $\frac{3}{8}$, $\frac{1}{2}$, $\frac{5}{8}$, and $\frac{3}{4}$ in.

A Toggler screw anchor is used to join something to a surface having a cavity behind it (Fig. 10-34). It is avilable for use in surface thicknesses of $\frac{1}{8}$, $\frac{3}{8}$, and $\frac{5}{8}$ in. A sheet metal screw is driven into the anchor to hold the item to be hung to the wall.

A Pronto block anchor is used in the web or hollow sections of hollow masonry. A $\frac{3}{8}$-in.-diameter hole is bored and the anchor is driven into the hole. The wedge on the end expands the end, holding it in place. A $\frac{1}{4}$-in. 20 hex head machine screw is fastened into the anchor (Fig. 10-35).

A Wedge Anchor is to fasten items to solid concrete. A hole the proper size is drilled. Its depth must exceed the minimum embedment desired. Assemble the anchor with the nut and washer. Drive through the material to be fastened so that the washer is flush with the surface. Then tighten the nut three to five turns to expand the anchor (Fig. 10-36). Wedge Anchors are available in diameters of $\frac{1}{4}$, $\frac{5}{8}$, $\frac{3}{4}$, $\frac{7}{8}$, $1\frac{1}{8}$, and $1\frac{1}{4}$ in.

There are many types of mechanical fasteners used to assemble furniture. These are used in place of the traditional wood joints (Fig. 10-37). Additional information is presented in Chapter 2.

A HOLLOW-WALL FASTENER

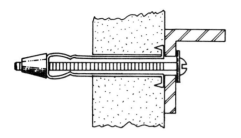

I. BORE A HOLE IN THE WALL. INSERT HOLLOW WALL ANCHOR.

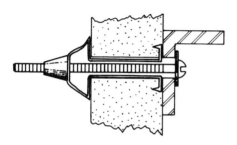

2. TIGHTEN SCREW TO BEND ANCHOR INSIDE OF WALL.

FIGURE 10-32
Hollow-wall fasteners penetrate the wall and bind against the inside surface.

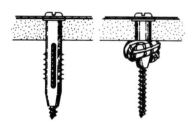

FIGURE 10-33
This Poly-Set hollow-wall anchor is plastic and forms a knot as the screw is tightened. (*Courtesy of ITT, Phillips Drill Division.*)

FIGURE 10-34
Toggler screw anchors can be used in hollow walls or as anchors in solid wall materials. (*Courtesy of ITT, Phillips Drill Division.*)

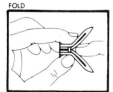

FOLD

Drill hole using 5/16" drill. Fold legs of the Toggler Screw Anchor together

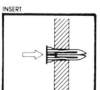

INSERT

Insert the Toggler Screw Anchor into the hole and tap flush to wall.

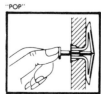

"POP"

In hollow walls, "pop" the Toggler Screw Anchor open with red key provided. Then install item and tighten screw.

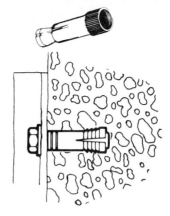

FIGURE 10-35
Pronto block anchors are driven into holes bored into solid masonry. (*Courtesy of ITT, Phillips Drill Division.*)

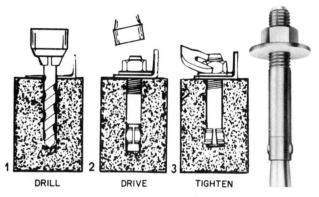

1 DRILL 2 DRIVE 3 TIGHTEN

FIGURE 10-36
Wedge anchors are made with a threaded shaft that extends out from wall. (*Courtesy of ITT, Phillips Drill Division.*)

FIGURE 10-37
Two types of multipiece mechanical fasteners used to assemble knock-down furniture and cabinets. (*Courtesy of H'a'fele America, 203 Feld Ave., High Point, NC 27261.*)

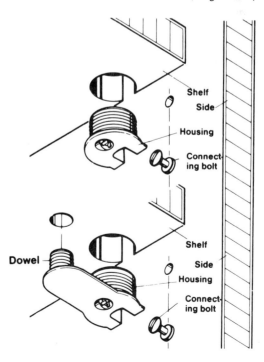

Shelf
Side
Housing
Connecting bolt

Dowel
Shelf
Side
Housing
Connecting bolt

PART **3**

Cabinet Construction

11

WOODWORKING JOINTS

Selecting which wood joints to use is part of a designer's work. There are many kinds of joints (Fig. 11-1). Each has advantages and disadvantages. As designers decide on joints, they consider the following factors.

Strength. Some joints are stronger than others. The joint selected must fit the job it is supposed to do. Joints must not separate during use.

Appearance. Sometimes, the joint should be hidden. A joint not visible is called a blind joint. Sometimes a joint is exposed so that it becomes part of the overall design.

Cost. A complicated joint is costly to cut. Is it worth the cost? Would metal fasteners give acceptable results for less money?

Difficulty. Select the simplest joint that will do the job.

Assembly. Ease of assembly influences the cost and time of production. Can the product be assembled easily and accurately?

Quality. A low-cost product often has joints that are not the best but that are the least costly. What is the quality of the product that you will be making?

Disassembly. Is the product one that will be taken apart for shipping? Knocked-down furniture has many joints that can be easily assembled. This feature makes it easy to move the product from a store to a home.

JOINT STRENGTH

The strength of a joint depends on a good fit. The contact area between mating pieces must be smooth and flat. This is necessary for maximum contact of glued surfaces.

The direction of the wood influences the strength of the joint. Wood is strongest in the with-the-grain direction. The strongest joints have edge or face grain as the contact surface. The end grain is weak and difficult to join by gluing or with mechanical fasteners.

CUTTING CONSIDERATIONS

The pieces to be joined are cut to their finished sizes before the joints are cut. All pieces having identical joint sizes are cut together. The power tools should be set so that the cuts are very accurately made. Use only sharp cutting tools.

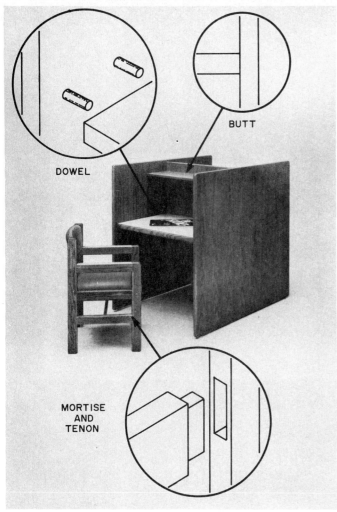

FIGURE 11-1
Joints are an important part of the design solution.
(*Courtesy of Worden Company.*)

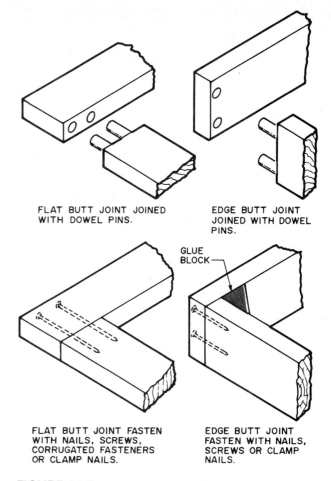

FLAT BUTT JOINT JOINED WITH DOWEL PINS.

EDGE BUTT JOINT JOINED WITH DOWEL PINS.

FLAT BUTT JOINT FASTEN WITH NAILS, SCREWS, CORRUGATED FASTENERS OR CLAMP NAILS.

EDGE BUTT JOINT FASTEN WITH NAILS, SCREWS OR CLAMP NAILS.

FIGURE 11-2
End butt joints are the easiest to cut.

FIGURE 11-3
This butt joint is being secured with wood screws.

BUTT JOINTS

The butt joint is the easiest to cut, but assembly can be difficult. One of the butting surfaces is end grain, and glues are therefore ineffective (Fig. 11-2). Butt joints can be joined using screws, nails, wood dowels, corrugated fasteners, Skotch fasteners, or clamp nails (Figs. 11-3 to 11-7). Glue blocks help stiffen butt joints (Fig. 11-8). Butt joints used in knock-down furniture are discussed later in this chapter.

EDGE JOINTS

Edge joints can be assembled using glue. The joining edges must be square and straight so that the glue contacts both surfaces and does not have to fill a crack between the boards. Wood can be joined edge to edge using only glue. If additional strength is

FIGURE 11-4
Butt joints can be secured with corrugated fasteners when strength and appearance are not important.

FIGURE 11-6
Skotch fasteners provide a quick way to secure a butt joint.

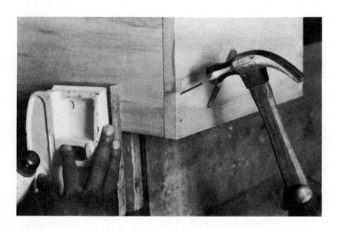

FIGURE 11-5
The easiest way to secure a butt joint is with nails.

FIGURE 11-7
Butt joints can be securely joined with clamp nails.

desired, dowels or some form of machined spline, tongue and groove, rabbet, or other shape can be used (Fig. 11-9). If it is desired that the spline or tongue not show, it can be stopped several inches from the edge (Fig. 11-10). A well-made edge joint is stronger than the wood itself. Edge joints can also be joined using corrugated fasteners, Skotch fasteners, or clamp nails (Figs. 11-3 to 11-7).

DOWELS

Wood dowel pins are widely used in joint construction. Dowel pins range in diameter from $\frac{1}{8}$ to $\frac{1}{2}$ in. by $\frac{1}{16}$ths and from $\frac{1}{2}$ to 1 in. by $\frac{1}{8}$ths. They are available

FIGURE 11-8
Glue blocks can be used to strengthen joints.

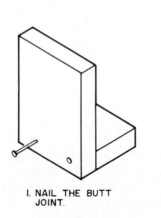

I. NAIL THE BUTT JOINT.

THEN GLUE THE GLUE BLOCK IN PLACE.

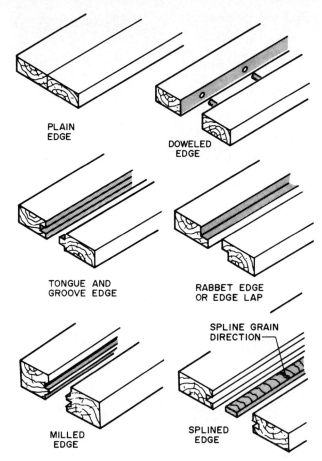

FIGURE 11-9
Stock can be joined edge to edge with these joints.

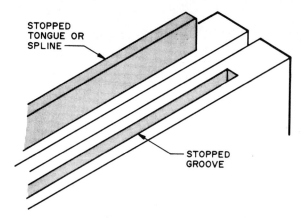

FIGURE 11-10
A stopped tongue or spline can be used on edge joints when it is desired that it not show on the end.

cut to standard length. Some have straight or spiral grooves in the side to help carry excess glue and allow air to escape as the joint is clamped (Fig. 11-11). They are also beveled on each end.

For most work the diameter of the dowel to use should be half the thickness of the wood. For example, a ⅜-in. dowel is used in wood ¾ in. thick. The spacing of dowels is a matter of judgment. Small

butt joints should have at least two dowels. On longer joints, as an edge joint, they should be 4 to 6 in. apart. The dowel should enter the wood at least two and one-half times its diameter. A ⅜-in. dowel should enter each piece of wood 15/16 in. or more. The dowel holes should be bored at least ⅛ in. deeper than the length of the dowel. This provides a pocket for excess glue (Fig. 11-12).

Dowel holes can be drilled one at a time on a

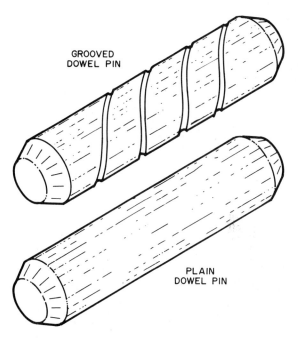

FIGURE 11-11
Dowel pins are chamfered on each end. Some have grooves to carry the glue.

FIGURE 11-12
This section through a dowel joint shows that the hole is deeper than the length of the dowel.

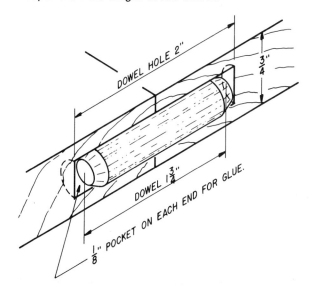

FIGURE 11-13
Several dowel holes can be drilled at the same time with a multiple drill head on a drill press. (*Courtesy of Forest City Tool Company.*)

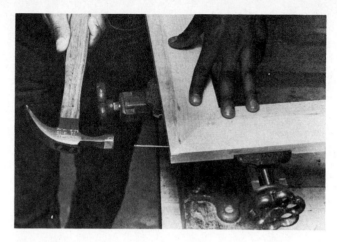

FIGURE 11-14
The use of a miter vise helps when fastening a miter joint with nails.

FIGURE 11-15
Flat miters can be fastened with corrugated fasteners.

FIGURE 11-16
Clamp nails can be used to produce a strong flat miter joint.

standard drill press, or several can be drilled with a multiple drill head (Fig. 11-13). Another dowel joint system, the 32-millimeter system, is discussed in detail in Chapter 2.

MITER JOINTS

A miter joint is much like the butt joint. The main difference is that the members are cut on a 45° angle. This joint has no end grain showing. It is a weak joint because both meeting surfaces are end grain. Plain miters can be fastened with some type of mechanical fastener. Those commonly used include nails, corrugated fasteners, clamp nails, Skotch nails, and wood and plastic dowels (Figs. 11-14 to 11-18).

Recommended joints for fastening flat miters are shown in Fig. 11-19, page 120. Notice the grain of the feather and spline runs perpendicular to the face of the miter. The half-lap miter can be joined by gluing because it has face grain exposed in the joint. Flat miters can be cut with a power miter saw or a radial arm saw (Fig. 11-20).

Recommended ways to join edge miters are shown in Fig. 11-21. In addition to using nails, dowels, or splines, various joints can be cut to increase the joining surface and lock the two pieces together.

1. CUT GROOVES FOR THE CLAMP NAIL.

2. DRIVE CLAMP NAIL IN THE GROOVES.

FIGURE 11-17
Edge miters can be fastened with long clamp nails. The kerf is perpendicular to the face of the miter.

FIGURE 11-18
Edge miters can be joined using plastic dowels that are formed at a 90° angle.

The rabbet miter should be glued and nailed. The lock miter does not require nailing. A glue block can be used to strengthen and stiffen the joint.

Edge miters can be cut using a table or radial arm saw (Fig. 11-22, page 121). Polygon miters are those cut on an angle other than 45°. To find the angle to cut the miter, divide 180° by the number of sides and subtract the answer from 90° (Fig. 11-23).

A compound miter forms products that have a tapered shape (Fig. 11-24). The angle may be 45° or one of the angles for a polygon miter. The joint is a combination of a miter and a bevel cut (Fig. 11-25, page 122). It is cut with a radial arm saw (Fig. 11-26).

GROOVES AND DADOES

A dado is a rectangular slot cut across the grain of a board. Use the *dado joint* for holding the ends of shelves, cabinet sides and bottoms, and partitions or dividers. It is a strong joint but must be cut so that the members fit snugly. The edge of the dado provides a lip on which a shelf can rest. It also helps align members as they are assembled (Fig. 11-27, page 122).

There are many variations of the dado. Examples are shown in Fig. 11-28. The through dado is exposed to view when assembled. If this is not desired, a blind, or stopped, dado can be used. The dado can be used with a rabbet joint. The rabbet should be one-half to two-thirds of the width of the board on which it was cut. The dovetail dado is strong and is cut with a router.

Dadoes on solid lumber are usually cut to a depth of half the thickness of the board. Dadoes in $\frac{3}{4}$-in. (19-mm) plywood should be only $\frac{1}{4}$ in. (6 mm) deep. If the dado is cut deeper, too many plies of veneer will be cut, thus weakening the board. They are often cut with a radial arm saw (Fig. 11-29).

Join dadoes by gluing. For additional strength, nail the glued joint or join it with screws. You usually do not need clamps when the joint is fastened with glue plus nails or screws.

A groove is a rectangular slot cut with the grain. A *groove joint* frequently is used to hold pan-

FIGURE 11-19
These are other ways of securing flat miter joints.

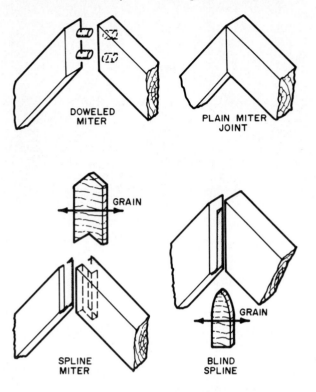

DOWELED MITER

PLAIN MITER JOINT

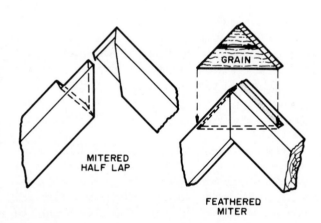

GRAIN

SPLINE MITER

GRAIN

BLIND SPLINE

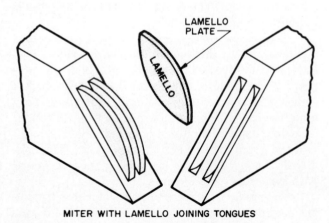

GRAIN

MITERED HALF LAP

FEATHERED MITER

LAMELLO PLATE

LAMELLO

MITER WITH LAMELLO JOINING TONGUES

FIGURE 11-20
A radial arm saw can be used to cut miters.

els. A drawer bottom usually is set in a groove. Grooves most often are cut to a depth of half the thickness of the board. Panels set in grooves, such as drawer bottoms, often are not glued. The assembled unit, the drawer, is thus permitted to expand and contract around the bottom of the unit. This prevents the wood from cracking or buckling. Grooves are often cut on a table saw or radial arm saw (Fig. 11-30, page 123).

RABBET JOINTS

A rabbet joint is used to form corners of cases and drawers and backs of cabinets. It is not a strong joint and must be glued and reinforced with nails or screws. It is stronger than a butt joint because it has a greater glue area. Commonly used rabbet joints are in Fig. 11-31.

The recess is usually cut about two-thirds of the thickness of the board. In a $\frac{3}{4}$-in. (19 mm) board this would be $\frac{1}{2}$ in. (13 mm). They are often cut on a table saw (Fig. 11-32).

LAP JOINTS

A lap joint is used when two pieces of wood meet or cross and their surfaces must be flush (Fig. 11-33). The half lap is used to join boards end to end. The end lap forms a corner. The middle lap forms a T.

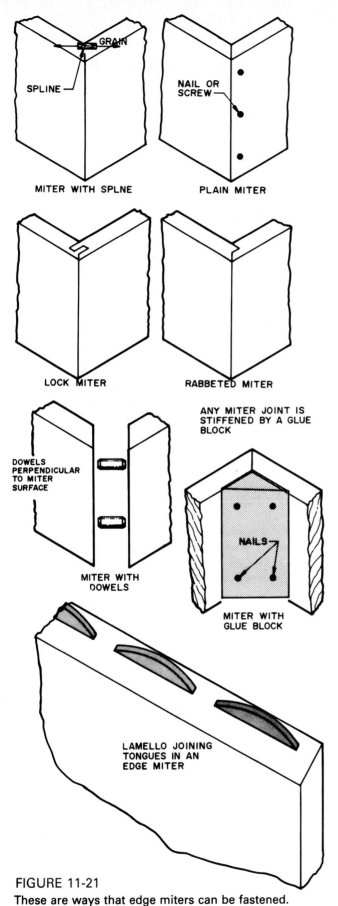

MITER WITH SPLNE

PLAIN MITER

SPLINE

GRAIN

NAIL OR SCREW

LOCK MITER

RABBETED MITER

DOWELS PERPENDICULAR TO MITER SURFACE

MITER WITH DOWELS

ANY MITER JOINT IS STIFFENED BY A GLUE BLOCK

NAILS

MITER WITH GLUE BLOCK

LAMELLO JOINING TONGUES IN AN EDGE MITER

FIGURE 11-21
These are ways that edge miters can be fastened.

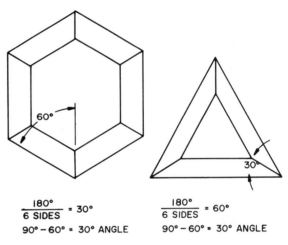

FIGURE 11-22
Edge miters can be cut with a table saw. (*Courtesy of Rockwell International.*)

60°

30°

$$\frac{180°}{6 \text{ SIDES}} = 30°$$

90° − 60° = 30° ANGLE

$$\frac{180°}{6 \text{ SIDES}} = 60°$$

90° − 60° = 30° ANGLE

FIGURE 11-23
How to find miter angles for any type of polygon.

FIGURE 11-24
The sides of this planter required that compound miters be cut.

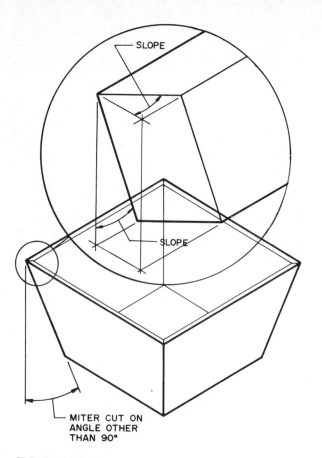

FIGURE 11-25
A compound miter is a combination of a miter and a bevel cut.

FIGURE 11-26
This compound miter is being cut on a radial arm saw.

FIGURE 11-27
The construction of this library carrel required the use of several dados. (*Courtesy of Library Bureau.*)

Usually, each member is cut one-half its thickness. They are joined by gluing. Nails or screws may be added if needed. Lap joints are most often cut with a radial arm saw or a table saw.

END-TO-END JOINTS

Two commonly used joints that unite two boards end to end are *scarf* and *finger joints* (Fig. 11-34, page 124). The scarf joint is cut at a low angle to provide maximum gluing surface. Sometimes, it is strengthened by adding dowels.

The finger joint is widely used in the construction industry. The joint is cut with special, powered cutters. It is used to join short pieces of wood to form longer pieces. The joint is then glued. This joint is as strong as or even stronger than the original board.

MORTISE-AND-TENON JOINTS

A *mortise* is a rectangular opening cut into the wood. A *tenon* is a projecting part designed to fit into a

FIGURE 11-28
Variations of the dado and groove joints.

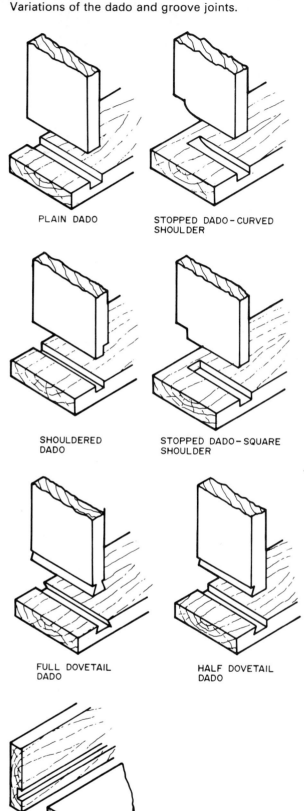

PLAIN DADO

STOPPED DADO – CURVED SHOULDER

SHOULDERED DADO

STOPPED DADO – SQUARE SHOULDER

FULL DOVETAIL DADO

HALF DOVETAIL DADO

GROOVE

FIGURE 11-29
A radial arm saw can be used to cut a dado.

FIGURE 11-30
Grooves can be cut with a radial arm saw.

FIGURE 11-31
End and edge rabbet joints are commonly used in furniture and cabinet construction.

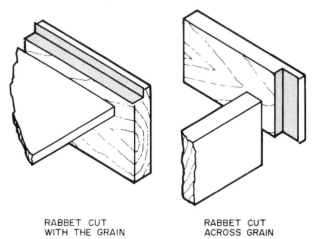

RABBET CUT WITH THE GRAIN

RABBET CUT ACROSS GRAIN

FIGURE 11-32
This rabbet is being cut on a table saw.

mortise. Together they make a strong joint. For maximum strength they must be accurately cut to size.

The mortise-and-tenon joint is widely used to join cross members—for example, a rail to the leg of a chair or table. It is used in high-quality cabinet and frame construction. There are many adaptations of this joint. The common ones are shown in Fig. 11-35.

The blind mortise-and-tenon joint is completely hidden. The shoulders cut around the tenon and cover the edges of the mortise. The open mortise-and-tenon joint is easier to cut. It is useful when joining members at corners. The haunched mortise-and-tenon is designed for frames that have a panel.

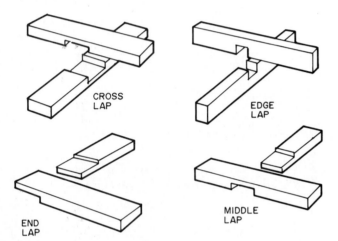

CROSS LAP
EDGE LAP
END LAP
MIDDLE LAP

FIGURE 11-33
Variations of the lap joint.

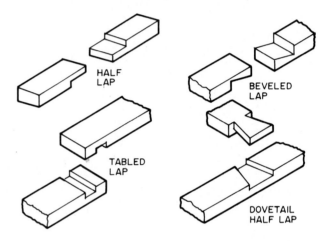

HALF LAP
BEVELED LAP
TABLED LAP
DOVETAIL HALF LAP

FIGURE 11-34
Scarf and finger joints are used to join stock end to end.

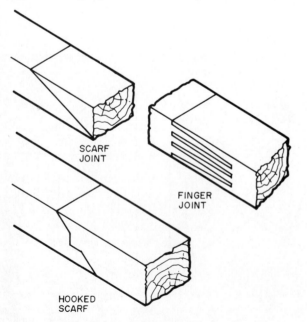

SCARF JOINT
FINGER JOINT
HOOKED SCARF

The haunch on top fits in the panel groove in the side rail. The stub joint has a short tenon that fits in a long groove. A plywood panel is held in the remaining portion of the groove. It does not have shoulders at top or bottom. The barefaced mortise-and-tenon places the tenon on one side of the rail. This is done when the rail is to be flush with the surface of the leg.

The tenon should be cut as large as possible without reducing the strength of the member containing the mortise. Generally, the thickness of the tenon is one-half the thickness of the piece on which it is cut. It is usually $\frac{1}{2}$ in. (13 mm) from the top of the rail and $\frac{1}{4}$ in. (6 mm) from the bottom of the rail. The length depends somewhat on the thickness of the piece to contain the mortise. Generally, the tenon length should be two and one-half times its thickness (Fig. 11-36, page 126).

The mortise should be no closer to the top of the part than $\frac{1}{2}$ in. (13 mm). It should be no closer to the face of the part than $\frac{5}{16}$ in. (8 mm) (Fig. 11-36). The joint will be stronger if these distances can be larger. Cut the mortise $\frac{1}{8}$ in. deeper than the length of the tenon. This forms a glue pocket. Cut the mortise

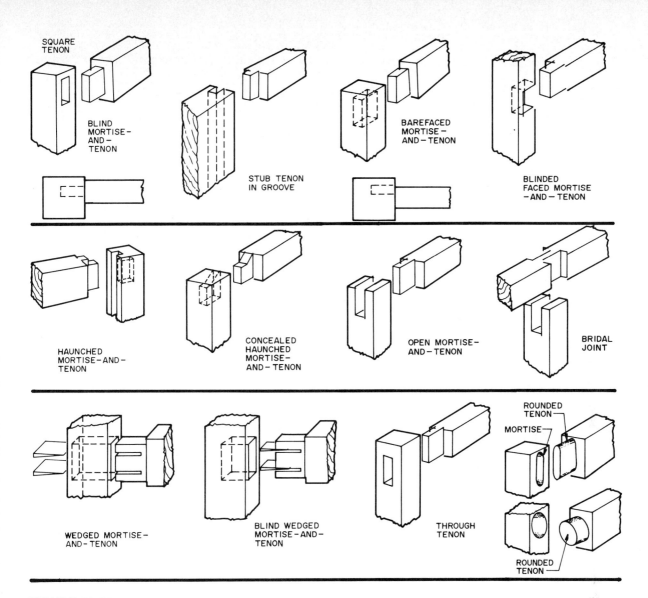

SQUARE TENON

BLIND MORTISE- AND- TENON

STUB TENON IN GROOVE

BAREFACED MORTISE- AND-TENON

BLINDED FACED MORTISE -AND- TENON

HAUNCHED MORTISE-AND- TENON

CONCEALED HAUNCHED MORTISE- AND- TENON

OPEN MORTISE- AND-TENON

BRIDAL JOINT

WEDGED MORTISE- AND- TENON

BLIND WEDGED MORTISE-AND- TENON

THROUGH TENON

ROUNDED TENON

MORTISE

ROUNDED TENON

FIGURE 11-35
Variations of the mortise-and-tenon joint.

before you cut the tenon. It is easier to adjust the size of the tenon to fit the mortise.

Tenons are cut with a table saw, radial arm saw or tenoner (Fig. 11-37). Mortises are cut with a mortiser or router (Fig. 11-38).

BOX AND DOVETAIL JOINTS

The dovetail joint is used to join drawer sides and fronts and forms a decorative way to join corners of chests. It is a strong joint but must be carefully cut. Several variations are in Fig. 11-39. The half-blind dovetail provides a corner where the joint does not show on the front. It is widely used on good-quality furniture construction.

The box joint is used to join corners of boxes and chests. It is a strong joint and easy to cut. The through dovetail is similar but stronger than the box joint.

The sizes of pins on a box joint will vary depending upon the desire of the designer. Generally, they are the same thickness as the wood on which they are cut. This produces a square pin. When cutting a box joint, remember that one side starts with a notch and the other a pin (Fig. 11-40).

Dovetail joints are usually sized by the size and selection of templates and router cutters available. Generally, they are on an angle of 80°. When cutting them, start with a half pin on one side and a half notch on the other (Fig. 11-41). It is best if the joint stops with a half pin on the bottom end of the wood.

Dovetail joints are cut with a router and a dovetail attachment (Fig. 11-42). Box joints are usually cut with a table saw.

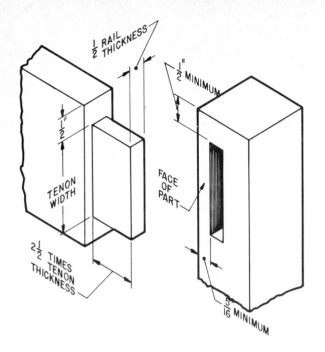

FIGURE 11-36
Recommended proportions for laying out mortises and tenons.

FIGURE 11-37
This tenon is being cut on a table saw. The guard has been removed so that you can see the relationship between the dado cutters and the wood. (*Courtesy of Rockwell International.*)

FIGURE 11-38
Mortises are cut with a mortiser.

FIGURE 11-39
Dovetail and box joints are strong and decorative.

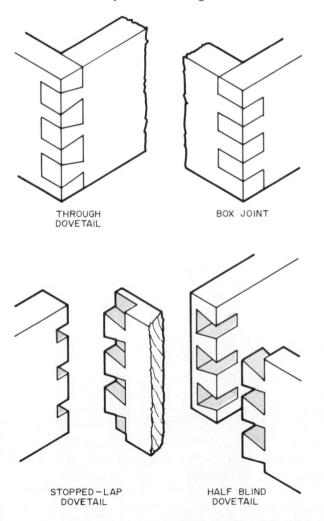

THROUGH DOVETAIL

BOX JOINT

STOPPED-LAP DOVETAIL

HALF BLIND DOVETAIL

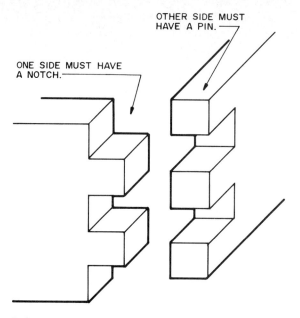

FIGURE 11-40
When laying out a box joint, alternate the notches and pins starting at the top of the stock.

FIGURE 11-41
Start the dovetail with a half pin on the top of one side and a half notch on the other side.

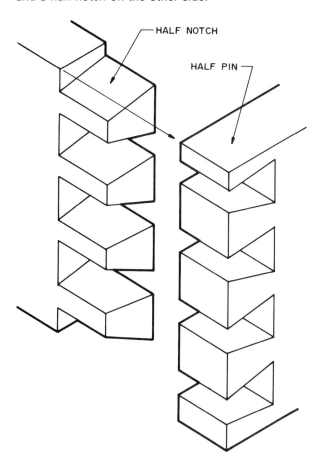

FIGURE 11-42
Dovetails are cut with a router and a dovetail template.

THE LEMON SPLINE SYSTEM

The lemon spline system can be used to join butt and miter joints, and install knock-down furniture fittings and special hinges (Fig. 11-43). The joints are joined using an elliptical plate that is set into slots cut to fit the plate (Fig. 11-44). A plate joiner machine is used to cut the curved bottom slot in both pieces to be joined. The adhesive is placed in the slot followed by the insertion of the plate (Fig. 11-45). After the joint is closed, the pieces may be slid $\frac{1}{8}$ in. (3 mm) in either direction to assure perfect align-

FIGURE 11-43
Typical applications of Lamello plates. (*Courtesy of Colonial Saw.*)

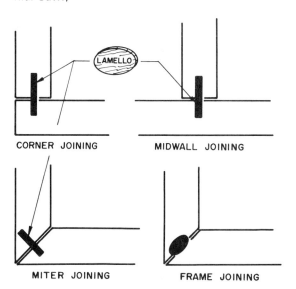

FIGURE 11-44
The Lamello plate is glued in the slot cut by the Lamello machine. (*Courtesy of Colonial Saw.*)

FIGURE 11-45
Lamello saw being used to cut slots in a table leg. (*Courtesy of Colonial Saw.*)

FIGURE 11-46
The Lamello Lamex is a mechanical fastener used to assemble knock-down furniture. (*Courtesy of Colonial Saw.*)

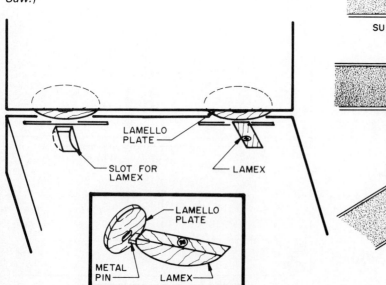

ment of the parts. The plate, which is manufactured in a compressed condition, expands when wetted by the adhesive. This ensures a tight-fitting strong joint.

The Lamello Lamex is a system for detachable wood joining. The Lamello plates have a slot in them. The Lamex is a wood mechanical fastener

FIGURE 11-47
These joints are used with mechanical carcass fasteners.

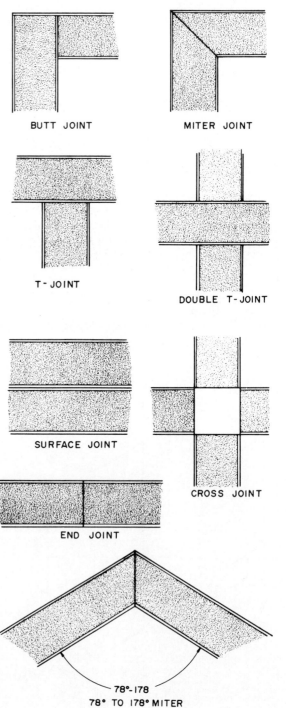

with a metal pin adjusted by a screw. The Lamello plate is glued as described earlier. The Lamex is glued in a curved bottom slot cut in the matching piece. A turn of the screw moves the metal pin into the slot joining the two wood members (Fig. 11-46).

MECHANICAL FASTENERS FOR JOINTS

A variety of mechanical fasteners that are finding extensive use in cabinet construction and furniture units use box-type carcass construction. The joints used include butt, miter, T-joint, end, cross, double T, and surface (Fig. 11-47). These can be joined by one of three types of fasteners, forming (1) rigid non-releasable joints, (2) rigid releasable joints, or (3) flexible releasable joints.

A rigid releasable joint can be secured using a special one-piece fastener (Fig. 11-48). Another type uses a fastener that goes through the one material to be joined and is secured in an insert set into the second piece (Fig. 11-49). Still another uses a cylinder head machine screw that is secured in a cross-nut in the second member (Fig. 11-50). Detailed information on these and other mechanical fasteners is provided in Chapter 2.

FIGURE 11-48
Butt joint secured with a one-piece fastener forming a rigid releasable joint. (*Courtesy of H'a'fele America, 203 Feld Ave., High Point, NC 27261.*)

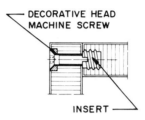

FIGURE 11-49
This two-piece mechanical fastener uses a decorative countersunk head machine screw and a threaded insert. (*Courtesy of H'a'fele America, 203 Feld Ave., High Point, NC 27261.*)

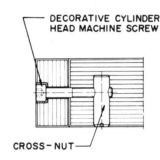

FIGURE 11-50
This mechanical fastener uses a decorative cylinder head machine screw and a cross-nut. (*Courtesy of H'a'fele America, 203 Feld Ave., High Point, NC 27261.*)

12

DOOR CONSTRUCTION

Doors serve functional purposes such as hiding the contents of a cabinet from view or protecting items from dust. They are also a part of the design and influence how people react to a furniture or cabinet unit. Doors are made in many different ways and from a variety of materials (Fig 12-1).

FRAME-AND-PANEL DOORS

Frame-and-panel doors have solid wood frames with panels filling the space between. Small doors have top and bottom rails and stiles on the sides. Larger doors will have a middle rail and perhaps a mullion (Fig. 12-2).

Panels are usually flush or raised (Fig. 12-3). The flush panel may be set in a groove or rabbet in the stiles and rails. It can have molding and decorative overlays bonded to it (Fig. 12-4). Raised panels are thick panels having the edges machined to fit into a groove in the edges of the rails and stiles.

Frame-and-panel doors can be built using a stub tenon, open mortise and tenon, dowel, or haunched mortise-and-tenon joint (Fig. 12-5). Good-quality factory manufactured cabinets use the stuck

FIGURE 12-1
The doors on this china cabinet form a major element in the design. The top doors have glass panels and the lower doors matched veneer panels. (*Courtesy of Drexel Heritage Furnishings Inc.*)

point shown in Fig. 12-6. The edge of the stile and rail is shaped to receive a panel, and the outer edge

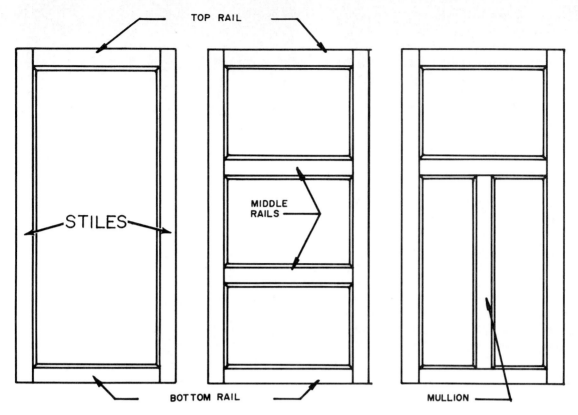

FIGURE 12-2
Parts of a paneled door.

FIGURE 12-3
Panels can be flush or raised.

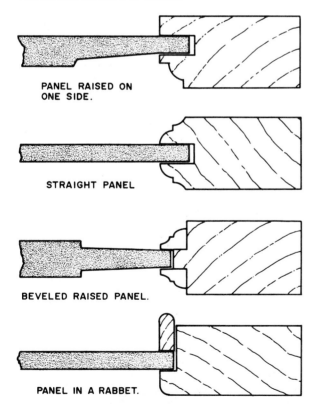

PANEL RAISED ON
ONE SIDE.

STRAIGHT PANEL

BEVELED RAISED PANEL.

PANEL IN A RABBET.

FIGURE 12-4
Decorative overlays are often used.

is rounded. This is referred to as *sticking*. The ends of the rail are cut in the shape of the reverse of the sticking so that they match when the door is assembled. This shaped end is referred to as *coping*. Another method of molding an inside edge is with a router (Fig. 12-7).

SOLID DOORS

Doors can be *solid wood*. If the wood is edge-glued lumber, it may be difficult to keep the door from warping. Cleats may be screwed to the inside of the door to help keep it flat.

Plywood is a good door material because it is stable. Veneer-core plywood shows the multiple plies along the edges unless it is banded. Hinges on these doors must screw into the face of the plywood. Screws do not hold well in the edge of the panel. Lumber-core plywood doors can have shaped or banded edges. Since the door has a solid lumber core, hinges can be screwed into the face or edge.

FIGURE 12-5
These joints are used to build frame-and-panel doors.

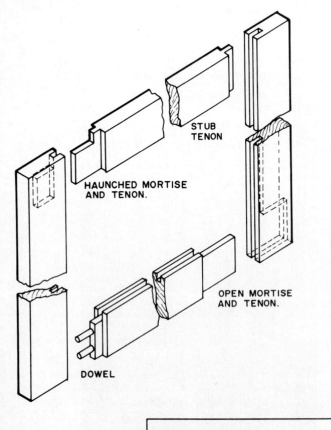

FIGURE 12-6
The stuck joint is used when manufacturing doors for good-quality furniture.

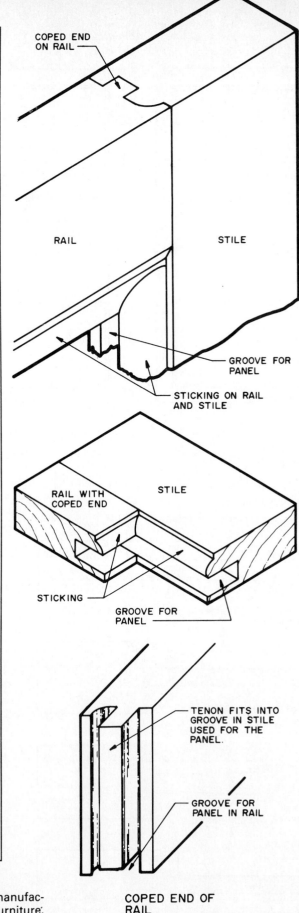

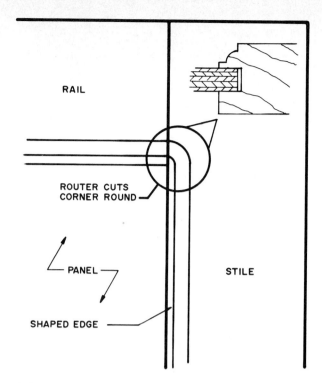

FIGURE 12-7
It improves the appearance of frame-and-panel doors if the square edge is relieved by shaping it.

Particleboard doors are stable but require that a plastic laminate be glued to them to improve their appearance. Painted, stained, or natural finish particleboard can be used for storage cabinets where a

FIGURE 12-9
Plastic hinges can be used to assemble a tambour door.

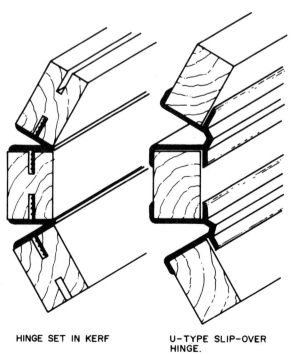

HINGE SET IN KERF   U-TYPE SLIP-OVER HINGE.

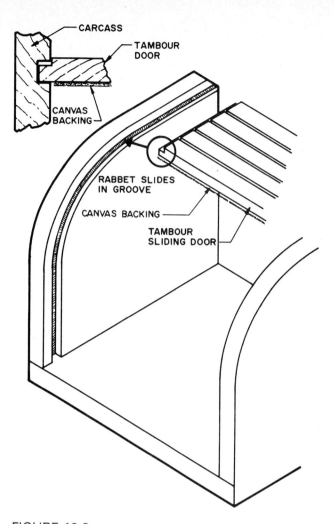

FIGURE 12-8
Tambour doors can slide in a groove cut in the sides of the cabinet.

high-quality grain is not necessary. Special screws are needed to secure hinges into particleboard.

Hardboard can be used for doors of all kinds. Wood or plastic laminates can be applied to the surface.

Many doors are *glass panels, plastic panels* that are translucent and opaque, and *metal grills* of various types. With special hinges or tracks, glass doors do not need a supporting frame.

TAMBOUR DOORS

Tambour doors are made of narrow wood strips fastened to heavy canvas, or flexible plastic hinges are used. The wood strips are cut to slide in a groove cut in the sides of the cabinet (Fig. 12-8). A canvas back is glued to the back of the tambour to hold the slats in place as the door is moved up or down. Plastic hinges are either set in a saw kerf or have a U-shaped channel that slips over the wood strip (Fig. 12-9). Tambour doors can slide vertically as in Fig.

12-8 or horizontally as in Fig. 12-10. These can slide in a groove or on a plastic track that is set in a groove in the cabinet bottom.

SLIDING DOORS

Sliding doors are often used on bookshelves, wall cabinets, and other furniture units. The simplest and least expensive way to do this is to cut grooves in the unit bottom and the rail above the door, or nail wood strips to them and slide the doors in between the strips (Fig. 12-11). Cut the bottom groove about $\frac{1}{4}$ in. deep and the top groove $\frac{1}{2}$ in. deep. To insert the door, slide the top up into the top groove and lower the door into the bottom groove. The height of the door should be $\frac{3}{16}$ in. higher than the opening. Plastic and metal tracks are available for this purpose (Fig. 12-12). They provide a superior means for sliding the doors. The doors can be of any

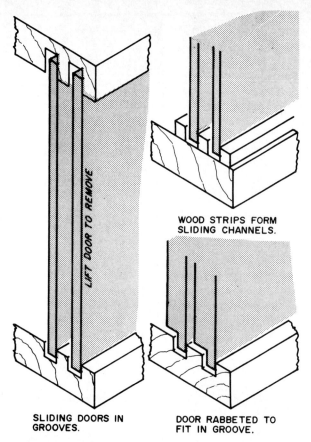

WOOD STRIPS FORM
SLIDING CHANNELS.

SLIDING DOORS IN
GROOVES.

DOOR RABBETED TO
FIT IN GROOVE.

FIGURE 12-11
Horizontal sliding doors can run in grooves or channels.

FIGURE 12-10
Horizontally sliding tambour doors can slide on plastic rails.

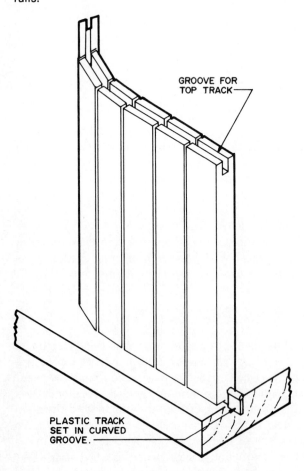

GROOVE FOR
TOP TRACK

PLASTIC TRACK
SET IN CURVED
GROOVE.

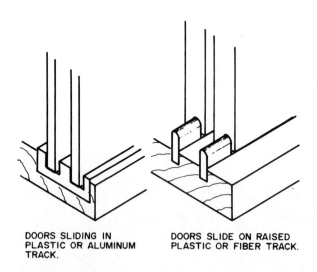

DOORS SLIDING IN
PLASTIC OR ALUMINUM
TRACK.

DOORS SLIDE ON RAISED
PLASTIC OR FIBER TRACK.

FIGURE 12-12
Aluminum, fiber, and plastic tracks are available for guiding sliding doors.

suitable material. They can be the same width as the groove or rabbetted on each end to fit the groove. Allow a generous allowance between the width of the groove and the part of the door to slide in it.

STYLES OF DOORS

The most commonly used styles of doors are the lipped, reveal overlay, flush overlay, flush with faceframe, and flush without faceframe. These are described in great detail in Chapter 2.

The *lipped door* has the advantage of covering the crack around the door opening, reducing the need for the accuracy required with flush doors. A rabbet is cut on three or four sides, depending on the design of the frame. The edge can be square, rounded, or shaped (Fig. 12-13).

A lipped door is usually mounted with semi-concealed hinges. These are made for a $\frac{3}{8}$-in. lip. These hinges are made in various styles, such as modern or colonial. Before installing the hinges, place the door in the opening to be certain it fits. Mount the hinges on the door first. Place it on the cabinet, and check to be certain that it is square and centered in the opening. Then fasten the hinges to the faceframe with screws.

Flush doors fit inside the faceframe, or if it has no faceframe, the front edge of the carcass. They must be made carefully so that the crack around the edges is uniform (Fig. 12-14). These doors use butt, wraparound, invisible, and European-style hinges.

Flush overlay doors cover the side of the carcass and any bulkheads between doors. They give a clean, modern look. Knife and invisible hinges are commonly used (Fig. 12-15). These doors use wraparound, pivot, and European-style hinges.

Reveal overlay doors are sized so that they partially overlap the end panels and bulkheads. This provides a three-dimensional appearance and an interesting shadow line around each. The amount of overlap is usually $\frac{3}{8}$ in. on end panels, which reveals

FIGURE 12-13
Lipped doors cover the crack between the door and faceframe.

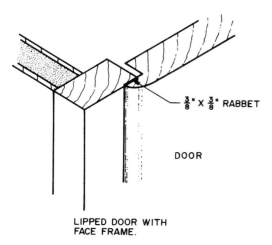

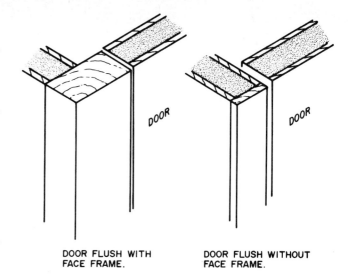

DOOR FLUSH WITH FACE FRAME.

DOOR FLUSH WITHOUT FACE FRAME.

FIGURE 12-14
Flush doors may be with or without faceframe.

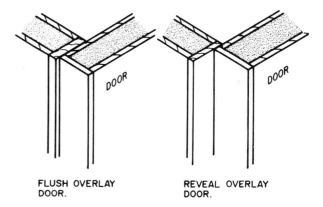

FLUSH OVERLAY DOOR.

REVEAL OVERLAY DOOR.

FIGURE 12-15
Flush overlay doors cover the end panels and bulkheads. Reveal overlay doors partially overlap the end panels and bulkheads.

$\frac{3}{8}$ in. of the end of the panel. When two doors meet on a bulkhead, the overlap is about $\frac{3}{16}$ in. for each door (Fig. 12-15). These doors use wraparound, pivot, and European-style hinges.

HINGES

There are many types of hinges available for use on furniture and cabinets. Some are visible and decorative and become a part of the design. Others reflect the hinges used at a certain period of history. Still others are hidden or partially hidden. The parts of a hinge are shown in Fig. 12-16. The door wing or leaf is fastened to the door. The frame wing or leaf is fastened to the frame. *Butt hinges* are available either swaged or unswaged. Swaging is a slight offset

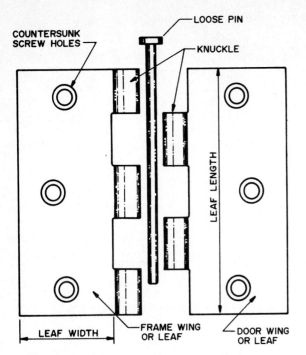

COUNTERSUNK SCREW HOLES
LOOSE PIN
KNUCKLE
LEAF LENGTH
LEAF WIDTH
FRAME WING OR LEAF
DOOR WING OR LEAF

HINGE WIDTH = 2 LEAVES PLUS KNUCKLE

FIGURE 12-16
Parts of a hinge.

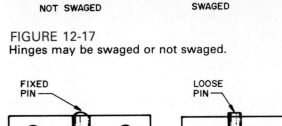

NOT SWAGED   SWAGED

FIGURE 12-17
Hinges may be swaged or not swaged.

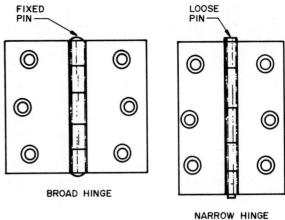

FIXED PIN   LOOSE PIN

BROAD HINGE   NARROW HINGE

FIGURE 12-18
Cabinet hinges are available in broad and narrow types.

of the leaf hinge at the barrel. This permits the leaves to come closer together (Fig. 12-17). *Cabinet hinges* are available with loose or fast pins in light narrow and broad hinge types (Fig. 12-18). *Plain* *steel hinges* are available in broad, narrow, and back flap types. *Continuous hinges* are also available in lengths from 30 to 72 in. They are available in steel, brass, aluminum, and stainless steel.

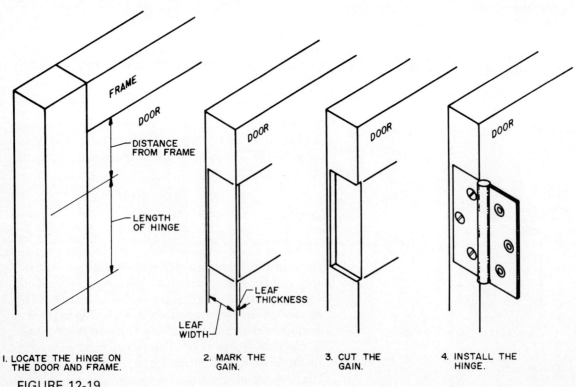

1. LOCATE THE HINGE ON THE DOOR AND FRAME.
DISTANCE FROM FRAME
LENGTH OF HINGE
FRAME
DOOR

2. MARK THE GAIN.
LEAF THICKNESS
LEAF WIDTH

3. CUT THE GAIN.

4. INSTALL THE HINGE.

FIGURE 12-19
How to install butt hinges.

Installing Butt Hinges

Butt hinges are usually installed on the edge of the door and faceframe. This sets the door flush with the faceframe (Fig. 12-19). First place the door in the faceframe. Mark the location of the hinge on both. Using a try square, mark the hinge location on the edges of the frame and door. Then mark the depth of the gain. A gain is a rectangular notch cut to receive the leaf of the hinge. The gain could be cut into the frame and door the thickness of one leaf. It could be cut into the frame the thickness of two leaves (Fig. 12-20). After cutting the gain, place the hinge in it to locate the screw holes. Drill the anchor holes and install the screws.

Decorative Butt Hinges

Decorative butt hinges are used to enhance the appearance of the furniture or cabinet unit. They are mounted on the face of the frame and door (Fig. 12-21).

To install, locate and install the hinges on the door. Place the door inside the frame and put one screw in each hinge. If the door moves freely, install the other screws (Fig. 12-22).

FIGURE 12-21
Decorative surface-mounted hinges enhance the appearance of the furniture or cabinet unit. (*Courtesy of American Plywood Association.*)

Mortiseless Hinges

Mortiseless hinges do not require a gain because the one leaf fits inside an opening in the other leaf (Fig. 12-23).

Pivot Hinges

Pivot hinges are used where it is desired to have the hinge less noticeable than with butt hinges. They are mounted to the stile or cabinet side and the back

FIGURE 12-22
How to install a door using surface-mounted hinges.

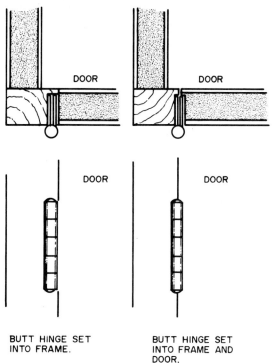

FIGURE 12-20
Hinges may be recessed into the door or faceframe.

BUTT HINGE SET INTO FRAME.

BUTT HINGE SET INTO FRAME AND DOOR.

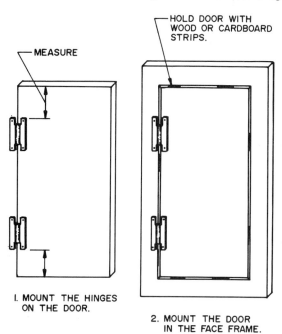

I. MOUNT THE HINGES ON THE DOOR.

2. MOUNT THE DOOR IN THE FACE FRAME.

HOLD DOOR WITH WOOD OR CARDBOARD STRIPS.

MEASURE

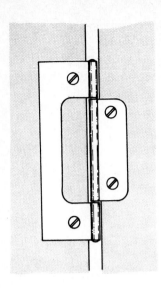
FIGURE 12-23
Mortiseless hinge.

FIGURE 12-25
This flush door is mounted using pivot hinges. (*Courtesy of American Plywood Association.*)

of the door (Fig. 12-24). Two types are available. One mounts on the vertical stile and the other on a horizontal rail. They are used on flush doors (Fig. 12-25).

Knife Hinges

A knife hinge is similar to the pivot hinge. It mounts on the horizontal frame and on top of the door. It is used on flush doors (Fig. 12-26).

FIGURE 12-24
The pivot hinge is designed to mount on the vertical stile. (*Courtesy of Stanley Hardware.*)

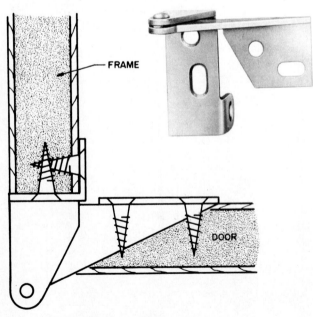

PIVOT HINGE FOR VERTICAL STILE.

Semiconcealed Hinges

Semiconcealed hinges are used for lipped doors and reveal overlay doors (Fig. 12-27). The lipped door hinge is formed to fit into the ⅜-in. rabbet on the door edge. The reveal overlay door hinge has a straight leaf (Fig. 12-28).

Wrap-Around Hinges

Wrap-around hinges are used on flush, lipped, and reveal overlay doors. They are called wraparound because the leaves wrap around the frame and/or the door.

Typical wraparound hinges are shown in Fig. 12-29, page 139. The lipped door hinge wraps around

FIGURE 12-26
The knife hinge mounts on the horizontal frame.

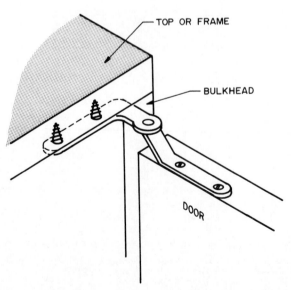

FIGURE 12-27
The semiconcealed hinge fits in the lip and is screwed to the inside of the door. (*Courtesy of American Plywood Association.*)

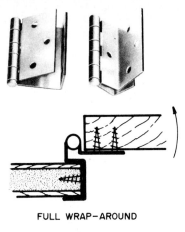

FULL WRAP-AROUND

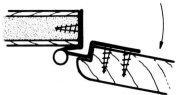

LIPPED DOOR FASTENED TO EDGE OF FRAME. (PARTIAL WRAP-AROUND)

FLUSH DOOR HINGE

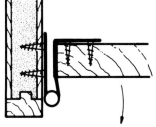

RECESSED FLUSH DOOR

FIGURE 12-29
These are typical of the wraparound hinges available. (*Courtesy of Stanley Hardware.*)

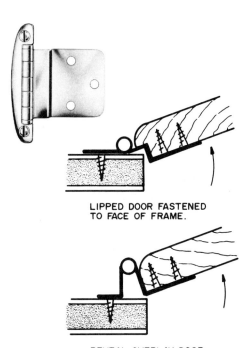

LIPPED DOOR FASTENED TO FACE OF FRAME.

REVEAL OVERLAY DOOR.

FIGURE 12-28
Two types of semiconcealed hinges. (*Courtesy of Stanley Hardware.*)

FIGURE 12-30
This wraparound hinge fits into a recess cut in the cabinet side panel. (*Courtesy of American Plywood Association.*)

the door and fastens to the edge of the frame. The flush door hinge fastens to the edge of the frame. The recessed hinge fastens to the inside face of the cabinet (Fig. 12-30). It can also be used without recessing the door.

Concealed or European Hinges

The trend toward European-style cabinets that do not have faceframes has led to an increased need for concealed hinges that are sometimes called European hinges. A number of designs are available.

The concealed hinge in Fig. 12-31 is designed for overlay and flush inset doors. The hinge has adjusting screws that permit lateral adjustment of the door after the hinge has been installed. The hinge requires a mortise hole in the door. A typical mortise is $1\frac{3}{8}$ in. in diameter and $\frac{1}{2}$ in. deep with a flat bottom. It can be bored with a multispur or Forstner bit. The hinge is fastened to the door with screws through the plate above the round part that fits into the mortise. It fastens to the cabinet bulkhead with a mounting base plate. The plate is screwed to the bulkhead. The arm of the hinge slides over the plate and is secured to it with setscrews. Installation locations for flush overlay and reveal overlay doors are shown in Fig. 12-31.

Various types of concealed hinges allow the door to open through a range of angles. These vary from 95 to 180° (Fig. 12-32). Some types of concealed hinges have a self-closing function.

Another type of concealed hinge is the invisible link-stop hinge. It is set in the edge of the door and cabinet frame in a mortise (Fig. 12-33). A no-mortise concealed-cylinder-type hinge is set into round holes bored in the door and frame edges. The outside of the round body is heavily knurled, so it binds tightly when inserted in the hole. No screws are necessary (Fig. 12-34).

FIGURE 12-31
This concealed hinge will mount flush and overlay doors. (*Courtesy of Stanley Hardware.*)

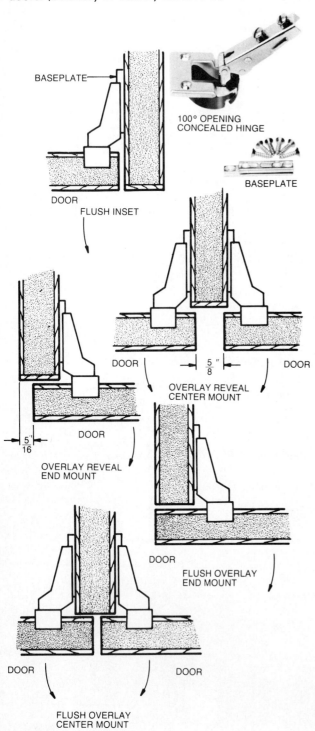

FIGURE 12-32
Concealed hinges are available that permit doors to swing through 180°. (*Courtesy of Grass America Inc.*)

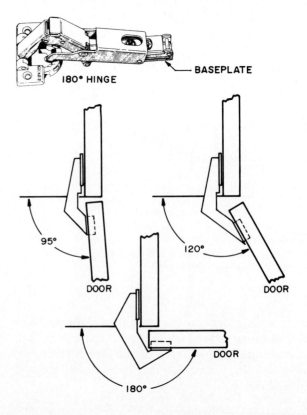

FIGURE 12-33
An invisible link-stop concealed hinge is mortised into the edge of the door.

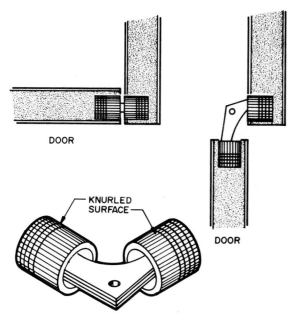

FIGURE 12-34
The no-mortise concealed cylinder hinge is set into round holes bored into the door and frame.

Glass Door Hinges

In Fig. 12-35 is shown a hinge for glass doors as found on stereo and television cabinets. The hinge mounts on the side of the cabinet and the glass door fits into a channel. It will hold glass up to $1\frac{1}{4}$ in. in thickness. A plastic spacer is inserted between the glass and the side of the channel. Screws in the channel press the plastic against the glass, holding it in place. This is designed for inset doors.

Plastic Hinges

Flat plastic hinges are available in coils up to 500 ft long. They are made from a tough extruded polypro-

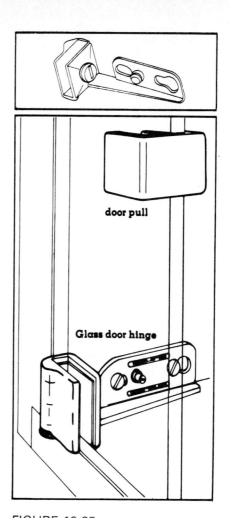

FIGURE 12-35
This glass door hinge holds the glass with setscrews. (*Courtesy of The Woodworkers' Store.*)

pylene. They are self-aligning and do not require mortising. They are attached with screws, nails, or staples. They are not recommended for outdoor use. Use with particleboard is especially helpful because they cover the edge grain (Fig. 12-36).

CATCHES

Some of the new hinges available are *self-closing* and do not require a catch. Self-closing hinges have

FIGURE 12-36
Plastic hinges are fastened to the surface of the door or frame.

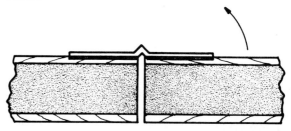

MAGNETIC CATCH

FRICTION CATCH

ROLLER CATCH

FIGURE 12-37
These are typical magnet and friction catches used to secure cabinet doors.
(*Courtesy of The Stanley Works.*)

a built-in spring that assists with the closing of the door. It also holds the door shut. If a catch is needed, the magnetic catch is most useful. There are a variety of friction catches available. These must be carefully installed so that they line up when the door is closed. They are made with elongated holes for the screws, which permits some adjustment to be made after they are installed. Some commonly used catches are in Fig. 12-37.

PULLS AND KNOBS

The style of pull or knob used must be in keeping with the design of the cabinet. Sliding doors usually use recessed pulls so that the doors slide freely past each other. The pulls and knobs should be coordinated with those used on drawers (Fig. 12-38).

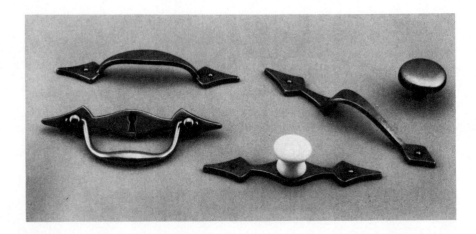

FIGURE 12-38
The knobs and pulls are designed so that they form a coordinated set. (*Courtesy of Amerock Corporation, an Anchor Hocking Company.*)

13

DRAWER CONSTRUCTION

There are many ways to build and install drawers. The type chosen depends on the quality of the cabinet being produced, the drawer size, the type of drawer guide to be used, the style of the cabinet, the load the drawer will be expected to carry, and the possible frequency of use (Fig. 13-1).

Good-quality drawers must be constructed so that they remain square even when loaded. They should slide out of the cabinet easily and not tip downward when pulled out to their full extent.

When choosing a drawer design, it is necessary to consider the type of drawer guide to be used and the requirements for the style of furniture. A drawer can be designed so that it can accommodate shop-made or commercial drawer guides. The type of commercial guide must be known before construction starts. Similarly, the type of drawer front required due to the furniture design must be known.

TYPES OF DRAWER FRONTS

There are four basic types of drawer fronts: flush with a faceframe, lipped, flush overlay and reveal overlay, and flush without a faceframe (Fig. 13-2). The front of the *flush drawer* is flush with the stiles

FIGURE 13-1
The drawers in this cabinet are sized to store items commonly kept in a storage/display cabinet. (*Courtesy of Yorktowne Cabinets.*)

143

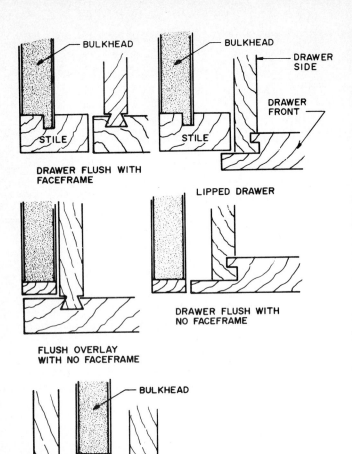

DRAWER FLUSH WITH FACEFRAME

LIPPED DRAWER

FLUSH OVERLAY WITH NO FACEFRAME

DRAWER FLUSH WITH NO FACEFRAME

REVEAL OVERLAY

FIGURE 13-2
Drawer fronts are made in four types.

and rails of the faceframe (Fig. 13-1) or with the exposed edge of the case if a faceframe is not used (Fig. 13-3).

The *lipped drawer* has a rabbet cut on the edges. The lip overlaps the stiles and rails. This enables the drawer front to cover the space between

FIGURE 13-3
These drawers are set flush with the edge of the case. (*Courtesy of Thomasville Furniture Industries, Inc.*)

FIGURE 13-4
The drawers on these cabinets have lipped edges to conceal the crack around their edges. (*Courtesy of American Woodmark Corporation.*)

the stiles and the sides of the drawer. While the lip can be any thickness desired, $\frac{3}{8}$ in. is frequently used (Fig. 13-4).

The *flush overlay drawer* front overlaps the sides completely, covering the front of the case. With this construction a faceframe is not needed (Fig. 13-5).

The *reveal overlay drawer* covers part of the stile and rail, or part of the side of the case if stiles and rails are not used. The edges of the drawer front can be left square, slightly rounded, or shaped.

DRAWER CONSTRUCTION

A drawer is made up of a front, bottom, back, and two sides. The requirements of the drawer and the quality of construction can vary and the actual design is influenced by these (Fig. 13-6).

Drawer Front

The front is the only part of a drawer that is exposed to view. The style of front and the material from which it is made must fit in with the style of the cabinet. The style of the drawer front will usually be the same as the adjacent doors. Most good-quality cabinets require drawer fronts made from wood that matches the outside of the carcass or cabinet in grain and color. These are usually $\frac{3}{4}$-in. solid wood, but thicker material could be used. The drawer front could be plywood with a proper wood veneer on the face and edges or solid-core plywood with a wood veneer on the exposed face. The drawer front can be covered with plastic laminate over plywood. If the edges are exposed or shaped, they can be painted to blend in with the basic color on the laminate. On some units, such as kitchen cabinets, the plastic laminate might be a color that is different from the basic cabinet producing a totally different appear-

FIGURE 13-5
These cabinets are made with flush overlay drawers and doors. (*Courtesy of Kleweno of Kansas City.*)

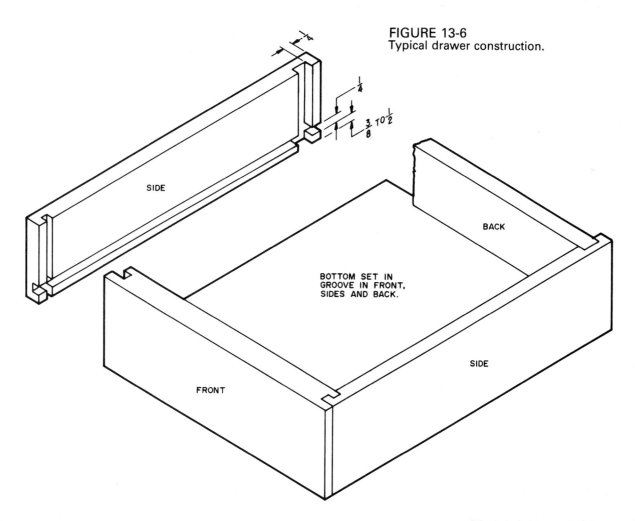

FIGURE 13-6
Typical drawer construction.

SIDE

BACK

BOTTOM SET IN
GROOVE IN FRONT,
SIDES AND BACK.

SIDE

FRONT

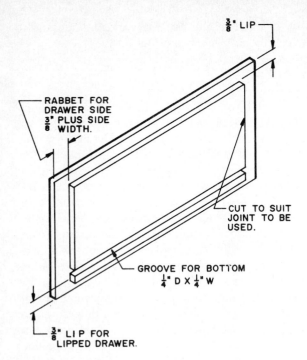

FIGURE 13-7
This lipped drawer front has a ⅜ × ⅜ in. lip.

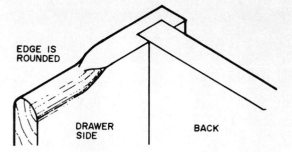

FIGURE 13-8
Drawer sides have the top rounded.

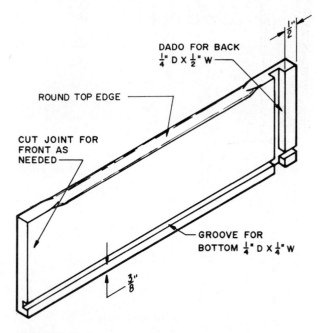

FIGURE 13-9
Drawer sides have grooves for the bottom and back.

ance. Drawer fronts can be decorated by adding molding on the surface or carving into them.

The drawer front has a groove cut across it to hold the bottom. The ends are cut to suit the type of drawer (flush, lipped, reveal, flush overlay) and the joint to be used (Fig. 13-7).

Drawer Sides and Back

Drawer sides are usually made from ½-in.-thick plywood or solid stock. If a side guide is to be used which requires that a groove be cut in the drawer side, use ⅝-in. (16-mm)-thick stock. Very small drawers can use ¼- to ⅜-in. (6- to 10-mm)-thick stock.

The wood used in the sides and back is usually less expensive than that in the drawer front. For lower-cost units, sycamore, poplar, and pine are used. For higher-quality units, maple, red oak, and mahogany are used.

To give a finished appearance, the *top edge* of the sides are rounded with a shaper or router to a ¼-in. radius (Fig. 13-8). In all but the lowest-quality units, the *sides of the drawer* are grooved to receive the bottom. The groove is usually cut ½ in. deep (Fig. 13-9). The *back* may also be grooved (Fig. 13-10). Sometimes the back and sides sit on top of the bottom and are nailed or stapled to it (Fig. 13-11). This is frequently used with the newer European hardware where the side-mounted drawer slides over the bottom edge of the side.

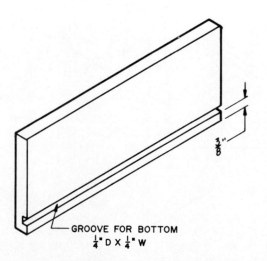

FIGURE 13-10
The back of the drawer is grooved to receive the bottom.

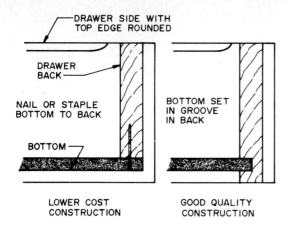

FIGURE 13-11
Drawer bottoms are stapled in place in low-quality drawer construction.

Drawer Bottom

The drawer bottom is usually made from $\frac{1}{4}$-in. hardboard or plywood. In small drawers $\frac{1}{8}$-in. hardboard could be used. The bottom is set in grooves and *not glued*. As the drawer expands and contracts, it can slide over the edges of the bottom. Plywood and hardboard expand and contract very little and provide a stable base.

Remember to cut the bottom $\frac{1}{16}$ to $\frac{1}{8}$ in. (2 to 4 mm) shorter in length and width than the distance from the bottom of the grooves. This allows $\frac{1}{32}$ to $\frac{1}{16}$ in. (1 to 2 mm) of clearance on all sides of the bottom in the assembled drawer. The bottom, if fit properly, should help to square up the drawer when it is assembled.

JOINTS IN DRAWER CONSTRUCTION

The strongest and also the most difficult joints to use to join the drawer front and sides are shown in Fig. 13-12. The French dovetail and multifinger dovetail are cut with router cutters. The blind French dovetail is cut with a dovetail router bit using a router table. The milled shaper joint requires a special shaper cutter. The others can be cut on the table saw. All these joints are assembled by gluing.

Other joints, which are easier to cut but not quite as strong or decorative, are shown in Fig. 13-13. They can all be cut easily on a table saw. The dado and rabbet joints are assembled by gluing. The rabbet butt and dado joints are glued and nailed.

Cutting a Milled Shaper Joint

This joint is usually cut on a shaper using a milled glue joint cutter. To cut this joint on a shaper, a

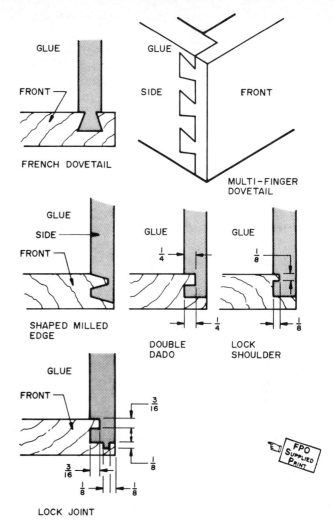

FIGURE 13-12
Strongest joints used in drawer construction.

special stubbed spindle must be installed. This allows the spindle nut to be recessed flush with the top of the shaper table.

The steps to cut a milled shaper joint are:

1. Adjust the spindle to cut the drawer sides as shown in Fig. 13-14, step 1. The distance A on the draw side must be cut exactly the same as B on the top of the cutter. Stand the drawer side on end and cut the joint on the inside face. For narrow drawer sides, use a tenoning jig to guide the material past the cutter.

2. Place the drawer front flat on the shaper table with the inside face down. Adjust the fence to give the desired depth of cut, and cut each end (Fig. 13-14, step 2). You will note that the drawer front extends over the top of the cutter.

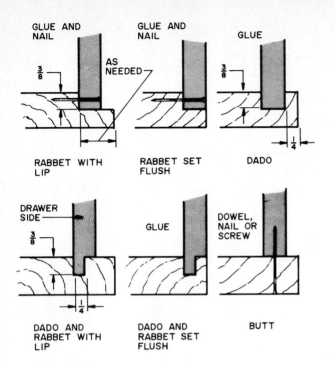

FIGURE 13-13
These drawer joints are easy to cut.

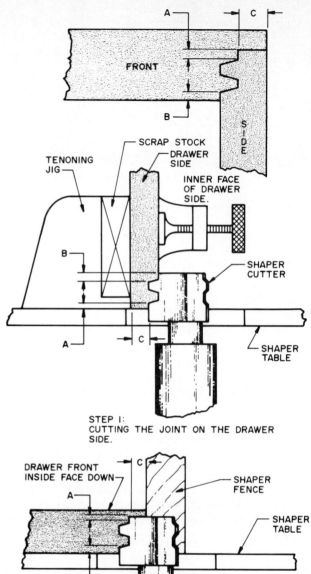

STEP 1:
CUTTING THE JOINT ON THE DRAWER SIDE.

STEP 2:
CUTTING THE JOINT ON THE DRAWER FACE.

FIGURE 13-14
Steps to cut a milled shaper joint.

Cutting a Locked Shoulder Joint

This joint is cut on a circular saw using a dado head. The following tells how to lay out and cut it on a drawer having $\frac{1}{2}$-in. sides and a $\frac{3}{4}$-in. front.

1. Use two $\frac{1}{8}$-in. dado cutters. Cut a dado in the side (Fig. 13-15, step 1). Cut the dado $\frac{1}{16}$-in. deeper than the length of the tongue to enter it.

2. Cut the $\frac{1}{4}$-in. (6-mm) dado in both ends of the drawer front (Fig. 13-15, step 2). Use a tenoning jig to guide the stock.

3. Set the dado head to cut slightly higher than $\frac{1}{4}$ in. Clamp a piece of stock to the fence. Butt the end of the drawer front against it with the inside face down. Position the fence so that the dado head cuts $\frac{5}{16}$ in. off the tongue on the inside face of the drawer front (Fig. 13-15), step 3). Use a miter gauge to guide the stock.

Assembling the Drawer

After cutting the drawer parts, assemble them without glue to make certain that they will go together. The joints should fit snugly but go together without forcing. Remember to assemble the sides around the bottom, which is not glued. After the drawer is clamped and before the adhesive sets, check it for squareness. It is best to measure across the diagonals or from corner to opposite corner. If they are the

same, the box is square. Place it on a flat surface while the adhesive is setting.

Drawer Supports and Guides

Some cabinets are made with dust panels. These provide support to the sides and back of the unit, and the drawer slides on top of them. The dust panel may be exposed or hidden by the drawer front.

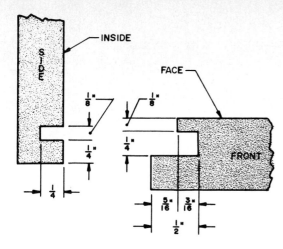

LOCKED SHOULDER JOINT

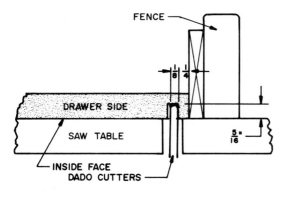

STEP 1: CUT THE DADO IN THE DRAWER SIDE.

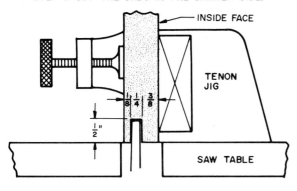

STEP 2: CUT A DADO IN EACH END OF THE DRAWER FRONT.

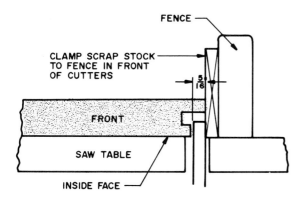

STEP 3: POSITION THE FENCE SO THE DADO CUTTERS REMOVES ⅜ in. OF THE TONGUE ON THE INSIDE FACE.

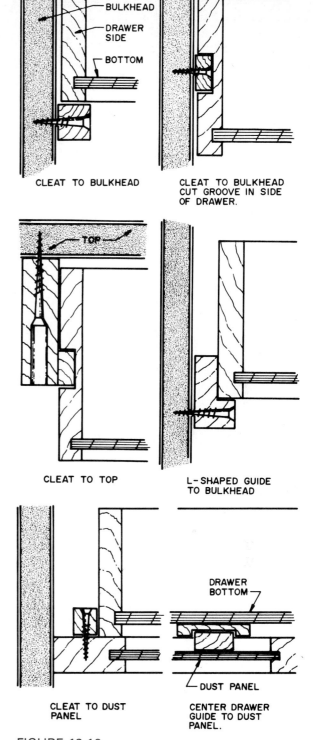

CLEAT TO BULKHEAD

CLEAT TO BULKHEAD CUT GROOVE IN SIDE OF DRAWER.

CLEAT TO TOP

L-SHAPED GUIDE TO BULKHEAD

CLEAT TO DUST PANEL

CENTER DRAWER GUIDE TO DUST PANEL.

FIGURE 13-16
Typical drawer guides.

Furniture and cabinets may or may not have a face frame. This will influence the drawer guides selected as well as the size of the drawer. A variety of wood guides are shown in Fig. 13-16. The simplest

FIGURE 13-15
Steps to cut a locked shoulder joint.

JOINTS IN DRAWER CONSTRUCTION   149

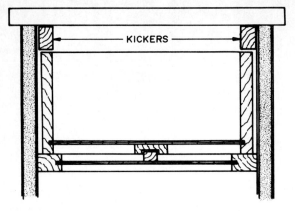

FIGURE 13-17
Cleats are the simplest form of a kicker.

FIGURE 13-18
A cleat in a groove in the drawer sides is a simple slide system.

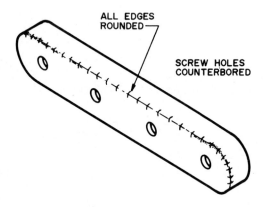

FIGURE 13-19
Slides from plastic cleats slide easily.

guides are cleats that may be fastened to the bulkhead. Cleats are satisfactory for work that will not carry heavy loads. When several drawers are one above the other, the cleat could also serve as a kicker. A kicker is a strip that keeps the front end of the drawer from dropping as it is opened (Fig. 13-17). Cleats should be of hard wood and heavily waxed.

Another simple drawer slide is to cut a groove in the side of the drawer. The cleat slides in this groove. Cut the groove wide enough so that the cleat slides freely in it (Fig. 13-18). A plastic drawer slide is available for drawers with side grooves. They could also serve as cleats. Because the plastic slides have rounded edges and ends, drawers slide easily, making plastic slides superior to wood slides (Fig. 13-19).

FIGURE 13-20
Typical wood center drawer guides.

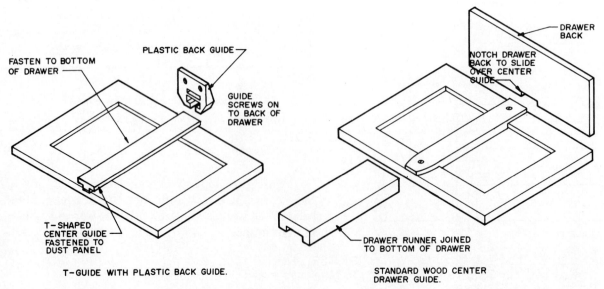

T-GUIDE WITH PLASTIC BACK GUIDE.

STANDARD WOOD CENTER DRAWER GUIDE.

Another shop-made drawer guide is an L-shaped strip that is fastened to the sides of the unit. It could be a single piece of stock with a rabbet or two pieces glued and nailed together. The actual size of the guide can vary. The method of securing it to the cabinet will vary with the design. The drawer face will have to be laid out to allow for the thickness of the vertical part of the guide. The L-shaped wood guide can also be used with a face frame.

The two common types of wood center guides are shown in Fig. 13-20. One type uses a wood runner fastened to the dust panel. It is rounded and tapered on the front end. A U-shaped channel is glued to the bottom of the drawer. Another type has a T-shaped hardwood runner fastened to the dust panel. A U-shaped runner is fastened to the bottom of the drawer. Screwed to the back of the drawer on the end of the runner is a plastic guide that fits into the T-shaped runner. This helps guide the drawer and serves as a kicker.

There are a variety of commercial drawer slides available. For commercially made cabinets a metal guide is generally used. The center rail of the one shown in Fig. 13-21 is screwed to the front rail and the back of the cabinet. It is often called a *monorail*. A metal guide that fits over the rail is screwed to the drawer back. This serves as a guide and a kicker. There are available plastic pads and rollers that can be mounted on the front rail for the sides of the drawer to slide upon. Although it is easy to mount, this slide has much side-to-side play and is somewhat noisy.

Furniture and cabinets which have drawers that could be expected to carry heavy loads will use side drawer slides. Office furniture is one type that generally uses these heavy-duty slides. A metal track is mounted on the sides of the cabinet. A metal rail is mounted on the sides of the drawer. The rail or track will have one or more rollers on which the drawer will move (Fig. 13-22). When designing pieces to use these units, be certain to get the design specifications telling the clearance needed for installing these guides.

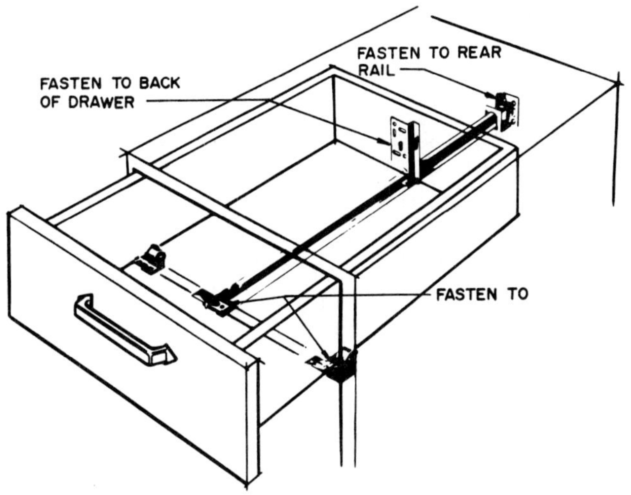

FASTEN TO REAR RAIL

FASTEN TO BACK OF DRAWER

FASTEN TO

FIGURE 13-21
A commercial center drawer guide using rollers fastened to the front stile. (*Courtesy of Knape and Vogt Manufacturing Co.*)

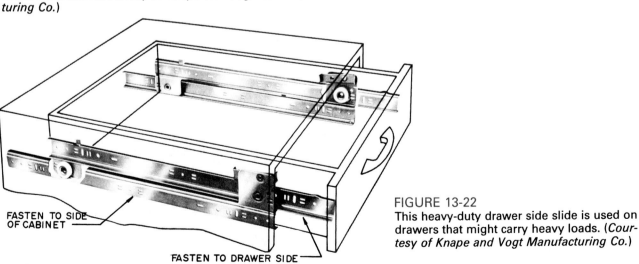

FASTEN TO SIDE OF CABINET

FASTEN TO DRAWER SIDE

FIGURE 13-22
This heavy-duty drawer side slide is used on drawers that might carry heavy loads. (*Courtesy of Knape and Vogt Manufacturing Co.*)

14

SHELF CONSTRUCTION

As cabinets are designed, the efficient use of the interior space should receive considerable attention. A flexible arrangement of shelves and the use of special-purpose accessories enables the designer to make use of all the enclosed space. It enables the user to adjust the interior arrangement to suit a variety of storage problems.

DESIGN CONSIDERATIONS

The following things must be considered as shelves are designed:

1. *Depth*. The depth must be great enough to hold the intended objects. Book shelves are usually 8 to 10 in. deep. Shelves in deeper units may be the same depth as the unit or in some cases less than this width. A series of shelves in a deep cabinet may be undesirable because items get pushed to the back and are not easily available. Kitchen wall cabinets are usually 12 in. (300 mm) deep on the outside, so the actual shelves will be closer to 11 in. (280 mm). Kitchen base cabinets are 24 in. (610 mm) deep on the outside. Shelves can range from 15 to 23 in. (380 to 585 mm) deep.

2. *Length*. The length of shelves is controlled by the size of the cabinet and the load it is expected to carry. A very wide cabinet with very long shelves presents some problems. First, the flexibility of arrangement is limited because when one shelf is moved, it changes a large part of the storage. If the long shelves were installed as two shorter shelves, greater flexibility is available. The long shelf tends to bend under a heavy load more readily than does a shorter shelf. If heavy loads are expected, the load-carrying capabilities of the shelf and the distance it must span need to be considered. Span data for hardboard and fiberboard shelves are given in Chapter 8.

3. *Spacing*. For greatest flexibility, shelving should use hardware that permits the spacing between shelves to be changed. If shelves are fixed, the spacing used must be chosen with care. In bookcases the lower shelf is spaced wider than those above it. The large books are placed here. This is normally 12 to 14 in. Spacing for regular-size books is usually $10\frac{1}{2}$ in. minimum. Again, consider the use of the unit. If it is to hold a television set, the space must be large enough to hold any of the portable television sets on the market. Examples of

fixed and adjustable-shelving are shown later in this chapter.

4. *Special accessories.* Hardware manufacturers have available a wide variety of special accessories for improving the efficiency of interior cabinet space. This includes items such as revolving shelves, wire and plastic storage racks, and shelves that slide in and out like a drawer (Fig. 14-1). Additional information on accessories for cabinets is given in Chapter 2.

5. *Material.* Shelving can be made from any material that will carry the loads and be pleasing in appearance. This usually includes solid wood, plywood, particleboard, hardboard, and fiberboard products. Glass shelves are used in china cabinets and display units.

FIXED SHELVING

Fixed shelves are attached using metal angles, shelf brackets, wood cleats, or dados. The metal angles and wood cleats are the easiest to use but are not attractive. The wood cleats can be glued and screwed to the sides. Metal shelf brackets are installed by screwing one leg to the cabinet or wall. The shelf is screwed to the other leg. They are available in several sizes with 6×8 in. and 10×12 in. being common (Fig. 14-2).

A stronger and more attractive way to install fixed shelves is with a plain or stop dado. The plain dado is the easiest to cut but is visible on the edge of the side. This can be covered with a molding glued to the edge or with a faceframe. The stop dado is more difficult to cut. The edge of the shelf must also be cut to fit into the dado (Fig. 14-3). When exposed joinery is to be used, other types of dados, such as a full dovetail or half dovetail dado, can be used.

ADJUSTABLE SHELVING

Most good-quality furniture and cabinets use adjustable shelving because of the advantages it offers. In

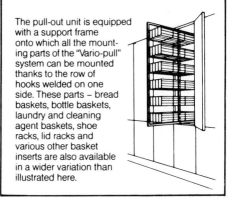

The pull-out unit is equipped with a support frame onto which all the mounting parts of the "Vario-pull" system can be mounted thanks to the row of hooks welded on one side. These parts – bread baskets, bottle baskets, laundry and cleaning agent baskets, shoe racks, lid racks and various other basket inserts are also available in a wider variation than illustrated here.

PULL-OUT STORAGE RACKS

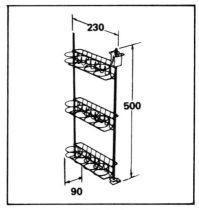

SPICE RACK

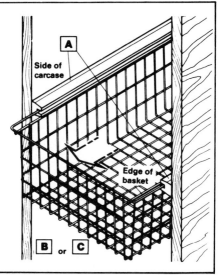

These steel wire baskets can be used for various applications since they have been surface treated, suitable for any type of material to be stored. They are also extremely easy to clean.

All baskets have overhanging edges on the sides so that they smoothly run in the guide strips. This not only facilitates easy installation but also provides a clear arrangement of the baskets in the frame of the cabinet.

The baskets can be stacked, saving space, due to their tapered walls.

The guide strips are available in three widths in order to be able to adapt to various cabinet widths without having to double the unit.

WIRE BASKETS THAT SLIDE ON SIDE TRACKS

FIGURE 14-1
Special accessories increase the efficiency of the use of interior cabinet space. (*Courtesy of H'a'fele America, 203 Feld Ave., High Point, NC 27261*)

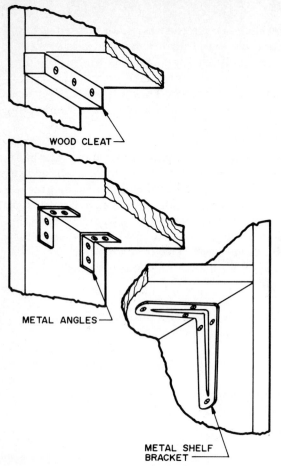

FIGURE 14-2
Ways to install fixed shelves.

WOOD CLEAT

METAL ANGLES

METAL SHELF
BRACKET

FIGURE 14-3
Fixed shelves can be set in dadoes.

addition to improving the efficiency of the unit, it is easy to install.

The least expensive adjustable way is to use wood dowel pins or metal or plastic shelf pins set in holes bored into the sides (Fig. 14-4). The metal and plastic pins are supplied by several hardware manufacturers. If using wood dowel pins, chamfer each end to help start the pins in the hole. A pencil sharpener is a good tool to use to chamfer wood dowels. The holes should be $\frac{1}{2}$ in. deep. Use $\frac{3}{8}$-in.-diameter wood dowels. The spacing between holes is in the range 1 to 2 in. Set the holes in about $\frac{3}{4}$ in. from the front and back of the edges of the shelf so that it will not tilt. The bored holes should be a little deeper than the length of the pin to be inserted in it. Remember when locating the holes to allow for the door as well as the set back from the edge of the shelf (Fig. 14-5).

Metal shelf standards provide the strongest support for adjustable shelves (Fig. 14-6). The perforated metal strips are screwed or nailed to the sides of the cabinet. The shelves are laid on top of adjustable clips that snap into the slots on the standard.

FIGURE 14-4
Shelf pins are an inexpensive way to provide adjustable shelves.

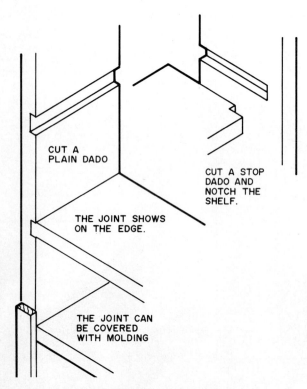

CUT A
PLAIN DADO

CUT A STOP
DADO AND
NOTCH THE
SHELF.

THE JOINT SHOWS
ON THE EDGE.

THE JOINT CAN
BE COVERED
WITH MOLDING

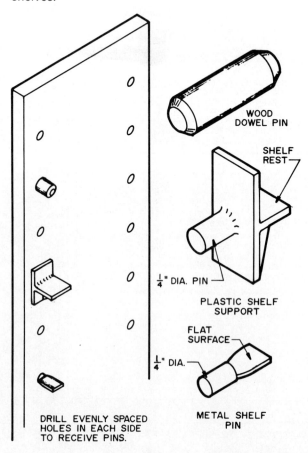

WOOD
DOWEL PIN

SHELF
REST

$\frac{1}{4}$" DIA. PIN

PLASTIC SHELF
SUPPORT

FLAT
SURFACE

$\frac{1}{4}$" DIA.

METAL SHELF
PIN

DRILL EVENLY SPACED
HOLES IN EACH SIDE
TO RECEIVE PINS.

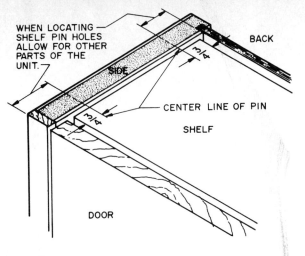

FIGURE 14-5
When locating holes for shelf pins, remember to allow for doors and the cabinet back.

FIGURE 14-6
Metal shelf standards provide the best way to support adjustable shelves. (*Courtesy of Knape and Vogt Manufacturing Co.*)

The standards are $\frac{5}{8}$ in. wide and $\frac{3}{16}$ in. deep and can be surface mounted or set flush by cutting a groove. Mounting holes are every 6 in. Use $\frac{5}{8}$-in. flat-head wood screws or special standard nails to secure it to the bulkhead. Be certain to install each strip so that the mounting screws are exactly in line. Otherwise, the shelf will slope or wobble. Every strip must also start with the same number at the bottom of the standard. If the standard is turned upside down or the numbers are not in the same order, the clips cannot be mounted at the same level.

Another system uses a metal standard that mounts on the back of the cabinet or on a wall. The shelves are held by metal brackets that extend out from the standard and hold the shelves. They are available in light and heavy-duty sizes. The brackets are available for various width shelves (Fig. 14-7).

Another type of shelf support is made from high-impact polyvinyl chloride. It is set into a groove cut into the sides of the shelving unit. The support is installed by driving it into the groove. Place a wood block over the support and tap on it to force the support into the groove. It can be glued in the groove if additional strength is needed (Fig. 14-8).

FIGURE 14-7
These metal standards mount on the wall and use metal brackets to hold the shelves. (*Courtesy of Knape and Vogt Manufacturing Co.*)

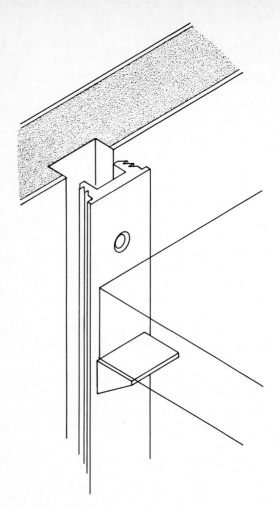

FIGURE 14-8
Polyvinyl chloride shelf supports are driven into grooves.

A shop-made system for adjustable shelves involves cutting $\frac{3}{8}$-in.-deep dadoes across the sides of the unit. Space them as desired, but 2 in. is a good distance. Cut the dadoes $\frac{1}{8}$ in. wider than the thickness of the shelf. This will allow for expansion and the finish on each part. The parallel dadoes provide an interesting pattern in addition to supporting the shelf (Fig. 14-9).

MAKING THE SHELVES

The shelves are normally $\frac{3}{4}$-in. solid wood or plywood stock. This will carry almost any load that can be placed on shelves found in most cabinets. Reconstituted wood products such as particleboard, hardboard, and fiberboard can also be used as shelving. Since the shelves are not fastened to other parts of the cabinet, they are most susceptible to warping. Be certain the moisture content is in the 6 to 8% moisture range. Each shelf should be finished on all sides, edges, and ends to keep out moisture.

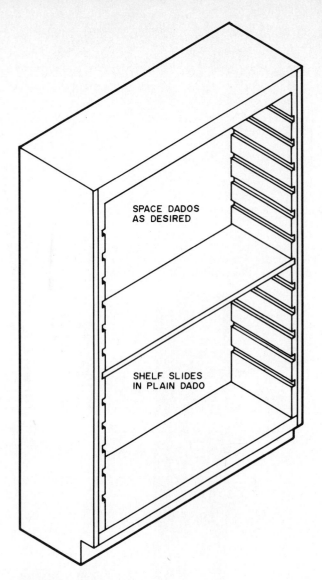

FIGURE 14-9
Adjustable shelves can be set in dadoes cut in the sides of the cabinet.

FIGURE 14-10
Shelves can be stiffened by adding wood strips on the edge.

Adjustable shelves should be cut $\frac{1}{4}$ in. shorter than the clear area between the actual supporting brackets or clips.

If a shelf is to be very long, it can be stiffened by installing $\frac{3}{4} \times 1$ in. or wider solid wood strips to the front and back edges (Fig. 14-10).

FIGURE 14-11
This small cabinet unit is set into the shelving unit and is held by the clips that hold the shelves.

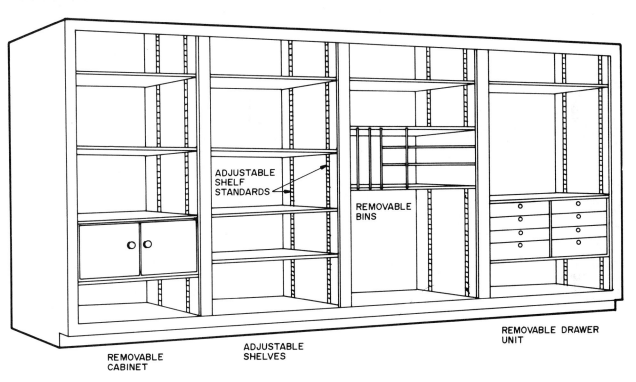

ADJUSTABLE
SHELF
STANDARDS

REMOVABLE
BINS

REMOVABLE DRAWER
UNIT

REMOVABLE
CABINET

ADJUSTABLE
SHELVES

FIGURE 14-12
This shelving unit has a variety of internal storage units.

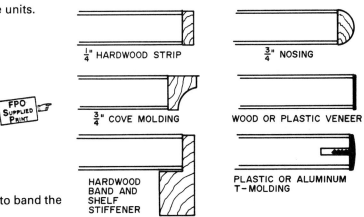

$\frac{1}{4}$" HARDWOOD STRIP

$\frac{3}{4}$" NOSING

$\frac{3}{4}$" COVE MOLDING

WOOD OR PLASTIC VENEER

HARDWOOD
BAND AND
SHELF
STIFFENER

PLASTIC OR ALUMINUM
T-MOLDING

FIGURE 14-13
These are a few of the ways to band the edges of shelves.

FPO
SUPPLIED
PRINT

Storage on shelves can be increased in efficiency by designing small cabinet units that will rest on the adjustable shelf clips (Fig. 14-11). These can give enclosed storage, provide small drawers, or be divided into horizontal or vertical compartments. Since they can be moved like a shelf, the flexibility of the storage unit is greatly increased. They can also be arranged to create interesting designs (Fig. 14-12).

SHELF EDGING

If the shelf is made from materials other than solid wood, it may be desirable to band the front edge to improve the appearance. Some of the frequently used methods are shown in Fig. 14-13. Additional information on banding these materials is given in Chapter 2.

15

GLUING AND CLAMPING

The permanent fastening of wood parts is often accomplished with some type of bonding agent, such as a glue, adhesive, or cement. *Glues* are made from natural materials, whereas *adhesives* are made from synthetic materials. *Cements* are rubber-based bonding agents.

When these are used properly, a strong and almost invisible bond is produced. The selection of the correct bonding agent, properly applied and cured, is vital to furniture and cabinet construction. There are many kinds of glues, adhesives, and cements. It is important to select the right one for each job (Fig. 15-1).

JOINT PREPARATION

Before even considering applying an adhesive to a joint, it must be checked to make certain that it is properly made. The joint must fit closely because most adhesives do not fill in large gaps between mating surfaces. It must not fit too tight because space must be left for the adhesive. If the joint is too tight, the adhesive is stripped away or squeezed out as it is clamped. Mating edges, as found in long boards, must be straight to get the maximum strength and have the smallest visible glue joint.

FIGURE 15-1
There are many types of bonding agents to choose from. (Courtesy of The Woodworkers' Store.)

Before starting to glue, make certain that everything needed is at the workstation. This includes adhesives, clamps, a mallet, and scrap stock to protect the work from the clamps.

Make certain that the wood has the proper moisture content. Wood that is too dry or has too high a moisture content will not bond properly. Generally, a 7 to 10% moisture content is satisfactory.

BONDING ACTION

Some agents bond by *mechanical adhesion*. The bonding agent is spread on a wood surface and that

TABLE 15-1
Characteristics of Bonding Agents

Type	Form	Mixing procedure	Color of glue line	Chief application
Glues				
Casein	Powder	Mix with water	Cream	Laminated timbers, doors, assembly edge gluing
Liquid hide	Liquid	None	Off-white-brown	Assembly, edge gluing and laminating
Adhesives				
Thermoplastics				
Aliphatic resin (yellow glue)	Liquid	None	Cream	Assembly, edge and face gluing, laminating
Hot melts	Solid	Melt with applicator	Varies	Quick assembly
Polyvinyl (white glue)	Liquid	None	Yellowish or whitish transparent	Assembly gluing, laminating, edge gluing
Thermosets				
Epoxy	Liquid	Mix with liquid catalyst	Varies	Quick assembly
Resorcinol resin	Liquid	Mix with powdered catalyst	Dark red	Laminated timbers, sandwich panels, general bonding, boats, skis
Urea-formaldehyde	Powder	Mix with water	Tan	Lumber and hardwood plywood, assembly gluing
Contact Cement	Liquid	None	Yellow-tan, red	Plastic and similar laminating

surface is brought into contact with another surface. As pressure is applied, the bonding agent enters into pores of the wood and hardens.

Materials are also bonded by *specific adhesion*. Materials without pores, such as glass and plastic, are also bonded by specific adhesion. This bonding is caused by the attraction of unlike electrical charges. Every material has an electrical charge. The positive (+) and negative (−) charges in the bonding agent are attracted by the electrical charges on the surface of the wood or other material. They are thus molecularly attracted to each other, providing the strongest possible holding force between the adjoining surfaces. Specific adhesion occurs when edge or face grain is bonded. Porous end grain cannot be successfully joined by either mechanical or specific adhesion. End grain joints, such as a miter, must be reinforced with splines, which provide face grain for bonding. In most cases apply the bonding agent to only one of the surfaces to be joined. This provides more cohesive force than when the agent is applied to both surfaces. On cements, follow the manufacturer's directions.

TYPES OF ADHESIVES

Adhesives are made from synthetic materials. They are the most commonly used bonding agents. They are divided into two types, thermosets and thermoplastics. A summary of the characteristics of woodworking bonding agents is presented in Table 15-1.

Thermosets

Thermosets produce a chemical reaction when they are mixed and therefore are water and heat resistant. Following are the four major types of thermosets.

1. *Epoxy* is used to bond almost any kind of material. It is not used in furniture and cabinet construction because it is expensive. It produces a very strong joint and is often used when regluing wood joints on furniture being restored. Epoxy is packaged in two tubes one containing a resin and one a hardener. To use, these are mixed in equal amounts. A thin coat is applied to both surfaces. The surfaces are clamped to-

Service durability	Application temperature	Clamp time	Brand names
Water resistant	32°F	2 hours	
Interior use	70°F	2 hours	Franklin Liquid Hide Glue
Interior use	45°F	1 hour	Titebond, Elmer's Carpenter's Wood Glue
Interior use	Determined by electronic welder	None	Thermogrip, Jet-Melt
Interior use	60°F	1 hour	Elmer's Glue-All
Interior use	60°F	2 hours	Elmer's Epoxy, Scotch-Weld Epoxy
Waterproof	70°F	16 hours	Weldwood Resorcinal Waterproof Glue, Elmer's Waterproof Glue
Water resistant	70°F	16 hours at 70°F	Plastic Resin, Elmer's Plastic Resin
Water resistant	70°F	No clamp time	Elmer's Contact Cement, Franklin Contact Cement

gether for at least 2 hours. Epoxy reaches full strength in 12 to 24 hours. Excess material is removed with nail polish remover or denatured alcohol while the epoxy is still tacky (Fig. 15-2).

2. *Phenol-formaldehyde* is used in the production of exterior plywood. It is not used for furniture and cabinet construction.

3. *Resorcinol-formaldehydes* are used where a waterproof glue line is needed, such as when building a boat or surfboard. They are sold in two parts: a resin and a catalyst. After thorough mixing they are ready for use, which must be within 8 hours after mixing. The material is applied to both surfaces in a thin coat. Since it stains wood a dark brown, hiding the glue line is difficult. It is slow to gain strength and must be kept clamped for about 16 hours.

4. *Urea-formaldehyde* is sold in powder form and is mixed with water to form a pastelike mixture. It is moisture resistant but not waterproof. Since it has poor gap-filling qualities,

FIGURE 15-2
An epoxy is packaged in two containers, the resin and a hardener.

joints must be very accurately made. The recommended clamp time is 6 hours. It is widely used with radio-frequency glue-drying equipment and will cure in a few seconds.

Thermoplastics

Thermoplastics are the most widely used bonding agent for wood products. Although most are resistant to moisture, they should not be used on products that will be exposed to moist conditions. Following are the four major types.

1. *Hot melts* are sold in solid form. There are different types for bonding plastics, particleboard, softwoods, and hardwoods. Hot melts are applied by placing the solid material in an electric applicator (Fig. 15-3). This melts the adhesive stick and applies it to the surface through a nozzle. The surface to be bonded must be free of dust and oily films. The viscosity of the adhesive must be thin enough to wet thoroughly the surface to be bonded. The viscosity can be lowered by raising the temperature of the adhesive. Other factors affecting viscosity are the amount of adhesive used, the temperature and type of material to be bonded, and the air temperature (Fig. 15-4).

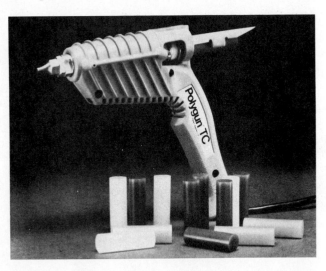

FIGURE 15-3
Hot melt adhesive applicator and samples of the adhesive, which is in stick form. (Courtesy of Adhesives, Coatings and Sealers Division/3M.)

FIGURE 15-4
The hot melt applicator melts the adhesive stick and applies it to the surface through a nozzle. (Courtesy of Adhesives, Coatings and Sealers Division/3M.)

The shorter the open time (time lapsed between applying adhesive and closing the joint), the better the bond. The firmer the pressure when the bond is closed, the stronger the bond. Firm hand pressure is usually adequate. Apply pressure from a few seconds with thin films to a few minutes with thicker films and larger areas.

Hot melts produce a wide glue line that may be objectionable if on a visible part. They are fast but not very strong. Their best use is in applying overlays to furniture exteriors (Fig. 15-5).

FIGURE 15-5
The decorative overlays on these doors can be bonded with hot melts. (Courtesy of Thomasville Furniture Industries, Inc.)

2. *Alpha-Cyanoacrylate* is used with metals, plastics, and other dense materials. It is not suited for use with porous materials such as wood. It is often called "superglue."

It dries very rapidly but does not reach full strength for 24 hours. Avoid getting it on your hands. If you do, it can be softened with fingernail polish or acetone.

3. *Polyvinyl adhesives* are often called white glues. They are the most widely used of the thermoplastic types. They are excellent for furniture and cabinet work. Although they are moisture resistant, they are not suitable for exterior use. Polyvinyls are sold premixed ready to use. Since the mix is creamy, it is easy to apply. Set-up time is 30 minutes, but stock should be allowed to cure for 24 hours before working it.

Since polyvinyl adhesives cure by the loss of moisture, the wood to be bonded must have a moisture content of 6 to 12% to get the maximum strength. Polyvinyl adhesives soften under heat and solvents such as lacquer.

4. *Aliphatic resins* are a form of polyvinyl resin and are yellow in color. They are stronger and more heat resistant than other polyvinyls and are not affected by lacquer finishes. These features make them superior to the white polyvinyl adhesives, and the choice of those making good-quality furniture and cabinets.

GLUES

Glues are made from vegetable and animal products, such as hides and bones. Although still an effective material, they have been largely replaced by adhesives and cements. The most commonly used glues are animal, casein, blood albumin, vegetable, and fish glues.

1. *Casein glue* is made from dried milk curds. It is sold in powdered form and is prepared by mixing with water until it forms a thick, creamy mixture. It must stand 15 minutes after mixing before it is applied to wood, to allow a chemical reaction to occur in the casein.

   Casein glue is water resistant and can be used for exterior work that will not be directly subjected to the elements. It can be applied in cold temperatures and will harden as long as the temperature is above freezing. It takes longer to set up in colder temperatures.

2. *Animal glue* is available as a hot glue or a ready-mixed liquid. *Hot animal glue* is sold as a dry powder or as large flakes. It is mixed with water in an electric glue pot. Here it is heated until it dissolves, forming a liquid. It is applied to the wood surfaces while hot. The joint must be clamped before it begins to chill, or a weak joint will result. This type of glue is not widely used anymore.

   Liquid hide glue is a ready-mixed form of animal glue. It is applied directly from the container to the wood. It is especially good for filling gaps in joints as well as small cracks and chips. When it dries it develops a dark glue line. Therefore, it is especially useful with dark woods such as walnut and mahogany. It is not waterproof and should be used for interior purposes. It sets best if temperatures are above 70°F. If used below this temperature, the glue must be kept warm. Normally, clamps can be removed in 2 hours.

3. Blood albumin, vegetable, and fish glues are not used in the assembly of furniture and cabinets. Blood albumin and vegetable glues are used in some types of interior plywood. Fish glues are used on packing tapes and for sealing cartons.

CEMENTS

Cements are made from synthetic rubber, such as neoprene, nitrile, or polysulfide, suspended in a liquid. Some are flammable and others are nonflammable.

1. *Contact cement* is used to adhere plastic laminates, veneers, and other surface decorations. It is applied to both surfaces and allowed to dry. When these surfaces are brought together, they bond instantly. It is not possible to slide or shift the position of a part. No clamping is necessary. Contact cement can be cleaned off surfaces with lacquer thinner. Since contact cement is flammable, the area in which it is being used should be well ventilated.

2. *Mastic* is a thick form of contact cement that is sold in tubes and is applied with a caulking gun. It is used in building construction to join sheathing to studs and floor joists and paneling to walls.

HAND CLAMPING TOOLS

There are a number of hand-operated clamping tools available (Fig. 15-6). These are too slow and inaccurate for use in mass-production situations, where power-operated clamping devices of great speed and accuracy are used.

The *hand screw* is used to provide clamping pressure over a broad surface with two parallel jaws. To adjust it rapidly, it can be held in two hands and spun like a propeller (Fig. 15-7). Final adjustments are made by turning each handle to apply pressure. Be certain the jaws are kept parallel as pressure is applied (Fig. 15-8).

Clamp sizes are specified by number. The larger the number, the longer the jaws and the wider they will open. The most commonly used sizes are listed in Table 15-2.

C-clamps, sometimes called carriage clamps, have a strong C-shaped frame and a threaded shaft that applies pressure. Since the clamping parts are metal, scrap stock is placed between them and the wood (Fig. 15-9).

They are specified by the size of the opening and the depth of the C-shaped frame, called the throat size. There are many different styles available with a wide range of opening and throat sizes. The larger sizes most commonly used in woodworking shops are listed in Table 15-3.

Press frames are used to apply pressure to large surfaces. An example is the need to apply pressure to hold the veneer on a tabletop (Fig. 15-10).

FIGURE 15-6
Basic hand clamping tools used in furniture and cabinet construction. (Courtesy of Adjustable Clamp Co.)

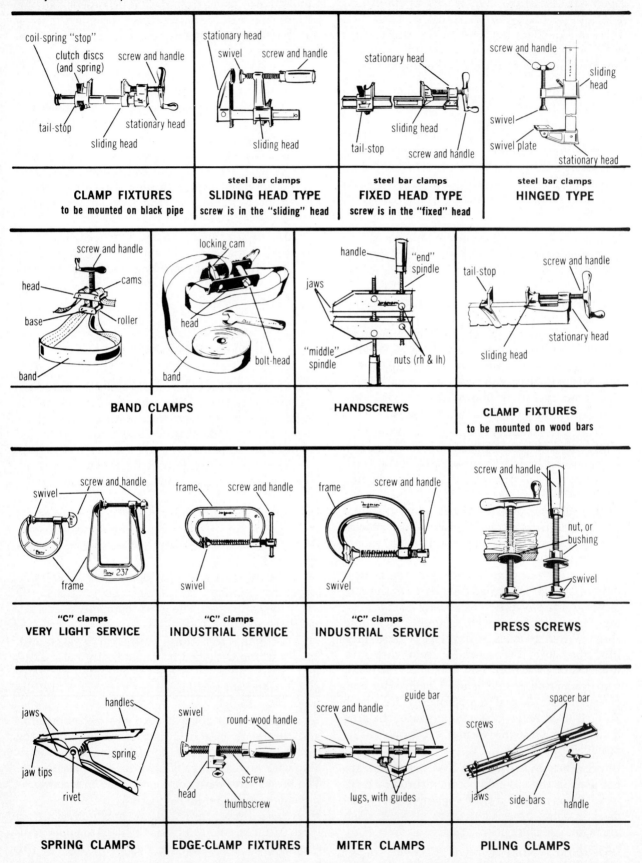

CLAMP FIXTURES to be mounted on black pipe	**steel bar clamps** **SLIDING HEAD TYPE** screw is in the "sliding" head	**steel bar clamps** **FIXED HEAD TYPE** screw is in the "fixed" head	**steel bar clamps** **HINGED TYPE**
BAND CLAMPS		**HANDSCREWS**	**CLAMP FIXTURES** to be mounted on wood bars
"C" clamps **VERY LIGHT SERVICE**	**"C" clamps** **INDUSTRIAL SERVICE**	**"C" clamps** **INDUSTRIAL SERVICE**	**PRESS SCREWS**
SPRING CLAMPS	**EDGE-CLAMP FIXTURES**	**MITER CLAMPS**	**PILING CLAMPS**

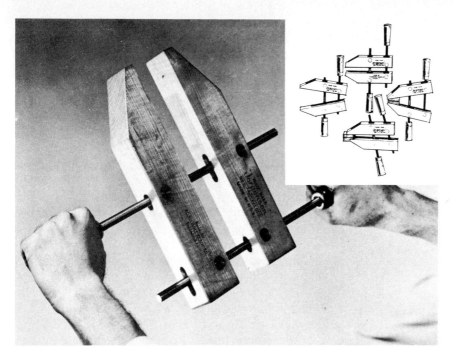

FIGURE 15-7
Hand screws are adjusted by turning the handles. (Courtesy of Adjustable Clamp Co.)

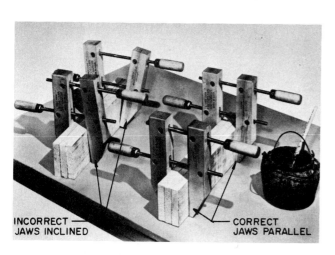

INCORRECT — JAWS INCLINED

CORRECT JAWS PARALLEL

FIGURE 15-8
When face clamping keep the jaws parallel. (Courtesy of Adjustable Clamp Co.)

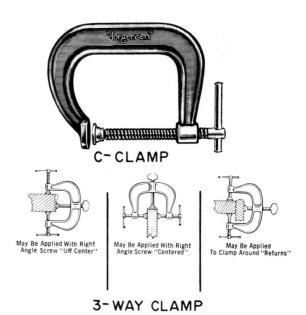

C-CLAMP

May Be Applied With Right Angle Screw "Off Center"

May Be Applied With Right Angle Screw "Centered"

May Be Applied To Clamp Around "Returns"

3-WAY CLAMP

FIGURE 15-9
Typical carriage clamps. (Courtesy of Adjustable Clap Co.)

TABLE 15-2
Handscrew Clamp Sizes

No.	Jaw length (in.)	Jaw opening (in.)
5/0	4	2
4/0	5	$2\frac{1}{2}$
3/0	6	3
2/0	7	$3\frac{1}{2}$
0	8	$4\frac{1}{2}$
1	10	6
2	12	$8\frac{1}{2}$
3	14	10
4	16	12
5	18	14

TABLE 15-3
C-Clamp Sizes

Opening (in.)	Depth (in.)
2	$1\frac{3}{4}$
3	$2\frac{1}{4}$
4	$2\frac{1}{2}$ and $4\frac{1}{2}$
6	$3\frac{1}{8}$ and $6\frac{1}{2}$
8	$3\frac{3}{4}$ and $8\frac{1}{2}$
10	4
12	$4\frac{1}{4}$

FIGURE 15-10
Press frames are used to apply pressure over a large area. (Courtesy of Adjustable Clamp Co.)

FIGURE 15-11
Types of bar clamps. (Courtesy of Adjustable Clamp Co.)

They are suspended over a sturdy wood base on which is placed the material to be clamped. This is covered with a sheet of plywood or caul board and pressure is applied to the top of the plywood.

Bar clamps have a long metal bar with an adjustable foot on one end and a foot moved with a screw on the other (Fig. 15-11). They are used to clamp stock for edge-to-edge assembly as well as to clamp cabinet and furniture carcasses together. A variety of sizes is available. The short clamps are available with opening sizes of 6, 8, 12, 18, 24, and 30 in. The long clamps have opening sizes of 2, 3, 4, 5, 6, 7, and 8 ft. One type has a 5 in. throat opening. It is available in opening sizes of 6, 8, 12, 18, 24, 30, and 36 in. A common style of bar clamp is a *pipe clamp;* ½- and ¾-in. black pipe is used to make up the clamps. Since the clamp mechanism is easily removed, different lengths of clamps can be made. Stock as narrow as 6 in. or as wide as 120 in. can be clamped with this style. Another type of bar clamp is a *piling clamp*. It has two sets of jaws facing in opposite directions. Each layer of wood is clamped from above as well as from below (Fig. 15-12). In this way each board is clamped twice—once below and once on top. This helps keep the stock from buckling during the clamping operation.

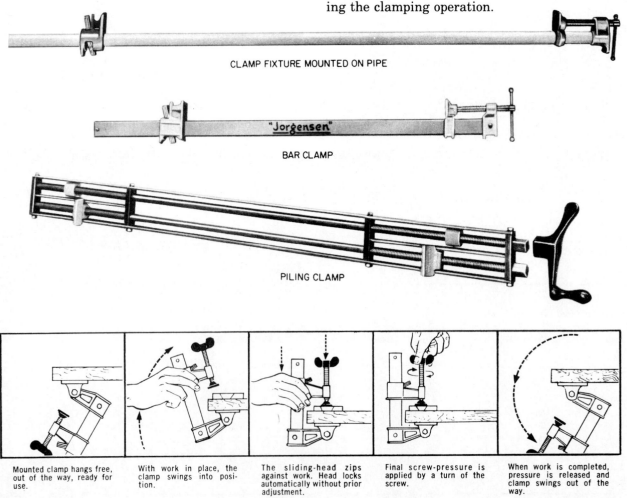

CLAMP FIXTURE MOUNTED ON PIPE

BAR CLAMP

PILING CLAMP

Mounted clamp hangs free, out of the way, ready for use.

With work in place, the clamp swings into position.

The sliding-head zips against work. Head locks automatically without prior adjustment.

Final screw-pressure is applied by a turn of the screw.

When work is completed, pressure is released and clamp swings out of the way.

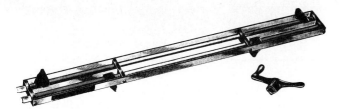

FIGURE 15-12
The piling clamp is used in production shops. (Courtesy of Adjustable Clamp Co.)

Spring clamps use a torsion spring to keep the plastic-covered jaws together. They are available with openings of 1, 2, 3, and 4 in. (Fig. 15-13).

Web clamps are made with a nylon band running through a metal clamping device. They are used to hold irregularly shaped objects (Fig. 15-14).

A *corner clamp* and a *miter frame clamp* are used to hold mitered corners as they are glued with splines or nailed together (Fig. 15-15). The corner clamp holds one corner at a time, while the miter frame clamp holds all four corners (Fig. 15-16). The miter frame clamp can be enlarged to hold any size frame by adding extension screws to each side. The miter vise will hold stock up to 4 in. wide.

FIGURE 15-13
Spring clamp. (Courtesy of Adjustable Clamp Co.)

FIGURE 15-14
Web clamps are used to hold irregular objects. (Courtesy of Adjustable Clamp Co.)

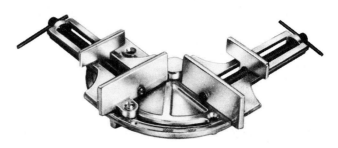

FIGURE 15-15
Corner clamp. (Courtesy of Adjustable Clamp Co.)

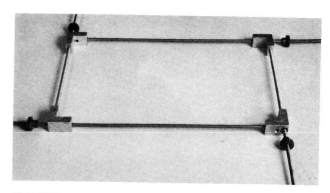

FIGURE 15-16
Miter frame clamp.

GLUING CONDITIONS

The surfaces to be joined must be clean, smooth, and free of defects. The joints should fit properly since most bonding agents cannot fill a gap in a poorly made joint. A joint could also be too tight, resulting in a starved glue joint.

The glue film should wet both surfaces to be joined. It must be a thin, uniform layer free of dust.

Dense woods such as maple require a thicker glue mixture. In more porous, lighter woods a thinner mixture is better because it absorbs some of the moisture in the glue, increasing its thickness.

Be aware of the *pot life* of the glue being used. The pot life is the length of time glue retains all its properties. It is a good practice not to mix any more than you think you are going to use. Select glues that have an open assembly time long enough to permit you to assemble the unit. Complex units take more assembly time and require bonding agents with a longer open assembly time. *Open assembly time* is the period from when the glue is first applied until the boards are brought together. Fast-setting glues enable you to free your clamps rapidly for additional work.

Consider the moisture content of the wood. Since a high moisture content weakens glue joints, consider using kiln-dried wood for all projects.

The clamping pressure should be enough to close the joint and hold it until the bonding agent has set. As a general rule, 100 to 125 lb of pressure should be used. Thinner glues, such as polyvinyl resins, require light clamp pressures. Thick glues, such as plastic resin, require higher clamp pressures. Clamping times vary with the bonding agent. Use the times recommended by the manufacturer.

FIGURE 15-17
After clamping stock mark the date and time it was clamped.

CLAMPING PROCEDURES

A joint attains its maximum strength when it is properly clamped and kept clamped during the entire recommended set time. The clamps must be placed to hold the joints together and keep the furniture or cabinet unit square. Following are some clamping recommendations.

Edge-to-Edge Clamping

1. Gather the tools needed for the job. Select bar clamps long enough to span the board to be assembled. Get blocks of scrap wood to use to protect the edges where the clamps will rest. A few hand screws or C-clamps will be needed to clamp the stock to the bar clamp to prevent buckling.
2. Place several bar clamps on a table and place the boards on top. Space the clamps not over 16 in. apart. Check to make certain that the boards are placed in the direction and order they were in when the edge joint was made. No board should be wider than 4 in., and the end grain should be reversed on each piece. They should have been marked on the face with chalk as shown in Fig. 15-17.

3. Assemble the boards *without adhesive*. This ensures that the joint will close properly before the adhesive is applied.
4. Loosen the clamps and separate the boards. Apply the adhesive to one edge and in the dowel holes. Slide the dowels in the dowel holes. Place the boards on the lower bar clamps, put scrap blocks in place, and lightly tighten to close the joint.
5. Put bar clamps on the top of the boards in between those on the bottom. Put scrap blocks under each jaw and start to tighten the clamps from one end. As the clamps are tightened, work from one end to the other.
6. It is important that the boards stay flat on the bar clamps. If they buckle, use hand screws or C-clamps to clamp the boards to the bar clamp.
7. Store in a flat condition to avoid twisting the assembled unit. Leave the clamps on for the full recommended clamp time for the adhesive used. An assembly for a faceframe is in Fig. 15-18. Notice the use of bar clamps in both directions.

FIGURE 15-18
This faceframe assembly requires the use of long bar clamps. (Courtesy of Adjustable Clamp Co.)

FIGURE 15-19
When clamping a case, gradually tighten the clamps in rotation until the joints are closed.

Case Assembly

1. Gather the tools needed for the job. This will normally include bar clamps, hand screws, C-clamps, scrap blocks, a framing square, and a measuring tape.

2. Make a trial assembly without the adhesive. The exact procedure will vary depending on the situation, but generally the corner joints will be assembled and bar clamps used to close the joints. Place the bar clamps 6 to 9 in. apart. Tighten each gradually rotating from one clamp to the other. If each is fully tightened before the others, the case may become warped. Check the squareness of the case by measuring the diagonals of each opening. If all joints close and the case is square, remove the clamps.

3. Apply the adhesive to the joints and reassemble the joints. Replace the bar joists and again tighten gradually in rotation until the joints are closed (Fig. 15-19).

4. Check the unit for squareness with a framing square (Fig. 15-20). Another check that can be used is to measure the diagonals. They should be exactly the same (Fig. 15-21). If the unit is out of square, place a bar clamp along the longest diagonal and tighten until the cabinet is square (Fig. 15-22).

ELECTRONIC GLUE CURING

Electronic glue curing is a way to speed up the initial set time of the adhesive. The joint is clamped in the normal manner. The controls on the electronic glue welder are set for the thickness of the wood and

FIGURE 15-20
Check the case for squareness.

FIGURE 15-21
Measure the diagonals to see if the case is square.

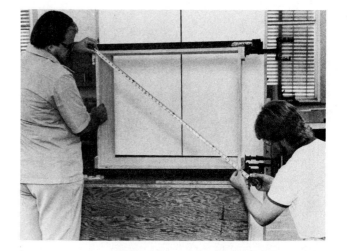

FIGURE 15-22
A bar clamp can be used to pull a case square.

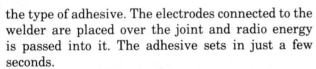

FIGURE 15-24
Straight electrodes are used to cure edge joints.

the type of adhesive. The electrodes connected to the welder are placed over the joint and radio energy is passed into it. The adhesive sets in just a few seconds.

The glue welders contain a generator that produces *high-frequency radio* energy (Fig. 15-23). The electrode is connected to it by a heavy cable. The welder works by generating a short-length high-frequency radio signal similar to that used by shortwave radios. This energy excites the adhesive molecules and heats the bonding agent to its polymerizing temperature, which is about 200°F (93°C). This cures the glue line in a few seconds. When this happens the clamps can be removed. The cabinet should be carefully set aside and allowed to cure for the recommended time specified by the adhesive manufacturer.

FIGURE 15-25
Inverted electrodes are used to cure inside joints.

FIGURE 15-23
Electronic glue welder. (Courtesy of Workrite Products Company.)

FIGURE 15-26
Outside electrodes are used on outside corners.

To operate the welder, it will have to be set for the adhesive used and the thickness of the stock. After the stock is clamped, place the electrodes across the glue line and pull the trigger. Keep it in place for the required time, usually 3 to 5 seconds. You will notice that the adhesive boils. Move the electrodes 3 in. down the glue line and pull the trigger again. Continue until the entire joint is cured.

A variety of electrodes are available. For edge joints straight electrodes are used (Fig. 15-24). Inverted electrodes are used on inside corners (Fig. 15-25). Outside electrodes are used on outside corners (Fig. 15-26). Roller electrodes are used on banding, moldings, and shelf edging. The most commonly used adhesive is urea-formaldehyde. Polyvinyls can be used but do not develop maximum strength.

There are several safety factors to consider. Do not pull the trigger on the electrode unless it is against the stock. Do not hold the stock being bonded in your hand. An electric shock could result. Do not touch the metal clamps while the welder is operating.

16

APPLYING PLASTIC LAMINATES

Plastic laminates are used for countertops and facings on bulkheads, drawer fronts, doors, and face frames. They are manufactured in a wide range of colors, designs, and reproductions of natural wood grains and colors (Fig. 16-1).

A standard plastic laminate sheet is made from five to seven layers of paper that are treated with a phenolic resin. The top layer of paper has the color, design, or printed grain pattern. This layer is protected with a translucent coat of melamine plastic which is tough and resists heat and chemical attack. The layers are bonded together at a temperature of 265 to 305°F and under a pressure of 800 to 1200 psi. The sheet is held in this condition for 60 to 90 minutes. It is then trimmed to size.

Plastic laminates are made with shiny, suede, embossed, and wood grain finishes. The shiny finish is referred to as a furniture finish. Since it has a high gloss it shows wear and scratches easier than the others.

Plastic laminates used for furniture and cabinet construction are used on the top and back of panels. They are available in several types and thicknesses. These are:

1. *.050-in. (1.27-mm) general purpose.* This is used for both exposed vertical and horizontal

FIGURE 16-1
Plastic laminates are manufactured in a wide range of colors and patterns.

surfaces. It is the most widely used type. It is the thickest type and has greater impact resistance and is more dimensionally stable than the thinner type.

2. *.030-in. (0.76-mm) vertical surface.* It is used on exposed vertical surfaces only, such as cabinet interiors and exteriors and wall panels. It

is not as desirable as the general-purpose type, so is used where usage is light. It is not recommended for use on surfaces over 24 in. (600 mm) wide.

3. *.025-in. (0.63-mm) cabinet liner.* This is used on the interior surfaces of cabinets, where it will not be subjected to wear.

4. *.040-in. (1.00-mm) postforming.* This high-pressure laminate can be heated and bent around curved surfaces such as a countertop. It serves the same purposes as the general-purpose type.

It is often necessary to apply a backing sheet to a panel to balance the construction. This reduces moisture absorption. Following are the types of plastic laminates used for backing purposes:

1. *.050-in. (1.27-mm) and .060-in. (1.52-mm) balancing sheet.* This type is used for large unsupported surfaces and wall paneling. It is the thickest and stablest of the backing sheets.

2. *.040-in. (1.00-mm) backing sheet.* This is made from sheets of .050-in. (1.27 mm) general-purpose sheets that are damaged in manufacturing. The melamine facing is removed.

3. *.020-in. (0.50-mm) and .030-in. (0.76-mm) backing sheet.* These are used on small unsupported panels which are attached to other structural members. They serve to inhibit penetration of moisture into the substrate and produce a balanced construction.

Another type of plastic laminate is available that has the color through the entire thickness. This means that when scratched a dark line will not appear as does on standard laminates. Also, the edge of the laminate does not appear as a dark line when it is exposed. These full-depth color laminates are more expensive than standard laminates.

TYPES OF CORES

Particleboard and plywood are the most commonly used substrate materials to which plastic laminates are bonded.

Particleboard is the type most commonly used in furniture and cabinet construction. It is stable and has a defect-free surface. It is low cost and available in a variety of sizes. Medium density (45 lb) is most often used. It can be used with rigid glue or contact adhesives.

Hard-faced fir-core plywood is also an excellent substrate. It usually has a Philippine mahogany face veneer upon which the plastic laminate is bonded. It costs more than particleboard but has

high structural strength. It can be used with rigid glue or contact adhesives.

Fir plywood finds some use as a substrate. However, the grain pattern of the face veneer often shows through the laminate. When contact adhesive is used, this is less noticeable.

If the plastic laminate product is to be used where it is exposed to the weather or other high-moisture conditions, use a waterproof-type plywood.

GLUES AND ADHESIVES

Several glues and adhesives can be used to bond plastic laminates to the substrate.

Rigid glues such as urea-formaldehyde and resorcinol develop a rigid glue line and have maximum bonding effectiveness and heat resistance. They require that the bonding be done in a press. Since they form a rigid glue line, any dimensional change in the panel must be absorbed by the substrate. It is important that the balancing sheet have approximately the same characteristics as the face laminate. Rigid glues are used only on flat pieces that will fit in a press.

Contact adhesives adhere when two coated surfaces are brought together. Pressure can be applied by a hand roller or power roller. This glue line is less rigid and will absorb some of the stresses due to dimensional change. Contact adhesives are universally used for applications to curved surfaces and those that cannot be press glued.

Hot melt glues are used to apply laminate edges. They are applied at very high temperatures and require immediate pressure. Specialized application is recommended for most efficient application.

POSTFORM AND SELF-EDGE TOPS

The two types of plastic laminate tops are postform and self-edge (Fig. 16-2). The postform top has a curved back and front edge. It uses the postforming grade of laminate and requires special equipment to do the forming and lamination. The self-edge top has square corners and can easily be produced.

PREPARING THE TOP

The surface to receive the plastic laminate must be flat and smooth. If the top is to appear thicker than the usual ¾-in. (18-mm) substrate glue and staple additional material to the bottom. On kitchen cabinet tops the front edge is usually 1½ in. (38 mm) thick (Fig. 16-3).

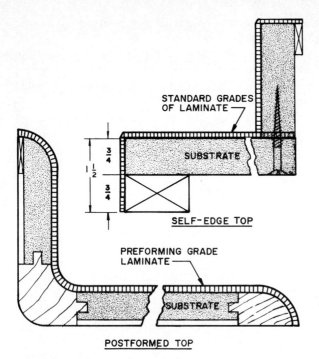

FIGURE 16-2
Laminate tops are available in postform and self-edge types.

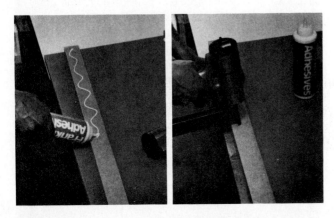

FIGURE 16-3
Apply adhesive to the ¾-in.-thick strip, place on the bottom of the cabinet top, and staple in place.

LAMINATING SELF-EDGE TOPS

1. Cut the substrate to form the top to size. This could be plywood, particleboard, or hardboard. For a kitchen cabinet this would normally be 25 in. (635 mm) wide by the length of the cabinet. Tabletops vary a great deal in size. Be certain to allow for the required overhang over the base cabinet or rails or carcass of furniture units. The substrate must be cut square and smooth.

2. Cut the sheet of plastic laminate for the top 1 in. (25 mm) wider and longer than the substrate. Cut the plastic laminate for the edges of the top ¼ in. (6 mm) wider and 1 in. (25 mm) longer than required. Cut on a table saw with a carbide-tipped blade. Cut with the good side up. Be careful that the laminate does not slide under the fence of the saw. If it does not have a tight fit, clamp a piece of wood to the fence that fits tightly to the saw table (Fig. 16-4). Laminate can be cut with a saber saw that has a fine-toothed blade, but the blade will get dull fast and it is difficult to cut a straight line.

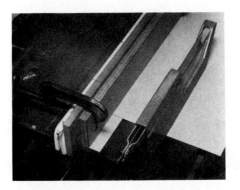

FIGURE 16-4
Clamp a wood strip to the rip fence to keep the laminate from sliding under it.

Laminates can also be cut by scoring a line with a carbide-tipped scoring tool. It looks like a utility knife but has a special carbide-tipped blade. To do this, place the laminate with the good side up. Score along a straightedge. It will take several strokes to cut into the dark material below. Hold the laminate firmly beside the score mark and *lift the edge of the sheet up* to break it on the score mark. A slitter is a tool used to trim off excess laminate after the sheet has been bonded to the substrate. The location of the blade is adjustable. It can also bevel the edge (Fig. 16-5).

3. Be certain that the substrate is free of dust. Brush it off carefully or blow it clean with compressed air. The back of the laminate should also be clean.

4. Apply the laminate to the edges first. Do this by applying contact cement to the back of the laminate edge strips and the edge of the substrate. A disposable paintbrush works well (Fig. 16-6). Be certain that all surfaces are covered with contact cement. After the cement has dried, apply a second coat on the substrate.

5. Allow both surfaces to dry. To test this apply a

FIGURE 16-5
Excess laminate is being removed with a carbide-tipped scoring tool.

FIGURE 16-7
Test the contact cement with paper to see if it is dry.

FIGURE 16-6
Apply contact cement to the edge of the substrate and the plastic laminate.

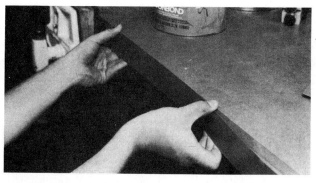

FIGURE 16-8
Let the plastic laminate extend a little above the top surface.

piece of kraft paper to each. If the surface is dry, the paper will not stick to it. If it feels sticky, wait 5 minutes and check again (Fig. 16-7).

6. Now apply the edge band. Remember, once the laminate touches the edge it will stick and cannot be moved. It requires two people to handle longer pieces. Line up the laminate with the edge and allow it to extend a little above the top. The excess will be trimmed off later. Place one end of the laminate against the edge and applying light pressure work toward the other end (Fig. 16-8). After it is in place, apply pressure with a "J" roller (Fig. 16-9).

7. Using a router with a special cutter that cuts the plastic flush with the top of the substrate, trim the edge to size (Fig. 16-10). A laminate router designed for this operation can also be utilized. It has a special base which controls the depth of cut.

8. To give the edge a final trim, run over it with a

FIGURE 16-9
Firmly press the laminate against the edge.

belt sander, being careful not to slant it and cut down into the edge of the laminate. Position the sander so that the belt rotation is inward toward the top. Keep it moving from side to side so that you do not cut too deeply into the top at any one place. This should be a very

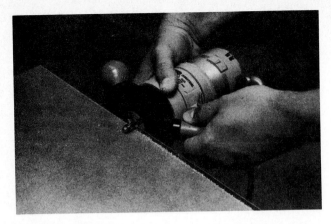

FIGURE 16-10
Remove the excess laminate with a router and a special laminate cutter.

FIGURE 16-12
Apply contact cement to the top surface and the bottom of the sheet of laminate.

light cut and should not be overdone (Fig. 16-11).

9. Clean the face of the substrate again and apply contact cement to it and the large sheet of plastic laminate. Let it dry as described above. Large surfaces can be coated with a small paint roller with a disposable sleeve (Fig. 16-12).

10. When the cement is dry place $\frac{3}{8}$-in.-diameter wood dowels across the top about 12 in. apart (Fig. 16-13). Place the plastic laminate on these with the cemented side down. The dowels keep the laminate from touching the substrate.

FIGURE 16-13
Place dowels across the dry contact cement on the top and lay the laminate on top of them with the glued side down.

FIGURE 16-11
Lightly sand the edge laminate flush with the top.

11. Line up the laminate so that it overlaps the substrate on each side. Start sticking the laminate to the substrate at one end by removing a dowel. Carefully remove each dowel as you press the laminate against the substrate. Press them together with hand pressure (Fig. 16-14).

12. Using a laminate roller apply pressure to the laminate starting in the center of the top and working toward the edges (Fig. 16-15).

13. The edges are trimmed using a router with a

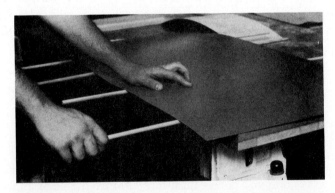

FIGURE 16-14
Position the laminate over the top. Then start removing the dowels. This permits the laminate to stick to the top.

bevel-cut bit (Fig. 16-16). This top edge of the laminate is cut on a bevel, so it does not present a sharp edge. Be careful not to cut too deeply (Fig. 16-17).

14. The mill marks left by the router bit can be

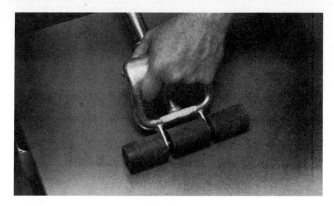

FIGURE 16-15
Press the laminate firmly against the top with a large roller.

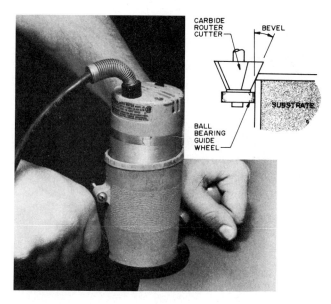

FIGURE 16-16
Trim the top laminate using a special bevel cutter.

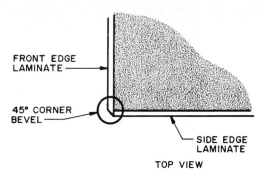

TOP VIEW

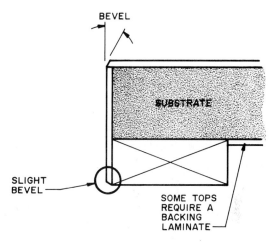

FIGURE 16-17
The top laminate is cut on a slight bevel.

FIGURE 16-18
The beveled edge can be smoothed with a very fine file if needed.

removed with a single-cut mill bastard file (very fine), but a plastic-cut file works the best. Work the file downward so that you do not pull the laminate loose (Fig. 16-18).

15. If contact cement has gotten on the laminate, clean it with a cloth dampened with lacquer thinner. Be careful not to soak the joints and loosen the laminate.

LAMINATE EDGE DESIGNS

In Fig. 16-19 is shown a typical application of standard laminates to countertops. They are applied as just described and the edge is cut on an angle. The edge shows as a dark line.

A top can be edged with a hardwood to give a rich look. One way to do this is to apply the plastic laminate to the edge and top as described earlier. Then using a rabbet router bit, take a very light cut along the edge, removing a little of the top laminate. A cut ⅜ in. (9 mm) wide is adequate. Take the first light cut by feeding the router *with the bit rotation.* This will produce a very light cut out of the lami-

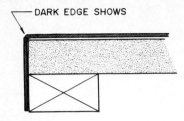

FIGURE 16-19
This edge design bevels both the edge and top laminates.

nate. Then take additional cuts against the rotation of the bit until the desired depth is reached. Usually, $\frac{1}{8}$ in. (3 mm) deep is enough. Cut and glue hardwood strips in this rabbet. Miter them at the corners (Fig. 16-20). Since the edges of the laminate are covered, standard laminate can be used.

Another way is to glue a strip of hardwood to the edge of the substrate. Trim it flush with the substrate. Apply the edge banding and top laminate as described earlier. Then using a router and bit that has the shape you desire, route the edge exposing the hardwood (Fig. 16-21). Apply a finish to the hardwood. Since the edge of the laminate is exposed, some prefer to use the color-through type.

The following procedures relate to the use of color-core laminates and take advantage of the full-depth color. When bonding these, it is important to use a transparent contact cement applied in a thin,

FIGURE 16-20
A hardwood edge is an attractive feature of this laminate top.

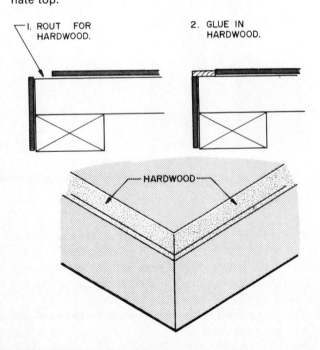

1. ROUT FOR HARDWOOD.

2. GLUE IN HARDWOOD.

HARDWOOD

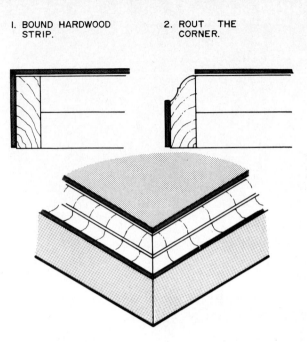

1. BOUND HARDWOOD STRIP.

2. ROUT THE CORNER.

FIGURE 16-21
This hardwood edge is shaped to produce a decorative edge.

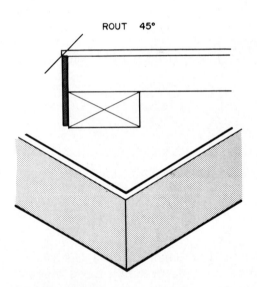

ROUT 45°

FIGURE 16-22
Beveling the edge that has two different color laminates produces two color corners.

even layer so that the glue line is not noticeable. In all cases apply uniform pressure on the glued laminate so that the glue line does not open up.

One procedure is to produce a two-color top. The edge is bonded in one color and the top in another. The edge can be shaped on an angle (Fig. 16-22). Another uses the same laminate on the edge and top, but the edge is rounded. Since the color is through the laminate, a single-color rounded edge is produced. The router bit should produce a $\frac{1}{8}$-in. (3-

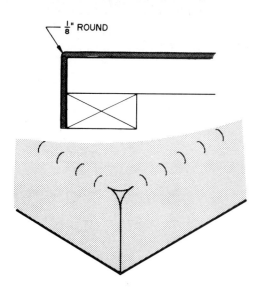

FIGURE 16-23
A slight rounding of the laminate will produce a solid-color corner.

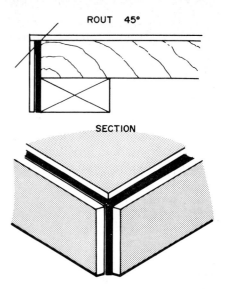

ROUT 45°

SECTION

FIGURE 16-24
Bonding a single layer of laminate of a different color under the edge laminate will produce a striking edge.

FIGURE 16-25
Multiple layers of different color laminates will produce a multistriped edge.

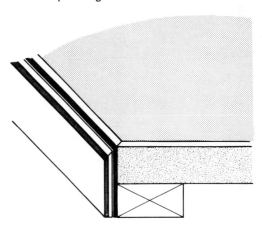

mm)-radius curve. If it is much larger, it will cut through to the substrate (Fig. 16-23). Polish any routed edge with 600-grit wet or dry abrasive paper.

Attractive striped edge designs can be obtained by combining laminates in layers. One technique is to bond one color to the edge. Than sand it to roughen the surface and bond a laminate of a second color to it. Then bond the laminate to the top. When the edge is cut on a 45° chamfer, the inner layer will appear as a strip (Fig. 16-24). Another approach is to apply the top laminate first. Then apply several layers of contrasting colors on the edge. Then trim on a 45° chamfer to produce a multistriped edge (Fig. 16-25).

PART 4

Portable Power Tools

17

PORTABLE ELECTRIC SAWS

Portable electric saws are utilized both in the home shop and on the job site. Because of their portability these saws can easily be moved to the project. There are two portable saws from which to select: the portable circular saw and the saber saw. The *portable circular saw* is used primarily for carpentry-type jobs such as cutting dimensional lumber to length (Fig. 17-1). A *saber saw* is designed to saw curves and to make internal cuts (Fig. 17-15).

PORTABLE CIRCULAR SAWS

Portable circular saws are used almost exclusively for cutting stock to width and length (Fig. 17-1). Because this type of saw can easily be moved, carpenters often prefer this machine to cut material. It also has the advantage of cutting boards that have already been installed. A carpenter, for example, may cut a sheet of plywood sheathing after it has been nailed in place.

A portable circular saw is used by industry that is much like that used in schools. Industrial saws may have larger-horsepower motors. They allow heavier cuts and continuous cutting. A *worm-drive portable saw* is specifically designed for this type of sawing (Fig. 17-2).

Parts of the Portable Circular Saw

The major parts of the portable circular saw are the handle, motor, base plate, and retractable guard (Fig. 17-1). The saw is controlled by the operator gripping the *handle*. Located on the inside edge of the handle is the *on-off switch*. It is spring loaded and will provide power to the motor when the switch is depressed.

To adjust the depth of the saw blade, the *motor* is moved up and down. The *depth-adjustment knob* is loosened to raise and lower the *base plate*. Moving the base plate will expose more or less of the blade. The base plate can also be angled up to 45° for bevel-type cuts. Loosen the *bevel-adjustment knob* to tilt the base plate.

To protect the blade, the *upper blade housing* covers the majority of the saw blade. The portion of the blade below the base plate is covered with the *retractable guard*. It is spring loaded and automatically moves out of the way as the saw blade is fed into the stock. After the cut is finished and the base-plate lifted from the board, the retractable guard must snap shut. A *retractable guard handle* can be used to pull the retractable guard out of the way for specialized cuts.

PORTABLE CIRCULAR SAW SAFETY RULES

1. Unplug the power cord before changing blades.
2. Before cutting any boards, clamp all small pieces to sawhorses or a workbench.
3. Keep the power cord away from the blade and cutting area.
4. Use both hands to hold the saw securely.
5. Hands should come no closer than 4 in. (102 mm) to the blade.
6. Keep from reaching under the stock while cutting.
7. Do not stand directly in line with the saw.
8. Make sure that the guard automatically covers the blade after the cut.
9. Retract the guard only with the retracting handle.
10. Do not set the saw down until the blade stops turning.

Selecting the Saw Blades

As with other circular saws, there are many different types of blades that can be used with the portable saw. Refer to Chapter 23 for all the tooling that can be utilized.

For rough construction work a rough-cut combination blade is recommended. Finish cuts can be made with a four-tooth combination blade. If you need to make a fine cut on plywood and other panel products, install a plywood blade. Carbide-tipped blades are ideal for cutting abrasive materials such as particleboard. These blades will also stay sharper longer.

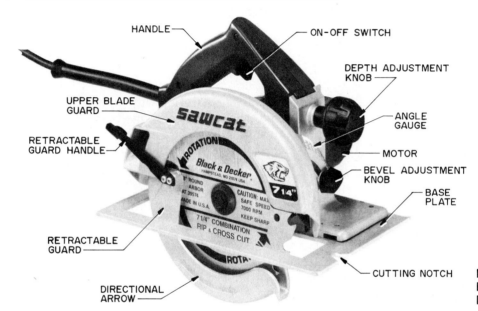

FIGURE 17-1
Major parts of the portable circular saw. (Courtesy of Black & Decker.)

Purchasing a Portable Saw

The first consideration when buying a portable saw is the size. The size of this machine is determined by the largest diameter of saw blade that can safely be mounted on the saw. General-purpose portable saws are typically $7\frac{1}{4}$ in. (181 mm) diameter in size. Saws as small as 4 in. (102 mm) are available for cutting wall paneling. Bridge timbers can be cut with the largest size, a $16\frac{5}{16}$-in. (414-mm) saw.

Portable saws are made with either direct-drive or worm gear design. *Direct drive* is the most common and may contain a friction clutch (Fig. 17-1). This allows the saw blade to slow to a stop when it becomes pinched or stuck in the stock. Having this feature prevents the saw motor from overheating. The *worm gear* drive provides a more positive drive that can make heavy cuts (Fig. 17-2).

FIGURE 17-2
Worm-drive portable saw. (Courtesy of Black & Decker.)

Installing the Saw Blade

To change the saw blade on a portable saw, you need to first unplug the power cord. Pull the retractable guard out of the way and secure the saw blade. Some models of saws have a blade lock for holding the

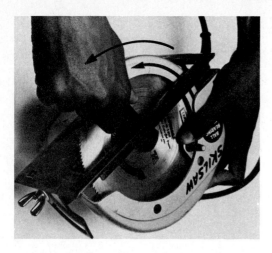

FIGURE 17-3
To change the blade, pull the wrench the same direction as the saw teeth are pointing.

FIGURE 17-4
Adjust the blade to ⅛ in. (3 mm) below the bottom surface of the stock.

blade. Other saws will have a shaft wrench to keep the blade from turning.

With the blade wrench, loosen the blade bolt by pulling the wrench the same direction as the saw teeth are pointing (Fig. 17-3). Remove the existing blade and install the new blade. Be certain that the teeth are pointing in the same direction as the rotation of the motor. Most saws will have a directional arrow to indicate the rotation.

Tighten the blade bolt and allow the guard to go shut. Turn the blade by hand to be certain that it will not rub against the guard. Plug in the power cord and make a trial cut. Check the accuracy of the cut by placing a square from face to face.

Setting Up the Portable Saw

To use the portable circular saw, first adjust the depth of cut. Loosen the depth-adjustment knob and place the base plate on the stock. Lower the blade until it is ⅛ in. (3 mm) below the bottom face of the board (Fig. 17-4). Tighten the depth-adjustment knob. Lift the saw from the stock and check that the retractable guard is working properly.

Next, set the saw blade to the desired angle. Although there is an angle gauge on the saw for establishing the approximate angle, cut a scrap piece to measure the angle (Fig. 17-1). Using a protractor to check this cut will assure an accurate cut.

Position the stock on a pair of sawhorses. Never hold the board with just your hands. For superior results the best face should be placed down against the sawhorses. Since the blade cuts on an upward swing most of the splinters will develop on the top surface.

Crosscutting

The most common operation with a portable saw is crosscutting stock to length. First position the material solidly on two sawhorses (Fig. 17-5). Clamp small boards to a sawhorse to keep them from moving. The point where the stock is to be cut should be approximately 12 in. (305 mm) from the edge of the horse.

Measure the stock to length and square a line at the point the board is to be cut. Place the base plate of the saw on the stock and align the *cutting notch* with the layout line (Fig. 17-6). This will position the saw blade in the same path as the layout line.

Make certain that the blade is not touching the stock, then turn on the power. Slowly push the saw forward checking that the blade is on the waste side of the layout line. After the cut is started, support the waste side of the stock with one hand (Fig. 17-7).

FIGURE 17-5
Positioning the stock on two sawhorses.

FIGURE 17-6
Place the cutting notch just to the side of the layout line to position the saw.

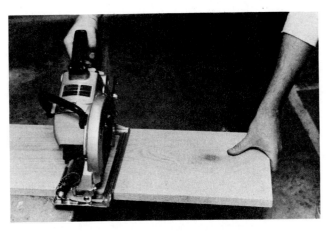

FIGURE 17-7
Use your free hand to support the waste side of the stock. Hands must come no closer than 4 in. (102 mm) to the blade.

FIGURE 17-8
Ripping a board using an adjustable fence.

FIGURE 17-9
Clamping a board to a sawhorse for ripping.

Do not allow your hand to come closer than 4 in. (102 mm) to the blade. Keep the waste from pinching the blade or a kickback will occur. After the cut is completed, remove the saw from the stock and release the on-off switch. Do not lay the saw down until the blade has stopped turning.

Ripping

Ripping stock to width can be completed using either an adjustable fence or with freehand techniques. An *adjustable fence* is attached to the base plate, which can be moved in or out. *Freehand techniques* require the operator to guide the saw skillfully along a layout line.

To rip a board using the adjustable fence, move the fence the same distance from the saw tooth set to the right as the width of the board. Position the fence along the edge of the stock and turn on the power. Use your right hand to keep the fence against the board and your left hand to push the saw for-

ward (Fig. 17-8). Your hand, however, must remain 4 in. (102 mm) from the blade.

To rip a board using freehand techniques, first scribe a line along the face of the board. Clamp the board to a sawhorse with one-half its length extending from the sawhorse (Fig. 17-9). Align the blade with the layout line and cut the board using the techniques discussed in the section "Crosscutting."

Stop the cut when the blade comes close to the sawhorse. Reposition the stock with the remaining end extending from the horse (Fig. 17-10). Place the saw blade back in the kerf. After making certain that the blade turns freely in the kerf, turn on the power and cut the remaining portion of the board.

Cutting Panel Material

Panel material can be cut using a portable saw. Most operators may have difficulty, however, in freehand sawing pieces that are straight and square. For beginners a straightedge can be used to guide the saw.

FIGURE 17-10
Ripping the second half of the board.

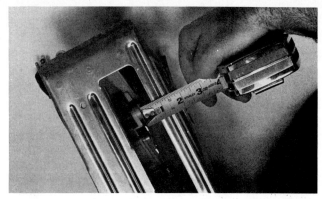

FIGURE 17-11
Measure the distance between the saw tooth set to the left and the base plate.

To cut a panel, first make a layout line where the cut is needed. Next measure the distance between the saw tooth set to the left and the outside edge of the base plate (Fig. 17-11). Measure and mark this same distance on the waste side of the layout line. Clamp a straight edge at this point and parallel to the layout line.

Position the base plate of the saw against the straightedge. Check that the blade is aligned with the layout mark (Fig. 17-12). By sliding the saw along the straightedge, a straight cut is made.

Pocket Cutting

Pocket cuts are internal cuts that do not touch an outside edge of the board. These may be utilized to cut windows in doors, make openings for utility boxes, or cut other inside holes.

To make a pocket cut, first lay out the desired pattern on the stock. With the retracting handle, pull the retractable guard up into the upper blade housing. Keeping the guard in this position, align the blade with the first layout line.

Place the nose of the base plate against the stock by tilting the saw forward (Fig. 17-13). Turn on the power and carefully pivot the blade down into the stock. The nose of the base plate must remain against the stock. Once the base plate is flat against the stock, release the retracting handle and continue the cut until the blade reaches the intersecting layout line. Repeat the process until all other cuts are made. Because the saw blade makes a circular arc as it enters the wood, use a handsaw to complete the cut at each corner.

Panel Saws

A useful attachment for the portable circular saw is the panel saw (Fig. 17-14). The saw is clamped into a frame that is mounted on a movable carriage. To use the panel saw, plywood and other panel material are placed on the incline table. Stock can be crosscut by

FIGURE 17-12
Cutting a panel using a straight edge.

FIGURE 17-13
Positioning the saw for a pocket cut. The nose of the base plate must be against the stock.

FIGURE 17-14
A panel saw uses a portable circular saw to cut plywood and particleboard. (Courtesy of Safety Speed Cut Manufacturing Co., Inc.)

SABER SAW SAFETY RULES

1. Unplug the power cord when installing the blade.
2. Select the correct blade for each material and type of cutting.
3. Before cutting any boards, clamp all small pieces to sawhorses or a workbench.
4. Keep the power cord away from the blade and cutting area.
5. Hands should come no closer than 4 in. (102 mm) to the blade.
6. Make a plunge cut on $\frac{1}{4}$ in. (6 mm) or thinner material.
7. Use both hands to hold the saw securely.
8. Keep from reaching under the stock while cutting.
9. Keep the base tightly against the stock.

pulling the carriage downward. By positioning and locking the carriage in place, the panel can be ripped by feeding it past the saw.

SABER SAWS

The saber saw is a portable power tool designed primarily to make curved cuts (Fig. 17-15). It has a blade that reciprocates or moves up and down much like the scroll saw. This saw is particularly suited for cutting irregular patterns that are too large to be placed on the table of a stationary power tool.

Parts of the Saber Saw

The major parts of the saber saw include the handle, motor, gearbox, and base plate (Fig. 17-15). The saw

FIGURE 17-15
Major parts of the saber saw. (Courtesy of Black & Decker.)

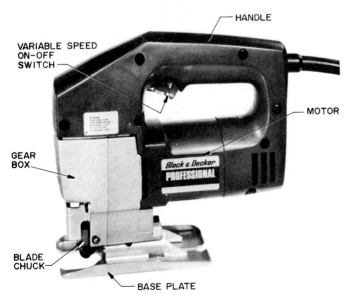

is controlled by the operator gripping the *handle*. Located on the underneath side of the handle is the *on-off switch*. Power is provided to the saw whenever the switch is depressed. A *switch lock* may also be located in the handle. It will hold the switch in the "on" position when lengthy cuts are required. Be careful, however, not to lock the power on when the saw may need to be quickly stopped.

The blade is driven by the *motor* located under the handle. A *gearbox* bolted to the front of the motor changes the rotary motion of the motor to the up-and-down movement of the blade. The blade located at the end of the *blade shaft* is held in place with the *blade chuck*. To operate the saber saw the *base plate* is positioned against the stock. Although the base plate is normally kept 90° to the blade, it can be angled for bevel cuts.

Purchasing a Saber Saw

There are not a great many features that can be selected with a saber saw. Although the size is not generally specified, it can best be found by checking the motor ampere rating. It varies from 2.5 to over 4.5 A. A general-purpose saber saw will have a motor of at least 3.5 A.

Some models of a saber saw have a *variable-speed on-off switch* (Fig. 17-15). This allows the blade speed to be regulated for different materials and types of cuts. The farther the switch is pulled, the faster the blade reciprocates. Fast speeds are used for softwoods and other easy-to-cut materials. Medium speeds work well for hardwoods. Slow speeds are selected for metal and plastics.

A few saws have an *orbital cutting action* feature. The blade not only moves up and down but also pivots forward and backward (Fig. 17-16). This cutting action produces a more aggressive cut which will saw the material at a much faster rate.

TABLE 17-1
Recommended Saber Saw Blades

	Blade type	Length (in.)	Teeth (per in.)	Applications
Carbide Coated Blades				
	Coarse— Tungston Carbide Grit	$2\frac{7}{8}$		Fiber Glass (Polyesters, Epoxies, Melamines, Silicones), Asbestos, Cement, Nail Embedded Wood, Plaster With Nails
	Medium—Tungston Carbide Grit	$2\frac{7}{8}$		Chalkboard, Carbon, Clay Pipe, Brick, Plywood, Hardwood Veneer Plywood.
	Fine— Tungston Carbide Grit	$2\frac{7}{8}$		Ceramic Tile, Slate, Cast Stone, Stainless Steel Trim, Sheet Metal to 18 ga., Ducting, Counter Top Materials, Tempered Hardboard.
Carbide-Tipped Blades				
	Carbide-Tipped	3	6	For cutting fiberglass and similar materials and all types of wood. Tooth configuration provides rapid cutting for production use.
High-Speed Metal Cutting Blades				
	Coarse-Set Tooth, Metal Cutting	3	14	Cuts steel—16 gauge (.059) to 10 gauge (.134). Cuts $\frac{3}{32}"$ to $\frac{3}{16}"$ aluminum, copper, brass. Cuts plastics, asbestos, Fiberglas, etc. $\frac{1}{2}"$ to $\frac{3}{4}"$ rigid conduit, 1/0 stranded cable and $\frac{3}{16}"$ buss bar.
	Coarse-Set Tooth, Metal Cutting	3	18	Cuts ferrous metals from $\frac{1}{8}"$ (.125) to $\frac{1}{4}"$ (.250) thick; Non-ferrous (aluminum, copper, brass, etc.) from $\frac{1}{16}"$ to $\frac{1}{4}"$; will cut pipe and tubing from $\frac{3}{64}"$ to $\frac{1}{4}"$ wall thickness.
	Medium-Set Tooth, Metal Cutting	3	24	Cuts ferrous metals from $\frac{1}{16}"$ (.059) to $\frac{3}{16}"$ (.187) thick; Non-ferrous metals under $\frac{1}{16}"$ thick. Suitable for pipe and tubing under $\frac{3}{64}"$ wall thickness.
	Fine-Set Tooth, Metal Cutting	3	32	Cuts steel—22 gauge (.023) to 13 gauge (.089). For cuts under $\frac{3}{32}"$ in aluminum, copper, brass. Cuts plastics, slate, formica, Fiberglas. Also $\frac{1}{2}"$ to $\frac{3}{4}"$ thin-wall conduit.
All-Purpose Wood and Composition Cutting Blades				
	Hollow-Ground, Fine-Tooth, Wood-Cutting	3	10	Deluxe series for faster, smooth scroll cuts in wood up to $\frac{3}{4}"$ thick. Precision-hollow-ground. Excellent for pocket cutting.
	Hollow-Ground, Medium-Tooth, Wood-Cutting	3	7	Deluxe series for faster, smooth scroll cuts in wood up to $\frac{3}{4}"$ thick. Precision-hollow-ground. Excellent for pocket cutting.
	Hollow-Ground, Coarse-Tooth, Wood-Cutting	3	5	Deluxe series for faster, smooth scroll cuts in wood up to $\frac{3}{4}"$ thick. Precision-hollow-ground. Excellent for pocket cutting.
	Knife Punch Blade	1		Especially useful to signmakers for scroll cutting all types of paperboard materials. Excellent for making intricate pocket cuts in vinyl floor tiles for inlay work.

Blade type	Length (in.)	Teeth (per in.)	Applications
Knife Edge Blade	2½		For smooth, fast cuts in leather, rubber, cork and other composition materials.
Fine-Tooth, M2 Steel, Hollow-Ground, Wood-Cutting	4	10	For fine finish scroll cutting in wood, plywood, Masonite, plastics, etc. Also for ⅛" to ½" soft aluminum, brass. Maximum cut in wood—3" thick.
Coarse-Tooth (Narrow) Hi-Speed Steel, Hollow-Ground, Wood-Cutting	4	6	For faster scroll cutting in wood, plywood, Masonite, etc. Maximum cut—3" thick.
Coarse-Tooth (Wide), M2 Steel, Hollow-Ground, Wood-Cutting	4	6	For fast "production" cutting. Handles wood and plywood up to 3" thick. Also cuts Masonite. Stays sharp longer. Saws through a 2 × 4 at 45°.
Fine-Set Tooth, Hi-Speed Steel, Wood-Cutting	4	10	For scroll cutting in wood, plywood, Masonite, plastics, etc. Maximum cut in wood—2". Set tooth designed for excellent sidecutting action.
Coarse-Set Tooth, M2 Steel, Wood-Cutting	4	6	Set tooth designed for excellent side-cutting action.
Coarse-Tooth, Plaster-Cutting	3⅜	9	For coarse, fast cuts in plasterboard and other highly abrasive materials.
Coarse-Tooth, Wood-Cutting	3	7	Makes fast cuts in wood, plywood, composition boards, etc.
Fine-Tooth, Wood-Cutting	3	10	For smoother cuts in wood, plywood, composition boards, etc.
Coarse-Tooth Hollow-Ground	3	7	For fast, very smooth cuts in wood, plywood, composition boards, etc.
Flush Coarse, Wood-Cutting	3	7	Very accurate flush cuts in corners and other tight spots permitted by projecting cutting area. Cannot be used with No. 3155.
Double-Edge Coarse, Wood-Cutting	3	7	Makes fast pocket cuts up to ¾" thick in wood, composition boards, etc. Exclusive: cuts forward and backward. Cannot be used with No. 3155, 3153-10, 3157-10, and 3159-10.
Double-Edge Fine, Wood-Cutting	3	10	
Scroll Fine, Wood-Cutting	2½	10	Makes intricate cuts, as small as ⅛" radius, up to ½" in wood, plastics, etc.
Skip-Tooth, Wood-Cutting	3	5	More efficiently cuts up to ¾" thick plywood, plastics, etc. due to extra space for chip clearance.
Coarse-Tooth, Wood-Cutting	6	4	For coarse cuts in wood over 2" thick. Also suitable for plastics and composition boards.
Medium-Tooth, Wood-Cutting	6	7	For smoother cuts in wood over 2" thick.

Source: Black & Decker.

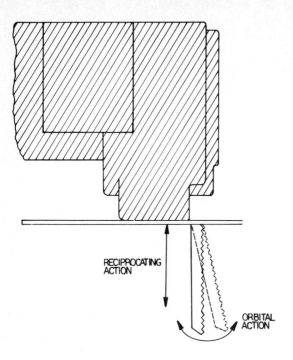

FIGURE 17-16
An orbital cutting action moves the blade up and down and forward and backwards.

Selecting the Saber Saw Blade

The primary reason the saber saw can cut a wide variety of materials is the large selection of available blades. Although there are general-purpose blades, there are also specialized blades for specific materials and types of cuts. Refer to a blade selection chart such as that in Table 17-1 to match the proper blade for your cutting. The blade package will also contain valuable information on recommended applications (Fig. 17-17).

FIGURE 17-17
Information contained on a saber saw package will include length, number of teeth, type of recommended cutting, and application.

It is important that the shank end of the blade fit the blade chuck. Although most of the saber saw blades will fit the majority of saws, there are some machines which require a specially designed blade shank. Always refer to the information on the blade package for the brands and models the blade will fit.

Installing the Saber Saw Blade

To install a saber saw blade, first be certain that the power cord is unplugged. Use a screwdriver or Allen wrench to loosen the chuck screws (Fig. 17-18). After removing the old blade, replace it with a new one. The teeth should be pointing forward and down. Replace the chuck screws and tighten them securely. Plug in the power cord and make a trail cut. You will need to use a square to check the squareness of the cut.

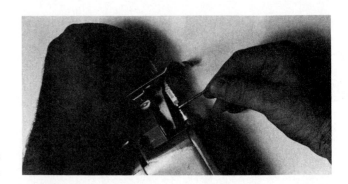

FIGURE 17-18
Loosening the chuck screws to remove the blade.

Setting Up the Saber Saw

Once the blade has been properly installed, a cut can be made. Start the setup by laying out the desired cut. Since the blade cuts on the upper stroke, place the best face down. The majority of the splintering will take place on the top face.

Use clamps or a bench vise to secure the stock (Fig. 17-19). Plan your cut so that the first portion of the cut is extended out away from the workbench or sawhorse. In many cases it will be necessary to saw up to the table and then reposition the stock for the remaining portion of the cut. Arrange the power cord so that it will not interfere with the cut.

Crosscutting and Ripping

Use a square to lay out the cut. Place the base plate against the stock and align the blade with the layout line. Turn on the power and apply light forward pressure. Allow the blade to do the cutting and do not force the saw. Too much forward or side pressure and the blade will break.

FIGURE 17-19
Secure the stock with either a bench vise or clamps before starting the cut.

Crosscutting is done with freehand techniques (Fig. 17-20). Ripping can be completed either using freehand techniques or with a rip guide (Fig. 17-21). The rip guide rides along the edge of the board to control the saw.

Cutting Curves

Curves can be easily cut with a saber saw using freehand techniques. After the pattern has been laid out, plan the best path for the saw to take. If there are any sharp or small curves, use a series of *relief cuts* to enable the blade to cut the curve (Fig. 17-22). Relief cuts are shortcuts made in the waste portion of the board, allowing the blade to saw sharp curves. Keep the cut as close to the layout line as possible without crossing over the line. If you do accidentally come too close to the layout line, back the saw up and restart the cut.

FIGURE 17-20
Crosscutting a board using freehand techniques.

FIGURE 17-22
Relief cuts allow small curves to be cut.

FIGURE 17-21
Ripping a board with a rip guide.

Internal Cuts

Internal cuts are openings made on the interior face of a board and do not extend to an outside edge. To introduce the blade into the stock, a hole is bored or the moving blade is plunged into the wood. If the material is thicker than $\frac{1}{4}$ in. (6 mm), bore a hole in each corner of the layout lines (Fig. 17-23). The blade can then be lowered through the hole. The hole should be larger than the width of the blade so that the saw can be turned once the blade reaches the corner.

To make a plunge cut, make certain that the material is $\frac{1}{4}$ in. (6 mm) or thinner. Pivot the saw up on the nose of the base plate and turn on the power (Fig. 17-24). Slowly lower the saw, introducing the blade into the stock. The saw blade will make its own hole.

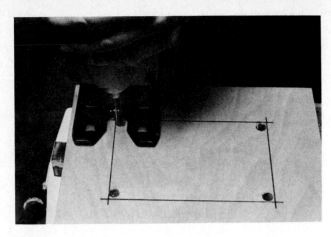

FIGURE 17-23
Introducing the blade through a hole for an internal cut.

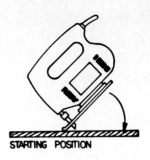

STARTING POSITION

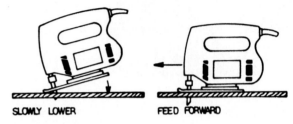

SLOWLY LOWER   FEED FORWARD

FIGURE 17-24
Plunging the blade into the stock for an internal cut.

18

PORTABLE POWER PLANES

A portable power plane is utilized primarily for planing the edges of boards (Fig. 18-1). This portable power tool is often used when it is not convenient to use a jointer, such as planing a door on a construction site. It is also useful for jointing the edges of long or extra large pieces that cannot be safely surfaced on a jointer. A carpenter, for example, may select this machine for planing the edge of a door.

PARTS OF THE POWER PLANE

The major parts of the power plane are the bed, motor, and handle (Fig. 18-1). There are two parts to the bed of the plane. A *rear* or *fixed bed* is set at the same level as the bottom of the cutting circle of the cutter. In front of the cutter is the *front* or *adjustable bed*. It is moved up and down and set at a level equal to the depth of cut. Mounted to the side of the two beds is the fence. The *fence* is set at the angle of the cut. Although the fence is normally adjusted to the 90° position, it can be tilted up to 45°.

The *motor* provides power to the cutter. To the top of the motor is the *handle*. The handle is gripped firmly to control the plane. On the underneath side of the handle is the *on-off switch*. Pulling in on the

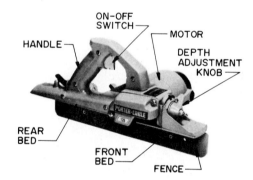

FIGURE 18-1
Major parts of a portable power plane. (Courtesy of Porter-Cable Corporation.)

switch turns on the plane. Releasing the switch automatically turns off the machine.

PURCHASING A POWER PLANE

The primary consideration when purchasing a power plane is the size. It is determined by the motor ampere rating and the size of the bed. Motors vary in size from 2.5 A to over 10 A. The larger the ampere number, the more powerful the motor. The size of

193

PORTABLE PLANE SAFETY RULES

1. When changing the cutter, always unplug the cord.
2. Before cutting any boards, clamp them to saw-horses or a workbench.
3. Use both hands to hold the plane securely.
4. Keep the power cord clear of cutter and cutting area.
5. Keep from reaching under the stock while cutting.
6. The maximum depth of cut is $\frac{1}{16}$ in. (2 mm).
7. Hands should come no closer than 4 in. (102 mm) to the cutter.
8. Keep the fence and rear bed against the stock until the cutter has stopped turning.

FIGURE 18-3
To change the cutter pull the wrench counterclockwise.

the bed varies from $1\frac{13}{16}$ to over $3\frac{1}{4}$ in. (45 to 82 mm) wide. The length of the bed also varies from $7\frac{1}{2}$ to over 18 in. (191 to 457 mm).

SELECTING AND INSTALLING THE CUTTER

The first consideration in the selection of the cutter is the number of cutting edges. The number of cutting edges varies from two to three or more. The more cutting edges, the smoother the cut will be. Some models of plane also have available carbide cutters. Carbide cutters will plane particleboard, high-pressure plastic laminates, and other abrasive materials (Fig. 18-2).

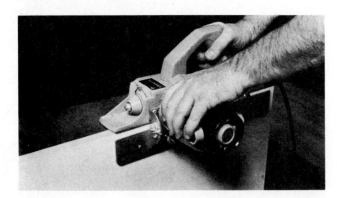

FIGURE 18-2
Planes with carbide cutters can be used to joint high-pressure plastic laminates.

To change the cutter, unplug the power cord. Use the correct size of wrench to fit the cutter nut. Wedge a piece of wood between the cutter and the bed and remove the cutter nut (Fig. 18-3). Replace the existing cutter with a newly sharpened cutter. Wedge a piece of wood against the cutter and tighten the cutter nut. Remove the wedge and check that the cutter turns freely.

SETTING UP THE PLANE

To set up the plane, unplug the power cord. Set the depth of cut by using the *depth-adjustment knob*. Refer to the owners' manuals for recommended maximum depth of cuts. Depending on the particular machine, recommended depth of cut varies from $\frac{1}{64}$ to $\frac{1}{16}$ in. (0.5 to 2 mm).

Next check the angle of the fence. Most planes contain an *angle gauge* to indicate the tilt of the fence (Fig. 18-4). For cuts requiring great accuracy, plane a scrap piece and check the cut with a square or protractor.

FIGURE 18-4
Setting the angle of the fence by using the angle gauge.

PLANING AN EDGE

To plane the edge of a board, secure it in a bench vise or clamp it to a sawhorse. Position the stock so that the clamps will not interfere with the travel of the plane. No matter how large or small the part, never hold the stock with your hands.

Adjust the depth of cut and check that the fence is at the desired angle. Plug in the power cord. Position the front bed on the edge of the board and the fence against the face of the stock (Fig. 18-5). If a bevel or chamfer is to be cut, the plane will be held at an angle (Fig. 18-6). It is important that the plane be held in a steady position if an accurate cut is to be made.

Grip the handle with your right hand and pull in on the power switch. Your hands must be kept up above the bed and away from the cutter. After the motor has gained full speed, push the plane forward.

FIGURE 18-6
The plane is positioned at an angle when jointing a bevel or chamfer.

FIGURE 18-5
The front bed and fence must be kept against the stock.

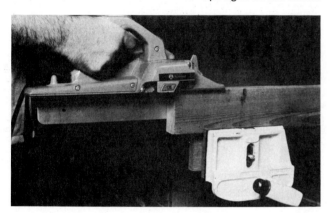

Feed the plane at a steady rate. Too fast a feed rate will cause the cut to be rough and the motor will be overloaded. If you use too slow a feed speed, however, the wood will be burned and the cutter prematurely dull.

Once the cutter has cleared the far end of the stock, release the on-off switch. Keep the plane in this position until the cutter has stopped turning. Remove the plane from the stock and repeat the planing process if additional passes are required. With each pass, be certain that the front and rear beds are kept against the stock. If the beds raise up off the stock, a bowed edge will be produced.

19

PORTABLE ELECTRIC DRILLS

The most versatile portable power tool is the electric drill (Fig. 19-1). It is available in many sizes and can be used with numerous attachments. Although it is most commonly used with drill bits, many other accessories are available. A few of these attachments include drill press stand, grinding wheel, sanding disk, and others shown in Fig. 19-2.

Industry utilizes many of the same electric drills as those used in schools and homes. They will, however, generally have continuous-duty motors. Some manufacturers prefer *pneumatic* or air-driven

drills (Fig. 19-3). These drills are cooler running and more compact.

PARTS OF THE ELECTRIC DRILL

The major parts of the electric drill are the handle, motor, and chuck (Fig. 19-1). Most drills will have either a pistol grip or a T-handle, The *pistol-grip* handle is the most common for small to medium-sized drills. Larger drills will typically have *T-han-*

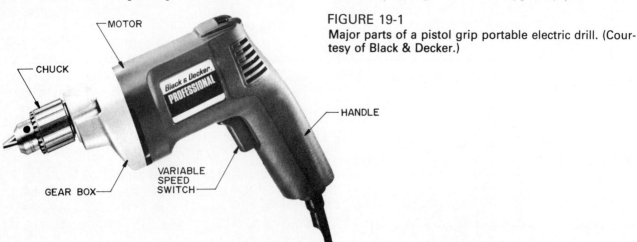

FIGURE 19-1
Major parts of a pistol grip portable electric drill. (Courtesy of Black & Decker.)

MOTOR

CHUCK

HANDLE

GEAR BOX

VARIABLE
SPEED
SWITCH

PORTABLE DRILL SAFETY RULES

1. Unplug the power cord before changing bits or tightening the chuck.
2. Remove the chuck key once the chuck has been tightened.
3. Before cutting small pieces, clamp them to saw-horses or a workbench.
4. Hold the handle securely when using the drill.
5. Keep the power cord clear of the drilling area and the drill bit.
6. Hands should come no closer than 4 in. (102 mm) to the drill bit.
7. Do not reach under the stock while cutting.

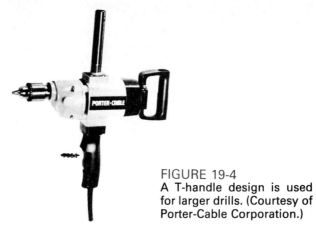

FIGURE 19-4
A T-handle design is used for larger drills. (Courtesy of Porter-Cable Corporation.)

FIGURE 19-2
Accessories for a portable drill.

FIGURE 19-3
Pneumatic drills are driven by compressed air.

dles for better control (Fig. 19-4). More pressure can also be applied for large holes or for drilling in very hard materials.

The motor and gearbox make up the majority of the drill. The motor provides power to the gear-box. The *gearbox* reduces the speed of the motor and increases the *torque* or turning power to the *chuck*.

At the end of the gearbox is the chuck. It holds the drill bit and can be adjusted to fit different shank diameters.

PURCHASING AN ELECTRIC DRILL

The first consideration in purchasing a drill is the size. The size is determined by the largest shank diameter than can be secured in the chuck. Drill chuck sizes include $\frac{1}{4}$, $\frac{3}{8}$, $\frac{1}{2}$, and $\frac{3}{4}$ in. (6, 10, 13, and 19 mm). A $\frac{3}{8}$-in. (10-mm) drill is recommended for general-purpose boring. Select a $\frac{1}{2}$-in. (13-mm) chuck size for large-diameter holes or for heavy boring.

Another consideration in buying a drill is the selection of an on-off switch. Simpler drills have switches that only turn the power on and off. A switch that provides more versatility is the *variable-speed switch*. The farther the switch is pulled, the faster the chuck will rotate. When boring in softer materials such as wood, a fast speed is selected. Use a slower speed for drilling in harder materials such as metal and plastic. A variable-speed switch is also convenient when slower turning speeds are required for installing screws (Fig. 19-14).

Drills may also contain a reversing switch. This feature allows the chuck to rotate either clockwise or counterclockwise. Although the clockwise rotation is generally selected, the counterclockwise direction is used when a bit becomes stuck or when removing wood screws. Do not move the reversing switch unless the chuck is not turning.

Portable drills are also available with rechargeable batteries (Fig. 19-5). This makes the drill highly portable and does not require a power cord to provide electricity. The battery is recharged in the charger once the power becomes weak.

SELECTING THE DRILL BIT

The portable electric drill can be used with most of the drill bits described in Chapter 30. Refer to this chapter for detailed information. Twist bits are the most common, however, and are utilized to bore holes $\frac{1}{2}$ in. (13 mm) and smaller in diameter (Fig. 19-6). Spade bits can be used to bore larger-diameter holes (Fig. 19-7).

FIGURE 19-5
A rechargeable drill requires batteries with a charger. (Courtesy of Black & Decker.)

FIGURE 19-6
Twist bits are generally used with a portable drill.

FIGURE 19-7
Spade bits work well for large-diameter holes.

INSTALLING THE DRILL BIT

To install a drill bit, insert the shank of the bit a minimum of 1 in. (25 mm) into the jaws of the chuck. Any less than this and the chuck will easily be worn. Hand-tighten the outside chuck sleeve until the jaws hold the bit. Make certain that the bit is centered in the opening of the chuck.

Next use the chuck key by first inserting it in one of the chuck key holes (Fig. 19-8). By turning it clockwise the bit will be secured in the chuck. For large-diameter bits, use the chuck key in all three holes. This will prevent the bit from spinning in the chuck.

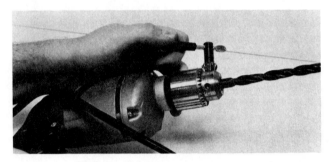

FIGURE 19-8
Securing the drill bit in the chuck with a chuck key.

BORING THROUGH HOLES

Holes that extend completely through the stock can be bored by first marking the center of each hole. Use an awl and make an indentation at these centers. This will provide a starting point for each hole and keep the bit from drifting away from the center.

Place the tip of the bit in the starting point and establish the desired angle to the surface of the stock. If an exact angle is required, use a square or a sliding T-bevel as a guide (Fig. 19-9). Commercial

FIGURE 19-9
Using a sliding T-bevel as a guide for boring an angular hole.

fixtures can also be utilized to give exact angles (Fig. 19-10).

Turn on the drill and apply light forward pressure. Drills having variable-speed switches should initially use a slow speed. Once the bit has fully engaged the material, additional forward pressure and rotation speed can be used. When boring deep holes, pull the bit back out of the hole to allow the chips to fall free from the bit.

As the bit approaches the far side of the stock, slow the feed rate and lighten the feed pressure. If no splinters are allowed on the back side of the stock, clamp a *backup board* to the stock before starting the hole (Fig. 19-11).

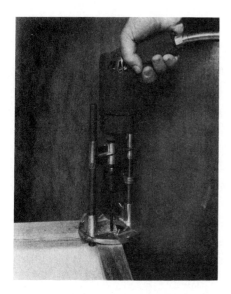

FIGURE 19-10
A commercial fixture guides the drill bit to the exact desired angle.

FIGURE 19-11
A backup board prevents splintering on the back of the board.

BORING STOPPED HOLES

Use the same techniques for boring stopped holes as recommended for through holes. Since the holes do not extend all the way through the stock, however, the bit must be marked in some fashion. The simplest method is to use a piece of tape at the desired length on the drill bit (Fig. 19-12). Commercial stops are also available which can be clamped on the bit (Fig. 19-13). They will keep the bit from going any deeper once the stop meets the surface of the board.

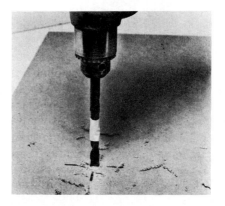

FIGURE 19-12
A piece of tape marks the desired depth of the hole.

FIGURE 19-13
A commercial stop keeps the bit from going too deep for a stopped hole.

INSTALLING WOOD SCREWS

A portable drill with a variable-speed switch can be utilized for installing screws. Start the process by boring the appropriate shank and pilot holes. A countersunk hole may also be necessary for flat-head and oval-head screws.

After lubricating the threads of the screw with paraffin wax, insert a screw into each hole. Place the

FIGURE 19-14
Installing a wood screw. Note the position of the hands of the operator.

FIGURE 19-15
A pneumatic screwdriver installs screws.

screwdriver bit squarely in the slot of the screw and slightly pull in on the switch (Fig. 24-14). Keep your fingers away from the end of the screwdriver bit and the stock surrounding the screw. Your hands will then be clear in case the bit should slip.

Once the screw has been started, the rotational speed can be increased. If the screw becomes stuck, reverse the rotation and remove the screw. Check that the shank and pilot holes are of the correct depth and diameter. Start the screw again and apply more downward pressure.

Specialized power screwdrivers can also be utilized to install screws (Fig. 24-15). They are designed only to drive screws and do not bore holes. Both pneumatic and electric models are manufactured.

20

PORTABLE ROUTERS

The portable router is a multifunctional machine that can be utilized for both joinery and decorative-type cuts (Fig. 20-1). Most shops have several routers because of this versatility. Shapes produced by the router are usually clean, splinter free, and require little sanding.

Industry uses many of the same routers as schools. They do, however, sometimes contain larger continuous-duty motors. The heavier motors can be utilized for long periods without overheating. Occasionally, industrial routers will be driven by air. This allows heavy cuts and cooler-running motors.

PARTS OF THE ROUTER

There are only two major parts to the portable router (Fig. 20-1). They are the motor and base. The motor powers the router bit. At the end of the threaded motor shaft is the collet and collet nut (Fig. 20-2). The *collet* is a tapered split sleeve that secures the router bit to the motor shaft. Most heavy-duty routers have $\frac{1}{4}$-, $\frac{3}{8}$-, and $\frac{1}{2}$-in. (6-, 5-, and 13-mm) collets. This allows any common bit shank size to be used with the router.

The base slides up and down on the outside of the motor unit. Once positioned, a *depth lock* secures

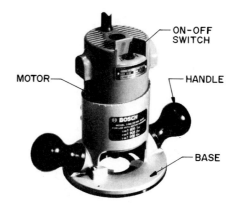

FIGURE 20-1
Major parts of a portable router. (Courtesy of Robert Bosch Power Tool Corporation.)

the base to the motor. Along the sides of the base are the handles. The handles are gripped by the operator to control the machine. Attached to the bottom of the base is the plastic base plate. This provides a smooth surface to slide along the stock.

PURCHASING A PORTABLE ROUTER

There is a wide range of costs for portable routers. The primary difference is the size and construction

201

PORTABLE ROUTER SAFETY RULES

1. Unplug the power cord when changing bits.
2. Before routing, clamp any board to sawhorses or a workbench.
3. Hold the router securely by both handles.
4. Hands should come no closer than 4 in. (102 mm) to the bit.
5. Keep from reaching under the stock while routing.
6. Make cuts that will not overload the router.
7. When routing an outside edge, move the router in a counterclockwise direction.
8. Keep the router away from your body and clothing.

FIGURE 20-3
A laminate trimmer is a specialized router used for cutting high-pressure plastic laminates.

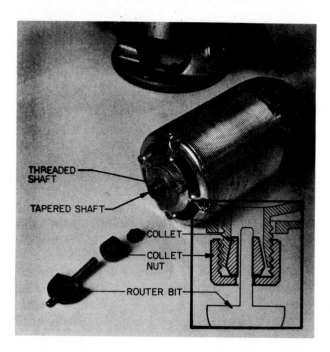

FIGURE 20-2
The motor unit contains a threaded shaft and collect.

FIGURE 20-4
A plunge router allows the router bit to be lowered into the stock.

of the motor unit. Horsepower ratings vary from $\frac{1}{4}$ to over 3 hp. Lower-horsepower routers are designed for light shortcuts. This may be ideal for a home handyman who does not utilize a router on a regular bases. A *laminate trimmer* is used to trim high-pressure plastic laminates (Fig. 20-3). It has a small motor because of the thin material.

Routers with motors larger than 1 hp can generally make most cuts. Heavy-duty motors are designed to be used continuously with little danger of overheating. Very deep cuts require a router of 2 hp and larger.

Some routers are available with a plunge base (Fig. 20-4). This allows the depth of cut to be locked at a specific level or for the rotating bit to be lowered into the stock. Once the bit reaches the desired depth, the downward travel is stopped. Blind grooves and other stopped cuts can be made without the base being lifted from the work.

FIGURE 20-5
A D-shaped handle provides ready access to the on-off switch.

Always purchase a router that feels balanced in your hands. You should be able to control it easily by gripping the handles. The on-off switch must also be readily accessible from the handles (Fig. 20-5). There should be no need to remove your hands from the machine to turn the router on or off.

A consideration when purchasing a router is the motor speed. The router spindle will generally turn at a constant speed between 15,000 to 30,000 rpm. Routers that turn at a fast speed will make a smoother cut and allow faster feed speeds. The horsepower of the motor, however, must be adequate to keep the bit turning at the desired speed.

SELECTING THE ROUTER BITS

There are hundreds of different router bits. Each style or pattern is available in several sizes. In addition, they are sold in a few different shank sizes and have cutting edges made from different materials.

The major parts of the router bit include the shank, cutting edge, and with some bits, a pilot (Fig. 20-6). The *shank* fits into the collet located in the threaded shaft of the motor. Shanks are made in ¼-, ⅜-, or ½-in. (6-, 10-, and 13-mm) diameters. Although the ¼-in. (6-mm) shank size is the most common for smaller routers, a ½-in. (13-mm) size is recommended. The ½-in. (13-mm) diameter will flex less and be less likely to break. The *cutting edge* contains the ground pattern to produce the router edge. Most router bits have two cutting edges. Bits designed to shape edges contain a pilot. The *pilot* controls the horizontal depth of cut. Pilots can be made either from solid steel or with a ball bearing. A solid pilot turns at the same speed as the rest of the bit and may burn the wood. A ball-bearing pilot will ride easily over the edge and turns only as fast as the feed speed. Bits that do not contain a pilot are designed primarily for interior cuts.

Cutting edges are either made of carbon steel or are carbide tipped. Although steel cutters are initially less expensive, carbide tipped will last much longer. Carbide will also shape hard abrasive materials such as plastic laminates and particle board.

FIGURE 20-6
The major parts of the router include the shank, cutting edge, and pivot. (Courtesy of Porter-Cable Corporation.)

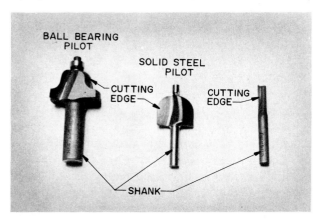

This type of bit, however, does require a diamond grinding wheel to sharpen the hard cutting edge.

Router bits will be used primarily to make decorative or joinery-type cuts. Decorative bits will enhance the appearance of a project (Fig. 20-7). The major styles are as follows:

1. *Rounding-over bits* round a corner, providing a smooth appearance. The diameter of the pilot will be the same size as the adjoining cutting edge.

2. *Beading bits* are often confused with the rounding-over bit. The pilot is, however, smaller in diameter than the adjoining cutting edge. This creates a step at the bottom of the radius.

3. *Cove bits* make a concave-shaped cut on the corner of the board. The pilot controls the depth of cut.

4. *Core box bits,* like the cove bits, make a concave cut. They do not, however, contain a pilot and can shape a rounded-bottom groove.

5. *Chamfer bits* make a 45° chamfer on a corner. Because of the pilot they are designed to run along the edge.

6. *V-grooving bits* make a vee-shaped groove generally on the face of a board. The sides of the bit are ground at a 45° angle.

7. *V-groover and scorer bits,* like the V-grooving bits, also shape a vee-bottomed groove. It does, however, have a longer cutting edge along the sides and is available only in narrow widths.

8. *Roman ogee bits* make a highly decorative cut along the edge. It is often used in traditional-styled furniture to add detail to the edge of a top or shelves. The pilot controls the horizontal depth.

There are also router bits, which are designed primarily for joinery-type cuts (Fig. 20-8). They are as follows:

1. *Straight bits* are used mostly for making grooves. They are available in several diameters from 1/16 to over 2 in. Straight bits are made in two styles, single flute and double flute. The *single flute* has only one cutting edge and contains the most metal to support the cutting edge. It is therefore the strongest of the two styles and less likely to break. The *double flute* has two cutting edges and produces the smoothest cut.

2. *Rabbeting bits* shape rabbets along the edges of boards. The pilot controls the horizontal depth of cut.

3. *Plunge bits* are similar to straight bits except that a vee-shaped starting tip is grounded into

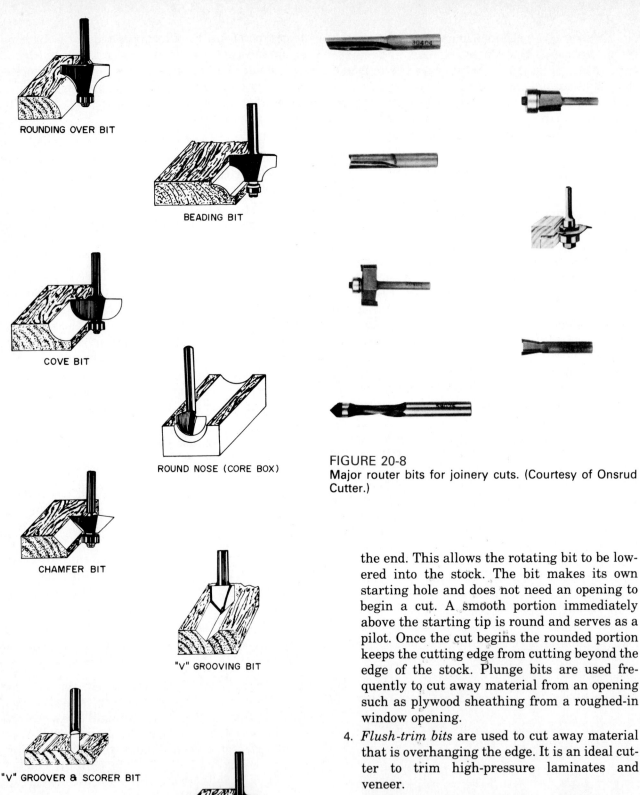

ROUNDING OVER BIT

BEADING BIT

COVE BIT

ROUND NOSE (CORE BOX)

CHAMFER BIT

"V" GROOVING BIT

"V" GROOVER & SCORER BIT

ROMAN OGEE BIT

FIGURE 20-7
Major router bits which produce a decorative cut. (Courtesy of Robert Bosch Power Tool Corporation.)

FIGURE 20-8
Major router bits for joinery cuts. (Courtesy of Onsrud Cutter.)

the end. This allows the rotating bit to be lowered into the stock. The bit makes its own starting hole and does not need an opening to begin a cut. A smooth portion immediately above the starting tip is round and serves as a pilot. Once the cut begins the rounded portion keeps the cutting edge from cutting beyond the edge of the stock. Plunge bits are used frequently to cut away material from an opening such as plywood sheathing from a roughed-in window opening.

4. *Flush-trim bits* are used to cut away material that is overhanging the edge. It is an ideal cutter to trim high-pressure laminates and veneer.

5. *Slotting bits* are utilized to make narrow grooves along the edge of the stock. The pilot controls the depth of cut. This cutter works well for installing tee molding and splines.

6. *Dovetail bits* are used to shape dovetail joints and often used in association with a dovetail fixture. Both are discussed in detail later in this chapter.

INSTALLING THE ROUTER BIT

To install a router bit, unplug the power cord. To have easier access to the collet, remove the motor unit from the base. After selecting the desired cutter, insert the shank of the cutter into the collet. If the collet size does not match the diameter of the shank, change the collet.

The shank of the router bit must fit into the collet a minimum of $\frac{1}{2}$ in. (13 mm). Any less than this and the opening in the collet will be enlarged (Fig. 20-9). This process is called *bellmouthing*. After a collet becomes damaged, it should be replaced with a new part.

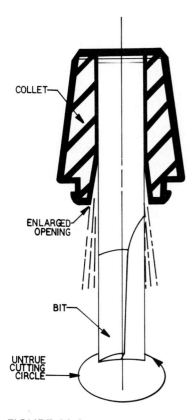

FIGURE 20-9
Bellmouthing occurs when the opening in the collect becomes enlarged.

Using the collet nut wrench and the collet wrench, tighten the collet nut. Reassemble the motor unit and base. With most models the bit can be raised and lowered in the base by turning the motor unit. Once the desired bit height has been set, tighten the depth lock. Be certain that the power switch is in the off position before plugging in the cord. It is also a good idea to make a trial cut on a scrap board before routing the finished stock.

SETTING UP THE ROUTER

Operating the portable router is relatively easy, but there are a few procedures that must be followed. First, solidly position the base against the stock. Arrange the power cord away from the path of the cutter. Holding the handles with both hands, check that the router bit is completely clear of the stock before turning on the power.

Turn on the power and move the router into the stock. Once the pilot or router guide reaches the material, immediately start moving it along the edge. If you are shaping the outside edge, move the router from left to right (Fig. 20-10). For inside edges move the machine from right to left. Always

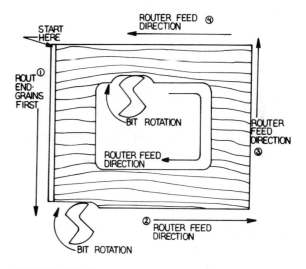

FIGURE 20-10
Proper feed directions for routing the outside and inside edges of stock.

keep the router bit moving. Allowing the router to stop will cause the cutter to overheat and severely burn the stock.

Use a consistent moderate feed speed. Too slow a feed speed and the bit and stock will burn. Too fast a feed speed and a rough cut will be produced.

If a large amount of material is to be removed, make the cut with several light passes. You can determine when the appropriate depth of cut and feed speed are being used by listening to the motor. If the motor pulls down considerably, reduce the depth of cut. When the sound level is not lowered, increase the feed speed or take a deeper cut.

Once the cut is complete, pull the router bit away from the edge, but the base must remain against the stock. Keep the router resting on the material until the bit has stopped turning. Never rest the router against your body.

ROUTING AN EDGE

As with any routed surface, first decide which method to be utilized to guide the router. In most cases, either a piloted router bit or a commercial fence are selected to shape the edge.

Piloted Router Bits

The most common method of routing an edge is with a router bit that contains a *pilot*. This smooth bearing surface rides along the edge of the stock (Fig. 20-11). It controls the horizontal depth of the bit. Some router bits have changeable pilots which can be unscrewed from the bit. This allows the depth to be varied by using a smaller- or larger-diameter pilot.

FIGURE 20-12
A commercial straight guide contains an adjustable fence to control the router.

FIGURE 20-11
A pilot of a piloted router bit rides on the edge to control the depth of cut.

With all piloted router bits, it is important that the edge be smooth and true. Any irregularities in the stock will be transferred to the routed shape. A ball-bearing pilot is less likely to burn the stock than a solid pilot.

Commercial Straight Guide

For router bits without pilot, a commercial straight guide can be used (Fig. 20-12). It contains two rods which are attached to the base of the router. The guide can be moved in and out on the rods to adjust the horizontal depth of cut. A wooden fence can be added to the front of the guide. This will increase the contact area with the stock and make it easier to guide the router.

ROUTING A CIRCULAR EDGE

Outside curves and circular disks can be shaped easily using a router. Piloted router bits are most frequently used for routing the edges. Utilize the same procedure with the piloted bits as given in the preceding section. For router bits not containing a pilot, a modified commercial guide can be used (Fig. 20-13). It is referred to as the *commercial circular guide*. In addition, large-diameter circular grooves can be made using a *pivot point* attached to the commercial guide (Fig. 20-14).

FIGURE 20-13
The commercial circular guide controls the router when routing a circular shape.

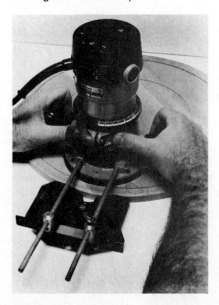

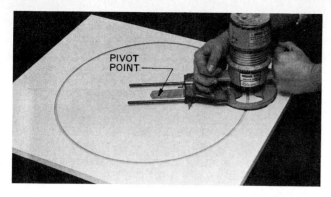

FIGURE 20-14
Attaching a pivot point to a commercial guide allows routing a circular groove.

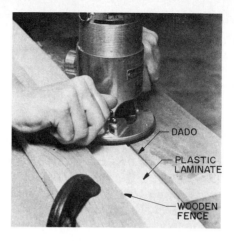

FIGURE 20-15
The plastic laminate on the custom wooden fence will automatically gauge the location of the fence.

FIGURE 20-16
A secondary fence will keep the router from drifting away from the fence.

Commercial Circular Guide

After the circular guide has been installed, adjust the guide the desired distance from the router bit. If the edge is to be shaped, adjust the guide so that the bit is on the outside of the stock. For interior circular grooves, the guide can be set farther from the bit. Be careful to keep the vee-shaped guide against the stock (Fig. 20-13).

Pivot Point

When several circular grooves are required, install a pivot point on the commercial guide. The guide can then be moved in or out to adjust the diameter of the groove (Fig. 20-14).

ROUTING DADOS AND RABBETS

The router produces splinter-free smooth bottom dados and rabbets. In certain cases, it is one of the few ways to dado hardwood plywood smoothly and cut arc-shaped grooves. Dados and rabbets can be routed with either a commercial guide or a wooden fence. For further information on the commercial guide, refer to the section "Routing an Edge."

Wooden Fence

The wooden fence provides a surface against which the router can be guided (Fig. 20-15). The distance the fence is from the dado layout line should be equal to the space between the outside edge of the router base and the cutting circle of the bit. Clamp the fence to the stock.

When several dados of the same width are to be cut, make a custom fence that can be used repeatedly. Glue to the bottom of a wooden fence a piece of high-pressure plastic laminate. Install the same

router bit as is to be used to make the dado. Carefully guide the router along the fence, trimming the laminate to width. To make a dado, align the edge of the laminate along the layout line for the dado (Fig. 20-15). The plastic laminate will automatically gauge the location of the fence. Any time a different-diameter bit is required, a new fence will need to be made.

To make certain that the router will not move away from the fence, use a secondary fence. A track is formed in which the router base just fits (Fig. 20-16). The double fence can be reused for other dados and rabbets.

ROUTING RABBETS

A rabbet can be routed with either a piloted rabbeting bit or with a straight bit and a commercial straight guide. Rabbeting bits will make either a $\frac{1}{4}$- or $\frac{3}{8}$-in. (6- or 10-mm)-wide rabbet. To make other sizes or rabbets, install a straight router bit larger in diameter than the width of the rabbet. Use a commercial straight guide to guide the router. A wooden fence attached to the guide will make it easier to keep the guide against the edge of the board.

ROUTING A MORTISE

Mortises can be accurately cut using a router. A spiral flute straight bit should first be installed. Use a bit that is one-fourth to one-third the thickness of the stock. Either $\frac{1}{4}$- or $\frac{3}{8}$-in. (6- to 10-mm)-diameter bits can be selected for $\frac{3}{4}$-in. (19-mm)-thick material. If a $\frac{1}{4}$-in. (6-mm)-wide mortise is required, however, make several shallow passes to achieve the desired depth. A $\frac{1}{4}$-inch bit breaks easily and should not be forced to make a deep cut. To guide the router a commercial straight guide can be utilized. Layout each mortise on the edge and best face of the stock. In addition, place an "X" on the best-face side of the boards.

Commercial Straight Guide

When the commercial guide is to be used, clamp to the faces of the stock two thick boards (Fig. 20-17). This will increase the width of the material on which to run the router.

Attach a long board to the fence of the guide for better control of the router. Always run the fence along the face that contains the "X" mark. Use the same procedure to route the mortises as described in the section "Routing an Edge."

FIGURE 20-17
Routing a mortise using a commercial straight guide. Note the extra boards clamp to the sides of the stock.

ROUTING HALF-BLIND DOVETAILS

Half-blind dovetails are frequently utilized in high-quality drawer construction. Wedge-shaped tenons are cut to fit into socket shaped mortises.

Industry uses a machine called a dovetailer to shape the dovetails (Fig. 20-18). It contains many dovetail bits and produces all the tenons and mortises with one pass of the machine. Home shops usually cut dovetails with a portable router, dovetail router bit, and a dovetail fixture.

To produce dovetails with a router first square all material to finish dimensions. In addition, make two more pieces from scrap material which will be the exact same thickness as the finished stock. Next, attach the template collar to the router base and install the dovetail bit. It is very important that the depth of cut for the bit be adjusted exactly $\frac{19}{32}$ inch (15 mm). Because it is difficult to measure the amount the bit extends below the base use a dovetail depth gauge (Fig. 20-19). The set screw of the gauge should just touch the end of the dovetail bit.

Clamp the dovetail fixture in a bench vise. Slip the scrap drawer side under the front bar of the fixture and let it extend beyond the top surface of the fixture by approximately $\frac{1}{2}$ inch (13 mm). Next slide the scrap drawer front under the top rail. Position the board against the front drawer side and against the indexing pin (Fig. 20-20). Tighten the top bar knobs. Loosen the front bar knobs and reposition the drawer side. Use a straight edge to flush the top end of the front piece with the face of the top piece (Fig. 20-21). The drawer side should be pushed against the front indexing pin and then tighten the knobs. Finish the set-up by placing the dovetail template over the two pieces of wood. Push the template tight against the top of the stock and tighten the template knobs.

Place the base of the router solidly on top of the template. Carefully check that the router bit will not cut into fixture base. Do not for any reason raise the router up off the template. This will cause the rotating router bit to cut through the template. Turn on the power and slowly trace around the fingers of the template (Fig. 20-22).

After the cut has been completed, turn off the power and allow the router to remain on the template until the bit has stopped turning. Remove the router and the boards from the fixture.

Check the fit of the two pieces. If the tenons do not fully engage the mortises, adjustments must be made. When there is too much play between the tenons and mortises, lower the dovetail bit $\frac{1}{64}$ in. (0.5 mm). When the mortise and tenons fit but the drawer side is not flush with the end of the drawer front, change the position of the template nuts located on the front of the template. Turn the nuts clockwise when the side extends too far into the front. Turn them counterclockwise when the side extends beyond the drawer fronts. Continue to make trial cuts until the joint fits perfectly. Make only one adjustment with each cut.

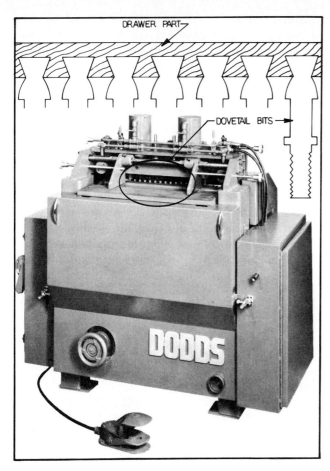

FIGURE 20-18
A dovetailer contains many dovetail bits.

FIGURE 20-19
Adjusting the depth of cut using a dovetail depth gauge.

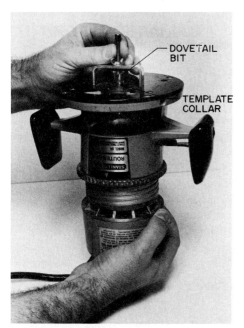

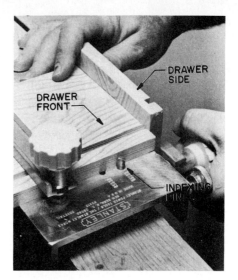

FIGURE 20-20
Locating the drawer front in a dovetail fixture.

FIGURE 20-21
Locating the drawer side in a dovetail fixture.

FIGURE 20-22
By tracing around the dovetail template the dovetails are produced.

After the settings have been made, make the dovetail joints. Cut the right front and left rear on the left side of the fixture. Make the left front and right rear on the right side. The inside surfaces of the drawer front and drawer side must always be facing out.

Rabbeted Drawer Fronts

Because of the $\frac{3}{8}$- $\times$ $\frac{3}{8}$-in. (10- $\times$ 10 mm) rabbet on a rabbeted-style drawer, a different procedure is necessary (Fig. 20-23). A *positioning block* is required to locate the drawer front. Without a positioning block the lip of the rabbet prevents the inner part of the drawer from being dovetailed. To make a positioning block select a $\frac{3}{4}$-in. (19-mm)-thick scrap the same width as the drawer front. Approximately $\frac{1}{2}$ in. (13 mm) from the end of the block, cut a $\frac{1}{2} \times \frac{1}{2}$ in. (13 $\times$ 13 mm) dado.

After the drawer front has been rabbeted, slide it under the top bar of the dovetail fixture. The outside face of the drawer must be against the fixture. Place the positioning block under the front bar and slide the rabbet of the drawer front into the dado of the positioning block (Fig. 20-24). Tighten the front bar knobs. Push the drawer front against the indexing pin and tighten the top bar knobs. After removing the positioning block and installing the dovetail template, route the dovetails.

To dovetail the mating drawer side, use a squared spacer of the same thickness as the drawer front. Place the spacer on top of the fixture and clamp the side on the front of the fixture. The end of the drawer side must be flush with the face of the spacer. Use the procedure to cut the dovetails recommended in the preceding section.

ROUTING A DESIGN OR RECESS

A decorative design or recess can be routed using a template and template collar. A template can be made from $\frac{1}{4}$-in. (6-mm) hardboard. Make the opening in the template the same size as the design plus twice the space between the cutting circle of the bit and the outside edge of the collar (Fig. 20-25). The template can either be held in place with small brads or by constructing a frame into which the stock can fit.

Once the template has been constructed, the routing can begin. Start the cut by positioning the template collar in the corner of the template. Ideally, use a plunge router to lower the bit into the stock. If a plunge router is not available, pivot the router bit into the stock. Keep the collar against the edge of the template or the desired pattern will not be produced (Fig. 20-26). For recesses, route around the perimeter of the template. Remove the interior area by making multiple passes.

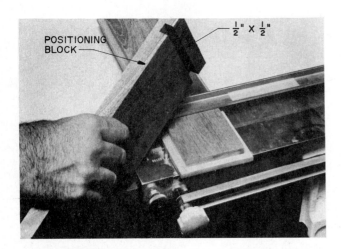

FIGURE 20-23
A rabbeted door front and positioning block.

FIGURE 20-24
Positioning the rabbeted drawer front in a dovetail fixture.

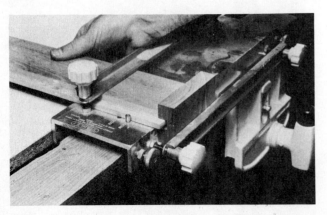

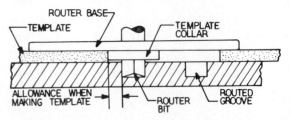

FIGURE 20-25
Make the opening in the template the size of the design plus twice the space between the bit and the collar.

ROUTING INLAYS

Veneer inlays add a great deal to the appearance of projects. Commercial inlays come in a wide variety of colors and patterns (Fig. 20-27). They are made

FIGURE 20-26
Routing a design with a template.

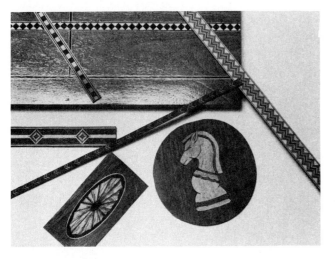

FIGURE 20-27
Inlays are available in many colors and patterns.

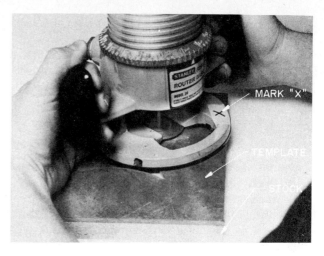

FIGURE 20-28
Routing an inlay to size using a template. Note the "X" on the base.

Remove the template and carefully slip a putty knife under the inlay to remove it from the plywood. Clamp the template on the finish-sanded stock and place the guide bushing on the template collar (Fig. 20-29). This guide bushing will automatically provide the proper spacing for the recess for the inlay. Set the depth of cut to be slightly less than the thickness of the veneer. Route all the material within the template opening. As with the first cut, keep the "X" on the router base to the outside of the work. Make certain that the bottom of the router area is smooth.

Remove the template and apply a thin coat of adhesive in the recess for the inlay. Glue the inlay in place with the paper side of the veneer facing up. After the adhesive has dried, carefully sand the face of the veneer even with the face of the stock.

FIGURE 20-29
Mounting the guide bushing on the template collar.

from pieces of veneer or dyed wood and are glued to a piece of paper to form a picture.

Once the inlay has been selected, lay out the desired outer circle, ellipse, or rectangle for the inlay on a piece of ¼-in. (6-mm) hardboard. This will serve as a template. Cut the template accurately and file the edges smooth.

With a few pieces of double-faced carpet tape, secure the inlay to a scrap piece of plywood. Center the opening in the template over the inlay and clamp it to the plywood. Using a template collar, trace carefully around the edge of the template (Fig. 20-28). To make the most accurate cut, place an "X" on the edge of the router base. As the router traces the template, always keep this "X" mark to the outside of the plywood. A plunge router with an ⅛-in. (3-mm) straight bit will work best to lower the bit easily into the inlay. The depth of cut should be set with the router bit just below the inlay.

ROUTING A DESIGN OR SIGNS

Because there are many decorative router bits, a broad variety of designs and signs can be produced. Either a duplicator or freehand techniques can be used to shape the desired pattern.

Duplicator

A commercial duplicator attachment has many stencils with cutouts of the alphabet and numbers. Custom stencils containing unique letter styles or patterns can be made out of hardboard. These stencils serve as a template that is clamped to the stylus table. After the stock is clamped to the machining table, a stylus is used to trace around the stencils. The letters, numbers, or patterns are then transferred to the board by the rotating bit (Fig. 20-30).

FIGURE 20-31
Routing a sign using freehand techniques.

FIGURE 20-30
Using a duplicator to produce a sign.

Freehand Techniques

The freehand technique requires first that the design be drawn on the stock. A router bit is installed and the depth adjusted. To keep the router from following the grain of the board, set the depth of cut to less than ¼ inch (6 mm). Start in the center of the pattern and route to the outside edge. It is best to introduce the bit into the stock at a corner of the design. If words are to be routed, start at beginning of the word and trace each letter (Fig. 20-31). Practice will be required to make smooth, even designs.

ROUTING A TAPER

Occasionally, a tapered shape is required such as for the recessed area in the bottom of a gun cabinet for the butts of the gun stocks. A template collar and

template are required as described in the section "Routing a Design or Recess." In addition, a rabbeted stop strip is attached to one side of the template to index the fixture on the stock (Fig. 20-32). The stop strip also elevates one side of the template. As the router is moved down the slope of the fixture, a recessed shape will be created.

To use the template, align the centerline drawn on the template with the centerline on the stock. Use two handscrews to secure the fixture to the stock. Using a spiral straight router bit, remove the material around the edge of the opening in the template. Make multiple passes to remove the rest of the material.

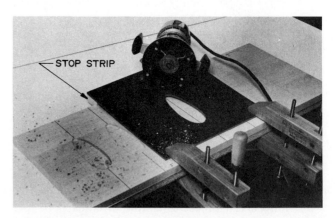

FIGURE 20-32
A slanted template will produce a routed taper.

ROUTER TABLES

The router table holds the router in a stationary vertical position. Stock can then be fed past the bit much like a shaper. The table can be either shop built or commercial in style (Fig. 20-33). Both require the router to be bolted to the underside of the

FIGURE 20-33
Commercial router table. (Courtesy of Porter-Cable Corporation.)

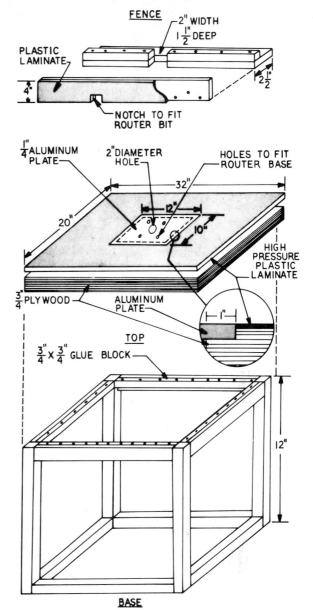

FIGURE 20-34
Shop-built router table.

FIGURE 20-35
Routing a through groove on a router table.

table. Cover the shop-built router table with high-pressure plastic laminate to provide a smooth, durable surface on which to guide the stock (Fig. 20-34). A tall fence should be constructed to support the stock.

After the bit has been installed, clamp the fence at the desired position on top of the table. Use featherboards and a push shoe to hold the stock against the table and fence (Fig. 20-35).

For stopped grooves or cuts that do not extend from end to end, make a layout mark at the beginning and ending of the cut. Draw an "X" on the best face of the board.

Place a pencil mark on the table at the beginning and ending of the cutting circle. Align the first layout on the stock with the far pencil mark on the table. Clamp a stop block against the leading end of the stock. Finish the setup by adjusting the bit to the proper height.

Turn on the router and place the stock against the first stop block (Fig. 20-36). The "X" mark should be facing out away from the table. Slowly lower the board onto the rotating cutter. After the face is against the table, feed the board forward. Once the leading end has reached the second stop block, pivot the stock off the bit. Run all identical pieces before removing the setup.

ROUTING RAISED PANEL DOORS

One of the newest router techniques is making raised panel doors. Refer to the section "Stuck Joinery" in Chapter 31 for details on how a shaper is used to make this style of doors. Many of the same concepts can be used with the router. With the avail-

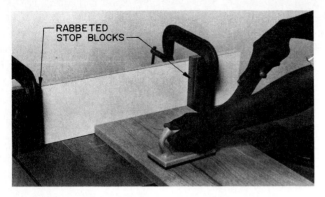

FIGURE 20-36
Routing a stopped groove with two stop blocks.

FIGURE 20-38
Coping the ends of the rails using a miter gauge.

ability of the specialized panel raiser, stile bit and cope bit doors can easily be constructed using the portable router (Fig. 20-37). These bits have $\frac{1}{2}$-in. (13-mm) shanks and usually are carbide tipped and contain ball-bearing pilots.

To make raised panel doors safely, you will need to use a $2\frac{1}{2}$-hp or larger router mounted to a router table. In addition, the router should have several rotational speeds available. Run the large bits on the slowest speed. Although the bits contain pilots, you will also need to install a fence on the router table. This fence will not only aid in guiding the stock, but also guard the cutter. Use a push stick and featherboards with each operation.

To make a raised panel door, work the stock to finish size. Check that the edges are jointed and the pieces are cut to accurate length. No single part should be narrower than 2 in. (51 mm) or shorter than 10 in. (254 mm). It may be necessary to combine individual parts into one wide, long piece. For example, if two $1\frac{3}{4}$-in. (44-mm)-wide rails are required, combine them into one $3\frac{3}{4}$-in. (95-mm)-wide

FIGURE 20-39
Routing the inside edge of the stiles and rails.

FIGURE 20-40
Producing the raised panel.

FIGURE 20-37
Router bits for making raised panel doors. (Courtesy of Freud Inc.)

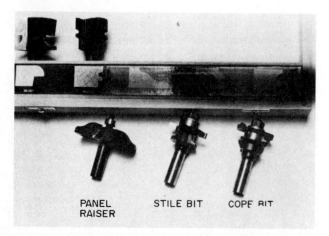

PANEL RAISER   STILE BIT   COPE BIT

board. Once routed, the stock can then be cut to finish size.

Mount the cope bit on the router first. Using the router table fence and a miter gauge, cope the two ends of each rail (Fig. 20-38). A backup board held against the trailing edge of the stock will greatly minimize grain tearout.

Next use the stile bit to route the inside edge of all pieces (Fig. 20-39). Check that the tongue of the coped end matches the groove in the edge. Once the stiles and rails are assembled, the faces of jointing pieces must be even.

The raised panel is produced with the panel raiser. Set the depth of the router bit so that the face of the raised panel is even with the faces of the stiles and rails. On dense woods or lower-horsepower routers, set the depth to one-half this amount. Route the ends first and then the edges (Fig. 20-40). The tongue of the raised panel should easily slide into the grooves of the stiles and rails.

21

PORTABLE
SANDERS

Most furniture, cabinets, and other wood products are sanded with portable sanders. These machines can easily be moved over the surface of a project and will rapidly remove any millmarks.

There are two major types of portable sanders. They include the portable belt sander and the portable pad sander. Both electric and pneumatic models are available. The *portable belt sander* is used primarily for sanding major millmarks and removing large amounts of material (Fig. 21-1). Woodworkers use the *portable pad sander* for finish sanding and sanding minor millmarks (Fig. 21-7).

PORTABLE BELT SANDERS

Portable belt sanders can be utilized to sand face-frames, flat panels, and other solid lumber parts. This sander can have either narrow or wide belts for sanding minor millmarks (Fig. 21-1).

Parts of the Belt Sander

The major parts of the belt sander are the motor, handles, pullies, and platen (Fig. 21-1). The *motor* provides power to turn the sanding belt. In the front and to the rear of the motor are the handles. The

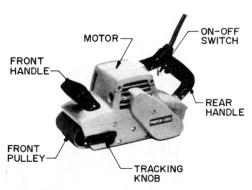

FIGURE 21-1
Major parts of the portable belt sander. (Courtesy of Porter-Cable Corporation.)

rear handle contains the *on-off* switch. Pulling in on the switch turns on the sander. The *front handle* is used to control the movement of the machine.

The belt is suspended between the power pulley and the front pulley. The belt is turned with the *power pulley* and is kept stretched tight with the pressure applied from the *front pulley*. To pull the front pulley back, use the *tension-release lever*. This will enable you to replace the belt. Between the two pullies is the *platen*. It provides a flat surface that the belt can run against.

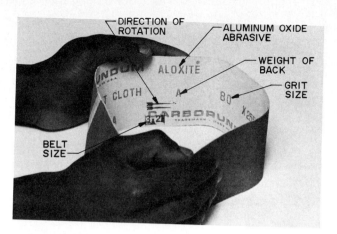

FIGURE 21-3
Refer to the inside of the belt for the belt size, grit size, type of abrasive, and direction of rotation.

PORTABLE SANDER SAFETY RULES

1. Unplug the power cord before changing the abrasive.
2. Clamp small pieces to sawhorses or a workbench.
3. Use both hands to hold the sander securely.
4. Keep the power cord away from the sanding area and sander.
5. Never set the sander down with the belt moving.
6. Check that the switch is off before plugging in the cord.

The *tracking knob* keeps the belt centered on the platen. By turning the knob, the belt can be moved from side to side.

Purchasing a Belt Sander

When purchasing a portable belt sander, the first consideration is the size. The size of the sander is determined by the length and width of the sanding belt. Sizes can range from 3×21 to 4×24 in. (76×533 to 102×610 mm). The larger the belt, the faster the belt will sand. Larger belts, however, cost more and require more strength to control.

A feature to consider when buying a sander is the dust bag attachment (Fig. 21-2). This accessory picks up any surplus sanding dust that is produced.

FIGURE 21-2
A dust bag attachment minimizes the sanding dust. (Courtesy of Porter-Cable Corporation.)

The dust bag is desirable when sanding large surfaces. It may, however, interfere with sanding small areas or inside projects.

Selecting the Sanding Belts

It is recommended that you have a wide selection of sanding belts from which to select. Be certain that the size of the belts fits the sander. You will be able to find this along with other information printed on the inside of the belt (Fig. 21-3). Aluminum oxide is

TABLE 21-1
Abrasives for Portable Belt Sanders

Application	Grit size	Abrasive
Removing paint, varnishes	60	Aluminum oxide
Rough glued-up panels, face frames, general rough sanding	80–100	Aluminum oxide
Removing minor defects, sanding planer marks, general smooth sanding	120	Aluminum oxide

generally used as the abrasive because of its ability to withstand the heat generated during sanding. Refer to Table 21-1 for specific grit sizes for each of your sanding operations.

Installing the Sanding Belt

To install the sanding belt, unplug the power cord. Pull back on the tension-release lever or with some models, manually push in on the front pulley. Remove the old belt and replace it with a new one. Be certain that the belt will rotate in the same direction as the printed arrow indicates on the back of the belt (Fig. 21-3).

After centering the belt on the platen, release the front pulley. Turn the sander over and hold it with the belt on top. Quickly turn the power on and off. The belt should remain centered on the platen. If it does not, turn the *tracking knob* a small amount (Fig. 21-4). Keep turning on the power and moving the tracking knob until the sanding belt stays centered.

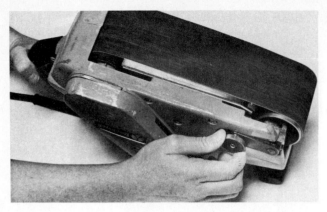

FIGURE 21-4
Tracking a sanding belt by turning the tracking knob.

Operating the Belt Sander

A great deal of damage can be done with the belt sander if it is not properly operated. Applying uneven pressure or using improper feeding techniques will cause the sander to dig rapidly into the wood. These sanding marks are very difficult to remove and will become apparent when the finish is applied.

To use the sander, select the proper grit size for your sanding job. Refer to Table 21-1 for the recommended grit size. Course belts will sand faster but will leave deep scratches. Finer grit belts will produce smaller scratches but may burnish the wood.

Clamp the stock securely to the benchtop. Because the sander is difficult to control, do not attempt to sand a vertical surface. Lay the piece flat on the workbench or sawhorses for best results. Position the sander flat on the stock and arrange the cord away from the path of the machine. Grip the handles firmly and turn on the sander. Start moving the sander immediately and use a sanding pattern as shown in Fig. 21-5. The strokes of the sander should be short, straight, and slightly overlapped. Always keep the sander moving with the grain and

FIGURE 21-5
Recommended pattern for guiding the belt sander.

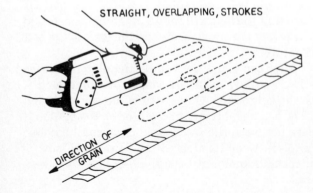

do not concentrate in one spot. This will produce a noticeable low area.

If the surface is large, divide the face into 24-in. (610-mm) squares. Sand each of these sections before moving onto the next. Because the sander cuts rapidly, be careful when sanding plywood and other veneered products. It is very easy to sand through the face and completely remove the face veneer.

Sanding Small Pieces

A portable belt sander can be clamped in a bench vise (Fig. 21-6). This allows small and irregular-shaped pieces to be sanded that are difficult to sand using conventional techniques. Cut wooden blocks to fit around the housing of the sander to prevent it from moving. Be careful not to get your hands close to the sanding belt.

FIGURE 21-6
Sanding small pieces by holding the sander in a bench vise.

FIGURE 21-7
Major parts of the portable pad sander. (Courtesy of Porter-Cable Corporation.)

PORTABLE PAD SANDERS

Portable pad sanders come in a variety of styles and sizes (Fig. 21-7). They are utilized primarily to finish sand projects before the finish is applied. Because of this some woodworkers call these machines *finish sanders*.

There are three different styles of pad sanders: vibrating, orbital, and straight-line (Fig. 21-8). The *vibrating sander* is the least expensive of the sanders, but places scratches across the grain. An *orbital sander* is the most popular and has the fastest sanding action. It does, however, produce small elliptical sanding scratches. The *straight-line sander* moves back and forth only, producing straight scratches. Although it is the slowest cutting of all sanders, it does produce the superior results of hand sanding.

FIGURE 21-9
Small sanders can be utilized to sand inside projects.

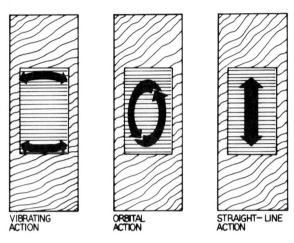

FIGURE 21-8
Pad sanders are either a vibrating, orbital, or straight-line style.

Parts of the Pad Sander

The major parts of a pad sander are the handles, motor, and sanding pad (Fig. 21-7). To use the sander, the *handles* are gripped by the operator. Some compact machines have the handle built into the motor housing (Fig. 21-9). This allows them to be used in small enclosed areas.

The *motor* frequently makes up the majority of the sander. It provides power to the sanding pad. Located under the motor is the *sanding pad*. It is generally covered with a soft rubber or felt. On each end of the pad are the *abrasive paper clips*. They are spring loaded and used to hold the abrasive paper on the pad.

Purchasing a Pad Sander

The major considerations when purchasing a pad sander are the sanding action of the pad and the size of the sander. As discussed earlier in this section, sanders are manufactured as either vibrating, orbital, or straight-line (Fig. 21-8). Each has its advantages. Select the one that is the most important to your woodworking.

The size of the pad sander is determined by the width and length of the pad. The most common sizes use either one-fourth, one-third, or one-half a sheet of abrasive paper. Select a large pad for sanding big surfaces. A smaller pad is desirable for sanding inside projects or vertical surfaces.

Another consideration when purchasing a sander is the number of strokes or *oscillations per minute*. They will range from 10,000 to over 20,000 oscillations per minute. The more strokes per minute, the faster the wood will be sanded.

Pad sanders are either powered by electricity or compressed air. The *electric* sanders operate on 110-V power. This is readily available and generally the most common form of power. A *pneumatic sander* runs with 60 to 76 lb of air pressure. These sanders are lighter in weight and do not overheat (Fig. 21-10). Although pneumatic sanders are more expensive, they generally last longer. Industry frequently utilizes this type of sander.

FIGURE 21-10
Pneumatic sanders are compact in size and run on compressed air.

Operating the Pad Sander

For most sanding operations, start with 100-grit abrasive paper. Follow this with 120- and then 150-grit paper. Do not skip a grit number or sanding scratches will remain in the wood. Most projects that are to receive a transparent finish can be finish sanded with 180-grit paper.

To sand a surface with a pad sander, place the stock on a workbench. If the piece will be exposed on both faces, lay the board on a blanket or another protective pad. Place the sander flat on surface and move the machine over the entire area. A vibrating and orbital sander can be moved in any direction. The straight-line sander must be moved only with the grain.

Allow the weight of the sander to do the sanding. Pressing down on the machine will produce a low spot and rapidly wear out the sander. If you concentrate the sanding on a dent or other defect, a noticeable low spot will also be sanded. Be certain to cover the entire surface equally.

22

LEMON SPLINERS

One of the newest forms of joinery requires the use of a lemon spliner (Fig. 22-1). This machine uses a sawblade type cutter to cut a short, circular kerf. In this groove is placed an elliptical spline which is used to reinforce miters, butt joints, and other assemblies (Fig. 22-2). Entire cabinets and pieces of furniture can be put together with this machine. It can take the place of dowels, mortise and tenons, and dados.

The lemon spliner is considered to be a very fast and accurate machine. It has the advantage over other forms of jointery because the parts can slide into alignment. The adjustment is made by cutting the kerfs slightly longer and deeper than the spline. This extra space allows the pieces to slide up to $\frac{1}{8}$ in. (3 mm).

PARTS OF THE LEMON SPLINER

The major parts of the lemon spliner are the motor, handle, and base (Fig. 22-1). The high-speed *motor* provides power to the 4-in. (102-mm)-diameter carbide-tipped cutter. Located below the motor is the *sliding base*. It allows the cutter to be moved into the stock. On the front of the base is the *indexing mark*. This mark indicates the center of the cutter. When

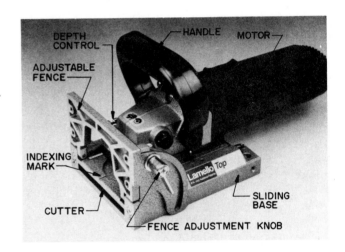

FIGURE 22-1
Major parts of the lemon spliner. (Courtesy of Colonial Saw.)

not being plunged into the work, the base is spring loaded and held in the forward position to keep from exposing the cutter. Attached to the base is the *adjustable fence*. It is tilted to the desired angle to establish the angle at which the cutter enters the stock. Located to the side of the base is the *depth control*. The depth control has three settings, one for

221

LEMON SPLINER SAFETY RULES

1. Unplug the power cord before changing the cutter.
2. Before cutting small pieces, clamp them to saw-horses or a workbench.
3. Keep the power cord away from the cutter and splining area.
4. Use both hands to hold the spliner securely.
5. Hands should come no closer than 4 in. (102 mm) to the cutter.
6. Keep from reaching under the stock while cutting.
7. Do not set the spliner down until the cutter stops turning.

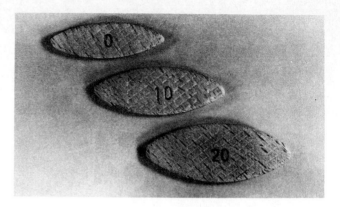

FIGURE 22-3
There are three sizes of compressed beech splines.

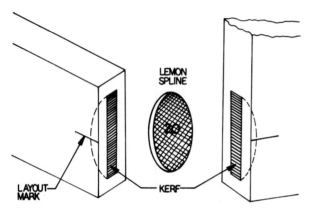

FIGURE 22-2
The lemon spline is inserted into the kerfs to reinforce the joint.

each size of splines. The *handle* is utilized to locate and control the spliner.

SPLINES

The splines, biscuits, or plates as they are sometimes called are made from die-cut compressed beech. The grain runs diagonally to the length of the spline. Once glue comes in contact with this compressed beech, it swells and locks it in the small circular kerf. This action occurs rapidly, so you must be ready to assemble your project quickly.

There are three sizes of splines from which to select (Fig. 22-3). They are numbered from smallest to largest: 1, 10, and 20. All of the plates are of the same thickness, but do vary in width and length. The dimensions of number 0 splines are $\frac{5}{8}$ in. wide by $1\frac{3}{4}$ in. long. A number 10 spline is $\frac{3}{4}$ in. wide by $2\frac{1}{8}$ in. long. Number 20 splines are 1 in. wide and $2\frac{1}{2}$ inches long. Use as large a spline as the stock will allow without the kerf breaking through the opposite side. Turn the depth stop to the same number as the number of the spline. If you are using a number 20 spline, for example, set the depth stop to 20.

The proper spacing between the splines depends on the application. In most cases the closer the

splines, the stronger the joint. As a general rule, however, place 5 in. (127 mm) between the centerlines of each spline.

SPLINING AN EDGE-TO-EDGE JOINT

To operate the lemon spliner, first cut the stock to exact size. Be certain that the cuts are made square and true. Any gaps between the mating pieces will be obvious when the parts are assembled.

Next dry assemble the parts and mark the center of each spline on the face of each piece (Fig. 22-2). In most applications, 5-in. (127-mm) centers provide adequate reinforcement. The layout line should extend onto each mating piece.

Place the stock flat against a true surface. A large piece of plywood or particleboard can be used for a work surface. Position the fence against the stock and center the cutter index mark on the first layout line (Fig. 22-4). Turn on the motor and

FIGURE 22-4
Cutting a groove by aligning the index mark on the layout mark.

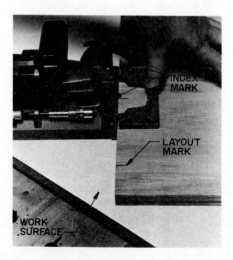

plunge the cutter into stock. Continue pushing the motor forward until the motor has reached the end of the travel for the base. Allow the motor to return to its original position. Continue cutting all the kerfs by following the same procedure. One-half of the elliptical groove is cut in each mating part.

After all the kerfs have been cut, apply glue in each of the kerfs. A special designed glue bottle will spread an even coat of adhesive along the length of the kerf (Fig. 22-5). Since the compressed splines expand rapidly, you must work fast. Slide a spline into one side of each joint and utilize standard assembly techniques. Because the compressed beech in the spline expands rapidly, however, it is only necessary to apply clamp pressure for 10 minutes.

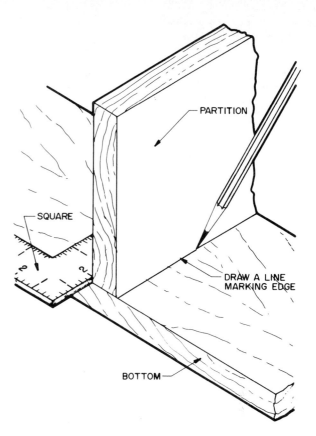

FIGURE 22-6
Laying out the position of the partition for a butt joint.

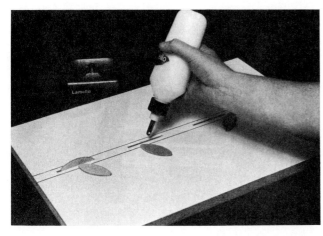

FIGURE 22-5
The special glue bottle will apply the adhesive evenly in the kerfs.

SPLINING A BUTT JOINT

Installing splines in a butt joint requires the pieces to be cut to exact size. Align the parts in their final position. Draw a line along one edge to lay out the position of the parts (Fig. 22-6). After determining the size of the splines, mark the desired centers of each spline. Either measure each center or use a template to locate the position of the splines (Fig. 22-7).

To make the kerfs for the splines, place the second piece along the layout line to serve as a guide for the lemon spliner (Fig. 22-8). Be careful that this guide board does not move or the kerfs will not be cut correctly. Cut each of the kerfs by placing the base of the spliner against the stock (Fig. 22-8). Next, position the fence in the 180° setting and cut the kerfs in the second piece (Fig. 22-9). The fence is kept flat against the face of the board. After all the kerfs have been made, the parts can be assembled.

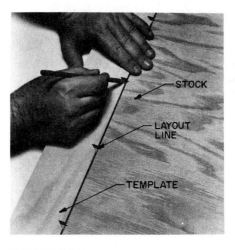

FIGURE 22-7
Drawing the centerlines for the splines.

SPLINING MITERS

The lemon spliner is an excellent machine for reinforcing miters. To make the grooves for the lemon splines, cut the miters to the desired angle. Select the largest spline size that will not break through the outside surface. If the contact area between the

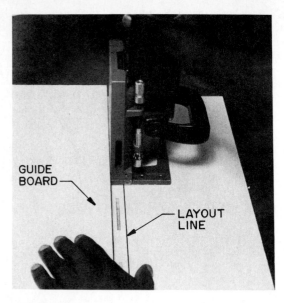

FIGURE 22-8
Splining the face of a board using the second piece as a guide.

FIGURE 22-9
Splining the end of a board with the fence in a 180° setting. (Courtesy of Colonial Saw.)

adjoining boards is large, use two or more splines. Thick material can be reinforced by stacking splines on top of one another (Fig. 22-10).

If a bevel has been cut along one edge, the adjustable fence needs to be set to the correct angle

(Fig. 22-11). Adjust the fence to position the cutter 90° to the beveled surface. Place the fence against the stock. Make certain that the fence is kept tight against the face of the stock before turning on the machine. Cut all kerfs and assemble the miters.

FIGURE 22-10
Use two splines on thick material for maximum support. (Courtesy of Colonial Saw.)

FIGURE 22-11
Splining a miter by adjusting the fence. (Courtesy of Colonial Saw.)

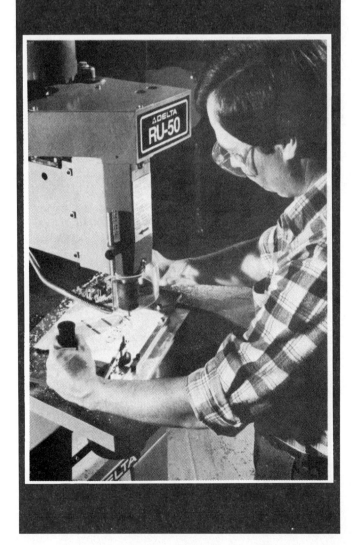

PART **5**

Stationary Power Tools

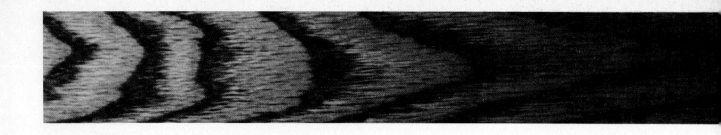

23

TABLE SAWS

In the opinion of most woodworkers, the table saw is the most basic and essential stationary power tool (Fig. 23-1). Most shops, both large and small, do have at least one of these machines. It is very versatile and capable of performing a broad variety of cuts. Although it is one of the best machines for ripping boards, the table saw can precisely crosscut, dado and make specialty cuts.

PARTS OF THE TABLE SAW

The major parts of the table saw include the table, miter gauge, rip fence, saw guard, and base (Fig. 23-1). Stock is placed against the *table*. It is usually a heavy casting which contains two *miter gauge grooves,* an opening for the saw blade, and the *rip fence guide rails*. Mounted on the table is the miter gauge, rip fence, throat plate, and saw guard. The *miter gauge* is used for crosscutting operations by sliding in one of the miter gauge grooves. The *rip fence* is used for ripping operations and is secured to the table by locking on the rip fence guide rails. In the middle of the table is the *throat plate*. It is usu-

ally made of metal and contains a slot through which the blade extends.

The *saw guard* consists of the blade guard, splitter, and antikickback pawls (Fig. 23-2). The blade guard covers the raised blade and rides on top of the stock. To keep the saw kerf open the splitter is positioned in line with the blade. The antikickback pawls ride on top of the stock and dig into the board if there is a kickback.

Located in the base are the ways and trunnions. The *ways* raise the blade when the *height adjustment handwheel* is turned (Fig. 23-3). To lock the blade at a specific height, tighten the *locking knob*. The *trunnion* tilts the blade when the *tilting handwheel* is turned. A *tilting gauge* on the front of the base indicates the approximate angle at which the blade is tilted. To lock the angle of the blade into position, tighten its *locking knob*.

The treaded shaft located inside the throat plate area is the *saw arbor* (Fig. 23-3). The saw blade is mounted on this arbor along with the stabilizing washer and arbor nut. Arbors range in diameter from $\frac{5}{8}$ to over 1 in. (16 to 25 mm). The arbor size must be included when ordering table saw tooling.

TABLE SAW SAFETY RULES

1. Your hands should be kept at least 4 in. (102 mm) from the blade.
2. The saw blade should project no more than ¼ in. (6 mm) above the stock to be cut.
3. When cutting stock, stand to the left or right side of the saw blade rather than directly behind it.
4. Avoid reaching over the saw blade at all times and use a guard and featherboards when possible.
5. Always use the miter gauge when crosscutting stock and the rip fence when ripping.
6. When crosscutting stock, there must be at least 6 in. (152 mm) of material against the miter gauge.
7. When crosscutting, material must be flat on the table and held firmly against the miter gauge.
8. When ripping, stock must be held flat on the table and firmly against the rip fence.
9. Use a push stick when ripping stock that has less than 6 in. (152 mm) of material between the rip fence and the blade.
10. Stock to be ripped must have at least ⅜ in. (5 mm) of material between the rip fence and the blade.
11. Stock to be ripped must be at least 10 in. (254 mm) long.
12. Cutting of cylindrical stock requires the use of special jigs and holding devices.

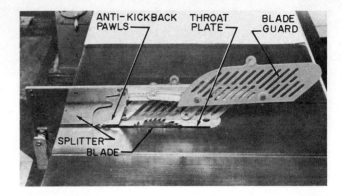

FIGURE 23-2
The saw guard contains the blade guard, splitter, and antikickback pawls.

common. It will use a 10-in. (254-mm) and smaller saw blade. The larger the saw blade, the thicker the board can be cut. A 10-in. (254-mm) saw can typically saw a 3⅛-in. (79-mm)-thick board in the 90° position.

Since it may be necessary to make heavy cuts, the motor size is also important. Most medium-size cuts can be made with a 1½-hp motor. If thicker material is to be machined or if the saw is to be used on a continuous basis, specify at least a 3-hp or larger motor.

A good-quality saw will also have a slotted miter gauge and micro-adjustment for the rip fence. The *slotted miter gauge* can be pulled beyond the edge of the table without it falling to the floor (Fig. 23-4). This also allows wider material to be crosscut. A *micro-adjustment* knob moves the fence in small

PURCHASING A TABLE SAW

In purchasing a table saw, first consider the size. The size is determined by the largest-diameter saw blade that can safely be mounted on the arbor. Although sizes as large as 18 in. (457 mm) are manufactured, the 10-in. (254-mm) table saw is the most

FIGURE 23-1
Major parts to the table saw. (Courtesy of Oliver Machinery Company.)

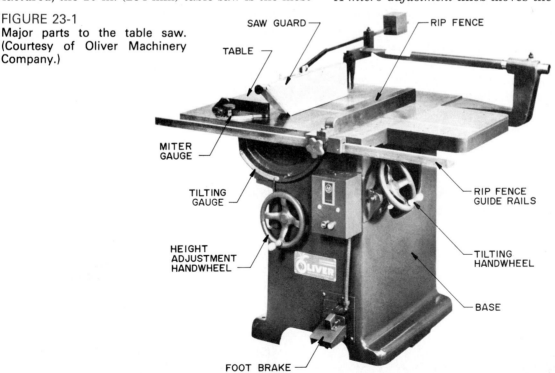

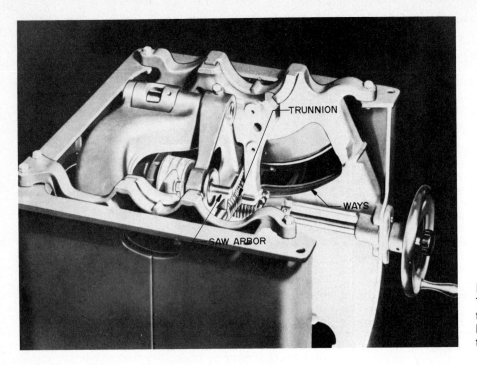

FIGURE 23-3
The ways raise the blade while the trunnion allows the blade to be angled. (Courtesy of Delta International Machinery Corp.)

amounts. This is particularly important when positioning the fence for a precise cut.

SELECTING THE TABLE SAW TOOLING

There are many different types of tooling which can be selected for use on the table saw. Some of them include saw blades, dado heads, and molding heads. Each of these types of tooling is available in a wide variety of styles.

Saw blades are made of carbon steel, high-speed steel, or have steel bodies with tungsten carbide tips. The carbon steel blades are the least expensive but dull rapidly. High-speed steel blades are

FIGURE 23-4
A slotted miter gauge allows wide material to be crosscut without the miter gauge falling to the floor.

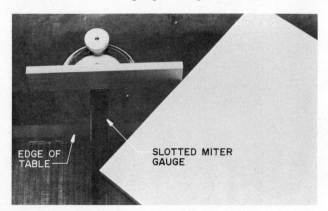

EDGE OF TABLE

SLOTTED MITER GAUGE

better than carbon steel and stay sharp longer. Carbide-tipped blades, however, have become the most popular style of blade today. This is because they stay sharp at least five times longer and can easily cut abrasive materials such as tempered hardboard, particleboard, and even high-pressure plastic laminates. Because the carbide material is so hard, a diamond grinding wheel is required to sharpen the blade.

Both *carbon and high-speed steel blades* are available in five tooth styles (Fig. 23-5). They are as follows:

> *Crosscut blades* have the smallest teeth and are designed to cut across the wood fibers. They will give the cleanest cut but require the slowest feed rate.
>
> *Rip blades* have the largest teeth that are designed to cut with the grain. Rip teeth are filed at a right angle to the face. These blunt chisel-shaped teeth, along with the large gullets, allow a fast feed speed. A rough cut, however, is produced.
>
> *Rough-cut combination blades* have teeth with the shape of a rip blade but have the top edges sharpened at an angle. This gives a smoother cut but with a fast feed speed.
>
> *Four-tooth combination blades* are best for general-purpose cabinet and furniture work. Each of the sets of four crosscut teeth cleanly sever the wood fibers, while the one raker tooth digs the sawdust out of the saw kerf.

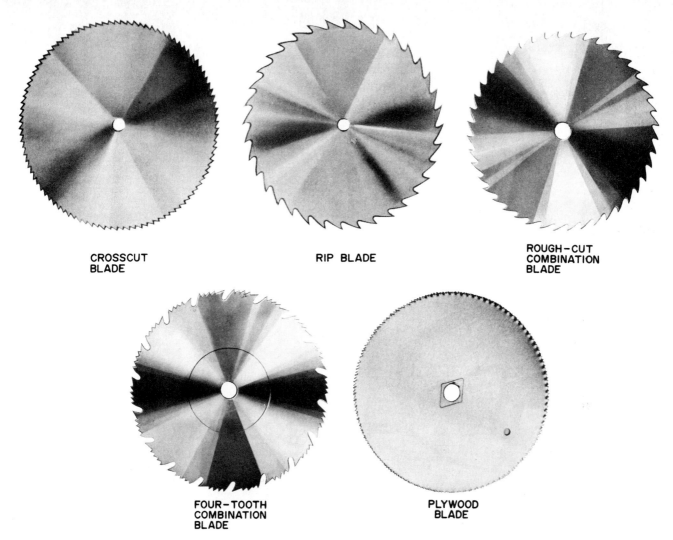

CROSSCUT BLADE

RIP BLADE

ROUGH-CUT COMBINATION BLADE

FOUR-TOOTH COMBINATION BLADE

PLYWOOD BLADE

FIGURE 23-5
Common carbon and high-speed steel blades. (Courtesy of Delta International Machinery Corp.)

Specialty blades are designed to cut a specific type of material. A plywood blade, for example, has very small teeth designed to cut plywood. It provides a splinter-free cut in hardwood plywood.

Carbide-tipped blades are sold in four major blade styles (Fig. 23-6). Although blade manufacturers commonly use their own brand names, they are as follows:

Alternate top bevel (ATB) blades are made with crosscut teeth. They give one of the smoothest cuts across the grain. As with all carbide-tipped blades, an ATB can be purchased with a varying number of teeth. The more teeth a blade has, the smoother the cut.

Flat top grind blades have rip teeth and are designed for cutting with the grain. When only this style of tooth is used, it will generally be used on an industrial ripping machine. A flat top grind tooth style however may be utilized with other teeth to assist with cleaning out the saw kerf.

Combination rip and crosscut blades have both alternate top and flat top grind teeth. The wood fibers are first sheared with the alternate top bevel teeth and then the kerf is cleaned out with the flat top grind tooth. It is the ideal blade for table saws that are required to perform general-purpose cutting.

Triple chip grind blades are specialty carbide-tipped blades designed for cutting aluminum and certain plastics. The triple chip grind teeth remove the majority of the material in the kerf.

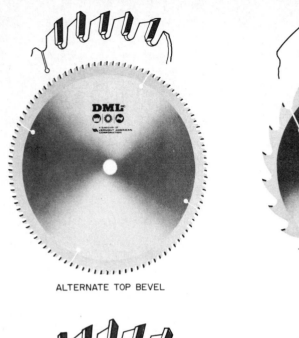

ALTERNATE TOP BEVEL

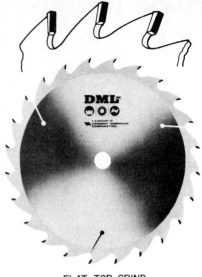

FLAT TOP GRIND

COMBINATION RIP & CROSSCUT

TRIPLE CHIP GRIND

FIGURE 23-6
Common carbide-tipped blades. (Courtesy of DML, Inc.)

The flat top grind then cuts chips on both sides of the saw kerf.

To provide clearance for the saw blade, there must be some type of *blade set* (Fig. 23-7). As the blade turns, the teeth overhanging the body of the blade create a groove or *saw kerf*. The saw kerf needs to be wider than the thickness of the blade. If the proper amount of set is not present, the sides of the blade will rub the wood, creating friction, and the blade will overheat. This will burn the wood and cause a kickback. It could also warp the blade, which must then be discarded.

With steel blades, there are three forms of set: spring, swaged, and hollow ground (Fig. 23-7).

Spring set has every other tooth bent to the left. The remaining teeth are bent to the right. *Swaged set* is rarely used. It has the tip of each tooth flared on both sides. Swaged set is utilized on the inside chippers of a dado head. *Hollow-ground* blades develop body clearance by having a small amount of spring set and a tapered body. The thin, tapered body provides a narrow saw kerf which reduces waste. The hub, however, limits the depth of cut; a four-tooth combination tooth style with a hollow-ground body is called a *planer blade*.

Carbide-tipped blades develop body clearance through the *carbide inserts* overhanging the body. The carbide is usually wider than the body. Even though there is body clearance on this type of blade,

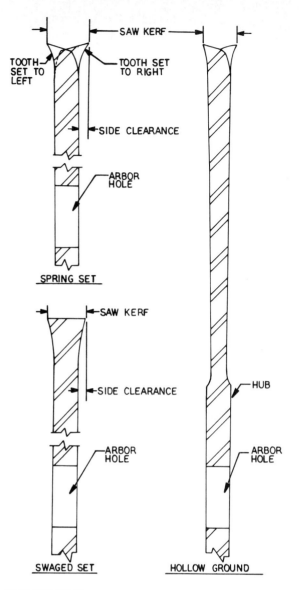

FIGURE 23-7
Body clearance is developed by spring set, swaged set, or having a hollow-ground body.

FIGURE 23-8
Adjustable dado. Note the width markings on the side of the cutting tool. (Courtesy of Delta International Machinery Corp.)

pitch and resin will still accumulate on the sides of the body. Keep the blade clean with oven cleaner or a solvent to prevent burning of the stock.

Dado heads are another major cutting tool utilized by the table saw. An 8-in. (203-mm) head will make most cuts. The larger the diameter, the deeper the cut it can make. There are two major styles: adjustable and standard. An *adjustable dado head* is a one-piece unit with graduated measurements spaced around the perimeter (Fig. 23-8). The outside sheaves are turned until the desired width of dado is aligned with the indicator mark. This method of width adjustment makes it easy to set the head to the exact dimension.

The *standard dado head* is more common and contains several parts (Fig. 23-9). The outside of the dado is made by the two *outside cutters*. Each is $\frac{1}{8}$ in. (3 mm) wide. To make wider dados, a variety of *inside chippers* are provided with the head. Most sets will contain one $\frac{1}{16}$-in. (2-mm) and four $\frac{1}{8}$-in. (3-mm) chippers. Larger dado heads may also have $\frac{1}{4}$-in. (6-mm) and $\frac{1}{2}$-in. (13-mm) wide inside chippers. The outside cutters are usually used in combination with the inside chippers to produce the desired dado. The standard dado head is sold in both high-speed and carbide-tipped varieties.

To make shaper-type cuts, a *molding head* can be used (Fig. 23-10). It contains a solid body and a set of three replaceable cutters. Allen setscrews hold the knives into the head. As many as 40 different patterns of knives are available.

FIGURE 23-9
A standard dado head contains outside cutters and inside clippers. (Courtesy of Delta International Machinery Corp.)

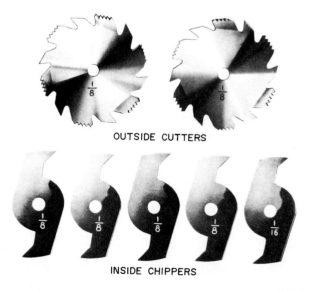

OUTSIDE CUTTERS

INSIDE CHIPPERS

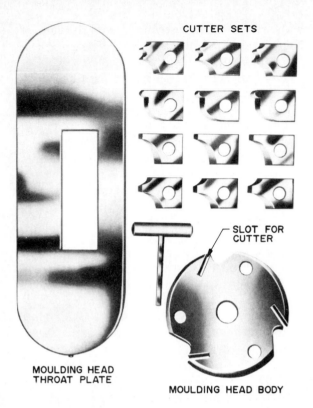

CUTTER SETS

SLOT FOR CUTTER

MOULDING HEAD THROAT PLATE

MOULDING HEAD BODY

FIGURE 23-10
A molding head contains a body and set of three identical knives. There are many knife patterns available. (Courtesy of Delta International Machinery Corp.)

INSTALLING THE SAW BLADE

After you have selected the desired blade, disconnect the power. Remove the throat plate and raise the blade. Holding a piece of scrap material against the front edge of the blade, place the arbor wrench on the arbor nut (Fig. 23-11). Pull the wrench forward in the same direction the teeth are pointing. Finish removing the arbor nut by placing your finger on the end of the arbor. Unscrew the nut onto your finger.

FIGURE 23-11
To remove a blade, pull the arbor wrench in the direction the teeth are pointing.

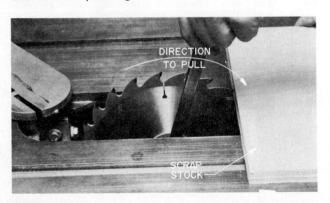

DIRECTION TO PULL

SCRAP STOCK

Holding your finger on the end of the arbor will prevent the nut from dropping to the floor. Remove the stablizing washer and blade. Do not place the blade on the saw table. Make certain that the blade is stored in a safe place where it will not come in contact with other metal objects.

Install the new blade with the teeth pointing forward and in the same direction as the rotation. The brand name of the manufacturer should be facing out and up. This will assure that the blade will rotate in a true circle. Replace the stablizing washer and hand tighten the arbor nut. Placing the scrap piece back against the blade, tighten the nut with the arbor wrench. Reposition the throat plate and rotate the blade by hand. Check that the splitter of the guard is immediately behind the blade with a straightedge. Reconnect the power.

SETTING UP THE TABLE SAW

After the saw blade has been installed and the guard checked for proper operation, the stock can be cut. Start the setup by placing the thickest board on the table next to the blade. Adjust the height of the blade so that it is approximately $\frac{1}{4}$ in. (6 mm) above the top surface of the board.

Next decide whether the miter gauge or the rip fence is to be used to guide the stock past the blade. Never cut freehand on the saw. In most cases, when cutting solid wood across the grain, use the miter gauge. This is called a *crosscutting operation*. When

FIGURE 23-12
Proper body position for operating the saw.

cutting solid wood with the grain and when cutting panel materials, use the rip fence. This is called a *ripping operation*. Be certain that the board is larger than the minimum dimensions given for either crosscutting or ripping.

After turning on the power, slowly feed the board forward. Your hands must never come any closer to the blade than 4 in. (102 mm). Do not stand directly in line with the blade because sometimes the wood is kicked back toward the operator. Position your body either to the left or right of the blade (Fig. 23-12). Use a push stick, push block, and featherboards whenever the operation allows.

CROSSCUTTING

Crosscutting on the table saw usually requires the use of a miter gauge to saw across the grain. The board must be at least 10 in. (254 mm) long with a minimum of 6 in. (152 mm) in contact with the miter gauge. The face against the table and the edge against the gauge must be straight. To keep the stock from slipping, screw an abrasive-covered board to the front of the miter gauge (Fig. 23-13).

To cut a board to length, move the rip fence to the far right of the saw. Next, check that the miter gauge is 90° to the blade. The fastest method to check the gauge setting is to turn over the miter gauge (Fig. 23-14). Place it back in the miter gauge slot and slide it against the rip fence rail. There should be no space between the rail and the miter gauge. With a square, also check that the blade is 90° to the table. Mark the point at which the stock is to be cut with a sharply drawn vee mark.

After adjusting the height of the blade, lower the guard. Although the miter gauge can be used on either side of the blade, most operators will prefer to place it in the slot to the left. Position the stock against the abrasive-covered board. Align the vee-

FIGURE 23-13
Screw a board to the front of the miter gauge. A piece of abrasive paper has been laminated to the face of the board.

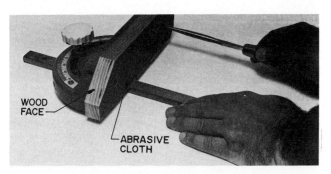

WOOD FACE

ABRASIVE CLOTH

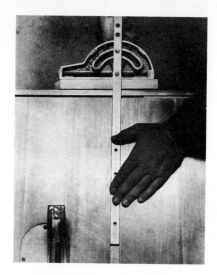

FIGURE 23-14
Squaring the miter gauge off of the front of the saw.

FIGURE 23-15
Crosscutting a board with the miter gauge.

shaped layout mark with the saw tooth set to the left. Turn on the power. Hold the stock with the left hand and push the miter gauge forward with the right hand (Fig. 23-15). Feed the stock forward until it completely clears the saw blade. Use a slow but smooth feed rate.

Once the stock reaches the far side of the blade, slide the board away from the blade. Pull the gauge back to the beginning position. Turn off the power and allow the blade to stop before removing any scrap material.

CROSSCUTTING IDENTICAL LENGTHS

When several parts of the same length are required, use a clearance block, stop rod, or stop block.

Clearance Block

A clearance block is a short planed board clamped against the fence. Measure the desired length between the face of this board and the saw tooth set to the right (Fig. 23-16). Lock the rip fence to the table. Move the clearance blocks back to the front of the fence and clamp it into position. The front end of the clearance block must be well in front of the blade.

Placing the miter gauge in the slot to the left, square the first end of each board. Position the squared end of the stock against the clearance block. Be careful not to bump the block (Fig. 23-17). Crosscut the stock. Move the board completely past the blade and remove it from the table. Pull the miter gauge back and cut the next piece. For short pieces, keep the miter gauge in the left miter gauge slot. Turn off the power and frequently remove the parts left between the blade and rip fence.

Stop Rod

The stop rod is an accessory that is sold with the saw (Fig. 23-18). It is attached to the miter gauge. To use the stop rod, square the first end of all the stock. Mark the first board to length. Align the mark with the path of the saw blade. Adjust the end of the stop rod against the squared end of the stock. This will gauge the length of the remaining pieces. Cut the pieces to length.

Stop Block

The stop block method requires an auxiliary fence to be screwed to the miter gauge (Fig. 23-19). Square the first end of each piece. Measure the length on the first board and align this mark with the saw blade. Clamp a stock block against the squared end. Cut

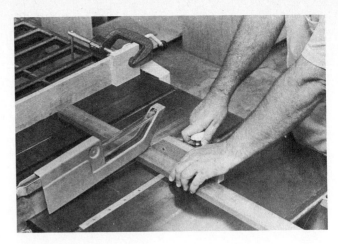

FIGURE 23-17
A clearance block allows duplicate pieces to be cut without binding the blade.

FIGURE 23-18
Cutting stock to length using a stop rod.

FIGURE 23-16
Measuring the desired length between the blade and clearance block.

FIGURE 23-19
Using a stop block to crosscut stock to length.

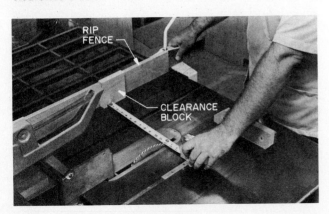

the first piece and check the length. The remaining stock can then be cut to length.

MITERING

Miters are used to make picture frames and other joints where end grain cannot be exposed. These joints are usually cut using crosscutting techniques.

Plain Miters

The first step in cutting a plain miter is determining the angle of the cut. Use the formula 90° − (180° ÷ number of sides in the piece). For example, the angle of a five-sided project would be calculated as follows:

$$180° ÷ 5 \text{ sides} = 36°$$
$$90° − 36° = 54°$$

The angle would be set at 54°.

Plain miters can be cut by using either the miter gauge or a mitering fixture. To use a miter gauge, set the desired angle on the angle gauge. If two miter gauges are available, angle one gauge to the left and the other to the right.

Miter one end of each piece. After cutting the first part, check the angle for accuracy with a protractor. To cut the remaining ends, attach to this gauge a long abrasive-covered auxiliary fence. Use the second miter gauge or angle the first gauge in the opposite direction.

Measure the desired length on one of the pieces of stock. Align the layout line with the tooth set closest to the miter gauge. Clamp a stop block against the mitered end and cut the first piece (Fig.

FIGURE 23-20
Mitering stock with a stop block attached to the auxiliary fence.

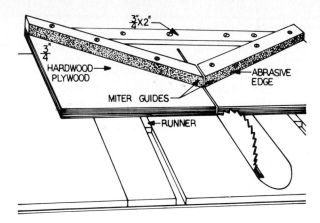

FIGURE 23-21
Construction of a sliding table mitering fixture.

23-20). Check that the part is to the desired length. After making any necessary adjustments, cut the remaining pieces.

Plain miters can also be cut with a sliding table mitering fixture (Fig. 23-21). The angle of the two fences has already been established on the auxiliary table. This makes the setup very fast and accurate. Most mitering fixtures are designed to make 45° miters. The guide rails on the bottom of the auxiliary table slide in the miter gauge grooves. Each piece is first cut using the left fence. The stock is then switched to the right fence and the second miter cut.

Compound Miters

Compound miters require that both the miter gauge and the blade be angled. Use Table 23-1 to establish the angles. Cut two mating pieces to check the accuracy of the joint. To provide a more finished appearance, bevel the top and bottom edges. The bevel will be the complementary angle of the angle of the sides.

Slip Feather Miters

A *slip feather* is a triangular piece that is used for reinforcement of the outside corner of a plain miter (Fig. 23-22). It exposes the face grain of the mitered frame to the face grain of the slip feather. This produces a very strong glue joint. The grain of the slip feather must run at a right angle to the miter joint. Ideally, it should be made from the same species of wood as the frame.

To make a slip feather miter, cut the frame pieces to size and assemble the frame using only adhesive. After the adhesive has dried, use a slip feather fixture to cut a groove across the corner of each miter.

TABLE 23-1
Recommended Angles for Cutting Compound Miters

Tilt of work	Equivalent taper per inch	Four-sided butt		Four-sided miter		Six-sided miter		Eight-sided miter	
		Bevel (deg)	Miter (deg)	Bevel (deg)	Miter (deg)	Bevel (deg)	Miter (deg)	Bevel (deg)	Miter (deg)
5	0.087	½	85	44¾	85	29¾	87½	22¼	88
10	0.176	1½	80¼	44¼	80¼	29½	84½	22	86
15	0.268	3¾	75½	43¼	75½	29	81¾	21½	84
20	0.364	6¼	71¼	41¾	71¼	28¼	79	21	82
25	0.466	10	67	40	67	27¼	76½	20¼	80
30	0.577	14½	63½	37¾	63½	26	74	19½	78¼
35	0.700	19½	60¼	35½	60¼	24½	71¾	18¼	76¾
40	0.839	24½	57¼	32½	57¼	22¾	69¾	17	75
45	1.000	30	54¾	30	54¾	21	67¾	15¾	73¾
50	1.19	36	52½	27	52½	19	66¼	14½	72½
55	1.43	42	50¾	24	50¾	16¾	64¾	12½	71¼
60	1.73	48	49	21	49	14½	63½	11	70¼

The fixture can be constructed from a piece of hardwood plywood (Fig. 23-23). To the back of this plywood, attach a cradle that will fit over the top of the rip fence. Attach two angled fences to the face of the plywood. They should each form a 45° angle with the saw table. A 90° angle is formed by the two fences on the plywood.

Carefully place the frame against the plywood back and on top of the fences. Secure the frame to the fixture with clamps. Adjust the blade height to cut into the frame equal to the width of the feather. Turn on the power and slide the fixture past the blade (Fig. 23-24). The groove will be made in the frame. If a wider groove is needed, the two outside

FIGURE 23-22
A slip feather or spline can be utilized to reinforce a miter.

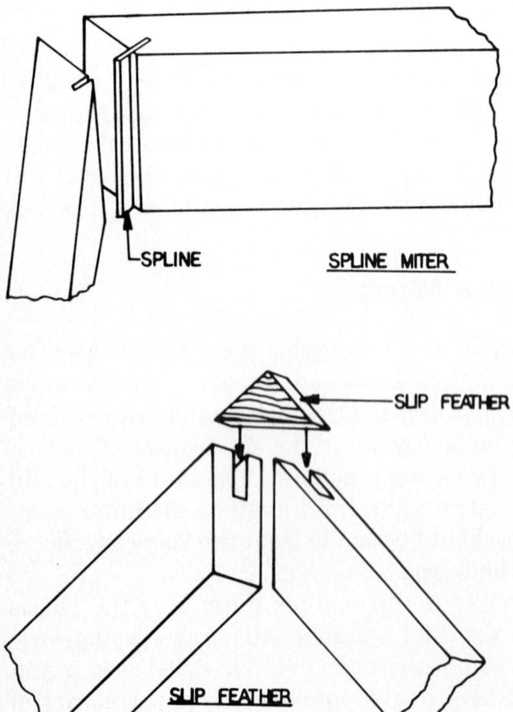
SPLINE
SPLINE MITER
SLIP FEATHER
SLIP FEATHER

FIGURE 23-23
Fixture for cutting a slip feather.

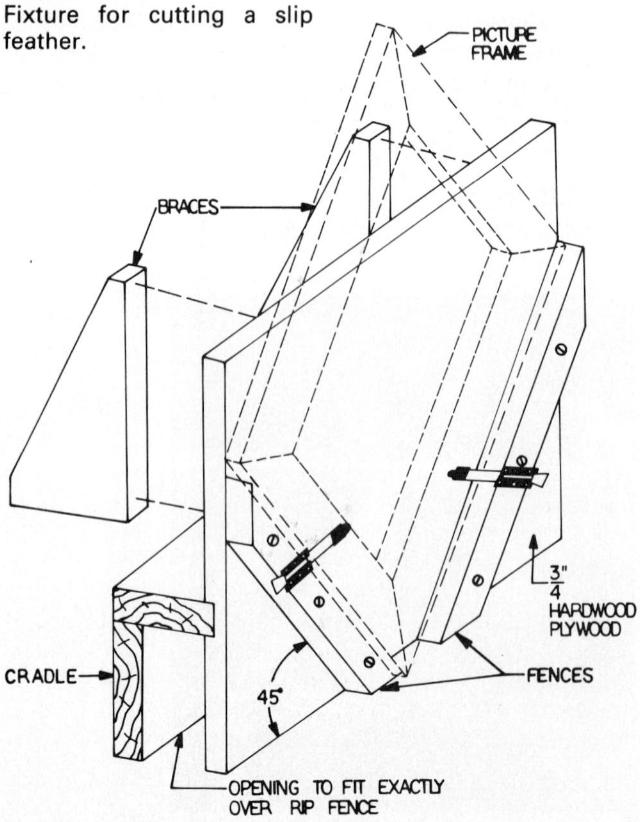
PICTURE FRAME
BRACES
3"/4 HARDWOOD PLYWOOD
FENCES
CRADLE
45°
OPENING TO FIT EXACTLY OVER RIP FENCE

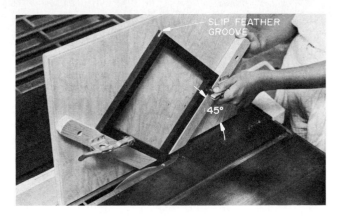

FIGURE 23-24
Cutting the groove for a slip feather using a fixture. The guard has been removed for demonstration purposes only.

cutters from the dado head can be used instead of a blade.

Cut rectangular pieces to fit into the grooves. This will serve as the slip feather. Wait until the adhesive dries and then trim the feathers flush with the sides of the frame. Finish by sanding the entire frame. The grain of the feathers should run parallel with the bottom of the triangle.

Spline Miters

Spline miters use rectangular pieces to reinforce a plain miter joint (Fig. 23-25). Unlike the slip feather, the spline extends along the entire edge or end of the miter. One-eighth-inch (3-mm) plywood will make excellent spline material.

Lay out the location of the spline on one piece. For spline miters that are cut along the edge of the stock, position the groove toward the heel of the miter. This will allow a wider spline and a stronger

FIGURE 23-25
Cutting the groove for a spline. The guard has been removed for demonstration purposes only.

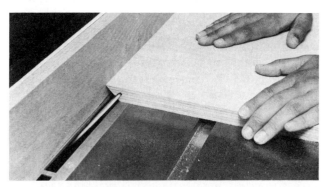

joint. Cut the groove for the spline by angling the blade so that it forms a 90° angle with the face of the miter (Fig. 23-25). Guide the toe of the miter along the rip fence.

For splines that are placed along the end of the stock, a fixture will be needed (Fig. 23-26). Cut each piece individually. The end of the miter should be positioned flat against the saw table. Keep the face of each part facing out away from the fixture. The spline should have its grain perpendicular to its long edge.

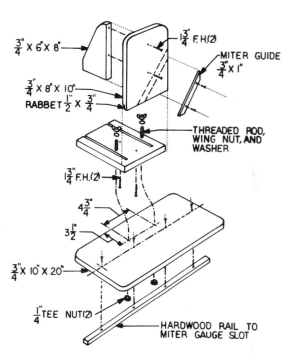

FIGURE 23-26
Universal fixture for cutting a spline on the end of a plain miter.

Rabbeted Miters

A *rabbeted miter* contains a rabbet and a miter. It is an easy way to assemble the joint that is utilized in cedar chests, jewelry boxes, and other box construction. The shoulders on the rabbet keep the frame members from slipping as clamp pressure is applied.

Start by laying out the rabbeted miter on the edges of one joint. The recommended dimensions for ¾-in. (19-mm) stock are given in Fig. 23-27. Cut the rabbets using the same techniques as given in the section "Rabbeting." You will note that the rabbets are cut differently on the mating pieces. Be careful that all cuts are made very precisely.

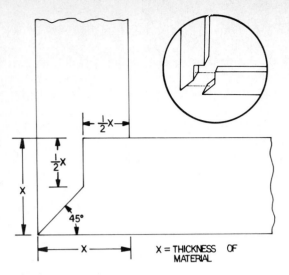

FIGURE 23-27
Recommended layout for cutting a rabbeted miter.

X = THICKNESS OF MATERIAL

Next, cut the miters by standing the stock on end. You will need to use a *support strip* clamped to the back to keep the pieces from dropping into the throat plate (Fig. 23-28). Follow the techniques given in the section "Beveling and Chamfering." After cutting the first two pieces of a joint, check the fit. Make any necessary adjustments before proceeding.

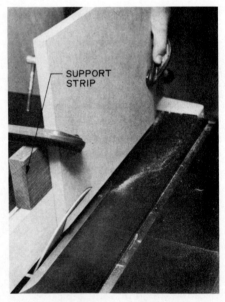

SUPPORT STRIP

FIGURE 23-28
Cutting a large bevel using a support strip clamped to the back of the stock. The guard has been removed for demonstration purposes only.

BEVELING AND CHAMFERING

An angle cut on an edge or end produces a bevel or chamfer. To make these cuts, the blade is tilted to the desired angle. The miter gauge can be used to make the cuts across the end grain. Most beveling and chamfering along the edge, however, is performed with a rip fence.

The blade can be set to the desired angle by one of two methods. The fastest method is to use the tilting gauge located on the front of the base. If an accurate cut is needed, however, use a combination square for a 45° angle or sliding T-bevel for any other angle (Fig. 23-29). Place the measuring device on the table and align the blade with it. Cut a scrap piece and check the angle with a protractor.

For angles greater than 45°, stand the board on end and set the blade to the complementary angle. For example, a 65° angle is needed, subtract 65° from 90°. Set the saw at a 25° angle. Clamp a *support strip* to the back surface of the stock (Fig. 23-28). It rides on top of the rip fence to keep the board from falling over and dropping down into the throat plate.

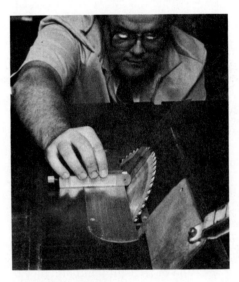

FIGURE 23-29
Accurately setting the blade to the desired angle with a sliding T-bevel.

CUTTING TENONS

A tenon is the peg portion that is inserted into the mortise (a rectangular opening) forming a mortise and tenon joint. Tenons are cut on the table saw using either a dado head or a single saw blade. Always make the mortise first using a mortising machine. It cannot be cut with a table saw.

To make a tenon, lay it out on a piece of stock cut to the finished size. Use a square to mark the *shoulder and cheek cuts* (Fig. 23-30). The tenon is then cut to fit the mortise. The tenon should slide into the mortise with a slight amount of hand pressure. If the joint must be driven together with a mallet, the tenon is too large.

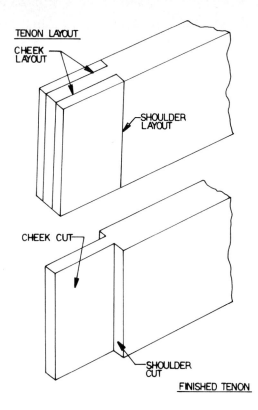

FIGURE 23-30
Lay out the shoulder and check cuts on a tenon.

Dado Method

To cut a tenon with a dado head, raise the cutter to the same height as the cheek layout line (Fig. 23-31). Adjust the rip fence so that the left outside cutter is in line with the shoulder layout line. Using the rip fence as a stop, feed the material across the dado head with the miter gauge. If the tenon is longer than the cutter can cut in one pass, make multiple cuts. Finish removing all the material from one side and then turn the board over and complete the tenon.

FIGURE 23-31
Making a tenon using a dado head. The guard has been removed for demonstration purposes only.

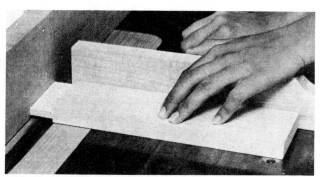

Single Saw Blade Method

To cut a tenon with a single saw blade, make the shoulder cuts first (Fig. 23-32). Raise the blade until it is the same height as the cheek layout line. Move the rip fence over until the saw tooth set to the left is in line with the shoulder layout mark. Keeping the stock against the rip fence, use the miter gauge to guide the material across the blade. Make all shoulder cuts on every tenon before going on to the next step.

The next step is to make the cheek cuts. Either a shop made or commercial *tenoning fixture* is required. The fixture safely holds the stock in a vertical position. Never attempt to hold the stock with only your hands. A kickback will occur. The commercial tenoning fixture slides in the miter gauge groove (Fig. 23-33). A shop-made fixture slides along the top and face of the rip fence (Fig. 23-34). It can be

FIGURE 23-32
Cutting the shoulder out using a single saw blade. The guard has been removed for demonstration purposes only.

FIGURE 23-33
Commercial tenoning fixture. (Courtesy of Delta International Machinery Corp.)

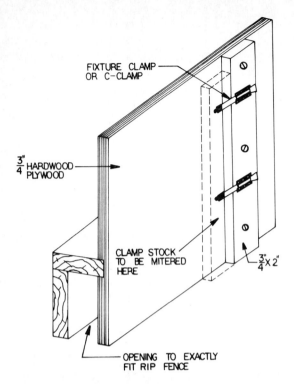

FIXTURE CLAMP
OR C-CLAMP

¾" HARDWOOD
PLYWOOD

CLAMP STOCK
TO BE MITERED
HERE

¾"X 2"

OPENING TO EXACTLY
FIT RIP FENCE

FIGURE 23-34
Shop-made tenoning fixture.

made with a backing board of hardwood plywood. A wooden fence is attached to the backing board, which is 90° to the saw table. The stock is secured to the fixture with clamps.

Raise the blade until it is even with the shoulder cut. Adjust the fixture until the saw tooth set to the right is in line with the outside layout cheek cut. The waste must fall to the outside of the blade. Make the first cheek cut (Fig. 23-35). Turn the board around and make the second cheek cut. Try the fit in the mortise before cutting any more tenons. Make any necessary adjustment and cut the remaining tenons.

FIGURE 23-35
Cutting the cheek cut with a tenoning fixture. The guard has been removed for demonstration purposes only.

OFF-FALL TO
OUTSIDE OF
BLADE

RIPPING STOCK TO WIDTH

Ripping material to width requires the use of the rip fence. Before ripping, check that the board will have a minimum of 10 in. (254 mm) in contact with the rip fence. To keep the stock from rocking, it must have a flat surface against the table and a straight edge to slide along the rip fence. Always adjust the blade height to no more than ¼ in. (6 mm) above the board. Position your body either to the left or right of the blade. Never stand in the path of the blade in case of a kickback.

Ripping Wide Boards

To rip boards 6 in. (152 mm) and wider, raise the blade guard. Measure the desired distance between the saw tooth set to the right and the face of the rip fence. If the stock is to be jointed later, add ⅛ in. (3 mm) to this distance. For minor adjustments, use the micro-adjustment knob to move the fence. Lock the rip fence to the rip fence guide rails.

Lower the guard and turn on the power. Position the stock against the rip fence. Use a slow, steady feed rate to push the board forward (Fig. 23-36). Feed it in a straight line with your right hand and use your left hand to keep it against the fence. Do not use your left hand once the trailing end comes close to the blade. Applying pressure on the outside of the blade will pinch the saw blade and cause a kickback.

As the stock clears the blade, continue to push it forward. Allow rough pieces to fall to the floor or be fed onto a cart. Have a tail-off person catch material that needs special handling. Never reach over the top of the blade to retrieve the stock.

FIGURE 23-36
Ripping a wide board.

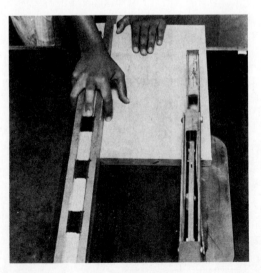

Ripping Narrow Boards

To rip boards less than 6 in. (152 mm) wide, use the same setup procedure as given in the section "Ripping Wide Boards." After the material has been started forward into the blade, pause and pick up a push stick with your right hand. Place it on the trailing end and against the rip fence (Fig. 23-37). Use the push stick to feed the material past the blade. In most cases, a $\frac{3}{4}$-in. (19-mm)-thick push stick will be used. For thin rippings, use a $\frac{1}{4}$-in. (6-mm)-thick push stick.

Use a second push stick in your left hand to keep the stock against the fence. Do not advance this second push stick past the front of the blade. It could cause the blade to be pinched and a kickback will occur.

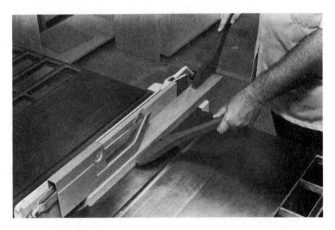

FIGURE 23-37
Ripping a narrow board using push sticks.

CUTTING LARGE PANELS

The table saw is an ideal machine for cutting plywood, particleboard, and other panel materials. In most cases, the rip fence is used with ripping techniques. Because the pieces are usually quite large, you should have a tail-off person assist you with cutting the material.

Push the panels past the blade primarily with your right hand. Only use your left hand to start the piece and keep it against the rip fence. Once the training end of the stock comes close to the saw blade, push only between the blade and the rip fence. Pushing to the left of the blade will pinch the saw blade and cause a kickback.

After the panels have been ripped to width, a shop-built sliding table can be utilized to crosscut it to lengths (Fig. 23-38). The two rails located on the bottom of the auxiliary hardwood plywood table slide in the miter gauge slot. The stock is positioned against the miter gauge slot. The stock is positioned against the auxiliary fence. To cut the stock, the entire sliding table is pushed forward. A stop block can be clamped to the auxiliary fence or a clearance block mounted on the rip fence can be used to cut duplicate pieces to length. Keep the guide rails and the bottom of the table waxed to minimize the amount of drag.

FIGURE 23-38
A shop-built sliding table can be used to cut ripped panels to length.

A smooth cut can be achieved by using a tight throat plate. This is done by making a throat plate out of wood. Clamp the plate in the throat plate opening in the table. Slowly raise the saw blade up through the wooden plate (Fig. 23-39). The blade will make a groove exactly the same width as the saw blade. This will keep slivers from developing on the bottom surface of the stock.

FIGURE 23-39
Raising the blade to produce a tight throat plate. Note that the throat plate is securely clamped into the table.

RESAWING

Resawing is the process of ripping stock on edge to produce two thinner boards. This process saves material and allows the grain in a panel to be book-matched.

Since the stock will not be completely sawed in half, the standard saw guard cannot be used. Set the distance between the rip fence and the blade equal to one-half the thickness of the board. To assist in holding the stock against the fence, install a featherboard. Place the featherboard on a thick piece of material to elevate the contact area on the stock (Fig. 23-40). The first finger on the featherboard

must be in front of the blade. Positioning it any farther forward will cause a kickback.

Adjust the height of the blade to $\frac{1}{2}$ in. (13 mm). Mark an "X" on one of the faces of the stock and always keep this surface against the fence. With a push stick, feed the material forward. Use a second push stick to assist the featherboard with keeping the material against the fence (Fig. 23-41). End for end the board and cut the other edge. Raise the blade an additional $\frac{1}{2}$ in. (13 mm) and repeat the process. Continue these steps until the stock is cut in half or until the blade is raised to its highest point. If the stock is not cut in half, finish separating the pieces with a bandsaw or handsaw.

TAPER CUTTING

Cutting a taper produces a slanted side with one end wider than the other. A fixture is needed to feed the stock at an angle. If only one side is tapered, an *adjustable tapering fixture* can be used. Small one-sided tapers can be cut with a *wedge fixture*. Tapers having two or more slanted sides require a *two-stepped taper fixture*.

One-Sided Tapers

If an adjustable tapering fixture is not available, start by constructing this device (Fig. 23-42). It con-

FIGURE 23-40
Proper setup for resawing stock. The guard has been removed for demonstration purposes only.

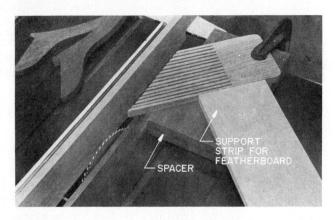

FIGURE 23-41
Resawing a board with a featherboard and push stick. The guard has been removed for demonstration purposes only.

FIGURE 23-42
Adjustable tapering fixture.

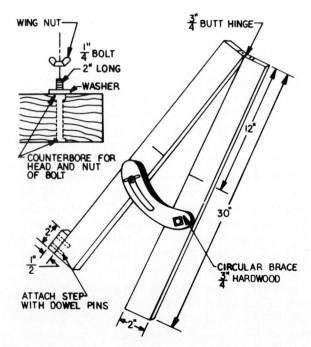

sists of two hardwood arms with a small butt hinge at one end. To provide a step to position the stock against, dowel a small block to the outside of one of the rails. The step should be the same distance from the hinged end as the length of the taper. A circular brace secures the two arms once they have been adjusted. To aid in the setting of the angle, a mark is scribed 12 in. (305 mm) from the hinged end.

There are two methods of adjusting this fixture. The fastest is the sighting method (Fig. 23-43). A line is drawn on the stock indicating the path of the taper. The stock is placed against the tapering fixture and the fixture against the rip fence. Move the arm in or out while sighting down the layout line. When the line aligns with the saw blade, tighten the wing nut on the circle brace. A scrap piece may need to be cut to check the setting.

The most accurate method of adjusting the fixture is to establish the amount of taper per foot of the finish part. Adjust the hinged arms the same distance apart as the amount of taper per foot (Fig. 23-44). Measure this dimension at the 12-in. (305-mm) mark previously drawn on the fixture. If a part, for example, has a taper of $\frac{1}{2}$ in. (13 mm) per foot, adjust the fixture with $\frac{1}{2}$ in. (13 mm) between the arms.

Once the fixture has been adjusted, lower the guard and place the stock against the fixture. Position the rip fence so that the beginning of the layout line is aligned with the saw tooth set to the right. Turn on the power and feed the fixture forward (Fig. 23-45). Keep the fixture against the rip fence and the stock on the step of the fixture.

FIGURE 23-44
Adjusting the angle of an adjustable tapering fixture using the amount of taper per foot.

FIGURE 23-45
Cutting a one-sided taper.

FIGURE 23-43
Adjusting the angle of an adjustable tapering fixture using the sighting method.

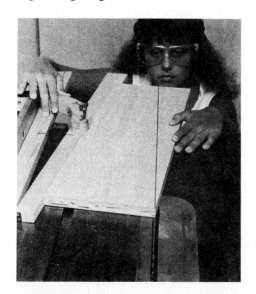

Wedges

A custom-made wedge fixture can be made if many wedges or one-sided tapered pieces are needed (Fig. 23-46). The outline of the tapered piece is first drawn on the face of a piece of $\frac{3}{4}$-in. (19-mm)-thick plywood. After the pattern has been bandsawed, glue a piece of $\frac{1}{4}$-in. (6-mm) plywood on top of the fixture. This will hold the stock against the table as it is being cut. To control the fixture, two handles are mounted on top.

Position the fixture against the fence and place the stock in the pocket of the fixture (Fig. 23-46). Cut the first piece by guiding the fixture against the rip fence. Do not pull the fixture back to you until an assistant has removed the tapered part. Turn the

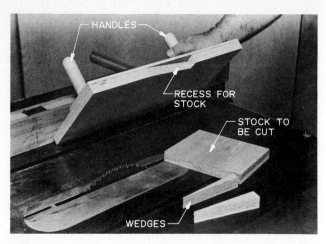

FIGURE 23-46
Using a custom-made wedge fixture for cutting wedges.

stock over with each cut. This will allow the grain to remain parallel with the edge and more parts to be cut from one piece of stock.

Four-Sided Tapers

A four-sided taper requires a custom two stepped taper fixture (Fig. 23-47). The arm is the same length as the length of the taper. A two-position step

FIGURE 23-47
Two-stepped taper fixture.

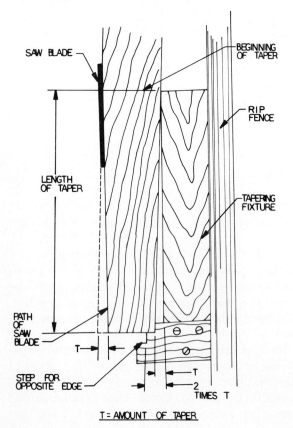

is attached to the trailing end of the arm. The first position is equal to the amount to be removed from one side of the stock. Make the second position twice this amount.

To use this fixture, cut the first two adjoining edges by placing the stock on the first position. The other two sides are cut on the second position (Fig. 23-48). Since part of the stock has already been cut away, it is necessary to move the leg over farther into the path of the blade. The second position automatically moves the board into the path of the saw.

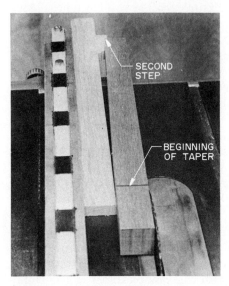

FIGURE 23-48
Cutting a four-sided taper with the stock on the second step.

SAWING TO A PATTERN

To make triangles, hexagons, and other multisided pieces, you can use a sawing to a pattern technique. First, make a pattern out of ¾-in. (19-mm) hardwood plywood the exact size and shape of the desired part. Drive at least three 1-in. (25-mm) screws through the plywood. The protruding tips should be filed to a sharp wedge. The wedge should point in the same direction as the grain of the stock. Install two 1-in. (25-mm) dowel handles to control the pattern.

Clamp to the rip fence an auxiliary L-shaped fence (Fig. 23-49). The horizontal piece of the fence must be wider than the widest piece of waste to be cut from the stock. Place the stock to be cut on the table with a piece of ¼-in. (6-mm) plywood on top to form a clearance spacer. Position the auxiliary fence on top of this. Using two clamps, secure the auxiliary fence to the rip fence. Remove the stock and spacer.

FIGURE 23-49
Setting up to saw after a pattern.

Adjust the fence so that the saw tooth set to the left is aligned with the edge of the auxiliary fence. Place the stock with the back facing up. After centering the pattern on the stock, drive the screws into the stock with a mallet. Turn on the power and slide the pattern along the auxiliary fence (Fig. 23-50). The waste extends under the fence. As the pattern is guided past the blade, the shape is cut. Stop the blade frequently and clean out any scraps left under the fence.

COVING

A *cove cut* produces a concave decorative shape. It is used most often to produce wide moldings such as used for bases on furniture. To make this cut, first layout the width and height of the cove (Fig. 23-51). Place the marks on the end of the board that will come in contact with the blade first. To make the cove, use either a rigid four-tooth combination blade

FIGURE 23-50
Sawing after a pattern. The guard has been removed for demonstration purposes only.

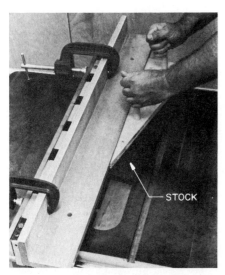

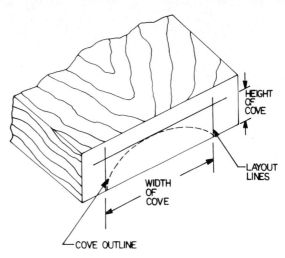

FIGURE 23-51
Layout of a cove cut.

or the outside cutter from a dado head. Raise the blade until it is even with the height layout line.

If an adjustable *parallel rule* is not available, construct one from hardwood lumber (Fig. 23-52). The legs are tied together with two diagonal pieces. As the rule is opened, the two legs will remain parallel. The legs can be secured by tightening the four wing nuts.

Set the legs of the parallel rule the same distance apart as the width of the cove. Place the rule over the raised blade and angle it until the rule comes in contact with the saw teeth (Fig. 23-53). The angle the rule makes on the table is the angle for the auxiliary fence.

FIGURE 23-52
Construction for a parallel rule.

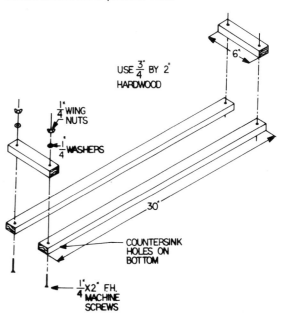

FIGURE 23-53
Establishing the angle of an auxiliary fence using the parallel rule.

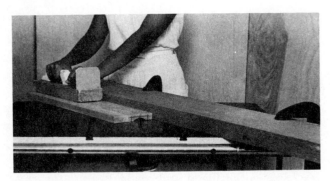

FIGURE 23-54
Cutting a cove cut using a push shoe.

With a pencil, draw a line on the table along the inside of the parallel rule leg closest to you. Measure back from this leg the same distance as the cove is from the edge of the board. Clamp the auxiliary fence along this line on the front side of the blade.

Lower the blade to $\frac{1}{8}$ in. (3 mm) above the table. Place the stock against the edge of the fence and turn on the power (Fig. 23-54). Using a push shoe, feed the board forward. Never place your hands on top of the board directly over or behind the blade.

After each pass, raise the blade an additional $\frac{1}{16}$ in. (2 mm). The cove will be completely shaped once the blade has been raised to the height layout line. Remove the saw marks with abrasive paper and hand scrapers.

GROOVING

There are different types of grooves that can be cut on the table saw: dado, plough and rabbet (Fig. 23-55). The dado is a rectangular groove that runs

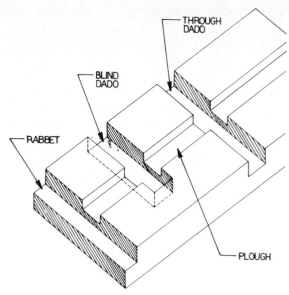

FIGURE 23-55
A groove can be either a through dado, plough, rabbet, or blind dado.

across the grain. A *plough* is also a rectangular groove, but it is cut with the grain. *Rabbets*, however, can be either with or across the grain but are cut along a face and edge or face and end. All can be made using a dado head as discussed in the section "Selecting the Table Saw Tooling."

Mounting a Dado Head

To mount a standard dado head, first determine the desired width of the dado. Next, select the outside cutters and inside chippers that will produce this cut. The two outside cutters, when mounted together, will make a $\frac{1}{4}$-in. (6-mm)-wide groove. Mount the cutters so that the teeth of one cutter fit into the gullets of the next (Fig. 23-56).

FIGURE 23-56
Mounting two outside cutters with the teeth of one cutter in the gullets of the second.

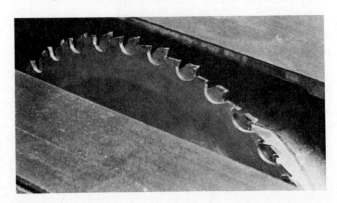

For grooves wider than $\frac{1}{4}$ in. (6 mm), add the appropriate size and number of chippers. Most dado sets include $\frac{1}{16}$ and $\frac{1}{8}$-in. (2- and 3-mm) chippers. To make a $\frac{1}{2}$-in. (13-mm)-wide dado, use the two outside cutters and two $\frac{1}{8}$-in. (3-mm) chippers. A $\frac{3}{4}$-in. (919-mm)-wide dado could be made with the two outside cutters and four $\frac{1}{8}$-in. (3-mm) chippers.

To mount the dado head, place the first outside cutter on the saw arbor. The teeth of this cutter and all others must point in the same direction as the rotation. Place the first inside chipper so that the tip is positioned in the gullet of the outside cutter. Balance the remaining inside cutters so that they are equally spaced around the arbor (Fig. 23-57). There should be equal space between each chipper. Bunching the cutters together will cause vibrations and wear on the bearings. The second outside cutter is mounted last on the arbor. The swaged teeth of the last chipper must fit into the gullets of the cutter.

Use the dado head throat plate with the extra-wide opening. A custom throat place can be made, however, by first making a blank the size of the opening in the table. Clamp it into the saw table and slowly raise the rotating head through the wooden insert (Fig. 23-39). This will leave no clearance between the dado head and the throat plate. The tight opening will eliminate most chipping that occurs on plywood and other veneered products.

Through Grooving

A through groove extends across the entire width or length of the piece. After the dado head has been mounted on the saw, raise it to the desired height. Install a guard to protect the area immediately surrounding the head. Some guards can be adjusted so they are wide enough to cover a dado head in the same manner as they cover a blade.

Cut a dado in a scrap piece of material. Check the fit and make any necessary adjustments. Paper washers can be placed between the chippers to make

FIGURE 23-57
Spacing the chippers evenly around the arbor.

FIGURE 23-58
Using paper washers to make small increases in the width of the dado head.

small increases in the width of the groove (Fig. 23-58). Do not place all the washers in one spot. They should be evenly distributed between all the chippers to prevent a ridge of wood from being left in the dado.

Grooves can be cut using either crosscutting techniques with the miter gauge or with ripping techniques on the rip fence. Use both the miter gauge and rip fence for wide material. The miter gauge helps guide the stock past the dado head. The rip fence also guides the stock but in addition serves as a stop (Fig. 23-59). This is helpful when cutting a pair of grooves. The rip fence assures that both dados will be the same distance from the ends.

Feed the stock over the dado head at a slow, steady rate. The larger the groove, the slower the feed rate. Never draw the stock back toward the direction of the operator. This will cause a kickback. Do not use your hand to hold the stock down directly over or behind the dado head. It is best to use a push stick or featherboard to keep the material against the table.

FIGURE 23-59
Making a through dado with the miter gauge and using the rip fence for a stop. The guard has been removed for demonstration purposes only.

Blind Dadoing

A *blind* or *stopped groove* conceals a dado once the project is assembled. It requires that the dado be stopped and not extended across the entire surface (Fig. 23-55). When laying out the dado on a pair of sides, it is important to determine the left and right side. With a square, transfer the stopping points of the dados on the top surface of each part.

Mount the dado head on the saw and raise it to the desired height. Move the rip fence against the cutter and with a square mark where the cut begins and ends (Fig. 23-60). This will be the point where the teeth first come up and go down into the table.

Adjust the rip fence the same distance from the dado head as the groove is from the end of the board. Lower the dado head below the table. Place the bottom surface of the board on the table with the end against the rip fence and align the front stopping point on the stock with the rear mark on the rip fence (Fig. 23-61). Clamp a stock block on the rip

FIGURE 23-60
Marking the beginning and ending points on the rip fence.

FIGURE 23-61
Setting up the saw to cut a blind dado for the right side. The guard has been removed for demonstration purposes only.

fence which is against the back edge of the stock. Slide a miter gauge up to the stock and clamp a second stop block against the end of the miter gauge rail.

Reset the dado head to the same height. Place the board on its edge and against the stop block on the rip fence and miter gauge. Turn on the power and lower the stock carefully down on to the rotating cutter. Once the board meets the table, feed it forward.

To dado the left sides of your project, lower the cutter and align the rear stopping point on the stock with the front layout line on the rip fence (Fig. 23-62). Clamp a stock block against the leading edge of the board on the rip fence. Clamp a stock block against the leading edge of the board on the rip fence. Clamp a second stop block against the front of the miter gauge bar. Raise the dado head back to the original height.

Position the stock against the rip fence and miter gauge. Turn on the power and push the miter gauge forward feeding the board into the cutter. Once the stock meets the stop blocks, turn off the power. If you cannot reach the switch while holding down the board, have an assistant turn off the power. The board must not be moved until the dado head has stopped turning.

FIGURE 23-62
Setting up the saw for a blind dado on the left side. The guard has been removed for demonstration purposes only.

Rabbeting

Rabbets can be cut with either a dado head or a single saw blade. With both cutters, be certain that the rip fence is covered with a piece of wood. This will protect the cutter if it comes in contact with the fence.

When several rabbets are needed, set up the dado head (Fig. 23-63). Adjust the rip fence just to

FIGURE 23-63
Cutting the rabbet with a dado head and using a feather-board.

FIGURE 23-65
Use a featherboard and push stick to make the second cut for a rabbet. The waste must fall to the outside of the blade.

the right of the cutter. Use a miter gauge to guide the stock past the dado head.

When just a few rabbets are needed, use a single saw blade. Layout the rabbet on the leading end of one of the boards. Place the face of the stock against the table and the marked end against the blade. Adjust the height so that it will be even with the horizontal layout line. Position the stock against the rip fence and move the fence over until the vertical layout line is aligned with the saw tooth set to the left. Feed each board over the blade using a push stick (Fig. 23-64). Do not place your hands directly over the blade or behind the blade.

Make the second cut by standing the stock on edge. Readjust the height of the blade and the position of the rip fence to be aligned with the layout lines. The waste from the rabbet must fall to the outside of the blade. If the waste is left between the blade and rip fence, a serious kickback will result.

Install a featherboard to keep the stock against the fence. Position it on top of a block so that the contact area of the featherboard is above the rabbet.

FIGURE 23-64
Make the first cut for a rabbet with the face against the table. The guard has been removed for demonstration purposes only.

Feed the stock across the rotating blade using a push stick (Fig. 23-65). Have a tail-off person catch the boards as they leave the saw table.

MAKING A RAISED PANEL

Raised panels are usually made from solid wood and are utilized in a door. They will have a decorative chamfer cut on the face of the panel. Although a shaper is used most commonly to mold the edges, a table saw can produce a pleasing appearance on a raised panel.

First, compute the size of the panel. It will be based on the overall width and length dimensions of the stile and rail frame. Refer to the section "Raised Panel Doors" in Chapter 31 for further information on how the frame is fabricated. A groove for the raised panel is cut on the inside edges of the frame. It will usually be $\frac{1}{2}$ in. (13 mm) deep. Calculate the inside dimensions of the frame and add 1 in. (25 mm) for the two grooves. This will give you the distance from the bottom of one groove to the opposite groove. Subtract from this amount $\frac{1}{4}$ in. (6 mm) for expansion and contraction of the panel.

Depending on the design of the door, the stock for the panel will be between $\frac{1}{2}$ to $\frac{3}{4}$ in. (13 to 19 mm) thick. Raised panels for $\frac{3}{4}$-in. (19-mm)-thick doors are generally $\frac{1}{2}$ to $\frac{9}{16}$ in. (13 to 15 mm) thick. Design your door so that the face of the panel and the face of the frame are even with each other.

To provide a shoulder and a straight line for the chamfer, make a $\frac{1}{8}$-in. (3-mm)-deep groove (Fig. 23-66). It should be $1\frac{1}{2}$ in. (38 mm) from each of the

FIGURE 23-66
Cutting a groove for a raised door panel.

four edges. If a wider chamfer is needed, make the groove farther from the edge.

Next, angle the blade to approximately 6°. Adjust the rip fence so that it is ¼ in. (6 mm) from the blade. Stand the stock on edge and clamp a support strip along the back (Fig. 23-67). The support strip will ride on top of the rip fence and keep the stock from dropping through the throat plate. Chamfer all four edges using the support board.

Finish the raised panel by sanding the saw marks. If the door is to be stained, stain the chamfer before the door is assembled. This will keep a white line from developing when the panel later shrinks because of the natural movement of wood.

FIGURE 23-67
Making a chamfer cut for a raised panel. Note the support strip on the back of the door. The guard has been removed for demonstration purposes only.

USING THE MOLDING HEAD

A molding head can be used to make many different types of decorative cuts. The parts of this cutter are discussed in the section "Selecting the Table Saw Tooling." There are several different patterns of shaper-like knives from which to pick.

After the three matching knives are selected, mount them in the molding head body. It is very important that each knife be mounted in the body so that the sharp edge is leading as the cutter rotates. Each Allen head bolt must be firmly tightened. Recheck each one several times before using. You will need to stop periodically during the cutting and re-tighten each bolt.

The miter gauge, rip fence, or combination of both can be used to guide the stock. Use the miter gauge when molding end grain and shaping small pieces (Fig. 23-68). A backup board screwed to the gauge will eliminate any tear out when shaping end grain. The rip fence works well for making long pieces of molding (Fig. 23-69). Cover the fence with a thick piece of wood. This allows only part of the cut-

FIGURE 23-68
Shaping the end grain using a miter gauge. The guard has been removed for demonstration purposes only.

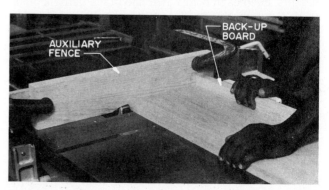

FIGURE 23-69
Shaping molding using the rip fence. The guard has been removed for demonstration purposes only.

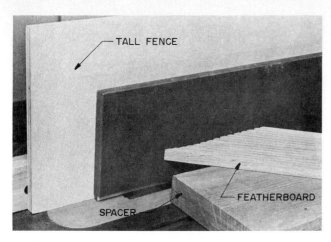

FIGURE 23-70
A tall fence allows the stock to be run on the edge.

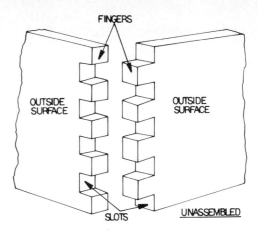

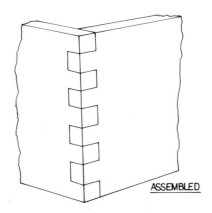

FIGURE 23-71
Layout of the box joint.

ter to be used while the remaining portion remains in the wooden fence. To cut a recess for the cutter to turn in, lower the head. Adjust and lock the rip fence in the desired location and bring the rotating cutter up into the wooden fence. Be careful not to hit the metal rip fence. Attach a tall piece of plywood to the rip fence when molding the edge of large stock (Fig. 23-70).

To set up the molding head, mount it on the arbor. Use a throat plate with a wide opening. Raise the cutter until it meets the layout drawn on the end of the board. If a heavy cut is necessary to shape the pattern, make the molding in several light passes. Use a push stick and featherboards whenever possible. Never place your hands on top of the stock when it is over the molding head.

BOX JOINERY

The box joint is a highly decorative joint that has a similar appearance to a dovetail (Fig. 23-71). It can be cut entirely on the table saw and when assembled is very strong. With the many fingers cut on each of the two sides, the gluing surface is more than twice the length of the joint.

To make a box joint, first lay out the fingers on one pair of sides. Each finger and slot are to be the same size. Ideally, a full-width finger will begin and end the joint. The layout should be made with the finger width $\frac{1}{8}$ to $\frac{1}{2}$ in. (3 to 13 mm) less than the thickness of the stock. Usually, the smaller the fingers, the more decorative is the appearance. Also, place an "X" on the outside surface of each piece. This mark will later be used to orient the stock when placed against the miter gauge.

Mount a dado head on the saw arbor. It should be the same width as the fingers. Raise the dado

head to just slightly more than the height of the slot. Cutting the slots slightly deeper will assure a flush box joint. After assembly, the overhang on the fingers can be sanded flush with the outside surface. Place an auxiliary fence against the miter gauge and cut a dado through the board. Glue into this dado a wooden guide pin which is the exact width and height as the finger (Fig. 23-72). It should ex-

FIGURE 23-72
Setup for making a box joint.

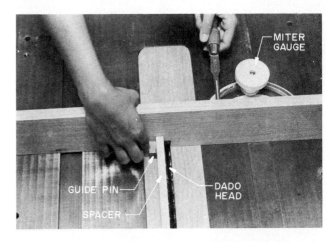

tend beyond the face of the fence at least the thickness of the stock.

To position the auxiliary fence on the miter gauge, place a spacer to the right of the dado head (Fig. 23-72). The spacer should be the exact same thickness as the width of the fingers. Slide the fence snuggly against the spacer. Attach the fence to the miter gauge with wood screws.

Place the inside surface of the first piece against the miter gauge (Fig. 23-73). Butt the edge

FIGURE 23-75
Making the first cut on the second side. The guard has been removed for demonstration purposes only.

FIGURE 23-73
Cutting the first slot on the first side. The guard has been removed for demonstration purposes only.

FIGURE 23-74
Use the guide pin to position the stock for the next cut. The guard has been removed for demonstration purposes only.

of the board against the guide pin and firmly hold it against the fence. Turn on the power and cut the first slot. Guide the stock past the dado head with the miter gauge. Once the stock has cleared the head, have an assistant remove it from the fence. Do not draw it back over the dado head.

Cut the remaining fingers by slipping the newly cut slot over the guide pin (Fig. 23-74). It will automatically position the board for the next finger. Use the same procedure as used for the first slot to feed the stock.

To cut the second mating piece, place the first board now with the outside surface against the fence (Fig. 23-75). The first slot that was cut should be over the guide pin. Position the second piece against the edge of the first piece of material. The inside surface should be against the fence. Remove the first piece being careful not to move the second. Feed the miter gauge past the dado head cutting the slot. Using the same procedure as for the first piece, make the remaining fingers.

After the first joint has been cut, check the fit. If the fingers do not easily slide into the slots, adjust the distance the guide pin is from the dado head or the width of the cut. You may also want to check that the dado head or miter gauge is perpendicular to the table.

24

RADIAL ARM SAWS

The radial arm saw is one of the most suitable pieces of woodworking equipment for cutting stock to length (Fig. 24-1). When crosscutting with this saw, the board is kept in a stationary position and the blade is drawn across the material. This allows accurate cutting and easier aligning of the layout line with the blade. Many woodworkers also utilize the radial arm saw for other purposes. It can dado, rip, miter, cut saucers, and perform many other specialized cuts.

PARTS OF THE RADIAL ARM SAW

The major parts of a radial arm saw are the arm, column, table, fence, and motor unit (Fig. 24-1). All of these components can be adjusted in several positions.

There are two styles of arms utilized with radial arm saws. The original style uses a single piece that is suspended over the table by the column. This is the simplest style and called the *single arm* (Fig. 24-1). A newer style has two arms and is called a *turret arm* (Fig. 24-2). The top arm remains stationary while the bottom one pivots. This allows for a larger mitering capacity. With either style the *miter*

clamp handle and *miter positive lock* secures the arm into either the crosscutting or mitering position.

Towards the rear of the saw is the *column*. It is a steel tube which is anchored to the base. An *elevation crank* raises or lowers the column to adjust the depth of cut.

Stock is positioned on top of the *table* against the *fence*. The blade should be adjusted so that it is $\frac{1}{16}$ in. (2 mm) below the top surface of the table. Occasionally, the blade may be lowered too far and the top weakened from too deep of a cut. Since the *table* is constructed from particleboard or plywood, it can be replaced with a new piece. The *fence* can also be replaced when it is cut away.

With most saws the fence can be positioned in several locations to the rear of the table. Although there must be space for the rotating blade next to the column, the farther back the fence is positioned, the wider the cutting capacity (Fig. 24-3). By moving it forward, a thicker board can be positioned against the fence (Fig. 24-3).

The motor unit is suspended from the arm by the *yoke*. Attached to the yoke is the motor. The blade is mounted directly to the shaft of the motor. On the front of the *yoke* is the *handle*. It is very important to always control the movement of the

RADIAL ARM SAW SAFELY RULES

1. Hands must be kept at least 4 in. (102 mm) from the blade.
2. Properly adjust the guard for each different type of cut.
3. Stand to the side of the blade and always keep your hands out of the path of the saw.
4. Stock must be held firmly against the table and the fence at all times.
5. Cut only one piece at a time.
6. When crosscutting, hold the stock firmly on the table with the first hand while pulling the feed handle across the stock with the second hand.
7. Obtain the instructor's permission before attempting to rip any stock on the radial arm saw.
8. When finished using the saw, return the carriage to the rearmost position and turn off the power.
9. Disconnect the power before making any adjustments or tooling changes.

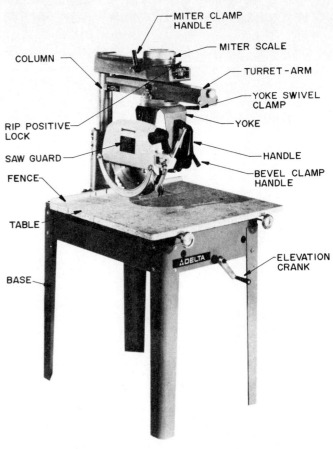

FIGURE 24-1
Major parts of the single-arm radial arm saw. (Courtesy of Black & Decker.)

FIGURE 24-2
Major parts of the turret-arm radial arm saw. (Courtesy of Delta International Machinery Corp.)

FIGURE 24-3
The position of the fence will determine the maximum width of the board that can be cut.

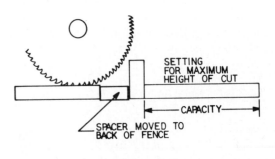

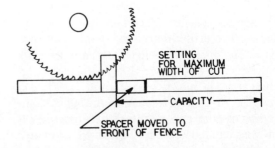

blade by grasping this handle. There are two adjustments for the motor unit (Fig. 24-4). The *yoke swivel clamp* and *rip positive lock* allow the blade to be swung into the ripping position. The *bevel clamp handle* and *bevel positive stop* are used primarily to set the saw in the bevel mode (Fig. 24-5).

An important part to this saw is the *blade guard* (Fig. 24-6). The guard is made of three major parts. An *upper blade housing* covers the top of the blade. It also contains the *sawdust spout*, which directs the sawdust away from the operator. The *ring guards* protect the operator from the bottom section of the blade when it is in the rearmost position.

FIGURE 24-4
Releasing the yoke swivel clamp and the rip positive lock allows the saw to be placed in the ripping position.

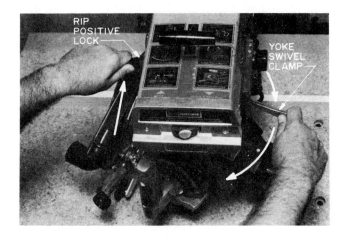

FIGURE 24-5
Releasing the bevel clamp handle and the bevel positive stop allow the saw to be placed in the ripping position.

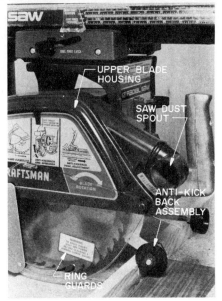

FIGURE 24-6
Major parts to a radial arm saw guard.

These ring guards may need to be removed in such operations as coving, resawing, and saucer cutting. The *antikickback assembly* covers the leading edge of the blade. It also keeps the boards from being thrown out of control when the saw is in the rip position.

PURCHASING A RADIAL ARM SAW

There are several items to consider when purchasing a radial arm saw. First select the size of the machine. Radial arm saws are sized by the diameter of the blade and the length of the arm. Diameters of saw blades range from 8 to over 20 in. (203 to 508 mm). Larger blades allow thicker boards to be cut. A good general-purpose size is 10 in. (254 mm). This will cut most boards 2 in. (51 mm) and thinner. The length of the arm is generally between 20 and 48 in. (508 and (1219 mm). Longer arms allow wider boards to be cut.

The horsepower of the motor is another aspect to consider when purchasing this machine. Generally, the larger the blade diameter, the bigger the H.P. of the motor. To make most cuts at least a 2-hp motor should be specified.

A good-quality radial arm saw will have adjustments that are easy to reach and solidly lock the movable parts in place. When pressure is applied to the end of the locked arm or other parts, they should not move.

SELECTING THE RADIAL ARM SAW TOOLING

Tooling for a radial arm saw includes saw blades, a dado head, a molding head, sanding disk, and many others. If the saw is used only for crosscutting, a carbide-tipped alternating top bevel blade will work the best. For crosscutting and occasional ripping, a carbide-tipped combination blade can make most cuts efficiently. Refer to the section "Selecting the Table Saw Tooling" in Chapter 23 for further details on tooling. These saw blades can also be used on the radial arm saw. In other sections of that chapter additional tooling is explained that can be utilized.

INSTALLING THE RADIAL ARM SAW BLADE

Always disconnect the power before changing any tooling. Next raise the column so that the blade is clear of the table and fence. Because the blade guard assembly surrounds the blade, it must be removed. Once the guard is taken off, both the blade and the *arbor* will be exposed. The *arbor* is the threaded shaft upon which the tooling is mounted.

Use either an Allen wrench or special arbor wrench to keep the arbor from turning (Fig. 24-7). You should never substitute a piece of wood wedged under the blade for a wrench. This will push the saw out of alignment when pressure is applied.

With the arbor nut wrench, loosen the arbor nut. The handle of the wrench should be pulled in the same direction as the saw blade teeth are pointing (Fig. 24-7). After the arbor nut has been unscrewed, remove the stabilizing washer and blade.

FIGURE 24-7
Removing the arbor nut.

PULL WRENCH

Select the new blade and slide it on the arbor. The teeth must point in the direction the arbor rotates. Place the stabilizing washer back on the arbor and tighten the arbor nut with the arbor nut wrench. Hold the arbor secure with the arbor wrench. Reassemble the guard and be certain the bottom on the upper blade housing is parallel with the table. The ring guards must cover the bottom cutting circle of the blade. For crosscutting operations, adjust the antikick fingers so that they are just above the top of your stock. Push the blade all the way back to the column and connect the power.

The blade should be adjusted to cut $\frac{1}{16}$ in. (2 mm) below the table. Occasionally, a groove will not be present in the table and fence at the desired location. If a new groove is needed, raise the blade up above the fence and turn on the power. Holding the motor unit securely in the rear most position have an assistant lower the rotating blade. Once it has cut $\frac{1}{16}$ in. (2 mm) into the rear table, stop lowering the blade. Pull the blade out until it reaches the end of the arm. Push the blade back to complete the groove.

To check the accuracy of the saw, select a scrap piece with a straight edge and a flat face. After cutting the board, check for squareness from edge to edge and face to face.

SETTING UP THE RADIAL ARM SAW

There are three basic adjustments for the radial arm saw. A few special cuts may require a combination of these. The power must always be turned off and the blade not turning any time an adjustment is made. With each setup make certain that no parts of the saw are forced into position and that all movable parts are locked after the adjustments are made.

The most common adjustment is the blade height. Make this adjustment when changing the depth of cut for regular cuts, making dados or other types of cuts. Use the *elevating crank* to raise or lower the column (Fig. 24-1). Turning the crank will then change the height of the blade.

Another common setup is the mitering adjustment. Miters are made with this setup by moving the arm either to the left or right. The arm can be moved by pulling up on the *miter latch,* loosening the *miter clamp handle* (Fig. 24-8). Saws will have a *miter scale and pointer* to indicate the angle of the blade to the fence. For fast adjustments a positive lock for the miter latch is provided at 90 and 45° to right and left. Tighten both the handle and latch before turning on the power.

To produce bevel cuts, use the *bevel clamp handle* and *bevel locating pin* (Fig. 24-5). Start by rais-

FIGURE 24-8
Releasing the miter latch and the miter clamp handle
allows the saw to be placed in the miter position.

FIGURE 24-9
Vee-shaped mark to indicate the location of the cut.

ing the blade well above the fence. Loosen the clamp handle and locating pin. The motor should then rotate in the yoke. Move the motor until it is at the desired angle indicated by the bevel scale. Most saws have a positive stop at 90, 45, and 180°.

The third adjustment involves placing the saw in the ripping mode. This allows the saw to be used for ripping operations. To pivot the *yoke* to the right or left, first raise the blade. Next release the *yoke swivel clamp* and lift up on the *rip positive lock* (Fig. 24-4). Turning the yoke clockwise places the blade in the *in-rip position*. Turning the yoke counterclockwise places it in the *out-rip position*. With either position the rip positive lock will automatically lock the yoke into position. Tighten the yoke swivel clamp to secure the yoke.

No matter which setup is selected, always cut a scrap piece and check it for the desired angle of cut. Minor changes may be needed in the adjustments to produce an accurate cut. Cut off a piece at least 1 in. (25 mm) long and then use a framing square or protractor on the remaining board. Check for accuracy not only from edge to edge but also from face to face.

CROSSCUTTING

The radial arm saw is ideal for crosscutting boards to length. There must be at least 6 in. (152 mm) of material to the left of the blade for the operator to hold. Any less than this and your hands come dangerously close to the blade. Before making this cut, make certain that the saw is setup correctly. The blade should be $\frac{1}{16}$ in. (2 mm) below the table and the guard properly adjusted. Cut a scrap piece of material and check the cut for squareness.

When cutting a board to length, crosscut the first 1 in. (25 mm) off the end. End-for-end the board, and measuring from the fresh cut, end-mark the piece to length. Use a vee-shaped mark to indicate the position of the cut (Fig. 24-9). Align this mark immediately to the left of the path of the saw blade. Hold the board firmly against the table and fence with the left hand. Grasp the handle of the radial arm saw with the right hand and push the saw all the way to the column. Turn on the power and slowly pull the motor unit forward (Fig. 24-10). Since the blade may have a tendency to grab the stock, be certain to control the movement of the saw. Once the saw blade has cleared the front edge of the board, push the motor back to the column. Make the next cut or turn off the power.

FIGURE 24-10
Crosscutting a board. Note position of hands.

CUTTING BOARDS TO IDENTICAL LENGTHS

When only a few boards are needed, it is usually best to mark each piece individually. Cut each board separately. For several pieces of the same length a stop block can be utilized. Each part will be of exactly the same length and much time will be saved.

When cutting several pieces, square the first end of one piece. Mark it to length. Align the mark with the path of the blade. Clamp a rabbeted stop block to the fence which has been placed against the end of the stock (Fig. 24-11). The rabbeted area will prevent sawdust from accumulating in front of the stop block. Cut the first piece to length and check the length with a tape measure. If the cut is not accurate, make any necessary adjustments. Industry frequently uses commercial stops and fences (Fig. 24-12). These have a built-in tape measure for easy setup. Often, spring-loaded stops allow several lengths to be set up at one time.

FIGURE 24-11
Use a rabbeted stop block to cut boards of identical length.

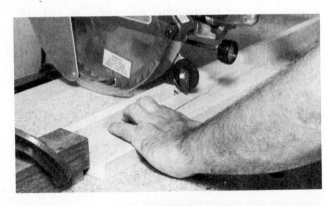

FIGURE 24-12
Commercial stops provide more than one length setting when cutting boards to length.

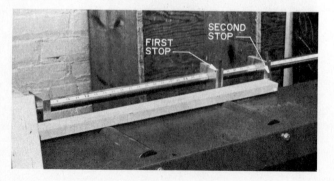

PLAIN MITERING

There are three major methods of cutting plain miters. Although they can be cut at various angles, most generally a 45° angle is utilized. This angle setting will produce a four-sided frame. To calculate the angle for any given frame, use the following formula:

$$\text{angle setting on saw} = 90° - \frac{180}{\text{number of sides}}$$

A hexagon or six-sided frame would require the miter scale pointer to be set at 60°. The formula above would be worked as follows:

$$\text{angle setting on saw} = 90 \text{ degrees} - 30 = 60$$

After setting the saw to the desired angle, always cut a piece of scrap to check the accuracy of the angle. Use a protractor or sliding T-bevel to measure the miter. Make any needed adjustments. If the angle is off by only a small amount, the miter will not fit properly.

Once the angle of the miter has been calculated it may be necessary to figure the length of the picture frame members. To find the length, measure the size of one side of the picture. Add to this twice the width of the frame material. Subtract from this amount twice the width of the rabbet.

An example of calculating a piece of molding as shown in Fig. 24-13 for a 10-in. (254-mm)-wide picture would be as follows:

picture width	= 10 in.	10 in.	width of picture
molding width	= 2 in.	+ 4 in.	twice width of molding
		14 in.	
width of rabbet	= ½ in.		
		14 in.	
		− 1 in.	twice width of rabbet
		13 in.	finish length of molding

METHOD 1. The first method requires the stock to be cut to rough length. Next, swing the arm to the right to the desired angle. If a 45° angle is desired, engage the miter latch. Always lock the miter clamp handle to secure the arm.

Miter all boards on the first end. Swing the arm to the left and set the miter scale pointer to the desired angle. Measure the length of the first piece and align the mark with the path of the blade. Clamp a stop block on the opposite end. Miter the second end of all pieces (Fig. 24-14).

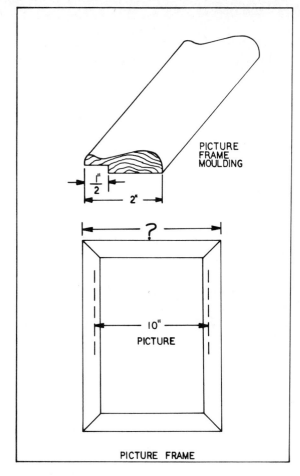

FIGURE 24-13
Picture frame molding.

METHOD 2. The second method of cutting plain miters requires the arm to be left at 90° angle. All pieces need to be cut to finish length. Install a mitering fixture on top of the table (Fig. 24-15). This requires the blade to be raised so that it will cut $\frac{1}{16}$ in. (2 mm) into the auxiliary table. Cut the first end by positioning the board against the left side of the vee.

FIGURE 24-14
Mitering stock with the arm set at the desired angle

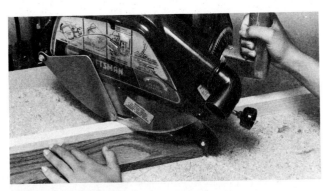

After cutting the first miter, end-for-end the board and cut the second end by placing the part against the right side of the vee. Be careful that the small piece that is cut away is not caught by the blade.

METHOD 3. The third method does not require stock to be precut to length. It will, however, work only for 45° angles. A large piece of squared plywood is clamped to the table (Fig. 24-16). This will serve as an auxiliary fence. Use a framing square placed against the saw fence to locate the auxiliary plywood fence. There should be just enough space left between the back edge of the plywood and the saw fence for the stock to slide.

Place the arm in the 45° position. Clamp a stop block to the right of the blade the same distance from the blade as the length of the finished board. Slide the stock against the stop block and miter the first end. Remove the piece and place it against the edge of the plywood. The second end can then be mitered.

FIGURE 24-15
Mitering with a vee mitering fixture.

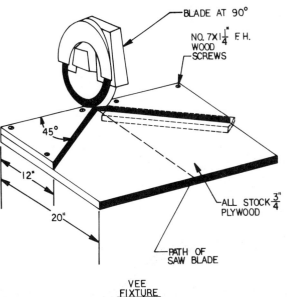

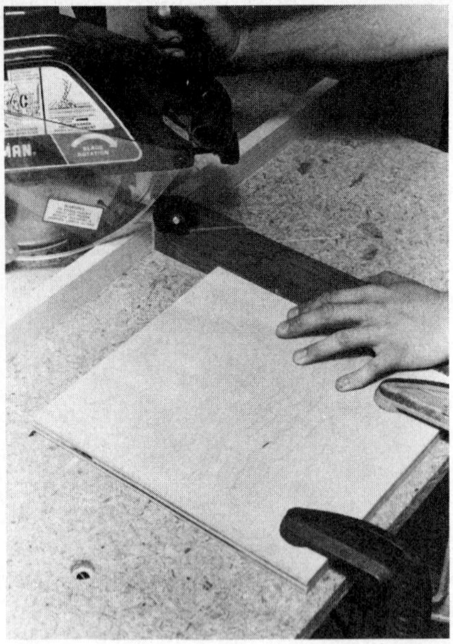

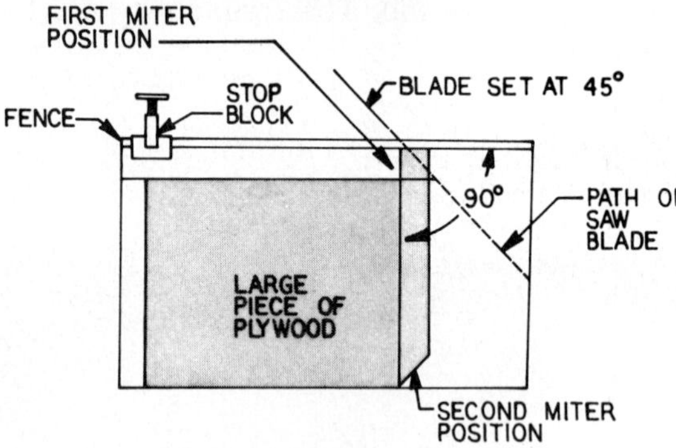

FIGURE 24-16
Mitering stock using an auxiliary fence.

COMPOUND MITERING

A compound miter is also called a hopper joint or bevel miter. The cut will produce a miter with sloping or angled sides. Use Table 24-1 to establish the angle settings for the arm and the motor unit. Both the arm and motor unit must be adjusted for this cut. After setting each to the desired angle, produce the compound miter using crosscutting techniques (Fig. 24-17).

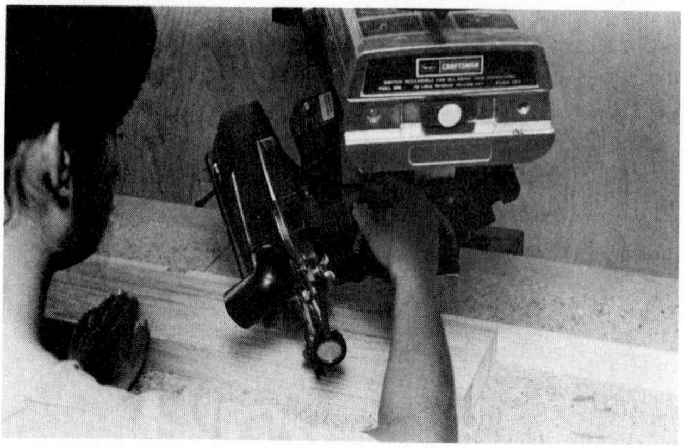

FIGURE 24-17
Making a compound miter.

RIPPING

Ripping should be done on the table saw if one is available. It is generally easier, faster, and safer than using a radial arm saw. If there is not one to

TABLE 24-1
Angles for Cutting Compound Miters

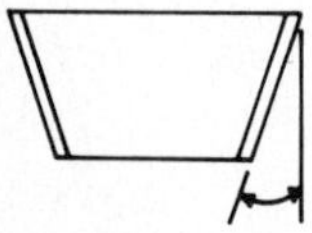

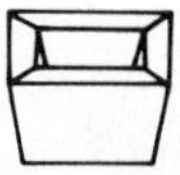

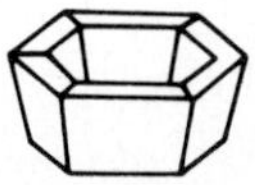

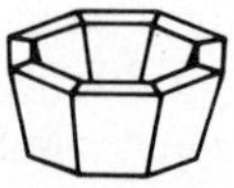

	Four sides		Six sides		Eight sides	
Work angle (deg)	Blade tilt (deg)	Arm setting (deg)	Blade tilt (deg)	Arm setting (deg)	Arm setting (deg)	Blade tilt (deg)
5	$44\frac{3}{4}$	5	$29\frac{3}{4}$	$2\frac{1}{2}$	$22\frac{1}{4}$	2
10	$44\frac{1}{4}$	$9\frac{3}{4}$	$29\frac{1}{2}$	$5\frac{1}{2}$	22	4
15	$43\frac{1}{4}$	$14\frac{1}{2}$	29	$8\frac{1}{4}$	$21\frac{1}{2}$	6
20	$41\frac{3}{4}$	$18\frac{3}{4}$	$28\frac{1}{4}$	11	21	8
25	40	23	$27\frac{1}{4}$	$13\frac{1}{2}$	$20\frac{1}{4}$	10
30	$37\frac{3}{4}$	$26\frac{1}{2}$	26	16	$19\frac{1}{2}$	$11\frac{3}{4}$
35	$35\frac{1}{4}$	$29\frac{3}{4}$	$24\frac{1}{2}$	$18\frac{1}{4}$	$18\frac{1}{4}$	$13\frac{1}{4}$
40	$32\frac{1}{2}$	$32\frac{3}{4}$	$22\frac{3}{4}$	$20\frac{1}{4}$	17	15
45	30	$35\frac{1}{4}$	21	$22\frac{1}{4}$	$15\frac{3}{4}$	$16\frac{1}{4}$
50	27	$37\frac{1}{2}$	19	$23\frac{3}{4}$	$14\frac{1}{4}$	$17\frac{1}{2}$
55	24	$39\frac{1}{4}$	$16\frac{3}{4}$	$25\frac{1}{4}$	$12\frac{1}{2}$	$18\frac{3}{4}$
60	21	41	$14\frac{1}{2}$	$26\frac{1}{2}$	11	$19\frac{3}{4}$

use, however, ripping can be done on the radial arm saw by following a specific procedure.

To rip a board, raise the motor unit well above the fence. Check that the arm is in the 90° setting. By loosening the yoke swivel clamp and lifting up on the rip positive lock, the motor yoke can be pivoted one-fourth of a turn into the rip position. The positive rip lock will automatically drop in a positioning hole once the blade is parallel to the fence.

By turning the motor to the left, the blade is placed in the *in-rip position* (Fig. 24-18). Use this position for ripping narrow-to-wide stock. Rotating the motor unit to the right places the blade in the *out-rip position* (Fig. 24-19). Use this position when ripping extra-wide material such as wide plywood. The saw should always rotate toward the stock as it is fed into it.

FIGURE 24-18
Ripping a board in the in-rip position

FIGURE 24-19
Ripping a board in the out-rip position.

Pull the motor unit out on the arm until the space between the fence and the saw tooth close to the fence is equal to the desired width of out. Tighten the rip lock to secure the motor unit to the arm.

Turn on the power and slowly lower the blade toward the table. Once the blade has cut $\frac{1}{16}$ in. (2 mm) into the table, stop turning the elevation crank. Next adjust the nose or front of the upper blade housing so that it is no more than $\frac{1}{4}$ in. (6 mm) above the stock (Fig. 24-20). The antikickback fingers are set $\frac{1}{16}$ in. (2 mm) below the face of the stock. To finish the guard adjustment, aim the sawdust spout toward the rear of the saw.

FIGURE 24-20
Proper setting for the blade guard when performing ripping operations.

Determine in which direction the stock is to be fed. The board must be directed against the rotation of the blade. When the saw is in the in-rip position, feed the material from right to left. The out-rip position requires the stock to be fed from left to right. Feeding a board from the wrong direction will lead to a serious kickback.

Turn on the power and feed the stock forward. Guide the stock along the fence and keep it flat against the table. Use a push stick to apply forward pressure between the fence and blade. Never place your hands in the path of the blade or closer than 4 in. (102 mm) to the cutting arc. Reaching under the arm can also lead to an accident.

CHAMFERING AND BEVELING

The saw is set up to make chamfers and bevels by raising the blade well above the fence. Next, swivel the motor unit. Use the bevel scale to determine when the blade has reached the desired angle.

On most saws there is a locating hole at the 30 and 45° settings. The bevel positive stop will automatically lock into these holes as the motor is swiveled. For angles other than these, use the bevel scale to set the angle.

With the blade in the rearmost position and the rip lock tightened, turn on the power. Slowly lower the blade until it is $\frac{1}{16}$ in. (2 mm) below the table. Securely holding the handle, loosen the rip lock and pull the motor unit out to the frontmost position. This will make a groove in the table.

When an accurate cut is required, cut a piece of scrap to check the angle (Fig. 24-21). Use a protractor to measure the angle cut on the board. Make any necessary adjustments. All cuts can then be made.

FIGURE 24-21
Cutting a bevel cut.

DADOING

The radial arm saw is ideal for cutting dados. Dados are grooves that run across the grain of the board and made use of crosscutting techniques. Layout lines are made on the top surface of the board. This makes them easy to see and for you to align the marks with the path of the dado head.

To dado a board, you will need to mount the dado head on the saw arbor. The procedure for attaching the dado head on the radial arm saw is the same as on the table saw. Refer to Chapter 23 for further details on this operation. Make certain that the inside chippers are equally spaced around the outside cutter and the teeth are pointed in the same direction as the direction of rotation. The guard assembly must be mounted and properly adjusted.

Lay out the lines on one board for each dado. Make the lines on the same side of the material as the dados are to be cut. Frequently, *blind dados* or *stopped dados* that do not extend across the entire face are made. Be careful that the two sides are laid out in pairs (Fig. 24-22). If the dados are not stopped at the correct edge, the two sides will not match up.

To make dados, adjust the depth of cut. Place the stock on the table and directly under the cutter. Lower the dado head until it just touches the top face. Pull the board back out of the way and lower the dado head the same amount as the depth of the dado. With most saws, each complete turn of the elevating crank will lower the dado head $\frac{1}{8}$ in. (3 mm). If the dado is to be $\frac{1}{4}$ in. (6 mm) deep, turn the crank two complete turns.

Next push the board against the fence and align the layout marks with the path of the dado head. If more than one dado is to be made in the same location, install a stop block against one end of the stock (Fig. 24-23). Turn on the power and firmly grasp the handle of the saw. Slowly bring the rotating head across the stock. Once the dado has reached the end of cut, push the motor unit back to the column. Check the cut for the proper depth and location. Make any necessary adjustments and proceed with the other dados.

Specialized Dados

Dados can take several forms, including blind dados, corner dados, and ploughs. Although the basic proce-

FIGURE 24-22
Lay the blind dados out in pairs to make a right and left side.

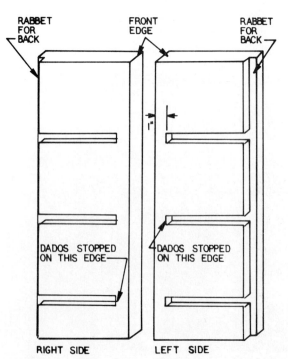

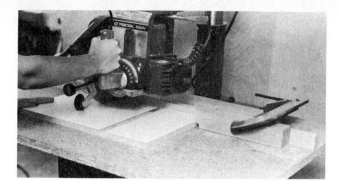

FIGURE 24-23
Cutting a through dado with a stop block.

FIGURE 24-25
Cutting a corner dado.

dure for each of these cuts is similar to that described in the preceding section, there are additional setup steps.

To make a blind dado, the forward movement of the dado head is stopped before it reaches the far edge of the stock. One method of making this dado is to mark the stopping point of each dado. You then carefully bring the rotating head up to these points as each dado is made. If several blind dados of the same length are to be cut, a stop clamp can be installed on the arm (Fig. 24-24). Once the yoke reaches the clamp, return it to the column.

Corner dados require that the stock be cradled in a 45° vee block (Fig. 24-25). Be certain that the vee block is large enough to support the stock and that the block is securely clamped to the fence.

Ploughing produces a cut running parallel with the grain. The saw is placed in the ripping mode for this operation. Refer to the section "Ripping" for the proper setup procedure. Be certain that the guard is adjusted and stock is fed from the correct side. Always use a push stick when the trailing end comes close to the cutter. If a stopped groove is needed install a stop block.

RABBETING

Cutting rabbets is very similar to making dados and grooves. For making rabbets along an edge or face, the saw is set up in the ripping position. The rip lock secures the motor unit to the arm. Remove the existing fence and replace it with a straight scrap piece. This will allow the rotating dado head to be lowered into the fence, exposing the desired amount of the dado head. Guide the stock past the dado head (Fig. 24-26). Always use a push stick. Utilize standard crosscutting techniques for producing rabbets across the end of the board.

COMBINATION RABBETING AND SAWING

By installing both a saw blade and a dado head, two operations can be accomplished with one pass of the saw. It is recommended that you use an 8-in. (202-

FIGURE 24-24
Cutting a stopped dado.

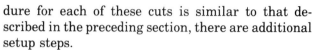

FIGURE 24-26
Cutting a rabbet.

mm) dado head with a 10-in. (254-mm) saw blade. Substitute one of the outside cutters on the dado head with the saw blade. This will allow the dado to make a groove while the stock is cut into.

When the stock is crosscut using this setup a rabbet will be made across the end and the stock cut to length (Fig. 24-27). By placing the saw in the rip mode, a rabbet is cut along the edge and the board is ripped to width. To prevent the blade from cutting into the table, an auxiliary table and fence can be installed.

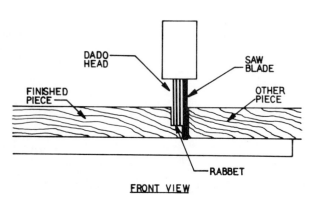

FIGURE 24-27
Making a combination rabbet and saw cut.

COVING

Cove cutting produces a recess or concave cut. Coves are sometimes used for decorative cuts on molding and trim. Either the outside cutter from a dado head or a molding head can be used to make this cut. You will need to start by laying out the desired depth and width of the cove (Fig. 24-28). Use a square to mark it on the end of the stock that will come in contact with the blade first.

Set up the saw by placing it in the bevel position. Raise the blade until the bottom of the cutting arc is equal to the depth of the cove. Pull the saw out on the arm until the blade is centered on the layout lines. Since only a light cut can be made with each pass of the board, raise the blade until only an $\frac{1}{8}$-in. (3-mm)-deep cut is made. Using ripping techniques, feed the stock past the angled rotating blade (Fig. 24-29). After each cut, lower the blade $\frac{1}{8}$ in. (3 mm). Continue this procedure until the cut has reached the width layout lines.

By varying the angle of the yoke and the diameter of the blade, different shapes of coves can be made. Using a smaller-diameter blade, for example, will produce a deeper recess for a fixed width of a cove. Angling the yoke at a larger angle will also make a deeper recess.

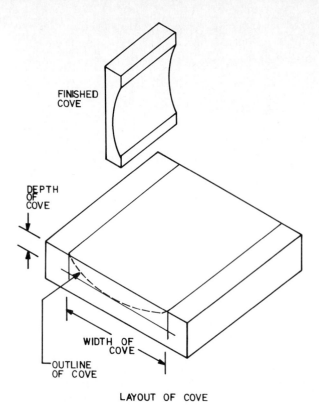

FIGURE 24-28
Layout the width and depth of the cove to make the concave out.

FIGURE 24-29
Cutting a cove.

SAUCER CUTTING

Saucer cutting is a form of cove cutting where the board is kept in a stationary position (Fig. 24-30). The cutting action will produce a dish-shaped recess.

Since the side ring guards will interfere with the cut, they must be removed. Select a board long enough to be securely clamped to the saw table. Next, raise the motor unit. Place the saw in a 45° bevel position. While holding out on the bevel positive lock, use your left hand to grasp the antikick-back rod or upper blade housing and pivot the motor

FIGURE 24-30
Making a saucer cut. (Courtesy of Black & Decker.)

FIGURE 24-31
Setting up to make a horizontal crosscut.

unit back and forth. Note where the bottom of the arc is made. Center the stock under this arc or move the board wherever the saucer is to be made. Pull the motor unit out on the arm if the cut needs to be farther out on the board. Tighten the rip lock to keep the motor unit from moving. Be certain to clamp the stock securely to the table.

Setting the blade to take a very light cut, turn on the power. Make the first cut by pivoting the motor unit back and forth. Lower the blade $\frac{1}{16}$ in. (2 mm) and repeat the process. Continue this until the desired depth is reached. The last pass should be an extra light cut to achieve the best-quality surface.

HORIZONTAL CUTTING
AND TENONING

To place the saw in the horizontal position, first raise the motor unit to approximately 4 in. (102 mm) above the table. Remove the standard blade guard assembly and install the special guard designed for this purpose. The motor unit is pivoted into the horizontal position. Once the blade is parallel to the table, the bevel positive stop will automatically slide into a positioning hole.

To make the cut the stock must be raised above the table and an auxiliary table must be constructed as shown in Fig. 24-31. It should be clamped securely to the radial arm saw table.

To make a tenon on the end of a board, use crosscutting techniques. Raise or lower the motor unit until the blade is in line with the layout lines on the sample stock. The depth of cut depends on how close the end of the board is to the blade. Keep your hands at least 4 in. (102 mm) from the path of the blade and make the cut.

To make a horizontal cut along the edge of a board, swing the yoke into the ripping position. A groove along an edge is shown in Fig. 24-32. Use an auxiliary table that extends across the entire length of the standard table. A push stick is required for narrow pieces. Use standard safe ripping techniques.

USING THE MOLDING HEAD

The molding head allows the radial arm saw to be used for shaper cuts. Because there are many different styles of changeable cutters for the molding head, the possible shapes you can produce are almost unlimited (Fig. 24-33). Trace around the cutter on the end of the stock to check the possible profile it

FIGURE 24-32
Making a groove in the horizontal cutting position. (Courtesy of Black & Decker.)

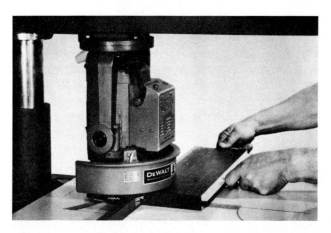

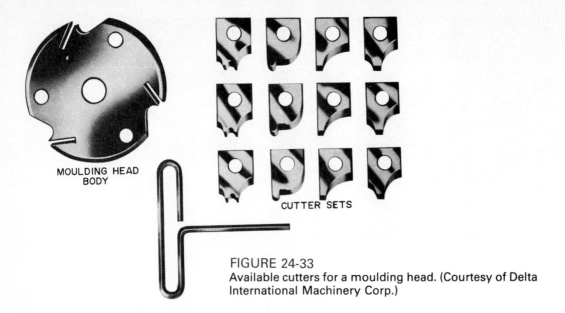

FIGURE 24-33
Available cutters for a moulding head. (Courtesy of Delta International Machinery Corp.)

can make. By adjusting the molding head from crosscutting to ripping to horizontal cutting positions, the same set of cutters will produce different-shaped patterns.

Crosscut molding cuts are done much like a dado cut. Remove the standard blade guard assembly and install the special guard. To prevent the edge of the stock closest to the fence from tearing out, a new fence which is taller than the top face of the stock should be installed (Fig. 24-34).

Sometimes horizontal-type cutting is used to shape the edges of the boards. An auxiliary molding table is used to raise the stock. Because the molding head is thick, a two-piece fence is required. Remove the standard fence and replace it with a shop-made two-piece fence. It must be tall enough to support

the entire edge of the stock but allow the cutter to extend through the face of the fence. The molding head can also be utilized to make specialized cuts. By building a vee-shaped fence the edges of a circular disk can be shaped (Fig. 24-35). The larger the diameter of the disk, the wider the vee will need to be.

Decorative molding strips can be produced by running the edge on a wide board. The shaped strip is then ripped from the board to make the molding.

SAWING TO A PATTERN

When several pieces are needed of the same shape, pattern sawing can be used. Each side of the piece must be no smaller than 10 in. (254 mm) long.

Make a pattern exactly the same shape and size as the desired pieces (Fig. 24-36). Drive three or more sharpened screws through the pattern. The

FIGURE 24-34
Crosscutting with the moulding head.

FIGURE 24-35
Shaping the edge of a circular disk.

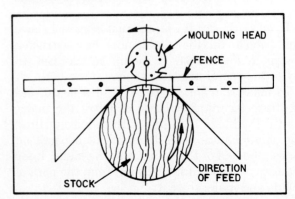

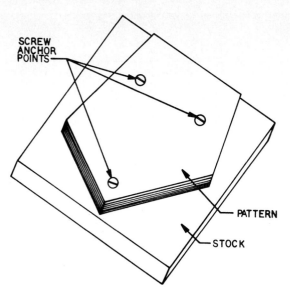

FIGURE 24-36
Attach the pattern to the bottom of the stock.

FIGURE 24-37
Set-up for sawing to a pattern.

points should extend through the pattern by $\frac{1}{8}$ in. (3 mm). Install a guide fence in place of the standard saw fence (Fig. 24-37). The height of the clamp guide fence should be the same as the thickness of the pattern. Clamp the guide fence to the standard fence. Set the saw in the out-rip position and align the saw blade exactly flush with the outside edge of the guide fence.

Cut the stock to rough size. Attach the piece to the pattern by tapping it lightly with a mallet. The tips of the screws must penetrate into the stock. Guide the pattern along the edge of the guide body. Any stock extending over the edge of the pattern will be cut away. Remove the pattern and attach the next piece.

25

BANDSAWS

The bandsaw is typically used to produce curves (Fig. 25-1). It is, however, well known for its large depth-of-cut capacity. This allows the machine to resaw thick stock into thinner boards. The bandsaw is unusual because the blade consists of a closed flexible band of steel with saw teeth cut on one edge.

PARTS OF THE BANDSAW

A bandsaw has two blade wheels which are supported by a heavy framework. There is an *upper blade wheel* mounted above the table (Fig. 25-1). It keeps the blade tight and centered in the bandsaw guides. It is not directly connected to the motor and serves as an idler wheel. There is also a wheel located below the table. This wheel is connected to the motor usually by V-belts and drives the blade. Both the upper and lower wheels are protected by a door guard.

The outer edge of the wheels is covered with a *rubber tire*. The tire protects the blade so that it will not come in contact with the metal wheels. Smaller bandsaws have tires made of a strip of rubber cemented to the wheel. Larger models have steel-reinforced tires, which will last longer.

The *table* provides a work surface to position the stock. It is most generally located at a 90° angle to the blade. For cutting chamfers and bevels the table can be tilted to the right up to 45° and 5° to the left by loosening the tilt knob. By tightening the *tilt knob,* the table is secured to the desired angle. The angle scale will give the angle at which the table is positioned. A slot is cut into the table to slide the blade though. A *throat plate* is also inserted in the middle of the table to fill in the hole.

To the rear of the upper blade wheel are the controls for tightening and tracking the blade (Fig. 25-2). The *tension handwheel* raises and lowers the upper wheel. The higher the wheel is raised, the tighter the blade will become. In addition, the raising and lowering of this wheel allows for slightly different lengths of blades and for the blade to be removed. The *tracking knob* tilts the wheel in or out. This will angle the blade forward or backward in order that the blade can be centered on the wheel.

The two *bandsaw blade guides* keep the blade from twisting and being pushed off the wheels (Fig. 25-3). One guide is attached to the movable arm above the table. The bottom guide is permanently mounted on the bottom side of the table. Both the upper and bottom guides contain guide pins and a

BANDSAW SAFETY RULES

1. Keep fingers at least 4 in (102 mm) away from the blade while cutting stock.
2. Set the saw guard and guide $\frac{1}{4}$ inch (6 mm) above the stock to be cut before turning on the power.
3. Avoid placing the fingers or hands in line with the blade.
4. Turn off the power and allow the blade to come to a full stop before backing out of a cut.
5. Make certain that the blade has come to a complete stop before making any adjustments on the machine.
6. If a blade should break, do the following:
   a. Turn off the power.
   b. Stand to the left of the machine.
   c. Notify the instructor.
7. Use a vee block when cutting a cylindrical stock.

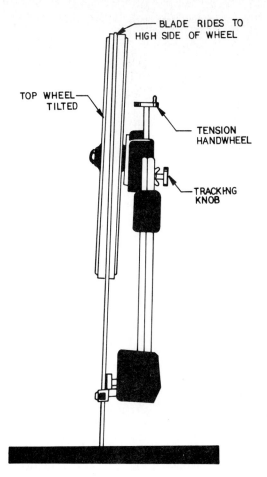

FIGURE 25-2
The tension handwheel and tracking knob keep the blade tight and centered between the two wheels.

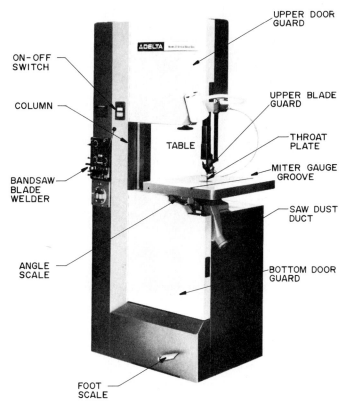

FIGURE 25-1
Major parts of the bandsaw. (Courtesy of Delta International Machinery Corp.)

thrust wheel. The *guide pins* are adjusted in or out to the side of the blade and keep the blade from being twisted. The *thrust wheel* is located directly behind the blade and supports the back edge of the blade. Without the thrust wheel the blade would be pushed off the wheels.

Some bandsaws contain a *footbrake* for rapidly stopping the blade. To use the brake the power is first turned off at the on-off switch. You can then step on the brake footpad which will stop the blade.

PURCHASING A BANDSAW

Always specify the size when purchasing a bandsaw. There are two considerations when determining size. The first is the distance or opening between the inside of the blade to the inside of the column. Most bandsaws have a throat size of 12 to 36 in. (305 to 914 mm). A good general-purpose bandsaw generally will have either a 14-or 20-in. (356- or 508-mm) throat size. The larger the opening, the wider a board can be cut between the blade and column. The second item in determining size is the maximum distance from the tabletop to the bottom of the raised upper blade guide. These heights range from $6\frac{1}{2}$ to 24 in. (165 to 610 mm). The larger size allows thicker or taller pieces to be cut.

A major consideration in the buying of a bandsaw is the blade guides (Fig. 25-3). The better the quality of the guides, the smoother the cut. They should have a large contact area to the sides of the blade and have a stable mounting. All parts should be replaceable to allow new components to be installed when they become worn.

FIGURE 25-3
A good-quality blade guide contains two guide pins and a thrust wheel.

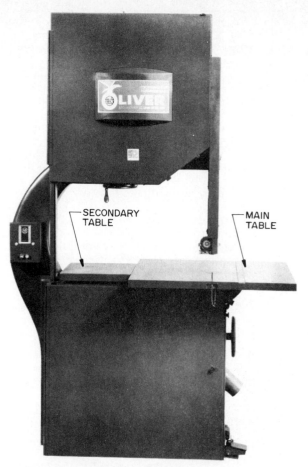

FIGURE 25-4
The secondary table provides support for extra wide material. (Courtesy of Oliver Machinery Company.)

The motor size for most general-purpose bandsaws should be at least $\frac{3}{4}$ HP. A larger motor size will allow thicker boards to be cut. Smaller bandsaws will have a 120-V motor which can be plugged into a conventional outlet. Larger bandsaws will have 220- or 440-V motors which are typically wired permanently to a junction box. The blade should travel at a rate between 1500 and 6000 feet per minute (fpm). For most general-purpose cutting the blade should travel at 4500 fpm.

Another item to consider in buying a bandsaw is the blade capacity. Although narrow blades are most often used, being able to utilize a wide blade is desirable for straight cutting. A long blade length is also beneficial. A longer blade will run cooler and stay sharper longer.

Purchase a miter gauge and rip fence with the bandsaw. They will increase the versatility and safety of the machine. Many straight cuts and some fixtures require the use of these accessories.

Table size can be a factor if larger pieces are to be cut. The larger the surface, the more support will be provided. Some commercial bandsaws have a secondary table which bridges the space between the column and the edge of the main table (Fig. 25-4).

SELECTING THE BLADE

Bandsaw blades are made from 100-ft-long coils of blade stock. The blade should be cut to proper length to fit around the bandsaw wheels according to the instructions of the machine manufacturer. The ends of the piece are welded with a band saw blade welder to form a finished blade (Fig. 25-5).

Blades can vary greatly in tooth styles and teeth per inch (Fig. 25-6). The most common tooth styles are the *skip, hook, buttress,* and *standard.* The set of the teeth provide clearance for the blade. Thick blades require more set than thin ones and are used primarily for making straight cuts. The additional set will produce a wide saw kerf and use up more material.

The number of teeth should also be specified. More *teeth per inch* will provide a smoother cut. It is important, however, to have large enough gullets to remove the sawdust. In specifying the number of teeth, the term *points per inch* is used. There will be one more point than the number of teeth per inch (Fig. 25-6). A five-tooth blade will have six points.

The width of the blade also can be varied. Blade widths start at $\frac{1}{8}$ in. (3 mm) and can reach over 1 in. (25 mm). The narrower the blade, the smaller the curve can be cut. Blades wider than $\frac{1}{2}$ in. (13 mm) work best for straight cuts. The most common bandsaw blade for general-purpose sawing is $\frac{3}{8}$ in. wide with five points per inch and having a hook set.

Most bandsaw blades are designed to be disposable. They are not resharpened or reset. Once the blade becomes dull, it is thrown away and a new one installed.

FIGURE 25-5
A bandsaw blade welder joins the two ends of the blade together.

REMOVING AND COILING THE BLADE

To remove a bandsaw blade, disconnect the power, remove the throat plate and open the door guards, then turn the tension handwheel counterclockwise. This will lower the upper wheel and loosen the tension on the blade. It can then be slipped from both wheels and passed through the slot in the table.

If the blade is to be stored, it should be coiled. This reduces the diameter of the blade. Start by holding the blade with the bottom of the loop just touching the floor (Fig. 25-7A). Place a foot on top the blade. The teeth should be pointing away from the operator. Bend the top of the loop downward by pushing the thumbs down (Fig. 25-7B). The teeth should point away from your body. Roll the hands outward until they face forward. Bend over and bring the hands together. The three smaller loops should form automatically (Fig. 25-7C).

If at any time the blade should start to knick or make a sharp bend, stop the procedure. Let the blade go back to the beginning step. Start the procedure over attempting to correct the mistake.

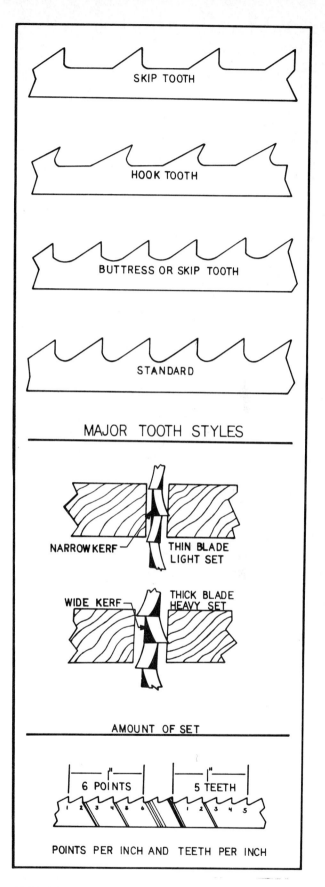

FIGURE 25-6
Styles of blade teeth and set.

(A)

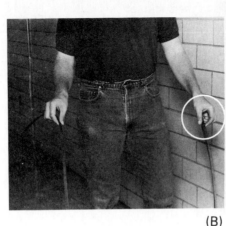

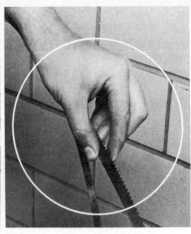

(B)

(C)

FIGURE 25-7
Steps in coiling a bandsaw blade: (A) starting position; (B) second step; (C) third step.

INSTALLING THE BLADE

Pull the bandsaw blade guides away from the sides of the blade and remove the throat plate. This will keep the guides from interfering with mounting the new blade. After uncoiling the new blade, hold it up in front of the bandsaw wheels. Make certain that the teeth next to the bandsaw guides are pointing forward and down.

Place the blade over the top of the upper bandsaw wheel. Slide the bottom of the loop over the bottom wheel. Center the blade in the middle of both wheels. Tighten the tension handwheel. This moves the upper bandsaw wheel upward and will tighten against the blade. Some bandsaws have a tension gauge (Fig. 25-8). This device indicates when the upper wheel has been raised the correct amount.

If a bandsaw does not have a tension gauge, tighten the blade until the blade deflects or moves to the side when pushed not more than ⅛ in. (3 mm). Too little tension will cause the blade to move or lead to one side while cutting. A blade with too much tension will break. Narrow thin blades require more tension than do wider thicker blades.

Next, check the tracking of the bandsaw blade. Proper tracking requires the blade to ride in the middle of the bandsaw wheels (Fig. 25-2). Rotate the upper wheel by hand. If the blade does not center itself on the wheel, turn the tracking knob a small

FIGURE 25-8
The tension gauge indicates when the upper wheel has been raised to the proper height.

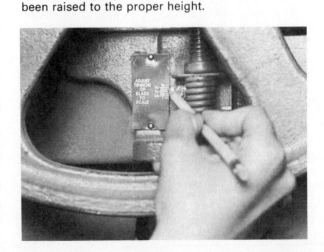

amount. Turn the bandsaw wheel again. Continue moving the tracking knob and turning the bandsaw wheel each time until the blade is centered.

Move the upper thrust wheel of the bandsaw guide in until it almost touches the back of the blade. Lock the guides into position. Do the same with the bottom thrust wheel. Turn the bandsaw wheels by hand. The thrust wheel should turn only when the blade is making a cut.

The side guides should be moved forward until the front edge of the guides are just behind the gullets of the blade. If the guides are too far forward, they will knock the set off of the blade. Place a piece of typing paper on each side of the blade (Fig. 25-9). Slide the side guides in until they just touch the paper. Lock into position. Remove the paper to provide the proper clearance. Repeat the procedure for the bottom set of guides.

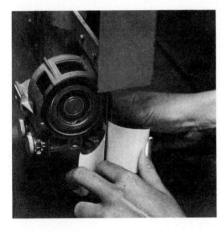

FIGURE 25-9
Paper spacers provide the proper side distance between the blade and guide pin.

Replace the guards and throat plate. Turn on the power by quickly switching the power on and off. This will cause the blade to coast. Check that the blade is properly tracking and make adjustments accordingly. Cut a scrap and check for squareness of cut with a square. If the cut is not square, adjust the table until it is perpendicular to the blade.

LAYING OUT THE PATTERN

Before laying out the pattern, plane the material to the desired finish thickness. Make certain that any surfaces which are not to be bandsawed are smooth and true. If the part requires straight edges and faces, it is better to use a tablesaw or jointer to produce these surfaces. It is much easier to do this ini-

tially when the board has square corners than after curves have been cut.

A major concern with laying out the material is achieving the maximum *yield* or usage from the material. If only one part is to be cut, select a piece of material that is slightly larger than the finished size. It is important always to have a small amount of waste on the outside edge of any curve (Fig. 25-10). This will prevent the blade from leaving the material and making it difficult to restart the cut. A great deal of waste material outside the cut, however, will only increase the cost of the project.

When more than one part is needed, layout becomes even more important. Study the shapes carefully and see how they can best fit on the stock to get

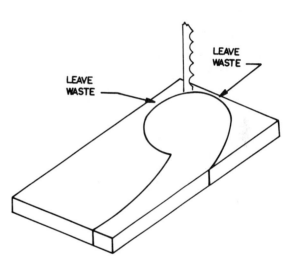

FIGURE 25-10
Lay out the pattern so that the blade will always be in contact with the material.

the best yield. It works best to cut patterns out of paper and then try different arrangements on the board. Sometimes the patterns can be angled to get a closer fit. Be careful, however, that there is sufficient room for the blade to pass between the pieces. Some pieces also require that the grain run in a certain direction. If this is the case, parts may need to lie in a particular direction.

When parallel curves are required, another form of stock utilization can be used. The size of the original board can be reduced considerably if the waste from the first cut is glued to the opposite straight edge (Fig. 25-11). After the adhesive dries, the second cut can be made. This is called *nesting of parts*.

Another consideration in layout is the face on which the pattern is drawn. This is particularly important with long boards. Marking it out on the wrong side will cause the board to strike the column as the cut is being made (Fig. 25-12).

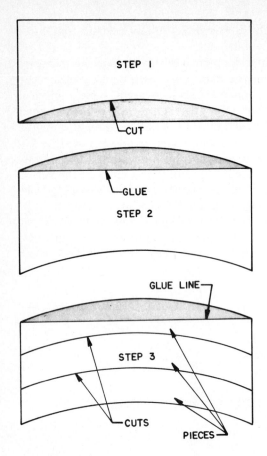

FIGURE 25-11
Nesting of parts saves a great deal of material.

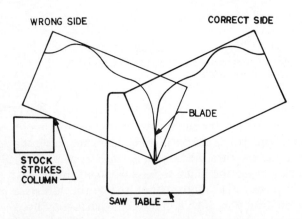

FIGURE 25-12
Laying the pattern on the right side of the board will prevent the stock from striking the column

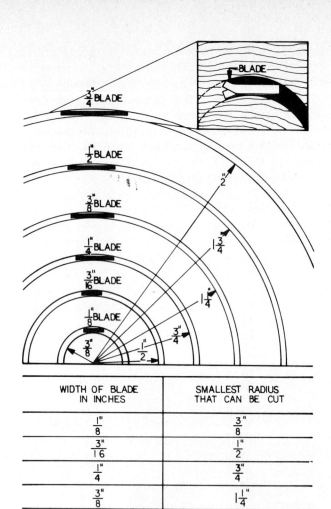

WIDTH OF BLADE IN INCHES	SMALLEST RADIUS THAT CAN BE CUT
$\frac{1}{8}$"	$\frac{3}{8}$"
$\frac{3}{16}$"	$\frac{1}{2}$"
$\frac{1}{4}$"	$\frac{3}{4}$"
$\frac{3}{8}$"	$1\frac{1}{4}$"
$\frac{1}{2}$"	$1\frac{3}{4}$"
$\frac{3}{4}$"	2"

FIGURE 25-13
Smallest radius that can be cut with each width of blade.

SETTING UP THE BANDSAW

Before turning on the power, first determine if the proper blade is mounted on the machine. Next establish what is the smallest radius on the pattern. Refer to Fig. 25-13 to see the maximum width of blade that can be used. The narrower the blade, the sharper the curve can be made. Wide blades will produce straighter cuts. Although relief cuts can allow smaller curves to be made, it is desirable to make the cut in one pass.

After the stock has been planed to thickness, place it on the table next to the blade. The material must have a flat surface to place against the table or be held in a fixture to keep it from rocking. Adjust the upper blade guide assembly to $\frac{1}{4}$ in. (6 mm) above the stock (Fig. 25-14).

OPERATING THE BANDSAW

After the pattern has been laid out, plan the order of cuts. There should be as little backing out of cuts as possible. Usually, it is best to cut the shortest distance first (Fig. 25-15). Also make straight cuts before cutting curves. It is easier to back out of a straight cut. If it is necessary to cut up to a line, turn

274   CHAPTER 25   BANDSAWS

FIGURE 25-14
There should be no more than $\frac{1}{4}$ in. (6 mm) between the guide and stock.

off the power, allow the blade to stop turning and then back out of the cut. It may be easier to cut through the waste and start the cut from the opposite end.

To feed the material forward, use a firm pressure. Feed the material as fast as the blade will efficiently cut. Too fast a rate will break the blade. Too slow a feed will overheat the blade and dull it. It is very important to keep the hands out of the direct path of the blade. If the board should accidentally split or the hands should slip, the hands should be on either side of the blade.

FIGURE 25-15
Make the shortest cuts first.

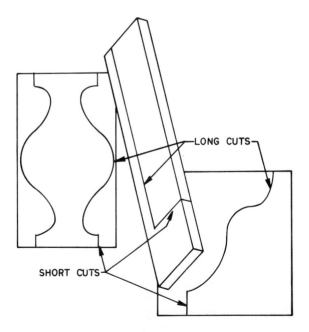

CUTTING CURVES

The major secret to cutting accurate curves is to achieve a high degree of skill. This comes through a great deal of practice. Since most are cut using free-hand techniques, the operator must be able to guide the stock successfully. With practice, the pattern can consistently be cut on the layout line in a minimal amount of time.

After the proper blade is selected, the machine adjusted and the best path for the blade selected, the cutting can begin. Although the blade must be kept in the waste area, stay immediately next to the layout line. This will reduce the amount of material that must be later sanded or filed away. If the blade wanders across the layout line, back the board up and recut.

If the pattern contains curves which are too small to cut with one pass, *relief cuts* are required (Fig. 25-16). These are short cuts through the waste within $\frac{1}{32}$ in. (1 mm) of the layout line. As the pattern

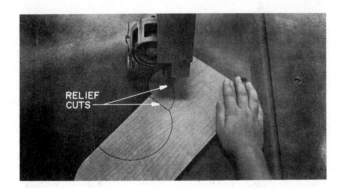

FIGURE 25-16
Relief cuts allow small curves to be cut with a wide blade.

is cut, the small pieces will fall free. This keeps the back of the blade from rubbing against the saw kerf. If internal circles or parts of circles are required, first bore them on the drill press using a drill bit of the same diameter as the layout (Fig. 25-17). This saves time and gives superior results.

MULTIPLE CUTTING

Several pieces of the same pattern can be cut at one time. Use a large bandsaw capable of making heavy cuts. Be careful not to cut more pieces than what can be easily cut. First layout the pattern on one piece. Stack two or more pieces on top of each other with the pattern piece on top. Drive nails through the

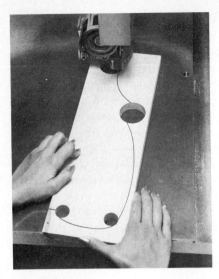

FIGURE 25-17
First boring holes will save a great deal of time.

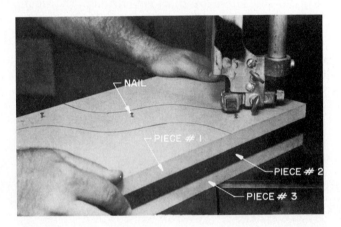

FIGURE 25-18
Cutting more than one piece at a time will speed production. Be careful not to saw into the nails.

waste portion. Cut the boards to pattern (Fig. 25-18). All pieces will be the exact same shape.

CUTTING TO A PATTERN

In some cases it is desirable to use a pattern to cut multiple parts. Cutting after a pattern has the advantages of producing identical parts and requiring a lower operator skill level. It does require time to set up and the curves must be moderate in size.

A modified *pivot block* is clamped to the table (Fig. 25-19). A step is made on the bottom side of the pivot block to allow the waste to pass under it. It has a curved end whose radius will match the smallest radius on the pattern. The center of the pivot block should be in the same line as the front edge of the blade. A notch is cut into the edge of the pivot block

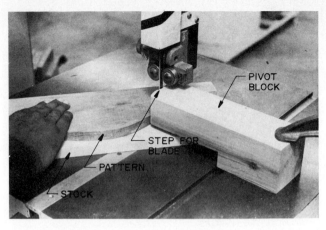

FIGURE 25-19
Proper set-up for cutting after a pattern.

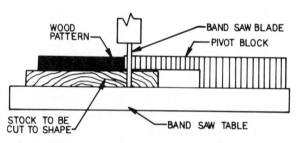

FIGURE 25-20
Cutting a piece using a pattern and pivot block.

for the blade to fit into (Fig. 25-19). It is very important that the teeth set to the left are exactly on a line even with the edge of the pivot block.

Make a pattern out of $\frac{3}{4}$-in. (19-mm) hardwood the exact same size as the finished piece. Place screws through the pattern which will extend into the stock $\frac{1}{4}$ in. (6 mm). Center the pattern over the stock and drive the screw into the back of the board. guide the pattern past the pivot block (Fig. 25-20). Keep the pattern at right angles to each curve. Remove the screws after the cut is made.

COMPOUND SAWING

Compound sawing requires that two adjoining surfaces be bandsawed to a curved pattern. The process produces a *compound curve*. Although there are many examples of compound sawing, the cabriole leg is the most popular.

To make a cabriole leg, square the stock to size and make any required mortises or dowel joints. Lay out and cut a full-size cardboard template (Fig. 25-21). This is the most important step when making a cabriole leg. Designing a leg that is both beautiful and strong can be a challenge.

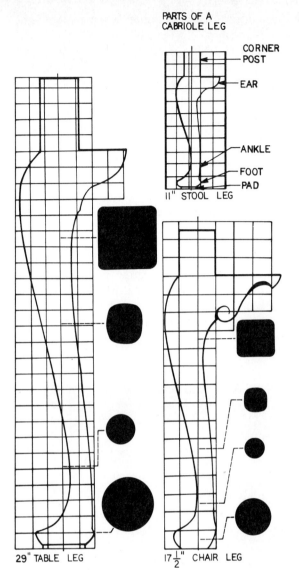

PARTS OF A
CABRIOLE LEG

CORNER
POST

EAR

ANKLE

FOOT
PAD

11" STOOL LEG

29" TABLE LEG

17½" CHAIR LEG

FIGURE 25-21
Design a cabriole leg with the foot centered.

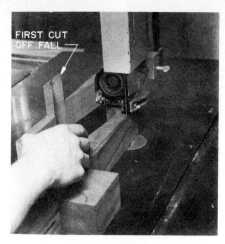

FIRST CUT
OFF FALL

FIGURE 25-22
Cutting the first side of a cabriole leg. The waste or off-fall is to the left of the blade.

and positioning against the bandsaw table. Roll the leg 90° and mark the second adjacent side.

Cut the second side using the same techniques as for the first (Fig. 25-23). After making the last cut, use rasps, files, and abrasive paper to smooth the surfaces (Fig. 25-24). The foot of the leg can be made round by also using hand techniques.

To give the cabriole leg a more flowing appearance, *wings* or *ears* can be added as a secondary operation (Fig. 25-21). These are small extensions doweled to the side of each leg. Use a file to blend the wings into the curved top of the cabriole leg.

Some compound curves are not symmetrical and require two templates. Examples of unsymmetrical compound curves include a boat hull and shoe blanks. They can be cut using the same techniques as discussed before except a different template is used for each cut.

FIGURE 25-23
Cutting the second side of a cabriole leg with the waste taped to the sides.

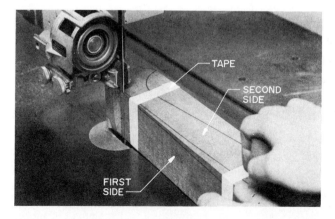

TAPE

SECOND
SIDE

FIRST
SIDE

If the cabriole leg is 15 in. (381 mm) or less in height, make the template no wider than 2¼ in. (64 mm). Legs that are longer than 15 in. (381 mm) can be made from a template up to 3 in. (76 mm) wide. It is of prime importance that the center line at the top of the leg pass through the foot. Ideally, the center line should pass through the center of the foot. After the cabriole leg has been cut, it should stand by itself.

Trace around the template on one of the sides. After installing a narrow blade, cut out the pattern on this side of the leg. Bandsaw each line with one smooth pass (Fig. 25-22). Do not make any relief cuts unless necessary.

Tape the waste or off-fall back on the leg. This will provide a flat surface for drawing the pattern

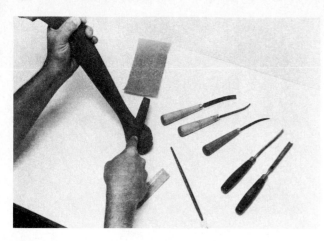

FIGURE 25-24
Work the cabriole leg smooth and to the final shape with files and abrasive paper.

CUTTING CIRCLES

Cutting a circle can be done in one of two ways. If only a few pieces are needed, first scribe the circle with a compass. The circles can then be freehanded on the bandsaw. This method requires a great deal of operator skill to produce a smooth true circle. A circle cutting fixture is recommended if a perfect circle or segment of a circle is required. Very little skill is needed to produce large quantities of circles with this technique. It does call for a sharp blade with even set.

To make a circle-cutting fixture, select a piece of plywood slightly larger than the right half of the bandsaw table (Fig. 25-25). Center a dovetail dado

FIGURE 25-25
Parts of a circle cutting fixture.

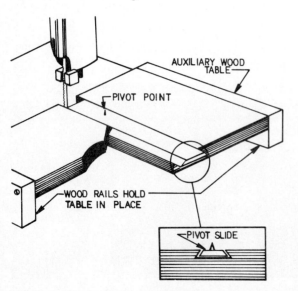

on the face of the plywood immediately to the right of the bandsaw blade. Insert a dovetail-shaped hardwood strip into the dado. Wax the strip so that it will slide in and out freely. Clamp the plywood to the tabletop. Scribe a mark from the leading edge of the blade across the *pivot strip*.

Remove the strip and from the bottom side drive a small flathead wood screw 1 in. (25 mm) from the end. The tip of the screw should extend through the face approximately $\frac{1}{4}$ in. (6 mm). File this tip to a sharply tapered point to serve as a pivot point. Slide the strip in the dado positioning it so that the pivot point is the same distance away from the saw tooth set to the right as the radius of the circle. Clamp the pivot strip in the dado with a C-clamp. Square the stock to rough width and length on the tablesaw. Center the board over the screw point and push down. If the wood is hard, use a mallet to tap the center of the board. One edge must be against the blade. Turn on the power and slowly turn the stock (Fig. 25-26).

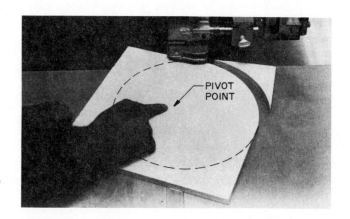

FIGURE 25-26
Making a circle with a circle cutting fixture.

CUTTING ROUNDED CORNERS

A corner can easily be rounded on the bandsaw using a pivoting fixture (Fig. 25-27). Mount a piece of $\frac{3}{4}$-in. (19-mm) plywood over the right side of the bandsaw table. Draw a line perpendicular to the front edge of the blade. Place a short $\frac{1}{2}$-in. (13-mm) dowel pin along this line (Fig. 25-28). The center of the dowel should be the same distance from the blade as the radius of the rounded corner. Construct a pivoting table to cradle the stock. It has a hole in it to fit over the dowel pin. Place a stop on the plywood to keep the stock from turning too far. Position the stock in the pivoting table and turn the table to cut the corner.

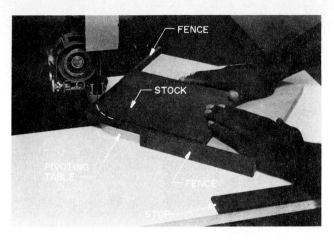

FIGURE 25-27
Rounding corners using a pivoting fixture.

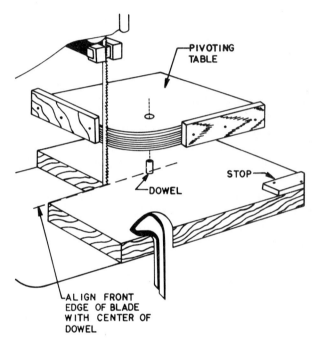

FIGURE 25-28
Parts of a pivoting fixture.

CROSSCUTTING A BOARD

To cut a board squarely across the end requires the use of a miter gauge. Place the gauge in the miter gauge groove to the right of the blade. The front of the gauge should be covered with a piece of wood (Fig. 25-29). Glue a piece of coarse abrasive paper to the face of the board. This abrasive-covered board will prevent the stock from slipping to the side.

Mount the widest available blade on the saw. The wider blade will prevent the cut from drifting when cutting a straight line. Square a line where the cut is to be made. Align the layout line with the

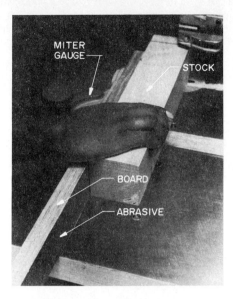

FIGURE 25-29
Crosscutting a board using a miter gauge. Note the abrasive covered board on the gauge.

saw tooth set to the right. Hold the board against the miter gauge as it passes the blade.

RIPPING STOCK

There are three methods of ripping stock on the bandsaw. Regardless of the method, use at least a $\frac{1}{2}$-in. (13-mm)-wide blade. The freehand method requires that a line be scribed where the cut is to be made. Place the left hand flat on the table and use the edge of the thumb as a guide. Slide the stock along the thumb (Fig. 25-30). Move the trailing end to the left or right to keep the blade centered on the layout line.

The second method requires the use of a rip fence. Place it to the right of the blade (Fig. 25-31).

FIGURE 25-30
Ripping a board using the freehand technique.

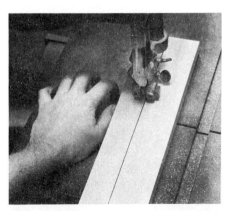

FIGURE 25-31
Ripping a board using a rip fence.

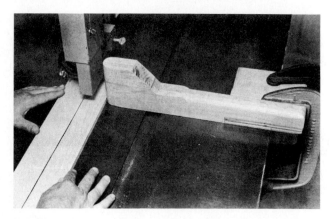

FIGURE 25-32
Ripping a board using a pivot block.

Clamp the fence down so that the distance from the saw tooth set to the right is equal to the width of the board. Use a push stick to feed the board.

The third method requires that a pivot block first be made (Fig. 25-32). Round one end and sand it smooth. The height of the pivot block should be slightly less than the stock to be ripped. Clamp the pivot block to the right of the blade. The rounded end should be in line with the leading edge of the blade. Feed the stock past the blade. If the blade starts to drift one direction or the other, move the trailing end of the board in the direction the cut is heading.

RESAWING A BOARD

Resawing lumber on the bandsaw allows two or more thin boards to be made from one thicker piece. Unlike the tablesaw, the bandsaw makes the cut in one pass. Because the bandsaw kerf is only $\frac{1}{16}$ in. (2 mm) wide much less waste is also generated. If book match grain is required for raised panel doors or in an attractive glue joint, resawing is an easy method of producing this material.

FIGURE 25-33
Resawing a board with a rip fence and featherboard.

To achieve the straightest cut, install the widest blade available. A $\frac{3}{4}$-inch (19-mm) blade works well. A wide blade will run cooler and not drift away from a straight line. Use a slow feed rate because of the heavy cut.

Resawing can be accomplished with either a rip fence or a pivot block. With the rip fence method, first clamp it to the table (Fig. 25-33). Stock is fed past the blade using a push stick. An elevated featherboard on the outside surface of the board will help keep the stock against the fence. Position the featherboard in front of the blade.

Resawing with a pivot block requires that a shop-made pivot block be constructed (Fig. 25-34). The device should be slightly less in height than the width of the board to be resawed. Bandsaw a curve on the front end of the pivot block. Sand this radius smooth.

Position the pivot block the same distance away from the blade as the desired thickness of the

FIGURE 25-34
Resawing with a pivot block.

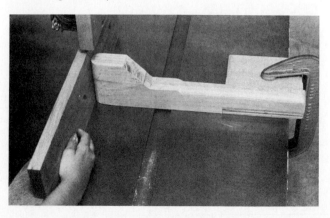

stock plus $\frac{1}{8}$ in. (3 mm). Since the bandsaw will not produce a finished surface, the extra $\frac{1}{8}$ in. (3 mm) will provide material to be planed. The front curve of the pivot block should be in line with the leading edge of the blade.

Turn on the power and push the stock forward. If the cut is not parallel to the face of the board direct the trailing end of the board to the right or left. Once the saw kerf returns to a straight line, move the trailing end back parallel to the blade.

CUTTING SQUARE INSIDE CORNERS

Square corners can be cut by a variety of methods. When several pieces are to be cut bore a large round turning hole in each corner (Fig. 25-35). This allows the blade to be turned without binding. A mortiser can also be used. It will give a square hole which needs no further attention.

A square corner can also be cut using only the bandsaw. Start by making a straight cut on each side of the board along the layout line (Fig. 25-36). On the second straight cut, saw up to the intersecting line and back out partway. Next cut a large-diameter curve over to the first cut. Remove the waste and cut away the remaining portion.

Method B of cutting a square corner requires sawing up to the intersecting line and backing up the blade a couple of inches (Fig. 25-36). Saw forward again but to the side of the first cut. Repeat the process until a large notch is made in the waste portion. Turn the blade in the notch and cut in the next direction.

FIGURE 25-35
A turning hole allows the board to be turned at the corner.

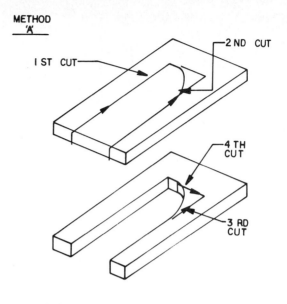

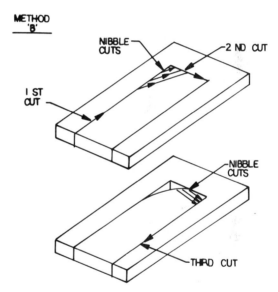

FIGURE 25-36
Cutting an inside corner using only the bandsaw.

FIGURE 25-37
Ripping a cylinder using a vee block.

CUTTING CYLINDRICAL STOCK

Because round stock such as dowel pins have a tendency to roll, they must be cradled in a vee block. Never freehand-cut round stock. Use the miter gauge and vee block to crosscut cylindrical stock.

To rip a round piece requires the use of a rip fence (Fig. 25-37). Position the rip fence so that when the vee block is positioned against the face of the rip fence, the blade is centered at the bottom of the vee. Cut into the vee block so that the blade is positioned halfway along the length of the block. Scribe a line along the length of the cylindrical stock. Rip the stock by using a push stick.

26

SCROLL SAWS

The scroll saw is best known for its ability to produce small intricately curved shapes in thin material (Fig. 26-1). Many woodworkers also call this machine a *jig saw*. The scroll saw has an unusual cutting action when compared to other equipment. It has a *reciprocating blade* or a cutting tooling that is moved up and down to saw the material. This cutting action can be compared to a hand coping saw.

PARTS OF THE SCROLL SAW

The major parts of the scroll saw are the overarm, blade chucks, table, and crank shaft drive (Fig. 26-1). To the rear of the saw is the *overarm*. It is a structural part that connects the base to the *tension sleeve* and *upper blade chuck*. The base holds the *table, motor,* and the *crank shaft drive*. The crank shaft drive is responsible for changing the circular motion of the motor to the reciprocating movement for the blade.

To keep the blade running in a straight line, the scroll saw has two *blade chucks* and one *blade guide* (Fig. 26-2). The upper blade chuck is attached to the end of the tension sleeve at the end of the

overarm. Located below the table is the lower blade chuck, which is attached to the crank shaft drive.

The upper guide assembly is located on the end of the guide post (Fig. 26-2). Both are adjusted up or down by loosening the guide post thumb screw. At the end of the guide assembly is the support disk and guide roller. They keep the blade from twisting and being pushed backwards.

Stock is positioned against the table in order to be machined. To cut a bevel, the table can be tilted to the left or right up to 45° (Fig. 26-3). Loosen the *tilt knob* to allow the table to move. An *angle scale* located below the table indicates the set angle. In the center of the table is a hole that holds the *table insert*. Removing the table insert allows a new blade to be passed through the opening in the table.

PURCHASING A SCROLL SAW

There are not a great many items to consider when purchasing a scroll saw. This is because there are few options from which to select. Most manufacturers offer only one size. The size of the scroll saw is determined by measuring the distance to the near-

SCROLL SAW SAFETY RULES

1. Always keep the fingers out of the line of the saw blade.
2. Disconnect the power before making any adjustments on the machine.
3. Make sure that the spring holddown is pressing lightly on the workpiece.
4. The surface placed against the table must be flat.

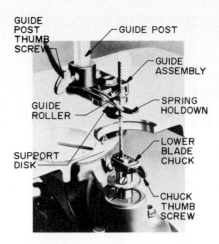

FIGURE 26-2
The blade is controlled by the blade chucks and blade guide. (Courtesy of Delta International Machinery Corp.)

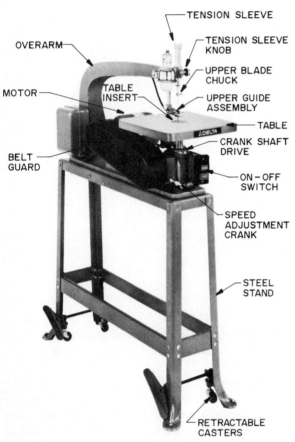

FIGURE 26-1
Major parts of a scroll saw. (Courtesy of Delta International Machinery Corp.)

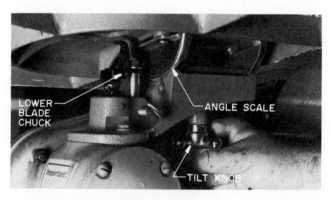

FIGURE 26-3
By loosening the tilt knob the table can be angled.

est inch from the front of the blade to the front of the overarm. This is called the *throat opening*. The most common size is 24 in. (610 mm). With a 24-in. (610-mm) scroll saw, the operator can saw to the middle of a 48-in. (1219-mm)-diameter circle.

Another feature to specify is the speed control. The speed of the reciprocating blade is controlled by one of three ways. The simplest and least expensive is a *cone pulley* (Fig. 26-4). A V-belt is moved from one step on the pulley to another to regulate the speed. Available speeds include 610, 910, 1255, and 1725 *cutting strokes per minute* (CS/M). The largest diameter pulley on the motor will give the *slowest*

speed. A more convenient method of adjusting the speed is with the variable speed pulley (Fig. 26-5). By turning the *speed-adjustment crank* the speed is changed. An infinite number of CS/M is available from 650 to 1700. Turning the crank to the clockwise will increase the CS/M rate. Only move the crank when the power is on. The newest method of varying the speed is with an *electronic system* (Fig. 26-6). By

FIGURE 26-4
A cone pulley allows the V-belt to be moved to change cutting speeds.

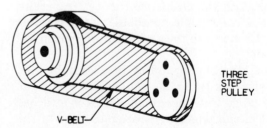

THREE STEP PULLEY

V-BELT

FIGURE 26-5
A variable-speed pulley changes the cutting speed by turning the speed adjustment crank.

simply turning a control knob, the up-and-down blade movement is changed. Any speed between 40 and 2000 CS/M can be selected. A lighted gauge indicates the cutting speed. For hard materials such as metals and plastics, select a very slow speed. Hardwood with large to medium-sized curves can be cut at a medium speed. Softwoods are cut at a fast speed. Other recommended speeds are given in Table 26-1.

Most scroll saws have available a steel stand. It provides a stable table that is relatively easy to move around. If a stand is not purchased, make certain that the saw is securely bolted to a sturdy tabletop.

FIGURE 26-6
The electronic system changes speeds by turning a control knob. (Courtesy of Delta International Machinery Corp.)

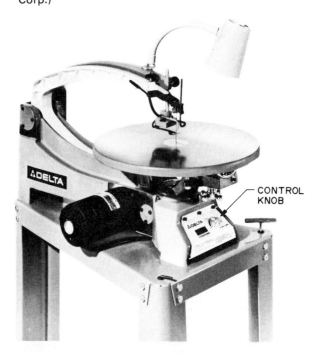

CONTROL KNOB

TABLE 26-1
Recommended Operating Speeds

Material or operation	General features of blade	Operating speed (rpm)
Hardwood		
¾-in. stock	Medium temper; set teeth; not over 15 teeth per inch	1000–1750
¼-in. stock	Medium temper; teeth need not be set	1750
Softwood		
¾-in. stock	Medium temper; set or wide-spaced teeth; not over 10 teeth per inch	1750
¼-in. stock	Teeth need not be tempered or set	1300–1750
Puzzles, inlays, marquetry	Not tempered; not set; blade must be thin	1300–1750
Soft metals		
Over ⅛ in.	Medium-hard temper; set teeth	650
Under ⅛ in.	Medium-hard temper; set or not set	650–1000
Iron and steel	Hard temper; set teeth	650
Plastic, bone, ivory		
Rough cut	Medium temper; set teeth	1000–1300
Finish cut	Medium temper; with or without set	1000–1750

SELECTING THE SCROLL SAW BLADES

Because there are numerous available blades, the scroll saw can cut many different materials. Blades can vary by length, width, thickness, and teeth per inch. Table 26-2 gives the recommended blades for various materials.

Select a thin narrow blade with many teeth for sharp curves or for cutting thin material. For thicker stock and larger curves, use a wider thicker blade with fewer teeth. The more teeth per inch, the slower the cut will be, but the smoother the surface. There should be at least three teeth in contact with the stock at all times. Blades are specifically designed to saw wood, plastic, metals, and many other materials. By referring to the information on the blade package, match the blade with the type of stock being cut.

Most blades are rectangular in shape and designed to be gripped by both the upper and lower blade chucks. They are called *jeweler's blades* (Fig.

26-7). Specialty blades can also be used. The *saber blade* is a *specialty blade* which is tapered and designed to be held only by the bottom blade guide. It is used for making internal cuts which do not contain many sharp curves. A *circular blade* is another specialty blade that can cut from any direction without turning the stock.

When not on the scroll saw, keep all blades in some type of storage rack or in a protective cover. This will keep them from touching each other and becoming dull.

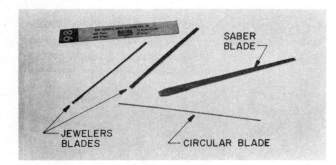

FIGURE 26-7
Styles of scroll saw blade.

INSTALLING THE BLADE

After selecting the best blade for the job, install it on the scroll saw. Start by unplugging the power cord. Remove the table insert in the middle of the table. With the teeth pointing downward and forward lower it through the hole in the table. Use a *guide board* to make certain that the blade is perpendicular to the table (Fig. 26-8).

FIGURE 26-8
A guide board assures that the blade is at a right angle to the table.

TABLE 26-2
Recommended Blade Styles

Material cut	Width in.	Teeth per inch	Blade full size
Steel ■ Iron Lead ■ Copper Aluminum	.070	32	▰▰▰▰▰
Pewter Asbestos Paper ■ Felt	.070	20	▰▰▰▰
Steel ■ Iron Lead ■ Copper Brass	.070	15	▰▰▰▰
Aluminum Pewter Asbestos	.085	15	▰▰▰▰
Wood	.110	20	▰▰▰▰
Asbestos ■ Brake Lining ■ Mica Steel ■ Iron Lead ■ Copper Brass Aluminum Pewter	.250	20	▰▰▰
Wood Veneer Plus Plastics Celluloid Hard Rubber Bakelite Ivory Extremely Thin Materials	.035	20	▱▱▱▱▱
Plastics Celluloid	.050	15	▱▱▱▱
Bakelite	.070	7	▱▱▱
Ivory ■ Wood	.110	7	◣◢
Wall Board Pressed Wood Wood ■ Lead Bone ■ Felt Paper ■ Copper Ivory Aluminum	.110	15	▰▰▰
Hard and Soft Wood	.110	10	◣◣◣
	.187	10	◣◣◣
	.250	7	◣◣
Pearl ■ Pewter Mica	.054	30	▱▱▱▱▱
Pressed Wood Sea Shells	.054	20	▰▰▰▰
Hard Leather	.085	12	▰▰▰▰

As a general rule, always select the narrowest blades recommended for intricate curve cutting and widest blades for straight and large curve cutting operations.

Source: Delta Internation Machinery Corp.

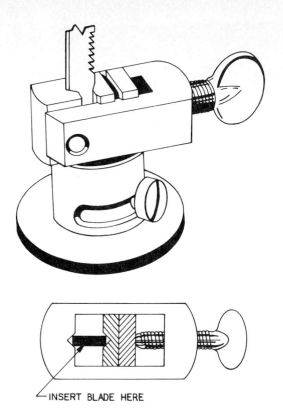

FIGURE 26-9
Position the blade between the chuck blocks.

INSERT BLADE HERE

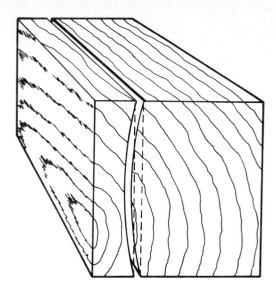

FIGURE 26-10
Drift produces a convex shape cut.

Insert the blade at least $\frac{1}{2}$ in. (13 mm) into the lower blade chuck. The blade must be placed between the chuck blocks before hand tightening the thumbscrew (Fig. 26-9).

Turn the motor shaft by hand until the blade chuck is at the bottom-most position. By loosening the tension sleeve knob, adjust the tension sleeve until the top blade chuck is approximately 1 in. (25 mm) above the top of the blade. This will provide the proper tension on the blade and keep it from flexing. Pull the chuck down over the blade. It, too, should cover the blade by $\frac{1}{2}$ in. (13 mm). Tighten the chuck thumbscrew.

The thinner and narrower the blade, the more tension is required. If the blade does have a tendency to bend, raise the tension sleeve an additional $\frac{1}{2}$ in. (13 mm). Occasionally, the blade will also *drift*. This creates a sideways convex type of cut along the edge (Fig. 26-10). To straighten the cut, increase the tension, use a wider blade, or select a blade with more teeth per inch.

Spaced around the *support disk* are several slots for supporting the blade (Fig. 26-11). Select the slot that allows the blade to move freely up and down. It should prevent the blade from twisting as curves are being cut. The disk should support the blade but not touch the saw teeth. Check that the front of the disk is located immediately behind the blade gullets. Always check the fit of the slot when installing a different blade. The support disk may need to be rotated to position a better-fitting slot to support the blade.

Move the *guide roller* out to keep the blade from bending backward (Fig. 26-2). Replace the table insert and position the stock to be cut next to the blade. By loosening the guide post thumbscrew, lower the upper guide. The spring hold-down must rest lightly on top of the stock. If the table is tilted, it is also necessary to angle the holddown to the same angle.

Turn the motor shaft by hand to check for proper adjustments. See that the table is set at the desired angle by checking the angle gauge. Plug in the power cord.

FIGURE 26-11
The support disk keeps the blade from twisting.

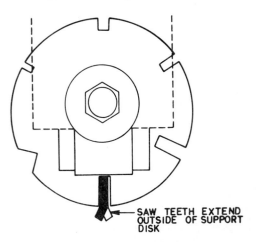

SAW TEETH EXTEND OUTSIDE OF SUPPORT DISK

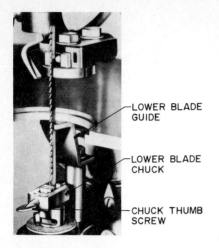

FIGURE 26-12
Installing a saber saw blade. (Courtesy of Delta International Machinery Corp.)

LOWER BLADE GUIDE

LOWER BLADE CHUCK

CHUCK THUMB SCREW

TEMPLATE

STOCK

FIGURE 26-13
Laying out a part using the template method.

To install a saber saw blade, install a *lower blade guide* below the table (Fig. 26-12). Since the upper blade guide is not used, this device will keep the saber saw blade from twisting. Rotate the lower blade chuck one-fourth of a turn. Insert the blade between the chuck thumbscrew. If much cutting is to be done with this type of blade, remove the overarm.

MAKING A LAYOUT

Before any cutting can be done, the pattern needs to be drawn or laid out on the stock. The simplest but slowest method is to draw the pattern on each piece. If only one or two parts are needed, this may be acceptable. A slightly faster method is to use a piece of carbon tracing over the drawing; the pattern will be transferred onto the material.

When several parts of the same shape are needed, the *template method* can be used (Fig. 26-13). First make a template out of cardboard, hardboard, sheet metal, or other long-wearing material. Place the template over the material and trace around it using a pencil. Keep the template from slipping as the pattern is being drawn. Using this piece will allow the original template to last longer.

Sometimes it is necessary to reduce or enlarge a pattern. The *graph method* allows the size of pattern to be changed easily (Fig. 26-14). Decide how many times smaller or larger the pattern should be than the original. If the pattern is to be made twice the size of the original drawing, draw ½-in. graph squares over the top of the drawing. Next draw 1-in. graph square on the stock. Wherever the object line of the pattern crosses a graph line on the drawing, place a corresponding mark on the same squire lo-

cated on the stock. After all points are transferred, use a French curve to connect the points. By changing the ratio of the size of the square, the size can be enlarged or made smaller.

If many patterns are to be enlarged an opaque or overhead projector can be used (Fig. 26-15). The master used in the projector can be an actual drawing, picture from a magazine, or photograph. By moving the projector in and out or by adjusting the focal length of the picture, the projected image can

FIGURE 26-14
The graph method allows patterns to be reduced or enlarged in size. This illustration shows a part being enlarged.

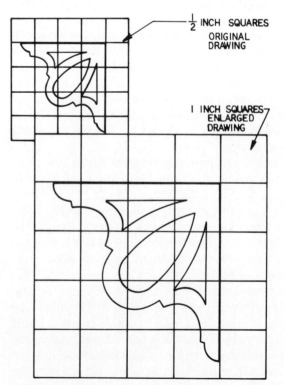

½ INCH SQUARES
ORIGINAL DRAWING

1 INCH SQUARES
ENLARGED DRAWING

FIGURE 26-15
Making a pattern with an overhead projector.

be adjusted in size. The image can be traced around onto the stock or onto a piece of cardboard. The piece of cardboard then becomes a template after it is cut to shape.

MAKING EXTERNAL CUTS

The most common operation with the scroll saw is cutting irregular shapes. This requires the outline of the shape to be drawn on the stock. Use one of the methods discussed in the section "Making a Layout."

Install the recommended blade and set the cutting speed to the proper cutting strokes per minute. Adjust the upper blade guide assembly. The spring hold-down must be positioned against the top surface of the stock.

Study the layout and determine the most efficient path to guide the blade (Fig. 26-16). Ideally, the entire shape can be cut with one pass of the blade. Very detailed complicated layouts, however, may need to be divided into sections and certain parts removed a section at a time. When small curves are required, *relief cuts* are necessary (Fig. 26-17). These short straight cuts are made in the waste portion of the stock. Relief cuts keep the blade from binding on sharp curves and eliminate having to back out of cuts. They divide the curve into sections and extend to within $\frac{1}{32}$ in. (1 mm) from the layout line. As the layout is then cut, small portions of the waste fall away, keeping the blade from binding.

Because the scroll saw is a very slow cutting machine, use a slow feed rate. The thicker the stock, the slower the feed rate should be. Keep the fingers and hands away from the path of the blade. Stay to the waste side of the layout line. If the blade drifts

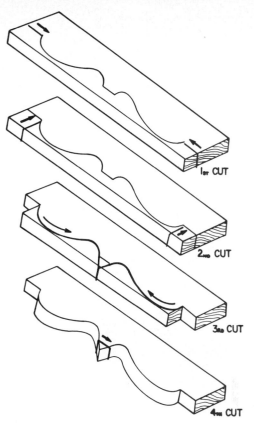

FIGURE 26-16
Proper cutting procedure for making an external cut. Make the shortest cut first.

across the line, back the board up and recut the stock.

A scroll blade is fragile and breaks easily. Applying too much forward pressure will bend the blade backward and it will snap. Turn the stock slowly when cutting curves. Forcing the blade around corners will cause the blade to twist and break. Never push the board sideways because this action will also damage the blade.

FIGURE 26-17
Relief cuts allow small curves to be cut.

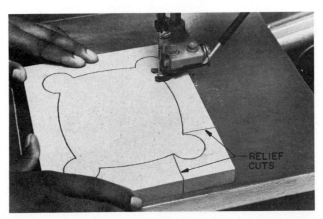

MAKING IDENTICAL PIECES

Many projects require more than one part of the same shape. Although pieces can be cut one at a time, the job can go much faster if several parts are cut at the same time. One method of producing several parts is called *stack cutting* (Fig. 26-18). Several pieces are first placed one on top of the other. A few small brads are driven through the waste area to hold the pieces together. As the top piece is cut, so will the stock below it.

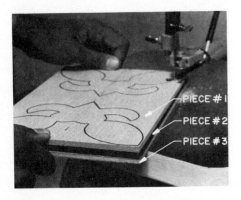

FIGURE 26-18
Stack cutting allows several pieces to be cut at one time.

MAKING IDENTICAL CURVED CUTS

If many identical curved cuts are required, a shop-built curved fence and template can be constructed (Fig. 26-19). The template is made from dense hardwood and is the exact size and shape of the finished product. The curved fence contains the opposite

FIGURE 26-19
Identical curved parts can be made with a shop-made fence and template.

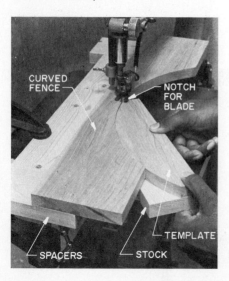

shape of the template. A notch is cut in the edge of this fence to position the blade. Spacers are attached to the bottom of the fence to raise it off the table. The distance from the bottom of the fence to the table should be slightly more than the thickness of the stock to be cut.

Clamp the curved fence to the table. Position the blade in the notch of the fence. The saw tooth set to the right must be exactly in line with the curved edge of the fence. Cut the stock to the finish size. Attach the stock to the template with nails or screws. Turn on the power and guide the template along the fence. As the stock passes the blade, the curve will be reproduced in the wood mounted on the bottom. Once the stock has cleared the blade, re-move the template and cut the next piece.

MAKING INTERNAL CUTS

An *internal cut* is required when a cutout is to be made that does not extend to an outside edge. Since this cut cannot be started on an edge, a hole is bored in the waste portion next to the layout line. If possible, make the hole part of the pattern. Use the same-diameter drill bit that will match a curve in the layout. Bore a hole in each corner to allow the board to be turned easily.

Remove the blade from the upper blade chuck. Raise the upper guide assembly to its topmost position. Feed the blade through the hole in the board (Fig. 26-20). Insert the blade into the upper chuck and tighten the thumbscrew.

Cut the pattern out staying on the waste side of the line (Fig. 26-21). If a piece is cut loose and lodges against the blade, stop the saw and remove it. Once the pattern has been completely cut out, remove the blade and take the finished piece from the table. If

FIGURE 26-20
The blade is fed through the hole bored in the waste area.

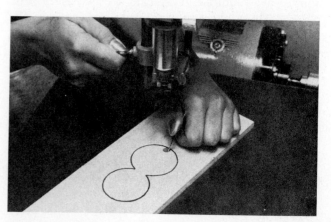

FIGURE 26-21
Making an internal cut. (Courtesy of Delta International Machinery Corp.)

no other internal cuts are to be made properly, install the blade.

SABER SAWS

Saber sawing utilizes a specialty blade that is held only by the bottom blade chuck. Saber saw blades are usually wide and have coarse teeth which have heavy sets (Fig. 26-7). This allows them to make heavier straighter cuts than that of the smaller jeweler blades. Most generally this cutting technique is utilized for internal cuts which contain large curves. Because the top end of the blade is free, stock can easily be lowered over the blade (Fig. 26-22). To al-

low the blade to enter the stock, a hole is first bored through the board for insertion of the blade.

Since only the bottom blade chuck secures the blade, an additional lower blade guide is installed (Fig. 26-12). The upper guide assembly should be moved out of the way. If much saber sawing is to be done, the entire overarm may be removed. This allows larger pieces to be cut and makes the blade more accessible for internal cutting.

MAKING STRAIGHT CUTS

There are other saws which are better suited than the scroll saw for making straight cuts. Because of the slow cutting and the narrow blade, it can be difficult to control the cut.

If the scroll saw should be selected, use the widest blade available that has coarse teeth. Clamp a wooden fence the same distance away from the blade as the desired width of the board. Use a slow feed speed and keep your hands out of the path of the blade.

MAKING BEVEL CUTS

A bevel cut on the scroll saw can be made simply by tilting the table (Fig. 26-23). Loosen the tilt knob and move the table to the desired angle. The angle scale will indicate the angle. Tighten the tilt knob to secure the table. To hold the stock against the table, also tilt the spring hold-down located on the end of the upper guide assembly. It should be the same angle as the table.

Since a different angle will be cut on each side of the blade, do all the cutting on only one side.

FIGURE 26-22
The saber saw technique is an ideal method of making internal cuts.

FIGURE 26-23
A bevel cut is made by tilting the table and the spring hold-down. (Courtesy of Delta International Machinery Corp.)

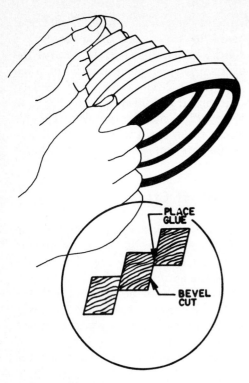

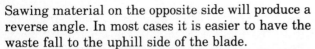

FIGURE 26-24
Producing a bowl using a bevel cut.

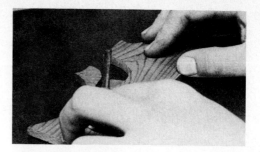

FIGURE 26-25
Filing on a scroll saw.

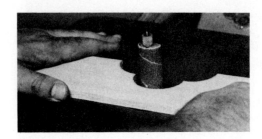

FIGURE 26-26
Using a sanding attachment.

Sawing material on the opposite side will produce a reverse angle. In most cases it is easier to have the waste fall to the uphill side of the blade.

A tapered cone or bowl can be made by cutting concentric circles from one piece of stock (Fig. 26-24). Although trial and error can be used, 5° is a good starting point to tilt the table. The final shape of the bowl depends on the thickness of the stock, wall thickness of the rings, and angle of the sides of the ring. Lay out the number of circles desired. Bore a small hole on each layout line. Use a very thin jewelry blade. Insert the blade through each bored hole and accurately cut the circles. The beveled sides of the rings are glued and then pushed outwards. The disks will tighten on each other.

SANDING AND FILING

Since the scroll saw uses an up-and-down cutting action, it can be converted for sanding and filing.

Small square, triangular, round, and other shaped files can be utilized (Fig. 26-25). These files should have either an ⅛-in.-diameter shank. A special sanding attachment is also available (Fig. 26-26). One side of this attachment is flat for sanding straight edges. The other side is semicircular for sanding curves.

To either sand or file, the tool is held only by the lower blade chuck. The shank of these tools is held between the vee slots in the chuck blocks. It is best to use the slowest available machine speed. Too fast a CSM will only damage the file or sanding attachment.

Since the sanding and filing tools are much larger in diameter than the regular blades, a custom-made table insert should be made. The opening in the insert should match the shape of the tool. If much work is to be done, remove the overarm to make the tool more accessible. Do not apply excessive pressure against these accessories. This will shorten their life considerably.

27

JOINTERS

The jointer is used primarily for straightening edges and flattening faces (Fig. 27-1). It can, however, make tapers and a few joints. The surfaces produced are usually smooth and require less sanding than with saw-cut surfaces.

PARTS OF THE JOINTER

The major parts of the jointer are the cutterhead, infeed table, outfeed table, fence, and guard. The *cutterhead* is a steel cylinder with slots cut across the surface (Fig. 27-2). In the slots are placed flat knives and gibs. Each knife is held into the cutterhead with the *gib*. Most jointers have three knives. Some commercial models may have up to six knives. The more knives contained in the cutterhead, the smoother the cut will be. As the cutterhead is turned by the motor, the tips of the knives produce a circle. This circle is called the *cutting circle*.

The *infeed* and *outfeed tables* are positioned to each side of the cutterhead. Each is mounted on a set of *incline ways*. These are angled castings that allow the tables to be raised or lowered with a handwheel. The infeed table often contains the *rabbeting arm*. This supports the stock during rabbeting operations.

```
JOINTER SAFETY RULES

1. Keep your fingers and hands at least 4 in. (102 mm) away from the cutterhead.
2. A cutterhead guard should be used at all times.
3. The maximum depth of cut in one pass is 1/16 in. (2 mm).
4. Stock must be at least 10 in. (254 mm) long before it can be face or edge jointed.
5. Stock that is less than 1 in. (25 mm) wide should not be edge jointed.
6. Stock that is less than 1/2 in. (13 mm) thick should not be face jointed.
7. Use a push shoe or push stick whenever possible.
8. Stock must be held flat on the table and firmly against the fence.
9. The outfeed table should never be adjusted unless you are a skilled operator.
10. Disconnect the power before getting your hands close to the cutterhead.
```

Mounted on the top surface of the tables is the *fence*. The fence can be moved anywhere across the table by loosening the fence handle. It can also be tilted for bevel cuts by loosening the *fence-tilting lock* (Fig. 27-3).

A *guard* must cover the cutterhead anytime a board is being jointed. It is retractable and kept under spring pressure. This allows the board to fit between the guard and fence but cover the remaining

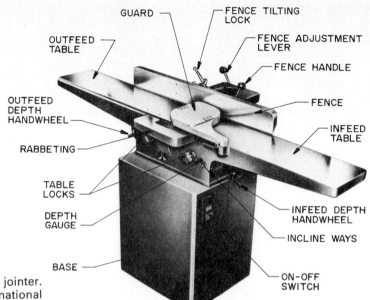

FIGURE 27-1
Major parts of the jointer.
(Courtesy of Delta International
Machinery Corp.)

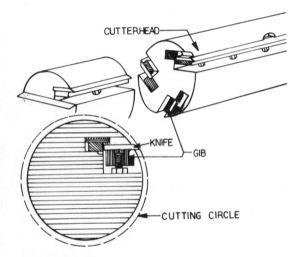

FIGURE 27-2
Parts of the cutterhead.

portion of the cutterhead. Never operate the jointer
without the guard properly positioned.

PURCHASING A JOINTER

One of the few items to specify when purchasing a
jointer is the size. The size of this machine is determined by the length of the knives. Smaller jointers
are from 4 to 6 in. (102 to 152 mm). Commercial
jointers may be as large as 12 to 24 in. (305 to 610
mm).

A general-purpose 6-in. (152-mm) jointer
should be equipped with a $\frac{3}{4}$-hp or larger motor.
Heavy cuts or continuous service may require a
larger motor.

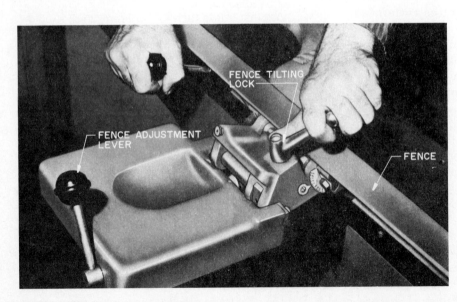

FIGURE 27-3
The fence can be tilted for the
bevel cuts. (Courtesy of Delta International Machinery Corp.)

SELECTING THE JOINTER TOOLING

Although it is desirable to have an extra set of knives, there is not a great deal of selection. Most jointer knives are constructed from high-speed steel. Carbide knives may be needed if a large amount of abrasive material such as particleboard is to be jointed. Refer to the owner's manual for the proper size to fit each machine.

SETTING UP THE JOINTER

The first step in setting up the jointer is to adjust the depth of cut. In most instances no more than $\frac{1}{16}$ inch (2 mm) should be removed with one pass. Certain cuts may require a shallower depth of cut. Consider using lighter cuts for face jointing, jointing a dense wood such as hard maple, working with irregular grain such as knotty pine, or when making a finish cut on an exposed edge. By turning the *infeed-depth handwheel,* the infeed table can be raised or lowered. The distance from the top of the cutting circle for the cutterhead to the top of the infeed table is equal to the depth of cut (Fig. 27-4). For most cuts, the depth gauge will be sufficient for indicating the depth of cut. When a high degree of accuracy is required, make a trial cut partway across a scrap board. The difference between the freshly machined edge and the original surfaces will equal the exact depth.

Although it is not necessary to check the setting of the outfeed table every time, you do need to know when it is out of adjustment. It should be set exactly in the same plane as the top of the cutting circle. Use a straightedge placed on top of the outfeed table to test for proper alignment. As the cutter head is turned by hand, the knives should just pass under the straight edge (Fig. 27-5).

FIGURE 27-4
Setting of the infeed table.

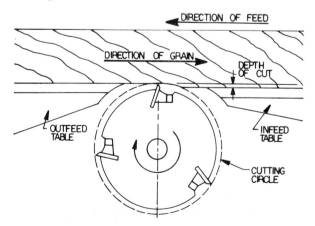

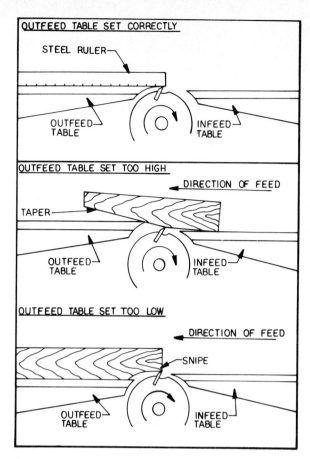

FIGURE 27-5
Correct and incorrect settings of the outfeed table.

The best clue for establishing when the outfeed table is not in adjustment is to evaluate a freshly made jointer cut (Fig. 27-5). If a taper is produced, the outfeed table is too high. Often with this condition, the leading end of the board will bump into the lip of the outfeed table. When the outfeed table is too low, a clipped end or *snipe* is produced on the trailing end of the board. This is caused when the board drops down over the cutterhead. Once both tables are adjusted to the correct height, they should be secured with the *table locks.*

There are also two adjustments to make on the fence. First see that the fence is at a 90° angle to the table. Use a square to check this setting (Fig. 27-6). If any adjustments are necessary, loosen the *fence tilting lock* and pivot the fence in or out (Fig. 27-3). Many jointers have a positive stop at 90 and 45°. The fence automatically stops at these settings as it is being pivoted. Move the fence across the table to expose a minimum amount of the cutterhead. Use the *fence-adjustment lever* to allow the lateral movement or in and out position of the fence.

Be certain that the retractable guard is working properly. It should spring shut covering the cut-

FIGURE 27-6
Checking the squareness of the fence with the table. The guard has been removed for demonstration purposes only.

terhead any time a board is not between it and the fence.

Once the adjustments are made, the cut can be made. Position yourself to the left of the infeed table. Your hands must not be placed within 4 in. (102 mm) of the cutterhead anytime it is turning. Place the board on the infeed table with the grain pointing away from the cutterhead (Fig. 27-7). If a square cut is to be produced, the stock must also be kept against the fence.

Feed the board forward into the cutterhead. Keep it tight against the fence and table. Use a slow, steady feeding rate. To keep your hands away from the cutter, use a push shoe or push stick (Fig. 27-8). Once the leading end of the board has cleared the cutterhead by at least 6 in. (152 mm), transfer the left hand over to the outfeed table (Fig. 27-9). As the hands are moved, be careful not to rock the board. If you hear a tearing or chipping sound, slow

FIGURE 27-7
Proper position of the operator to feed the stock.

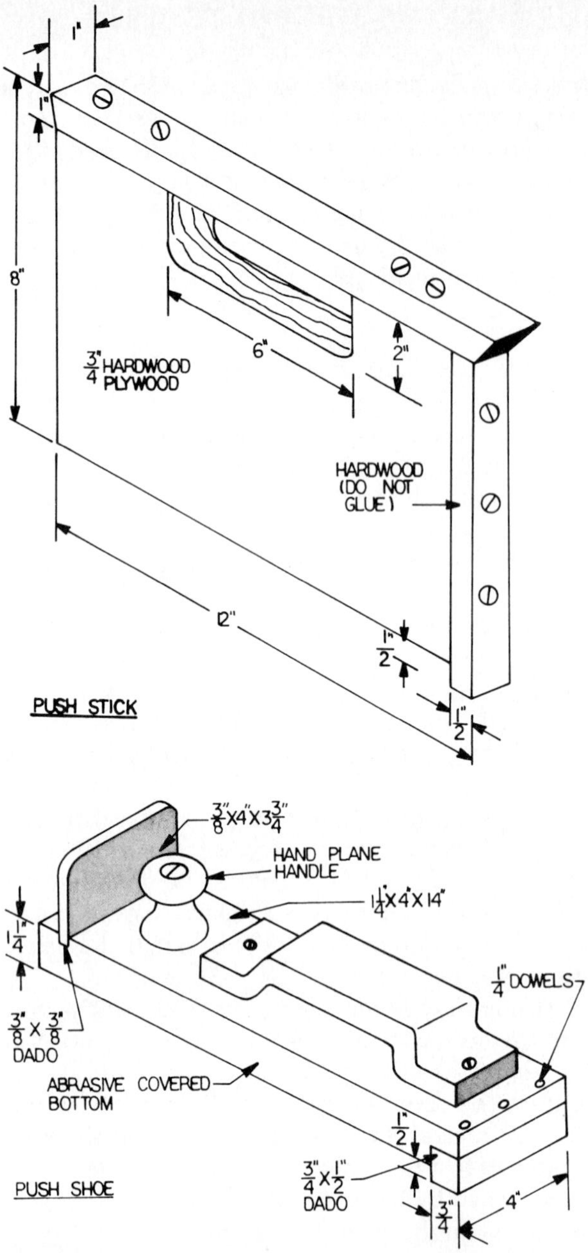

PUSH STICK

FIGURE 27-8
Push stick for edge jointing and push shoe for face jointing.

the feed rate. Finish feeding the board forward by pushing with the right hand and holding it against the fence and outfeed table with the left hand. Never hook your thumb over the end of the board. It may slip into the cutterhead as the board clears the jointer.

JOINTING THE FACE

When squaring a rough board, the first surface to be jointed is the face. Inspect both faces and select the one that is the flattest. If it is cupped, place the

FIGURE 27-9
Move the left hand to the outfeed fence to support the board.

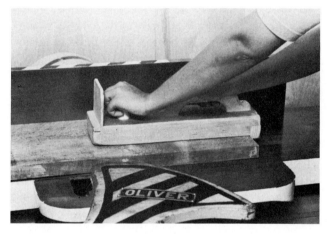

FIGURE 27-10
Face jointing a short board with a push shoe.

FIGURE 27-11
Face jointing a long board with a push shoe and a foam-covered pusher.

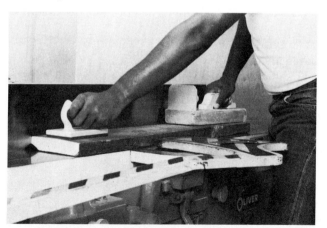

concave side down. Set the depth of cut to no more than $\frac{1}{16}$ in. (2 mm). For dense woods or extra-wide boards, reduce this amount. Position this surface on the outfeed table. Place a push shoe over the trailing end and push forward with the right end (Fig. 27-10). Grasp the knob on the front of the push shoe with the left hand. If the board is long, use a foam-covered pusher to keep it against the table (Fig. 27-11). Keep pushing the board forward until it has cleared the guard.

Even if it is covered by the board, never place your hands directly over the cutterhead. After the first pass, inspect the jointed surface. If the face is chipped from the jointer cut, end-for-end the board and joint from the opposite direction.

JOINTING THE EDGE

The second surface to be jointed on a rough board is the edge. Sight down both edges and select the straightest edge. If both are very crooked, scribe a straight line on the face and bandsaw to the line.

Position the board on the infeed table with the jointed flat face against the fence. The grain should point toward the front end of the infeed table. If the edge is bowed with the length shorter than the infeed table, place the concave side down. When the stock is narrower than the jointer fence is high, a push stick is required (Fig. 27-9). Use it in the right hand to feed the stock forward. With the left hand, hold the board firmly against the fence. Allowing the board to lean away from the fence will cause a bevel to be jointed.

Never place your hands within 4 in. (102 mm) of the cutterhead. It is important to keep the stock against the outfeed table. If the board should raise up off of the table, a straightedge will not be produced.

JOINTING THE END GRAIN AND PLYWOOD

It is best to cut the board to the correct length with a fine-cutting saw blade than to joint to finish length. Accuracy is difficult to maintain when jointing across the ends of wood fibers. If the correct procedure is not used, the edge will be chipped off as the end clears the cutterhead.

When jointing end grain select one of two available methods. The first method requires that the first 1 in. (25 mm) be jointed and then pivoted off the cutterhead (Fig. 27-12). Turn the board around and joint from the opposite direction. Due to the material being jointed away from the trailing end, the last 1 in. (25 mm) will clear the cutterhead.

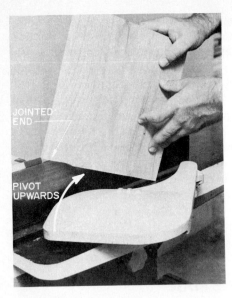

FIGURE 27-12
Pivoting the stock off of the cutterhead after the first 1 inch has been jointed.

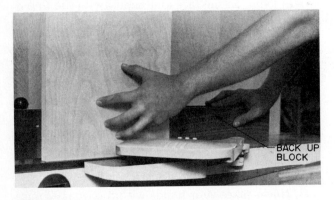

FIGURE 27-13
Supporting the trailing of the stock with a back-up block while jointing end grain.

The second method of jointing end grain is to support the trailing end with a backup block (Fig. 27-13). As the stock is fed forward, the backup block is pushed immediately behind the stock. The backup block keeps the fibers from being chipped out.

JOINTING THROUGH BEVELS AND CHAMFERS

To produce a bevel or chamfer on the jointer, the fence is tilted to the desired angle. It can be angled either in or out. In most cases placing the fence in the in-position is safer and easier to control the stock (Fig. 27-14). Angling the fence out may allow the board to slide down as it is jointed. Mark on the leading end of the stock the desired bevel or chamfer.

FIGURE 27-14
Beveling with the jointer fence in the in-position.

The angle of the fence can be determined in one of two ways. For most bevels and chamfers using the angle gauge is a precise enough of a method (Fig. 27-15). When the angle needs to be very accurate, use a T-bevel set to the desired angle (Fig. 27-16). To verify the setting, joint an edge and check its accuracy with a protractor.

Most bevels and chamfers should not be made with one pass. The maximum depth of cut should be $\frac{1}{16}$ in. (2 mm) deep. Multiple passes can then be made to produce the necessary width. Since the chamfer is a narrower cut, fewer passes are needed. In either case continue to make cuts until the jointed edge meets the layout line.

JOINTING A STOPPED CHAMFER

A *stopped chamfer* is a decorative type of cut that does not extend along the entire length of the board. Making a stopped chamfer on the jointer will give a

FIGURE 27-15
Setting the fence using an angle gauge.

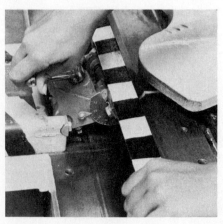

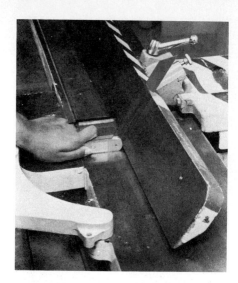

FIGURE 27-16
Setting the fence using a sliding T-bevel. The guard has been removed for demonstration purposes only.

gentle curve at the beginning and ending of the chamfer. Start by marking the starting and ending points on the stock. Angle the fence to the desired angle. Most stopped chamfers are made at a 45° angle.

Since the chamfer is stopped, both the infeed and outfeed tables must be lowered to the same depth (Fig. 27-17). First lower the infeed table to the correct depth. Place wooden blocks of equal thicknesses on each table and bridge the two tables with a level. Lower the outfeed table until the level indicates both tables are in the same plane. Move the fence over to expose a minimum amount of cutterhead.

Place the stock on the infeed table with the first layout line on the lip of the outfeed table (Fig. 27-18). Clamp a stop block against the trailing end of the stock. Slide the stock forward until the second layout line is on the lip of the infeed table. Clamp a stop block against the leading end.

FIGURE 27-17
Setting up the jointer tables for making a stopped chamfer. The guard has been removed for demonstration purposes only.

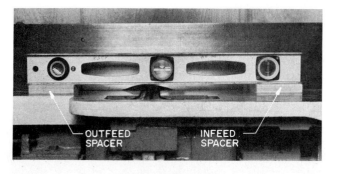

Make certain that the guard is operating properly and place the trailing end of the board against the first stop block. Have an assistant turn on the power and then draw the guard back only enough to lower the board into the revolving cutterhead. Release the guard once the board touches the tables. Feed the board forward with a push stick and foam-covered pusher. Once the stock reaches the second stop block, have the assistant turn off the power. Do not move the board until the cutterhead has completely stopped turning.

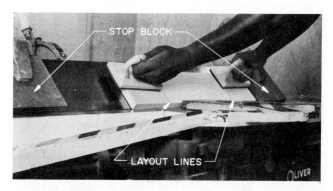

FIGURE 27-18
Making a stopped chamfer.

JOINTING A RECESS

A recess can be made much the same way as a stopped chamfer is cut. The major difference is that the fence is kept at a 90° angle. Once the infeed and outfeed tables have been brought to the same level, install the stop blocks. Pivot the stock onto the rotating cutter (Fig. 27-19). Because of the stock having a tendency to chip out, feed the board forward only a short distance. Have an assistant turn off the power while the stock is held completely still. Do not move the board until the cutterhead stops turning.

Reverse the board and pivot it again onto the rotating cutterhead. Feed the stock forward until the leading end comes in contact with the stop block. Stop the jointer and allow the cutterhead to stop turning before removing the board.

JOINTING AN OCTAGON

Clamp a long vee block over the cutterhead and against the fence (Fig. 27-20). A dado has been cut on the bottom of the vee block to allow the cutterhead to extend up through the vee groove. Lower the infeed and outfeed table to the desired level. Enough of the cutterhead should be exposed in the

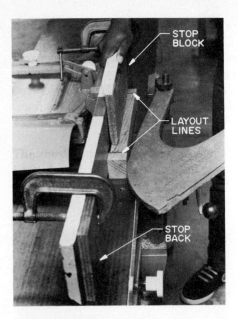

FIGURE 27-19
Jointing a recess in a square to produce a decorative leg.

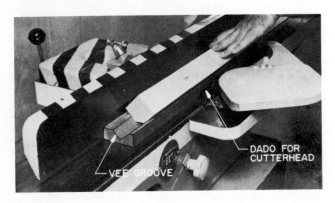

FIGURE 27-20
Setup for jointing an octagon.

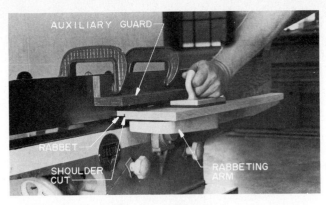

FIGURE 27-21
Jointing a rabbet. Note the rabbeting arm supporting the stock.

opening of the vee block to remove the desired amount of material.

A wood square is fed over the vee block to joint the bottom corner. The sides of the vee block form a trough for the square to slide along. The width of each flat of the octagon should be the same size. If they are not equal, adjust the depth of cut for the infeed and outfeed table. Always use a push shoe and keep your hands at least 4 in. (102 mm) from the cutterhead. This is particularly important because the guard cannot be utilized. After each corner has been jointed, an octagon is formed.

JOINTING A RABBET

The major advantage of jointing a rabbet is that it produces a smooth surface. This may be important when making an exposed rabbet such as for a lipped door. On dense woods and plywood, make a shoulder cut with the table saw. This will eliminate any grain tearout on the face produced by the jointer (Fig. 27-21). The jointer must have a rabbeting arm and with the knives extending the same distance from the edge of the cutterhead.

To set-up the jointer for rabbeting, remove the guard. For maximum protection, an auxiliary guard can be clamped to the fence. Move the fence over until the exposed knives are equal to the width of the rabbet. Set the depth of cut to $\frac{1}{16}$ in. (2 mm). Since most rabbets are deeper than this, multiple passes will need to be made. After each cut the infeed table will need to be lowered an additional $\frac{1}{16}$ in. (2 mm).

Stabilize the board on the front of the rabbeting arm and turn on the power. Feed the board across the cutterhead. Never place your hands within 4 in. (102 mm) of the cutterhead. Always use a push stick and do not reach under the stock or auxiliary guard.

JOINTING A SHORT TAPER

For tapers shorter than the length of the infeed table, lay out a line around the stock at the beginning of the taper. Lower the infeed table the same amount as that to be jointed from one surface. Move the fence over exposing only the necessary cutterhead.

A stop block must be clamped to the fence on the infeed table (Fig. 27-22). The layout line should be located immediately over the top of the lip of the outfeed table. Place the stop block against the trailing end of the stock.

Remove the stock and turn on the power. Have an assistant pull back the guard only enough to lower the stock onto the cutterhead. Keeping the end of the stock against the stop block, carefully lower the board into the cutterhead. The assistant

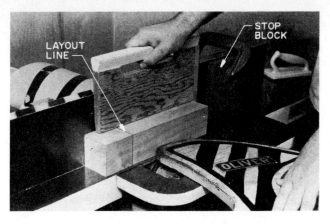

FIGURE 27-22
Making a short taper.

should release the guard once the board touches the outfeed table. With a push shoe feed the material forward until it clears the guard.

JOINTING A LONG TAPER

Long tapers are longer than the length of the infeed table, and require a two-step process. The key to producing a long taper is using the correct layout method (Fig. 27-23). Place the first layout line

FIGURE 27-23
Layout for a long taper.

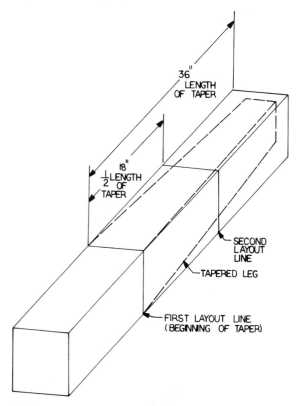

36"
LENGTH OF TAPER

18"
$\frac{1}{2}$ LENGTH OF TAPER

SECOND LAYOUT LINE

TAPERED LEG

FIRST LAYOUT LINE (BEGINNING OF TAPER)

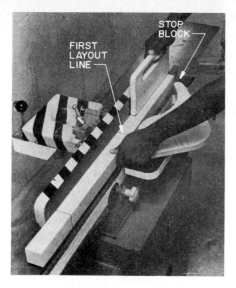

FIGURE 27-24
Making the first series of cuts for a long taper.

around the stock at the beginning of the taper. Mark a second layout line halfway between the first line and the end of the square. This distance must be less than the length of the infeed table.

To cut the first part of the taper adjust the depth of cut to one-half the total amount to be taken off one side at the deepest point. Use the same procedure for jointing the first section as previously given for jointing a short taper (Fig. 27-24). The cut starts at the halfway point.

Leaving the depth of cut the same, remove the stop block. Turn on the power. Have an assistant pull the guard back enough to allow the stock to once again be lowered onto the rotating cutterhead. As the material is being slowly lowered, sight the first layout line so that it will be placed on the lip of the outfeed table (Fig. 27-25). Since the stock may have a tendency to kickback, grip the material firmly and stay at least 4 in. (102 mm) from the cutterhead. Feed the stock forward with a push shoe.

FIGURE 27-25
Making the second series of cuts for a long taper.

JOINTING A STOPPED TAPER

Although a stopped taper can be utilized for other items, it is generally used to make a *spade foot leg* (Fig. 27-26). This is a leg having a long stopped taper with a short taper at its base. A layout line is required at both the beginning and ending of the taper. Adjust the depth of cut to the same amount as to be removed from one side at the deepest point.

Set up the jointer as recommended in the section on jointing a short taper. A stop block must be

FIGURE 27-27
Making a stopped taper.

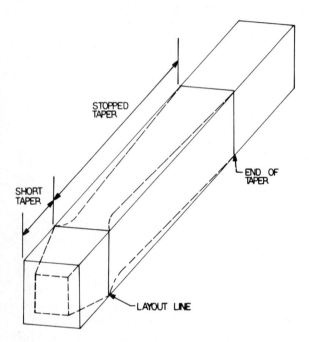

FIGURE 27-26
Typical layout for a spade foot.

positioned against the trailing end of the stock. Move the stock forward until the second layout line is even with the lip of the infeed table. Install a second stop block at the leading end of the board.

Remove the stock and turn on the power. Using a push stick feed the board forward (Fig. 27-27). Once the leading end meets the front stop block, have an assistant turn off the power. Do not move the board until the cutterhead has come to a stop. If the part requires tapering on the remaining sides, rotate the board and repeat the process. When a spade foot is to be made, the short taper can be cut with the bandsaw. It is then sanded to smooth the saw cut.

28

PLANERS

The *planer,* or as it is sometimes called the *surfacer,* is primarily a single-purpose machine (Fig. 28-1). It is used almost entirely for surfacing boards to a desired thickness. Occasionally, it may be utilized for planing boards on their edges and a few other operations. Many shops, however, may use the planer only for face planing.

PARTS OF THE PLANER

The major parts to a planer include the feed system, chipbreaker, cutterhead, and pressure bar (Fig. 28-2). Those machine components located on the front of the cutterhead are on the *infeed side* of the machine. The remaining parts located to the rear of the cutterhead are on the *outfeed side.*

A very important part to the planer is the *feed system* (Fig. 28-2). It is made up of several rollers and drive components. There are two rollers located in the bed. They are called the *bottom smooth infeed roller* and *bottom smooth outfeed roller.* The tops of these rollers are slightly above the *platen* and help the board move over the top of the bed. Many planers have adjustable rollers which can be raised and lowered with the *adjustable bed roller handle* (Fig.

28-1). The rougher the board, the higher they should be raised. Those planers with fixed rollers and set for general-purpose planing are set at a height of 0.005 in. above the bed.

Another roller located above the bottom infeed roller is the *corrugated infeed roller.* The corrugations in the outer surface help to grip and feed the stock forward.

The fourth roller is located immediately above the *bottom outfeed roller.* It is called the *top smooth outfeed roller,* and like the corrugated infeed roller, is power driven. Once the board leaves the cutterhead, it is pulled out of the planer by this roller.

The drive system powers the corrugated and top outfeed rollers. On some planers the bed rollers will also be driven. The *feed handwheel* regulates how fast the rollers rotate.

Located immediately in front of the cutterhead is the *chipbreaker.* It is responsible for holding the stock down and preventing the knives from tearing out the grain (Fig. 28-2). The chipbreaker is set at the same level as the bottom of the cutting arc.

To remove the material a circular *cutterhead* is utilized. It is a steel cylinder that holds the knives. Most planers have a conventional cutterhead with three or more straight knives. To reduce noise and

PLANER SAFETY RULES

1. Keep fingers and hands at least 4 in. (102 mm) away from the front of the infeed and outfeed on the machine.
2. Always stand to one side of the bed and never directly behind it.
3. Stock should not be surfaced across the grain or on the end grain.
4. The face of the stock placed on the table must be flat and true before being surfaced.
5. The maximum amount of material to be removed in one pass is $\frac{1}{16}$ in. (2 mm).
6. Stock to be planed should be at least $\frac{1}{2}$ in. (13 mm) thick, 2 in. (51 mm) wide and at least 2 in. (51 mm) longer than the distance between the feed rollers.
7. Use a backing board whenever stock is less than $\frac{3}{4}$ in. (10 mm) thick.
8. If a board becomes stuck, the following should be done:
   a. Stop the machine and allow the cutterhead to come to a full stop.
   b. Lower the bed.
9. Disconnect the power before making any adjustments on the machine.

provide a more efficient cut, several new cutterhead designs have been developed. The knives on these planers are either made in short segments or mounted in a spiral pattern (Fig. 28-4).

Located immediately behind the cutterhead is the *pressure bar*. It rides on top of the surfaced material and keeps it from vibrating. If not properly adjusted, the planer will produce *chatter marks*. This produces a washboard affect.

To regulate the depth of cut, the bed is raised and lowered. The level of the bed is adjusted by turning the *height-adjustment handwheel* (Fig. 28-1). The *depth gauge* indicates the current depth setting that the planer will surface material.

PURCHASING A PLANER

The planer is generally one of the more expensive pieces of woodworking equipment for many wood shops. This is because it must be heavy to absorb the vibration and contains a feed system to feed the stock through the machine. It is wise, therefore, to

FIGURE 28-1
Major parts to a single planer. (Courtesy of Oliver Machinery Company.)

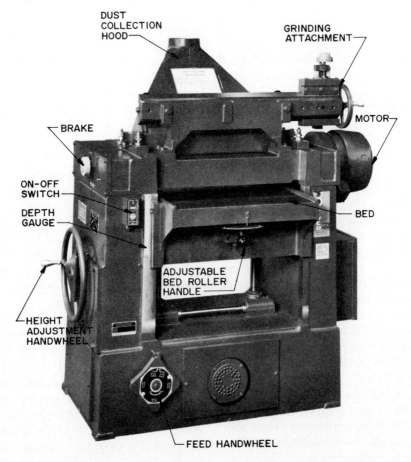

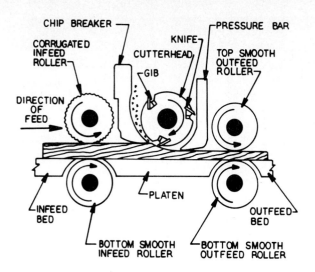

FIGURE 28-2
Internal parts of a planer.

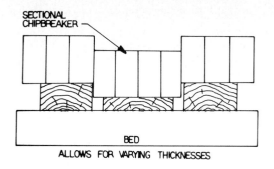

ALLOWS FOR VARYING THICKNESSES

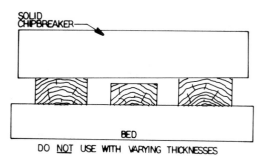

DO NOT USE WITH VARYING THICKNESSES

FIGURE 28-3
A sectional corrugated infeed roller is made of separate sections that move independently. A solid chipbreaker moves as one unit.

FIGURE 28-4
The knife sharpener is used to grind the knives in the cutterhead. (Courtesy of Oliver Machinery Company.)

make a very careful decision as to which model to purchase.

One of the first considerations is the size of the planer. The size is determined by the widest board that can be surfaced which is measured to the nearest inch. You can find the size by measuring the width of the bed. Sizes of planers range from 12 to over 60 in. (305 to 1524 mm). A good general-purpose size is 24 in. (610 mm).

Several features are available. The first you may like to consider is a *sectional* corrugated infeed roller and sectional chipbreaker (Fig. 28-3). These spring-loaded sectional parts enable several pieces of slightly different thicknesses to be fed into the planer at the same time. Each section will give as much as $\frac{5}{16}$ in. (8 mm).

Another optional feature is the variable feed system. An adjustable feed rate allows the operator to select how fast the stock is fed through the machine. The feed handwheel regulates the speed the material is fed through the machine (Fig. 28-1). Slow feed rates should be utilized for woods that are difficult to machine. Fast feed speeds are needed for roughing cuts.

You may also want to specify *adjustable bed rollers* (Fig. 28-1). They can be raised and lowered to reduce the drag on the bed. A rough board that has not been face jointed requires the rollers to be raised. For best results a finish cut or the final pass on a board needs to have the bed rollers lowered.

Other optional features include a *grinding attachment, brake,* and *dust collection hood.* The grinding attachment allows the knives to be sharpened in the cutterhead (Fig. 28-4). This is faster and usually more accurate than having the knives sharpened outside the machine. A brake will stop the machine

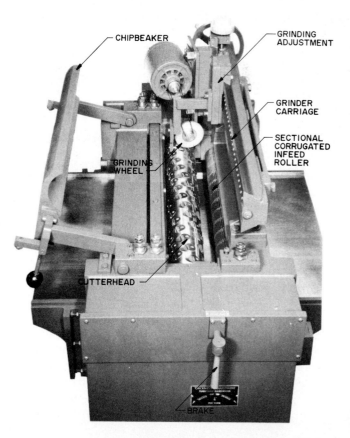

in a matter of seconds if an emergency should arise. The dust collection hood directs the planer shavings to a pipe. The planer shavings can then be sucked away by the dust collector.

SELECTING THE PLANER CUTTERHEADS

The tooling used in a planer is not frequently changed as it is with many woodworking machines. This makes it very important to select the best cutterhead design at the time the machine is purchased.

Most planers have a solid steel cutterhead with rectangular slots which house the knives and gibs (Fig. 28-2). The *gib* and *locking nuts* hold the knife in the cutterhead. If the planer has a traditional cutterhead, it will contain three flat knives which reach across the entire cutterhead.

The newer planer cutterhead designs will have a knife configuration which provides a more efficient cut at a lower noise level. Some planer manufacturers mount their knives in a spiral pattern around the perimeter of the cutterhead (Fig. 28-4). The spiral pattern provides a quiet slicing pattern rather than the loud hammering which occurs with the traditional flat tooling. Rather than having a knife which extends across the cutterhead, these are made from many individual short knives. This allows only one or two small pieces of tooling to be sharpened if a nick is developed in the cutting edge. The many separate knives are often of carbide, which allows them to stay sharp much longer.

PLANING STOCK TO THICKNESS

To plane stock to thickness, determine which face is the straightest and flattest. With most planers it is desirable to flatten this face on a jointer to make a smooth true surface. This is particularly important when dealing with warped material. A planer will not flatten warped material that does not have one true surface to place against the planer bed.

Measure the stock at the thickest point and set the depth gauge to $\frac{1}{16}$ inch (2 mm) less this amount. For example, if the board measures 1 in. (25 mm) at the thickest point, the pointer for the depth gauge should be set at $\frac{15}{16}$ in. (24 mm). To set the height of the bed or depth of cut, turn the height-adjustment handwheel (Fig. 28-5).

For planers with adjustable bed rollers, set their height by using the bed roller handle. Use a

FIGURE 28-5
Adjusting the depth of cut with the height adjustment handwheel.

setting of 0.9 to 0.6 in. (0.035 to 0.024 mm) for boards which are rough and relatively flat. A setting of 0.6 to 0.3 in. (0.024 to 0.012 mm) is selected for boards that have previously been surfaced or for the final pass.

If your planer has an adjustable feed rate, you will need to set the feed speed. Feed rates can be varied from 15 to 130 feet per minute (fpm). The faster the feed rate, the quicker the board will be planed but the rougher the cut. A slow feed speed will produce a smooth cut but reduces the production rate. For the first few passes through the machine or for a part that is not exposed, use a feed rate of 38 fpm. Use a 20-fpm feed rate for a high-quality cut or stock that has irregular highly figured grain.

Check that the stock to be planed is at least 2 in. (51 mm) longer than the distance between the bed rollers. The boards must be free of excess glue, metal fasteners, dirt, and any other foreign material. Any of this will dull and possibly nick the knives.

Turn on the power and stand to the left of the bed (Fig. 28-6). Position the stock on the infeed side

FIGURE 28-6
Proper position for the operator when surfacing a board to thickness.

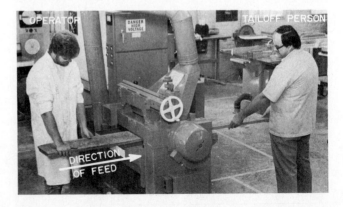

of the bed with the grain pointing toward the operator. Planing material with the grain pointing in the opposite direction will cause wood fibers to tear out. Placing the flattest, smoothest face down, slowly feed the material forward. Keep your hands from the underneath side of the boards and away from the throat of the machine. After the infeed roller starts to feed the board forward, continue to support the trailing end. If the board starts to be pulled at a slant, use a quick jerk to straighten it.

Have a tail-off person support the leading end of the board once it clears the bed. You should not allow long boards to hang from the outfeed bed.

When a board becomes stuck in the planer, apply forward pressure to the board. Keep hands clear of the throat of the machine and never look into the machine. If the board does not feed forward immediately, turn off the machine. After you are certain that the cutterhead has stopped turning, lower the bed and remove the board. Reset the depth of cut to one-half of the material being removed. Attempt to feed the board again. If it does not feed itself through the machine, check the machine adjustments.

When a great deal of material is to be removed, attempt to take equal amounts off of each side of the board. Once the face has been mostly cleaned up, turn the board over with each pass through the machine. Planing the board on only one side may release the internal stress or *casehardening,* which will cause the board to warp.

If several boards are to be planed to the same thickness, begin by planing the thickest piece first and measure the thickness after each pass. As the depth setting comes within $\frac{1}{16}$ in. (2 mm) of the remaining boards, start planing them. Working the boards down as a group will save a great deal of time and produce stock all of the same thickness.

PLANING BOARDS ON EDGE

If a planer comes equipped with a sectional corrugated infeed roller, boards can be planed on edge (Fig. 28-3). The advantage of using the planer over the jointer for this operation is that the two edges will be perfectly parallel. Do not attempt to plane boards on edge that are wider than 3 in. (76 mm) or shorter than 24 in. (610 mm).

It is recommended to joint the straightest edge of each board on a jointer. Rip the stock to $\frac{1}{8}$ in. (3 mm) oversize by positioning the jointed edge against the rip fence.

Set the planer to $\frac{1}{16}$ in. (2 mm) over the desired final width. Use the slowest available feed speed. Hold at least three of the boards together face to face with the saw cut edge facing up (Fig. 28-7). The

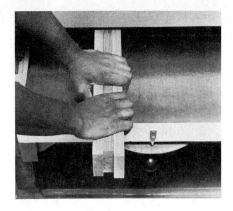

FIGURE 28-7
Holding the boards to be edge planed.

grain must point toward the operator. There must also be a minimum of $2\frac{1}{4}$ in. (57 mm) of stock in contact with the table. Standing to the left of the planer, feed the boards through the machine.

As the material moves forward, continue tightly holding the boards together. Once the leading end has cleared the machine, have a helper on the outfeed side of the planer also squeeze the boards together. If the pieces are allowed to spread apart, they may tend to lean over.

To remove the remaining $\frac{1}{16}$ in. (2 mm), adjust the depth of cut to the desired finish width of the board. Inspect both edges of each board and place the poorest edge facing up. Plane the stock as previously stated.

FACE PLANING THIN BOARDS

Planing stock less than $\frac{3}{8}$ in. (10 mm) thick can be dangerous unless a *backup board* is utilized. The backup board raises the stock up off the planer bed (Fig. 28-8). If this board is not used, the cutterhead may come dangerously close to the planer platen.

FIGURE 28-8
Using a backup board to plane thin boards.

Material as thin as $\frac{1}{16}$ in. (2 mm) can be surfaced with this technique.

To surface thin boards, select a piece of $\frac{3}{4}$-in. (19-mm)-thick hardwood plywood 1 in. (25 mm) wider and longer than the material to be planed. Place the stock on top of the backup board and measure the total thickness of the two pieces. Set the depth of cut to $\frac{1}{16}$ in. (2 mm) less than this amount. Center the stock on the backup board and feed the material through the machine. Continue adjusting the depth of the cut with each pass through the machine and feed the stock and backup board forward.

PLANING SHORT STOCK

Short boards which are at least as long as the distance between the bed rollers can be planed. Feed them one at a time through the machine. Butt each piece against the trailing end of the preceding piece (Fig. 28-9). This part will then push the board in the planer clear of the planer.

FIGURE 28-9
Planing short boards by butting one against the other.

After the last short piece has started through the planer, place a board at least 2 in. (51 mm) longer than the distance between the bed rollers against its trailing end. This longer board will push the last short piece through the planer.

PLANING SQUARES

A planer can produce squares that are very accurate and contain surfaces that require minimal sanding. Start by ripping stock to rough thickness and width. It should be $\frac{1}{8}$ in. (3 mm) larger than the finished dimensions.

Joint the flattest face using a jointer. Next place this freshly jointed surface against the jointer fence and joint the straightest edge. Place an "X" on the end of the stock next to the jointed surfaces (Fig. 28-10). This will allow you more easily to identify

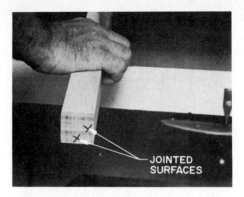

FIGURE 28-10
Planing a square. Note the "X" is against the planer bed.

these surfaces at a later time. Using a square, check that the jointed surface forms a 90° angle. Move to the planer and set the depth of cut equal to the final dimensions. Placing one of the jointed surfaces indicated with an "X" against the planer bed, feed the material forward (Fig. 28-10). Rotate the stock 90° so that the second jointed edge is now against the bed. Feed the last surface past the cutterhead at the same depth of cut.

PLANING OCTAGONS

Small octagons or eight-sided pieces can be produced with the planer. First prepare the stock by planing a square of the desired size. Make certain that the square is 12 in. (305 mm) longer than the length of the bed. Mark out on one end the shape of the octagon. Make a vee fixture to fit against the planer bed

FIGURE 28-11
A vee-fixture allows octagons to be planed.

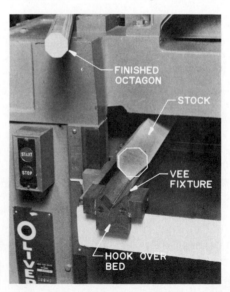

(Fig. 28-11). The end of the fixture on the infeed side of the planer must have a flat piece to hook over the end of the table. This keeps the fixture from feeding through the planer with the square. Keeping the fixture stationary allows unlimited lengths of stock to be fed through the machine.

Because the bottom feed rollers are not used, the stock may not totally feed itself. The stock may be carefully pushed and pulled through the planer.

Do not stand behind the stock. A tail-off person is needed on the outfeed side to pull the stock out.

If the planer has a bed roller adjustment, lower the rollers below the table. Position the vee fixture to one side of the bed. Pass the stock through the planer with the square cradled in the fixture. Rotate the board 90° and plane the remaining corners. If a larger octagon is being made, several passes are needed for each side.

29

LATHES

The spindle lathe is designed primarily for making spindle and faceplate turnings (Fig. 29-1). Parts produced on the lathe include chair and table legs, decorative spindles, and fruit bowls. Although the machine is relatively easy to operate, it does require more skill than most pieces of woodworking equipment.

PARTS OF THE LATHE

The major parts of the lathe are the headstock, bed, tool rest, and tailstock (Fig. 29-1). To the left side of the lathe is located the *headstock*. It contains the *spindle,* which is a hollow, number 2 Morse tapered shaft with external threads. The inside of the spindle holds the *live center* (Fig. 29-2). This center has four spurs and a pointed center which dig into the spindle. A *faceplate* can be screwed onto the headstock spindle. This attachment is available in several diameters. Large-diameter stock is attached to the faceplate with wood screws. The face of the headstock closest to the bed is called the *inboard side*. All spindle and most faceplate turnings are made on this side of the lathe. The opposite surface is called the *outboard side*. Very large diameter turnings are made on the outboard side.

WOOD LATHE SAFETY RULES

1. Be certain that stock to be turned is free of cracks, knots, or improper glue joints.
2. Rough and large diameter turnings should be turned at the slowest possible lathe speed.
3. Hold all lathe turning tools securely with both hands.
4. The distance between the tool rest and the stock should be adjusted so that it is not less than $\frac{1}{8}$ in. (3 mm) or more than $\frac{1}{2}$ in. (3 mm).
5. Position the tool rest $\frac{1}{8}$ in. (3 mm) above the lathe centers.
6. Rotate the stock by hand before turning on the power to be certain that it will clear the tool rest and lathe bed.
7. Be certain that the tailstock, tool rest, and tool post are securely fastened before turning on the power.
8. Stand to one side of the machine rather than directly in front when turning on the power.
9. The faceplate must be securely fastened to the work before turning on the lathe. Care must be taken when turning to avoid cutting too deep and striking screws.
10. Remove the tool rest and tool post before sanding or polishing on the lathe.

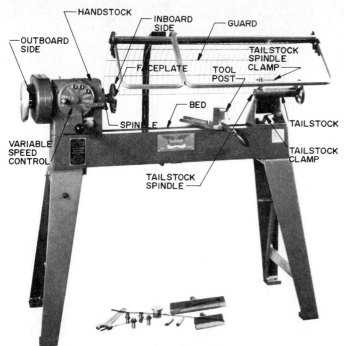

FIGURE 29-1
Major parts of the spindle. (Courtesy of
Oliver Machinery Company.)

The headstock is mounted to the *bed* along which the *tool post* and *tailstock slide*. If there is a recessed area immediately adjacent to the headstock, it is called a *gap bed* (Fig. 29-3). This allows larger-diameter faceplate turnings to be made.

The *tool post* is bolted to the bed but is adjustable anywhere along its length by loosening the *tool post clamp* (Fig. 29-4). It holds the *tool rest*, which provides a ledge to support the lathe chisels. Tool rests come in various straight lengths ranging from 3 to 48 in. (76 to 1219 mm). For faceplate turning, tool rests are also available in different shapes. The "L" and "S" shapes allow turning on both the side and face without adjusting the rest.

The *tailstock* is also bolted to the bed and can be clamped anywhere along its length (Fig. 29-1). It is moved close to the end of the stock and secured to the bed with the *tailstock clamp*. By turning the *tailstock handwheel*, the *tailstock spindle* is brought forward. The *tailstock spindle clamp* secures the spin-

FIGURE 29-3
The gapped bed allows large-diameter stock to be turned. (Courtesy of Delta International Machinery Corp.)

FIGURE 29-2
Accessories for the lathe include: live center, faceplate, ball-bearing cup dead center, solid dead center, ball-bearing cone dead center.

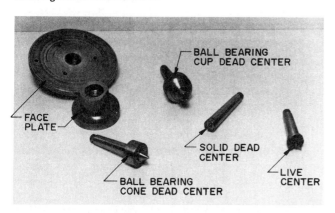

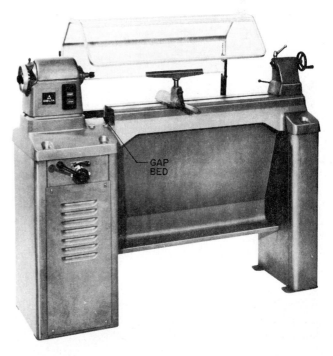

dle and keeps it from moving. The tailstock holds the *dead center* (Fig. 29-2). It is either a cup or cone design which holds the end of the stock. Dead centers are either solid or ball bearing. Although not as costly, solid dead centers can easily burn the end of the rotating stock. The ball-bearing dead center turns with the stock and eliminates any burning.

An important part of the lathe is the *guard* (Fig. 29-5). It is either made of a plastic or a metal

FIGURE 29-4
The tool post and tool rest are adjustable and can be positioned anywhere along the bed. (Courtesy of Delta International Machinery Corp.)

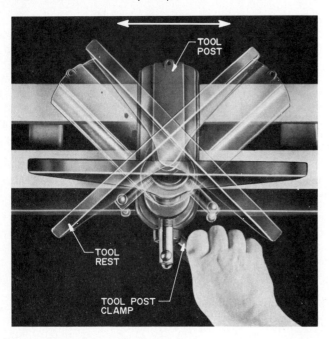

FIGURE 29-5
The guard protects the operator during turning operations. (Courtesy of Delta International Machinery Corp.)

wire shield. The guard should fit over the top of the stock and will confine any flying chips or broken pieces of wood. Do not operate the lathe unless the guard is in the closed position.

PURCHASING A SPINDLE LATHE

To purchase a spindle lathe, first specify the size. There are two points to consider. The first item is the distance between live and dead centers. The longer the distance, the longer the stock that can be turned. The next item to specify is the *swing*. The swing is the maximum diameter of stock that can be mounted on the lathe. A general-purpose lathe will have a length of 38 in. (967 mm) and a swing of 12 in. (305 mm).

Another aspect to consider in purchasing a lathe is the speed control for the spindle. The simplest and least expensive is a step pulley. The step pullies on the motor and headstock have several levels. To change speeds, the spindle is stopped and the belt is manually lifted to another level. Most operators prefer a *variable-speed control* (Fig. 29-1). This is a more expensive system, but allows the speed to be changed rapidly without stopping the lathe. The variable-speed control has a spring-loaded pulley that is mounted on the motor to change the speed. The *variable-speed control lever* is simply rotated to select the desired speed.

Buy a lathe with at least a $\frac{3}{4}$-hp motor. The larger the motor, the larger the stock can be turned. To do large-diameter and long spindles, at least a 1 HP is recommended.

SELECTING THE LATHE CHISELS

The basic lathe chisel styles are the gouge, skew, round nose, spear point, and parting tool (Fig. 29-6). They all have long handles and blades. This allows better leverage and control of the cut. The chisels come in a variety of styles, and each can make more than one type of cut. Operators develop their own turning techniques and select which specific chisel to utilize for each type of cut.

The *gouge* is used initially to work a turning square into a cylinder. Some operators also utilize this chisel for shaping coves. It is the only one that has a rounded body and cutting edge. Gouges are sold in widths of $\frac{1}{4}$, $\frac{3}{8}$, $\frac{1}{2}$, $\frac{3}{4}$, 1 in. and wider (6, 10, 13, 19, and 25 mm).

The *skew* is used mainly to smooth a cylinder, turn beads, and shape vees. It can cut from either direction by placing either face of the chisel against

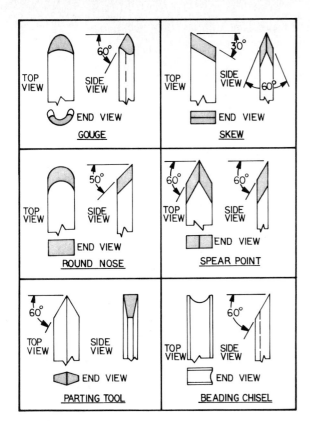

FIGURE 29-6
Basic lathe chisel styles.

FIGURE 29-7
A lathe chisel holder protects the tools when not in use.

the lathe bed. This keeps the holder from being knocked off accidentally during use. When the lathe is not being used, the holder can be hung on the wall.

MEASURING TURNINGS

There are several general-purpose and specialized measuring tools used to measure turnings. Never use any of these tools while the stock is rotating. The rotating stock may grab them and throw them from the lathe.

An *outside caliper* can be utilized for checking the outside diameters of turnings in progress and when they are finished (Fig. 29-8). *Inside calipers* check inside dimensions such as on the inner spaces of a bowl (Fig. 29-9). Both of these calipers are adjusted to the desired dimension using a ruler. They can then be tried on the lathe turning to check

FIGURE 29-8
Outside calipers measure outside diameters of turnings.

the tool rest. It is available in ½, ¾, and 1 in. (13, 19, and 25 mm) and wider widths.

A *round nose* has a flat body and a rounded cutting edge. This makes it ideal for forming coves and other concave cuts. Widths of this chisel include ½, ¾, and 1 in. (13, 19, and 25 mm).

The *spear point,* or as it is sometimes called the *diamond point,* has a very sharp tip and flat body. It has a cutting edge on each side of the chisel. This allows cutting from either direction in small areas. Spear points are usually sold only in one width.

A *parting tool* is a multisided chisel used to layout depths of cuts and mark lengths of parts. It is rarely used to make a finish cut. The parting tool is only available in one size.

Lathe chisels are made from either steel or are carbide tipped. Most are made from a high grade of steel. The advantage of the steel tool is that it can easily be ground and honed to a keen edge. Carbide-tipped chisels are very hard and will hold a sharp edge longer. However, they will be severely damaged if dropped.

Both types of chisels should be properly stored when not in use. A holder such as that shown in Fig. 29-7 provides an individual space to place the chisels both on a temporary and a long-term basis. The block on the bottom of the fixture is placed between

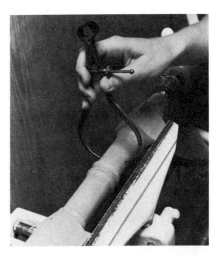

FIGURE 29-9
Inside calipers measure inside diameters of turnings.

FIGURE 29-11
Dividers mark off distance.

the fit. The workpiece is at the desired dimension when the caliper just slips over the stock.

A *wooden or steel rule* is a convenient measuring instrument for transferring key dimensions to a turning (Fig. 29-10). It can be laid on the tool rest and a pencil placed at the desired point. As the spindle is slowly turned by hand, a line will be scribed around the stock. The *dividers* can also be used to transfer measurements (Fig. 29-11). After setting them to the desired distance, the point can scribe a mark on the board.

When several identical turnings are required, time can be saved by making a layout board and template. The *layout board* has the profile drawn on its face (Fig. 29-12). Major dimensions are then drawn from the profile to the edge of the board. By laying it on the tool rest and rotating the spindle, a pencil mark can be scribed around the cylinder. The *template* has the reverse shape cut along one edge (Fig. 29-13). As the turning takes shape, the template is used to check the accuracy of the pattern.

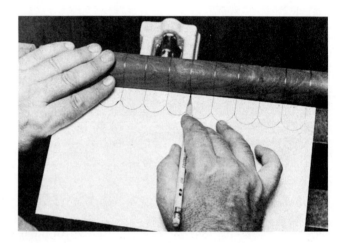

FIGURE 29-12
Layout boards can be used to quickly transfer measurements.

FIGURE 29-13
A template checks the progress of the turning. The edge of the spindle should match the profile on the template.

FIGURE 29-10
A rule can be used to transfer measurements.

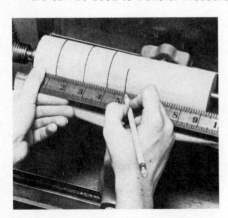

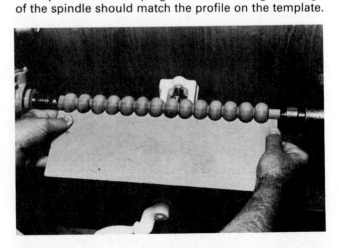

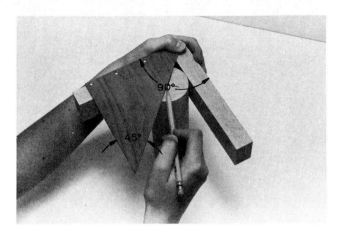

FIGURE 29-14
Use a centering jig to locate the center of a turning.

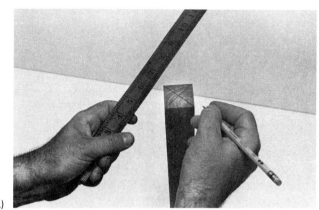

(A)

(B)

FIGURE 29-15
Sequence of mounting a turning square: (A) locating the center; (B) cutting the diagonal center lines; (C) boring for the dead center; (D) driving in the live center.

Occasionally, the center must be found on a square or turned cylinder. To locate the center on a square, drawn a diagonal line connecting opposite corners. Where the two lines intersect indicates the center. For cylinders use a *centering jig* to make several arcs around the edge of the stock (Fig. 29-14). Where the lines cross will mark the center.

MOUNTING THE STOCK

The first step in mounting the stock is preparing the material. Ideally, the turning square should be a solid piece without any glue joints. In most cases this is not practical, and the turning is made of several pieces. When glue joints are made, they must be of the highest quality. None of the wood should have knots, splits, or other defects.

Cut the stock to 1 in. (25 mm) longer and at least $\frac{1}{4}$ in. (6 mm) larger than the largest diameter of the turning. The ends should be square. If any of the original edge will remain in the finished spindle, it should be planed to the final dimensions. When the diameter is larger than $2\frac{1}{2}$ in. (64 mm), use a jointer or table saw to remove the four corners of the square. This will produce an octagon. An octagon will be safer and faster to turn into a cylinder.

Find the center of both ends (Fig. 29-15A). On the end that will hold the live center, cut $\frac{1}{8}$-in. (3-mm)-deep grooves on the diagonal center lines (Fig. 29-15B). This can be done with a backsaw or by placing the square in a vee block and cutting it on the bandsaw. The grooves will allow the spurs of the live center to be driven into the stock. On the end next to the dead center, bore an $\frac{1}{8}$-in. (3-mm)-diameter hole that is $\frac{1}{4}$ in. (6 mm) deep (Fig. 29-15C). The hole will hold the center of the dead center.

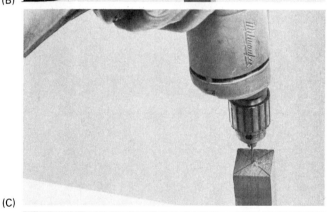

(C)

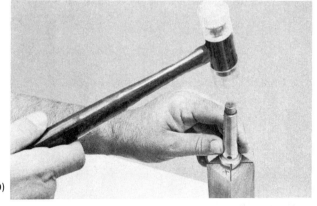

(D)

Slide the dead center into the tailstock spindle and raise the tool rest to $\frac{1}{8}$ in. (3 mm) above the tip of this center. Slide the tool rest out of the way and with a mallet, drive the live center into the stock with the diagonal cuts (Fig. 29-15D). In case the stock will need to be removed from the lathe and remounted, place an "X" on the end of the stock next to the groove which has been filed into the live center. This will assure that the stock will turn true between centers.

Slide the live center and square into the headstock spindle. Bring the tailstock up to within 1 in. (25 mm) of the stock. Secure the tailstock to the bed with the tailstock clamp. If a solid dead center is used, place a small amount of beeswax in the previously bored hole to serve as a lubricant. Bring the dead center forward until it penetrates the wood. Back off the tailstock handwheel one-quarter of a turn to release some of the tension on the center. Tighten the tailstock spindle clamp.

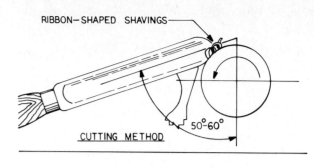
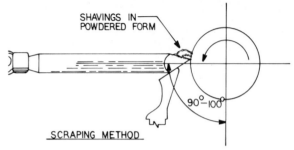

FIGURE 29-17
Material is removed on the lathe using either the cutting or scraping method.

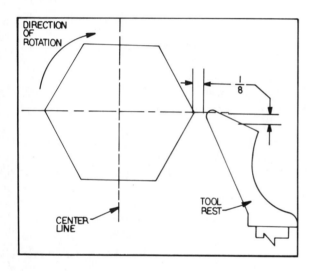

FIGURE 29-16
Proper location of the tool rest should be $\frac{1}{8}$ in. above the center of the stock and $\frac{1}{8}$ in. away from the outside corner.

Bring the tool rest forward and adjust it to within $\frac{1}{8}$ in. (3 mm) of the corner of the stock (Fig. 29-16). Rotate the square at least one complete turn by hand to see that it turns freely and does not hit the tool rest. There should be no side-to-side movement. Adjust the guard to complete the setup.

REMOVING THE STOCK

There are two methods of removing material on the lathe. A skilled lathe operator will use both the *cutting method* and *scraping method* (Fig. 29-17). Each has its own advantages.

The *cutting method* is performed with the gouge, skew, and parting tool. As the stock is turned, thin shavings are formed. It produces the cleanest cut with the least amount of grain tear-out. The cutting method is performed by lowering the lathe chisel handle to approximately a 50° angle. Move the handle up and down until the best angle is achieved. Shavings should be removed in long, thin ribbons.

The *scraping method* can be done with any of the lathe chisels. The material is removed in the form of sawdust or fine particles. This is the simplest method and the best for beginning operators. It is considered to be the most accurate. To use the scraping method, the hand of the chisel is held at a 90° angle to the stock.

TURNING A STRAIGHT CYLINDER

After the stock has been properly mounted on the lathe, the first step is to turn a straight cylinder. Position the tool rest to the far left of the square. Take a large skew and place it on its edge. Turn on the power and select the turning speed indicated in Table 29-1. This initial setting usually will not exceed 600 rpm. Place a nick in the material every 2 in. (51 mm) (Fig. 29-18). This will cut the wood fibers and prevent long pieces from flying off of the square.

Select a wide gouge and grip it firmly with one hand at the end of the handle (Fig. 29-19). With the other hand, grasp the blade immediately next to the

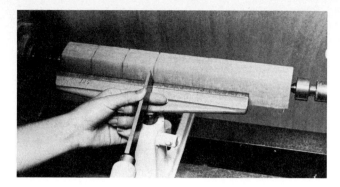

FIGURE 29-18
Nicking the corners of the square with a skew. The guard has been removed for demonstration purposes only.

FIGURE 29-19
Roughing out a cylinder with a gouge. The guard has been removed for demonstration purposes only.

tool rest. Use the index finger to slide along the rest to control the depth of cut. Lower the handle and slowly bring the cutting edge into the turning stock. Lean the handle in the direction the gouge is to be moved. This will expose the proper point to the stock.

With the gouge to the left of the tool rest, slowly start the cut 1 in. (25 mm) from the end of the stock. Not starting the cut right on the end will prevent the chisel from catching the corner and being thrown from the lathe. Carefully push the chisel inward until the cut begins. Once the chisel reaches the end of the rest, move the handle to the left and make a pass toward the tailstock. Next make a cut all the way back to the headstock. After making a few passes, stop the lathe and inspect the work. Adjust the tool rest in when $\frac{1}{2}$ in. (13 mm) space develops between the edge of the rest of the stock.

Continue roughing the square into a cylinder until all the flat areas have disappeared. Be careful not to remove too much stock and make the cylinder too small. Next, use a parting tool to turn several grooves to $\frac{1}{16}$ in. (2 mm) over the finished diameter (Fig. 29-20). The grooves should be placed every 2 in. (51 mm). Use a pair of outside calipers to check this diameter. The skew can then easily connect the

grooves to make a straight cylinder. Move the tool rest to the right and work the remaining sections of the cylinder.

After the cylinder has been roughed to size, select the widest skew. Place the face of the skew against the tool rest and make the finishing cuts (Fig. 29-21). Keep the leading edge away from the stock. Either a cutting or scraping action can be used.

Frequently, turn off the power and check the diameter with a pair of outside calipers. They should be set to $\frac{1}{16}$ in. (2 mm) larger than the finished diameter. This last $\frac{1}{16}$ in. (2 mm) is for sanding. Once the cylinder is smooth, increase to a medium speed. The faster speed will produce a smoother surface. Continue working the cylinder until it is to the desired diameter set on the calipers. A straightedge placed along the turning will indicate any low or high points.

FIGURE 29-20
Use the parting tool to make depth grooves along the length of the spindle. The guard has been removed for demonstration purposes only.

TABLE 29-1			
Straight Cylinder Turning Speed			
Wood diameter (in.)	Roughing cut (rpm)	Shaping cut (rpm)	Sanding (rpm)
Up to 2	910	2590	4250
2 to 4	810	2375	3380
4 to 6	600	1825	2375
6 to 8	600	1200	1825
8 to 10	600	910	1025
Over 10	600	600	650

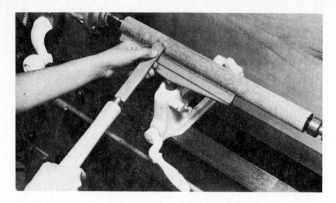

FIGURE 29-21
Smoothing the cylinder with a skew. The guard has been removed for demonstration purposes only.

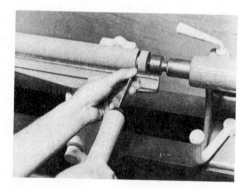

FIGURE 29-22
Use a parting tool to cut the stock to length. The guard has been removed for demonstration purposes only.

Start sanding the cylinder using 100-grit abrasive cloth. Refer to the section "Sanding Turnings" for further details. Measure the length of the cylinder and scribe a line around the two ending points. With the parting tool, cut along the waste side of the line (Fig. 29-22). Continue cutting until only $\frac{1}{2}$ in. (13 mm) of material remains. If the turning is large in diameter, make two cuts side by side. This will reduce friction and keep the tool from overheating. Remove the stock from the lathe and cut off the tails of the turning with a back saw.

TURNING A TAPER

To turn a taper, first draw a full-scale pattern (Fig. 29-23). It should show the slope of the sides and the smallest and largest diameters. Make a straight cylinder the same size as the largest diameter of the pattern. Measure the length of the taper on the spindle and scribe a line at each ending point. With a parting tool, make a groove equal to the smallest diameter along the last layout line.

Scribe additional lines around the cylinder 1 in. (25 mm) apart. Taking the measurements from

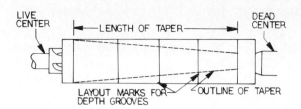

FIRST:
TURN STRAIGHT CYLINDER AND LAYOUT

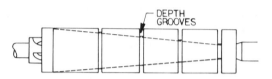

SECOND:
TURN DEPTH GROOVES

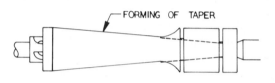

THIRD:
CONNECT DEPTH GROOVES

FIGURE 29-23
Steps in turning a taper.

the drawing, cut a groove to the depths equal to the slope of the taper. Use a gouge to connect the bottoms of the grooves (Fig. 29-24). Smooth the taper with a skew and sand the taper to the finished diameters.

FIGURE 29-24
Turning a taper. The guard has been removed for demonstration purposes only.

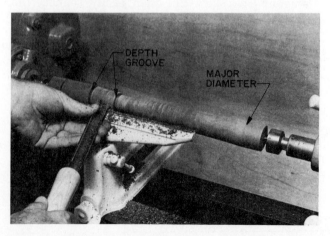

TURNING A VEE

Start making a vee by drawing a full-sized pattern (Fig. 29-25). Measure the largest diameter. Turn a cylinder to $\frac{1}{16}$ in. (2 mm) larger than this dimension. Using the pattern, scribe on the spindle the center and ending points of each vee.

With a spear point, cut down on the centerline to the smallest diameter of the pattern. If the vee is relatively small, finish the vee with this chisel. Larger vees can be made at a faster rate with the toe of the skew (Fig. 29-26). Only one-half of the vee is made at a time. Pivot the chisel from side to side to connect the ending points with the center groove.

TURNING A COVE

To turn a cove, first draw a layout pattern (Fig. 29-27). Measure the largest diameter and make a cylinder $\frac{1}{16}$ in. (2 mm) larger than this dimension. Using the pattern, scribe a line around the cylinder at the ending points and center of each cove.

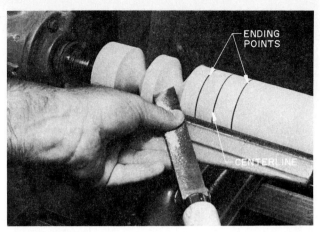

FIGURE 29-26
Turning a large vee with a skew. The guard has been removed for demonstration purposes only.

Take a parting tool and cut down to the depth of the smallest diameter along the centerline. Check the diameter with a caliper set to $\frac{1}{16}$ in. (2 mm) larger than that indicated on the pattern. With a round-nose chisel, connect the ending points and the bot-

FIGURE 29-25
Steps in turning a vee.

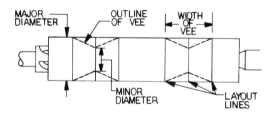

FIRST:
TURN STRAIGHT CYLINDER AND LAYOUT

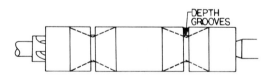

SECOND:
TURN DEPTH GROOVES

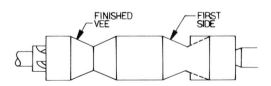

THIRD:
CONNECT LAYOUT LINES AND BOTTOM OF GROOVE

FIGURE 29-27
Steps in turning a cove.

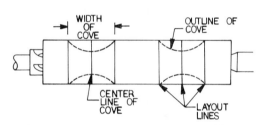

FIRST:
TURN STRAIGHT CYLINDER AND LAYOUT

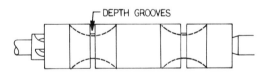

SECOND:
TURN DEPTH GROOVES

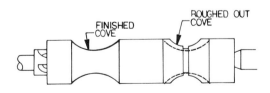

THIRD:
CONNECT LAYOUT LINES AND BOTTOM OF GROOVES

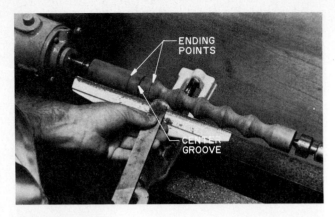

FIGURE 29-28
Turning a cove with a round nose. The guard has been removed for demonstration purposes only.

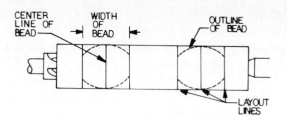

FIRST:
TURN STRAIGHT CYLINDER AND LAYOUT

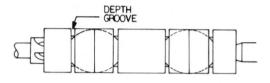

SECOND:
TURN DEPTH GROOVES

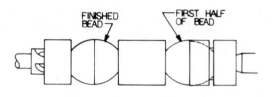

THIRD:
CONNECT CENTER LINE AND BOTTOM OF DEPTH GROOVES

FIGURE 29-29
Steps in turning a bead.

tom of the groove (Fig. 29-28). Use a small round nose for small coves. A larger round nose should be selected for coves that have more space between the ending points.

Using a scraping action, place the chisel at an ending point. Pivot it toward the centerline making a smooth concave cut. Be careful not to remove the pencil marks at the ending points or turn deeper than the groove in the center. Match the two halves of the cove so that the cut will appear uniform.

TURNING A BEAD

To turn a series of beads, make a full-sized pattern of the layout (Fig. 29-29). Measure the outside diameter of the largest bead. Turn a cylinder to $\frac{1}{16}$ in. (2 mm) larger than this diameter. From the pattern, transfer to the cylinder the ending points and the center of each bead. With a pencil, scribe a line around the turning at each of these marks.

Set a pair of outside calipers to $\frac{1}{16}$ in. (2 mm) larger than the small diameter of the bead. If the beads are at least $\frac{1}{4}$ in. (6 mm) apart, use a parting tool to cut down to the measurement of the caliper. When the beads are closer than $\frac{1}{4}$ in. (6 mm), select a small skew or spear point to make a vee-shaped groove (Fig. 29-30). Cut into the cylinder equal to the depth set on the caliper.

To shape the head, use either the skew or spear point (Fig. 29-31). A skew works well for larger beads. Using a cutting action, start at the center point penciled on the bead. Roll the skew over with a smooth motion. For small or closely spaced beads, use a spear point with a scraping action. Be careful not to remove the pencil mark at the centerline.

If many small beads are required, you may like to use a specialty tool (Fig. 29-6). It is named the

FIGURE 29-30
Making the shoulder cuts for a bead. The guard has been removed for demonstration purposes only.

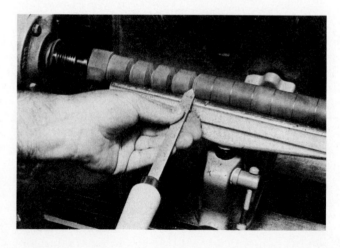

FIGURE 29-31
Turning a series of beads with a spear point. The guard has been removed for demonstration purposes only.

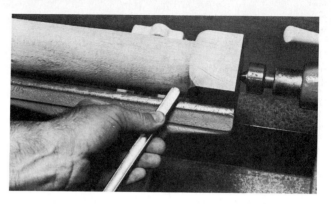

FIGURE 29-33
A gouge rounds the corners on a square section. The guard has been removed for demonstration purposes only.

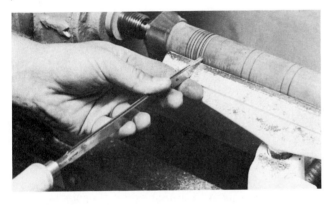

FIGURE 29-32
A beading chisel automatically shapes beads by holding it against the turning spindle. The guard has been removed for demonstration purposes only.

beading chisel. They come in various radiuses from $\frac{1}{8}$ to $\frac{5}{8}$ in. (3 to 16 mm). To use a beading chisel, simply hold the tool against the rotating stock (Fig. 29-32). The preshaped cutter automatically makes the bead.

TURNING A SQUARE SECTION

When a square section is required, make certain that the turning square is first planed on all four sides. Since part of this surface will be left, it should be free of chips and other defects. Lay out the location of the corner with a square.

Using a skew placed on its edge, nick the corners of the square. Next, turn a groove with a parting tool immediately next to the nick. Increase the width of the groove to $\frac{1}{4}$ in. (6 mm) by making another cut with the parting tool. If you desire, round the corners over with a gouge (Fig. 29-33).

TURNING OFF CENTER

Off-center turning produces a very attractive leg with a *clubfoot*. A clubfoot leg has tapered sides except for the back surface. The bottom part or *foot* extends toward the front much like a cabriole leg.

Cut the material to exact size and make a layout as shown in Fig. 29-34. A line is extended through the first *true center* to locate the *offset center*. This second center should be $\frac{1}{4}$ to $\frac{3}{8}$ in. (6 to 10 mm) from the true center (Fig. 29-35). The farther the distance between the two points, the larger the foot will be.

Mount the stock on the lathe with the end containing the layout marks against the tailstock. Turn a straight cylinder and make a small radius where the squared portions join the cylinder. Sand the spindle smooth and true.

Remove only the end of the stock next to the tailstock. Remount the material but with the dead center located in the offset center hole. Check that stock will not strike the tool rest. With the lathe set at no more than 600 rpm, carefully turn the bottom portion of the leg (Fig. 29-35). The leg will initially turn in a jump-rope fashion and the chisel may be difficult to control. Hold it firmly and take light cuts. Blend the sides of the two turnings together by sanding it on the lathe. Any additional blending can be accomplished by hand sanding.

DUPLICATING TURNINGS

In most cases, it is necessary to make more than one spindle of the same shape and size. As a result, identical turnings are required. This can be difficult if the proper procedure is not used.

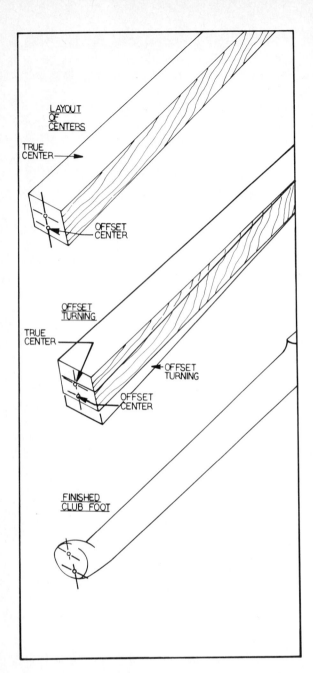

FIGURE 29-34
Layout for a clubfoot.

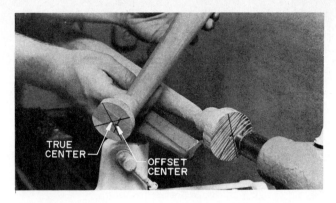

FIGURE 29-35
A clubfoot will have a true center and offset center. The guard has been removed for demonstration purposes only.

FIGURE 29-36
A duplicator is used to produce multiple spindles. The stylus is used to trace the pattern spindle. (Courtesy of Toolmark Company.)

To make duplicate turnings, draw a full-sized pattern on lightweight cardboard. Cut the pattern in half along the centerline of the spindle. Extend major measuring points from the drawn profile to the edge of the first half of the pattern. This portion of the pattern can be used as a layout board and to transfer these layout lines onto the turning (Fig. 29-12). The second half of the pattern is used as a template to check the development of the spindle (Fig. 29-13). Since the outline of the spindle has been cut out, the turning should match the pattern exactly.

Another method of producing multiple spindles is with a commercial *duplicator* (Fig. 29-36). It is an attachment which is mounted on the bed of the lathe. A hardboard template or pattern spindle is made of the profile of the finished spindle. The template or pattern spindle is then clamped to the duplicator. A movable arm containing a stylus is traced along the edge of the pattern spindle. As the stylus follows the spindle, the arm moves with it. The chisel mounted at the end of the arm then shapes the turning spindle.

TURNING SLENDER STOCK

Turning slender or long small-diameter stock can be difficult. These turnings are often used for decorative spindles on chairs, beds, and other furniture. When this type of work is machined, it has a tendency to "jump-rope" or vibrate. Unsupported, the spindle will often chatter and then break.

FIGURE 29-37
Shop-made steady rest supports slender turnings.

A support called a *steady rest* can be utilized to back up the slender spindle and keep it turning true. Although there are commercial models available, a shop-made steady rest can be utilized. The version shown in Fig. 29-37 is constructed of hardwood and is adjustable to various diameters of work. A metal model can also be made which will be sturdy and contain three rollers having ball bearings (Fig. 29-38). The rollers turn with the stock and reduce friction.

To use a steady rest, turn the cylinder down to $\frac{1}{8}$ in. (3 mm) oversize approximately in the middle of its length. Bring the rest up to the turned area and adjust the supporting arm to just touch the stock. Too much pressure will cause friction and burning. Using beeswax as a lubricant or wrapping the spindle with heavy cloth tape will eliminate any friction.

FIGURE 29-38
A metal steady rest uses ball bearings to eliminate any burning.

After the rest has been properly adjusted, turn the stock located between the steady rest and tailstock. Make light cuts and do not force the chisel inward. Next, turn the material between the headstock and rest. To finish the turning, remove the steady rest and finish the cut where the arms were touching the stock. Use even lighter cuts and on a very delicate turning, support the backside of the spindle with your left hand.

SPLIT TURNINGS

Split turnings are fabricated with standard spindle turning practices but later separated into halves, quarters, or other pieces (Fig. 29-39). It can be used to make furniture overlays, corner post, and other moldings.

FIGURE 29-39
Split turnings are made in three-quarters, halves, and quarters for decorative pieces on furniture.

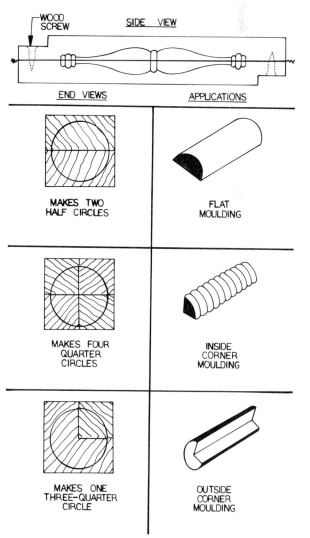

To prepare the stock, determine what shape is desired and the location of the finished flat sides. A layout such as shown in Fig. 29-39 will aid in determining the size of the stock and the location of the flat sides. All parts should be 3 in. (76 mm) longer than the finished length. This will provide an area to later install wood screws. Glue the pieces together but with a glossy magazine cover in the glue joints that are later to be separated. Adhesive is applied to both sides of the joint. To prevent the spindle from splitting during turning, place a screw in each piece at each end of the square. Be careful not to hit these screws, however, with the lathe chisel.

After the square has been turned, remove the screws. Place a wide chisel on the glue line and drive the tip into the glue joint (Fig. 29-40). Slowly work the chisel down into the joint. Once the parts have been separated, remove the paper and glue.

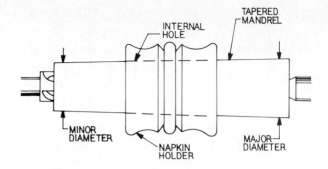

FIGURE 29-41
A mandrel allows the outside of a hollow cylinder to be turned.

FACEPLATE TURNING

Faceplate turning is used to machine work that cannot be accomplished between centers. This major division of turning primarily applies to large-diameter stock and turnings which are shaped on their faces. Products will include fruit bowls, trays, goblets, and circular picture frames.

Preparing the Stock

It is difficult and expensive to find stock thick and wide enough to use for most faceplate turnings. Because of this, most projects require glued-up stock. Use a thermoset adhesive such as *urea-formalde-hyde* to prevent the adhesive from melting out of the joint during sanding.

The first method of gluing up material calls for the boards to be edge glued to the rough width. After the adhesive has cured and the stock surfaced to thickness, face-laminate the pieces. Match the layers for color and grain. To minimize warping, the end grain of every other layer should be reversed.

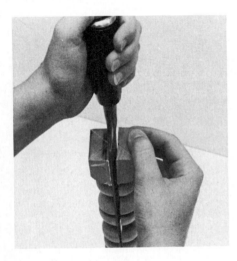

FIGURE 29-40
Dividing a split turning with a wide chisel.

MANDREL TURNING

Mandrel turning is utilized when a hole is first bored in the stock and then the outside is turned. Napkin rings are often made with this technique.

First, bore a hole through the stock of the desired finished diameter. Next, turn a mandrel on the lathe which has a slight taper to match the diameter of the bored hole. The stock should start to slip over the mandrel but must wedge against the spindle.

The mandrel can be mounted on the lathe and the material turned to the desired shape (Fig. 29-41). After it has been sanded and finished, tap the turning from the mandrel. It should slide off the small end.

FIGURE 29-42
Gluing up rings for a faceplate turning. The rings are placed against a flat board for better clamping force.

Allow the adhesive to cure for at least 24 hours and bandsaw the blank to the rough diameter.

The second method requires more time to assemble, but it does save a great deal of material. Rings are first cut from three to four boards. Each ring is smaller than the previous one. Depending on the shape and size of the turning, the waste from the inside of each ring can then be used for smaller rings or to make the bottom solid piece. Stack the rings in ascending order of size (Fig. 29-42). After matching them for grain and color, glue them together. Because the blank is already to rough shape, much time will be reduced in turning.

Faceplates, Screw Centers, and Chucks

The work is held on the machine with either a faceplate, a screw center, or a chuck (Fig. 29-43). *Face plates* are sold in a variety of diameters from 3 to 12 in. (76 to 305 mm). They are screwed onto the headstock spindle. Mount the faceplate on the stock with flat-head wood screws. A *screw center* is a small faceplate with a permanently mounted screw. Because there is not space for wood screws, one screw holds the stock in place. *Chucks* are custom or commercially made fixtures which hold the turning after one of the surfaces has been shaped.

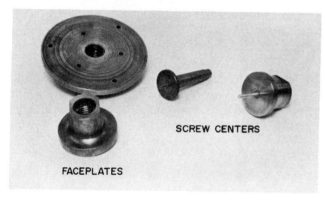

FIGURE 29-43
Stock can be mounted on the lathe spindle using a faceplate or screw center.

Mounting the Stock

Once the stock has been glued and cured, locate the center on the end to be positioned against the faceplate. Scribe a circle for the outside of the turning and also a circle the same diameter as the faceplate. Use a bandsaw to cut the outside circle. It should be $\frac{1}{4}$ in. (6 mm) larger than the largest diameter in your piece. Center the faceplate over the faceplate circle and install the wood screws (Fig. 29-44). These screws should be of the proper shank size that just fits the holes in the faceplate. To hold the faceplate

FIGURE 29-44
Install large wood screws to attach the scrap to the faceplate.

and stock together securely, several screws should enter the wood a minimum of 1 in. (25 mm). Be careful, however, that the lathe chisels will not touch these screws as the stock is turned.

If the bottom is to be thin, the wood screw will break through exposing the screw holes from the faceplate. To eliminate this problem, use a *backing block* (Fig. 29-45). This is a scrap piece of material which is glued to the bottom of the lathe stock. A magazine cover is placed in the glue joint. This allows the scrap piece to be removed once the turning is complete. Upon removing the glue, the bottom is left clean and hole free.

Place a thick leather washer on the lathe spindle (Fig. 29-45). This acts as a shock absorber to

FIGURE 29-45
A backing block allows the bottom of a faceplate turning to remain free of holes.

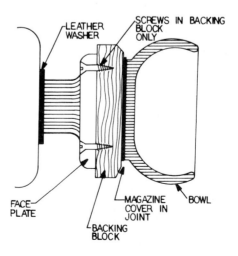

FIGURE 29-46
Use scraping techniques to turn the outside of a bowl. The guard has been removed for demonstration purposes only.

keep the faceplate from becoming locked on the spindle. Screw the faceplate all the way onto the spindle. Use the spindle lock to secure the spindle and the faceplate wrench to tighten the faceplate.

Turning the Stock

After positioning the tool rest along the side of the material, rotate the spindle at least one complete turn. This will assure that the wood does not strike the tool rest. Bring the tailstock against the stock to support the work. Turn on the power using the slowest rpm and use scraping techniques with a round nose chisel to turn the stock to a cylinder (Fig. 29-46). Use calipers and a template to establish depth grooves at key points. Connect the points us-

FIGURE 29-47
Boring a hole on the face of a bowl to gauge the inside depth. The guard has been removed for demonstration purposes only.

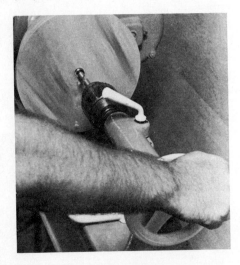

ing the chisels that will match the shape of the pattern. They can include the round nose, skew, or spear point. Completely turn and sand the outside before moving onto the inside.

Move the tailstock back and install a drill chuck. Bore a hole into the material equal to the depth of the turning (Fig. 29-47). Use a 1-in. (25-mm) Forstner bit. Position the tool rest across the face and use the round nose chisel only on the front half of the rest. Placing the chisel on the back half will cause the chisel to be thrown from the lathe.

Turn on the power and turn the inside. Keep the tool rest within ⅛ in. (3 mm) of the stock. As the inside area takes shape, it will be necessary to extend the rest inside of the turning (Fig. 29-48). Check the development of the shape often with inside calipers and a template. Sand the inside surface until it is free of defects.

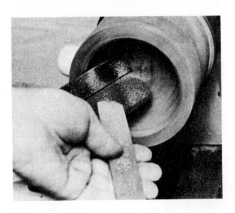

FIGURE 29-48
Extend the tool rest inside the turning to support the chisel. The guard has been removed for demonstration purposes only.

CHUCKING

Chucking can be used to shape the bottom of surfaces which have been previously turned with a faceplate. Unless a commercial, universal chuck is available, a custom wooden chuck will need to be constructed (Fig. 29-49). The commercial chuck can be adjusted to many sizes. The custom chuck should be made from a medium-density hardwood such as poplar. Each different-diameter turning will require a new chuck to be constructed. There are two different forms of chucking, inside and outside. *Inside chucking* holds the turning from the inside. *Outside chucking* secures the turning from the outside edge.

The stock to be used for the recessed block of the chuck is bandsawed to a rough size. A 1-in. (25-mm)-diameter hole is bored through the center. This will be used later to remove the finished piece from the chuck. Attach the recessed block to the faceplate with wood screws. For outside chucking, turn a recess in the chuck which is slightly larger than the outside diameter of the lip of the turning. In most cases, a ½-in. (13-mm)-deep cavity is sufficient. For inside chucking, turn a plug that will fill the inside cavity of the turning.

Press the turned piece into the chuck. There must be a tight fit between the chuck and the turning. With the chuck rotating at a slow speed, use light scaping techniques to remove the material (Fig. 29-50). After sanding the bottom, the turning can be removed from the chuck. Use a large dowel rod to push the turning gently out of the recessed block.

FIGURE 29-49
A chuck holds the turning so that the bottom surface can be shaped.

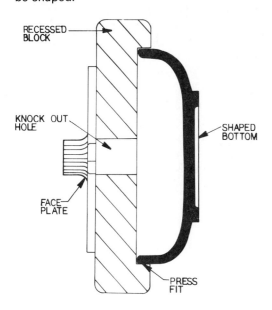

FIGURE 29-50
Turning the bottom of a bowl using an outside chuck. The guard has been removed for demonstration purposes only.

BORING HOLES

Occasionally, it is helpful to bore holes using the lathe. This is particularly true when the stock is already mounted on the lathe.

A drill chuck containing a tapered shaft is inserted into the tailstock. For small holes, use a brad point drill bit. Larger holes can be made with either Forstner or multispur bits.

Make certain that the stock is securely attached to the headstock. Turn on the power and slowly turn the tailstock handwheel to bring the bit into the stock (Fig. 29-47). Use a slow turning speed. Back the bit out often to clean the sawdust.

TURNING LARGE-DIAMETER STOCK

Most projects can be turned on the in-board or live center side of the lathe. There are, however, some turnings which are very large in diameter and will not fit between the spindle and the bed. In this case, stock can be turned on the *outboard side* of the lathe or to the left of the headstock (Fig. 29-1).

Use a heavy-duty lathe and bolt the machine to the floor. Large turnings will create vibrations, and this will stop the lathe from moving. To hold the chisels, a *floor stand* is used (Fig. 29-51). It is separate from the lathe and can be positioned next to the stock.

FIGURE 29-51
A floor stand supports the tool rest on the outboard side of the lathe. (Courtesy of Delta International Machinery Corp.)

Because the stock is large, select the slowest available speed. Use scraping techniques and take light cuts.

SANDING TURNINGS

Before sanding spindles or faceplate turnings, make certain that they are turned to the desired size and shape. Sanding should not be relied on to substitute for removing stock with a lathe chisel. To minimize the amount of sanding, carefully shape the stock with a sharp chisel with proper turning techniques.

Before turning on the power, be certain to remove the tool post. If there are no major defects or torn grain, start sanding with a 100-grit abrasive cloth. Old sanding belts work well for this abrasive. Serious defects can be removed with 80 grit.

With the lathe turning at the speed recommended in Table 29-1, bring the abrasive cloth against the rotating stock (Fig. 29-52). Use medium pressure and keep the abrasive moving from side to side. Do not hold it in one spot. This will create friction and a low area. Be careful not to round over any shoulders or other sharp details.

FIGURE 29-53
Sanding a small recess with a folded piece of abrasive paper. The guard has been removed for demonstration purposes only.

For small recesses, fold the abrasive and use your fingers to hold it against the stock (Fig. 29-53). For general sanding, hold the abrasive cloth between your hands and bring it in contact with the turning on the top surface. Do not wrap the abrasive around your hands. It is very easy to remove more than the excess $\frac{1}{16}$ in. (2 mm) left from turning. If the dimensions are critical, stop the lathe often and check your measurements with calipers.

Finish sanding the turnings with 120-grit and then 150-grit abrasive cloth. If any sanding scratches remain, stop the lathe and sand them by hand with the grain. Do not use the lathe chisels after sanding. The abrasive worked into the wood will rapidly dull the tools. Be certain that the turnings are completely sanded before removed from the lathe.

FIGURE 29-52
Sanding a spindle with a piece of abrasive cloth. The guard has been removed for demonstration purposes only.

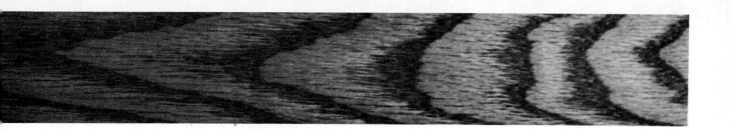

30

DRILL PRESSES

Although the drill press is a multifunction machine, it is designed primarily for boring holes (Fig. 30-1). It can, however, perform many other jobs. With the proper setup the drill press can make circular disks, produce plugs, route shapes, and even sand curves.

PARTS OF THE DRILL PRESS

There are two types of drill presses, a floor model and a table model. Most woodworkers prefer a floor model because it can bore holes in the ends of long pieces (Fig. 30-1). A table model is fastened to a bench. It is generally not as expensive as the floor model.

The main parts of a drill press are the *base, table,* and *head* (Fig. 30-1). The *column* is anchored in the base and supports the head and table. The table can be moved up and down the column by loosening the *table locking clamp*.

The head of the drill press consists of several parts. The hollow shaft that contains the rotating *spindle* is called the *quill* (Fig. 30-2). The quill raises and lowers the *spindle*. Attached to the end of the spindle is the chuck. Chucks are sized according to the largest diameter bit shank it can hold. Most woodworking drill presses have a $\frac{1}{2}$-in. (13-mm)

DRILL PRESS SAFETY RULES

1. Keep hands and fingers out of the 4-in. (102-mm) safety area surrounding the boring tool.
2. Remove the chuck key before turning on the power.
3. Use recommended speeds when boring any material.
4. Always center the bit in the chuck. Tighten the chuck by using the chuck key in all three holes.
5. Clamp small work and all metal pieces to the drill press table or in a drill press vise.
6. Clamp cylindrical stock in a vee block.
7. Disconnect the power before changing bits or working near any cutting tool.
8. Use only bits designed for use in a drill press.

chuck. This allows the operator to use a drill bit of shank diameter of $\frac{1}{2}$ in. (13 mm) or less.

At the top of the spindle is a drill pulley (Fig. 30-2). A V-belt is used to connect this pulley to the motor pulley at the top of the motor. The motor at the rear of the head provides power to drive the chuck. It is generally a 110-V motor which is plugged into a wall outlet. A pulley guard surrounds the pulleys and belt to protect the operator. Never turn on the power unless the guard is in place. Most drill presses will contain an on-off switch conveniently located on the front of the head.

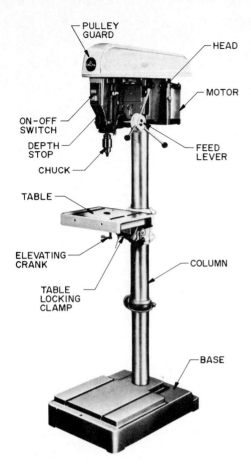

FIGURE 30-1
Major parts of a floor model drill press. (Courtesy of Delta International Machinery Corp.)

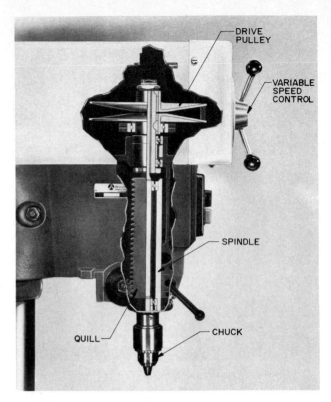

FIGURE 30-2
The spindle rotates inside the quill. (Courtesy of Delta International Machinery Corp.)

The *feed level* is manually turned to lower the quill and the drill chuck (Fig. 30-3). A spring automatically returns the quill to the topmost position once the feed lever is released. To keep the quill and chuck at a particular height, the *quill lock* is tightened. The *depth stop* allows the chuck to be lowered to the same depth every time. It consists of two threaded nuts on a graduated shaft. The nuts can be turned toward each other to lock them into position. Some drill presses have an automatic feed feature. Once the machine is setup, the chuck is lowered by a power drive.

PURCHASING A DRILL PRESS

There are several items to consider when purchasing a drill press. The most important is the size. The size of a drill press is first determined by measuring the distance from the center of the bit to the front of the column. This amount is then doubled. For example, if there is $7\frac{1}{2}$ in. (188 mm) from the center of the bit to the front of the column, the drill press would be rated at a 15-in. (381-mm) size. It would bore

holes in the center of a 15-in. (381-mm)-wide piece of stock. Another indication of size is the stroke length. The *stroke length* is the amount the chuck can be lowered from its highest position. Most drill presses have a stroke length of 6 in. (152 mm). The longer the stroke length, the deeper a hole can be bored.

In purchasing a drill press, always consider the motor size. Purchase a motor that will have enough horsepower to perform the jobs required. For most wood boring operations, a $\frac{3}{4}$-hp motor is sufficient. If it is anticipated that routing, shaping, or other heavy-duty jobs are to be performed, buy a heavier motor.

The method of changing the chuck speed must also be selected. The speed can be varied by either a stepped pulley or variable-speed control. The *stepped pulley* is the least expensive and generally will have only three to five speed selections (Fig. 30-4). This many speeds are usually enough, but it does take time to move the pulley from one leve to another. The *variable-speed control* is preferred but does cost more money (Fig. 30-3). Any speed between 200 and 4600 rpm can be selected. Only change speeds on a variable-speed pulley when the motor is running.

A drill press can also be purchased with a variety of table designs. A simple utility table has a hole in the center for the drill bit to pass through (Fig.

FIGURE 30-3
The feed lever lowers the quill while the depth stop controls the depth of the hole.

FIGURE 30-4
Changing the speed on a stepped pulley. Disconnect power before attempting this operation. (Courtesy of Delta International Machinery Corp.)

(A)

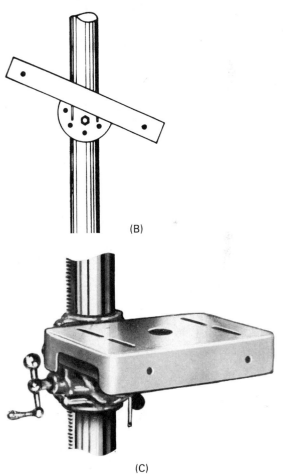

(B)

(C)

30-5A). Two other sets of slots are in the table to aid in clamping stock. A tilting table can be tilted for boring holes at an angle (Fig. 30-5B). Production tables provide larger surfaces for boring holes in big pieces (Fig. 30-5C). Many of this type will also include an *elevating crank* for raising and lowering the table.

FIGURE 30-5
(A) A utility table contains slots for clamping down work and a bit hole to allow the drill bit to pass through the table. (B) A tilting table can be angled to bore holes on an angle. (C) A production table has a large surface and an elevating crank to raise and lower the table. [(A) and (C) courtesy of Delta International Machinery Corp.]

SELECTING THE DRILL BIT

The secret to any boring operation is the proper selection of the drill bit. There are many to pick from but only one right bit for each job.

Twist Drill

The most common boring tool for a drill press is a *twist drill* (Fig. 30-6). It is used primarily for boring holes less than $\frac{1}{2}$ in. (13 mm) in diameter in wood, metal, or plastic. General-purpose twist drills have a spiral groove for removing waste from the hole and a tip ground at 118°. Twist drills designed for boring only in wood are ground at 60°. They are available in sizes from $\frac{1}{32}$ to $\frac{1}{2}$ in., varying in increments of 32nds. These bits are also sold in metric sizes of 1 to 13 mm.

Twist drills are kept in a metal storage box called a *drill index*. It can be kept close to the drill press by attaching it to the column with hose clamps. Although twist drills are available in different lengths, the most common length is specified as jobbers length.

Recommended speeds vary depending on the diameter of the bit. Table 30-1 gives speeds for boring in wood.

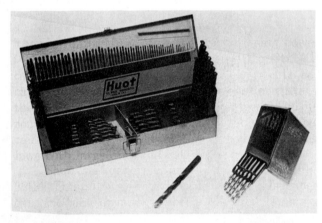

FIGURE 30-6
Twist drills for woods are kept in a metal drill index.

TABLE 30-1 Twist Drill Speeds for Boring in Wood	
Tool diameter (in.)	Spindle speed (rpm)
Up to $\frac{1}{4}$	3800
$\frac{1}{4}$ to $\frac{1}{2}$	3100
$\frac{1}{2}$ to $\frac{3}{4}$	2300
$\frac{3}{4}$ to 1	2000
Over 1	700

FIGURE 30-7
A spur bit is recommended for dowel holes and boring in plywood.

Spur Bit

A bit that looks similar to the twist drill but with a different point is the *spur bit* (Fig. 30-7). It is sometimes called a *brad point*. Two outside cutting lips produce a clean hole and the centering tip prevents it from following the grain of the wood. This is particularly desirable when boring dowel holes. The spur bit will also eliminate surface chip-out in material such as plywood. Use the same boring speeds as recommended for twist drills. Sizes range from $\frac{3}{16}$ to $1\frac{1}{4}$ in. (31 mm) by $\frac{1}{32}$ in. (1 mm). They are to be used on wood products only.

Machine Bit

A *machine bit* is sometimes used in a drill press (Fig. 30-8). More commonly, however, they are used in industrial boring machines. An auger bit with a tang or an enlarged end should not be used in a drill press. Machine bits are similar in appearance but

FIGURE 30-8
A machine bit contains a lead screw which pulls the bit into the stock.

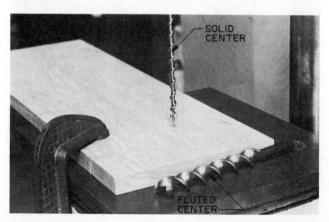

have smooth, straight shanks. These bits have a self-feeding screw center that pulls the bit into the wood. Stock being bored with a machine bit must be clamped to the drill press table. The positive feed action of the screw may throw the stock from the table. The body style may be either fluted or solid center. The *fluted center machine bit* will provide the smoothest hole because it contains the most spirals. The *solid center* is the stiffest and will take the most abuse. Use boring speeds of less than 700 rpm. Sizes of machine bits range from $\frac{1}{4}$ to over 1 in. (6 to 25 mm) by increments of $\frac{1}{16}$ in. (2 mm). They are to be used on wood products only.

Forstner Bit

Large-diameter holes with a flat bottom can be bored with a *Forstner bit* (Fig. 30-9). The small centering tip is very short. It will not break through the bottom surface when boring a stopped hole until the hole gets very close to the bottom surface. It should be used at speeds given in Table 30-2 and at a slow constant feed speed. Forstner bits work well for boring a hole for a dowel pin or other round work. Sizes range from $\frac{1}{4}$ to 2 in. (96 to 51 mm) by $\frac{1}{16}$ in. (2 mm). They are to be used on wood products only.

FIGURE 30-9
Forstner bits have a smooth cutting lip and make flat-bottomed holes.

Multispur Bits

Multispur bits look very similar to Forstner bits (Fig. 30-10). They do, however, have teeth ground into the outside cutting lip. This allows them to cut at a faster feed rate. Although it appears that they would make a very rough hole, the cut is actually smooth. Speeds should be as given in Table 30-2. Sizes range from $\frac{1}{2}$ to 4 in. (13 to 102 mm) by $\frac{1}{16}$ in. (2 mm). They are used in wood products only.

TABLE 30-2 Recommended Speeds for Forstner and Multispur Bits			
Soft (low-density) wood		Hard (dense) wood	
Tool diameter (in.)	Spindle speed (rpm)	Tool diameter (in.)	Spindle speed (rpm)
$\frac{1}{4}$–$\frac{5}{8}$	2400	$\frac{1}{4}$–$\frac{5}{8}$	1800
$\frac{11}{16}$–1	1800	$\frac{11}{16}$–1	1400
$1\frac{1}{16}$–$1\frac{7}{16}$	1200	$1\frac{1}{16}$–$1\frac{7}{16}$	900
$1\frac{1}{2}$–over	600	$1\frac{1}{2}$–$2\frac{1}{8}$	450
		$2\frac{1}{4}$–over	250

FIGURE 30-10
The teeth in the outside lip make a multispur bit cut rapidly and cleanly.

Spade Bit

A *spade bit* is used to make large-diameter holes with flat bottoms (Fig. 30-11). It is less expensive than the multispur or Forstner. The spade bit gives good results if only a few holes are needed. Because it heats up rapidly, it should not be used for heavy

FIGURE 30-11
Spade bits are recommended for boring small numbers of large-diameter holes.

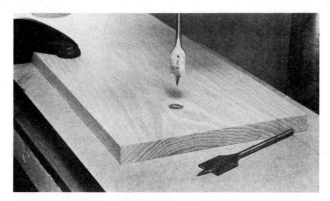

boring. It has an extra-long tapered centering point which may break through the bottom surface of a stopped hole. Chuck speed should be less than 1000 rpm. Sizes range from $\frac{1}{4}$ to 2 in. (6 to 51 mm) by $\frac{1}{16}$ in (2 mm). They are used on wood products only.

Hole Saw

Hole saws produce large-diameter holes (Fig. 30-12). As they cut a hole, they also cut out a circular disk which is the inside of the hole. This is an ideal method of making wooden wheels for toys. The hole saw has a $\frac{1}{4}$-in. (6-mm) twist drill in the center which bores a lead hole in the wood. After boring each hole the drill press is turned off and the circular disk removed from inside the hole saw. The chuck speed should be less than 800 rpm. Sizes range from $\frac{9}{16}$ to 6 in. (15 to 152 mm). They can be used on wood or plastic.

FIGURE 30-12
Hole saws produce a large diameter hole and a circular plug.

Circle Cutter

The *circle cutter* makes the largest-diameter hole of all boring tools (Fig. 30-13). It consists of a $\frac{1}{4}$-in. (6-mm)-diameter guide bit and an adjustable arm with a cutter. The arm can be adjusted in or out to make various diameter holes. It is secured to the cutter body with a setscrew. Because the bit is aggressive in its cutting, the stock to be bored must be clamped to the drill press table to keep it from being thrown. Most generally, the hole must be bored from both sides of a thick board to produce a through hole. A circular plug is produced from the operation. Rotate the cutter less than 500 rpm. Holes can be made from 1$\frac{1}{8}$ to 8$\frac{3}{8}$ in. (28 to 213 mm). They are used on wood and plastics.

FIGURE 30-13
Circle cutters are adjustable and make the largest of all holes.

Counterbore

Counterbores are used to make two holes with one pass of the bit (Fig. 30-14). Normally, the counterbores are attached to a twist drill. The hole in the counterbore must match the outside diameter of the twist drill. The twist drill enters the wood first and produces the small-diameter hole. As the chuck is lowered further, the counterbore makes the larger hole at the top of the surface. They can either produce a flat bottom hole for a bolt or a tapered bottom hole to match a flat-head wood screw. Select a chuck speed recommended for the twist drill being used. Sizes range from $\frac{3}{8}$ to 1$\frac{1}{2}$ in. (10 to 38 mm) by $\frac{1}{8}$ in. (3 mm). They are utilized only in wood products.

Screw Bit

Screw bits are specialized boring tools for making a combination of holes for a wood screw (Fig. 30-15). They will produce the countersink, shank hole, and pilot hole in one pass. Most are made from light-gauge material and are not meant for heavy use. Some have a positive stop which limits the depth of the hole to equal the length of the screw. Other

FIGURE 30-14
Counterbores make two holes with one pass.

FIGURE 30-15
Screwbits make the countersink, shank hole, and pilot hole in one pass.

FIGURE 30-17
Countersinks make the tapered holes to match the head of oval- or flat-head wood screws.

styles allow the bit to go deeper, requiring a plug to cover the surface opening. Sizes of screw bits are designated by flat-head wood screw sizes. Chuck speed should be less than 1000 rpm. They range from $\frac{3}{4}$ in. × 6 to 2 in. × 12. Use this bit only with wood products.

Taper Point Bit

Taper point bits are tapered bits specially designed for wood screws (Fig. 30-16). The angle on the sides of the bit closely matches the taper of the threads of a screw. The tapered hole will give the screw maximum holding power. An adjustable countersink head allows a combination hole to be bored. Boring speeds are the same as given in Table 35-1. Sizes range from $\frac{1}{8}$ to $\frac{3}{8}$ in. (3 to 10 mm).

Countersink

Countersinks can produce the tapered hole for the head of an oval- or flat-head wood screw (Fig. 30-17).

The shank hole is first made with a twist drill. The countersink then enlarges the top of the hole to an 82° angle. Chuck speed should be less than 1500 rpm. The diameter of these boring tools are $\frac{1}{2}$, $\frac{5}{8}$, and $\frac{3}{4}$ in. (13, 16, and 19 mm). Depending on the type of material from which the countersink is made, it can be used in wood, plastic, or metal.

Plug Cutter

A *plug cutter* is used to make wood plugs to cover the heads of flat-head wood screws (Fig. 30-18). Before the screw is inserted a counterbore hole is made the same diameter as the inside diameter of the plug cutter. A thick scrap of matching color and grain is selected and a plug is cut. The plug cutter is not used to bore all the way through the waste piece of stock. A chisel is used to break off the plug produced in the block of wood. Adhesive is applied to the hole to fasten the plug. Use a chuck speed of 500 rpm, or less. Plug cutters commonly come in $\frac{3}{8}$-, $\frac{1}{2}$-, $\frac{5}{8}$-, $\frac{3}{4}$-, and

FIGURE 30-16
Taper-point bits have the same taper as the threaded portion of a wood screw.

FIGURE 30-18
Plug cutters produce short wooden plugs for screw holes.

1-in. (10-, 13-, 16-, 19-, and 25-mm) diameter. Sizes up to 2 in. (51 mm) are available. Use plug cutters only on wood products.

SETTING UP THE DRILL PRESS

The first step to setting up a drill press is to install the bit. After selecting the desired drill bit, unplug the drill press. Insert the shank of the bit into the drill chuck a minimum of 1 in. (25 mm) and center the bit in the chuck. Hand tighten the chuck collar and then tighten the chuck using the chuck key. Insert the key into each of the three holes in the chuck and tighten. If the chuck is not tightened using each hole, the bit may slip in the jaws. This will damage the bit and may cause the bit to seize (stick) in the hole. Be certain to remove the key after tightening at each hole.

Next select the boring speed that the bit should turn. As a general rule, the larger the diameter of the bit, the slower it should turn. Use the recommended speeds given for each type of drill bit shown earlier in this unit as a starting point. Harder, denser materials require a slower speed than softer materials. If the chips are not smooth or if burning occurs, reduce the speed.

The speed can be changed on some drill presses by moving the position of the belt on a stepped pulley (Fig. 30-4). By changing the belt to pulleys of various diameters, the boring speed is changed. Consult the owner's manual for speeds and procedure of changing pulleys. When the belt is on the largest pulley on the motor and the smallest pulley on the arbor, the chuck will run at the fastest speed. When it is on the smallest motor pulley and the largest arbor pulley, it will be at the slowest revolutions per minute position.

Some drill presses have a variable-speed selector on the front of the head (Fig. 30-3). The boring speed is changed simply by turning the speed selection knob. Any speed is available between 200 and 4600 rpm. By turning the knob a spring-loaded pulley mounted on the quill will get smaller or larger. Move the selection knob only when the motor is running.

The height of the drill press table needs to be adjusted each time the bit or thickness of stock is changed. By loosening the table locking clamp, the table can be raised or lowered on the column (Fig. 30-1). Larger production tables have an elevating crank to move the table more easily (Fig. 30-5C). Since the table is a heavy casting, be careful not to allow it to drop to the floor. If not held up, it will fall as soon as the lock is loosened. A 6-in.-long board should be permanently attached at the bottom of the

FIGURE 30-19
A wood pad protects the tabletop.

column. This will prevent the table from striking your foot if it is ever dropped accidently. The table should be adjusted until the distance between the bit and the work is $\frac{1}{2}$ in (13 mm). Secure the table to the column with the table lock clamp.

Always cover the drill press table with a flat scrap piece or *wood pad*. This will protect the metal table top and keep the stock from breaking out when the bit comes through the bottom surface (Fig. 30-19). Make certain that the hole in the table is centered under the bit so that if a bit does reach the table it will enter the hole.

SECURING THE STOCK

Unless the stock to be bored is large and can be safety held, it should be secured to the drill press table. A commercial hold-down clamp works well (Fig. 30-20). C-clamps or hand screws are also used

FIGURE 30-20
Commercial hold-down clamps secure the work to the drill press table.

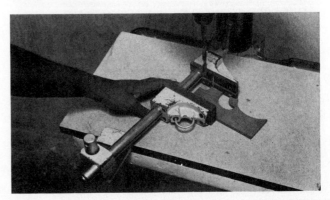

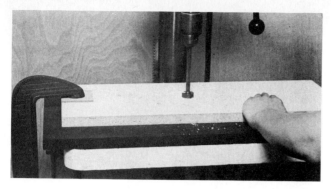

FIGURE 30-21
(A) C-clamps work well to keep the stock from moving. Note the protective block to keep the clamp from marring the panel.

FIGURE 30-22
(B) A hand screw supports small pieces.

FIGURE 30-23
A V cut into a handscrew holds cylindrical shape stock.

RADIUS CUT
IN CLAMP

to secure stock to the table (Fig. 30-21). When boring into the end of a cylinder, a modified hand screw is used to hold the stock (Fig. 30-22).

BORING THROUGH HOLES

To bore a *through hole,* first install the correct drill bit in the chuck. Raise the table to the proper height and position the hole in the table immediately below the bit. Cover the table with a wood pad. Lower the bit until the tip is just below the top surface of the scrap. Set the depth stop to this level by turning down the depth stop nuts to the depth stop flange (Fig. 30-3).

Lay out the center of the hole on the stock by using two intersecting lines at right angles to one another. Mark the center with a awl to start the bit more accurately. Center the cross marks of the layout lines under the tip of the bit (Fig. 30-24). It may be helpful to lower the bit to bring the bit closer to the marks before turning on the power. Clamp the stock to the table if it is small or any piece that has a rounded surface. Always clamp metal or plastic pieces to be drilled to the table.

Turn on the power and with the right hand, lower the feed lever. Steady the stock with the left hand but keep the hand at least 4 in. (102 mm) from the bit. Continue lowering the bit into the stock at a slow constant speed. Too rapid a feed rate and the bit may grab and throw the stock. Too slow a feed rate and the bit will burn and become dull.

If the hole is deep, back the bit out occasionally to allow the bit to clean itself of chips. Keep feeding the bit downward until the depth stop meets the bottom flange. The bit should have cut through the

FIGURE 30-24
The two intersecting lines show exactly where the tip of the bit should be located.

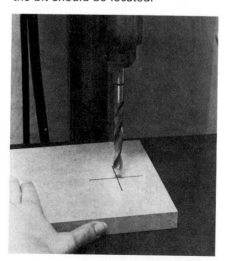

stock and cut into the scrap piece. Remove the chips from the table with a brush or compressed air before boring the next hole.

BORING STOPPED HOLES

Holes that do not extend completely through the stock are called *stopped holes*. First mark the desired depth of the hole on the side of the stock. Then place the stock on the drill press table. Lower the bit until the tip is level with the depth layout mark (Fig. 30-25). Secure the quill with the quill lock. Set the depth stop and release the quill lock.

Start the motor and bore the hole in the same manner as a through hole. Once the depth stop reaches the bottom flange, return the quill to the top position. Measure for the correct depth of the first hole before boring any others.

FIGURE 30-25
Lower the bit until it is level with the layout mark.

BORING DEEP HOLES

Most drill presses have a stroke length of 6 in (152 mm). A hole up to twice the distance of the stroke length can be bored by using a three-step method. Use a spur bit because it has less tendency to follow the grain.

Bore the desired hole in one end of the stock as deep as possible. Then bore another hole in a ¾-in. (19-mm)-thick scrap piece to serve as a base board. Clamp this base board to the table. To line up the hole with the drill, replace the drill bit with a straight dowel of the same diameter as the original bit (Fig. 30-26). The dowel must be as long as the total depth of the deep hole plus the length of the drill.

Lower the chuck and center the hole in the base board on the end of the dowel. Lock the table in this position. Put a 1-in. (25-mm) length of dowel in

the hole in the base board and place the first hole in the original piece over this dowel (Fig. 30-27). The third and last step is to bore the hole from the opposite end of the stock (Fig. 30-28).

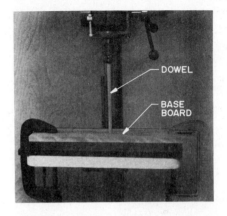

FIGURE 30-26
The dowel rod centers the scrap board on the drill press table.

FIGURE 30-27
Place the previously drilled hole over the short dowel.

FIGURE 30-28
Boring through the first hole to complete the deep hole.

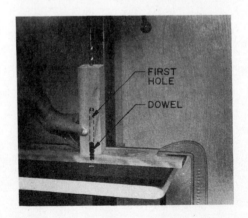

BORING HOLES SPACED EQUALLY APART

Holes that are to be equally spaced can be made with a variety of methods. Laying out the holes each time takes time and leaves room for error. It may be justified, however, if only a few pieces are to be bored.

The centers of the holes can be located using a *template*. Carefully mark the centers of the holes on a cardboard, plastic, or sheet metal template. Arrange it so that two edges of the template line up with two adjoining edges of the stock. Place the template on the stock and mark through each hole to locate the center (Fig. 30-29).

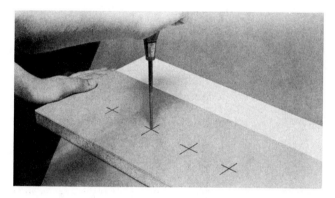

FIGURE 30-29
A cardboard template is used with an awl to locate the center of the hole.

The *auxiliary fence method* of spacing holes requires that a wooden fence be constructed. Holes $\frac{17}{32}$ in. (14 mm) in diameter are bored into a straight fence the same distance apart as the holes of the finished product (Fig. 30-30). Turn the fence on edge and position the edge of the first hole the desired distance away from the side of the bit. Clamp the fence in place with C-clamps. Insert a $\frac{1}{2}$-in (13-mm) dowel pin into the first hole. Butt the end of the

FIGURE 30-30
The dowel is moved from hole to hole in the fence. The holes in the stock will be the same distance (2 in.) apart as those in the fence.

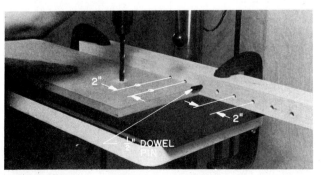

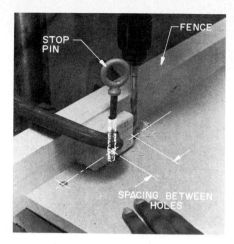

FIGURE 30-31
The distance from the center of the bolt to the center of the bit is equal to the space between the holes.

board against the dowel and bore the first hole. By moving the dowel and the board, the series of holes can be bored.

A *stop pin technique* can also locate equally spaced holes. A bolt of the same diameter as the desired hole is clamped to a fence attached to the table (Fig. 30-31). The inside edge of the bolt is the same distance away from the side of the bit as the space between holes. After measuring and boring the first hole, slide the stock along the fence until the pin drops into the bored hole. As many holes as are necessary can be made by repeating the process. This is an excellent process for boring holes for adjustable shelving.

BORING ANGULAR HOLES

Holes at an angle can be made by first tilting the table. This requires a drill press with a tiltable table (Fig. 30-5B). A sliding T-bevel set to the desired angle serves as the gauge (Fig. 30-32). Some tables have a positive stop at 45°.

FIGURE 30-32
Use a sliding T-level to set the drill press table to the desired angle.

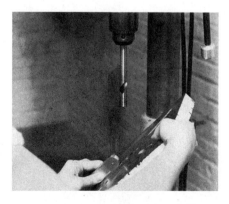

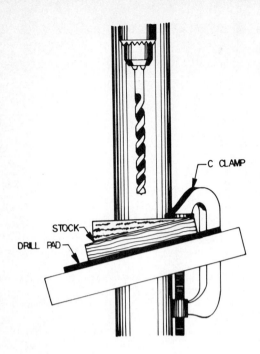

FIGURE 30-33
The triangular wedge keeps the bit from slipping to the downhill side.

Since the stock will have a tendency to slide off the table, clamp the material into position. Use a stiff shank bit such as a Forstner. If a small-diameter hole is to be bored or a sharp angle is necessary, cut a corresponding triangular wedge to be clamped on top of the stock and bore through it (Fig. 30-33). The level top surface of the triangular piece will keep the bit from bending when the hole is started.

For drill presses without tiltable tables construct a tilting fixture (Fig. 30-34). *Pocket holes* used for attaching tabletops to aprons can be made using a tilted drill press table or tilting fixture. The angled screw holes are an excellent method of securing most tops (Fig. 30-35).

FIGURE 30-34
The tilting fixture allows angled holes to be bored on a drill press table that does not tilt.

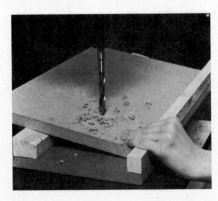

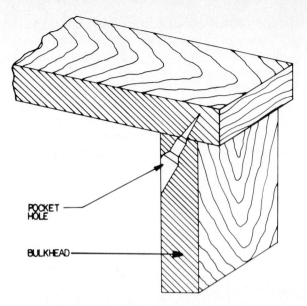

FIGURE 30-35
Pocket holes are angular screw holes used to attach tops.

COUNTERBORING AND PLUGGING HOLES

A *counterbore* is a large-diameter circular hole placed on top of a smaller hole. It is used primarily for sinking the heads of screws and bolts below the surface of the board. A wooden plug is often glued into the counterbored hole (Fig. 30-36). If the hole is to blend into the surrounding wood, select a piece of wood for the plug with the same color and grain characteristics as the piece it is to be glued. Contemporary furniture often used plugs with contrasting color and grain which is run at right angles to the surrounding wood. Use a plug cutter to produce the plugs.

FIGURE 30-36
A wooden plug is glued into a counterbored hole.

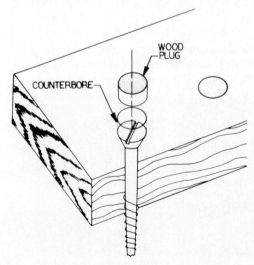

To counterbore a hole, always make the larger-diameter hole first. This will leave a center point for the smaller bit to follow. A Forstner or multispur bit works the best for the largest hole. Counterboring bits can be attached to a twist or spur bit (Fig. 30-14). This will allow both the large and small hole to be bored at the same time.

If for some reason the smallest hole is bored first, it will be difficult to bore the largest hole. The material needed to locate the center of the bit has been removed. Insert a dowel pin of the same diameter as the drill bit into the hole and then bore the larger hole (Fig. 30-37). This method also works well when it is necessary to enlarge a hole.

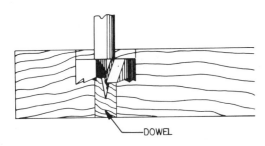

FIGURE 30-37
A dowel glued into the small hole will provide a center for the counterboring bit.

BORING HOLES IN CYLINDRICAL STOCK

Because a cylinder or round does not have a flat bottom, it requires a vee block holding fixture (Fig. 30-38). The fixture can easily be made by making two 45° cuts in a block of wood.

FIGURE 30-38
The V-block cradles the cylinder and keeps it from turning.

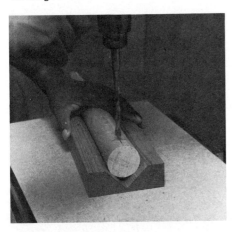

Place the cylinder in the vee groove and bore the desired holes. Locate the centers of the holes with an awl mark to keep the bit from sliding to the side.

BORING HOLES IN A CIRCULAR PATTERN

To bore a series of holes in a circular pattern, first attach an auxiliary table to the drill press (Fig. 30-39). A pivot point is established at a distance from the bit equal to the distance from the center of the circle to the center of the holes. The pivot point may be a dowel pin which extends completely through the board. If a through centering hole is not acceptable, use a wood screw with an exposed tip that has been filed to a sharp point. The screw is

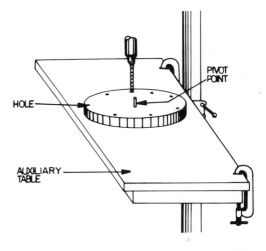

FIGURE 30-39
An auxiliary table with a pivot point provides a method of producing holes in a disk.

driven through the auxiliary table from the bottom until the tip protrudes slightly above the top surface. Center the stock over the pivot point and drill the desired holes. The holes may have their centers marked on the surface or some form of stop can be made.

Use a vee block clamped to a vertical table for boring holes on the edge of a disk (Fig. 30-40). The face of a circular part can be bored with angular holes by tilting the table (Fig. 30-41). A fixture with a matching curve cradles the disk.

BORING HOLES IN ODD-SHAPED STOCK

Stock that cannot be placed flat against the horizontal drill press table must be secured by some other means. A special fixture or holding device generally

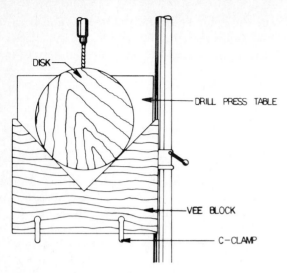

(A)

FIGURE 30-40
Holes in the edge of a disk can be made by using a vee block and tilting the table.

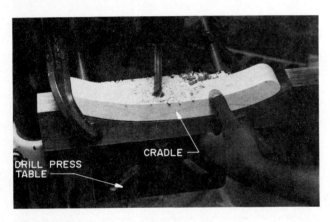

FIGURE 30-41
Boring holes on the inside of an arc requires a curved cradle board.

(B)

needs to be constructed. It is often helpful to be able to tilt the table to assist with the setup. Several possibilities are shown in Fig. 30-42.

BORING SCREW HOLES

A shank and anchor hole are required for installing a wood screw. The flat head and oval head also require a countersink hole. Use a twist drill for making the shank and anchor holes. A countersink bit will make the countersink hole. A spur or Forstner bit can make the counterbore hole.

Screw bits and specialized boring bits can be used as a quick method of making all three screw holes with one pass of the boring tool (Fig. 30-16). The best method of selecting the correct size of standard twist drill bits for a screw is by using a screw chart (Table 30-3).

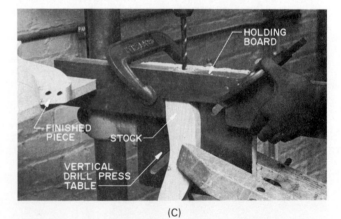

(C)

FIGURE 30-42
(A) Two intersecting V-grooves can steady ball-shaped pieces. (B) Ends of long pieces can be bored by securing them in a hand screw. Make certain that the board is parallel with the top of the clamp. (C) Ends of curved pieces can be bored by using a holding board.

TABLE 30-3
Recommended Hole Sizes for Wood Screws[a]

Screw no.	Pilot holes: twist drill (nearest size, in.)		Shank clearance holes: twist drill (nearest size, in.)	Countersink: twist drill to counterbore (in.)
	Hardwoods	Softwoods		
0	$\frac{1}{32}$	$\frac{1}{64}$	$\frac{1}{16}$	—
1	—	$\frac{1}{32}$	$\frac{5}{64}$	—
2	$\frac{3}{64}$	$\frac{1}{32}$	$\frac{3}{32}$	$\frac{3}{16}$
3	$\frac{1}{16}$	$\frac{3}{64}$	$\frac{7}{64}$	$\frac{1}{4}$
4	$\frac{1}{16}$	$\frac{3}{64}$	$\frac{7}{64}$	$\frac{1}{4}$
5	$\frac{5}{64}$	$\frac{1}{16}$	$\frac{1}{8}$	$\frac{1}{4}$
6	$\frac{5}{64}$	$\frac{1}{16}$	$\frac{9}{64}$	$\frac{5}{16}$
7	$\frac{3}{32}$	$\frac{1}{16}$	$\frac{5}{32}$	$\frac{5}{16}$
8	$\frac{3}{32}$	$\frac{5}{64}$	$\frac{11}{64}$	$\frac{3}{8}$
9	$\frac{7}{64}$	$\frac{5}{64}$	$\frac{3}{16}$	$\frac{3}{8}$
10	$\frac{7}{64}$	$\frac{3}{32}$	$\frac{3}{16}$	$\frac{3}{8}$
11	$\frac{1}{8}$	$\frac{3}{32}$	$\frac{13}{64}$	$\frac{7}{16}$
12	$\frac{1}{8}$	$\frac{7}{64}$	$\frac{7}{32}$	$\frac{7}{16}$
14	$\frac{9}{64}$	$\frac{7}{64}$	$\frac{1}{4}$	$\frac{1}{2}$
16	$\frac{5}{32}$	$\frac{9}{64}$	$\frac{17}{64}$	$\frac{9}{16}$
18	$\frac{13}{64}$	$\frac{9}{64}$	$\frac{19}{64}$	$\frac{5}{8}$
20	$\frac{7}{32}$	$\frac{11}{64}$	$\frac{21}{64}$	$\frac{11}{16}$
24	$\frac{1}{4}$	$\frac{3}{16}$	$\frac{3}{8}$	$\frac{3}{4}$

[a] Sizes of holes are recommended for average application. Slightly larger or smaller holes may be required.

When a chart is not available, make the shank hole slightly larger than the shank of the wood screw. It should slip through the hole with little pressure. The anchor hole size can be determined by holding drill bits against the thread portion of the screw. Select the bit whose diameter is equal to the root or small diameter of the wood screw roughly one-third up the length of the threads. For dense hardwoods or with brass screws, make the anchor hole slightly larger.

If possible, position the two boards to be joined as they are to be assembled. Bore the anchor hole through the top piece and into the bottom board. Follow this by boring the shank hole by enlarging the anchor hole through the first piece.

When the two pieces cannot be placed together on the drill press, bore the shank hole first. Put the top board over the bottom piece and with a scratch awl mark the location of the anchor hole. Bore the anchor hole separately.

MORTISING ON THE DRILL PRESS

To cut mortises on the drill press, first install the yoke around the drill chuck (Fig. 30-43). Slip the mortising bit into the chisel. Place the shank of the chisel into the yoke and bit into the drill chuck. Position a dime between the top shoulder of the chisel and the bottom of the yoke (Fig. 30-44). Push

FIGURE 30-43
Major parts to a mortising attachment for a drill press (Courtesy of Delta International Machinery Corp.)

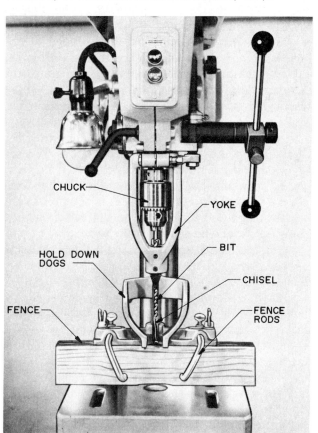

CHUCK

YOKE

HOLD DOWN DOGS

BIT

CHISEL

FENCE

FENCE RODS

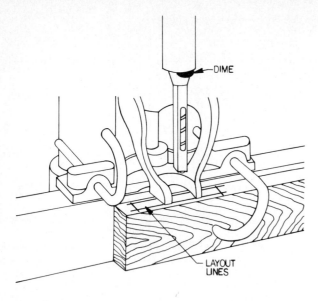

FIGURE 30-44
Use a dime as a spacer when installing the chisel.

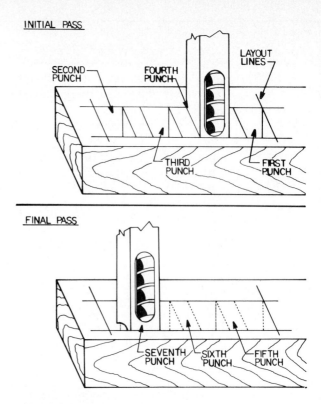

FIGURE 30-45
To prevent bending the chisel use this sequence in making the mortise.

the bit all the way up into the chisel. Tighten the chuck securing the bit. Position the slot in the side of the chisel facing toward the front of the drill press. Remove the dime and push the chisel up tight against the yoke. Tighten the yoke nut to secure the chisel. This procedure will provide the proper clearance between the flared end of the bit and the inside edge of the chisel. The slot in the side of the chisel is used to remove the chips.

Mark out each mortise on the edge of the board. Bolt the mortising fence to the drill press table. Place the stock against the fence. Raise the table until the end of the chisel is ½ in. (13 mm). from the top of the stock. Place a square against the chisel and fence to square each.

Position the stock against the fence with the face side out. Adjust the fence in or out so that the layout marks are centered under the bit. If the mortise is to be punched completely through the stock, place a scrap piece on the table. This will protect the chisel and minimize chip-out on the bottom side of the stock when the chisel breaks through.

Mark on one end of the stock the desired depth of the mortise. After placing the board against the fence, lower the chisel until the tip is level with the layout line. Secure the quill with the quill lock. Adjust the depth stop to this level. Release the quill lock. Position the hold-down dogs and fence rods against the stock. These two devices will hold the stock against the fence and table.

Adjust the chuck speed to 1500 rpm and turn on the power. Check that the clearance between the tip of the bit and chisel are maintained. They must not rub against each other. Make the first punch to

the extreme right of the layout (Fig. 30-45). Move the board to the right and make the second punch to the extreme left. Remove the rest of the mortise using the steps shown in Fig. 30-45. This procedure will prevent the chisel from being bent to one side.

ROUTING ON THE DRILL PRESS

Routing on the drill press should only be attempted on a heavy-duty machine. No less than a ¾-hp motor should be used. The chuck should rotate no slower than 15,000 rpm. Use the fastest speed available.

FIGURE 30-46
An auxiliary table and sliding fence are used for routing.

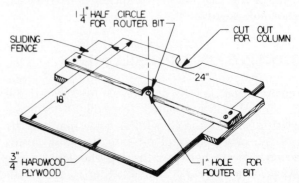

Make an auxiliary wood table from plywood and bolt it to the regular drill press table (Fig. 30-46). An adjustable wooden fence with a 1¼-in. (31-mm) half circle at the cutter location is attached to the top surface and serves as a guard and an edge to guide the stock against.

Insert the router bit a minimum of ½ in. (13 mm) into the chuck. Tighten the chuck securely with the chuck key. Lower the bit to the desired depth and lock into position with the quill lock. Clamp the wooden fence to the plywood table.

Routing Straight Edges

Clamp the wooden fence the desired distance from the router bit. Start the drill press and shape any end grain first. Edge and face grain are shaped last. On all surfaces use a slow feed speed. Keep hands at least 4 in. (102 mm) from the router bit (Fig. 30-47). Use a push stick whenever possible.

Take only very light cuts. If a great deal of material is to be routed, make multiple passes setting each to cut deeper than the previous cut. Raise the chuck so that no more than ¼ in. (6 mm) material is removed in one pass. Lower the chuck to take a deeper cut after all edges have been routed with the first-depth setting.

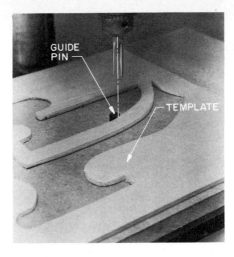

FIGURE 30-48
Auxiliary table with a guide pin centered under the bit.

Position the stock and pattern over the pin. Use a router bit the same diameter as the pin in the table. Lower the turning bit into stock (Fig. 30-49). Use the quill lock to secure the quill. Move the stock keeping the template against the pin. This routes a groove in the stock the same shape as the template. Do not take any cut deeper than ¼ in. (6 mm). Keep the hands at least 4 in. (102 mm) away from the bit.

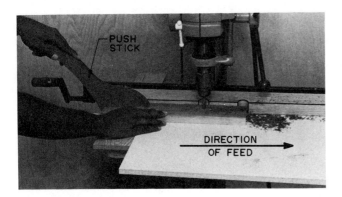

FIGURE 30-47
Use a push stick and keep hands at least 4 in. (102 mm) from the router bit.

FIGURE 30-49
Keep hands at least 4 in. (102 mm) from the router bit.

Pin Routing

A drill press can also be turned into a pin router. Refer to unit on the pin router for details of what this machine can do. Attach a short bolt to the auxiliary table to serve as a guide pin (Fig. 30-48). It is important that the center of the bolt and the center of the router bit be exactly in the same line (Fig. 30-48). Make a template from hardboard the same size and shape as the finish piece. Use small brads to attach the template to the bottom of the stock.

SPINDLE SANDING

The drill press makes an excellent spindle sander. This type of sander works best on inside curves. Commercially manufactured sanding drums with abrasive sleeves of many diameters can be purchased (Fig. 30-50). Shop-made drums can be made by first turning a hardwood cylinder on the lathe (Fig. 30-51). Cut a ¼ in. × ¼ in. groove the length of the cylinder. Insert a ½-in. carriage bolt through the

FIGURE 30-50
Commercial sanding drums come with abrasive sleeves.

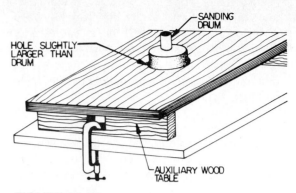

FIGURE 30-52
The auxiliary table allows the sanding drum to be raised and lowered.

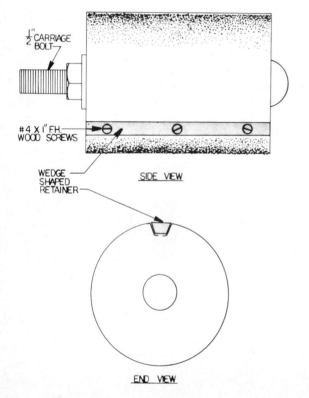

SIDE VIEW

END VIEW

FIGURE 30-51
A shop-made drum uses abrasive cloth wrapped around the outside.

FIGURE 30-53
Stock can be sanded on the face using a drum. Take only light cuts feeding the board from the right direction.

FIGURE 30-54
Setup for sanding stock to a pattern.

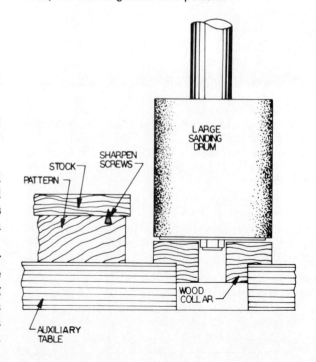

center for a shaft and wrap abrasive cloth around the outside. The cloth is held in place with a recessed strip of wood in the $\frac{1}{4} \times \frac{1}{4}$ in. groove. Several screws secures the wood strip. Set the strip and screws a little below the surface of the drum.

Select a sanding drum that is slightly smaller than the diameter of the curve to be sanded. Set the chuck speed between 1000 and 2000 rpm. If burning occurs, lower the chuck speed and use a new position on the abrasive. Install an auxiliary table with a hole in the center slightly larger than the drum (Fig.

30-52). Lower the sanding drum into the table and secure with the quill lock. Sand the curve. Raise or lower the drum once a section of the abrasive becomes clogged or burned.

There are several fixtures that increase the versatility of the sanding drums. Stock can be sanded to size by using a large-diameter drum (Fig. 30-53). Clamp a fence the same distance away from the surface of the abrasive as the desired size of stock. Cut the material to $\frac{1}{64}$ in. (0.5 mm) over the desired size on the table saw. Feed the stock only from the direction where the drum is turning into the board. Do not sand more than $\frac{1}{64}$ in. (0.5 mm) at a time.

Stock can be sanded to a pattern using the setup shown in Fig. 30-54. A wooden collar of exactly the same diameter as the drum is inserted into the table. Make a hardwood pattern of exactly the same shape and size as the desired product. Bandsaw the stock to shape, but do not cut into the layout line. Attach the stock to the pattern with wood screws. Push the pattern against the collar in the auxiliary table. Any stock extending over the pattern will be sanded away.

31

SINGLE-SPINDLE SHAPERS

A single-spindle shaper is typically utilized to make moldings and other decorative cuts (Fig. 31-1). Occasionally, it is also used for jointery-type cuts such as rabbets and stuck joints. Some woodworkers feel this machine is an unimportant accessory. Advanced furniture, cabinets, and architectural woodwork, however, often cannot be constructed without the shaper.

PARTS OF THE SINGLE-SPINDLE SHAPER

The major parts of the single-spindle shaper consists of a fence, table, spindle, and base (Fig. 31-1). There are also a few other secondary parts which are necessary for safe operation: the motor, height-adjustment system, and power switch.

Although there are several fences that can be installed on the shaper, the most common is the *commercial split fence* (Fig. 31-2). Stock is guided against the fence to control the depth of cut. The fence is bolted to the table with the *fence studs*.

The table provides a surface to lay the material. It will be made from a piece of cast metal and contains a milled slot and several holes. The slot or *miter gauge groove* guides the miter gauge. In the center of the table is the large spindle hole where

SHAPER SAFETY RULES

1. Keep fingers and hands at least 6 in. (153 mm) away from the rotating cutter.
2. Stock to be shaped on an edge must be at least 2 in. (51 mm) wide and 10 in. (254 mm) long.
3. Use a holding device whenever shaping end grain that is less than 10 in. (254 mm) wide.
4. Whenever possible, use guards, hold-down devices, and featherboards.
5. Remove all wrenches and other tools from the table before turning on the power.
6. Have the instructor check all setups before turning on the power.
7. Whenever possible, shaping should be completed from the bottom side of the board to minimize cutter exposure.
8. Stock should always be cut by moving it forward into the cutter.
9. The cutter must always rotate into the stock.
10. Use a push stick whenever possible.
11. Disconnect the power before making any tooling changes or major adjustments.

the threaded *spindle* is found. The other smaller holes are for the *fence studs* and *starting pin*.

The vertical spindle holds the *cutter, collars* and *spindle nut* (Fig. 31-3). It is either direct or belt driven by the motor. Most medium-size to large

348

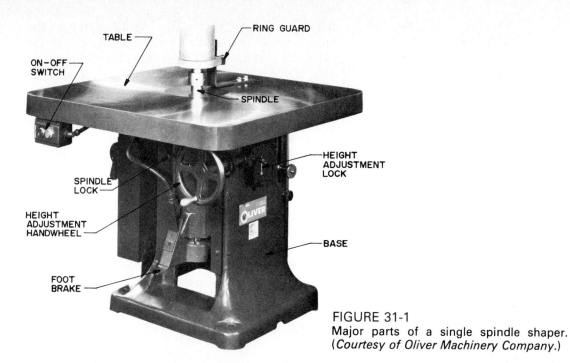

FIGURE 31-1
Major parts of a single spindle shaper.
(*Courtesy of Oliver Machinery Company.*)

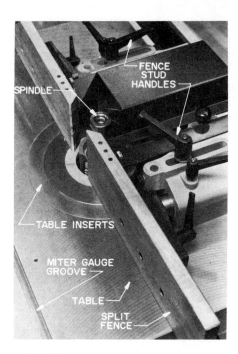

FIGURE 31-2
A commercial split fence is bolted to the table with fence studs.

shapers will have changeable spindles. They can be unscrewed from the shaper shaft and then a different-sized spindle is mounted (Fig. 31-3). Standard spindle sizes are $\frac{1}{2}$, $\frac{3}{4}$, 1, $1\frac{1}{8}$, and $1\frac{1}{4}$ in. (13, 19, 25, 28, and 31 mm).

The *base* is located below the top. It houses the height-adjustment system, shaper shaft, and *on-off switch*. The height-adjustment system raises and

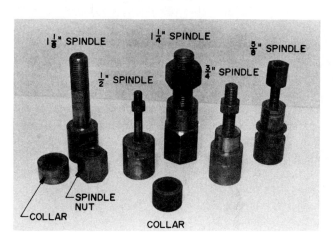

FIGURE 31-3
Shaper spindles can vary in size from $\frac{1}{2}$ to $1\frac{1}{4}$ in.

lowers the spindle with the *height-adjustment handwheel*. Heavy shapers may have a second handwheel for tilting the spindle. Once the desired spindle height has been reached, it can be secured into place with the *height-adjustment lock*. The *on-off switch* turns the power on or off to the motor. Some machines will also have a *reversing switch* which changes the direction of spindle rotation from clockwise to counterclockwise.

PURCHASING A SHAPER

The first thing to consider when buying a shaper is the size. Shapers are sized by spindle diameter and motor horsepower rating. Smaller shapers come equipped only with a $\frac{1}{2}$-in. (13-mm) diameter spindle. This size of spindle will work well on most small cutters with relatively light cuts. Medium- to heavyweight machines will have changeable spindles which range from $\frac{1}{2}$ to $1\frac{1}{4}$ in. (13 to 31 mm). This allows larger cutters to be used and deeper cuts to be made.

Motor sizes range from a $\frac{1}{2}$ to over 5 hp. The larger the horsepower rating, the heavier the cut can be made. Deep cuts should be made on shapers with a motor of at least 3 hp.

There are many other features available for this machine. A reversible power switch allows the spindle to be rotated in either direction. Some shapers come equipped with a router collet attachment. This allows router bits to be used with the shaper.

SELECTING THE SHAPER CUTTERS

There are literally hundreds of different cutters which are available for the shaper. A cutter can be used individually where the entire cutting edge is used or only a portion of the cutter is utilized to shape the whole pattern. When a more complex shape is required, several cutters can be selected to develop the edge. Make a separate pass for each cutter that is required.

Shaper cutters are either of a multiwing style or loose-leaf style. Multiwing shaper cutters contain two, three, or more cutting edges or *wings* (Fig. 31-4). They are commercially made and are available in all standard patterns. The more wings a cutter contains, the smoother the cut will be and the faster the feed rate is required. Three wing cutters are the most common.

Loose-leaf shaper knives are made from several parts (Fig. 31-5). The assembled cutter consists of a top and bottom collar which holds the two custom-ground knives. Two bolts are used to hold the collars together and secure the knives in the assembly. Knife stock is either plain or notched. The notched style is considered to be safer because the small notches are locked in between the collars and the setscrew allows small adjustments on extending the knives.

Knife blanks are cut from a bar. Using special layout techniques, the desired shape is drawn on the back side of the piece of steel. Next, the shape is freehand ground on a pedestal grinder (Fig. 31-6). The two knives should weigh within 0.5 g of one another. If one is heavier than the other, the assembled cutter will run out of balance. This will create vibration which will lead to excessive wear on the spindle bearings and could produce an uneven cut.

After the two knives are installed between the notched collars, the assembly can be placed on the spindle. The knives should not extend beyond the edge of the collar more than three times the thickness of the knife. Any more than this amount and the knife may break. Always use a dial caliper to check that both knives extend the same amount past the collar (Fig. 31-7). The setscrew can be turned in or out to adjust the amount of extension.

All shaper tooling is either made totally of high-speed steel or contains carbide-tipped cutting edges. The steel cutters are the least expensive and can be easily sharpened. Use a flat oil stone to hone the back side of the knife. Never sharpen the beveled edge because the contour of the pattern will be altered. Carbide-tipped cutters stay sharper longer and work the best when machining abrasive materials such as particleboard.

INSTALLING THE SHAPER CUTTER

To install a shaper cutter, make certain that the power has been disconnected and the fence removed. If the spindle has a cutter on it, raise the cutter well above the table and lock the spindle so that it does not rotate. On some commercial machines there is a spindle lock for this purpose (Fig. 31-8A). By engaging the lock, the spindle will not turn. On other machines a wrench is utilized to hold the spindle secure. In this case the wrench is placed either at the base of the spindle or on the flattened area at the very top of the spindle (Fig. 31-8B and C).

Use a second wrench and turn the nut in a counterclockwise motion to loosen the spindle nut. Finish unscrewing the nut and remove the collars and shaper cutter. Because the cutter can easily be damaged off the machine, store it in the original container or in a shaper cutter cabinet. It must not touch other cutters or any metal objects.

Next select the shaper cutter that will produce the desired shape. Check that the bore hole in cutter is the same diameter as the spindle. If it is not, remove the existing spindle and replace it with the correct size following the instructions of the machine manufacturer. When the cutter is mounted on the spindle, determine which side of the cutter should be facing up. If at all possible, have the largest portion or biggest diameter of the tool on the bottom side (Fig. 31-9). This will expose the least amount of the cutter to the operator.

There are four pieces that are generally mounted on the spindle (Fig. 31-10). A *collar* is first placed on the spindle to provide the accurate machined surface to place the cutter against. Next position the cutter next to the first collar. After inserting another collar on top of the cutter, tighten the spin-

3-LIP SHAPER CUTTERS

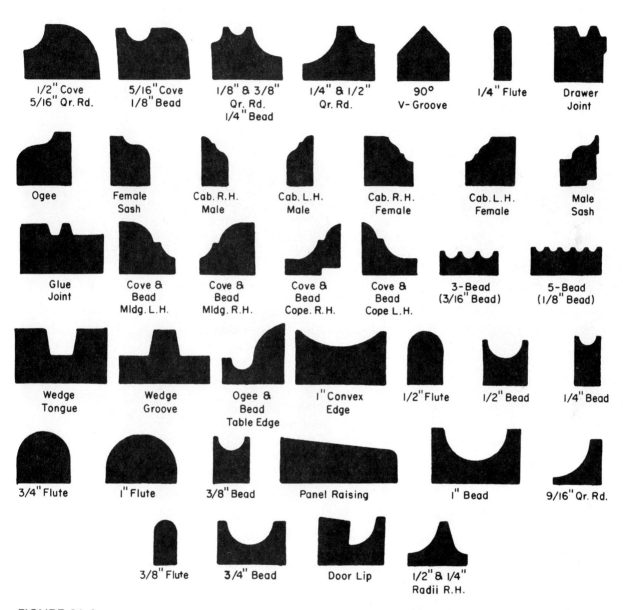

FIGURE 31-4
Commercial multiwing shaper cutters are available in a variety of sizes. (*Courtesy of Delta International Machinery Corp.*)

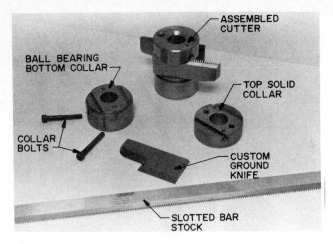

FIGURE 31-5
Parts to a loose-leaf shaper knife assembly.

FIGURE 31-6
Grinding a knife blank.

FIGURE 31-7
Use a dial indicator to set the loose-leaf shaper knife in the knotched collars.

(A)

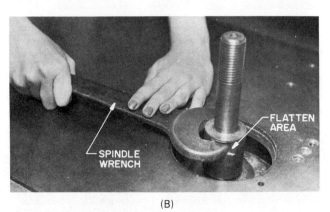

(B)

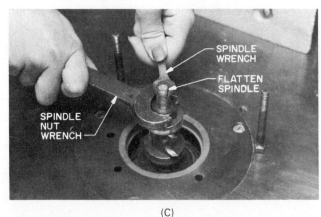

(C)

FIGURE 31-8
Secure the spindle by the (A) spindle lock, (B) wrench at the base, or (C) wrench at the top of the spindle.

dle nut. While keeping the spindle from turning, use the spindle wrench to secure the nut. If the spindle has a keyway cut along its length, install a *keyed washer* before screwing on the spindle nut. This will keep the nut from loosening once the power is turned on. Be certain to remove all wrenches and other parts from the shaper table before starting the machine.

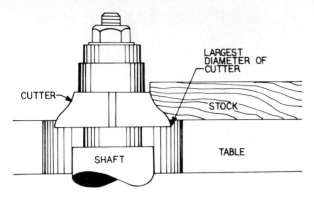

FIGURE 31-9
Mount the cutter with the largest portion below the table.

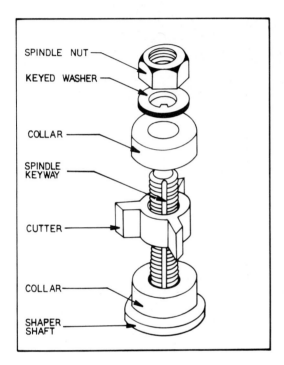

FIGURE 31-10
Correct order of parts in the mounting of a cutter.

Unlock the spindle and install the proper fence and guards. Turn the cutter by hand to be certain that the knives will not strike anything. Connect the power.

SETTING UP THE SHAPER

After tracing around the cutter on the end of the board and installing the shaper cutter, the machine setup can be completed. Next determine which direction the cutter must rotate (Fig. 31-11). Most shapers have reversible spindle which allows them

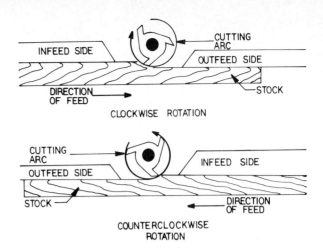

FIGURE 31-11
The rotation of the cutter will determine the direction of feed.

to rotate in either direction. The cutter must be turned so that the cutting edge is leading and the beveled edge is trailing. Quickly turn the power on and off to determine which direction the spindle is rotating. If the cutting edge is not leading, place the reversing switch in the opposite position.

By using the height-adjustment handwheel, adjust the height of the spindle. Raise or lower the spindle until the outline of the cutter aligns with the layout lines on the end of the board (Fig. 33-12). Tighten the height-adjustment lock once the position is established. To serve as a guide, a fence is usually installed. There are several styles from which to select. Most fences are held in place on the table with either fence studs or clamps. The fence studs are threaded rods which are screwed into the table (Fig. 31-2). The fence is then mounted over the top of these studs. When clamps are utilized, they are used to secure the fence to the underneath side of the table.

FIGURE 31-12
By raising the cutter, align the cutter with the layout lines.

SHAPER FENCES

Any time a straight edge is to be shaped, a fence should be installed. This forms a surface to guide the stock along and also protects the operator from the rotating cutter. In addition, it provides a surface to which hold-downs and featherboards are attached.

With all fences it is important that the fence halves are as close together as possible. The closer they are, the less likely the stock will dip into the opening and less chipping of grain. On some fences, the two halves can be adjusted inward so that the rotating cutter just clears the tips of the fence.

To provide the least amount of clearance, first attach a piece of scrap material to the face of the fence (Fig. 31-13). Clamp one half of the fence to the table and turn on the power. Slowly pivot the free end of the fence into the rotating cutter. The knives will cut its pattern through the scrap piece. Stop moving the fence once the cutter is extending through the fence the desired amount.

There are several different styles of fences. They include the wooden fence, the commercial split fence, and specialized fences. Each has certain advantages. All of these are secured to the table with either two fence studs or by C-clamps.

Wooden Fence

Wooden fences are made in the shop and come in several versions (Fig. 31-14). This fence is the best style when only a portion of the edge is removed. The face of the fence shown in Fig. 31-14 is made from one piece of hardwood. This assures that both fence halves are even with each other. An extension is added to the back of the fence to provide an area to clamp the fence to the table. Covering the face of the fence with high-pressure plastic laminate will form

FIGURE 31-14
A wooden fence can be attached to the table with fence studs.

a hard, smooth surface. This surface will allow the stock to be fed more easily across the machine.

Commercial Split Fence

Shapers are generally sold with a split fence (Fig. 31-2). Although it can be used as a guide to remove a portion of the edge, the split fence is ideally suited for shaped surfaces that cover the entire edge. The two fence halves can be adjusted independently. By turning the depth-adjustment knob, one-half of the fence can be moved in or out. This allows the outfeed portion of the fence to be moved forward to support the freshly shaped edge.

Specialized Fences

Specialized fences are designed for a specific purpose. The only limitations are the creativity of the operator and the safety requirements of the machine.

A few of the specialized fences include a high fence, long fence, miter fence, strip molding fence, and circular fence. With all of these fences, remember to have a minimal opening between the fence halves. To keep from making a new fence for each cutter, a replaceable insert can be used to fit into the specialized fences (Fig. 31-15). When a new cutter is to be used, install another insert and allow the cutter to cut through the insert.

FIGURE 31-13
Pivoting the fence into the rotating cutter to provide a minimum amount of clearance.

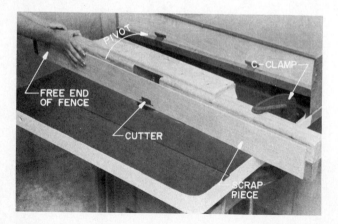

FIGURE 31-15
A replaceable insert provides a new throat opening without making a new fence.

HIGH FENCE. A high fence is utilized primarily for shaping wide pieces that are shaped on their faces (Fig. 31-16). The tall vertical fence provides support for the stock and also gives a large surface to clamp featherboards.

LONG FENCE. A long fence is used primarily on small shapers with short tables (Fig. 31-17). This fixture not only makes a long fence but also provides a base or table to feed the stock against. This makes it ideal for long boards or for attaching stop blocks.

MITER FENCE. A miter fence will shape a bevel or chamfer on the edge or end of a board (Fig. 31-18). The incline base holds the board at the desired angle. If a different angle is required, a new fence is made.

FIGURE 31-16
A high fence provides additional support for large pieces. Note that the featherboard also adds more support.

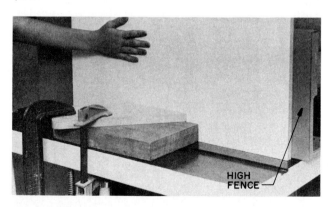

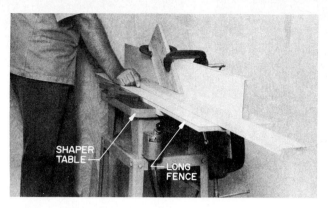

FIGURE 31-17
A long fence provides support for extra long stock.

FIGURE 31-18
A miter fence angles the board for a bevel or chamfer cut.

STRIP MOLDING FENCE. Thin pieces of molding can be made by either of two methods. When a wide board is available, the edge can be first shaped and then the molding ripped to thickness on a table saw. The second method is to construct a strip molding fence (Fig. 31-19). This allows thin pieces to be fed

FIGURE 31-19
A strip molding fence allows the material to be shaped.

safely past the cutter. The featherboard holds the stock against the fence while the top piece keeps it against the base. Make certain that the stock is long enough to be pushed and pulled past the fixture.

OPERATING THE SHAPER

After the cutter has been mounted and the fence adjusted, featherboards must be installed. Featherboards are shop-made wooden hold-downs which keep the board against the table and serves as a barrier against the rotating cutter. Figure 31-20 shows the recommended dimensions for featherboards that are used with the shaper.

Position a piece of stock of the same thickness as the material to be shaped against the fence. A featherboard is to be mounted on each side of the fence and as close to the rotating cutter as possible (Fig. 31-21). With a C-clamp, secure each one in place. Rotate the cutter by hand to be certain that the cutter does not come in contact with the featherboards.

Check to see that the stock is at least 2 in. (52 mm) wide and 10 in. (254 mm) long. Never shape a piece with less than 10 in. (254 mm) in contact with fence unless a special holding device is used. The sliding miter gauge with hold-downs works well when shaping the end grain on narrow boards (Fig. 31-22). Turn on the power and slowly feed a scrap piece forward into the cutter. After the piece has reached the outfeed fence, pivot the board away from the cutter. Check that the shaped surface matches

FIGURE 31-21
Use two featherboards to hold the stock down and to guard the cutter.

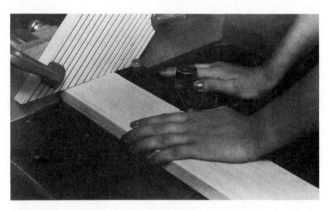

FIGURE 31-22
A sliding miter gauge can be selected to hold small stock or when shaping end grain.

FIGURE 31-20
Construction details for a featherboard.

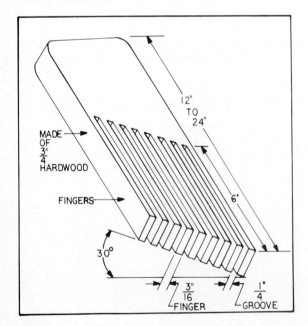

the desired profile. If the cut is too heavy for the machine to make in one pass, adjust for a lighter cut. Make the shaped edge in two or more passes.

Use a push stick to guide the boards past the cutter. Your hands must not come within 6 in. (152 mm) of the cutting circle. Use a slow constant feed speed. To minimize the torn grain at the corners of the board, always shape the end grain first. Any chipping that occurs will usually be removed when the edges are shaped.

SHAPING PART OF AN EDGE

When only part of the edge is to be shaped, start by jointing the surface. Since part of the edge will not be removed and left exposed, make certain that this jointed edge is straight and free from chipped grain (Fig. 31-23).

Install either a commercial split fence or a wooden fence to guide the stock. If a split fence is

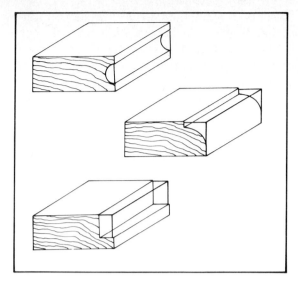

FIGURE 31-23
Part of the original edge may be left with some types of cuts. The colored lines indicate the original edge that has been shaped away.

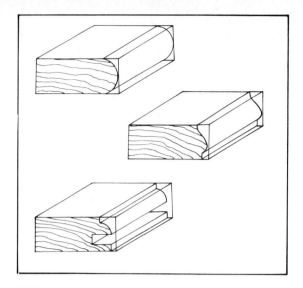

FIGURE 31-24
Some shapes require that all of the original edge be machined. The colored lines indicate the original edge that has been shaped away.

utilized, use a long, straight edge to align the two fence halves. A wooden fence, as shown in Fig. 31-14, does not need to be aligned.

Raise the cutter to the desired height and move the fence to expose the correct amount of the cutter. Fasten the fence to the table using the fence stud. Next, determine which direction the cutter must rotate (Fig. 31-11). If it does not rotate opposite the direction of feed, reverse rotation. Complete the remaining setup and follow the operating procedure as given in the section "Operating the Shaper."

SHAPING THE ENTIRE EDGE

Many profiles require that the whole edge be shaped (Fig. 31-24). To produce this type of a cut, mount the desired cutter and adjust it to the correct height. Determine which direction the cutter is to rotate and set the rotation switch to the proper position.

The split fence next needs to be mounted in the proper position. To do this, place the stock on the infeed side of the fence and slide the fence in or out until the desired amount of the cutter extends past the face of the fence. At least $\frac{1}{16}$ in. (2 mm) should be removed from all areas of the edge. Tighten the fence stud nut on the infeed side of the fence and install a featherboard (Fig. 31-25).

Turn on the power and check that the cutter is rotating the opposite direction of the feed (Fig. 31-11). Slowly feed a large scrap piece forward until the leading end is approximately 3 in. (76 mm) past the cutter. Pivot the stock away from the cutter and

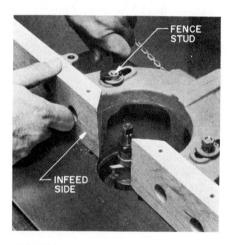

FIGURE 31-25
Tighten the fence stud on the infeed side of the fence to secure that half of the fence.

turn off the power. Make any necessary adjustments to produce the desired shape.

By turning the depth-adjustment knob, move the outfeed side of the fence forward until it just touches the newly shaped edge (Fig. 31-26). If it is brought too far forward, the stock will hit the lip of the outfeed fence and a taper will be shaped. Not bringing it far enough forward will produce a snipe at the end of the board. Lock the fence with the depth-locking handle and then tighten the remaining fence stud nut.

Install a featherboard on the outfeed fence and feed a large scrap board across the rotating cutter. Check that the fence has been properly adjusted and

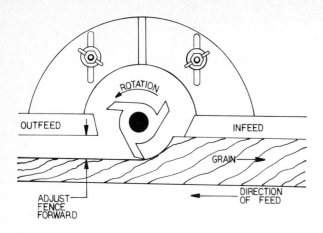

FIGURE 31-26
Adjust the outfeed side of the fence up to support the freshly shaped edge.

the cut is correct. The stock can then be shaped. Remember each time the boards are passed over the shaper, it becomes smaller. If the stock is run more than once, it may become too small. Use the operating instructions as given in the section "Operating the Shaper."

COLLAR SHAPING

Curved or irregularly shaped stock can be shaped by using a contact collar (Fig. 31-27). The precut piece is simply fed against this special collar. Make certain that the piece is large enough to allow you to keep your hands a minimum of 6 in. (152 mm) from the cutter. In addition, with this method only part of the edge is shaped. Since a portion of the original edge will remain, it must be perfectly smooth and true. This edge also serves as a pattern to run the stock against. Any irregular surfaces will be transferred to the shaped edge.

FIGURE 31-27
Collar shaping utilizes a contact collar to control the depth of cut.

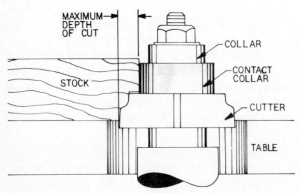

To set up the machine, install the cutter in the normal manner with the largest diameter of the cutter on the bottom side. It is recommended to place a contact collar immediately on top of the cutter against which to run the stock. The collar can also be placed under the cutter or mounted between two cutters. These last two positions, however, leave more of the shaper knife exposed. Contact collars can be either a *highly polished solid collar* or a *ball-bearing collar*. The solid collar is the least expensive but does tend to burn the stock. The ball-bearing collar does not spin with the spindle once it comes in contact with the stock. This prevents burning from occurring. Keep both types of collars smooth and shiny.

The amount the cutter overhangs the contact collar determines the depth of cut (Fig. 31-27). The smaller the collar, the heavier the cut. If a great deal of material is to be removed, initially use a larger-diameter contact collar or lower the spindle.

To protect the operator and cutter, install either a *plastic shield* or a *ring guard* (Fig. 31-28). Both are suspended over the top of the cutter and should extend farther out than the cutting circle.

FIGURE 31-28
Use (A) a plastic shield or (B) a ring guard when a fence is not used.

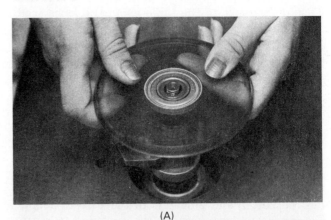

(A)

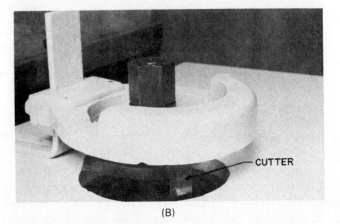

(B)

358   CHAPTER 31   SINGLE-SPINDLE SHAPERS

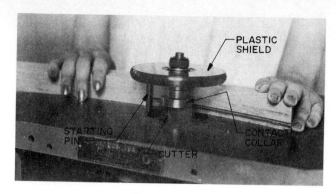

FIGURE 31-29
Collar shaping with a starting pin.

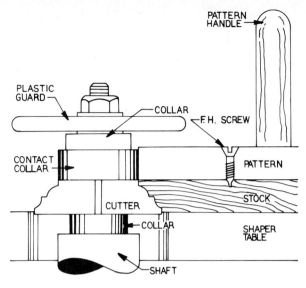

FIGURE 31-30
Proper setup for pattern shaping.

These guards will protect you only from the top side of the cutter. Be careful that your hands do not slide into the cutter from the side.

Never attempt to perform collar shaping without a starting pin. A *starting pin* acts as a fulcrum point for the material to be pivoted into the cutter (Fig. 31-29). It generally fits into a tapered hole which is located on the infeed side of the shaper.

Once the shaper has been set up, raise the cutter to the desired height. Check that at least $\frac{1}{4}$ in. (6 mm) is against the contact collar. Any less, and the stock may plunge into the cutter.

Turn on the power and firmly grip the stock. Place the board against the starting pin and slowly pivot it into the rotating cutter. Plan the cut so that it will not start on the corner. The cutter should first come into contact with the stock immediately behind the corner. This will keep the cutter from grabbing the work.

After the stock has come against the contact collar, feed it forward. Swing the board off the starting pin and use only the collar to guide the stock. Once a corner is reached, rotate the stock to the next edge and continue shaping until the entire board is shaped. As the board is being fed forward, keep working your hands back away from the cutter. After the shaped edge is complete, pivot the stock away from the cutter.

PATTERN SHAPING

Pattern shaping can be used when the entire edge is to be molded on a curved or irregular shaped piece. Industry often uses this method because it is one of the fastest methods of producing parts such as plaque backs, mirror frames, and other curved furniture parts. Pattern shaping does require a pattern or form to produce the part. This requires time and skill to produce.

To produce parts using the pattern-shaping technique, first make the pattern (Fig. 31-30). For a small number of parts, $\frac{3}{4}$-in. (19 mm) dense hardwood such as northern hard maple works well. If a large number of pieces are required, the pattern will wear much longer if it is made from tempered hardboard, plastic, or metal. After the outline of the part has been laid out, carefully use a scroll saw to cut out the form. With files and other hand tools, work the edge until it is smooth and true. The pattern will be complete when it is exactly the same size and shape as the finished part. Any remaining imperfections will be reflected in the shaped parts.

To secure the stock to the pattern, use at least three flat-head wood screws. The larger the part, the more screws should be utilized. File the first $\frac{1}{8}$ in. (3 mm) of each screw to a flat chisel shape. Drive the screws through the patterns until the $\frac{1}{8}$-in. tip is extending through the face of the pattern. To achieve maximum holding power, the flatten tip should be oriented parallel to the grain of the part.

Finish the pattern by attaching two handles to the back of the pattern and gluing 100-grit abrasive paper to the face. The handles provide a method of safely holding and controlling the pattern. The abrasive paper provides more gripping power and the stock is less likely to twist off the pattern.

After the pattern is finished, install the cutter and set up the shaper as described in the section "Collar Shaping." Ideally, the contact collar should be just slightly smaller in diameter than the deepest part of the cutter (Fig. 31-31). Always mount the contact collar on top of the cutter to provide maximum safety. A ball-bearing collar is less likely to burn a groove in the pattern.

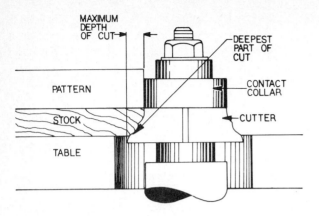

FIGURE 31-31
Select a collar that is slightly smaller in diameter than the deepest part of the cutter.

The pattern and stock can be run much like a part as described in "Collar Shaping." The stock, however, is first roughly sawed to shape. After placing the pattern on top of the stock, draw around the outside edge. Cut each piece to within $\frac{1}{16}$ to $\frac{1}{8}$ in. (2 to 3 mm) of this layout line. Place the precut piece with the face against the shaper table and the back or poorest side facing up. After centering the pattern over the stock, use a mallet to drive the screw tips into the board. Check that the stock and pattern are firmly seated together.

Place the pattern against the starting pin and pivot the pattern into the rotating cutter. Begin the cut in the middle of one of the edges (Fig. 31-32).

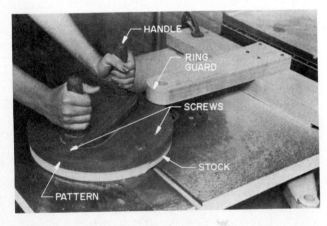

FIGURE 31-32
Shaping a circular edge with a pattern.

Pivot the pattern away from the starting pin keeping it against the rotating cutter. Keep the stock moving at all times, and your hands on the handles. Once the cut is complete, slide the pattern away from the cutter.

STUCK JOINERY

Stuck joinery is commonly found on good-quality traditional furniture and cabinets (Fig. 31-33). This joinery is frequently used on raised panel doors and frame plywood bulkheads. It requires a matched set of cutters that will cut the molding on the inside edges of stiles and rails and the shaped end on the mating ends of the rails. The shaped edges on the inside edge are called *sticking*. The shaped ends are referred to as *coped ends*. There are many different styles of cutters available which will provide different patterns.

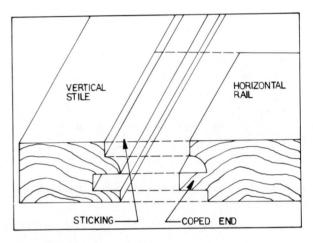

FIGURE 31-33
Stuck joint sticking and coped ends.

Because grain tear-out is always a problem, the ends of the rails are shaped first. Cut the material to the finished length and $\frac{1}{4}$ inch (6 mm) wider than the finished widths. The length can be determined by establishing the inside dimension of the panel. This is called the *between the shoulder length* (Fig. 31-34). To this amount, add the length of the two tenons. With most cutters, this is a total of 1 in. (25 mm). For example, if there is 10 in. (254 mm) between the stiles, add 1 in. (25 mm). The finished length of the rails will then be 11 in. (279 mm).

Set the shaper up with a wooden fence (Fig. 31-35). Ideally, a $\frac{1}{4}$-in. (6-mm)-thick piece of plywood should be attached to the face of the fence. After the cutters have been adjusted to the proper height, the fence should then be pivoted into the rotating cutter (Fig. 31-13). This will provide a minimum of clearance between the cutting circle and the fence. Having this small space will make coping much safer and reduce grain tear out.

As the fence is installed, it must be mounted parallel to the miter gauge groove. Check that the distance between the face of the fence and the edge

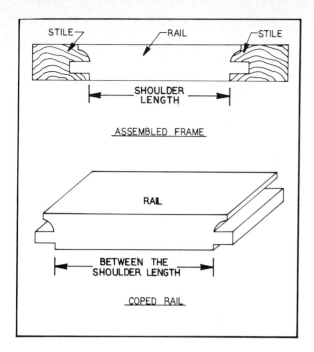

FIGURE 31-34
Check the between the shoulder length to determine the overall width of the frame.

of the miter gauge groove is the same at each end of the shaper table. Once the fence is secure to the table, attach featherboards to the face of the fence.

To the face of the miter gauge, screw a piece of squared stock to serve as a backup board (Fig. 31-35). It will extend to the fence. It should be at least 12 in. (305 mm) longer than the longest rail. This serves as an additional surface to hold the material but also prevents grain tear-out. After it has been attached to the gauge, turn on the power and run the miter gauge past the cutter. This will cut the shape into the end of the stock. Check that this profile is correct. If not, make any necessary adjustments.

FIGURE 31-35
Shaping the coped ends of stuck joint.

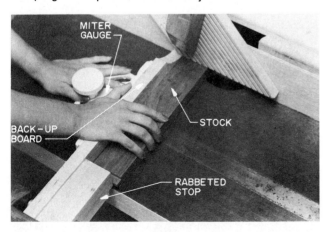

Place the first piece of material with the edge against the miter gauge and the end against the fence. There must be a minimum of 10 in. (254 mm) in contact with the gauge. Clamp a rabbeted stop on the backup board and against the other end of the stock. Turn on the power and grip the board securely against the miter gauge. Feed the stock slowly past the cutters. End for end the piece and cope the remaining end. After this first piece has been run, check that between the shoulder dimension is correct. Run all the remaining pieces.

Tear the setup down and install the matching cutters for the sticking (Fig. 31-36). Place a rail on the table to determine the correct height of the cutters. Match the cutters up with the coped end of the rail. Place the split fence on the shaper and adjust it to remove $\frac{1}{16}$ in. (2 mm) from the original edge. Finish the set up by installing featherboards.

FIGURE 31-36
Match the sticking cutters with the coped end by raising the spindle.

Stock for the stiles should be the same thickness as the rails and $\frac{1}{4}$ in. (6 mm) wider than the finished width. This extra width will allow the pieces to be run a second time if there is any chipped grain. Stiles will need to be cut to the finished length.

For the sticking operation, feed the stock past the cutters with a push stick. Be careful not to push in on the stock immediately around the throat of the fence. A sniped end is very likely to occur.

After the first piece is run, check that the rails properly fit into the sticking. The faces of the two pieces should be even, and there should be a slight amount of drag as the tenon is inserted. If the fit is correct, run the remaining pieces. Any shaped edges that develop torn grain can be rerun. Feed the piece at a slower rate. After all parts have been shaped, rip them to rough width and joint the outside edge to finish width.

GLUE JOINERY

One method of adding quality to a solid wood panel is to make the edge glue joints on the shaper. A special glue joint cutter is used to make both mating surfaces. It provides a decorative tongue and groove appearance on the end grain while assuring the alignment of the boards. Because the stock does overlap on each joint, it requires an additional $\frac{1}{4}$ in. (6 mm) of material per joint.

To run this glue joint, first rip all material to width and surface it to thickness. In addition, plane a piece of scrap material to this exact thickness to be used for setup. Install the cutter and adjust the height where the top shoulder (surface A) and the bottom shoulder (surface B) will be *exactly* the same width (Fig. 31-37). Unless this is done, the face of the boards will not be even.

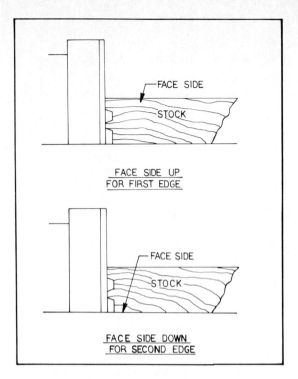

FIGURE 31-38
Run a shaped glue joint with the face up of the first edge. Turn the board over to shape the second edge.

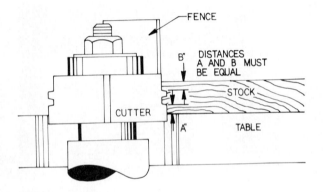

FIGURE 31-37
Setup for shaping a glue joint.

Place the split fence on the shaper and adjust the fence halves to remove $\frac{1}{16}$ in. (2 mm) with the smallest diameter of the cutter. The outfeed fence will need to be moved forward to support the newly shaped surface. By removing the entire edge, not only is the joint cut but also the boards will be straightened.

After installing featherboards, run the scrap stock. Crosscut the piece in half and fit the two halves together. Make any necessary adjustments so that the faces are even and a straight edge is produced. Shape the stock following the recommended procedure as given in the section "Operating the Shaper." Run one edge of each board with the face side up (Fig. 31-38). Then turn the boards over and shape the mating edges with the face side down. To glue the panel up, be certain a glue brush is used to work the adhesive into the grooves.

SHAPING WITH SPECIALIZED FIXTURES

Using a fixture to hold and guide the material allows custom patterns to be made and undersized material to be run. They should be made so that the stock is held firmly and that the hands of the operator do not come within the 6-in. (152-mm) danger zone of the cutter.

A few of the possible specialized fixtures are as follows:

Circular Fixture

The circular fixture provides full support on stock that is a true circle or a segment of a true circle (Fig. 31-39). A fixture is made the reverse shape and same diameter as the piece to be shaped. Since featherboards are not used, install a ring guard or other form of protection.

Fretting Fixture

To make an ornamental piece of molding, a fretting fixture can be utilized (Fig. 31-40). Although there are many variations possible, one method of producing the required template is to bore a series of holes.

FIGURE 31-39
A circular fixture provides a method of shaping circular parts.

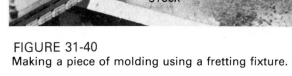

FIGURE 31-40
Making a piece of molding using a fretting fixture.

The template is then ripped in half leaving one-half of each hole.

An indexing pin of the same diameter as the template holes is installed in the table on the infeed side of the cutter. After the cutter and contact collar are mounted, screw the stock to the template. The part can then be run. The indexing pin determines the distance between the cuts. The contact collar sets the depth of cut. Move the template to the first hole and pivot the stock into the rotating cutter. Once the contact collar meets the template, swing the work back away from the cutter. Move the template to the next hole and repeat the process until all the notches are made. The cutter can be raised and another row of cuts can be made.

32

PIN ROUTERS

The pin router is one of the newer stationary power tools to be used in the woods industry (Fig. 32-1). It can make both joinery and decorative-type cuts. Because this machine utilizes router bits for cutters, there are many different available patterns. The pin router has the advantage over a portable router because the cutter is held in a fixed position. This allows both large and small stock to be shaped.

Shops will generally have a *shaper-router* (Fig. 32-2). This allows the motor unit to be suspended over the table or mounted below the table. To make heavier industrial cuts, a larger *pin router* is used (Fig. 32-1). It may have a floating head which moves up and down over the top of curved stock.

PARTS OF THE PIN ROUTER

There are relatively few major parts to the pin router (Fig. 32-1). It is made from a base, column, and arm. An *arm* is suspended over the top of a table. Inside this arm is located the motor and drive system. At the end of the arm is the *spindle*. On most routers, the spindle moves the router bit up and down and rotates the cutter in a clockwise direction.

The *table* holds the stock while it is being machined. In the center of the table will be the *pinhole*.

FIGURE 32-1
Major parts of the pin router. (*Courtesy of Ekstrom, Carlson & Co.*)

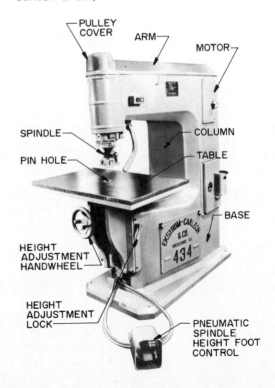

PIN ROUTER SAFETY RULES

1. Your hands and fingers must be kept at least 4 in. (102 mm) from the router bit.
2. Keep your hands out of the path of the router bit.
3. Utilize guards and featherboards whenever possible.
4. Before working around or changing the router bit disconnect the power.
5. Lower the table before bringing the bit down for the first time.
6. Always feed the material against the rotation of the router bit.
7. When using a fixture keep your hands on the handles.

manually steps down on the peddle to raise the table. This second technique uses a *pneumatic spindle height control* (Fig. 32-1). A foot control switch activates an air cylinder which raises and lowers the spindle. This is much faster and easier than with a foot treadle. With both methods a *height-adjustment handwheel* moves the table up and down to regulate the depth of cut. The *height-adjustment lock* secures the table once the desired depth of cut has been set.

PURCHASING A PIN ROUTER

An important consideration when purchasing a pin router is the size. It is determined by three items. The first is the *motor horsepower rating*. Larger motors allow deeper and heavier cuts. A good general-purpose size is 3 hp. The second item in establishing the size is the *throat dimension*. This is the distance from the center of the spindle to the front of the column. The larger this space, the wider the stock or pattern that can be run. The last item in determining size is the *collet size*. The collet holds the shank of the cutter. Sizes of collets include $\frac{1}{4}$, $\frac{3}{8}$, $\frac{1}{2}$, and $\frac{3}{4}$ in. (6, 10, 13, and 19 mm) (Fig. 32-3). Although some routers have only $\frac{1}{4}$-in. (6-mm) collets, they can still perform a great deal of work. Those having up to $\frac{1}{2}$-in. (13-mm) collets allow larger bits to be used. Only the very large pin routers have $\frac{3}{4}$-in. (19-mm) collets.

Another item to specify when purchasing a pin router is the *spindle speed*. Most pin routers will rotate at 20,000 (rpm) or faster. This is ideal for most router bits. Larger machines, however, may have a spindle speed selector which provides either 10,000 or 20,000 rpm's. The slower setting is for shaper cutters and other larger-diameter tooling.

The last item in purchasing a pin router to consider is the method the router bit is to be introduced into the work. As described in the section "Parts of the Pin Router," either a foot-operated treadle or the pneumatic spindle height control can be specified. The treadle has the advantage of the operator controlling the rate at which the table is raised toward the cutter. A pneumatic control is faster and less tiring for the operator to work.

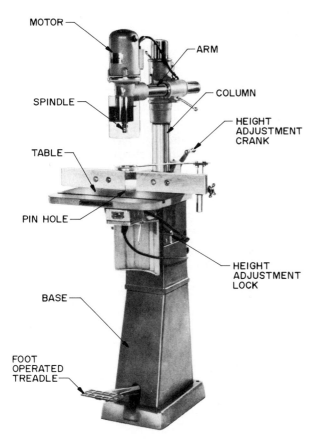

MOTOR
ARM
COLUMN
SPINDLE
HEIGHT ADJUSTMENT CRANK
TABLE
PIN HOLE
HEIGHT ADJUSTMENT LOCK
BASE
FOOT OPERATED TREADLE

FIGURE 32-2
A shaper-router can have the cutter mounted either above or below the table. (*Courtesy of Delta International Machinery Corp.*)

A *guide pin* is inserted through this hole against which the patterns can be run.

There are two methods of introducing the router bits into the stock. The simplest technique employs a *foot-operated treadle* to raise and lower the table (Fig. 32-2). With the treadle, the operator

SELECTING THE ROUTER BITS

Any router bit that can be used with a portable router can also be run on a pin router. Refer to the section "Selecting the Router Bits" in Chapter 20 for

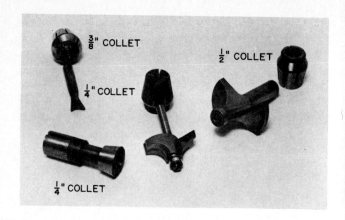

FIGURE 32-3
Collet sizes vary from $\frac{1}{4}$ to $\frac{3}{4}$ in.

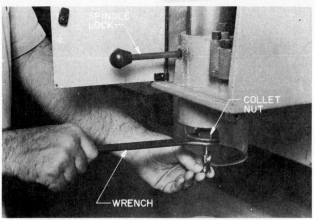

FIGURE 32-4
Changing a router bit using the spindle lock.

detailed information. There are, however, a few additional important points to remember when working with a pin router.

For joinery cuts, such as rabbets and dados, use as large a straight bit that will produce the cut. With larger sizes, a higher-quality cut is made and there is less chance of chattering. *Chattering* is created when the tip of the bit turns in an untrue circle and the bit flexes as it cuts. This produces a rough cut and will eventually lead to the bit breaking.

Whenever possible, select a bit with a $\frac{1}{2}$-in. (13-mm) shank. This will provide a stronger bit which is less likely to break. For example, a $\frac{1}{4}$-in. (6-mm) straight bit with a $\frac{1}{2}$-in. (13-mm) shank will last six times longer than the same bit with a $\frac{1}{4}$-in. (6-mm) shank.

INSTALLING THE ROUTER BIT

To install a router bit, first secure the spindle. On some models, a spindle lock is provided (Fig. 32-4). Other spindles are secured with a spindle wrench. Check that the tapered internal hole inside the spindle is clean and free of corrosion. Select the desired router bit and the matching collet. Be very careful that you do not drop or abuse either of these precision made items.

Insert the collet into the spindle and screw on the collet nut. Next, place the shank of the router bit into the collet. It must extend into the collet a minimum of $\frac{1}{2}$ in (13 mm). If this is not done, the collet will become enlarged at the shank hole opening. This is called *bellmouthing* (Fig. 32-5).

Using a collet nut wrench, tighten the collet nut. Free the spindle and check that the bit is secure and turns freely. Lower the guard and make certain that the operator is protected from the rotating cutter.

SETTING UP THE PIN ROUTER

To set up the pin router, install the router bit according to the directions given in the section "Installing the Router Bit." Next, lower the table to the lowest point with the depth-adjustment handwheel. This will prevent the bit from accidentally being driven into the table. Step down on the foot treadle or the pneumatic spindle height control. Depending on the

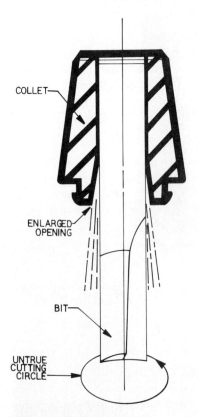

FIGURE 32-5
Bellmouthing is created when the shank is not inserted in the collet at least $\frac{1}{2}$ in.

drive system mounted on the machine, this will either raise the table or lower the spindle.

Mark on the end of the stock the desired depth of cut. Place this board on the table and raise the table until the tip of the bit is aligned with the layout mark (Fig. 32-6). If a fixture is being used, position the stock on top of it and then adjust the depth. Secure the depth of cut setting by tightening the height-adjustment lock.

Adjust the guard so that it provides full protection surrounding the cutting circle (Fig. 32-7). The height of the guard should be set so that the stock will just pass under the bottom edge. After the fence or guide pin is installed, release the treadle or pneumatic spindle height control. Rotate the spindle by hand to check that the cutter will not strike the guard or fence.

FIGURE 32-6
Aligning the end of the router bit with the layout mark.

FIGURE 32-7
Properly adjusted guard. Note the stock will just pass under the bottom edge.

ROUTING THROUGH STRAIGHT EDGES

A pin router is an ideal machine for making dadoes, gains, and rabbets. Because of the cutting action of the router bit, the groove will be free of torn grain and provide a smooth bottom. This is particularly important when machining plywood and other easily chipped materials.

To cut a groove, set up the pin router as described in the section "Setting Up the Pin Router." Prepare the stock to finish size. The edge against the fence must be straight and the flat face against the table. Mark the depth and width of cut on the leading end of a piece of the stock. Place this on the table and adjust the router for the proper depth of cut. For a deep cut, make the groove with multiple passes.

If part of the original edge is to remain, use either the commercial fence or a wooden fence for guiding the material. A wooden fence will assure you that both the left and right fence halves will be in a straight line (Fig. 32-8). When the commercial split fence is utilized, a straight edge can be used to align the two fence halves. Secure the wooden fence to the table with C-clamps. Fence studs work well for attaching the commercial fence.

When the entire edge is to be routed, a commercial split fence is needed (Fig. 32-9). Adjust the left side of the fence to remove the desired amount from the edge. After positioning the guard, feed the board past the cutter until it reaches the outfeed side of the fence. Pivot the stock away from the cutter and turn off the power. When the bit has stopped turning, move the right side of the fence to support the freshly cut edge. Make certain that both fence studs are tightened before running the material.

Once the fence is positioned, the stock can be run. Be certain to have a push stick within reach of the operator and that the guard has been properly adjusted. Stock must be at least 12 in. (305 mm) long

FIGURE 32-8
Routing a groove with a wooden fence.

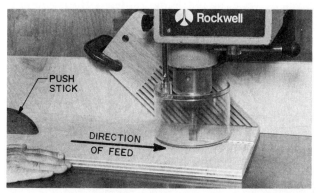

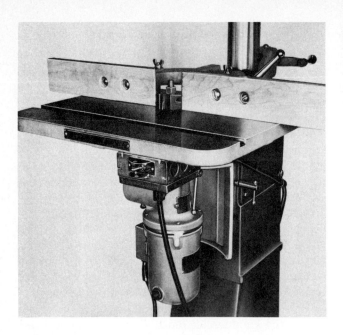

FIGURE 32-9
An entire edge can be routed using a commercial split fence. (*Courtesy of Delta International Machinery Corp.*)

FIGURE 32-10
Setting up to route a stopped groove.

and 4 in. (102 mm) wide. To keep the stock from raising off of the table, install featherboards on both sides of the cutter (Fig. 32-7). Turn on the power and slowly feed the stock from left to right. When running a shape on the edge, cut only on the front side of the cutter. Keep your hands at least 4 in. (102 mm) from the cutting circle. Once the trailing end comes close to the cutter, use a push stick to guide the stock past the cutter. On long material, have a tail-off person assist with supporting the stock as it leaves the table.

ROUTING A STOPPED GROOVE

To route a stopped groove, set up the router as directed in the section "Routing through Straight Edges." The fence must be at least 12 in. (305 mm) longer than twice the length of the stock. This extra length allows stop blocks to be installed at either end of the fence. Lay out on the face of the stock the starting and stopping points of the cut. Position the piece against the fence and table. With the height-adjustment handwheel, bring the tip of the bit to the top surface of the board. Move the board to the starting point of the groove and align the edge of the cutting circle with this mark (Fig. 32-10). Clamp a stop block to the fence at the trailing end of the material. Move the board along the fence until the second stopping point of the cut is aligned with the cutting circle. Clamp a second stop block against the leading end of the board. Remove the stock and reset the depth of cut for the router bit. If the groove is stopped at only one end, install only one stop block.

After the guard has been adjusted and featherboards installed, position the board against the stop block on the infeed side of the fence. Turn on the power and hold the stock securely against the fence and table. Using either the foot treadle or pneumatic height control, plunge the bit into the stock. Do not move the board until the bit has stopped moving downward. Push the stock forward along the fence until the leading end meets the second stop block. Hold it in a stationary position and withdraw the bit to its original position. Remove the stock from the table. With compressed air blow the router table free of chips before running the next piece.

PATTERN ROUTING

Pattern routing can be used to produce plaque backs, picture frames, highlight furniture parts, and make internal cuts. This method requires a fixture on which to mount the material and to be guided against a pin mounted in the center of the table. Because of the fixture, small parts and pieces having a great deal of detail can be run.

Making the Fixture

The first step in pattern routing is to develop the fixture. It is made of several parts as shown in Fig. 32-11. They are the *template, fixture body, hardwood rails, spacer, handles,* and *fixture clamps.* All should be made of high-quality materials and with high craftsmanship.

A template is cut out using a scroll saw or band saw. The template should be the exact size and shape of the path the router bit is to travel. Be careful to follow the layout marks precisely so that little filing is required. Any irregularities left in the template will be duplicated in the routed part. Although

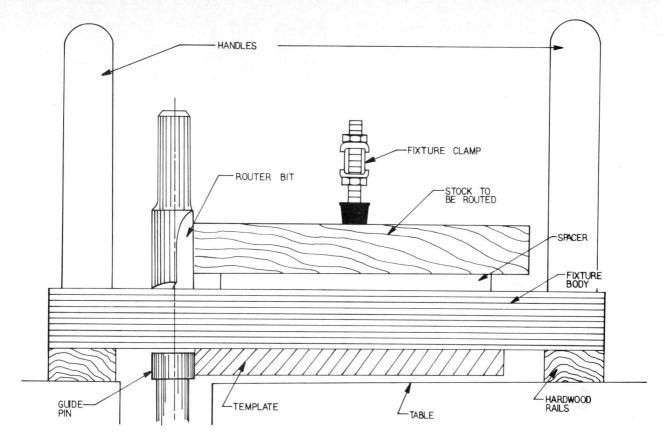

FIGURE 32-11
Parts to a pin router fixture.

several different materials can be used for this part of the fixture, tempered hardboard works and wears well.

The template is next glued to the bottom of a fixture body. This is usually a piece of ¾-in. high-quality hardwood plywood. It must be large enough to hold the stock, fixture handles, and fixture clamps. To raise the template up off the router table, hardwood rails are mounted around the outside edge of the body. This reduces drag as the fixture is moved over the table and eliminates the accumulation of sawdust around the template.

On the top surface of the fixture body is a spacer and handles. The ¼-in. (6-mm) spacer raises the stock up off of the body. This prevents the router bit from cutting into the plywood body. There should be at least two handles to control the movement of the fixture. They provide a place to keep your hands and to keep them from the cutter.

There are a variety of techniques utilized to secure the stock to the fixture. Study the path of the router bit and be certain that the holding devices will not interfere with the cutter. If the fixture clamps come too close to the bit, two fixtures may be needed. Part of the cut is made with the first fixture. The part is then moved to the second fixture, which

has the clamps located in different positions than the first. This allows the cut to be completed.

The simplest method of holding the stock is to use wood screws placed through the fixture and into the stock (Fig. 32-12). If the shape of the part will

FIGURE 32-12
Using screws to hold the stock on the fixture.

allow, homemade cam clamps can apply pressure to the side (Fig. 32-13). Two sides of the stock are held with rabbeted fences. In addition, there are commercial fixture clamps that are sold in a variety of sizes (Fig. 32-14). They apply pressure either from the side or top.

FIGURE 32-13
Cam clamps apply side pressure towards the rabbeted fences.

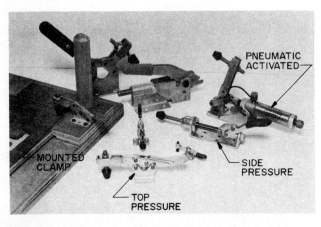

FIGURE 32-14
Commercial fixture clamps apply pressure either from the side or top.

Routing the Pattern

After the fixture is completed, the stock can be routed. Install the router bit and guide pin on the router. If a straight edge on the stock is desired, an upward spiral straight router bit is recommended (Fig. 32-15). It will produce a high-quality cut and remove the chips from the routed groove. For most general-purpose straight routing, a $\frac{1}{2}$-in. (13-mm) diameter router bit works well. Pattern bits can also be used if they do not contain a pilot.

The diameter of the guide pin can also be var-

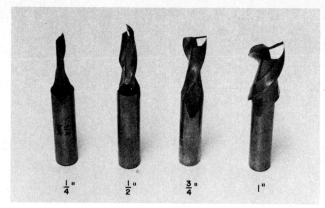

FIGURE 32-15
A spiral straight router bit lifts the chips up and out of groove.

ied (Fig. 32-16). To make the stock the same size as the template, use the same-size diameter bit and pin. If the piece is too small, the outside dimensions can be increased by using a larger-diameter pin. For parts that are larger than the desired size, the dimensions can be decreased by a smaller pin. After the correct size of pin is selected, secure it in the table so that it comes in contact with the template by at least $\frac{1}{4}$ in. (6 mm).

Clamp the stock to the fixture, making certain that it will not move. Adjust the guard and, without turning on the power, trace around the template with the guide pin. This will give you an indication of how the pattern should be run and which direction it should be moved. Check that the handles and clamps do not interfere with the machine. Continue practicing until you are confident of how to move the fixture. It is best to start and end the pass on an inside corner. The starting and stopping point are therefore less likely to show.

Turn on the power and adjust the depth of cut. If the bit is to extend all the way through the stock, be certain that it does not cut into the fixture body. Firmly grasp the handles of the fixture and always keep your hands on these handles while the cutter is turning (Fig. 32-17, page 371). Plunge the bit into the work. Move the fixture slowly around the pin, going against the rotation of the cutter. Once the pass is complete, retract the cutter from the material. Inspect the first part for quality of cut and dimensions. Once any needed adjustments have been made, run the remaining pieces.

PIN ROUTING

Irregular shaped stock can be routed on its edges by using a pin installed in the table (Fig. 32-18). The

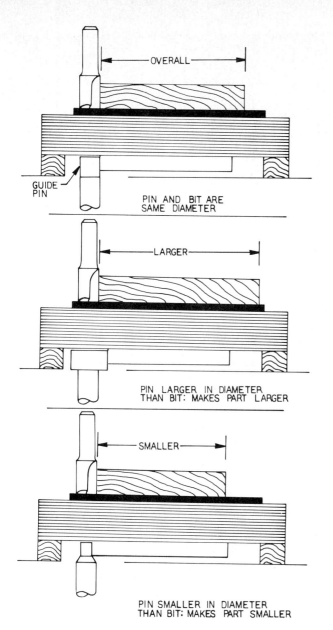

FIGURE 32-16
Varying the diameter of the guide pin changes the size of the finished piece.

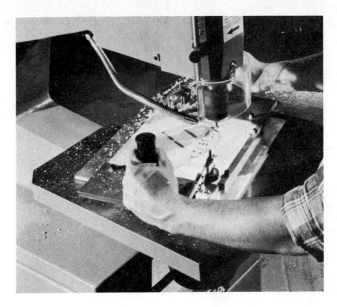

FIGURE 32-17
Routing with a pin router fixture. (*Courtesy of Delta International Machinery Corp.*)

FIGURE 32-18
Routing an irregular shape with a guide pin. (*Courtesy of Delta International Machinery Corp.*)

material must first be bandsawed to shape and the edges worked smooth with files and abrasive paper. Select the desired router bit and install a pin with a diameter that is equal to the smallest diameter of the router bit.

After adjusting the guard, turn on the power and slowly pivot the stock into the cutter. Do not start the cut on the corner of the board. Your material must be large enough to keep your hands at least 4 in. (102 mm) from the cutter. Once the cut is complete, move the piece away from the cutter.

33

SANDING MACHINES

There are many different types of sanding machines utilized in the woodworking field. There are specialized machines which are designed to sand faces of flat panels, edges of boards, and even curves.

You should remember that this equipment is not designed to remove large amounts of material. Before using a sander, your wooden parts should be machined closely and accurately. Sanders are not meant to sand joints or substitute for a cleanly cut surface.

ABRASIVES FOR SANDING MACHINES

Most sanding machines require belts, disks, or sleeves which are ordered for each specific piece of equipment. Aluminum oxide is the most common abrasive. It is very hard and resists breaking down with high temperatures. This is important because of the friction developed while sanding hardwoods.

The backing materials used with machine abrasives are usually either cloth or synthetic materials. Since most machines require a flexible backing, a J-weight cloth is commonly furnished.

Another item to specify is the grit size or coarseness of the abrasive. Refer to Table 33-1 for information concerning the sizing. The smaller the

GENERAL SANDER SAFETY RULES

1. Always wear eye protection. Use an approved respirator when sanding dust becomes a problem.
2. Keep fingers at least 4 in. (102 mm) from the abrasive materials or the throat of the machine unless otherwise noted.
3. Hold the stock firmly on the table and against the fence.
4. Do not operate a sander if the abrasive material is loose, torn, or worn excessively.
5. Devise special holding fixtures for sanding small pieces.
6. Apply firm and even pressure on the stock.
7. Applying excessive pressure will result in torn abrasive material.

grit number, the larger the individual particles or abrasives. Smaller grit numbers will cut faster but leave deeper sanding scratches.

DISK SANDERS

Disk sanders are made with vertical metal disks which are covered with abrasive (Fig. 33-1). Because it sands with a circular action, sanding scratches will be developed across the grain. If these scratches

TABLE 33-1

Recommended Abrasive Grit Sizes for Sanders

Sanding operations	Garnet and aluminum oxide grit sizes
Fine	180
	150
	120
Medium	100
	80
Coarse	60
	50
	40
	36

DISK SANDER SAFETY RULES

1. Follow general saftey rules.
2. Sand only on the downward rotating half of the disk.

are not removed or covered, they will become very obvious when the finish is applied. This sander is used primarily for rough sanding and sanding end grain. The size of the disk sander is determined by the diameter of the disk. Although the size can range from 12 to over 36 in. (305 to 914 mm), most general-purpose disk sanders are 12 in. (303 mm) in diameter.

The abrasive disks for the disk sander are usually purchased precut to the proper diameter. Be-

cause the disk sander is designed primarily for rough sanding, coarser grits are utilized. They cut faster and are less likely to load up and burn. Grits range from 36 to 60.

To use a disk sander, first lay out the desired pattern on the board. Use a square to mark out straight lines. If more than $\frac{1}{8}$ in. (3 mm) is to be removed, bandsaw or otherwise cut the pattern close to the layout. Position the stock flat against the table on the downward side of the rotating disk (Fig. 33-2). Sanding on the opposite side of the disk will cause the stock to be thrown from the table. Hold the stock firmly against the rotating disk and move it from side to side. Because the disk cuts faster toward the outer rim than the center, apply slightly more pressure on the left side of the board. Be careful not to sand beyond the layout line.

Straight edges can be sanded with the aid of a miter gauge. The gauge fits into a *miter gauge groove* and can be adjusted to any angle from 90 to 45° (Fig. 33-3). Angle the table for sanding bevels and chamfers (Fig. 33-4). The *angle gauge* will indicate the tilt of the table.

If a disk sander is not available, a disk attachment can be purchased for a radial arm saw or table saw. It is mounted in place of the saw blade (Fig. 33-5). Use the same sanding procedure as with the disk sander.

As the abrasive disk is used, it becomes loaded with material. An abrasive cleaning stick can be utilized to remove resin and minor burn marks. Move the stock back and forth against the rotating

FIGURE 33-1
Major parts to the disk sander. (*Courtesy of Delta International Machinery Corp.*)

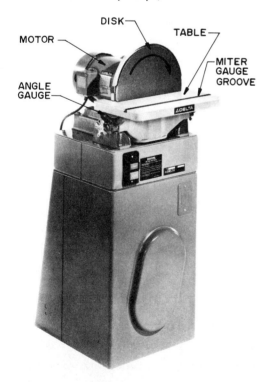

FIGURE 33-2
Sand the stock only on the downward side of the disk.

FIGURE 33-3
Sanding an angle with the assistance of a miter gauge.
(*Courtesy of Delta International Machinery Corp.*)

FIGURE 33-6
An abrasive cleaning stick will extend the life of the abrasive paper.

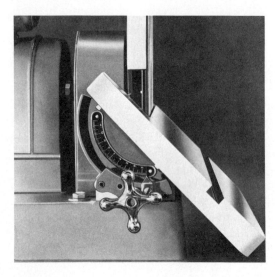

FIGURE 33-4
Use the angle gauge to set the table for sanding bevels and chamfers. (*Courtesy of Delta International Machinery Corp.*)

FIGURE 33-5
Using a disk sanding attachment on a table saw.

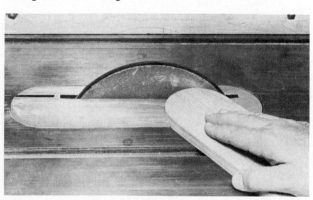

disk (Fig. 33-6). When the abrasive paper becomes severely worn, however, it must be removed and replaced with a new disk. Abrasive paper that is not easily removed can be soaked. Remove the metal disk from the sander and place it in a container filled with warm soapy water. After the paper has softened, scrape it clean with a putty knife.

The new abrasive paper can be applied with either stick cement or a polyvinyl adhesive. To use the stick cement, turn on the power (Fig. 33-7). Press the stick against the cleaned disk and apply a thin even coat of adhesive. Turn off the power and allow it to stop turning. Use your hands to press a new disk onto the metal plate. The polyvinyl method requires the use of a shop-made press (Fig. 33-8). Spread polyvinyl adhesive evenly over the entire face of the disk. Position the disk over the metal plate and clamp it in a press overnight.

FIGURE 33-7
Apply a new thin coat of stick cement while the disk is turning.

FIGURE 33-8
Clamping the metal plate and abrasive disk in a shop-made press.

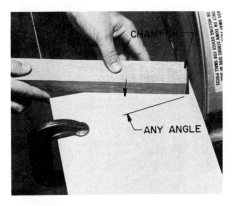

FIGURE 33-9
The chamfer fixture allows corners to be sanded.

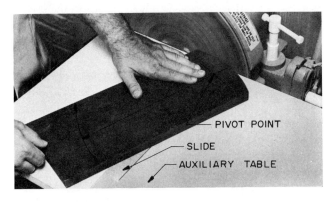

FIGURE 33-10
A radius can be sanded using a pivot fixture. Stock is swung from side to side.

A variety of fixtures can be utilized on the disk sander. A chamfer fixture aids in sanding chamfers on the corners of a post (Fig. 33-9). Each side of the stock is placed against the side of the fixture. A pivot fixture allows a smooth radius to be sanded (Fig. 33-10). Use a sharpened nail driven through a move-

SPINDLE SANDER SAFETY RULES
1. Follow general sander safety rules.
2. Disconnect the power before changing the spindle.

able slide as the pivot point. The distance from the disk to the nail should be equal to the radius of the curve. Use a mallet to tap the stock onto the pivot point. Move the slide toward the revolving disk until the stock touches the abrasive. Hold the slide in a stationary position and pivot the stock back and forth.

SPINDLE SANDERS

The spindle sander contains a cylinder that has been covered with an abrasive sleeve (Fig. 33-11). These *abrasive sleeves* are professionally made tubes of a heavy backing material covered with either aluminum oxide or garnet abrasive (Fig. 33-12). Although

FIGURE 33-11
Major parts of a spindle sander. [*Courtesy of Robert A. Martin Co. (RAMCO).*]

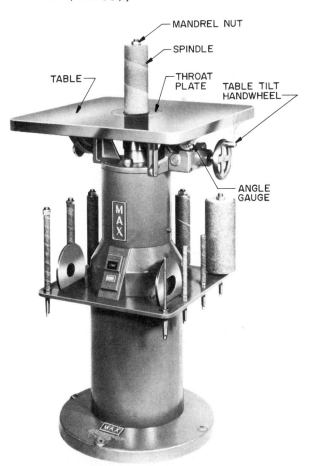

FIGURE 33-12
Abrasive sleeves are available in a variety of diameters.

grit sizes range from 60 to 220, for general-purpose sanding, use 100 grit.

Because of the shape of the spindle, this sander is ideal for sanding inside curves. Select the spindle that most closely matches the diameter of the curve. Most sanders will have spindles that range from ½ to 3 in. (13 to 76 mm) in diameter (Fig. 33-12). Using too small of a spindle will create small dips. They will become quite obvious when the finish is applied.

After selecting the proper spindle, slide the abrasive sleeve over the rubber mandrel. To hold the sleeve in position, tighten the *mandrel nut*. Place the assembled spindle on the sander and turn on the power. Position the stock on the table and move the piece side to side against the rotating abrasive (Fig. 33-13). Use moderate inward pressure and keep the stock moving at all times. Sand along the entire edge of the curve. Concentrating in one area will create a low spot. Stop sanding once you have reached the layout line.

FIGURE 33-13
Sanding an inside curve on a spindle sander.

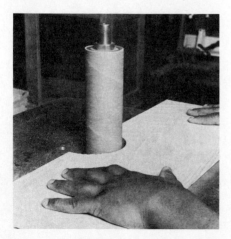

Some spindle sanders are *oscillating*. Their spindles not only rotate but also move up and down. This distributes the wear over a larger area making the life of the sleeve longer. Other sanders may have the tiltable tables. This enables bevels and chamfers to be sanded.

For those shops who may not have a spindle sander, inside curves may be sanded with a drill press or lathe. Refer to Chapters 29 and 30 for detailed information concerning sanding. A wooden mandrel mounted between lathe centers can be used on the lathe (Fig. 33-14). Abrasive cloth is wrapped around the mandrel and tacked in place on each end.

FIGURE 33-14
Using a wooden mandrel to sand on the inside curve on the lathe.

SMALL STATIONARY BELT SANDERS

The small stationary belt sander is one of the most versatile sanding machines (Fig. 33-15). Although belts are available from 60 to 220 grits, most sanding can be done with 100-grit belts.

Because the belt and table can be placed in three different positions, it is capable of sanding many different shapes. Most work is positioned against the table. A miter gauge can be used to aid in guiding the stock. Sanding outside curves, edges and ends can be accomplished with the belt in the

SMALL STATIONARY BELT SANDER
SAFETY RULES

1. Follow general sander safety rules.
2. Disconnect the power before changing the belt or making other adjustments.

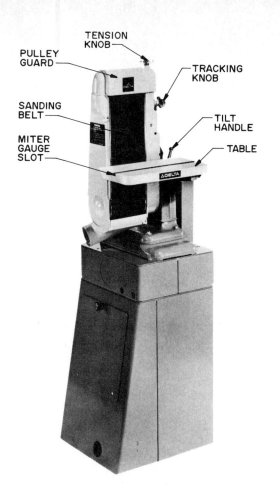

FIGURE 33-15
Major parts of a small stationary belt sander. (*Courtesy of Delta International Machinery Corp.*)

vertical position (Fig. 33-15). Use a miter gauge as a guide when sanding straight lines (Fig. 33-16). The belt can be angled for bevels and chamfers (Fig. 33-17). Faces and edges of stock can be sanded with the belt in horizontal position (Fig. 33-18). Inside

FIGURE 33-16
Sanding end grain using a miter gauge with the belt in the vertical position.

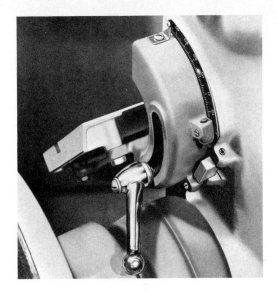

FIGURE 33-17
The table is tilted by loosening the tilt handle. (*Courtesy of Delta International Machinery Corp.*)

FIGURE 33-18
Sanding the face with the belt in the horizontal position. (*Courtesy of Delta International Machinery Corp.*)

FIGURE 33-19
Sanding an inside curve using the exposed pulley. (*Courtesy of Delta International Machinery Corp.*)

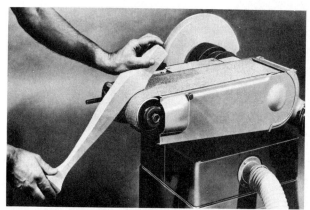

curves can be sanded on the exposed pulley (Fig. 33-19). Remove the pulley guard to expose this pulley. Fixtures can also be used to hold the stock. The chamfer fixture forms a trough in which the stock is placed (Fig. 33-20). The far side of the trough serves as a stop to make the same width chamfers. The angle of the sides determines the angle of the chamfer.

Small, narrow-belt sanders are also used in woodworking shops (Fig. 33-21). They work well to sand small curves and sharpen tools.

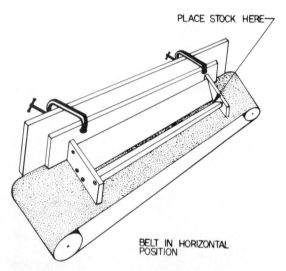

FIGURE 33-20
The chamfering fixture positions stock for sanding chamfers.

FIGURE 33-21
A small belt sander can reach into small area. (*Courtesy of Delta International Machinery Corp.*)

WIDE-BELT SANDER SAFETY RULES

1. Follow general sander safety rules.
2. Check the belt for breaks or tears before starting the machine.
3. The guard doors must be closed while the belt is turning.
4. Keep hands at least 6 in. (152 mm) away from the throat of the sander.
5. Hands should be kept above the stock and away from the edge of the sanding table.
6. If any irregularities occur when operating the machine, push the emergency stop. Notify the instructor.
7. Aways release the air pressure once the belt has stopped rotating.

WIDE-BELT SANDERS

A wide-belt sander is utilized to sand the faces of boards, faceframes, and other flat panels (Fig. 33-22. It will remove torn grain, millmarks, and other minor defects. Most wide-belt sanders have a single belt which is run on one head.

The major parts of a wide-belt sander include the contact drum, idler drum, platen, and endless feed belt (Fig. 33-23). The *contact drum* is a steel cylinder which is coated with rubber (Fig. 33-23). It is responsible for bringing the abrasive belt against the stock. Some sanders have in addition to the contact drum a *polishing platen* (Fig. 33-24). This

FIGURE 33-22
Major parts of a wide-belt sander. (*Courtesy of Time-savers, Inc.*)

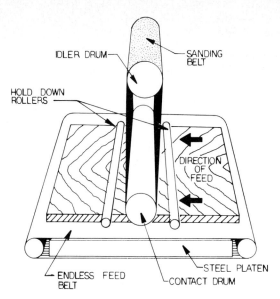

FIGURE 33-23
The contact drum brings the abrasive belt against the stock.

platen produces a longer sanding scratch pattern and polishes the surface. Above the contact drum is the *idler drum*. It applies upward tension on the abrasive belt. Associated with this drum is the *tracking system*. The belt is tracked or kept centered on the drums by either a photoelectric cell or a pneumatic cylinder.

To feed the stock forward, the board is placed on the rubber *endless feed belt* (Fig. 33-23). Immediately under the belt is the steel *platen*. It provides a

FIGURE 33-24
A polishing platen is mounted immediately behind the contact drum. It increases the area where the belt comes in contact with the stock.

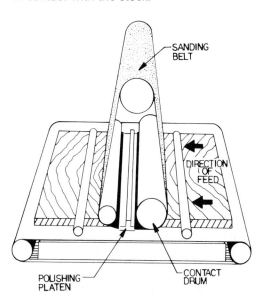

flat surface to feed the material over. Stock is held against the platen with *hold-down rollers*.

The size of the sander is determined by the width of the belt. Sanders can be purchased which have belts from 6 to 106 in. (152 to 2692 mm). Most shops need a sander that is 24 to 37 in. (620 to 939 mm) wide. Larger belts are more expensive but do allow wider pieces to be sanded.

For most freshly planed material, select a 100-grit belt for the initial passes. If a smoother sanding finish is desired, use progressive finer belts. Do not skip a grit number or the sanding scratches may not be removed. Most stock will be adequately sanded with the final passes made with a 120- or 150-grit belt. Hang new belts for a minimum of 48 hours from a rack as shown in Fig. 33-25. This will allow them to equalize and straighten.

Depending on the brand and model of wide-belt sander, the procedure for changing the belt varies. On most sanders, however, the tension is released on the belt by lowering the idler drum. After the safety bar is removed, the belt can be slid from the sander. Store the belt on a rack as shown in Fig. 33-25. Large cardboard tubes should be mounted on the top of the rack arms. This prevents the belts from developing a sharp bend. Replace the belt with another and check which way the directional arrow points on the back of the belt. Mount the belt on the sander with the directional arrow pointing the same direction as the rotation of the belt (Fig. 33-23).

To operate the wide-belt sander with a contact drum, measure the stock at the thickest point. Set the depth gauge to this dimension minus 0.010 to 0.015 in. Use less than this amount for 120-grit and finer belts. The sander is not designed to remove a great deal of material with one pass. Apply tension

FIGURE 33-25
A storage rack properly holds the belts when not in use.

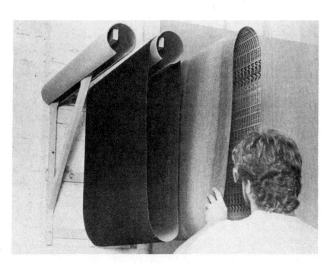

FIGURE 33-26
Sanding a faceframe.

to the belt and turn on the power. Place the stock to the left of the feed belt with the grain pointing in the same direction as the direction of the feed. Start it through the machine. The material must be supported and not allowed to hang off the table on either the infeed or outfeed side (Fig. 33-26). If more than one pass is required, position the stock to the right of the first location. Continue moving the board to the right with each pass until the entire width of the belt has been utilized. This will provide more even wear and longer life to the belt. After the last pass, stop the machine and release the tension on the belt.

STROKE SANDERS

A stroke sander uses a narrow belt to sand flat surfaces (Fig. 33-27). It is a sander that requires some skill to operate. The operator must move the *shuttle*

STROKE SANDER SAFETY RULES

1. Follow general sander safety rules.
2. Position stock against the fence and table before operating the machine.
3. Apply firm and even pressure with the pressure block.

table in and out while pushing down on the top of the belt with the *pressure block* (Fig. 33-28).

A *pressure block* is moved along the belt. Powdered graphite can be worked into the block to reduce the drag. Operators need to practice to keep their two hands working together. If the pressure block and shuttle table are not kept moving, a low spot will develop.

Most stroke sanders utilize either 120- or 150-grit abrasive-cloth-backed belts. To sand the shaped edges, make a custom pressure block (Fig. 33-29). It should have the reverse pattern of the shaped edge. Use a flexible back belt and release some of the tension on the belt. If you sand the edge for too long a time, some of the sharp detail will be sanded away.

FIGURE 33-28
The shuttle table is moved in and out while the pressure block is moved side to side.

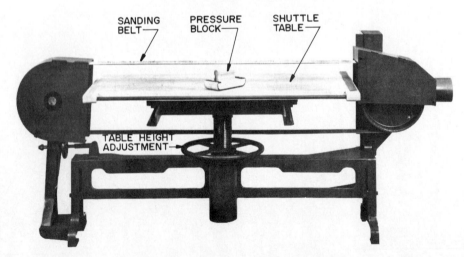

FIGURE 33-27
Major parts of a stroke sander. (*Courtesy of Oliver Machinery Company.*)

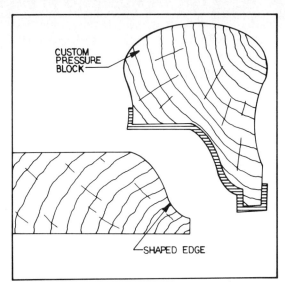

FIGURE 33-29
Shaped edges can be sanded with a custom pressure block.

EDGE SANDERS

Edge sanders are utilized for sanding the edges and ends of flat panels (Fig. 33-30). Inside curves can also be sanded on the *exposed pulley* (Fig. 33-31). A cloth-back abrasive belt is mounted vertically between two pulleys. Stock is placed on the table and gently pushed against the moving belt (Fig. 39-32). A fence is attached to the table to keep the stock at an accurate angle. Although the fence is normally kept at the 90° position, it can be angled for miter.

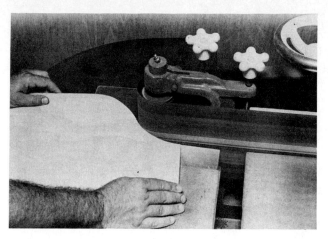

FIGURE 33-31
Sanding an inside curve on the exposed pulley.

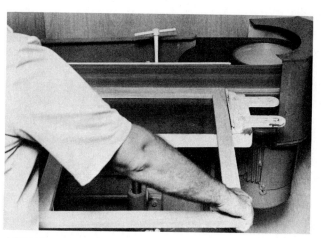

FIGURE 33-32
Sanding the edge of a panel.

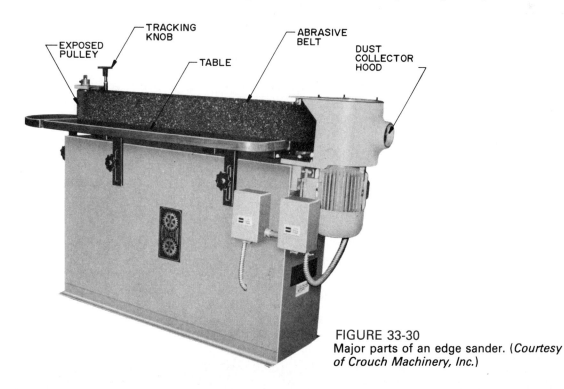

FIGURE 33-30
Major parts of an edge sander. (*Courtesy of Crouch Machinery, Inc.*)

EDGE SANDER SAFETY RULES

1. Follow general sander safety rules.
2. If the stock vibrates, pull it back clear of the belt and refeed.

Depending on the material being sanded, an 80- to 120-grit belt is used. Beginners should scribe a line along the edge to indicate the amount of material to be sanded. It is easy to sand away more stock than what is desired. Once the belt becomes worn, lower the table to another position to expose a new area of the belt.

PART **6**

Finishing

34

PREPARATION FOR FINISHING

One of the most important steps in producing a project is the finishing process. Even the best constructed piece of furniture or cabinet can be ruined if a high-quality finish is not applied. To develop a superior finish, you must first repair or remove defects. This can be accomplished by utilizing a variety of techniques, including applying wood dough or simply steaming out a dent. Minor defects such as torn grain can often be removed by sanding with coarse abrasive paper. After the defects have been dealt with it is extremely important that you sand the project thoroughly. This requires you to have a complete knowledge of abrasives and sanding techniques.

REPAIRING DEFECTS

Open defects become very apparent when the finish is applied. Any opening, whether a dent or a nail hole, should be repaired. There are several methods from which to select.

A small dent or other defect where the wood fibers have not been removed or torn can be raised with steam (Fig. 34-1). Dampen a piece of cloth and fold it into several layers. Position the cloth immediately over the defect and place a heated soldering

FIGURE 34-1
Removing a dent using a soldering iron to produce steam.

iron on top. Keep the iron moving over the cloth. Occasionally, stop and check to see if the dent has disappeared.

Large open defects such as knotholes can be patched with *water putty* (Fig. 34-2). This is an inexpensive powder that is mixed with water. Powdered pigments may be mixed with the putty to match the color of the wood more closely. Mix only what you can use in a short period of time. It cannot be reused.

A filler that is more likely to match the surrounding wood is *putty filler* (Fig. 34-3). It is sold in a variety of colors to match the major species of wood.

FIGURE 34-2
Using water putty to repair a large open defect.

FIGURE 34-3
Putty filler dries rapidly and blends with the surrounding wood.

Most putty fillers become very obvious when stains and other finishing materials are applied. There are a few brands, however, that will absorb stain and more closely match the finished wood.

A shop-made filler can also be used to repair defects. This filler is composed of sanding dust and a mixture of adhesive and water. It is frequently called cabinetmaker's filler. To make *cabinetmaker's filler*, take sanding dust from your project and mix it with a small quantity of polyvinyl adhesive and water. Once mixed, the filler should form a thick paste. Carefully apply it to the defect, being careful not to wipe it on the surrounding area. When dry, sand all excess from the surface.

Small defects, nail holes, and open joints can be filled with a *putty stick* (Fig. 34-4). These contain a pigmented wax that will blend with the surrounding wood. However, the stick must be rubbed into the defect after the last coat of finish has been polished. Two or more colors can be combined to form an exact match.

FIGURE 34-4
Putty sticks are rubbed into open defects on a finished wood.

The best method of repairing an open defect is the *stick shellac* or *lacquer stick* (Fig. 34-5). It does require the most skill. Select the stick or sticks that best match the wood. Use stick shellac for varnish finishes and lacquer stick on lacquer. With a hot *burn-in tool*, melt the stick into the defect. Be careful not to smear it on the surrounding wood. Once cooled, the filler can be sanded level with the surface. With practice you will be able to match the finished wood exactly.

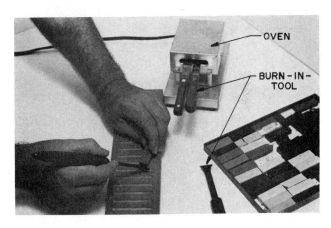

FIGURE 34-5
Lacquer sticks require burn-in tools and a knife oven to melt the lacquer into the defect.

SANDING TECHNIQUES

To further prepare a surface, start by working out any defects, such as small knots, checks, or raised surfaces. If a wide-belt sander or other power sanders are available, use them to remove the torn grain and other minor defects. Refer to Chapters 21 and 33 for proper safe operating procedures on power sanders. A hand scraper can also be used to work the stock. Be careful, however, that too much material is not sanded or scraped. This will affect the appearance and fit of adjoining pieces.

Apply the selected filler to repair any open defects. After it has dried, sand the surfaces with 100-grit abrasive paper. Use a sanding block or portable pad sander to keep the surface flat (Fig. 34-6). Never use just your hand because the softer spring wood will be sanded away faster than the denser summerwood. This will produce high and low spots on your boards. Sand only with the grain. Sanding across the grain will produce noticeable cross scratches. Because it is difficult to sand inside corners, sand inside surfaces before they are assembled. Be very careful to remove equal amounts over the entire surface. Sanding only the defects will produce low areas that will be very noticeable.

FIGURE 34-6
Sand flat surfaces using a sanding block.

After the millmarks have been removed with the 100-grit abrasive paper, you will need to sand all surfaces with 120 grit. Use the sanding techniques discussed in the preceding paragraph. Continue sanding until all the sanding scratches created by the 100 grit have been removed. Next sand the exposed surfaces with 150-grit, and finally, 180-grit abrasive paper. Do not skip a grit number in your sanding procedure. Sanding scratches will be left in the wood, which will be very difficult to sand away with the finer abrasive. Blow off the surface with compressed air to remove all sanding dust that is left in corners and in the pores of the wood.

Just before you apply the finish, use a damp sponge to wipe down your project (Fig. 34-7). This will raise loose fibers, which will cause problems when the finish is applied. After the surface has dried, use a sanding block and resand all areas with 180-grit abrasive paper.

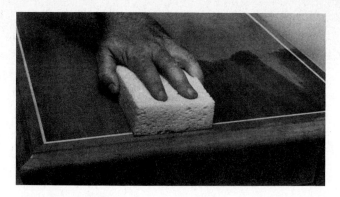

FIGURE 34-7
Sponging the surface with water to raise the grain.

ABRASIVES

Abrasives are available in a broad variety of types and degrees of fineness. You will need to know the abrasive material, backing material, and grit size so that you can select the correct material for your job. This information will be printed on the back of the sheet of abrasive (Fig. 34-8). Information generally given includes the abrasive material used, type of backing, backing weight, density of coverage, and grit size.

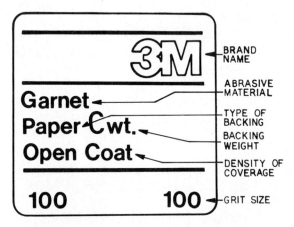

FIGURE 34-8
Information on the back of abrasive paper.

Abrasive Materials

When selecting abrasive paper or sanding belts, first pick the type of abrasive mineral that will best suit your job. For sanding most wood projects either garnet or aluminum oxide is used. *Garnet* is usually reddish brown in color and ideal for hand sanding. *Aluminum oxide* is typically brown or black in color and withstands the heat generated during machine sanding. Because of this, it is the most commonly used abrasive in the woods industry. Another abrasive is *silicon carbide;* it is bluish black in color and utilized for sanding finishes on wet or dry abrasive paper.

Backing

The backing materials commonly used include paper, cloth, and synthetics. Paper is selected for most hand sanding and for pad sanders. It is specified by A, B, D, or E weights. A weight is very thin and is the most flexible. E weight, the heaviest, is similar to light cardboard and rarely used in woodwork. C weight, sometimes called *cabinet paper,* is well suited for hand sanding and for use with portable electric sanders.

Cloth backing is more durable than paper. It is, however, more expensive. Cloth backing is sold in either J or X weight. J weight is the most common and the more flexible of the two.

Synthetics are the newest backing materials. They are used exclusively for machine sanding. This material is very resistant to wear and is quite durable.

Grit Sizes

The *grit size* determines the relative diameter of each particle of abrasive. The larger the particles, the faster the abrasive will remove the material. It will, however, leave deep scratches in the stock. Smaller particles produce a smoother surface, but sand the wood at a slower rate.

You can determine the grit size by finding the *grit number* or *ough size* printed on the backing. The larger the grit or ough number, the finer or smaller the particle size. For example, 220 grit is finer than 100 grit. Refer to Table 34-1 for recommended grits.

An additional item to consider is the spacing between the particles (Fig. 34-9). When little space is found between particles, it is labeled closed coat. Closed coat is selected for sanding dense hardwoods.

TABLE 34-1
Available Grits for Abrasives

	Garnet	Aluminum oxide	Silicon carbide
Very fine	—	600–12/0	600
(sanding	—	500–11/0	500
between	—	400–10/0	400
coats of	—	—	360
finishing	—	320–9/0	320
or polishing)	280–8/0	280–8/0	280
	240–7/0	240–7/0	240
	220–6/0	220–6/0	220
Fine	180–5/0	180–5/0	180
(final	150–4/0	150–4/0	150
sanding)	120–3/0	120–3/0	120
Medium	100–2/0	100–2/0	100
(rough	80–1/0	80–1/0	80
sanding	60–1/2	60–1/2	60
Coarse	50–1	50–1	50
(abrasive planing)	40–1½	40–1½	40
Very coarse	36–2	36–2	36
(grinding	30–2½	30–2½	30
or rough	24–3	24–3	24
shaping)	20–3½	20–3½	20
	—	16–4	16
	—	12–4½	12

Open-coat abrasives have additional space between the particles. Approximately 50 to 70% of the backing will be covered with open coat. It works best when sanding softwoods and other materials that are prone to load or fill in the abrasives.

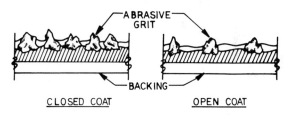

FIGURE 34-9
Spacing between abrasive particles is labeled as either closed coat or open coat.

35

FINISHING EQUIPMENT

There are two primary methods of applying finishing materials, brushing and spraying. Both require specialized equipment to work with the finishing material. There are several types of brushes and many different spray guns from which to select. In addition, you will need to consider related equipment that must be utilized to control the fumes and overspray produced in the finishing process. You should not proceed with your finishing until you have an understanding of finishing equipment.

FINISH BRUSHES

There are several items to consider when selecting a brush. If you purchase a high-quality brush, it will allow you to apply a superior finish with a minimum amount of effort.

The first consideration will be the kind of bristles used to make the brush. Pure bristles, nylon bristle, and polyester bristles are available. *Pure bristles* are made from the hair of an animal, the China boar. These bristles make a brush that is used almost exclusively for varnishes. *Nylon bristles* will wear longer and are designed primarily for water-base or latex finishes. *Polyester bristles* can be used for almost all finishes. They will outlast a pure-bris-

tle brush and apply a high-quality finish. Most recently, brushes have been developed with a *sponge pad*. The brushes are inexpensive and most are thrown away after one use.

All high-quality brushes should have bristles with *flagged ends* (Fig. 35-1). These split ends will hold more finish and produce fewer brush marks.

A good brush should also contain a *chisel-shaped edge* composed of many bristles. The best brush will develop the chisel shape by having the

FIGURE 35-1
Parts of a good-quality finish brush.

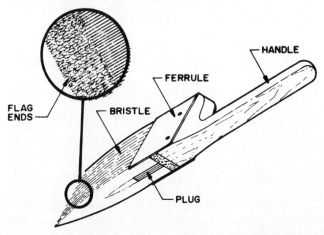

longest bristles in the center. Shorter bristles are utilized toward the outside of the brush. The more bristles a brush contains, the longer it will last and the more finish it will carry to the surface.

Another item to select is the width. Finish brushes range from $\frac{1}{2}$ to 8 in. (13 to 203 mm). The wider the brush, the faster the surface can be covered. Wide brushes do become awkward, however, when finishing smaller projects. Most projects can be finished with a 2- or $2\frac{1}{2}$-in. (51- or 64-mm) brush.

The handle is also important when selecting a brush (Fig. 35-2). The handle should fit your hand comfortably. Some finishers prefer an oval shape, while others prefer round shapes. To reach into corners use a *sash brush,* which has a long handle. *Trim brushes* have angled bristles for comfortably holding the handle at a slant.

FIGURE 35-3
Pour the finish material into a brush cup.

FIGURE 35-2
Brushes are available in various styles.

BRUSHING TECHNIQUES

To brush a project properly, start by slowly pouring a small amount of the finish material into the brush cup (Fig. 35-3). Only pour the amount of finish that is required to coat your project. Do not put the brush in the original can. The brush may deposit dirt and other foreign material in the can. This will contaminate the material remaining in the can. Any finish left in the brush cup should be disposed of properly, not poured back into the finish can. Never pour the remaining finish down a sink drain.

Dip the brush into the finish until approximately one-third of the length of the bristles extends into the finishing material. To remove the surplus finish from the brush, draw the bristles across the strike wire of the brush cup. Place the loaded brush in an uncoated area and brush toward the coated surface. To prevent runs from occurring near the

edge, work from the center out. Hold the brush at approximately a 45° angle and lightly draw the tips of the brush across the surface (Fig. 35-4).

For large areas first brush across the grain. Follow the cross brushing by brushing with the grain. As you are applying the finish it is best to flow the coating onto the surface. Overbrushing the finish will leave brush marks. Avoid putting too thick a coating on the surface. This might cause runs and drying problems. After you have completed an area, inspect the surface for holidays. *Holidays* are small areas that have not been coated with finish. They will usually appear as dry, nonglossy areas.

FIGURE 35-4
Hold the brush at a 45° angle.

Cleaning and Care of Finish Brushes

A high-quality brush will last only as long as it is properly cared for and cleaned. It is very important that you clean your brush immediately after each use.

Brushes used only for varnish can, however, be stored in a *brush keeper* (Fig. 35-5). This is a con-

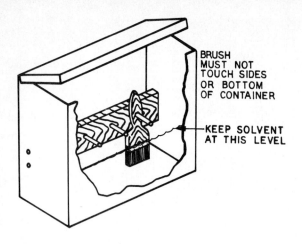

FIGURE 35-5
A brush keeper can be used to store varnish brushes.

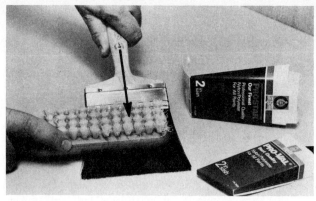

FIGURE 35-7
Comb and wrap the brush bristles for proper storage.

tainer in which the brush is suspended in a solution of one-half varnish and one-half turpentine. The bristles must remain submerged in the solution. After a period of time the solution becomes thick and must be replaced.

To clean a finishing brush for storage, use a three-container wash (Fig. 35-6). The first container has solvent which contains some finish from previous cleanups. The second container is filled with cleaner solvent. Your last container should have new solvent. When the solvent becomes dirty in containers 2 and 3, it can be used to replace the dirtier solvent in the next-lower-numbered container.

Work the bristles back and forth in container 1. Continue cleaning the brush in container 2 and finally, in container 3. Use your hands to work the finish from the bristles. The solvent in 3 should remain relatively clean if the brush has been cleaned properly in 1 and 2.

Use a stiff bristle brush or a brush comb to comb the bristle away from the handle (Fig. 35-7).

For long-term storage, work a small amount of turpentine into the bristle's brushes. All brushes must be wrapped in their original package or paper.

SPRAY GUNS AND RELATED EQUIPMENT

To spray a finish you will need a compressor, extractor, air hose, spray booth, and respirator. The *compressor* produces the pressurized air to spray the finish (Fig. 35-8). You need to select a compressor which is large enough to provide continuous dry air for your particular gun. The *extractor* adjusts the amount of air entering the spray gun and removes

FIGURE 35-8
A compressor provides pressurized air. (*Courtesy of Binks Manufacturing Co.*)

FIGURE 35-6
Use a three-container wash to clean brushes.

moisture from the compressed air (Fig. 35-9). An *air gauge* on the extractor indicates the pounds per square inch (PSI). To connect the extractor and spray gun, an *air hose* is utilized (Fig. 35-10). To prevent a serious loss in air pressure, the hose must be no longer than 96 in. (2400 mm) and contain no air leaks.

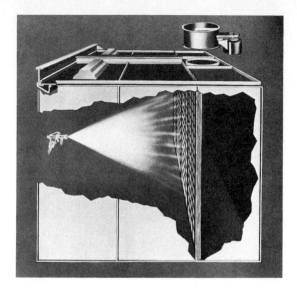

FIGURE 35-9
The extractor regulates the amount of pressurized air entering the spray gun. (*Courtesy of Binks Manufacturing Co.*)

FIGURE 35-10
An air hose connects the extractor to the spray gun. (*Courtesy of DeVilbiss Co.*)

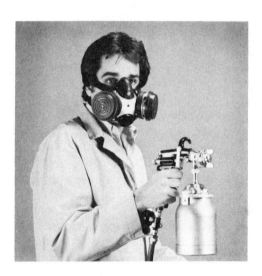

FIGURE 35-12
Use a respirator any time the spray gun is used. (*Courtesy of Binks Manufacturing Co.*)

Spray operators must protect themselves by using a spray booth and wear a respirator. The *spray booth* is a sheet metal enclosure in which the project is placed to be sprayed (Fig. 35-11). It will contain some type of filtering system to remove the excess finish from the exhausted air. The spray booth and filters must be kept clean. The walls of the booth can be protected with a stripable paint. This is a special paint that can be peeled off once it becomes covered with overspray. The *respirator* covers the face of the finisher and filters out harmful vapors (Fig. 35-12). You should frequently check that the filter cartridges are working properly.

There are several parts to a conventional spray gun. They are shown in Fig. 35-13. The *gun body* contains all the working parts. Once the *trigger* is pulled, pressurized air enters the bottom of the handle and the finish enters through the opening under the nozzle. The air and finish are mixed either in or immediately outside the *fluid nozzle*. The stream of air and finish are directed by the *air nozzle*. Adjustments are made with the *pattern control* and *fluid control knobs*. The *pattern control knob* shapes the spray pattern. Patterns will vary from a round to an oval shape. The *fluid control knob* adjusts the amount of finish allowed to pass through the nozzle. Adjusting these two knobs will provide the proper

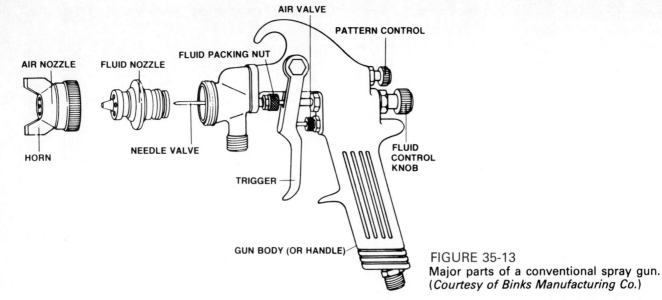

FIGURE 35-13
Major parts of a conventional spray gun.
(*Courtesy of Binks Manufacturing Co.*)

spray pattern. Refer to Fig. 35-14 for common spray pattern problems and their remedies.

A smaller spray system may use a *bleeder gun*. It allows the air to pass continually through the gun. Most systems, however, utilize a *nonbleeder gun*. Initially, pulling the trigger will release only the air. When the trigger is pulled all the way to the rear finish will also then come out of the nozzle.

Spray guns can also vary by the way the finish is fed into the gun. *Siphon feed guns* create a vacuum and the finish is sucked into the gun (Fig. 35-15). It is used primarily for thinned lacquers. The *pressure-feed gun* keeps the finish under pressure and forces the coating material up into the gun (Fig. 35-16). It can spray thicker materials such as paints.

One of the newest spray systems is the *air-assisted airless* concept. With this spray gun the finish is atomized for a full spray pattern at low pressures. This minimizes overspray and the amount of finish that stays on the project.

Spray Techniques

To spray a project, adjust the gun. Refer to the section "Spray Guns and Related Equipment" for the parts of the spray gun and their adjustments. Then practice on a piece of paper to learn how to control and trigger the gun. Make any necessary adjustments to achieve an even oval spray pattern.

The spray gun should be held 6 to 8 in. (152 to 203 mm) from the item to be finished (Fig. 35-17). Hold the gun at a right angle to the surface. Rotate the horns of the air nozzle horizontally when moving the gun from side to side. Move the horns vertically when you direct the gun up and down.

Plan the path that the spray gun will take. Start by coating each edge (Fig. 35-18). The trigger

should be squeezed and the finish material started through the nozzle before the spray pattern reaches the project. Next coat the part of the surface closest to you and work to the farthest side (Fig. 35-19). The overspray should fall on the uncoated area. Each pass of the gun should overlap the previous pass by one-half the width of the pattern.

The gun must be kept moving at all times. If you do not keep it moving for even a second, too heavy a buildup will occur and a run will develop. Keep your wrist stiff and move the gun in a straight line. Swinging the gun in a natural arc will produce light and heavy spots (Fig. 35-20, page 395).

Cleaning a Suction-Fed Gun

It is extremely important to keep your spray gun very clean. Any finish left in the gun will cause future problems. Allowing lacquer, stain, or other material to remain in the gun may require that the components be completely disassembled and several parts replaced.

Once you are through spraying, empty the fluid cup and allow it to drain completely. While it is draining, unscrew the air cap a few turns and place a folded rag over the air cap (Fig. 35-21, page 395). Pull the trigger to drive the finish back through the gun. Never attempt to hold anything in front of the air cap unless you are certain that it is a conventional gun.

Refill the fluid cup approximately one-half full of solvent and attach it to the gun. Screw the air cap back on the nozzle. Pull the trigger several times and allow the solvent to spray through the gun. Turn the horns of the air cap to several positions and pull the trigger each time.

Unscrew the air cap and fluid cup and place the

Faulty Patterns and How to Correct Them

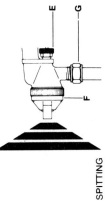

CAUSE
Dried material in side port "A" restricts passage of air through port on one side. Results in full pressure of air from clean side of port in a fan pattern in direction of clogged side.

REMEDY
Dissolve material in side port with thinner. Do not use metal devices to probe into air nozzle openings.

CAUSE
Dried material around the outside of the fluid nozzle tip at position "B" restricts the passage of atomizing air at one point through the center ring opening of the air nozzle. This faulty pattern can also be caused by loose air nozzle, or a bent fluid nozzle or needle tip.

REMEDY
If dried material is causing the trouble remove air nozzle and wipe off fluid tip, using rag wet with thinner. Tighten air nozzle. Replace fluid nozzle or needle if bent.

CAUSE
A split spray pattern (heavy on each end of a fan pattern and weak in the middle) is usually caused by: (1) atomizing air pressure, too high (2) attempting to get too wide a spray with thin material, (3) not enough material available.

REMEDY
(1) Reduce air pressure. (2) Open material control "D" to full position by turning to left. At the same time turn spray width adjustment "C" to right. This reduces width of spray but will correct split spray pattern.

CAUSE
Air entering the fluid supply.
Dried packing or missing packing around the material needle valve which permits air to get into fluid passageway.
Dirt between the fluid nozzle seat and body or a loosely installed fluid nozzle.
A loose or defective swivel nut, siphon cup or material hose.

REMEDY
Be sure all fittings and connections are tight.
Back up knurled nut "E", place two drops of machine oil on packing, replace nut and finger tighten. In aggravated cases, replace packing.
Remove air and fluid nozzles "F" and clean back of fluid nozzle and nozzle seat in the gun body, using a rag wet with thinner. Replace and tighten fluid nozzle using wrench supplied with the gun. Replace air nozzle.
Tighten or replace swivel nut "G".

CAUSE
A fan spray pattern that is heavy in the middle, or a pattern that has an unatomized "salt-and-pepper" effect indicates that the atomizing air pressure is not sufficiently high, or there is too much material being fed to the gun.

REMEDY
Increase pressure from air supply. Correct air pressures as discussed elsewhere in this manual.

Jerky or fluttering pattern. Check for:
Air leaking into fluid line or passageway.
Lack of paint.
Loose or cracked fluid siphon tube.
Loose fluid nozzle.
Loose fluid packing nut or worn packing.

SPITTING

FIGURE 35-14
Faulty patterns and how to correct them. (*Courtesy of Binks Manufacturing Co.*)

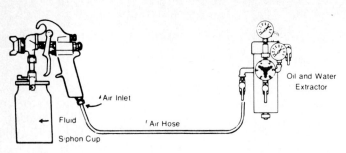

FIGURE 35-15
Atmospheric pressure is utilized with a siphon feed gun to create a vacuum. (*Courtesy of Binks Manufacturing Co.*)

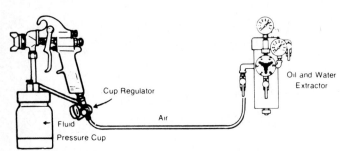

FIGURE 35-16
Pressure feed guns have an airline to the pressure cup. (*Courtesy of Binks Manufacturing Co.*)

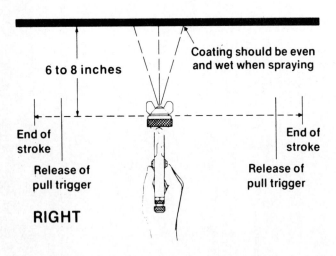

FIGURE 35-17
Position the gun 6 to 8 in. (152 to 203 mm) from the project. (*Courtesy of Binks Manufacturing Co.*)

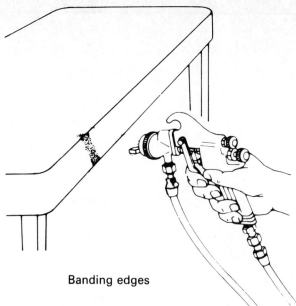

Banding edges

FIGURE 35-18
Coat each corner before spraying the larger flat areas. (*Courtesy of Binks Manufacturing Co.*)

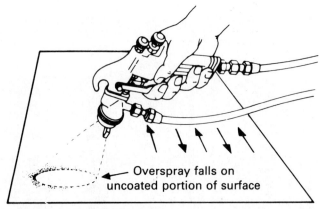

FIGURE 35-19
Allow the overspray to fall on the uncoated area. (*Courtesy of Binks Manufacturing Co.*)

cap in the cup. There should be at least 1 in. of solvent remaining in the cup. Wipe the outside of the gun clean with a solvent-soaked rag. In addition, check that the vent hole of a siphon feed gun is free of any finish. It may be necessary to unclog the hole with a wooden toothpick (Fig. 35-22, page 395); never use any metal object.

Leaving approximately 1 in. (25 mm) of solvent in the fluid cup, reassemble the gun. Occasionally, lubricate the points identified in Fig. 35-23 with light machine oil to prevent excessive wear. Hang the gun in a safety cabinet until you are ready for it again.

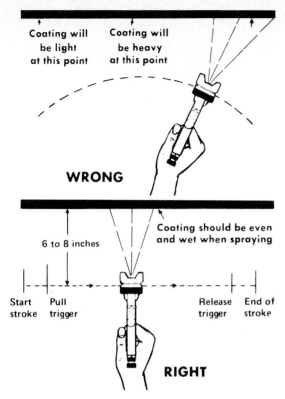

Coating will be light at this point

Coating will be heavy at this point

WRONG

6 to 8 inches

Coating should be even and wet when spraying

Start stroke | Pull trigger | Release trigger | End of stroke

RIGHT

FIGURE 35-20
Do *not* swing the gun in an arc but move it parallel to the surface. (*Courtesy of Binks Manufacturing Co.*)

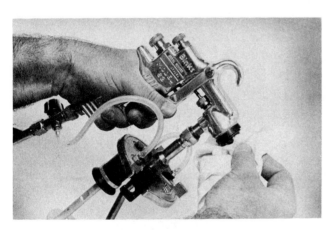

FIGURE 35-21
Hold a rag over the air cap to force the finish material back through the gun.

FIGURE 35-22
Clean the vent hold with a wooden toothpick only.

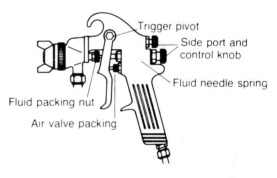

Trigger pivot

Side port and control knob

Fluid needle spring

Fluid packing nut

Air valve packing

FIGURE 35-23
Lubrication points for a spray gun. (*Courtesy of Binks Manufacturing Co.*)

36

FINISHING SCHEDULES

There are hundreds of different types of finishing materials from which to select. As a finisher you will need to pick the various components that will produce the desired effect. The finishing materials chosen determine color, the degree of gloss, durability, and the depth of finish.

DEVELOPING A FINISHING SCHEDULE

Your first step in finishing a project is to develop a finishing schedule. A *finishing schedule* is a list of the steps and the materials necessary to produce the desired effect. Not only should the stains, lacquers, and other coatings be included but abrasive paper and rubbing steps as well.

It is very important to try the finishing schedule on a small piece of wood of the same species as your project. The finished piece is called a *finish sample* (Fig. 36-1). The sample will allow you to practice applying the finishing materials. It will also indicate how the final finish will appear. Be sure to place the finish schedule on the back of the finish sample. This will allow you to use the sample later and know how the finish was produced.

The selection of the finishing schedule will depend largely on several items. The first consider-

FIGURE 36-1
Finishing samples show the final results of each finish schedule.

ation is the species of wood used in the project. Ring porous or open-grain woods, for example, may require a contrasting stain and filler to emphasize the wood pores. Another item to consider is the durability of the finish. An exterior door will require a finish that will weather. Novelty items, however, may only require a simple wax finish. Always evaluate your available time and skill level. Some finishes dry rapidly and require a minimum effort to apply. The last item to consider is the available finishing equipment. Having a spray booth with a spray gun allows many more finishing materials than if the finish must be applied in a dusty environment.

Although there is no all-purpose finish schedule, there is a checklist that you can utilize to develop your own. Table 36-1 includes most of the items that may be used in your finish. Although items 1 through 3 should always be practiced, it is not necessary to select every step listed in the illustration.

TABLE 36-1
Steps for Complete Finishing Schedule

1.	_____	Repair major open defects (knots, cracks)
2.	_____	Scrape or machine sand millmarks
3.	_____	Sand with 100, 120, 150, and 180 grit abrasive paper (some concealed areas may not require the finer grits)
4.	_____	Bleach (optional)
5.	_____	Stain—water, penetrating oil, pigmented oil, nongrain-raising
6.	_____	Wash Coat
7.	_____	Paste wood filler (primarily open grain woods)
8.	_____	Sealer—shellac, lacquer sealers
9.	_____	Glaze (optional)
10.	_____	Topcoats—lacquer, varnish, oil, wax
11.	_____	Rubbing—320 wet or dry abrasive paper
12.	_____	Polishing—for high gloss finishes; pumice, rottenstone, rubbing compound
13.	_____	Waxing (optional)

STEPS IN A FINISHING SCHEDULE

As indicated in Table 36-1, there are numerous steps that can occur in a very complete finishing schedule. In this section we describe briefly the major items that may or may not be included in your schedule. The remaining chapters in Section V will provide you with a more detailed description of the various finishing materials.

Bleaching

Bleaching is the process of chemically lightening the color of the wood. It is utilized to produce "blond" finishes and to remove the major differences in colors found in some wood. Bleach wood is often called harvest wheat, honey maple, or amber walnut.

A two-part commercial bleach is utilized to bleach wood (Fig. 36-2). Be extremely careful of these strong chemicals and wear protective clothing. Rubber gloves, safety goggles, and an apron must be worn.

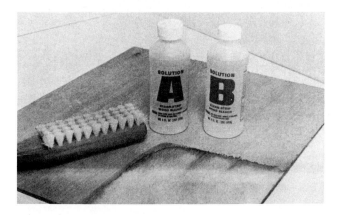

FIGURE 36-2
Bleaching removes the color from wood.

Staining

Although many projects are left *natural* and not stained, staining does add color. Staining the surface will also bring out the grain, emphasizing the pores and latewood. Staining is discussed in Chapter 37.

Washcoating

A *washcoat* is utilized after staining and before filler and sealers are applied. This step in the finishing schedule prevents stains which are prone to bleeding from leaching into the finish (Fig. 36-3). In addition, the washcoat keeps the wood from turning gray after being filled.

FIGURE 36-3
Apply a washcoat to prevent the stain from eventually bleeding.

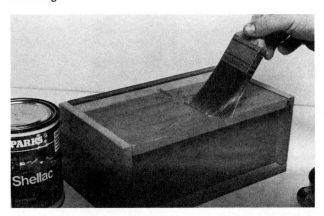

Filling

Woods with visible pores are usually filled with a paste wood filler. *Paste wood filler* levels the surface of the wood and adds color. Some coarse-grained woods are left unfilled to allow a more natural-appearing project. Filling is discussed in Chapter 38.

Sealing

Sealing is the step in which shellac or lacquer sealer is applied to keep the stain and filler from bleeding into the topcoat. Because it is easy to sand, some finishers utilize sealers to fill the pores of the wood. This gives the project a more natural appearance. Because this will require several coats, it is important that each be sanded until very little remains on the surface. Allowing the sealer to build up on the surface will cause the topcoat to chip easily. Sealing is described in Chapter 38.

Glazing

Glazing applies an additional coat of color to the surface which shades or darkens portions of the project (Fig. 36-4). Areas such as edges and flat surfaces are wiped more than others to produce an antique appearance. The glaze will add depth and interest to the finish.

FIGURE 36-4
Glazing gives a new piece of furniture an antique appearance.

Topcoating

Topcoats are most commonly varnish, lacquer, or some type of synthetic finish. Each has its own characteristic as described in Chapter 39. the more coats that are applied, the thicker the topcoat will be. In most cases it is better to apply several light to medium coats rather than a few thick layers. Remem-

ber, however, that the thicker the topcoat, the more likely it will crack and the more difficult it is to repair.

Rubbing

The finish must be rubbed between coats. Rubbing the finish levels the surface and removes any dust and other foreign material that may have become trapped in the wet finish.

For rubbing between the coats select 320 wet or dry abrasive paper (Fig. 36-5). To keep the abrasive paper from loading with finish, frequently dip the abrasive in water. Utilizing a felt pad or cork sanding block will produce a flatter surface than just using your hand to hold the abrasive paper. Be very careful about sanding through the finish along corners and edges.

FIGURE 36-5
Rub the finish between top coats with 320-grit wet or dry abrasive paper.

Polishing

After the last coat of finish has cured it can be polished. Be certain, however, that the finish has totally cured or you will develop white areas. Polishing is used to remove any defects from brushing or spraying and produces a smooth, slick surface. Not polishing your project will leave it with an unfinished appearance that still needs additional attention.

The first step in polishing is to work the finish with pumice and water (Fig. 36-6). Sprinkle a small amount of pumice onto the surface and dip a felt pad into water. Rub the pad back and forth with the grain. A slurry of pumice and water should be developed to polish the finish.

After the finish has been thoroughly rubbed with the pumice, rottenstone can be used (Fig. 36-7). Rottenstone will produce an even higher polish. Se-

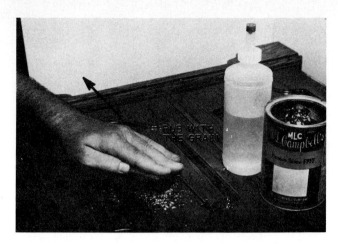

FIGURE 36-6
Polishing the surface with pumice and water.

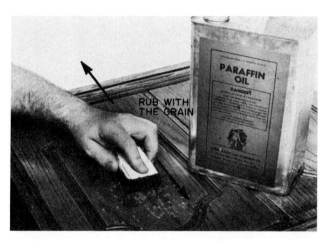

FIGURE 36-7
Rottenstone and rubbing oil will produce a deep shine.

lect the same procedure as recommended for pumice stone except use a lightweight rubbing oil as a lubricant. Clean the surface with mineral spirits once the job is completed.

For very high quality finishes, further polishing can be completed with rubbing compounds. These are very fine abrasive materials that are rubbed over the finish with a soft cloth. Use a clean cotton cloth to polish the surface and remove the excess compound.

Waxing

To protect the finish further, a coat of paste wax can be applied. Rub the wax on with a circular motion, but polish the finish by rubbing with the grain (Fig. 43-8). Waxing a surface will repel dirt and moisture, but it does make it very difficult to apply another coat or finish at a later time.

FIGURE 36-8
Waxing the project to provide additional protection.

A FURNITURE FINISHING SCHEDULE

Now that you are more familiar with some of the items in a finishing schedule, one is listed below that you may like to use as a pattern. The final results should produce a deep-looking finish that will add greatly to a high-quality piece of furniture.

To apply a furniture finish:

1. Prepare the surface by thoroughly sanding all exposed areas with 100-, 120-, 150-, and 180-grit abrasive paper. No millmarks should remain. Inspect the various surfaces by reflecting a light at a slight angle to the exposed areas. Note any defects that need additional attention. After the last sanding, clean the entire project using compressed air and a soft brush.

2. Moisten the surfaces with a sponge that has been dipped in water. After the wood has dried, lightly sand the raised grain with 220-grit abrasive paper.

3. After mixing the stain thoroughly, apply it following the instructions given in Chapter 37. Before proceeding, allow the stained project to dry for the period recommended.

4. Apply a wash coat of shellac if there is danger that the stain may bleed.

5. If the project is constructed from one of the woods requiring a paste wood filler (Table 38-1). Use the procedure given in Chapter 38.

6. Spray on a lacquer sealer to provide a proper base for the lacquer topcoat.

7. Lightly sand the project with 320-grit wet or dry abrasive paper. Do not sand the outside corners or areas where the stain may easily be removed. Blow off the project with compressed air. Clean the surface with a new tack rag (Fig.

36-9). A *tack rag* is a cloth that is sticky and easily picks up any remaining loose dirt.

8. Using a spray gun, apply the first topcoat of lacquer. First test the spray gun, however, on a piece of paper to be certain that the spray pattern is correct. Refer to Chapter 35 on how to adjust the gun. Spray a full wet coat in order that the lacquer will level itself. Be careful to prevent runs and sags.

9. Lightly sand the surface using water and 320-grit wet or dry abrasive paper. Always wet sand with the grain. Wipe the surface clean and dry with a lint-free cloth.

10. After allowing the last coat to cure for a minimum of 24 hours, rub the surfaces with pumice stone and then rottenstone. For an even deeper finish, polish the project further with extra-fine rubbing compound.

FIGURE 36-9
A clean tack rag will remove any remaining loose dirt.

37

STAINING

Staining is the process of applying a dye or pigment that modifies the color of the wood. Finishers will use stain to bring out the grain in the wood, add color, or to imitate a more expensive species. On simple finishes it is often the first step in the finishing schedule.

Stains consist of either a *soluble dye* or *insoluble pigment* and a *vehicle*. The dye and pigment contains the color, while the vehicle keeps the colorants in liquid form. The *vehicle* allows the stain to be spread on the surface and to penetrate into the wood.

Always read and follow the directions given on the label of the stain container. The directions will provide specific information on application and cleanup procedures. It will be very important that you note the proper length of drying time. Thoroughly stir the stain to mix the dye or pigments into the liquid. Not stirring the stain will cause the wood to vary in color. It is also recommended that you pause periodically and restir the stain, to keep the colorants from settling to the bottom of the container.

The most common stains are water stains, penetrating oil stains, pigmented oil stains, and non-grain-raising stains. Each has certain advantages and disadvantages to be considered. General characteristics are given in Table 37-1.

It is a good practice to wear rubber gloves when working with stains. Eye protection is also recommended.

WATER STAINS

Water stain is sold as a powder that is mixed with water. It is known for a fade-resistant, clear permanent color. You should sponge the surface with warm water, allow it to dry, and sand before applying the stain. This stain streaks easily and also requires light sanding after the stain has dried to remove the raised grain. Do not attempt to wipe on the wet stain unless the project is quite small (Fig. 37-1). Always wipe with the grain and do not overlap any of the passes. Ideally, use a spray gun to apply water stain. Stain applied with a spray gun should have stainless steel passages to prevent corrosion.

PENETRATING OIL STAINS

Penetrating oil stains are sold premixed in a variety of colors. They are very likely to fade and bleed into other coats of finish. Penetrating stains are not recommended for most applications.

TABLE 37-1
Characteristics of Stains

Stain	Characteristics	Application methods	Drying time
Water stain	Produces one of the clearest color; nonbleeding; raises grain, which requires light sanding	Wiping Spraying	12 hours
Penetrating oil stains	Non-grain-raising; likely to bleed; fades	Wiping Brushing Spraying	24 hours
Pigmented oil stains	Easiest to apply; non-grain-raising; hides grain	Wiping Brushing Spraying	3 to 12 hours
Non-grain-raising stains	Dries rapidly; nonbleeding non-grain-raising; clear colors; streaks easily	Spraying	15 minutes to 3 hours

FIGURE 37-1
Only wipe one water stain when the project is quite small.

PIGMENTED OIL STAINS

Pigmented oil stains are ideal for finishers who need an easy-to-apply stain. This stain is available in a broad variety of colors and is sometimes called a *wiping stain* (Fig. 37-2).

Pigmented stains can be applied by wiping, dipping, brushing, or spraying. Brushing or wiping is often used for small to medium-sized projects. Use short overlapping strokes from the bottom of the surface to the top (Fig. 37-3). After five to ten minutes, use a lint-free cloth to remove any excess stain. Rub across the grain and be certain that all corners are free of surplus stain. The longer the unwiped stain is allowed to stay on the surface, the darker the wood will become. Once the stain is applied, wait at least 24 hours before applying any other finish. Because the end grain tends to darken rapidly, the penetrating process can be slowed by first rubbing linseed oil into the pores.

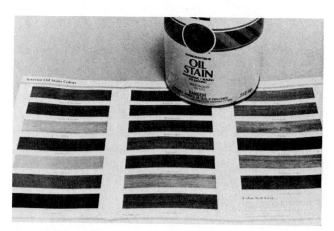

FIGURE 37-2
Pigmented oil stains are available in a broad variety of colors.

FIGURE 37-3
Brushing on a pigmented oil stain.

NON-GRAIN-RAISING STAINS

Non-grain-raising (NGR) stains are made from a dye base and a fast drying vehicle. This stain is best known for its rapid drying characteristics and clear transparent colors. It does not "muddy" the wood grain, giving the finish a clear appearance.

NGR stains are difficult to apply evenly except with a spray gun (Fig. 37-4). Any overlapping will cause dark streaks. Apply a light coat and be careful that the project does not become too dark. You can always apply additional coats to achieve a darker color.

FIGURE 37-4
Spraying NGR stains to develop an even color.

38

FILLING AND SEALING

After a project has been stained, it can be filled and sealed. Each of these is an important step which is often found in a finishing schedule. Not all finishes, however, require filling and sealing. Paste wood filler will aid you in developing a flat surface on woods containing visible pores. Sealing the project will provide a good base on which to apply most top-coats.

PASTE WOOD FILLERS

Paste wood filler is utilized to fill the small recesses created by the pores in wood. Open-grained woods such as oaks, ash, and mahogany need a paste filler (Table 38-1). Birch, red gum, and cherry have smaller pores and require liquid filler, which is thinner than the paste filler. Poplar, willow, and pine have no visible pores and do not need any type of filling. Paste wood filler should not be confused with wood putty. Wood putty is designed to fill larger recesses and defects.

Most finishers purchase the paste wood filler already mixed in a neutral color. For darker-colored woods concentrated oil pigments should be thoroughly mixed with the filler (Fig. 38-1). A color of filler can be made that matches the surrounding

TABLE 38-1		
Woods Requiring Filling		
No filler needed	Liquid filler	Paste filler
Basswood	Beech	Ash
Fir	Birch	Butternut
Hemlock	Cherry	Chestnut
Holly	Cottonwood	Elm
Larch	Gum, red	Hickory/pecan
Magnolia	Maple, hard	Locust
Pine, white	Maple, soft	Mahogany
Pine, yellow	Sycamore	Red and white oak
Poplar		Walnut
Willow		

wood. You may wish to use a contrasting color filler to highlight the pores.

Applying Paste Filler

To apply the paste filler, completely mix the required amount to a uniform creamy consistency. A *wash coat* should have been applied previously to seal in the stain. Not using a wash coat of thinned shellac or lacquer sealer will lighten the stain and make the color irregular.

404

FIGURE 38-1
Use concentrated oil pigments to color paste wood filler.

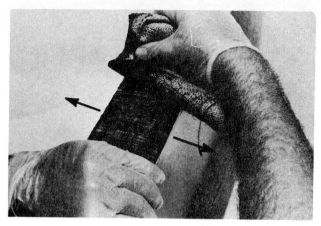

FIGURE 38-3
Remove the excess filler by rubbing across the grain.

Use a stiff-bristle varnish brush to work the filler into the grain. Brush across the grain to achieve the maximum penetration (Fig. 38-2). Some finishers prefer to rub the filler into the pores by using a circular motion with their hands. You may want to wear rubber gloves to prevent your hands from being stained. The more filler worked into the pores, the leveler the finish will be.

FIGURE 38-2
Brush filler across the grain.

After the filler has turned from a glossy wet appearance to a dull color, the excess can be removed from the wood. Rub the filler across the grain with a folded pad of burlap (Fig. 38-3). Frequently refold the pad to expose a clean area of the burlap to better remove the excess material. Use a sharpened dowel rod with a rag covering the point to dig out the filler in corners and other recesses (Fig. 38-4). Use a soft cotton cloth to clean the surface further by rubbing with the grain.

It is extremely important that all wood filler left on top of the surface be removed. Any remaining

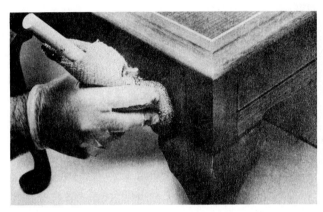

FIGURE 38-4
Use a sharpened dowel rod to remove filler from corners.

material will turn gray and require a great deal of effort to remove. After waiting for 24 hours, inspect the surface. If the pores are still somewhat open, repeat the process using a liquid filler.

LIQUID FILLER

For woods with smaller pores, use a liquid filler. (Table 38-1). Being a thinner-bodied material, the liquid filler will penetrate smaller pores and fill them more easily than with the thicker paste wood filler. Use the application techniques recommended for paste wood filler.

SEALING THE SURFACE

A very important step in finishing a project properly is the application of sealer. Sealers are typically utilized as the last step before the application of the topcoat. This coating should be utilized to serve as a barrier between the filler, stain, and the remaining layers of finish. Sealers will keep stains from bleeding and fillers from eventually turning gray. A coat of sealer will also provide a good base for topcoats in order that they may have proper adhesion to the wood substrate. They will also cause loose wood fibers to stand up in order that they be later sanded away.

Select the type of sealer based on the kind of topcoat finish. Varnish finishes are generally sealed with shellac. A mixture of 7 parts of alcohol with 1 part of 4-lb-cut white shellac will seal a stained and or filled surface which is to be varnished. Lacquer sealers are utilized for lacquer finishes. They are usually thinned in a sufficient amount to be sprayed. Polyesters, polyurethanes, and other synthetic finishes often require specialized sealers. For any finish, always read and follow the instructions on the topcoat container for the exact recommended sealer and method of application.

To seal most surfaces properly, two coats of sealer are required. Apply the first coat of sealer across the grain. After the sealer has been allowed to dry thoroughly, sand the surface. Lightly sand with the grain using 180-grit abrasive paper. It will remove any raised wood fibers. Be very careful about sanding through the stain, exposing the raw wood. You may find that you should not sand on or near the corners. The sealer will be very thin at these locations and can easily be sanded through. Follow the same procedure for the second coat of sealer, but apply with the grain.

Be careful about applying an excessive amount of sealer. Being a soft coating, it will cause cold cracking and chipping of the topcoat. Ideally, the majority of the sealer should be left in the wood with very little remaining on the surface.

39

TOPCOATS

The most common topcoats include penetrating finishes, varnishes, and lacquers. Like the other finishing materials discussed in this section, there are advantages and disadvantages to each. Your selection will depend on the final desired appearance, amount of skill required, available time, and existing equipment and facilities.

SOLVENTS

Solvents are used to dissolve topcoat materials such as those needed for cleaning finishing equipment. Some solvents are also utilized as thinners to reduce the viscosity of the topcoat material. Thinning allows the finish to penetrate the wood better when applying the first layer of the topcoat, and can also be more easily sprayed. Be certain to select the proper solvent for each application. A solvent that will dissolve one material may not affect another. Refer to Table 39-1 for recommended solvents, or more important, use the exact solvent indicated on the printed instructions on the finish can. Some topcoats require a specific type and brand of solvent.

TABLE 39-1
Finishes and Their Solvents

Finish	Solvent[a]
Lacquer	Lacquer thinner
Latex paint	Water
Oil paint and enamel	Turpentine or mineral spirits
Oil stain	Turpentine or mineral spirits
Oil varnish	Turpentine or mineral spirits
Polyurethane varnish	Mineral spirits
Shellac	Alcohol

[a] Always read the directions on the finish container for the recommended solvent.

LACQUERS

Lacquers are one of the most common wood finishes. Many woodworkers select this finish because it dries rapidly, is widely available, and comes in a broad variety of colors and sheens. The *sheen* indicates the amount of gloss or the degree of shine. Lacquers are available in gloss, semigloss, dull, and flat sheens.

Lacquers do have some disadvantages that you should consider. This finish should never be applied

407

over other coatings. It will soften paint and varnishes. Lacquer is likely to check and crack if the substrate or wood expands or contracts a great deal. Once cured the lacquer becomes quite hard and inflexible.

There are several varieties of lacquer-based materials from which to select. In addition, you will want to purchase the type and size of container that will best suit your application. Since it is possible to buy lacquer in containers ranging from small aerosol spray cans to rail tank cars, there is no need to purchase more than you can use in a reasonable period. Most woodworkers find 1- or 5-gallon containers to be the most convenient.

Lacquer Sealers

Lacquer sealers are applied to the raw wood surface and form a base for the other coats of lacquer. Because of its softness, it should never be used as a finish by itself. Many people prefer a *water-white lacquer sealer* because it darkens the wood less than do standard lacquer sealers (Fig. 39-1).

FIGURE 39-1
Water-white lacquer sealer darkens the wood very little.

Clear Lacquers

Although there are several different kinds of clear lacquer, finishes made from *nitrocellulose* remain the most popular. Clear lacquer is utilized as the topcoat and applied over the lacquer sealer. You will need to select the sheen that will provide the desired luster on your project.

Shading Lacquers

Shading lacquers are tinted with a dye and will change the color of the wood (Fig. 39-2). The more shading lacquer that is sprayed, the darker the wood will become. This lacquer can be utilized for making different colors of wood a more uniform color.

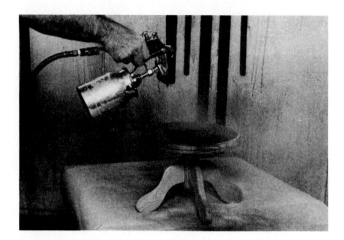

FIGURE 39-2
Shading lacquer tints the wood.

Opaque Lacquers

Opaque lacquers are utilized as fast-drying paints (Fig. 39-3). They will completely hide the grain. Most generally, opaque lacquer will be purchased in an aerosol container.

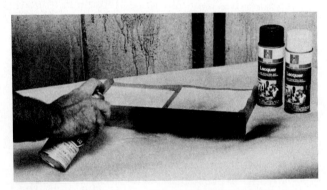

FIGURE 39-3
Opaque lacquers serve as a fast-drying paint.

Brushing Lacquer

Brushing lacquer is a slower-drying lacquer which is applied with a brush (Fig. 39-4). Because these lacquers dry at a slower rate, it is possible to brush the finish without developing brush marks.

FIGURE 39-4
Brushing lacquers are slower drying and can be brushed.

Water-Reducible Lacquers

One of the newest lacquers is acrylic based and thinned with water. Water-reducible lacquer has the advantage of being less polluting to the environment and less flammable. To prevent corrosion, you will need to use spray equipment with stainless steel passages.

Procedure for Spraying Lacquer

Before applying a lacquer finish, check that the stain, filler, and other preliminary steps in the finishing schedule are thoroughly cured. Use the spraying techniques discussed in Chapter 35. Spray on the lacquer sealer or sanding sealer. If you choose a natural appearance, select a water-white lacquer sealer. Sealers fill the pores and provide proper adhesion for the remaining coats of lacquer.

After the sealer has dried, select the lacquer to build up the desired depth of finish. Depending on the amount of lacquer sprayed with each coat, you may want to consider applying two to three coats of lacquer. The more coats applied, the deeper appearing the finish. Too much lacquer, however, will produce a finish that fractures easily. The last coat of lacquer should be the desired sheen. Remember, however, that the higher the gloss, the more the imperfections and defects will show. Be certain to sand lightly with 320-grit wet or dry abrasive paper between each coat of lacquer.

PENETRATING FINISHES

Penetrating finishes soak into the wood rather than building up a substantial layer on top of the surface of the wood. Examples of penetrating finishes are oils and waxes. They will produce a low sheen which gives a hand-rubbed appearance. Both can be applied with a soft cloth and do not necessarily require any other application equipment. Some woodworkers prefer waxes and oils because they do not require a dust-free finish room for their application. It is also easier to repair a penetrating-finished project than those finished with other topcoats.

Oil Finishes

Oil finishes are available as Danish oil, boiled linseed oil, and most recently, Food and Drug Administration (FDA)-approved wipe-on oil. Danish oil is the most common and frequently utilized for school mass-production projects and contemporary walnut furniture (Fig. 39-5). Boiled linseed oil is no longer popular because of its lengthy drying time and odor. The FDA-approved wipe-on oil is designed to be applied on fruit bowls and other wooden articles that will come in contact with food.

FIGURE 39-5
Danish oil produces a hand-rubbed appearance.

Procedure for Wiping Oil

To finish a project with Danish oil, soak a soft cloth in the finish and rub it into the pores of the wood. Use a circular motion (Fig. 39-6). The more oil worked into the surface, the better the project will be protected. After 30 minutes rub the surface dry with a clean cloth. Wipe with the grain. After 1 hour repeat the process to work more oil into the wood. Once the oil has cured completely, you may want to use a paste wax to develop a deeper-looking finish.

FIGURE 39-6
Rub the oil into the wood with a circular motion.

Wax Finishes

Wax finishes are sold either as pigmented or unpigmented rubbing waxes. Pigmented waxes contain a colorant and will tint the wood. Unpigmented waxes are an amber color and leave the surface a natural color. Although both varieties require a great deal of rubbing, they will produce a defect-free finish.

Procedure for Applying Wax

To apply wax, finish thoroughly and clean the project with pressurized air. Using a soft clean cloth, rub the wax into the pores of the wood with a circular motion. For maximum penetration, heat the wax in a double boiler and apply the wax hot (Fig. 39-7).

FIGURE 39-7
Heating the wax in a double boiler will increase the penetration.

Because the wax is highly flammable, apply only enough heat to melt the wax. After 5 minutes buff the surface thoroughly with a folded soft cotton cloth. Rub with the grain until the entire surface achieves a dull luster. Repeat the process if additional protection is needed.

VARNISHES

Varnishes are one of the oldest finishes utilized for wood surfaces. Over the years many different types have been developed for a variety of applications. Although this type of finish requires several hours and even days to dry, there are types which are water resistant and very durable. The four major categories of varnishes include spirit varnishes, linseed oil varnishes, tung oil varnishes, and synthetic varnishes.

Spirit Varnishes

The most common spirit varnish is *shellac*. (Fig. 39-8) Although at one time utilized as a complete finish, it is used primarily today as a barrier coat and sealer. When used as a finish, shellac yellows and tends to *water spot* if a wet dish is left standing on the surface. Water spotting leaves a white ring in the finish. Denatured alcohol should be used to thin the shellac and clean brushes.

FIGURE 39-8
Shellac is frequently utilized as a barrier coat.

Linseed Oil Varnishes

Linseed oil varnishes can be purchased in three varieties: short-oil, medium-oil, and long-oil. *Short-oil varnishes* are rarely used for furniture. *Medium-oil*

FIGURE 39-9
Medium oil varnishes can be used on kitchen cabinets.

FIGURE 39-10
Spar varnishes are recommended for exterior applications.

varnishes, however, are commonly used for interior furniture and cabinets. (Fig. 39-9). *Long-oil* varnishes are marketed as *spar varnishes* and ideal for wooden surfaces exposed to the exterior. (Fig. 39-10) Outside doors, lawn furniture and boats should be finished with this type of linseed oil varnish.

Tung Oil Varnishes

Tung oil varnishes, the third type of varnish, are designed for high demand areas such as children's

furniture and lawn furniture. They are, however, difficult to find.

Synthetic Varnishes

Synthetic varnishes are known for their toughness and durability. Although there are several types, polyurethane, alkyd and epoxy are the most common (Fig. 39-11). Alkyds and epoxies are limited primarily to industrial production. They along with polyurethanes dry to such a hard film that unless recoated within 24 hours, additional coats may not adhere.

FIGURE 39-11
Polyurethane varnish produces a very hard, durable finish.

Procedure for Brushing Varnish

After the project has been stained, filled, and sealed, a varnish finish can be applied. Read the directions carefully on the varnish container and follow them exactly.

Slowly stir the varnish and after it is completely mixed, gently pour a small amount into a brush cup. You must be very careful not to develop any air bubbles in the finishing material. Thin the varnish for the first coat by 25 percent. The thinner varnish will more readily penetrate the wood. Stir the mixture to completely disperse the thinner.

Because varnish is very slow drying use a dust free environment to apply the finish. The room must be completely dust free before brushing on the finish and at least two hours after the varnish has been applied. Wipe the project with a clean tack rag and flow on the varnish. Use the brushing techniques as given in Chapter 35, Finishing Equipment.

Be certain the finish is dry before lightly sanding with 320 wet or dry abrasive paper. Three coats of varnish will most generally coat a project. If the initial layers of varnish are sanded flat the last coat should produce a glass-like appearance.

INDEX

Stop pin technique, 339
Stop rod, 233
Straight bits, 203
Straight-line sanders, 219
Strip molding fences, 355
Stroke length, 330
Stroke sanders, 380
Structural particleboard, 87
Stuck joinery, 360
Surfacer (see Planers)
Swaging, 135–36
Swing, lathes and, 312
Sycamore, 72
Synthetic varnishes, 411

T

Table saws:
  beveling and chamfering, 238
  blades for, 228–29
  box joints with, 251
  cove cuts with, 245
  crosscutting with, 233
  cutting grooves with, 246
  cutting panels with, 241
  cutting tapers with, 242
  cutting tenons with, 238
  dado heads for, 239
  how to buy, 227–28
  installing blades, 232
  mitering, 235
  molding heads, 250
  parts of, 226
  pattern techniques for sawing, 244
  raised panels with, 249

resawing with, 242
ripping stock with, 240
safety rules for, 227
Tack rag, 401
Tambour doors, 133
Tangential surface, 68
Tapered shapes, routing, 212
Taper point bits, 335
Tapers:
  cutting, 242
  jointing, 300–01
  turning, 312
Tape rule, 50
Teak, 72
Tee nuts, 108
Templates, 56, 288, 313, 339
Tenons, cutting, 238, 265
Thermoplastics, 161–62
Thermosets, 160–61
32-millimeter construction, 25–32
Threelayer particleboard, 94
Toenailing, 102
Toggle bolts, 109
Toggler screw anchors, 110
Topcoating, 398, 407–10
Transverse surface, 68
Try square, 50
Tung oil varnishes, 410
Turning(s):
  beads, 320
  coves, 319
  duplicating, 321
  faceplate, 324
  large-diameter stock, 327
  mandrel, 324
  measuring, 313
  off-center, 321
  sanding, 327

slender stock, 322
split, 323
squares, 321
straight cylinders, 316
tapers, 318
vees, 319
(see also Lathes)
Twist drill, 332

U

U.S. Product Standard PS 1-83, 85
Urea-formaldehyde, 161, 173, 324

V

V and herringbone matching, 79
Varnishes, 410
Vees, turning, 318
Vehicle, 401
Veneer-core plywood, 80
Veneers, 72, 77–79
  construction and industrial plywood, and grades of, 85
  hardwood plywood and grades of, 81
Vertical butt and horizontal book leaf matching, 77
V-grooving bits, 203
Vibrating sanders, 219

W

Waferboard, 87, 94
Wall anchors, 109

Wall cabinets, 16–31
Walnut, North American, 72
Washcoating, 396
Water putty, 384
Water spot, 410
Water stains, 401
Water-white lacquer sealer, 408
Wax finishes, 410
Waxing, 339
Wedge anchors, 110
Wedge fixtures, 243
Wet process, 90
Willow, 72
Wiping stain, 402
Wire brad nails, 102
Wood:
  hardwoods, 68
  kiln dried, 72
  ordering, 79
  pad, 336
  sawing of, 68
  softwoods, 70
  structure of, 66
  veneers, 72, 77–79
Wooden fences, 354
Wood screws:
  diameters of, 106
  face framing, 106
  head types, 105
  installing, 107–08, 199
  particleboard, 106
  sizes of, 106
Work triangle, 3
Worm-drive portable saw, 182
Wrap-around hinges, 138

Z

Zebrawood, 72